A GLORIOUS EXTRAVAGANZA:
THE HISTORY OF MONKSTOWN PARISH CHURCH

A GLORIOUS EXTRAVAGANZA:

The History of Monkstown Parish Church

Étain Murphy

Wordwell

First published in 2003 by
Wordwell Ltd
PO Box 69, Bray, Co. Wicklow
www.wordwellbooks.com

Published with the financial assistance of
The Heritage Council and
The Select Vestry of Monkstown Parish Church

The quotation on pp xxi–xxii is from *Gothic Revival Architecture in Ireland* (Volume 1) copyright (© 1983) by Douglas Scott Richardson. Reproduced by permission of Routledge/Taylor & Francis Books, Inc.

Endpaper illustration of the Dublin and Kingstown Railway courtesy of the National Library of Ireland (see also page 309).

Library of Congress Cataloging-in-Publication Data is available for this book.

A CIP catalogue record for this book is available from the British Library.

ISBN 1869857 63 1

Cover design: Rachel Dunne.

Editor: Carole C. Devaney.
Copy editing: Wordwell Ltd.
Typesetting and layout: Wordwell Ltd.
Repro: Andrew Gregory.

Book design: Nick Maxwell.

Printed by E. G. Zure, S.A. Bilbao

Contents

This work would probably have had fewer imperfections, had it been produced beneath the calm shade of retirement; but it was not; it was written amidst the distracting scenes of a busy life, and by one unpractised in the art of composition.

Preface to *Historical memoirs of the Irish bards* (1786) by Joseph Cooper Walker,
great-great-grand-uncle of C. Garrett Walker,
chairman of Monkstown Finance Sub-committee, 1975–89

Old churches ... alone remain islands of calm in the seething roar of what we now call civilisation. They are not backwaters — or they shouldn't be, if the clergy and people love them — but strongholds ... A church isn't just an old building which interests pedantic brass-rubbers; but a living building with history written all over it and history that, with very little practice, becomes easy and fascinating reading.

Sir John Betjeman, patron of the Friends of Monkstown

*However interesting the church, it is only a building. Although it can be toured like a museum or an art gallery, everything in it should point towards heavenly things, because 'a church built with hands ... is the outward expression here on earth of that spiritual Church built of living stones, the bride of Christ ...
To enter therefore a Christian church is to enter none other than the House of God and the Gate of Heaven'.*

Ninian Cooper, *Of the atmosphere of a church*

History is the essence of innumerable biographies.

Thomas Carlyle

Foreword

For many centuries, as Étain Murphy has shown in this magnificent account of the history of Monkstown Church and parish, there has been a strong link with Christ Church Cathedral. In medieval times the cathedral priory had been one of the major landowners in Ireland — its granges (or farms) can still be seen in titles such as Dean's Grange and Grangegorman. The greater Monkstown area and the many parishes since formed from it are all part of the general southwards move of the city as the eighteenth century came to an end. Nineteenth-century innovation (the development of the port of Dunleary/Kingstown/Dun Laoghaire), the ease of travel provided by Ireland's first railway line, which ran through the parish, and the alleged health values of sea air for an increasingly prosperous middle class all ensured a rapid rise in population and the need for unprecedented church-building.

Interestingly, the rapid rise of Monkstown coincided with the rapid nineteenth-century decline of the fortunes of the cathedral. The move of the Four Courts from the cathedral precincts to Gandon's new building and the increasing disrepair of the fabric both increased its decline. Yet in that same period, at a time when the cathedral was falling into serious structural decay, and from which it was not saved until 1870, the daughter parish rebuilt its church on a new site and then enlarged it on a number of occasions. The link, of course, was essentially the right of the dean to appoint the perpetual curate of Monkstown. The position of dean of Christ Church, one of the wealthiest freeholds in Ireland, had in 1686 been given to support the poverty-stricken diocese of Kildare, the two offices to be held *in commendam*, and each successive bishop-dean continued to appoint each successive incumbent until the 1833 Church Temporalities Act. This added Kildare diocese to Dublin on the death of Bishop Lindsay in 1846 and gave the right of appointment to the archbishop. Disestablishment in 1871 abolished even this patronage and the cathedral's links with its prosperous daughter ceased.

This book, however, is far more than a history of church re-building. It bursts with vivid stories about the people of the parish — both laity and clergy — and the stories indicate that not all those eulogised on the many mural monuments were quite the knights in shining armour that their elegantly scripted memorials might have us believe. The author has done us a real favour by giving us history that includes warts and all.

Monkstown on the whole was a parish of the wealthy, with pew rents in operation until well into the twentieth century. Not that there was any shortage of poor Protestants in the parish. Indeed, we are told that at the reopening of the 1831 church there were 400 poor people who attended. There was even the establishment of a parish poor fund from which people of all denominations were supposed to be given aid. The author, late in the book indicates that Roman Catholics, as a percentage of the poor, may just possibly have received less than a percentage share of such funds. Today's splendid ecumenical relations with nearby St Patrick's are, however, a fine example of how things can change for the better.

Étain Murphy has done her parish great service in the writing of this history. It is not just a gripping read: it is more. She has meticulously uncovered even the minutest details concerning the people and places of the parish and has assembled them for us in a comprehensive volume that few parishes will be likely to be able to emulate. Both author and parish deserve our thanks.

John Paterson
Dean of Christ Church Cathedral
Dublin, 1 October 2003

Preface

Here's the church
And here's the steeple …
Traditional nursery rhyme

The name 'Monkstown' is first mentioned in 1539–40 at the time of the Dissolution of the Monasteries — ironically, just as the curtain fell on the monks' jurisdiction in Monkstown. Among the lands, possessions and revenues of St Mary's Abbey was the 'Villa de Caribrynan alias Monketon', or 'the town of Carrickbrennan alias Monkstown' (Gilbert 1884). The 'town of the monks' was aptly named since no less than *three* religious orders had determined its origins and growth. The 'white' Cistercians (of Monkstown Grange, or Castle) and the 'black' Canons Regular of St Augustine (of Holy Trinity Priory, the predecessor of Christ Church Cathedral), both from continental Europe, replaced the early Irish monks who had built the first little wooden church, dedicated to St Mochonna, as early as the sixth or seventh century at Carrickbrennan. The ruined stone church we see today in Carrickbrennan Graveyard was built on the original site.

The name 'Carrickbrennan' means 'Brennan's Rock'. Bishop Donnelly suggested that Brennan might be St Brendan ('Brendan the Navigator') because of the fact that St Brendan had a friend called Macud, who founded a church at Kilmacud nearby. Another suggestion was that Brennan may have been Broen, the king of Leinster, who ruled in *c.* 1052 (Donnelly 1907).

The little church at Carrickbrennan, or Monkstown, was to see cataclysmic changes both inside and outside its walls. Rebellions threatened it, successive rulers imposed their particular denominational stamps on its liturgy, while the ravages of time, neglect and vandalism assailed it.

The small area around the church in Monkstown has been affected to a greater or lesser extent by every turning point in the wider history of Ireland. Viking raids *may* have led the first monks to Carrickbrennan; Monkstown Castle was built in the wake of the Norman invasion and the arrival of the Cistercians; the Dissolution of the Monasteries and the Reformation saw frequent interruptions in ownership and allegiance; the 1641 uprising and subsequent Cromwellian invasion caused even more upheaval — and bloodshed. But in the middle of all this apparent chaos, the church survived somehow and continued to function and grow.

The stone church that had replaced the wooden one was virtually rebuilt in 1668. A new curate was appointed in 1670 and new registers begun. These are the earliest surviving records. As the surrounding population grew, Carrickbrennan Church was enlarged, with a new north–south aisle built in 1748. Within 40 years this building had become too small for the congregation and the decision was made to build a larger church on a different site. This 1789 church, located on the Dublin to Dunleary road (the present site), accommodated 340 worshippers. But within 40 years it was outgrown again — business was booming in the Dunleary area, the harbour was being built (with 1,000 labourers involved) and people from all walks of life were flooding into the new houses mushrooming up everywhere.

Thus this Georgian church was rebuilt during the years 1829 to 1831 by John Semple & Son, Architects, transforming the 'rectangular preaching box' to the 'Lusitanian marvel' that is our present church (De Breffny and Mott 1976). It was four times larger and could seat 1,200 worshippers.

The church in which people worship today is probably the fifth parish church of Monkstown. It was opened on Christmas Day 1831, which happened to fall on a Sunday. Because the church was an enlargement of the 1789 Georgian church, rather than a new building, it was not reconsecrated. As described in the *Evening Packet* of 31 December 1831:

> 'On Christmas Day, this splendid Church was opened for the celebration of divine worship — the former building having been found inadequate to contain one half the Protestant population of this extensive and rising parish … The Rev. Archdeacon Lindsay, Minister of the parish, preached; his text having been — "Lord, I have loved the habitation of thy House, and the place where thine honor dwelleth" — 26th psalm.
>
> 'The young gentlemen of the choir of Christ Church sang the Te Deum and Jubilate. A solo, by Master Dudgeon, "There were Shepherds abiding in the fields", produced a fine effect. We do not remember ever to have witnessed greater anxiety in worshipping the Lord, than the poorer brethren manifested on Sunday last, when they, for the first time during a period of three years, were accommodated properly; there were fully four hundred poor present. The Church was crowded in every part, and looked particularly well; it is modelled from the *moresco* style of *architecture,* and is well aired and comfortable. The greatest praises were bestowed on the Church-wardens, Fenton Hort and John Murphy, Esqrs., for their unremitting zeal and activity in the discharge of their important duties.'

'Open the doors — And here are the people'

Monkstown parishioners have played their part in the history of Ireland and of the world. They supported both sides of the Rebellion of 1798; they fought in the Peninsular War, at the battle of Waterloo, in the Crimea and during the Indian Mutiny. They emigrated and died during the Great Famine. They joined up in their dozens in the two world wars.

They have come from every walk of life, from the 'rich man in his castle' to 'the poor man at his gate'. The judge and the plaintiff, the sheriff and the bankrupt, the doctor and the patient, the soldier and the civilian, the minister and his congregation — all are here.

John Mapas tried to help the victims of the Famine. William Digges La Touche fought poverty and ignorance. The three Pim sisters tried to limit the ravages of leprosy. Lord Ranelagh set up the Blackrock Association to protect the civilian from footpads and highwaymen. Dr William Plant spent his life ministering to the poor and underprivileged sick of Monkstown and the surrounding area. The historian Charles Haliday spent much of his life trying to help the poor and died from an infection probably caught from one of them.

These people have left a remarkable legacy behind. Some of them were truly 'great' in the sense that, in some way, they changed the course of history. Had it not been for a Monkstown parishioner, Lieutenant Robert Oliver, the seventeen-year-old Francis Beaufort would have drowned in Portsmouth Harbour in 1791 and we would not have the Beaufort Scale of today, invented by him to measure wind speeds. The Mission to Lepers was founded from Monkstown by the three Pim sisters and inspired Mother Teresa of Calcutta to begin her work. Sir William Betham single-handedly was responsible for the preservation of a huge volume of Irish wills and archives, and for the setting up of the Public Record Office. The charity schools and societies founded or supported from Monkstown (from the Anti-duelling Society to the Society for Lending Musical Instruments to the Poor) have helped thousands over the years in ways that will never be known. The Monkstown Poor Fund saved hundreds of lives and eased the hardship of thousands more. Robert, Louisa and James Stewart willingly gave their lives and left an enduring influence on the educational and medical systems in China. The Rev. Billy Wynne, when incumbent of Monkstown, founded the Samaritans in the south of Ireland and ran the operation virtually on his own from 1959, which led to the opening of the Dublin Samaritan Branch in 1970; he also set up the 'Friendly Room' in the Knox Memorial Hall, a place of friendship and counselling that was years ahead of its time. Until recently, the church vaults provided a venue for the Parish Youth Club and later opened at lunchtime to feed the homeless. A Diocesan Employment Bureau operated from the Knox Hall for almost 20 years and found jobs for up to 1,000 people.

The parishioners of Monkstown were — and are — sinners as well as saints. Many were bigoted and intolerant, like Sir Harcourt Lees; some were dishonest frauds, like Sir John Lees; and Sir Robert Day's judgement on a prisoner in 1798 seems harsh and inhumane to us today. For better or worse, they have all left us some part of themselves in Monkstown. This is their story and the story of their church — all part of our common heritage.

Étain Murphy
Monkstown
September 2003

A note on style and usage

Piecing together the story of Monkstown Church was like doing an old jigsaw puzzle since many of the key documents are either lost or missing. Chief among these are the Vestry minutes for the formative years of 1778–1804 (when the Georgian church was built) and from June 1829 right through to 1870 (when Semple's church was being planned and completed, and when McCurdy's chancel was added). This made the task of filling in the gaps more difficult and many circuitous routes were taken. Most of these were dead ends, while others, unpromising at first, yielded valuable information which, when weighed against other sources, produced a clearer picture of events. I have attempted to try and follow the example set by Professor John Oulton, former incumbent of Monkstown, in whose work, in the words of Dr George O. Simms, 'every point was verified, references were fully provided, evidence was never strained'. I have done my best to ensure the accuracy of the text, but any mistakes remaining are my responsibility alone.

I have used the name 'Dunleary' where the text refers to the town before 1821, 'Kingstown' for the town from 1821 (when it was renamed to mark the visit of George IV) to 1920, and 'Dun Laoghaire' for the town since 1920.

There are many quotations in the text, taken from the Vestry minutes of Monkstown and other churches, letters, newspapers and documents. The original spelling and punctuation have been reproduced, except in cases where an obvious or misleading error has occurred. I have used the convention of round brackets to fill in a missing word or words for the sense and flow of a passage, while square brackets are used to provide an explanation or additional information.

For those readers who may be unfamiliar with the pre-decimal system, pounds (£), shillings (denoted by 's') and pence (denoted by 'd') were the denominations used up to 1972. There were 12 pence (12d) in one shilling (1s or 1/-) and 20 shillings (20s) in one pound (£1). Since quoting from old documents, this nomenclature is used throughout the text.

I have attempted to explain technical terms as they arise in the text, rather than referring the reader to a glossary. Also, to avoid distracting footnotes, I have arranged all the notes (numbered in the text) in a section at the back of the book, called 'Endnotes'.

The Select Bibliography contains details of the sources used, including published and unpublished works, archive material, websites, and the newspapers and journals of the day.

Acknowledgements

The original idea for this book came from the Rev. Stephen Neill, who suggested it while curate of Monkstown in 1994 and then left the following year without realising what he had unleashed.

Full of optimism in my new venture, I visited Dr Michael Ryan, director of the Chester Beatty Library, in order to show him some of my early work. In about twenty minutes he had expertly brought me down to earth, signed a form recommending associate membership of the Royal Irish Academy and sent me on my way with these words ringing in my ears: 'Facts! Facts! Facts!' As a result, I scrapped everything I had already written and began afresh, with Dr Ryan's mantra as my inspiration.

This book would not have been written but for the many old and new friends whom I have been privileged to meet through my research — in person, by letter, on the telephone or in cyberspace. Possibly more than anyone else, I am greatly indebted to Roger Hill for his quiet encouragement and for repeatedly pointing my research in the right directions.

I am especially grateful to the individual members of the Select Vestry for their interest, support and great generosity, without which this book would not have been published. In particular, I would like to thank the Rev. Kevin Dalton for his encouragement throughout the project and for allowing me access to all relevant material.

I would also like to thank the Heritage Council for their flexibility and generous financial assistance for this publication.

I cannot thank John Paterson enough. At a time when he was supposed to be 'off duty' in his capacity as dean of Christ Church, owing to recuperation after illness, he agreed to write the Foreword, which necessitated reading the manuscript. Not only did he meet the deadline but he also checked the text in detail and saved me from making some thoughtless mistakes. Any remaining errors are mine alone.

I am indebted to Michael Merrigan whose enthusiastic ten-week genealogy course opened the doors of the main Dublin repositories to me and taught me how to find my way around them. I was welcomed into the Maritime Museum by the late Robbie Brennan, shown the historic registers of St Iberius, Wexford, by John Bayley and allowed into Carrickbrennan Graveyard by its diligent caretaker, Pat Walsh.

Monkstown opened the door to new experiences and delights: Betty Balcombe and her daughter, Amanda, kindly organised an exhilarating trip to Church Island (Inis Patrick), with Ray, Owen and Conor McGonagle; Brian Coleman invited me to a wreath-laying ceremony in Mount Jerome on the centenary of the death of George Fitzgerald, neglected scientist and son of a Monkstown rector; Br Cornelius Horgan showed me around St Helen's, York Road, Dun Laoghaire, the 'Fairyland' home of John Semple, Senior, architect of Monkstown Church.

I am grateful to the following, who are experts in their own field and who have been open-handed with their help and advice: Tom Burke (the Royal Dublin Fusiliers); Dr Maurice Craig (the architecture of John Semple); Trevor Crowe (the history of the organ); Stephen Devaney (historical and architectural technical advice and digital reprocessing of certain old prints, photographs and maps); Patrick Farrell (John Semple and his churches); Prof. Padraig Ó Riain and Dr Ailbhe Mac Shamhrain (early Irish hagiography); Gerald O'Carroll (Judge Robert Day); and Dr Michael Wynne (Irish stained glass).

I am indebted to the following people who allowed me to use their work: Cormac Allen, Ann Brady, Rob Goodbody, William Morgan, W.J. Smyly, C. Garrett Walker and Ronnie Wallace.

I must thank the following for their invaluable help: Tom Aplin, Stephen Devaney, Violet and Ronnie Elder, Canon Adrian Empey, Jarlath Glynn, Mr David Lane, Dr Gerald Morgan, Shirley O'Brien, J.J. O'Connor, Ré Ó Laighléis, Mr R.K.C. (Dickie) and Mrs Pilkington, Evelyn and William Richardson, the Rev. Patrick Semple, Mrs Una Semple, Mary Stuart, Diane Swift and the Rev. Jack Teggin.

I would have remained ignorant of many sources and documents were it not for Colm Breathnach (the Harbour Commissioners' files); Frieda Carroll (Mrs Jordan and her family); Prof. Davis Coakley (the Graves family); Patrick Cronin (Trinity History Workshop on World War I); the Rev. Kevin Dalton (letter from Sir John Betjeman); Mr William Ebbs (organs); Roger Hill (Brian Bolger papers, Scalé's edition of Rocque's map); Philip Lecane (Henshaw's *The sky their battlefield*); Dr Freddy O'Dwyer (Cormac Allen's thesis); Rachel and Henry Pollard (newspaper references to Monkstown); Celestine Rafferty (Lacy's *Sights and scenes of our fatherland*); Prof. David and Mrs Margaret Ride (Arthur Stewart's autobiography); John Stafford (the location of the Knox family tree); Canon Albert Stokes (the work of Gerald O'Carroll on Judge Day); and Mrs Cecil Wynne (Billy Wynne and the Samaritans).

I have been able to include photographs and illustrations, many previously unpublished, through the help and generosity of Carole Cullen; Janet Cooke (the senior class of Monkstown School); Julian Deale (the visit of George IV); Dr Desmond de Courcy-Wheeler (Monkstown Hospital); Stephen Ferguson (John Lees); Margaret Garrett (Louisa Stewart); Pauline Holland (John Lees); Liz Neill-Watson (Monkstown parish); Mr Michael Pegum (War Memorial windows); Mrs Elizabeth Sharp-Paul (the Dowse family); Dr Philip Crampton Smyly (Smyly and Stewart families); and the late Brian Taylor and Mrs Phyllis Taylor (Miss Edith Dowse). Brian Carnegie must be especially commended for his enthusiastic tracking down and identification of the 'Class of '59' (*see p. 221*).

I must also thank Dr Anthony Harvey, Roger Hill, Dr Susan Hood, Dr Fergus O'Ferrall, John Quin and David Quin for reading the manuscript and for their constructive suggestions and advice. In particular, I must single out David for his encouragement and skilful corrections of my early attempts, which gave me the confidence to continue.

As a 'blow-in' of only twelve years, I was not that familiar with Monkstown, but this was amply compensated for by the reminiscences of the late Ronnie Blay, Ken Bray and Miss Edith Dowse.

I would like to thank Mr Arthur Ogilvie and Tommy Walsh for their artistic expertise in photographing Monkstown Church.

It was always a pleasure to visit Nick Maxwell and his talented team at Wordwell in the run-up to publication. I am grateful to Nick, Niamh, Rachel, Emer and Andrew for their unfailing help and unruffled good humour while working towards a tight deadline.

I owe an enormous debt of gratitude to Carole Devaney for her huge input into this book over and above what should be expected of any editor. Her scrupulous attention to detail and sympathetic editing transformed my original text.

I should also like to thank the staff of the Civic Museum, Cork Public Museum, Dúchas, Dun Laoghaire Library, the Gilbert Library, the Irish Architectural Archive, the Library of the Royal College of Physicians of Ireland, Marsh's Library, the National Archives, the National Library, the Office of Public Works, the Religious Society of Friends Library, the Representative Church Body Library, the Royal Irish Academy, Trinity College Library and Richview Library (Architecture) at University College, Dublin.

Finally, I cannot thank my own family enough. Raymond has been an extraordinary tower of strength throughout these past nine years. He has been constantly supportive of his preoccupied wife, in spite of a heroic struggle to prevent his eyes glazing over when Monkstown Church came up in conversation. I dedicate this book to him. Meanwhile, my children — Sinéad, Catherine, Edward, Susanna, Madeleine and Alexandra — undemandingly allowed their mother to indulge what they considered to be her rather strange pastime.

What they have said about Monkstown Church

It is a characteristic evil habit of smart Dublin people to be Heaven-born critics
of architecture as of other arts of which they are particularly ignorant.
Sir Thomas Drew, 1899

When Semple's Monkstown was completed in 1831, in its spectacular position at the end of Monkstown Road, people were utterly bemused. This type of architecture was completely outside their experience. People either loved it or hated it — everyone had an opinion. The following gives a taste of 'what they said' at the time.

The 'amused'

A satirical poem in 1832 by Nicholson Numskull, in his *Essay on the rise and progress of architectural taste in Dublin*, suggested the inspiration for Monkstown Church:

> Time honoured Semple! are you blam'd alone,
> Or is this pile the dandy sheriff's own;
> This *tasteless frittered* fane — some people say —
> That seated at the board on Lord Mayor's day,
> Ere first the civic chain adorned his breast
> When dining with 'their honours' and the rest,
> A *pastry* ornament was plac'd on high,
> The pride of cooks — admir'd by every eye;
> He caught the *sweet* idea — hastened home,
> And there designed a what! — a moorish dome!
> Semple, thy genius left thee in the lurch
> When that design was made for *Monkstown Church*.

A woman's magazine of the day, *The Lady of the House*, wrote on 15 February 1909, 'We have heard Monkstown Church irreverently called the "Sponge Cake", owing to the likeness between its much crocketed exterior and the old-fashioned sponge cake made in a mould'.

The church organist, B. Warburton Rooke, in a lecture in 1923 recalled, 'We have constantly heard it called the cruet stand [a stand for holding bottles with stoppers, containing oil, vinegar, etc. for the table] and even the sponge cake'.

The 'not amused'

The *Dublin Penny Journal* of 12 July 1834 of gave a detailed, but biting, description of the new church:

'It is difficult to fix on the order of architecture of the present gorgeous edifice, it is *sui generis*; outside it looks somewhat of a *mule* between the Gothic and the Saracenic: the steeple is surmounted by a cross, but the minarets have something of the crescent, though on the whole it has not an unpleasing effect.

'The interior is of the oddest *fancy*, we will not call it *taste*. — It is of plaster made to represent immense blocks of granite, and even *the galleries* !! are of the same character, *to keep the congregation in awe*, we suppose. Immense blocks are represented ready to tumble on their heads, and crush them to atoms. Were they really granite, no earthly power could prevent the attraction of gravity from pulling them from their places. Perhaps the architect, as the whole inside is in the Arabesque style, wished, by the position of these ponderous blocks, to give the idea of the Prophet's tomb suspended in the air.

'Altogether, we never saw a greater perversion of judgement and taste, than is displayed throughout the entire building. Many other equally preposterous defects will at once strike an attentive observer — there is not a spot in the church where the eye can rest without pain. From the cross-lights behind the pulpit, *where there should be no light*, is a large window of three divisions, so that it is impossible to see the preacher; and under, and in the recess of the same window, the space is occupied by a curious sort of falling roof, *somewhat like the top of a cow-shed, with battlements* in the front!'

John D'Alton, in his 1838 book *The history of County Dublin*, wrote: 'A modern church, striking in its distant aspect, but faulty in its details, announced Monkstown … The interior … presents a grotesque, heavy and miscellaneous aspect.'

When a new chancel was suggested in 1857, a 'parishioner' wrote to *Saunders's News-Letter* (25 September 1857 issue), saying 'I noticed in your journal a proposal to enlarge and alter this beautiful church, so much admired by every stranger. Would it not be much better to build a new one in the locality?' Another 'parishioner' promptly wrote (in the 30 September issue), 'To anyone even slightly acquainted with the principles of church architecture, (Monkstown Church) cannot but appear simply hideous; and being built in defiance of those acknowledged principles, it is notoriously ill adapted for a larger congregation'.

The *Irish Ecclesiastical Gazette* of 20 March 1880 (before Drew's refurbishment of the chancel and the raising of the galleries) reported:

'We cannot say that we admire it as a whole, or think its style suitable for a Christian place of worship; but, anyhow, there it stands, it must be admitted, an imposing piece of architecture, and capable of holding about a thousand persons …

'Having (spoken) of the outside … we come to speak of the interior, and here we cannot praise as we would wish. On entering, one does not well know where to turn as being north, south, east or west. Each of the transepts seems as much the east as that which has the Holy Table. There are also deep galleries perched up close to the ceiling, under which we should be sorry to sit on a close summer's day. And as for the walls — we fancied ourselves inside Glasnevin or Mount Jerome mortuary chapels. We have seen many churches, churches dating centuries back, but we never saw any with the walls studded over to an equal extent with those sad memorials of the departed worthies of the place. Monkstown Parish must have been one of the most exceptionally favoured places in the world if all that is carved upon those stones be true!'

Again, the *Irish Ecclesiastical Gazette* of 14 January 1898 had this to say:

'Monkstown church … is said to combine sumptuousness with oddity more than probably any other ecclesiastical edifice in the empire … Monkstown Church will always retain a quaintness of its own, which we should be sorry to see it lose, and with the new galleries just finished [they had just been raised by several feet], it possesses all that modern taste and comfort demand in the interior; while externally it forms a conspicuous and interesting, if perhaps curious-looking object, on the main road from Dublin, on the east side of the village, facing an open space locally termed the "Place de la Concorde".'

Francis Elrington Ball, in his *A history of the County Dublin* (1902–20), did not mince his words: '(It) continued the parish church until superseded, about 1832, by the present grotesque structure'. In similar vein, D.A. Chart, in his *The story of Dublin* (1907), says, 'Here we have a church of singular not to say grotesque architecture, adorned with curious little pinnacles, the rounded curves of which recall the familiar pawn at chess, while the late Sir Thomas Drew declared that he couldn't worship in Monkstown Church because if the galleries were true to their pretensions, they should fall'. Weston St John Joyce, in *The neighbourhood of Dublin* (1912), deplored 'the nondescript edifice (which) disfigures its site …'

The impressed

In the October 1835 issue of *The Architectural Magazine,* London, a certain 'R.V. Worcester' wrote, in the 'Queries and Answers' section:

'There are some Buildings in Ireland that I was highly pleased with, one in particular, a modern church near Kingstown Moneton, or Monefort [Monkstown]. I had not time to sketch it, but doubt not you have some Dublin correspondent who will do so, and send it, with a description, to the *Architectural Magazine,* as it appears to me to be well worthy of a place there.'

In the December issue of the same journal, another writer replied:

'Buildings in Ireland — I quite agree with your correspondent, R.V., in his admiration of the church near Kingstown, having been equally struck by the originality and beauty of its style'.

In 1836, the 'Domestic Notices, Ireland' section of *The Architectural Magazine* (Vol. III) stated:

'Fig. 208 is the elevation of Monkstown Church, close to Kingstown … which is built of granite in uncoursed rubble. The exterior of this church is remarkably rough, but the interior is groined and plastered in imitation of granite. Both these edifices are from the designs of _____ Temple, Esq., architect to the First Fruits for the province of Leinster …' ('Temple' here is obviously a misprint for 'Semple', as he and his son were the diocesan architects to the Board of First Fruits during the years 1824–34.)

Meanwhile, the British *Building News* of 1857 called Monkstown Church Semple's 'chef d'oeuvre' and advised against tampering with his masterpiece.[1]

The admirers

The architectural historian Maurice Craig, in his book *Dublin 1660–1860* (1992), said of the church that

> 'scholarship and orthodox notions of scale are flung to the winds, but not constructional integrity … the astonishing example at Monkstown, facing up Monkstown Road, adorned with towers and turrets for all the world like chessmen …'

Sir John Betjeman always admired Monkstown Church; indeed, he became the patron of the Friends of Monkstown Church when the scheme was set up in 1974. In an address given to Church of Ireland clergymen in 1943 on *Fabrics of the Church of Ireland*, he spoke enthusiastically of 'Monkstown Church, laughed at today, a source of wonder and admiration tomorrow, for its originality and romantic outline' (Lycett-Green 1997). Again, in the 1958 *Monkstown Review*, he wrote how Semple's work

> 'now seems bold, modern, vast and original … I think Semple's idea was to provide a striking general skyline and an arresting termination to the roads that lead to his church. It was to be a cheerful Irish castle with a seaside rather than a fortress flavour. Why I like one building and not another I cannot always say. But in a life spent looking at buildings, the bold turrets so suited in their mouldings and terminations to the beautiful granite of which they are constructed, the plain walls with their deeply splayed window openings and the solid-looking base of the whole building make Monkstown Church one of my first favourites for its originality of detail and proportion … Only today is the original genius of Semple beginning to be appreciated.'

In his article 'South Dublin revisited' in the February 1959 issue of *Focus*, W.J. Grey described how

> 'Nelson-period terraces led the eye straight to the Portuguese Gothic of Monkstown Parish Church. The years between dropped away. I saw it now as first I knew it: its curious biretta-crowned walls pale beige in the declining light, its narrow portcullis windows gleaming bronzely athwart the last of the trees which framed its central tower. It stands in my mind as the lodestone of

the period evocations of this part of South Dublin.'

Brian de Breffny and George Mott, in their *The churches and abbeys of Ireland* (1976), wrote:

'John Semple … was unaffected by the current movement towards orthodoxy and historicism in Gothic buildings. His work is at once accomplished and highly original. Semple's eccentricity is by no means a mere urge to startle; his stranger designs were a real *tour de force* combining uncommon engineering skills, intellectual curiosity and aesthetic sensitivity … Semple's Monkstown is a glorious extravaganza; it would be less amazing if it were in Portugal than in alien majesty in the middle of genteel Monkstown. The retired judges and conservative ladies and gentlemen who worshipped there must have felt out of place inside their Lusitanian marvel, the subject of much criticism.'

Douglas Scott Richardson, in Volume I of his *Gothic Revival architecture in Ireland* (1983), stated:

'The last of Semple's churches is … the most majestic of all … Semple apparently removed the side walls of the old church in the last three bays to the east and built two huge transepts. He built these of Dalkey granite and recased the remnant of the old church in the same material, completely metamorphosing its appearance in the process. What emerged was an enormous T-shaped church with the orientation preserved on what was now the short axis of the building and a broad frontage spread magnificently across the vista in the fork at the end of Monkstown Road.'

Richardson describes the exterior in some detail and then turns to the interior:

'The interior is dominated by its stupefying ceilings. Enormous fan vaults fill the transepts and crossing, while the west arm has a plainer ceiling. Fortunately, the scheme of the painted plaster was preserved in the alterations of 1862 (and even extended into the new, matching chancel), although the rust-coloured stripes are distinctly High Victorian and must date from that period.

'We again glimpse the Sublime — with its immensity, its abrupt changes in scale and its delight in terror — in the interior. The *Dublin Penny Journal* was sensitive to this but did not like it … [Richardson quotes the passage above, of 12 July 1834] What bothered the writer was not that the vaults were plaster — that would be the reaction of a Victorian realist a decade later. It was rather the lack of apparent support.

'Semple eliminated almost all the structural and ornamental detailing of fan vaults, whether stone or plaster, apart from four giant corbels and some much smaller ones in juxtaposition. To achieve a more spectacular effect he concentrated on the overall shape, not the component part. There is a voluptuous quality to his massive fan vaults. He loved these forms for their fullness, heaviness, and pendulousness. Unlike [Francis] Johnston, he was not interested in the surface decorations. Semple reduced all that to a few radiating lines at the bottom of the fans and then his attention jumped across the smooth planes to a few concentric wavy bands at the upper edges. He showed his utter

'A glorious extravaganza' or 'a mule between the Gothic and the Saracenic'? Monkstown Church, pictured here in c. 1940, dominates the village and its surroundings in this designated Architectural Conservation Area.

disdain for the correct minutiae of Gothic by inserting the acanthus leaves of Neo-Classical furniture-makers around the strange orifices in his fan vaults.

'As the *Dublin Penny Journal* noted in the review just quoted, "even the galleries !! are of the same character". A series of hairpin forms under a separate arcading decorates the gallery fronts. These lines sweep from one side to the other with constantly changing inclination as if they took their origin from some point well beneath the floor of the church. Yet visually they connect with the elements at the centres and edges of the fan vaults above.

'What results is an interior of forms as arbitrary, abstract and homogeneous as those of the exterior. They are equally pulsating, radiant and vibrant …

'He [Semple] tried to produce a new Gothic by analytic means, observing Gothic structure, stripping it down, and enlarging certain details to a new scale … Semple's designs are the result of the selective subtraction of elements, and their austerity is one of abstention, not deprivation. [His] output undoubtedly influenced Irish architects for many years.'

M.J. McDermott, in the September/October 1990 issue of the *Irish Architect* on 'The Semples', wrote:

'Although Monkstown Church is more conventional, its size and character makes it, externally, more expressive than St. Mary's ("the Black Church"). It owes much to the tall central tower, and serrated skyline of battlements, turrets and pinnacles which make it not only a well-known landmark but a striking example of what used to be called "Carpenter's Gothic". Like the "Black Church", its originality may perhaps be regarded as Semple's free adaptation of an imported style.'

The fond

Other, more personal impressions exist, like those of Kenneth Bray, son of William Bray (the sexton during 1928–56). He recalls how he spent most of his youth

'on top of the church catching pigeons to keep as pets. At that time — late '40s, early '50s — my father was the Sexton, so access to the church roof was a daily routine to feed and catch the pigeons. I suppose in my own way and without knowing it, I kept the pigeon population under control until that strict disciplinarian, the Rev. Arthur Butler, found out and ordered the access trap to be locked. Of course, my father had a key, so nothing changed! Except it was then nightly visits for catching instead of during the day. I still have racing pigeons today and some race from the South of France to their lofts here'.[2]

Sir John Betjeman

29, Radnor Walk,
London, SW3 4BP

9.1.81

Dear Rector,

It is very refreshing to hear from Monkstown, the Brighton of Ireland, whose Parish Church like a huge chessman dominates the Dublin sky. I love the building inside and out and I am glad it is 150. Do you remember how marvellous it used to look from the top of a tram as it bulked on the horizon? Only Tallaght and Rathmines (IC) equalled it, though the Black Church was the strangest of all Semple's buildings.

I am afraid I must now tell you I can't trust myself to travelling long distances so cannot come to your celebrations.

Yours sincerely,

[signature]

Letter from Sir John Betjeman to the Rev. Kevin Dalton, dated January 1981, about the 150th anniversary celebrations for the opening of Semple's church in Monkstown.

A more recent view is given by Carole Cullen, a parishioner and member of the Choir. As an artist, she has many reasons for loving Monkstown Church, not least its colours and the small details that tell their own story:

'The inspired geography of the church, centred at the end of Monkstown Road, with the evening light gilding its mellow stonework — this sight delights and refreshes me on driving home, traffic-weary, at the end of the day. There is a feeling of tranquillity and spirituality experienced when worshipping in the church. The decorative detailing inspired by the Arts and Crafts Movement — the red and green marble 'buttons' of the stone flowers decorating the pulpit; the chancel panels with their paintings of pomegranates, passion flowers, sheaves of wheat, purple grapes, lilies and green olives; the off-white, duck-egg blue, terracotta red and gold organ pipes. Walk up to the balconies on elegant spiral staircases. Examine closely the filigree lamp roses in the soaring vaulted ceilings, plastered in authentic shades of beige, umber and ochre. Enjoy the little white enamel dishes designed to collect droplets of rain from Victorian umbrellas. Kneel on remnants of Turkish carpets that once covered the floorboards of the grand villas of Monkstown. These are but a few of the reasons why I am fond of Monkstown Parish Church.'

PART 1:
EARLY HISTORY OF MONKSTOWN

CHAPTER 1

Origins of Monkstown

According to the grace of God which is given unto me,
as a wise masterbuilder, I have laid the foundation,
and another buildeth thereon.
I Corinthians 3:10

The event 'Monkstown 1200' was celebrated on Saturday 26 September 1998 as a Village Day to commemorate the coming of the monks to Monkstown. The highlight of the day was when President Mary McAleese, as guest of honour, went to the Coal Harbour in Dun Laoghaire. There, she greeted the 'monks' who had just arrived by sea from Inis Patrick, a small island off Skerries, to the north of Dublin. A short ecumenical service was held at the quayside, in which all three Monkstown churches were represented (St Patrick's Roman Catholic Church, the Friends' Meeting House and Monkstown Parish Church). Later, the president spoke from the steps of Monkstown Church and presented prizes for the Children's Art Competition. Festivities continued, with 'monks' and 'Vikings' mingling with the crowd afterwards, as stalls, jugglers, model railway exhibition and puppet show vied for attention.

The monks of Inis Patrick

In the aftermath of 'Monkstown 1200', every schoolchild in the parish had supposedly become an authority on its history. Each could tell you that Monkstown was 1,200 years old, having been founded in AD 798 by monks who had made their way in currachs from Inis Patrick, fleeing from Vikings who had just ransacked their monastery. The monks brought with them the bones of their founder, St Mochonna, and established a new church there, dedicated to the saint.

But this particular school of thought, or slight variations on it, has only existed for less than a hundred years. Is it fact or fiction? If we examine the Annals of Ulster, we find the following statement:

Anno domini dcc xc uii:
Combustio inse Patraicc o genntibh, ⁊ borime na cric do breith, ⁊ scrin Doconna do briseadh doaibh, ⁊ innreda mara doaib cene, eitir Erinn ⁊ Albain.

3

President Mary McAleese speaking from the steps of the south transept on the occasion of 'Monkstown 1200', celebrated on 26 September 1998. (From left to right) 'Monks' from Inis Patrick (Michael Johnson, Joe Buckley, Fergus Merriman); Fr Maurice O'Moore of St Patrick's Roman Catholic Church; Kevin O'Sullivan, County Manager of Dun Laoghaire County Council; the Rev. Kevin Dalton of Monkstown Parish Church; and (seated) Donal Swift, joint organiser of event.

Translated, this means 'AD 797: Burning of Inis Patrick by Gentiles; and they carried off the preys of the districts; and the shrine of Dochonna was broken by them; and other great devastations [were committed] by them both in Ireland and Scotland.' (The Annals of Ulster are actually a year out; the correct date is AD 798, according to Dr Ailbhe Mac Shamhráin.) Thus it is recorded that the Vikings plundered the island monastery of Inis Patrick, torched its wooden buildings and broke the reliquary of Dochonna, its sixth-century founder. It does not say whether any of the monks survived the attack and there is no mention of a flight to Monkstown.

In the nineteenth and early twentieth centuries, well-known historians such as Ball (1902), Joyce (1912) and D'Alton (1838) wrote books about Dublin and its suburbs, including sections on the history of Monkstown. Monkstown itself had at least two keen amateur local historians: its organist, Bartholomew Warburton Rooke, who gave 'magic lantern' illustrated lectures on the local history, and its 'Jack of all trades', Alexander Downs, who worked variously as an undertaker, estate agent, coal-merchant, insurance agent, local postmaster and shipping agent for Cunard.[1] These historians reckoned that one of two religious orders had founded Monkstown — either the Canons Regular of St Augustine of Holy Trinity Priory (who served Monkstown Church) or the Cistercians of St Mary's Abbey (who had their grange at what we now call Monkstown Castle). The popular opinion was that the Cistercians were the founding fathers of Monkstown.

The evidence, however, suggests that these two orders were not the first religious to come to Monkstown since it has a pre-Norman foundation, thus pre-dating both. This means that the story of the Inis Patrick monks, fleeing in 798, is a possibility. As far as can be ascertained, the first person who propounded the theory (and he did stress that it was only a theory) was Bishop Nicholas Donnelly, who wrote histories of nearly all the Dublin parishes, published in 1907. He wrote rather tentatively: 'It may be that some of the Monks [from Inis Patrick], escaping across the bay, put in at Carrickbrennan, and settling down there, dedicated their church to their holy Patron'.

Bishop Donnelly knew that the old church in Carrickbrennan Graveyard, dating from the sixth or seventh century, was dedicated to Mochonna. He made the reasonable suggestion that the monks of Inis Patrick might have fled to Monkstown, where they founded another church dedicated to their original founder. He obviously regarded 'Dochonna' of Inis Patrick and 'Mochonna' of Monkstown as one and the same person.

The next time the story appeared in print, Donnelly's theory had become more substantial. The Rev. Albert E. Stokes in his book *Where monks walked*, published in 1950, wrote: 'One dark night we see the old Irish monks slipping out of Skerries in a currach, bringing with them the bones of the old Saint, St Mochonna, who had founded their monastery … Round the coast they came to the little creek at Dun Leary … Up the valley we can see them coming … until they reach a spot … in what is now known as Old Monkstown Graveyard, where they set up their monastery once more. They dedicated their church to St Mochonna, but popularly it was known as Carrickbrennan Chapel.'

Some years later, this story was reiterated by the Rev. Vincent Quilter, parish priest of St Patrick's Roman Catholic Church in Monkstown, included in a short history of Carrickbrennan and its graveyard (English 1987): 'It would appear that some of the monks escaped across Dublin Bay and put in at Carrickbrennan, where they were afforded the security of Laoghaire's Fort … Having reached Carrickbrennan, the monks resettled their monastery and built a church … They dedicated the new church to St Mochonna, their founder, but despite this it came to be known popularly as Carrickbrennan Church.'

The story has been retold in later publications, sometimes with embellishments or even marked differences from the original. For example, the date has been advanced to AD 900 (instead of AD 798), Mochonna has been incorrectly called 'Mochannta' and he even accompanies his monks to Monkstown (although he had been dead for 200 years by that

The three churches of Monkstown today — the Friends' Meeting House (Quakers, designed by Papworth, built 1832) in foreground, St Patrick's Roman Catholic Church (designed by Pugin and Ashlin, built 1866) and Monkstown Parish Church (designed by Semple & Son, built 1831).

The east coast of Ireland, as it is today, showing the island monastery of Inis Patrick off Skerries, the great monastic settlement of Glendalough in County Wicklow and the parish of Monkstown, south of Dublin.

time). The only writer I have come across who mentions searching for documentation that might support the original assumption is Kathleen Turner. In her 1983 book, *If you seek monuments: a guide to the antiquities of the Barony of Rathdown*, she relates the received wisdom on the story of the monks who fled from Inis Patrick, but does add, in a footnote, 'I have not been able to trace the source of this'.

On the available evidence, therefore, we cannot assume that the monks of Inis Patrick founded Monkstown. But we do know of two, perhaps isolated, events — first, the burning of the monastery on Inis Patrick and the theft and breaking open of Dochonna's shrine there, and secondly the founding of a church at Carrickbrennan dedicated to St Mochonna. On the first, we have the account in the Annals of Ulster mentioned above. In addition, the Annals of the Four Masters relate 'The age of Christ, 793 … Inispadraig was burned by foreigners, and they bore away the shrine of Dochonna', while the Annals of Clonmacnoise record 'the breaking of Dochonna's shryne by them'.

On the second event — the founding of a church at Carrickbrennan dedicated to St Mochonna — this church was first mentioned as such in about 1294 when, in a taxation of the diocese of Dublin, it was stated that the 'temporalities [property] of the monks at Kylmohennok [Kill Mohonnóc] waste, and of same monks at Karrygbrekane [Carrickbrennan] nothing on account of war' (McEnery and Refaussé 2001).[2] (Kill Mohonnóc means 'the church of Mohonnóc', or Mo Chonnóc or Mochonna, as we shall see.) In 1577, in one of Elizabeth I's fiants, or decrees, the church was described as the 'Church of St Mochonna of the Grange of Carrickbrennan, alias Monkstown, County Dublin'.

Although the first mention of St Mochonna's Church was in about 1294, it is fairly safe to assume that Carrickbrennan was a pre-Norman foundation (established before the Norman invasion in 1172 and the coming of the monastic orders from the Continent) because it was dedicated to an *Irish* saint. Similarly, there are other pre-Norman ecclesiastical sites in south Dublin (some seventeen in all, in the half-barony of Rathdown) with eleventh- or twelfth-century stone churches mostly dedicated to sixth- or seventh-century Irish saints, such as Kill-of-the-Grange (St Fintain), Dalkey (St Begnet), Tully (St Brigid) and Killiney (Iníon Léinín). This would indicate that many of these ancient churches, including that at Carrickbrennan, were built on the sites of earlier foundations, dating from the seventh century or earlier (O'Brien 1988).

Of saints and cults

Before coming to any conclusion about the monks of Inis Patrick and their connection with Monkstown, a brief digression is needed to explain some of the background of monastic Ireland in Early Christian times. Among the interesting aspects is the proliferation of cults devoted to saints, whose names could get changed, sometimes radically, over the centuries — a fact on which even scholars of the subject differ widely.

From the time of St Patrick, an episcopal church (one based on bishops), like the Roman system, existed in Ireland. But from quite an early date there was also a great surge towards monasticism in the Irish church. This was widespread, affecting whole families and communities. According to the secular law, inherited land had to be kept in the family, yet many wealthy families gave their lands to found monasteries. The law was circumvented by founding a monastery, endowing it with land and then choosing the first head of the church, or abbot, from among the donor family, who soon became the founding saint. Successive heads of churches usually belonged either to the family of the land-donor or to the patron of the church, and thus began a hereditary system. (Interestingly, one Irish term for the head of a church was *comarba*, which means 'heir'.) In some cases, different family groups, or dynasties, attempted to take over from ecclesiastical lineages. The larger monastic settlements, such as Glendalough or Clonmacnoise, were attractive prizes.

It was important to have written genealogies for the founding saints so that the relationships of future potential abbots could be checked. However, some of these genealogies were 'cooked' in order to prove the apparent entitlement of a particular dynasty to the abbacy. Ireland is unique in western Christendom in the antiquity and number of these genealogies.

As monasteries became larger, small groups of monks (thought to be thirteen in number, symbolising Jesus and his twelve disciples) were sent off to found communities of their own. The mother-house kept in touch with its offspring, which belonged to its *familia,* or federation of monasteries. Every few years, the chief abbot would visit all his daughter-churches. This helped to strengthen links between communities, besides being a way of collecting tribute and reminding them of the presence and importance of the parent monastery.

As we have already seen, the name of the founding saint associated with Inis Patrick and with Monkstown seems to be slightly different. 'Dochonna' seems to be associated with Inis Patrick, while 'Mochonna' occurs in Monkstown. But it is clear from hagiographical sources (the study of the saints) that the names Mo-Chonna, Do-Chonna, Mo-Chonnoc (and others) were used interchangeably.

The linguistic derivation is simple: *mo* and *do* mean 'my' and 'your', respectively, in Irish; placing *mo* or *do* in front of a name such as Conna changes it to Mo Chonna and Mochonna, or Do Chonna and Dochonna — a pet-name form of Conna. The original name of a saint often went through a bewildering variety of forms.

Professor Padraig Ó Riain of the Department of Early and Medieval Irish in University College, Cork, has some startling ideas on this subject. His arguments would make us rethink all our assumptions, if we have any, about Mochonna. Plucking his evidence from a labyrinth of early Irish texts, Ó Riain suggests that Mochonna was none other than one of Ireland's most important saints — Columcille (Ó Riain 1983).

It seems that only 100 years after he died, Columcille was called by a plethora of different names. Some sounded like Columcille, but many did not. Ó Riain's list includes Cainneac, Colmán, Cumma(e), Come, Commae, Coimme, Caimme, Cuimmíne, Mocholmóc, Mochommóc, Mochumma(e), Conna(e), Canna, Cunnu, Coinne, Cainne, Cuinne, Mochonne, Mochonna, Dochonna, Mochonóc, Conóc, Cainneóc and Cainnech. These are what are academically called hypocoristic (or pet-name) forms of the name 'Columcille'.

It is thought that these name variations could have developed over a relatively short period of time. The first step in the process was that, after Columcille's death, a monastic cult evolved in his honour. Over the years, this group divided into daughter-groups, as monks dispersed all over Ireland, founding churches and monasteries. Nearly everything then was passed on by word of mouth and, as many of us will have actually seen demonstrated in the old whispering parlour game, a word constantly repeated often becomes subtly altered. An additional factor was that, around this time, changes were occurring in the Irish language. Thus, 100 years after his death, two groups, separated geographically but united in their dedication to the saint called, for example, Mochonna and Caimme, might not have realised their original common link to Columcille.

Therefore, based on Ó Riain's arguments, the little ecclesiastical settlement at Monkstown could well have been founded by a group of devotees of St Columcille, the original name for Mochonna. This would be considered the 'minimalist' view.

However, there is another option. And, again, the experts differ. Mochonna is thought by, among others, the historian Dr Ailbhe Mac Shamhráin (1996) to have been a sixth-century British or Welsh holy man by the name of Colmán the Briton. (Although Ó Riain's theories carry the name-changing to their ultimate conclusion, even his dissenting colleagues would agree that the name-changing system of the early Irish saints is a can of worms. And, as Ó Riain has already demonstrated, Colmán is one of the alternative hypocoristic forms of Mochonna.) The cult of Colmán is thought to have originated in Cornwall (Broconnoc) or in Wales, where Mo Chon(n)óc, according to one folk story, was said to be the nephew of St David (Mac Shamhráin 1996). The cult came to Ireland, to Glendalough and its environs, where one of Glendalough's abbots (AD 687) is chronicled as 'Do Chuma(e) Chonóc', possibly a student or follower of Mo Chonnóc or Mochonna. Whether this is accurate or not, it shows that the cult reached Glendalough and became important there. Mochonna also appears in the *Vita S. Coemgeni* ('Life of St Kevin'), where Mochonna refers to St Kevin as *noster pater* ('our father').

From Glendalough, the spread of the cult of Mochonna can be traced through placenames and dedications, such as Kilmacumma in County Waterford. It may have been brought to Inis Patrick (as Dochonna) and to Carrickbrennan (the old name for Monkstown), where the church was dedicated to St Mochonna. A church at Kilmacanogue (derived from *Cell Mo Chonnóc*, meaning 'the church of Mo Chonnóc') in County Wicklow was also dedicated to Mochonna (or Mo Chonnóc). Here there is another link to Glendalough, since Kilmacanogue was a twelfth-century possession of Glendalough. The cult then returned, via north-east Ulster, to northern Britain and Scotland, where it can be traced in the obsolete placename 'Kilmachonock' — almost identical to the Irish 'Kilmacanogue'.

This, then, is our second possibility — that the cult of the original 'Colmán the Briton' spread via Glendalough to Carrickbrennan (through followers of 'Mochonna') and to Inis Patrick (through followers of 'Dochonna').

In conclusion, we can see from the above that recent studies in the field of Irish hagiography may throw new light on the early history of Monkstown. But, as yet, the evidence is inconclusive. However, there are valid alternatives to the original story of 'the monks from Inis Patrick'.

Monkstown could have been founded by devotees of Colmán the Briton or, possibly, more intriguingly, by those of the great Columcille himself. Instead of the Church of Mochonna in Monkstown being founded by monks from Inis Patrick, it seems more likely that *both* foundations were set up by members of the same cult — either followers of Colmán the Briton or of Columcille.

CHAPTER 2

Carrickbrennan Church (*c.* sixth century–1785)

North of [the castle] is the Church, very plain and small.
On the Weather Cock is cut '1668 E:C:'. Here are no Old Tomb Stones
or any thing in that way, but a very Old Yew Tree,
mostly decayed, & measuring in Diamr. 3 ft. 6 In.
Austin Cooper, antiquarian, visiting in 1780

The present church in which people worship today is probably at least the *fifth* parish church of Monkstown. It was built by John Semple in 1831 and was a spectacular modification of the earlier Georgian church on the same site, completed in 1789.

But before that, for anything between 800 and 1,000 years, the church of Monkstown was located in what we now call Carrickbrennan Graveyard, a quarter of a mile away, on the present Carrickbrennan Road. The ruined stone church now standing there is just over 300 years old. It was built by Edward Corker in 1668, using stones from an even earlier church on the same site. And that stone building, in turn, probably replaced a simple wooden church, which must have been built before the coming of the Normans because of its dedication to an Irish saint, St Mochonna.

Churches of Mochonna

The founding of St Mochonna's, the first church at Carrickbrennan, could have come about in one of three ways. It could have been founded as early as the sixth or seventh century by followers of Do Chuma(e) Chonóc, an abbot of the great monastic settlement at Glendalough in AD 687. Or monks from the small community of Inis Patrick, north of Dublin, could have founded it at the end of the eighth century (*see Chapter 1*). It is also possible that the church was founded by a third group of monks whose affiliation is unknown.

Such early churches in the wooded east of the country were usually made of oak planks (and thus were called *dairtheac*, meaning 'oak house') or of wattle and daub, interlaced branches plastered with mud (Edwards 1990). The roof may have been either steeply pitched and covered with shingles of overlapping pieces of split oak or yew, or flatter and simply thatched. If the walls were made of wattle they could not have supported a roof, so a separate system of strong wooden posts, driven into the ground at intervals around the perimeter, would have been used to support it.

This simple wooden church was replaced, in the eleventh or twelfth century, by a stone church, called the Chapel of Karibrenan (or Carrickbrennan) or the Church of Mochonna. It was made of limestone and granite, the local stone, and, being a pre-Reformation church, would have had a stone altar and rich furnishings, consisting of a decorated altar cloth, statues and shrines, candlesticks and a gilded cross. By this time it was being served by Cistercian monks from St Mary's Abbey, on the north bank of the River Liffey. (The church and land at Carrickbrennan, originally owned by the Mac Gillamocholmog family, Leinster chieftains, had been given to St Mary's soon after its foundation in 1139.)

In 1220, St Patrick's Cathedral took over the advowson (the right to choose a vicar) of Carrickbrennan, although the land was still owned by St Mary's. This complicated situation only lasted for twenty years, until 1240. Then the Augustinian Priory of the Holy and Undivided Trinity (the forerunner of Christ Church Cathedral) acquired Clonkeen (the original name for Kill-of-the-Grange) and its chapels, which included Carrickbrennan. Thus, for the next 300 years, the chapel of Carrickbrennan was served by the Augustinian community of the Priory of the Holy Trinity (*see Chapter 3*).

The Reformation and its aftermath

At the time of the Dissolution of the Monasteries in 1539 by order of Henry VIII, the Priory of the Holy Trinity was dissolved and reconstituted as Christ Church Cathedral, with the prior becoming the first dean. The church of Clonkeen (Kill-of-the-Grange), formerly owned by the priory, became the property of the dean, hence 'Dean's Grange'. Meanwhile, Henry VIII gave the Cistercian grange of Monkstown (Monkstown Castle) to Sir John Travers, master of the king's ordnance in Ireland. His Roman Catholic descendants (the Eustaces and the Cheevers) inherited the castle, the land and the advowson of Carrickbrennan Church.

At about this time, in 1540, there were some twenty buildings in Monkstown (White 1943), consisting of Monkstown Castle, four large houses or 'messuages', and fifteen cottages. At a conservative estimate of four or five per household, and assuming that everyone went to church, there might have been a congregation of 80 to 100 people attending Carrickbrennan. By the time of Elizabeth I (1558–1603), the church would have been in the Protestant tradition — stripped of its rich furnishings and statues, a plain wooden table placed nearer the nave serving as the altar, and the Lord's Prayer and biblical texts fixed on the walls. By 1630 the church was said to be 'in good repairacon, but wants decencie and some necessaries within'.[1] But by the end of the Cromwellian period (1649–58) it was 'ruinous'. Although some clergy carried on regardless, using the Book of Common Prayer (abolished by Cromwell in 1647) and other traditional rites, Carrickbrennan Church was uncomfortably close to Monkstown Castle, which had been taken over by Cromwell's general of horse, Edmund Ludlow, a strict Puritan (Seymour 1921). The owner of the castle, Walter Cheevers, had been evicted and transplanted to Connaught.

In the immediate post-Reformation period, the future of the church at Monkstown hung by a thread. At the Reformation, the existing clergy were allowed to stay on and very little change would have been apparent to the ordinary man in the pew. Few clergy were university graduates and few would have been enthusiastic about their new role. As they grew older and died, gaps were left in the ministry, with no body of trained graduate Protestant clergy to take their place.

So, in Monkstown, for 50 or 60 years, the 'cure of souls' (the religious duties in a parish), if it existed at all, was in the haphazard charge of occasionally employed, underpaid and unlearned curates. The lay Catholic patrons of the parish (called 'rectors' then; *see Chapter 3*) were not keen to support a curate and had ceased to employ one at all by 1615,[2] when it was recorded *Carragh Brennan Nullus curatus comparuit, ergo sequestratur* ('Carrickbrennan: No curate in charge, therefore [the parish] was sequestered').[3] It was probably around this time that the dean of Christ Church took over the patronage of Carrickbrennan.

Beset by financial problems, a hostile, largely Irish-speaking population and ruined empty churches, it was an uphill struggle for the ailing Protestant church to attract trained clergy of sufficient quality. Trinity College, Dublin, had been founded in 1591 by Elizabeth I, principally to train Irish clergy for the new Protestant church. But by 1615 only 23 Trinity graduates were serving in the 24 dioceses surveyed (Ford 1997). The Irish church was an attractive prospect for many totally unsuitable English clergy, some renegades from the law, others bigamists. The Ecclesiastical Commissioners in their survey of 1615 admitted: 'We have been hitherto driven to accept of, and to employ, such as come out of England unto us being admitted unto orders there, whom we have at first taken on trust, but in trial have found many of them very offensive and scandalous'. In 1622 there were 2,492 parishes in the Church of Ireland, manned by only 380 certified 'preaching ministers'; most were in the charge of unqualified 'reading ministers' (Clarke 1989).

William Morris Lloyd was the first perpetual curate appointed to Monkstown at some point between 1621 and 1630, and was also responsible for the parishes of Killiney and Dalkey.[4] His previous parish had been Dromore in the diocese of Clogher. It is probable that he was not a properly qualified 'preaching minister', but 'no scholar' and 'a reading minister' who actually lived in Dublin and paid someone else, probably another unqualified curate, to do his duty in Dromore (Leslie 1929). Non-residence was one of the many abuses highlighted by the Commissioners in their 1615 survey.[5]

Up to 1621 it was obligatory for people to attend the State church services, and a recusancy fine of twelve pence (more than the price of a pair of shoes) was still exacted from those who disobeyed. Conformity was rare in Clogher, so Lloyd's income from recusancy fines alone may have been considerable (Ford 1997). The immigrant clergy (and Lloyd may have been Welsh) were said to be much more assiduous about collecting their tithes than the native Irish had been, even to the extent of sending out proctors. This caused considerable resentment and would not have encouraged church attendance. Perhaps the fact that the recusancy fines dried up in 1621 was the nudge that persuaded Lloyd to move to Dublin, to an apparently wealthier group of parishes within the Pale.

But if he did move to Dublin in the hope of securing a better income, Lloyd soon found his situation just as precarious. He had to look after three parishes in order to have enough income. The tithes (one-tenth of the produce from church lands) for Monkstown alone amounted to £100 a year, which would have been a fortune if he had been paid them. But

13

these tithes belonged to three members of the Catholic gentry (Henry Cheevers of Monkstown, James Goodman of Loughlinstown and Henry Walshe of Dalkey), who allowed Lloyd only £5 or £6 a year. He also got £4 from Dalkey and £6 from Killiney, so his total income for the year was about £15 or £16.

In the ruined church in Dalkey, with its chancel open to the sky, Lloyd held morning and evening services on Sundays, using the Book of Common Prayer. In autumn and winter there was no one to give the responses except his wife and children. But during the spring and summer the congregation swelled, when the better weather enticed fishermen, from the coastal villages of England and as far afield as Scotland, to the good fishing grounds off Dalkey.[1] Lloyd's other parishes were faring less well. The church at Killiney was completely ruined and without any congregation at all, while Monkstown was in better repair but fighting a losing battle to keep its congregation.

Lloyd's predicament, with his ruined empty churches, was in striking contrast to the situation in the thriving Catholic church, 'a house in ye town of Mounctown tenanted from a Dwelling house, to be a Mass-house', where Father Turlagh Reyly said Mass and was openly supported by the local gentry.[1] The Irish-speaking villagers would have found Lloyd's English service incomprehensible. Their grandparents had noticed hardly any difference at the Reformation because Henry VIII had kept the familiar Latin service, only inserting prayers for the king instead of the pope. During Edward's short reign, things were tightened up and the Book of Common Prayer introduced. Rather than pay the recusancy fines, most people attended church. But since 1621 the fines had been relaxed, so the people had returned to 'the Mass-house' in droves and the Protestant churches were almost empty.

Lloyd, in his lifetime, lived through the crucial years when the Protestant State church failed to win over the majority of the Irish people. In spite of giants ahead of their time — such as Bishop Bedell who, in 1634, asked that the services should be translated into Irish — Protestantism was seen as a religion imposed by imported clergy, speaking a foreign tongue. Monkstown was typical of Irish churches in general. Even in the central Dublin parishes Protestants were in the majority in only three, and two of these were immediately beside the castle.

The 'new' church of 1668

In about 1667–8, Edward Corker, member of parliament for County Dublin, rented Monkstown Castle and its land from Walter Cheevers. (Cheevers had been reinstated as owner at the Restoration of Charles II in 1660; on renting Monkstown, he moved to Goat Castle, his tower house in Dalkey.) On that land stood the ruined eleventh- or twelfth-century church of Carrickbrennan in the old graveyard, which had been 'in repair' up to about 25 years earlier, but apparently (like so many others) became 'utterly broken down, ruined, and demolished' over the Cromwellian period owing to a combination of neglect and deliberate vandalism.

Corker rebuilt Carrickbrennan Church in 1668, using stones from the old ruined church. He placed a weathercock over his 'new' church, signing it with his initials and the

A sketch on the cover of *The Dublin Penny Journal* shows Carrickbrennan Church in a ruinous state, c. 1829, prior to the building of the watch-house to guard against 'body-snatchers'.

date, 'EC 1668'. The old west door was reconstructed, using some of the original carved limestone, but where the stones were missing, sandstone, a much softer non-local stone, was substituted. High in the east end was a round-arched window, matching that over the west door.

Even though the building was not strictly new, it is almost certain that the church was consecrated afresh. So many churches had to be repaired or built from scratch at the Restoration that, in 1666, 'A Form of Consecration or Dedication of Churches and Chappels, Together with What may be used in the Restauration of Ruined Churches, and Expiation of Churches Desecrated or Prophan'd' was prepared. Inside the cover, the imprimatur was officially licensed by the archbishop of Armagh and also by Michael Boyle, archbishop of Dublin (1663–78), who was also the chancellor of Ireland. It was probably Archbishop Boyle himself who consecrated the church at Carrickbrennan, using this new rite. Ten years later (*c.* 1678), Boyle bought Monkstown Castle from Cheevers; his descendants, Lords Longford and de Vesci, thus became the 'lords of the soil' (or ground landlords) of Monkstown.

Walter Cheevers died in Dalkey and was buried on 20 December 1678 in Carrickbrennan Graveyard. Even though he was a 'papist', his family had been the lay patrons of the church for generations and so he was buried there. He was the last of his line of Cheevers, or *Chievres*, a Flemish family who had first come to Ireland with Strongbow. (Goat Castle derives from the family name of *Chievres*, meaning 'goat'.)

In 1723, 55 years after its consecration, the perpetual curate of Carrickbrennan, Allan Maddison (1691–1741), gave a detailed description of the church and churchyard for the Visitation return.[5] He reported that the church was still in good repair; the churchyard was 'well enclosed' on the west with 'a large ditch' and on the other three sides with 'a stone and brick wall'. A bell hung in the belfry. Inside, 'a fair [Communion] table with a decent velvet Carpet & fair linnen Cloath' was railed in. There was a pulpit and reading desk, and a chest to collect alms for the poor. The aisles were paved with flagstones. There was a register for baptisms, marriages and burials, a book for the Vestry minutes and a surplice for the perpetual curate.

Maddison acknowledged that there was no book of Homilies or 'table of prohibited degrees hanging up', but that 'ye Church-wardens will soon provide' them. In addition, there was no font and 'no plate or other utensils' for Communion (the latter was remedied in 1737 when the first silver chalice and paten were provided).

Over the following years, various repairs were made to the church, all noted in detail in the Vestry books of the period, which began in 1744. Some sample entries illustrate the extent of the work involved and the maintenance carried out:

1744: 'For glazing ye Church Windows, paid Thos Seymor … £1-2-8; For flooring 2 seats and sceiling ye church, paid Joseph Smith … £1-0-3; For whitewashing and painting the Church, 11s 4½d'.

1746: 'For flagging the 2 seats adjoyning the Communion Table, £1-10-0; For a New Gate & Lock to the churchyard Door, £1-3-0; For a Matt for the Communion Table floor, 5/5'.

1747: 'For a pair of Stocks at Monkstown … £1-10; For Repairing the seat near the Bellrope, 6/6; For gravelling the way to the church … 3/3'.

1748: A new north–south aisle is built 'for the more convenient accomodation of the parishioners'.

1750: 'For the flooring the Communion Table with Boards, for flooring the restor'd seats in the old Isle in the same manner, to build a pair of Peers of stone in the Avenue to the Church yard, to clear the Church yard of rubbish, and to make such boarded floors in all the seats of the old work as they the said Church wardens shall think necessary, and particularly to provide proper steps at the entry into the Church — the sum by them to be expended not exceeding twelve pounds sterl'.

1751: 'That the sum of three guineas be raised for building a seat for the Church wardens at the righthand entry into the Church, opposite to and in the likeness of the seat built by Mr. Lord, and for the purchase of two quarto prayer Books for the Churchwardens' use, which are to be left in their seat … That the sum of eleven shill. and four pence halfpenny be collected for to buy a decent Copper Bason, in which to receive the Alms of the Parishioners'.

1752: 'That a further sum of one pound ten shillings be Added to a sum of one pound ten shillings formerly applotted for a pair of peers of Mountain Stone for the Church Yard Gate'.

Mr. Christr. Dalton   2 . 5 . 6

Brought from ye. other side £ 23 . 17 . 9
           42 . 18 . 3

Total Subscriptions Recd. from 21st. Martch 1748. to 21st. Augt. 1751. £ 66 : 16 : –

List of those who Built and Paid for Pews and Flagging in the New Isle —

North

West   *New Isle —*

Mr. Charles Coleman | James Maddock Esqr.
Christr. Dalton | Mr. William Fenner
Sr. George Ripton | Mr. Petr. Edkins
Robt. Roberts Esqr. | Mr. Hen: Gaven
Mr. Thos. Burrows | Mr. Edmond Shanley

South

At the bottom of a page in the Vestry minutes is a rough plan of the new north–south aisle, built in 1748, with a 'List of those who Built and Paid for Pews and Flagging in the New Isle'.

1753: 'Ten pounds … for the payment of the workmen employed in putting up the Sash windows in the Old Isle; whereas … ten pounds … is not sufficient … for repairs of the Old Isle … agreed … that … one pound twelve shills sterl … be … added … A stocks … in the parish of Monkstown, £2-10'.

1755: 'Ten shills sterl be Cess'd for repairing the Wall of the Churchyard … which is now in a ruinous Condition'.

1757: 'Two shill. and two pence were ordered to be collected and paid to John Marsden for clearing the Church yard of its weeds, and thirteen shill. and four pence to be collected in the Parish of Monkstown singly, and paid to the Coroner for holding an Inquest on the Body of Henry McGan'.

1760: 'For white-washing the Church, 10/-'.

1762: 'The sum of two pounds ten shills be rais'd on the united Parishes for providing a surplice and making an aditional seat in the Desk; 28/- … for clearing of Church yard of the Weeds and mending three Large Gaps in the Church yard fence'.

1763: 'Whereas the fence … on the East Side (of the church yard) is now quite out of repair, we … agree that the sum of six pounds sterl.g be applotted and raised upon the Union to be paid to the sd Lord Visct

Ranelagh … to build a good Wall at least six foot High … and to keep the same … in proper Repair at his own Expense, and we do consent … that (he) shall have power to make use of the Brick of the old Vestry Room and all other materials belonging to the old fence'.

1764: 'For Cushions for the Communion Table, £3-0-0; To a Funeral Pall … £2-18-4; To a bag for hold.g same, 1-7½; For a New Surplice, £2-10s'.

1767: 'Seven pounds … for building 24 Perch of Wall between the passage to the Church and Mr. Robert White's Garden by which means sd Passage will be widened four foot and for gravelling and filling the same'.

1769: 'For a Matting for the Communion, 5-6'.

1772: 'Rebuilding the Parish Pound of Monkstown, £4-13'.

1774: 'For Repairing the Church Roof and Whitening such parts of the Walls as have been Damaged by Rains, 10/-'.

1776: 'Towards a New mat and leveling the flags of the Church' £1-2-9'.

1777: 'To rebuilding the belfry, £2-10; To slating the Church, £1-10; To a New Axletree for Do, 2-8½; To Smith's Work for Do, 11-6½; To 2 Cut Stones for the belfry, 5/5'.

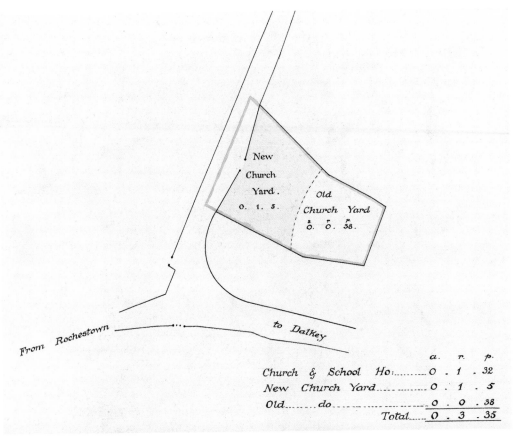

Lower section of the 1806 survey of Sherrard and Brassington, showing the site of the 'old' Carrickbrennan churchyard (38 perches), originally accessed by a laneway opposite Monkstown Castle, and the additional grant of land in 1806 (of 1 rood 5 perches) for the 'new' churchyard, fronting onto Carrickbrennan Road. The whole is the present site of Carrickbrennan Graveyard.

18

In 1780, Viscount Lifford, the lord chancellor, signed an Act of Council for the Perpetual Union of Monkstown, in which he '(did therefore) hereby Order and Direct that the ... parishes of Kill, Dalkey, Killeeny otherwise Killeen, Bullock and Carrickbrennan be united for ever to ... Monkstown and erected into one parish by the Name of the perpetual Cure or Parish of Monkstown with all Parochial Rights'. The Act was made law in 1781.

In 1787, it was declared that Carrickbrennan Church was 'by no means sufficient' for the congregation and 'out of repair'. The decision was taken to 'build a large and handsome Church in a more convenient situation'.[6] Five other perpetual curates succeeded Maddison (*see Appendix 3*) and then, under William Jephson (1782–91), the foundation stone for the new parish church of Monkstown was laid in 1785 by the duke of Rutland at the spectacular new site acquired further down the hill, where the roads met (the site of the present church; *see Chapter 4*). The old Carrickbrennan Church was allowed to fall into ruin once again.

CHAPTER 3

Patrons of Monkstown (1139–1870)

On 14 August 1846, the longest-serving rector of Monkstown was buried with great pomp and ceremony in the Royal vaults of Christ Church Cathedral.[1] His imposing black marble monument, sculpted by Joseph Kirk, now stands in the north aisle. A venerable gentleman, wearing a full rochet (surplice worn by bishops) and buckled shoes, lies with his head resting on a tasselled pillow. This is the Hon. Charles Dalrymple Lindsay, DD, the longest-serving dean of Christ Church, the last bishop of Kildare and the rector of Monkstown from 1804 to 1846.

How did the dean of Christ Church Cathedral, in the heart of the old city of Dublin, come to be the rector of Monkstown, a suburban seaside parish? The meaning of the word 'rector' has changed since Bishop Lindsay's day; it was not then synonymous with 'vicar' or 'incumbent'. Before Disestablishment of the Church of Ireland in 1871, the 'rector' was the patron of a parish and owned the advowson or right to choose the vicar, who was responsible for the 'cure of souls' or religious duties in that parish.

Incredibly, from its pre-Norman foundation until Disestablishment, the responsibility for choosing the vicar of Monkstown has been in the hands of *eight* different individuals or groups:

sixth–eighth centuries	Irish monks who built the first church at Carrickbrennan;
c. 1139–1220	St Mary's Abbey;
1220–40	Ralph de Bristol, treasurer of St Patrick's Cathedral;
1240–1539	Augustinian Priory of the Holy and Undivided Trinity;
1539–*c.* 1615	Sir John Travers and his successors, the Eustaces and Cheevers;
c. 1615–1846	dean of Christ Church;
1846–57	archbishop of Dublin;
1857	the Crown;
1858–70	archbishop of Dublin.

The black marble monument of the Hon. Charles Dalrymple Lindsay, DD, sculpted by Joseph Kirk, in the north aisle of Christ Church Cathedral.

Patronage from 1139 to 1846

St Mary's Abbey in Dublin was founded in 1139 by the Benedictines, a daughter-house of Savigny in France. Eight years later, in 1147–8, Savigny became united to the Cistercians, and St Mary's, therefore, followed suit (Gwynn 1949). The fact that it was originally a Benedictine monastery may account for its atypical location, on the north side of the River Liffey, opposite the walled city of Dublin. It was one of the very few urban foundations; Cistercian monasteries were typically built in isolated places, 'off the beaten track', such as Ballintubber, Co. Mayo, or Corcomroe, Co. Clare.

In spite of the Cistercians' original disapproval of power and wealth, St Mary's owned vast estates, presented to it over the years by Norman lords and Irish chieftains, amounting to over 17,000 acres by the time of the Dissolution of the Monasteries in 1539. The abbey owned much of Dublin itself and some of the surrounding villages. Carrickbrennan, with its church and lands, was probably given to St Mary's by Mac Gillamocholmog, a Leinster chief. These wholesale gifts of land and money came with certain conditions. Most of the grants stated that they were for the benefit of the donors' souls. Some asked to be interred in the abbey church, while others left money for perpetual prayer for the repose of their souls.

In 1220 Ralph de Bristol, first treasurer of St Patrick's Cathedral, held the prebend and tithes of Clonkeen and its five chapels — 'the church of Clunken [Clonkeen] with the chapel of Carrigbrenan [Carrickbrennan], the church of Kilbekennet [Dalkey], the church of Killeny [Killiney], the church of Tilach [Tullow] and the church of Staclorgan [Stillorgan]'. Although he owned the tithes of Carrickbrennan (the forerunner of Monkstown), he did not own the 'cure', or the right to appoint the vicar or curate. This

22

belonged to the Cistercian monks of St Mary's Abbey, who owned the land of Carrickbrennan. Since it made sense not to separate the tithes and the cure, de Bristol claimed the tithes of land near the grange of Monkstown, together with the small tithes to support a chaplain. St Mary's agreed to pay him half a mark of silver each year and five marks for his legal expenses. Thus de Bristol now owned the cure, although the monks of St Mary's still owned the land and the great tithes.

In about 1240 the Augustinian Priory of the Holy and Undivided Trinity (the forerunner of Christ Church Cathedral) substituted Ballymore (owned by the priory) for Clonkeen (owned by St Patrick's Cathedral). Thus Clonkeen, with the chapel of Carrickbrennan, its tithes and its cure, came into the possession of Holy Trinity and, ultimately, of Christ Church after the Dissolution of the Monasteries (McEnery and Refaussé 2001; Mason 1820).[2]

Then, in 1546, Sir John Travers was given the Cistercian grange of Monkstown (Monkstown Castle) in return for his services to the king (Fiants of Henry VIII 1875). After Travers's death, the castle, its lands and the advowson of Carrickbrennan (Monkstown) were inherited by his Catholic descendants. In 1577, 'the advowson of the church of S. Machona of the grange of Carrickbrenan alias Monkton, co. Dublin, which were the heritage of Sir John Travers' was confirmed to James Eustace, Viscount Baltinglass and owner of Monkstown (Fiants of Elizabeth I 1890). (Eustace had married Mary Travers, one of the two grand-daughters of John Travers.) As the patron of Monkstown, Eustace was supposed to pay a curate to serve the church, but it is probable that, as a Catholic, he neglected to do so.

In about 1615, the dean of Christ Church, as successor to the prior of Holy Trinity, may have seized his opportunity — while Monkstown parish was vacant — to establish his right to the advowson (Ball 1902). At that time Henry Cheevers, the great-great-grandson of Sir John Travers, was living at Monkstown Castle and, although he owned the advowson and tithes of Carrickbrennan Church, he too, like Eustace, conveniently 'forgot' to appoint a curate. The census that year found no one in charge at Carrickbrennan: *Carragh Brennan Nullus curatus comparuit, ergo sequestratur* ('Carrickbrennan: No curate in charge, therefore [the parish] was sequestered').[3] Sequestration meant confiscation of the profits or of the income of the benefice while the parish was vacant. As owner of the advowson, it was now the dean's prerogative to appoint the first perpetual curate, William Morris Lloyd, at some point between 1621 and 1630 (*see Chapter 2*).

After 1681 the dean of Christ Church was invariably also the bishop of Kildare. This curious situation evolved during the Cromwellian regime, when the Church of Ireland was persecuted and dispossessed, and the bishopric of Kildare was deprived of its property. When Charles II was restored to the throne, the Church tried to re-establish its former structure. But there was no money to maintain the bishop of Kildare. A solution was found in 1681 when the impoverished bishopric of Kildare was joined to the wealthiest deanery in Ireland — Christ Church Cathedral. William Moreton was the first to hold the combined position, being appointed dean of Christ Church in 1677 (with a stipend of £600) and bishop of Kildare in 1681.

Since that time, the bishop of Kildare, as dean of Christ Church, has had close ties with Monkstown. In fact, the influence of the dean of Christ Church can be seen behind every

The Down Survey of 1657 shows the parishes in the half-barony of Rathdown, including those of Kill (Dean's Grange) and Monkstown.

major move in Monkstown over the centuries; nothing happened without his approval. For example, he gave permission for the Perpetual Union of Monkstown, which was made law in 1781 (to consist of the six parishes of Monkstown, Kill, Dalkey, Killiney, Bullock and Carrickbrennan), and the consecration of the new parish church in 1789. The Act of Council for the Perpetual Union of Monkstown declared: 'That the Right Reverend Father in God, Charles [Jackson], Lord Bishop of Kildare, Dean of the Cathedral church of the Holy Trinity Dublin, Patron of the said several parishes in Right of the said Deanery … (has) also given (his) consent to the Union'.[4]

The dean nominated every incumbent to Monkstown. The nomination papers of the Rev. James Dunn, 20 July 1802, state: 'You are presented to us by the Right Reverend Father in God, George Lewis, by Divine Permission Lord Bishop of Kildare, Dean of our cathedral church of the Holy Trinity Dublin, in whose patronage as Dean thereof the said Union belongs'.[4]

The patron — or 'rector' in the old meaning of the word — of Monkstown about whom we know the most is the last bishop of Kildare, Charles Lindsay. He kept a particularly close eye on Monkstown, presumably because his son, also called Charles, was the perpetual curate there (1815–55). Bishop Lindsay was also the longest-serving dean of Christ Church. In 1832, at the consecration of the new organ in Monkstown, Bishop Lindsay preached the sermon. He brought with him 'the young gentlemen of Christ Church choir' to sing 'the choral part of the service', as reported in *Saunders's News-Letter* of 12 September 1832.

24

The last act in this peculiar alliance between Christ Church and Monkstown came with certain reforms of the Church of Ireland in 1833. The Church Temporalities Act of that year resulted in 22 dioceses being reorganised into twelve. But many bishops of these dioceses were still in office and could not be summarily ejected. The union of neighbouring dioceses did not take place until one of their bishops died. So Bishop Lindsay continued as dean of Christ Church and bishop of Kildare — and patron of Monkstown — until his death in 1846 (Wallace 2001). The 50th clause in the Church Temporalities Act stripped his successors of their ecclesiastical patronage. (The Oxford Movement in England was founded by Keble as a direct result of these 'reforms' of the Irish Church; *see Chapter 7*.)

A brass plaque on the wall opposite Bishop Lindsay's monument in Christ Church Cathedral informs us that, as dean of Christ Church, he 'presided over this cathedral for 42 years … till 8th August 1846 … faithful in the discharge of his duties, firm in his principles, clear in intellect, and sound in doctrine he retained all his energies to the end of his protracted career in the devout exercise of his sacred functions which he continued to discharge even to his 86th year. His aspect was so benign and venerable that all acknowledged his presence to be the best comment upon Leviticus … "Thou shalt rise up before the hoary head and honour the face of the old man and fear thy God".'

Patronage from 1846 to 1870

On Lindsay's death in 1846, all the revenues that had belonged to the bishop of Kildare went to the Commissioners of Church Temporalities. There was no money left to support a dean. The solution was found by combining the deaneries of St Patrick's *and* Christ Church — a situation which was to last for only 26 years (Lewis-Crosby, n.d.). Meanwhile, the patronage of the dean of Christ Church was vested in the archbishop of Dublin, and Kildare was united to Dublin and Glendalough.

Richard Whately, archbishop of Dublin, Glendalough and Kildare, stated that the Union of Monkstown 'is in our patronage' in the document appointing William Fitzgerald to Monkstown after the death of Charles Lindsay in 1855. He then formally 'commit[ted] unto our Wellbeloved in Christ, the Reverend William Fitzgerald … the care and cure of the souls of the parishioners within the … United parishes'.[4]

Two years later, in 1857, the patronage of Monkstown passed to the Crown. Where the incumbent had been elevated to a bishopric, the Crown had the right to appoint the next incumbent. The official appointment read: 'Whereas by the promotion of the Reverend Dr Fitzgerald to the Bishopric of Cork, Cloyne and Ross, the perpetual curacy of Monkstown … has become, and is now vacant, and the appointment thereto has become, and is vested in Her Majesty — We do hereby nominate and appoint the Rev. R.M. Macdonnell, Clerk, to the said Perpetual Curacy of Monkstown … to hold the same with all rights, stipends, profits and advantages thereunto belonging. Given at Her Majesty's Castle of Dublin this 6th day of April 1857, By His Excellency's Command [signed — illegible signature].' Underneath, Archbishop Whately had written, 'Let a license issue, 8th April 1857'.[4] After MacDonnell's appointment, the patronage of Monkstown reverted to the archbishop of

Dublin once again. This continued until Disestablishment in 1871, when most patronage ceased.

It is understandable that even church bureaucrats could not keep up with all these erratic turnabouts. Twenty years after the dean's patronage of Monkstown had officially ended, the registrar of the diocese of Dublin and Glendalough was unaware of the fact. On 11 June 1866, the short-tempered rector of Monkstown, the Rev. Ronald MacDonnell, wrote a tetchy letter to the registrar (obviously in reply to one of his), pointing out that 'as the Dean of Christchurch has ceased to be patron of Monkstown, it is not merely "unnecessary" but inaccurate to speak of him as still such'.[4]

PART 2:
HISTORY OF THE PRESENT CHURCH

CHAPTER 4

The Georgian church
(1785–1823)

The fairest country church in Ireland …
Hibernian Magazine, 5 September 1800, talking about Monkstown Church

Monkstown Parish Church originally stood in what is now called Carrickbrennan Graveyard (*see Chapter 2*). The Vestry minutes of 4 July 1808 record three reasons for moving the church to a different site (today's location) in 1785: the existing small site and confined situation, which did not allow for enough space to build a larger church or extend the old one; the increased population of the parish; and the fact that for several years the church had fallen 'into ruin and decay'.[1]

In his petition to parliament in 1785 for £1,000 to rebuild the church, Sir Nicholas Lawless (the first Lord Cloncurry), a parishioner of Monkstown, stated that 'great numbers of people every Sunday came out from Dublin to attend public worship … He had no doubt that the wisdom of parliament would deem it proper to aid an undertaking, which had for its object to promote religion, morality and health'.[2]

Acquisition of spectacular new site

The lords of the manor (also known as the 'lords of the soil'), who owned nearly all the land in the parish of Monkstown, were the Right Hon. Thomas Lord Viscount de Vesci and the Right Hon. Edward Michael Lord Baron Longford. In 1785 the churchwardens of Monkstown, Sir John Lees and Ralph Ward, approached them for 'a convenient and suitable piece of ground for a new Church and Church Yard'. Longford and de Vesci were amenable: they offered an excellent site 'adjoining the Road of Monkstown', on condition that it was 'properly inclosed and planted'. (This is the site of the present church.)

This arrangement was set out in an indenture, signed on 30 July 1785 by the various parties.[3] The churchwardens had to pay the nominal sum of £29 to Lords Longford and de Vesci, and ten shillings to the tenants of the church site, the Rev. Philip Tracy and his wife, Anne. The original name for the church site was mentioned in the indenture as 'that parcel of land … (which was) known by the name of Brickfield and Little Meadow'. The churchwardens 'and their successors for ever' were 'to have and to hold' this plot of land 'to the use and for the better convenience of the Inhabitants of the said parish in the worship and service of God, and that the same may be set apart for a church yard for the Burial of the dead'. However, if the land was 'disposed of, altered, employed or converted to any other use, intent or purpose', the original owners would be entitled 'to have, hold, possess and enjoy as in their former Estate and ancient right'.

Now that the site was available, the change had to be ratified by order of the lord lieutenant and privy council. A petition was made to the latter body, signed by prestigious residents of Monkstown, including Lord Longford, Lord de Vesci, Lord Ranelagh, Sir John Lees, John Mapas and Robert Byrne of Cabinteely. Thus, on 1 October 1787, the lord lieutenant and privy council 'ordered and directed that the Site of said parish or Union of Monkstown be changed to the piece of ground granted by the Lord of the Manor for the purpose of building a New Church and for a Churchyard, and that said Church should be for ever after deemed and taken to be the Parish Church of the said parish and always repaired at the common expense and charges of the parishioners of said parish or union'.

The Act of Consecration in 1789 gives the dimensions of the new church and churchyard:

> 'And Whereas the Minister and Churchwardens ... have Erected and Built a Church ... containing within the Walls thereof in Length from the West to the East 89 feet ... and in Breadth from the North to the South 31 feet ... and have also set apart ... a church yard and Burial Ground which ... area in the whole Circumference thereof contains 700 feet ...'[4]

The whole site was said to measure 'half an acre'. (According to an estate map of 1791 and a survey in 1806 by Sherrard and Brassington, the area was actually 1 rood 32 perches, a little less than half an acre.) A schoolhouse was also built on the church site in 1791, originally intended to educate 'the distressed offspring of Protestant Parents', but later it came to accommodate both Catholic and Protestant children of the parish (*see Chapter 16*).

Funding for the new Monkstown Church was organised. This was usually the stumbling-block for most church buildings. For example, in 1792 repairs to Christ Church Cathedral ground to a halt for 'a year or two' when money ran out. Similarly, in the same year the archbishop of Dublin, Robert Fowler, complained bitterly that 'not a shilling (was) granted to save' his St Patrick's Cathedral from destruction; he warned that the 'venerable fabric in a very few years to the disgrace of the Kingdom will be an entire ruin'. Again, extraordinarily, in 1792, the marquis of Downshire found it extremely difficult to wangle any donations from the Irish bishops for the rebuilding of Down Cathedral (Rankin 1997).

But fund-raising was not a problem in the wealthy parish of Monkstown. Sir Nicholas Lawless (created Lord Cloncurry in September 1789) had asked parliament for a grant of £1,000. It is not clear whether this was granted; the Vestry minutes of 4 July 1808 only record that £300 was raised on the parish by applottment (a tax from householders according to the value of their property) and 'the remainder ... by private subscriptions'.

From foundation to consecration

The site was now agreed, money was in hand to pay the architect and builders, and all the legalities were complete. The building of the new church could begin at last. Determined to do its very best, the Building Committee asked the most prestigious person possible to lay the foundation stone. The obvious choice was Charles Manners, the duke of Rutland and lord lieutenant for the past eighteen months — a handsome young man of 31 and a popular dignatory. It may also be relevant that among his friends was Lord Ranelagh, one of Monkstown's most loyal and enthusiastic parishioners. Rutland was described by Judge Robert Day, another Monkstown parishioner, as 'a viceroy whose affection for this country is indisputable ... whose administration will form a brilliant era in our history'.[2]

On 1 September 1785, the duke laid the first stone of the new church on its new site. Monkstown was an important parish and the presence of the lord lieutenant drew an astounding collection of VIPs. Besides Lord Ranelagh, they included the Right Hon. John Beresford, described ten years later as 'filling a situation greater than that of the Lord Lieutenant ... and to be virtually the King of Ireland' (Beresford 1977); John Foster, the chancellor of the exchequer and keeper of the great seal; Charles Agar, the archbishop of Cashel (later the earl of Normanton and archbishop of Dublin); and William Preston, the bishop of Killala. We may be sure that Dublin's aristocracy, and Monkstown's in particular, its judges and its generals came to watch the ceremony. Although it is not recorded, traditionally a silver trowel was specially fashioned and engraved for the occasion, and presented to the person who laid the stone. The duke gave a generous donation of £50 'in aid of this pious and necessary work', reported *Walker's Hibernian Magazine* of the day.

The minister, William Jephson, was a pluralist cleric who apparently spent most of the time at his living in the diocese of Raphoe and had to be summoned by letter to attend the consecration of his own church at Monkstown.[6] Thus most of the credit for overseeing the building of the new church must apparently go to Jephson's hard-working curate, Dr John Burrowes, the churchwardens and the Building Committee. Unfortunately, the architect's identity is unknown to us. But possibilities are Ralph Ward (churchwarden in 1768, 1784 and 1785) or Christopher Myers, the architect of Rathfarnham Church, a similar building. Both lived in the parish — Ward in 'Newtown House' on Newtown Avenue and Myers in 'Myersville' on Stradbrook Road. (Ralph Ward, sadly, never saw the completion of the church — he committed suicide in 1788; *see Chapter 14*.)

Four years after the laying of the foundation stone, the new church was consecrated on Sunday 30 August 1789 (the year of the French Revolution and the Mutiny on the *Bounty*) by Robert Fowler, archbishop of Dublin.[7] According to the preacher John Wesley, later founder of the Methodist Church, Archbishop Fowler was 'unrivalled' in 'his solemnity of manner in reading the service of the church'. The archbishop's son, the Rev. Robert Fowler, attended him. Other guests included Dr Henry Walsh, Archbishop Fowler's nephew, and his vicar general, Dr Patrick Duigenan, a doctor of law and a politician, who, although born a Catholic, was vehemently opposed to Catholic Emancipation. (He was known in the House of Commons for his eccentric dress, which included an 'antiquated bob-wig and Connemara stockings'. He died in 1816 and is buried in Carrickbrennan Graveyard, with

'A View of Montpelier Parade' in 1802 shows the Georgian church of Monkstown, 'commanding an enchanting prospect'. This engraving by S. Close was reproduced in *Walker's Hibernian Magazine* of March 1802. The building had been described as 'the fairest country church in Ireland'.

the epitaph 'An upright man', but apparently unaccompanied by his — Catholic — wife.)

Dr John Burrowes, Jephson's curate, took the service. He had come to Monkstown a few months after the foundation stone was laid and had watched the church building rise over the following four years. While a curate, he was awarded the degrees of LL.B and LL.D, so, on paper, he was better qualified than Jephson (Wallace 2001). He ran 'Prospect', a private school at Blackrock, where 80 to 100 sons of the nobility and gentry were instructed, including Valentine Lawless, son of Lord Cloncurry, who attended the school for two years from the age of twelve (Cloncurry 1849).

Richard Graves (1764–1829) gave the sermon — an onerous task for one who had only been ordained two years. But he was wise for his years: he had been made a junior fellow at Trinity at the age of 22 in 1786. The following year, he married Eliza Drought, but was obliged to keep the marriage secret since Trinity fellows had to remain unmarried or forfeit their fellowship. Eliza's father was also a fellow and professor of divinity, and therefore did not feel he could attend his own daughter's wedding.[8] So Graves had to keep his wife and ten children under wraps, as far as officialdom in Trinity College was concerned, until he resigned his fellowship 26 years later. Subsequently, he became professor of laws, Regius professor of Greek and Regius professor of divinity in Trinity, and dean of Ardagh. One of the east windows in Trinity Chapel was installed in 1866 in his memory.

One of Richard Graves's children was Dr Robert Graves (1796–1853) of the Meath Hospital, who instituted the bedside teaching of medical students and after whom Graves Disease of the thyroid is named. Richard's daughter, Jane, married Dr Richard MacDonnell, provost of Trinity College; of their nine children, one son, Ronald, became incumbent of Monkstown (1857–78) and two others, Charles Eustace and Frederick James, were killed during the Indian Mutiny. (There is a wall monument to their memory in the north transept of Monkstown Church today.)

32

In its brief report on the laying of the first stone, *Walker's Hibernian Magazine* had stated that the church was called St Mary's. This 'fact' has been repeated to the present day and is incorrect.[9] According to the Act of Consecration of 1789, Monkstown was *not* consecrated to St Mary:

> 'We ... Robert, by divine Providence Archbishop of Dublin ... Do separate the said Church and Church yard forever from all Common and profane Uses and Consecrate, Devote and Dedicate the same forever to the worship of God alone and the Celebration of Divine Service and the Burial of the Dead ... We also Consecrate the said Church and Church yard to the honour of God and Holy Uses *by the Name of the Parish Church and Church yard of the Parish or Union of Monkstown* [author's emphasis]. And We do Pronounce, Decree and Declare that the same hath been and is so consecrated and that it ought so to remain to future Times.'[4]

Archdeacon Charles Lindsay (1815–55) may have been responsible for perpetuating the incorrect name for Monkstown Parish Church. In 1836, when he had been the perpetual curate of Monkstown for over twenty years, he described the church as 'St Mary's' in a letter to the archbishop of Dublin, Richard Whately. Whately crossed out the words and wrote 'Monkstown' underneath.[10]

'A neat model of modern architecture'

Unlike the later Semple church of 1831, the church of 1789 broke no rules, raised no eyebrows. If it had, more might have been written about it. But it was generally approved of and even admired. Eleven years after its completion, the *Hibernian Magazine* of 5 September 1800 gave Monkstown Church high praise, describing it as 'the fairest country church in Ireland, containing a good organ, and two very fair mural monuments, on Doctor Domville [*sic*] who died in 1774, and Lieut. Col. Stewart of the Royal Irish Dragoons who died in 1798'.

A guidebook of the period, *The traveller's new guide through Ireland* (1815), described the location:

> '... on an eminence about half a mile beyond the Rock [i.e. Blackrock] is Montpelier, a most healthy and delightful spot, commanding an enchanting prospect; at the termination of this road or avenue, at the distance of three-quarters of a mile, is Monkstown church, a neat model of modern architecture, ornamented with a square steeple of hewn stone; round the church two roads sweep, one to the right leading to Roaches-town, the other on the left leading to Dunleary hill, and thence to Dalkey, by Bullock'.

A later guide, Brewer's *Beauties of Ireland* (1825), unfortunately, got the main date wrong: 'The church is a spacious building of stone, plain, but respectable in design, erected in 1797.' (The correct date was, of course, 1789.)

View of the New Church near Monkstowne, within 4 Miles of Dublin

The church, built in 1789 and reproduced in the *Gentleman's Magazine* of October that year, was a 'rectangular preaching box', typical of the day.

Taney Parish Church, opened in 1818, was designed along the same lines as the 1789 Monkstown church. The tower at Taney is remarkably similar to that shown in the engraving from the *Gentleman's Magazine* of October 1789.

Taney Parish Church, Dundrum, gives some idea of the external appearance of the 1789 Monkstown Church. In 1813, a new church was planned for Taney and a design drawn up by the architect, Mr William Farrell. However, after the design had been sanctioned, the Vestry had second thoughts and appointed a committee to visit Monkstown Church. Three weeks later, the committee reported that 'the plan of Monkstown would be more eligible than that drawn up by Mr Farrell', who had then to change his original design to resemble Monkstown (Ball and Hamilton 1895). (Taney has had frequent alterations since, including a complete change in its orientation.)

An engraving of Monkstown Church, reproduced in the *Gentleman's Magazine* of October 1789, shows a simple rectangular church with a square tower, very like that of Taney today. There are six lancet windows on both the north and south sides, and one on either side of the west door. The church stood on an open site, with fields sweeping down to the sea. Some sixteen years after the church was completed, the Easter Vestry of 1805 decided to build a wall around it in order to comply with their original agreement with Lords Longford and de Vesci in 1785. They had already asked 'Messiurs' Sherrard and Brassington to survey the church lands of both the present site and also of 'the old Churchyard' (Carrickbrennan). Sherrard and Brassington's 1806 map (*see below*) showed that the route of the road needed to be changed in order for the wall to be built, otherwise it would be too close to the church and school. This presented a problem, so once more the churchwardens, Colonel William Browne and John Armit (accompanied by the perpetual curate, the Rev. Singleton Harpur), approached the 'lords of the soil' — this time to ask for 'Permission to avail the parish of the Grant of the Ground in the Front of the Church'. This was agreed and in the resulting indenture of 1 July 1806 Lords Longford and de Vesci 'did thereby Grant, Release and Confirm unto the said Minister and Church wardens and their successors for ever, the said Resited Premises in Trust for the use of said Parish'.[5]

The indenture gave a new five-year deadline to the original conditions of 1785. This time, the 'lords of the soil' spelt out these conditions in detail: the church grounds were to be enclosed 'with a neat stone wall not less than four feet and an half high above the Road, the same to be capped with cutstone coping'. In addition, the parishioners were to 'plant the said ground so enclosed (except the burying ground) with a sufficient number of Ornamental Trees and ... Improvements shall (be carried out) ... from time to time for ever hereafter'. If this was not done to the letter within the timeframe specified, the covenant would be 'absolutely null and void', and Lords Longford and de Vesci would 'again repossess and enjoy as in ... their first and former Estate'.

The Sherrard and Brassington map of 1806 (*see below*) clearly shows that before the extra land was given the road ran uncomfortably close to the church building. More land was needed to allow the symmetrical, semicircular wall to be built in front of the church. As Lord Cloncurry had stated, Monkstown Church was a popular Sunday outing for Dubliners, who needed to 'park' their carriages on the roadway. Two entrances in the new wall, at approximately the same location as those of today, would allow vehicles to drive through the church grounds. (As the Vestry minutes of July 1808 record, 'In order to make the churchyard commodious, it was necessary to take in a part of the Road'.) The solution was to move the road southwards (as shown on the map). This did not present a problem

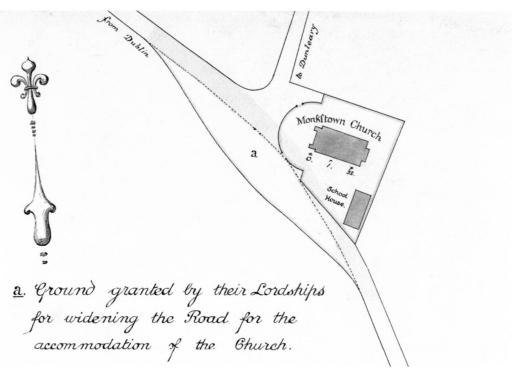

a. *Ground granted by their Lordships for widening the Road for the accommodation of the Church.*

Upper section of the 1806 survey of Sherrard and Brassington, showing the site of Monkstown Church (with an area of 1 rood 32 perches), the route of the original road (shaded) and the line of the new road, with 'a' being the ground granted for widening the road to accommodate the church.

because at that time Monkstown was a 'country' parish; the nearest houses around were at Old Dunleary (in the vicinity of the Purty Kitchen today) and, in the opposite direction, those in the fashionable 'village' of Montpelier, half a mile away.

Given a second chance, the Vestry took the 1806 indenture seriously: work began immediately, using money (£542) advanced by John Armit, one of the churchwardens, and repaid to him, free of interest, over the following three years. Before starting on the wall itself, the new road had to be finished and 'made passable for the Publick'. By July 1808 the 'improvements' were complete — with the road widened, gravelled and levelled, the wall built and all the 'ornamental timber trees' planted 'in fulfillment of the Covenant'. (The total cost, of £542, was practically as much as it had cost to build the church itself, almost twenty years earlier.)

George Smith, a parishioner and the future stone contractor for the new harbour at Dunleary, supplied the materials and built the wall. According to his estimate, there was already part of an 'old wall' that needed coping. He made a 'new Built surrounding wall' of rubble stone on the foundations of this old wall and put 'dashing on new and old walls'. He also carried out some cut-stone work on the church steps and the gate piers, and supplied the two iron gates, iron chains and other sundries. Bryan Bolger — probably the most important measurer in Dublin at the time — measured up the wall and produced the estimate on 6 February 1810, apparently retrospectively.[11]

We can more easily imagine the internal appearance and dimensions of the Georgian church when we remember that a third of it is still there, *inside* the later church designed by John Semple in 1831 (the present building). The original west end, up to where the north and south transepts begin, is practically untouched. Details have changed, but the little

The west end of Semple's 1831 church incorporates part of the earlier 1789 Georgian building. The width remains unchanged, but the ceiling is considerably higher. The height of the original Georgian church is marked by the cornices, still in place on the walls of the west gallery.

rooms, with their simple coving, are still there on either side of the octagonal porch, as is the elegant spiral staircase on the south side of the porch. There were originally two staircases at the west end: the north one has been removed, but its door to the gallery can be seen high up on the wall (it is hidden on the other side by a curtain). The lancet windows on either side of the west door were blocked up by Semple, but their faint outlines can still be made out — one on the way upstairs to the south gallery and the other in the little storeroom to the north of the porch.

The church was small and rectangular, measuring 31 feet wide (the width of the present west end), 70 feet long (from the main west door to just in front of the present chancel steps) and 23½ feet high (to the height of the Georgian cornices, still in place today and seen on the north and south walls of the west gallery). The west gallery was 16 feet deep, with twelve pews, holding 56 people in total. At the back, the organ (12 feet high and 9 feet wide) was housed in a handsome mahogany case. As regards the length of the church, Semple measured it as 70 feet, while the 1789 Act of Consecration states that it was 89 feet. This difference of 19 feet in the overall length fits in with the presence of a small extension containing a vestry or robing room beyond the main east wall of the original Georgian church. (This extension can be seen on Sherrard and Brassington's 1806 map.)

In the main body of the church there were a further 42 pews, holding 284 worshippers. Thus, with the twelve pews in the organ gallery, the seating capacity was 340. Of these 54 pews, 48 were 'allocated', or private; only six were public and these were so narrow (only 2½ feet deep) that 'grown up persons' could not kneel in them.[12] The private pews were high 'box' types, with doors. Some may have carried coats of arms (the Espinasse pew carried such a 'device', in either the old church at Carrickbrennan or in the 1789 church).[13]

At the east end, near the Communion table, which was covered with a blue cloth, were '3 Boards painted with the Ten Commandments, the Lord's Prayer and Creed in gold letters'. (The gold lettering had cost £22-15-0 in 1817, according to the Ecclesiastical Commissioners' report of 1824.) There was a 'Reading desk and Pulpit', a marble font and a 'hot air stove'. Other items in the church were '3 copper collecting boxes' and '6 plated plates for collecting'. On the walls of the nave were six tablets — to the memory of Dr Benjamin Domvile, General James Stewart, William Digges La Touche, William Browne, Judge Alexander Crookshank and Sir Joseph Atkinson. (All of these were moved to the transepts in Semple's later church.)

'The church is always much crowded'

In 1818, Warburton *et al.* wrote that, although the church was 'perhaps one of the largest and finest edifices erected for a country congregation in Ireland', it was 'always much crowded'. A footnote adds: 'The want of churches is much felt and complained of in this neighbourhood, where there is a more numerous population of the established religion than in any other part of Ireland. Yet, with the exception of Stillorgan, this is the only church from Ringsend to Bray, the extremity of the county, an extent including eleven populous villages, and a very thickly inhabited country.'

They wrote this one year after the first stones of the new Kingstown Harbour had been laid. Dublin's genteel suburbs were spreading rapidly southwards as the population grew. Even though it was not the universal practice then to attend church, enough new parishioners meant that Monkstown Church was uncomfortably crowded and a lack of ventilation made services unpleasant. Even the Communion chalice ('The gift of ye Parishioners of Monkstown and ye United Parishes to ye Parish Church of Monkstown, July ye 30th, 1737') was no longer adequate for the congregation, so Archdeacon Lindsay donated another one ('Presented to the Parish of Monkstown by their affectionate friend and Pastor in the year of Our Blessed Lord, 1824').

All the evidence confirmed that a larger church was needed. The new church, in its spectacular new location, had outgrown itself in less than 40 years. The impetus for innovation came in 1823 from outside the parish — from the new archbishop of Dublin, William Magee.

CHAPTER 5

The archbishop and the architect (1823–31)

A sea of troubles …
Shakespeare's *Hamlet*

This is a blow-by-blow description of the planning and building of Monkstown Church. Among the many fascinating details is the fact that only two of the 'prime movers' — Archdeacon Charles Lindsay and Judge Robert Day — saw the building of the church through from beginning to end. Although we can only guess what the archdeacon thought of the judge, we do know that the elderly judge (76 in 1823) thought that the young archdeacon (32 in 1823) was 'wrong-headed' (*see Appendix 1*).[1] In the eight years it took for the church to be completed, the site or design of the church changed at least seven times, no less than four Building Committees were appointed, the builders downed tools when money ran out, plans were unaccountably lost, funds were hard to raise from unenthusiastic parishioners, personalities clashed and, to cap it all, the central character in this catalogue of disasters, Archbishop Magee, lost his much-loved wife, battled with his final illness and died before the project was complete. This was, indeed, 'a sea of troubles'.

Archbishop William Magee

William Magee became archbishop of Dublin in 1822 at the age of 56. During his relatively short occupancy of nine years, he caused more than eighteen churches to be built or enlarged. Monkstown was among the first of these to be proposed and, as we shall see, he dominated the project's planning and funding for years.

Magee was a clever and gifted preacher, but he launched a religious war in his primary charge. At his enthronement in St Patrick's Cathedral, he announced that the Church of Ireland was 'hemmed in by two opposite descriptions of professing Christians: the one, possessing a church, without what *we* can properly call a religion [i.e. Roman Catholics]; and the other, possessing a religion, without what *we* can properly call a church [i.e. Presbyterians]'. Roman Catholics felt threatened by such words, which were said to herald the beginning of a 'Second Reformation' (Bowen 1978).

He was either liked or loathed: one contemporary 'authority' described him as 'a perfect *petit maître* in appearance … fond of daily parading his little person on horseback through the most fashionable streets'. He was said to love ostentation and pomp, spending a great deal of money on gilded decorations in his palace at 16 St Stephen's Green, which his successor, Whately, threatened to have whitewashed. Magee's life was said to be 'all work and worry, plot and counterplot'. Others, however, saw him in a different light: although his income was £7,000 a year (almost €700,000 in today's money), 'of this he set apart £2,000 a year for charitable and public uses' (*Dublin University Magazine*, Vol. 28, 1846). He was also a man of principle who, unusually for his time, refused to advance the careers of his own family through patronage; his family of fifteen children included four sons and two sons-in-law in the church (Wills 1875).

Marble bust of Archbishop William Magee by Thomas Kirk, exhibited in 1840 in the Royal Hibernian Academy and now in the Long Room of Trinity College, Dublin. (Courtesy of the Board of Trinity College, Dublin.)

Perhaps both versions hold some truth. Maybe Magee's personality changed towards the end of his life, so that he became somewhat erratic and unreasonable. It was said that he refused to consecrate a church that was not capable of being used as a fortress; perhaps this notion stemmed from the 'arrow slits' and battlements in Semple's Monkstown. On the other hand, it was true that he interrupted a Catholic funeral in a 'Protestant graveyard', refusing permission for the burial to go ahead (D'Alton 1838a). Magee, however, was a leading player in the building of Semple's enlargement of Monkstown Church. It was he who suggested a 'new' church in 1823, looked at the proposed plans and tried to bulldoze the Vestry (which had ideas of its own) into adopting his decisions, which seemed to change with the wind.

The first mention of a new church in Monkstown (or, rather, an enlargement of the existing church *and* the building of a new chapel of ease for the overflow of parishioners) is in an undated letter written by Archdeacon Charles Lindsay to John Radcliffe, judge of the prerogative court and vicar general, asking for advice about the salaries of church officers, to see if the parish outgoings could be reduced in any way. (Radcliffe's reply is dated 18 February 1823, which gives some idea of the timing.) Lindsay writes:

'An enlargement of our Parish Church is now in contemplation — Besides which it is proposed to erect a Chapelry … I have therefore represented to His Grace the Archbishop that a careful regulation of our parish affairs is necessary before we enter upon such difficult undertakings.'

Even though the church was crowded during services (it accommodated about 340 seated worshippers), the overall impression is that, otherwise, the vast majority of parishioners were not particularly involved in their church. Ratepayers of all denominations in the parish could attend and vote at general Vestry meetings, where secular matters were discussed. It is difficult to know how many attended these meetings because the usual practice was for only a few of the leading parishioners to sign the minutes. (Between 1820 and 1822, only three or four signed besides Archdeacon Lindsay, and only one person in two Vestries held in June and July 1822; at the Easter Vestries for 1820, 1821 and 1822, five, twelve and nine respectively signed their names.)

Although the unprecedented number of 20 were listed in the Easter Vestry minutes of 31 March 1823, discussion about a new church does not appear in the minutes until five months later, on 12 August 1823. Magee, as the new archbishop of Dublin, attended this meeting and 36 parishioners signed the minutes. One wonders if there is a whiff of dissent implied in the entry, 'His Grace the Archbishop of Dublin having been invited to explain his reasons why it is expedient to enlarge the mother church …'. Magee announced that a new or enlarged church was necessary since the present church had 'not … sufficient Accommodation for the parishioners'. He was formally thanked for 'his condescension and kindness in attending'.

Why was Archbishop Magee so interested in Monkstown? It was certainly one of the first — if not the very first — of the new churches mooted during his archbishopric. If we look at how Monkstown contrasted with other parishes, as Magee must have done, we may have a clue to his thinking. Of the 2,000 parishes of the Church of Ireland in 1830, 425 had less than 100 parishioners; 23 had less than ten; and 40 had none. Meanwhile, Monkstown was bursting at the seams — one of the few parishes with a growing congregation of well over 1,000. It was also in one of the most concentrated Church of Ireland enclaves in the country and it had some extremely wealthy and influential parishioners, who would surely know how to raise money.

It is obvious, looking at the church outgoings listed in the Vestry minutes of 8 April 1822, that a new church was the last thing parishioners were contemplating:

Geo. Simpson for keeping the slating of the Church in repair 1 year to 28 May 1822,	£3-8-3
James Tutty for Mason work done at Church,	£2-3-2
John Peppard for Carpenter work, etc.,	15/-
Willie Maguire for Window Cord,	10/9
Michl. Fannin painting Church Yd door,	3/4

Nevertheless, the archbishop's directive had to be followed. Funding was discussed: the Board of First Fruits, the body responsible for financing church buildings, had promised £2,000 and it was reckoned that a further £3,000 could be 'assessed on the Union' (raised from the parishioners of Monkstown). A Church or Building Committee of eight laymen was duly appointed to look after the project. They were Judge Robert Day (chairman), Robert Ashworth, Sir Richard Steele, Sir William Betham, George Smith, W.H. Carter,

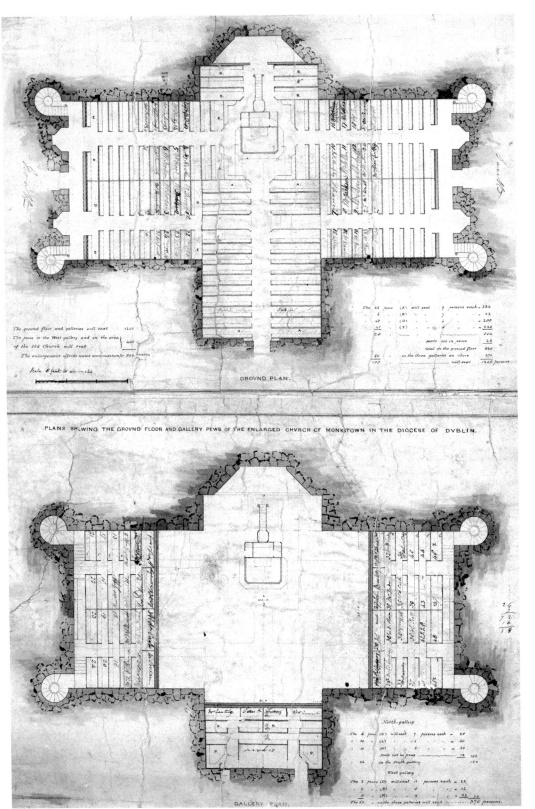

Semple's 'transeptal plan' for Monkstown Church, presented in 1823 and accepted in 1829 by the Vestry. (Top) Ground-plan of church, showing layout of pews (with some allocated), central three-decker pulpit, vestiary at east end and corner towers with spiral staircases. (Bottom) Gallery plan, showing seating accommodation in the three galleries, including the west gallery where the organ was housed.

GROVND PLAN.

PLANS SHOWING THE GROVND FLOOR AND GALLERY PEWS OF THE ENLARGED CHVRCH OF MONKSTOWN IN THE DIOCESE OF DVBLIN.

GALLERY PLAN.

William Disney and John Armit. Four others, from the clergy and churchwardens, made up the committee of twelve.

At the Building Committee's meeting on 30 November 1823, work had obviously progressed since it was reported that 'the transeptal plan' had been 'adopted at a former meeting' and a second option, the 'abbey' plan, was about to be studied, with 'Mr Semple' being asked for estimates for the two options.

The 'Mr Semple' referred to was John Semple, Senior, diocesan architect (*see Chapter 6*). He worked with his son, John Semple, Junior, from their Dublin office at 21 Marlborough Street.

Semple's plans of 1823

On 20 December 1823, John Semple, Junior, met the Building Committee and 'produced on the part of Mr Semple … estimates of two plans … He also presented a report on the peculiar advantages of each plan'. The report went into great detail, giving the present dimensions of the church, followed by those of each plan. The 23-year-old architect made his presentation to a depleted committee of only six members.

The 'transeptal plan' involved knocking down the east end of the Georgian church and adding transepts onto the existing west end, to finish up with a T-shaped building. The church would be lengthened by half as much again, while each transept was to be approximately the width of the main church. Galleries 20 feet deep in each transept would mean extra seating, thereby trebling the capacity of the church. Although not specified in his report, the 'transeptal plan' also included a shallow extension at the east end, leading into a 'vestiary' (vestry or robing room) below the east window. All this would cost £3,000. Semple reminded the committee that the 'stile [*sic*] and character of the enlargement' should be in keeping with the original building or there would be 'discord', and he complemented the committee for their 'good sense' in 'instantly detect(ing)' this aspect of the design.

Semple had done some homework already: he had knocked two holes through the church walls. One wall was sound, but the other was so 'loosely built' that it would not be advisable to use the walls 'as a vital or an important part' of the new church. But neither was it a good idea to 'raze' the church to the ground and build the new church on the same site, since the 'old materials' would only fetch 'a few hundreds of pounds' and also there would be the problem of finding alternative accommodation for services while the church was being built.

There were other problems, too. Galleries were necessary in order to hold such a large congregation, but a church with galleries did not have enough space for 'the existing cenotaphs'. Semple knew that moving these could be upsetting — 'even the temporary violation of these monuments of living recollections ought not to be undertaken without caution, and could not be accomplished without regret'.

All these stumbling-blocks had led to the second or 'abbey' plan, which Semple Junior presented in 'Vol. No. 2'. Although this plan was more complicated than the transeptal, it meant that the wall monuments could remain undisturbed, while galleries to fit the extra numbers could be built as well. The idea was that the existing church was to form a 'cenotaphed nave' to a brand-new church extension with galleries on each side. The capacity of the church would still be trebled, as in the transeptal plan. The roof was to be 'supported by six gothic arches whose vertices (were) 60 feet above the floor'. These arches, in turn, were to be supported by 'buttresses … perforated by doorways'. The organ gallery was to stay in its current position, in the west gallery over the main door. A 'great arch' between the old and the new parts of the church was to be 'decorated with ornamental groups of gilt organ pipes'. Four of the old church windows were to be blocked up and the robing room was to be in 'the space screened off under the eastern window'. This is all rather difficult to visualise since the plan has not survived.

Semple stressed the importance of the building's being in proportion. If the nave was to be enlarged, the height of the tower had to be increased to remain in proportion. He put it this way: 'As the building is raised to a dignity of altitude, it becomes necessary to increase the tower and its appendages'. He proposed doubling the height of the tower, from 77 feet to 145 feet. This new church would fit '1,200 persons seated with convenience and propriety' and would cost £8,000, which, he reminded the committee, was only £6 for each person. He said that this was not as expensive as might appear on first sight since 'a plain substantial Dublin church' cost about £10 for each person.

This momentous meeting with Semple Junior, reporting on behalf of his father, ended with the members of the Building Committee formally tendering their 'best thanks' to the young architect 'for having laid before (them) such elegant plans and so satisfactory a report'.

Over the following two months, the Building Committee decided against the transeptal plan, while they 'highly approved' of the abbey plan. However, they considered that it was too expensive and suggested that Semple scale it down to fit 800 worshippers instead of 1,200, mentioning a desirable cost of £5,000. On 24 February 1824, the Vestry approved the Building Committee's report (four of the Vestry members were also on the Building Committee — Lindsay, Mahaffy, Day and Gregg — so this was simply a formality) and it was decided that £5,000 for 'the New Church should be assessed upon the Union of Monkstown'. (They obviously thought an additional £2,000 was necessary since making their decision in August 1823, when £3,000 was to be assessed on the Union.)

Changing sites and plans

Fourteen months later, by April 1825, everything had changed. The Vestry had decided to abandon 'the present site of the Parish Church and (to build) the New Church on part of a certain piece of land in the parish of Monkstown commonly known by the name of "The Lime Kiln Field" '. This site, according to John Rocque's 1760 map of the coastline, was at Salthill (somewhere in the vicinity of the present Salthill Apartments or possibly even on the other side of the present railway line, on the higher ground). The Vestry appointed John Armit as treasurer[2] and Arthur Jones as their law agent, and a new Building Committee was

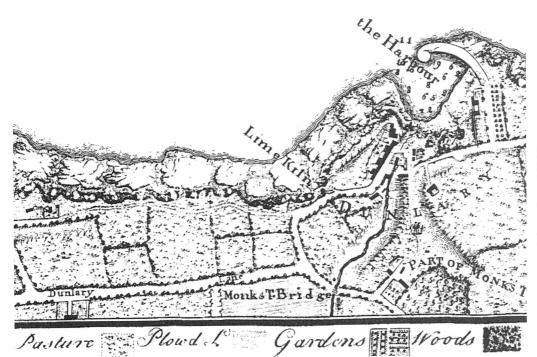

Location of the Lime Kiln Field, proposed site for Monkstown Church in 1825, from a 'Plan of the City, Harbour, Bay and Environs of Dublin' by John Rocque, 1760 (corrected 1773 by Bernard Scalé).

formed (consisting of the clergy, churchwardens and three others — John Armit, Alderman Cash and James Price) to organise fund-raising and 'all business connected with the building of the New Church'.

The new Building Committee decided that £600 should be raised before building started and they proposed to do this by selling pews to private individuals or families, at a cost of between £10 and £50 each. Parishioners would pay more for the status connected with a well-placed pew (*see Chapter 18*). Anyone who already owned a pew was entitled to one in the new church that was 'at least equal in dimensions and as nearly as possible in the same relative position'. Strict resolutions were drawn up on the type and price of various kinds of pew (*see Appendix 6*) and 500 copies were printed and circulated in the parish, with the auction or ballot being organised for 12 o'clock on 13 June 1825 in the schoolhouse. Also on view that day would be the plans for the new church and its seating arrangements.

The legal niceties had now to be organised. The Building Committee asked Arthur Jones, their law agent, to obtain written permission from the 'lords of the soil' (Lords Longford and de Vesci) for the site of the church to be changed. This was duly received and the committee thanked their lordships 'for their very liberal conduct to the parish' and recommended that 'the 2 pews unmarked in the Gallery of the New Church be allotted and presented' to them.

But by the end of 1825 the situation had changed again. The Vestry minutes of 26 December that year (an unusual date for a meeting) record, 'Resolved, that in consequence of the Archbishop of Dublin's disapprobation, we abandon the plan of enlarging the present church'. The minutes over the intervening months had given no indication of this return to the original plan — that of enlarging the church. At some point in between, obviously, the plan to build in the Lime Kiln Field had been dropped. The possibility of building a railway line or a ship canal along the coast from Dublin to Kingstown was being actively discussed in and around this time; if the Lime Kiln Field was on the seaward side of this proposed development, the site would have been quite unsuitable for a church. (The act of parliament for the building of the railway was passed in 1831 and the line, the first in Ireland, was opened in 1834.) At least one member of the Dublin and Kingstown Railway Company was also a Monkstown parishioner (Joseph Kincaid, churchwarden in 1834).

However, it would seem that Archbishop Magee was not happy with the Vestry's latest resolution to enlarge the church, despite his directive back in August 1823 that it was 'expedient' to do so. Trying to accommodate the archbishop, the Vestry said that it was 'willing to build a spacious and commodious new church either on the site of the present church, or in the old burial ground at Monkstown, whichever may appear to his Grace most expedient and satisfactory'. (The 'old burial ground' referred to Carrickbrennan Graveyard, where the ruins of Corker's 1668 church stood; *see Chapter 4*.) The Vestry added the rider that it would prefer the site at Carrickbrennan because 'by that plan, Divine service would not be interrupted'.

In the meanwhile, however, tragedy had struck the archbishop. His beloved wife, Elizabeth, had died only three months earlier, on 27 September 1825, aged 54. According to his biographer, James Wills (1875), Magee 'never was the same again … old age seemed to fall upon him instantaneously'. He shut himself away for weeks and would not see anyone; he could not even exert himself enough to perform the marriage ceremony of the lord lieutenant, Marquis Wellesley. It was said that, were it not for his Christian beliefs, 'he would hardly have ever again gone forth from his house of mourning'. As a result, the archbishop was not thinking straight on many matters, including Monkstown and its new church.

Early the following year, on 14 February 1826, the two churchwardens delegated by the Building Committee to discuss the issue with the archbishop reported a difference of opinion between him and the Board of First Fruits. Magee wanted the existing parish church to be enlarged and a new chapel of ease to be built 'in the old Church yard' (i.e. Carrickbrennan) for the overflow of parishioners. On the other hand, the Board of First Fruits — which had the final say since it held the purse strings — had dug its heels in and would grant no money if the new parish church was built on its present site; the Board wanted the new church to be built at Carrickbrennan and the existing church to be retained as a chapel of ease.

Instead of sending the same two churchwardens back to confront Magee, the Building Committee sent their most formidable member, Judge Robert Day (chairman of the first Building Committee of 1823), to inform the archbishop of the Board's stance. Magee seemed to accept the position and, soon afterwards, wrote to the committee with the welcome news that the Board of First Fruits had decided to grant them a loan of £5,000.[3] Thus a new chapel of ease was to be built in the old churchyard of Carrickbrennan and the existing parish church was to remain unchanged, on its present site. A generous offer then came from Bishop Charles Lindsay, dean of Christ Church, who, as patron of Monkstown, promised to endow a curate to serve in the new chapel of ease, thereby alleviating the parish's financial burden.

Plans now seemed to be settled. In April 1826, the Vestry responded with a formal

46

resolution of thanks to Bishop Lindsay. With John Armit appointed as treasurer, the parish was given notice of the decision 'to assess the 5000£ on the Parish Union to be repaid by Instalments without interest at the rate of four pounds by the hundred in each successive year until the whole be repaid'. The Semples were then asked to draw up new plans 'for a church similar to that now building at Donybrook [*sic*]' and to get estimates for same. (This church was costing £4,843-11-2, so it was within Monkstown's budget, but, as we shall see, Monkstown was to cost nearly twice as much.)

While the archbishop, the Building Committee, the Vestry and the Board of First Fruits were all trying to decide on what to do at Monkstown (remember that discussions had started in November 1823), the Semples had been supervising the construction of numerous other churches, including the one at Donnybrook, or Simmonscourt (*see Chapter 6*). The Monkstown Vestry had been watching this project with great interest and obviously approved, possibly because they thought it would be cheaper.

Semple's advertisement for estimates for the new chapel of ease at Carrickbrennan cannot, unfortunately, be traced.[4] But it was probably similar to the request for tenders for St Mary's, 'the Black Church' (completed in 1830), advertised in *Saunders's News-Letter* of 3 November 1827, which reads:

> To competant and Experienced Builders.
> Proposals will be received for Building a Chapel of Ease in the Parish of St. Mary, Dublin, according to the Plans and Specifications to be seen at the office of John Semple & Son, No. 21, Marlborough Street.
> The Proposer is to refer to some Public Building or Gentleman's Residence, as specimens of skill, and to seal and send his proposal (containing the names of two solvent securities for the due performance of his Contract) as above, on or before Tuesday, the 20th instant.

Meanwhile, since the Monkstown church was not going to be enlarged after all, the Vestry got on with some long-overdue improvements. As there was only one main church door, that at the west end, a second door was made in 1826 'to facilitate the egress and regress of the congregation' at a cost of £24-18-4. The windows and doors of the church and schoolhouse were painted, as were the gates and chains (two coats for £6-17-3), and 'lamps for lighting the Church' were acquired for £35. A sum of £40 was assessed on the parish 'for the purpose of repairing the church'. In 1828 heating was improved: 'Resolved that £46 be the rate for erecting a stove flue and chimney and all things belonging thereto in the church'. The sash-cords on the windows were repaired and 'white linen blinds' bought at a cost of £10.

Confusion reigns

There is now a frustrating silence in the Vestry minutes for over a year on the subject of the new church, until June 1829. By this time, the builders had already started on the church, probably around February of that year.[5] But everything had changed again. The new church was being built *not* in the 'old Church yard', as demanded by the Board of First Fruits (and apparently settled in the Vestry minutes of April 1826), but on its existing site, as Archbishop Magee had wanted from the beginning. He had had his way after all. The church plans, showing the transeptal design, are dated 30 April 1829.

Services were continuing in a 'temporary church' in the meanwhile. We do not know where this building was, except that it was only big enough to seat those who could pay for their pews. It seems that 'the poorer brethren', who sat in the 'free' pews, either could not attend church or had to stand for those three years (1829–31).[6] This temporary accommodation may have been a church since it seems to have possessed an organ: both the organist and the organ-blower were paid their salaries of £40 and 6 guineas, respectively, for both the years 1828–9 and 1829–30. (Such temporary arrangements were not unusual at the time: when St Bride's was undergoing extensive repairs over a ten-month period in 1828–9, its services were held in St Patrick's Cathedral.)

But all was not going smoothly with the building. Some months after work had begun on the church (in about February 1829), Edward Carolin & Sons, the builders, downed tools because they were not being paid. It is estimated that a total outlay of £3,400 had been expended by June of that year and only another £703 was needed to finish the church. But at their meeting on 9 June members of the Vestry received a shock. In their progress report, the architects, Semple & Son, estimated that another £4,000 would be needed to complete the work. This was a serious situation. Since the last Building Committee had been disbanded, a new one was appointed to decide on ways and means of raising this extra money.

Even more serious was the fact that the Vestry was still undecided on its final plan, even though building had begun. This strange anomaly was complicated further when the Building Committee met with the Vestry one week later, on 16 June 1829, and reported that it '(could not) trace (the 'second plan') [presumably the 'abbey' plan] ... alluded to in conversation ... in any tangible shape in the Report'. However, the committee was satisfied that 'a church completed according to (the transeptal plan) would in (their) opinion be a handsome and creditable Building and amply sufficient for the accommodation of the Protestant parishioners of Monkstown'.

Besides being unable to find some of the original plans, the committee was also unable to find a detailed estimate of all the costs involved and why the Semples should be asking for another £4,000. It was decided to report back to Archbishop Magee and ask him to negotiate an extension of the loan from the Board of First Fruits. Meanwhile, the committee thought that selling or letting more pews would cover the interest involved.

After some discussion, the Vestry made some formal — and courageous — resolutions. They agreed with the Building Committee and gave the 'go-ahead' to Semple's original 'transeptal plan'. Furthermore, it was *not* to be scaled down, as had been suggested at one point in order to save money. The minutes of that meeting of 16 June 1829 record: 'Resolved ... that the Church now building at Monkstown is well adapted to the magnitude and importance of the parish, and ought not to be lessened in its extent or in the accommodation it is calculated to afford'.

A meeting was arranged between the Building Committee and Archbishop Magee on 19

June 1829 and another one with Mr Semple one week later. Then, on 30 June, the Vestry met to hear the committee's report of these two meetings. But, unfortunately, this meeting was abandoned since there was not 'an attendance of Parishioners sufficiently numerous for the importance of the business' (only Archdeacon Lindsay and four others had turned up to hear the report). The meeting was rescheduled for the following week and the Vestry clerk in the meanwhile was instructed to 'send circular letters to the Parishioners giving them notice … and requesting particularly their attendance, and that said letters be pointed'. 'Pointed' they must have been since there were fourteen signatories at the next meeting, on 7 July.

The report of the Building Committee said that Archbishop Magee had 'entered very warmly into their views and (had) directed Mr Semple to give a more distict [*sic*] Estimate of what could be done for the money in hand and how much would be required to complete the Building according to his Plan'. Semple had subsequently produced a report detailing what would be done for another £4,000:

> To continue the present walls up to the intended height of forty feet.
> To complete the roof, ceiling and plastering …
> To erect the great supporting beams of the three Galleries.
> To give seats upon the floor, by the old pews (which are preserved) and by new forms for the remainder of the span.
> To complete the side doors of entrance with their steps and platform, and erect the reading desk, pulpit and communion rails, will amount to £2,500 in addition to the present fund.
> To complete the Galleries and their stairs, the pewing on the ground floor — the exterior masonry — and to finish the building in all respects, will amount to the further sum of £1,500.
> The money in hands, the second instalment and half the last instalment (making together five sixths of the loan) is sufficient to carry up the walls to their intended height, to put on the roof, slates and Gutters, and leave the building secure from the weather.
>
> Dublin 26th June 1829
J. Semple

The Vestry clerk noted that 'much discussion ensued' about getting the extra £4,000 necessary. The Vestry members knew that they could not realistically hope to raise this much by 'voluntary subscription' and were obviously not as convinced as the archbishop that the Board of First Fruits would lend them the money. The Building Committee recommended that this money should be assessed on the parish. Everyone, however, was agreed that building must begin again, so that the church would be safe from the elements. Thus, 'His Grace was pleased to say he would give directions, that the Building should proceed', suggesting that the builders should be paid most (i.e. five-sixths) of the £4,615-7-8 already lent by the Board of First Fruits.

The next sentence in the record of the meeting reveals how intensely the archbishop wanted to be in control of the entire project: 'His Grace likewise informed the Committee that as the entire Power of directing the Building of the Church was lodged in Him, He was solely responsible for the conduct of it, and that the Parish could not legally interfere with Architect or Contractor'. There is certainly an implication here that the archbishop suspected the Building Committee or the Vestry of negotiating with the Semples or the builders behind his back, possibly in order to scale down details of the church to save money. (This had happened at Whitechurch, where the Vestry tried to pass plans for a church with a capacity of less than the 300 specified by the archbishop.[7]) Magee wanted to be closely involved in every stage of the building and was determined that nothing should be changed at the last moment. His close involvement was remembered even 50 years later, when a writer in the *Irish Ecclesiastical Gazette* of 20 March 1880 wrote that Archbishop Magee 'took a great interest in its erection, constantly driving out [from his palace at 16 St Stephen's Green] to see how it was progressing'.

But the archbishop's health was failing. In June 1829, around the time he was meeting the Building Committee, he developed a 'strange sleepy feeling in his left hand'. This may have been a transient ischaemic attack (TIA) due to hypertension; he was also suffering from nose-bleeds, which would support this diagnosis. There were conflicting reports about his health. It must be remembered that Magee's religious intolerance had gained him many enemies and it suited some camps to believe that he was no longer mentally responsible. The eminent physician Dr John Cheyne (after whom Cheyne–Stokes Respiration is named) was satisfied that the archbishop's 'intellect is as clear as ever it was. His powers of calculation are impaired …', and he warned that any stress or agitation could be dangerous. This sounds as if Magee had had a right parietal stroke, which would impair numeracy but leave speech and intellect intact. Magee, however, refused to give up any of his duties and, although much weaker physically to the extent that he could no longer ride or climb stairs without help, he was determined to see through the building of Monkstown Church, so much his project from the start (Wills 1875).

Endless negotiations, eventual triumph

There is a frustrating gap in our knowledge of what happened next since the Vestry minute books are missing for the period July 1829 to 1871. (The last entry was on 7 July 1829, approving the 'transeptal plan'.) But, fortunately, the Easter Vestry minutes, covering the period 1858 to the present, contain extracts from Vestry minutes that help to fill in some of the main events.

Sometime between February and June 1829, work had ceased on the church since the builders had not been paid. The church was in 'a very unfinished state' and it was crucial that the parishioners should raise enough money so that work could continue. The Building Committee came up with several ideas to gather funds quickly. One suggestion was to build twenty vaults under the new church and to sell each for £130: £30 would cover its expense and the remaining £100 would go towards the completion of the church. This scheme should bring in £2,000. Another suggestion was to sell the pews in the new galleries at between £30 and £60 each, raising a potential further £1,500. However, the committee's optimism did not match reality and, by August or September, the cost of the vaults had dropped to £50 each and the pews to £20–£25 each. In the end, a good proportion of this sum had been realised — by 15 February 1831, £2,980 had been raised (including £100 from the vaults and the rest from the pews).

Some documents in the Representative Church Body Library helpfully take over the saga at this point. These include letters from John Armit, dating from October 1830.[8] As treasurer of the Monkstown Church Fund, Armit had a difficult role — treading a tightrope between the temperamental archbishop, the go-slow builders and the frustrated Building Committee. Two short letters (on 7 and 11 October) tell of his first visit to the archbishop's palace in order to collect the promissory note for £1,200, which Magee had generously offered to donate and which was much needed to spur on the builders. It seems that his visits were not fruitful and he came away empty-handed. (Magee did eventually pay up; *see below*.) Perhaps the Building Committee resigned in protest at this stage, for it is recorded that another committee was appointed on 8 November 1830. Its members agreed (on 27 December) to lend £426 between them in exchange for the unsold pews as security.

A copy of a letter dated 18 November 1830 (probably from John Armit, but with its last page or pages missing) sheds a little more light on the funding situation:

> Messrs. Caroline [*sic*], contractors for building the church ... propose to complete that structure on the sum of £4,000 being paid or secured to them as follows:
>
> £1,200 — a Donation from His Grace the Archbishop to be lodged in Trust with Doctor Radcliff and Mr. Armit, to be paid on completion of the work;
>
> £1,000 — in solvent Parishioners Bills payable in three Months after such completion; and
>
> £1,800 — the Balance, to be paid as the work proceeds ...

The Building Committee could not agree to these proposals, however: it 'found that, under circumstances which it (was) not in their power to remove, they could not close to these terms'. Poor Armit had to approach the builders again and negotiate further. The final agreement was for '£600 in cash, £1,200 proportioned as the work proceeds, and the Balance being £2,200 in Notes payable within Three Months after completion'. Although the committee was able to pay the £600 deposit, it found that the sum of £1,200 could not be raised in time to pay the builders. The sale of pews was not proceeding as planned.

Furthermore, the committee was most unhappy with 'a statement' in the builders' letter to Semple:

> 'It is there mentioned that the Plan and Estimate of the Church as approved of by the Parish in Vestry amounted to £8,615. This Statement the Committee must altogether contradict. The Parish never did approve ... of there being any greater Expenditure on the intended Church than a sum of £4,615 — with which Sum the Parish now stands assessed, the Board of First Fruits having agreed to a Loan to that amount.'

The committee insisted that they had neither seen nor approved of the 'detailed Plan and Estimate' mentioned in the letter. These had been 'entirely arranged and agreed upon between His Grace and Messrs. Semple and hence has arisen all the difficulties with which

Semple's Monkstown Church in 1834, shown in an idyllic rural setting (sketched by E. Heyden and engraved by R. Clayton, reproduced in *The Dublin Penny Journal* of 12 July 1834). Despite the odd perspective and inaccuracy of architectural detail, note the massive string-coursed window-sill and the ogee door of the north transept (to left of picture), which matches the main west door; both transept entrances were modified in 1890.

the Erection of the new Church of Monkstown has been attended'.

Here we come to what the Building Committee felt was the root cause of all the problems associated with the building — the fact that Archbishop Magee had been dealing directly with the architects, as he had insisted upon in June 1829, and had made agreements over the heads of the committee. At this point, the writer of the letter dated 18 November 1830 (probably Armit; *see above*) reminded his reader that 'His Grace proposed to give a sum of £1,200 … towards making up the deficiency between the Parish Grant and the Plan he had himself approved'. He seemed to be suggesting that Magee should now produce this amount, so badly needed, if work was to proceed: 'The Committee feel that they have therefore a peculiar claim on His Grace, to assist them now to meet his own Contractors' views, when, so far from the Parish having approved of the Plan, as asserted in Messrs. Caroline's letter, the Committee have never …' [tantalisingly, the rest of the letter is missing].

Carolins, the builders, sent their 'final proposal' to the Building Committee on 5 January 1831. This was a 'take-it-or-leave-it' letter. The builders must have been utterly frustrated with all the changes and stoppages over the years (building had commenced in about February 1829). Archbishop Magee was now ill and out of action, and they were dealing directly with the Building Committee at last. In their letter, the builders undertook 'to complete the building, according to the original designs, in a substantial and workmanlike manner'. This was on condition that they were guaranteed further payments of '£709-0-5 in cash and £1,918 in solvent parishioners' bills and £1,931 cash … from time to time as the work proceeds'. They had already been paid £2,532-19-7.

In return, the builders promised that the church would be 'fit for divine service in 8 months and completed in 12 months from the date (they received) directions to proceed'. They promised that there would be no 'further demands on the parish' and assured the Building Committee that they would be 'quite safe in agreeing to the terms proposed'. We know that the builders fulfilled their promise — Semple's Monkstown Parish Church opened for worship on Christmas Day 1831.

Funding had at last come together. Archbishop Magee had donated his promised £1,200 and it was lodged in the Bank of Ireland. The Board of First Fruits had also promised another £731, 'not to be paid us till the entire works shall be completed according to the designs, estimates and specifications and … the architect's certificate to that effect'. An extract from the Easter Vestry minutes of 31 March 1831 relates, however, how 'persons of responsibility' had to be persuaded to part with cash or 'promissory notes' so that the builders could be paid. 'To achieve this important object, every exertion was devoted.'

In their final proposal, the builders gave a copy of 'the Architects memorandum and report of the entire cost of the building':[9]

The cost of the foundations and work done according to the corrected measured bill dated the first of September 1829		£1,112
Amt. of Messrs. Carolin's first proposal dated 2nd Sept 1830	£5,925	
Second ditto dated 5th January 1831	£1,048	
To Reerecting the monuments	£118	
		£7,091
Measuring fees on first estimate as above		£50
Architects fees being 1/21 part of £8,665		£412
Cost of the building exclusive of the vaults		**£8,665**
Ways and means		
Cash from the Board of First Fruits	£4,615	
Ditto from His Grace the Archbishop	£1,200	
Cash and bills to be paid by the committee exclusive of the discount on the bills	£2,800	
Cash from sale of some old materials	£50	
Total		**£8,665**

Archbishop Magee never saw the completed church. He died, aged 65, on 18 August 1831 at 'Redesdale', Stillorgan, the neighbouring parish to Monkstown, probably as the result of a final stroke. He is buried in Rathfarnham Old Churchyard (Blacker 1874).

The extraordinarily metamorphosed Monkstown Parish Church was at last a reality. The following notice appeared on Tuesday 13 December 1831 in *Saunders's News-Letter*:

The Minister and church wardens of the Union of Monkstown have the gratification of informing the parishioners that the interior of the parish church being now completed it will be opened for the celebration of Divine Service on Christmas Day next. There are some pews still undisposed of, both in the galleries and body of the church.

CHAPTER 6

Who designed Monkstown Church?

Die two months ago, and not forgotten yet? Then
there's hope a great man's memory may outlive his life
half a year; but by'r lady, he must build churches then.
Shakespeare's *Hamlet*

My father once described Monkstown Church as 'peculiar' and, indeed, it is. I have never seen a church that is so idiosyncratic. Stand for a moment outside Goggin's, the pub opposite, and look at its mix of themes from early English, Moorish and even ancient Irish. And yet it works. All of the quirky fragments hang together to make a distinctive whole. There is something quite majestic about the sheer scale of the building, with its battlemented skyline and the corner turrets with their arrow slits, as it stands, slightly skewed, facing down Monkstown Road. And, when you first step through the oddly narrow entrance at the west end and look up — and try to do this with fresh eyes, if the church is familiar to you — at the vast vault of the ceiling, it can take your breath away.

You cannot stand on the sideline and be neutral about such a building. You will either love it or loathe it — with passion. And that has been the reaction to Monkstown Church from its very inception. The Vestry of 1826 had actually asked for something quite different. They had watched another Semple church being built nearby, at Simmonscourt (Donnybrook), and wanted something along the same lines for their parish. So they asked the Semples, the diocesan architects, to 'forthwith … furnish plans and specifications for a church similar to that building at Donybrook [*sic*]'.

But, instead, they got Monkstown — one of Sir John Betjeman's 'first favourites for its originality of detail and proportion' (*Monkstown Review*, 1958), while a writer in the *Dublin Penny Journal* (12 July 1834) declared that 'there was not a spot in the church where the eye could rest without pain'. And what of the reaction of contemporary Dublin? Sadly, its citizens did not appreciate such original work: they scoffed at the Semple buildings, according to the available evidence. On the other hand, English visitors were 'struck by the originality and beauty' of the building (*Architectural Magazine*, October 1835). For a more detailed description of 'what they have said about Monkstown Church', *see pp xvii–xxiv*.

It is well known that John Semple was the architect of Monkstown Church. This may sound simple, but it is, in fact, rather complicated, as my research has shown. There were actually four 'John Semples' around at the time. Two of them were Dublin architects, a father

The spectacular ceiling of Monkstown Church — its corbelled fan vaulting, like giant shuttlecocks, rising to the heavens. The scalloped plasterwork and decorative gallery fronts all combine to give a Moorish air to the interior of this unique building. Picture taken from chancel looking towards south gallery.

and son partnership. A third John Semple was also an architect, who did some work in Galway. A fourth man of the same name was an engineer from 'Burros' (Borris), Co. Carlow, who built Graiguenamanagh Bridge and possibly Bagnalstown Bridge. (He is also known for making the 26th largest claim, of £2,441-17-0, during the 1798 Insurrection for the loss of his furniture, books, papers and bonds.[1])

We are only concerned here with the father and son from Dublin — John Semple, Senior and Junior — the architects who worked together and designed Monkstown Church and a string of some sixteen other churches in the 1820s and early '30s in Dublin, Kildare, Offaly, Laois and Wexford. To discover which of these two men was the mastermind behind Monkstown is a fascinating study for, as Maurice Craig (1982) admits, 'We know nothing of (Semple) as a man and he remains the most enigmatic of architectural personalities'. He was referring to John Semple, Junior, who was almost always assumed to be the architectural genius behind the partnership.

John Semple, Senior (1763–1840)

The Semples came originally from Scotland, of Presbyterian or 'dissenter' stock. The vast majority of Semples still live in Scotland and the north of Ireland. However, as early as the seventeenth century, Semples had moved to Dublin to work in the building trade, as plasterers and stuccodores, masons and carpenters. One of the family, George Semple, recalled how his father, a workman in about the year 1675, 'often told me … (about a method of making mortar that) will … petrify, and … turn to the consistence of stone' (Semple 1873). This George Semple had put the spire on the square tower of St Patrick's Cathedral in 1749, designed Swift's St Patrick's Hospital in 1750 and rebuilt Essex Bridge in 1752–4 (where Grattan Bridge is now).

John Semple, the nephew of George, was probably 'John Semple, brick-layer, of Abbey Street'. He married Lydia Dryden in about 1755. Twelve children were born to the couple between 1756 and 1774, as they moved from house to house around the crowded streets on the north side of the River Liffey, with addresses in Abbey Street, Mecklinburg Street, Marlborough Street, Sackville Street and Gloucester Street. John and Lydia called their fourth son 'John' and he was baptised, like all the others, in St Thomas's Church on 6 April 1763 (Refaussé 1994). This is our 'John Semple, Senior, Architect'. As he grew up, he would have gained valuable hands-on experience working with his father, and probably other members of the family, in the building trade. There was still no formal training for architects (a student would simply 'sit at the feet' of a practising architect) and there was often no distinction made between architects and builders.

In 1788, at the age of 25, John married the seventeen-year-old Mary Russell.[2] By now he must have been doing well; he was fortunate to find himself in the middle of the boom period of Georgian Dublin. The houses of Merrion Square, Fitzwilliam Square and Gardiner Street were all being built, and skilled architects and builders could make good money. John was also closely associated with Dublin Corporation. On 28 April 1797 the sheriffs and commoners nominated eight men to the lord mayor and aldermen, who were to choose two of them as high sheriffs. These eight men included four merchants, a cooper, a cutler, a smith and a plasterer (the latter was the 34-year-old John Semple). Each was a holder of the ancient Freedom of Dublin, lived in the city or its Liberties, and was worth '£2,000 sterling, over and above all their just debts' (Lady Gilbert 1891–1944, Vol. XV).

The two high sheriffs appointed on that occasion were the merchant Robert Shaw and the 'plasterer' John Semple. A month later, on 29 May, both men bowed out, 'praying to be excused from serving the office'; their resignations were accepted, provided that they each pay a fine of 300 guineas, which was donated to the Blue Coat Hospital (the present King's Hospital School). Instead, Shaw and Semple became 'sheriff's peers' in 1798. Semple was elected to the same office for every year after that, for the next 42 years until his death in 1840. Against his name in the Dublin directories of the period there is a mark, indicating that he had been 'fined'.

Being a sheriff's peer opened doors for John Semple: he was elected to the Dublin City Grand Jury in 1807 (as reported in the *Correspondent*, 16 April 1807) and to a subcommittee for the Gaols of the City of Dublin in 1809 (Lady Gilbert 1891–1944, Vol. XVI). In 1804, now established and prosperous, he joined others of the new middle class who were moving out of Dublin to the suburbs growing up south of the city. (Others of the family were also doing well: his youngest brother, Anthony, was admitted to King's Inns in 1808, subsequently becoming a barrister.) Dunleary was still an undeveloped fishing village, but plots of land were being leased and houses built all around the area. John Semple leased 18 acres 2 roods, at a rent of £129-10 per year, for 70 years, from 1 May 1804, at the top of the present York Road, which from the 1820s was known as Kingstown Hill (Brady 2000).[3]

'Fairyland', the home built by John Semple, Senior, in c. 1804, as it is today (now called 'St Helen's'). Built to an L-shaped plan, the original façade faced down Kingstown Hill (now York Road), towards the sea. Surprisingly plain, its main features are the full-height bow on the west side and the paired sprockets under the eaves. The present porch is a later addition, but the original Georgian doorcase and fanlight are preserved inside.

Here, on a plot of 11 acres on the higher ground, he built a comfortable family home, which he called 'Fairyland'.[4]

Although it was not the only house in this vicinity (the premises known as 'Racefield', 'Primrose Hill' and 'Tivoli Parade' pre-dating it), 'Fairyland' was certainly the only house on the west side of Kingstown Hill for almost 50 years and would have had an uninterrupted view of both the sea and Monkstown village from this vantage point. About twenty years after it was built, an eye could also have been kept on the development of Kingstown and the progressing construction of the great harbour during this period.

Considering Semple's profession, the house was surprisingly simple in design, consisting of a plain-rendered two-storey building over a part-sunken basement, built to an L-shaped plan. Externally, the only features of decorative or architectural note are contained in the paired sprockets under the eaves of the main roof, which is conically slated at one end above a full-height bowed wall, rising from basement level. This was originally on the west side of the house, facing the small, stone-walled private garden away from the road; the main façade, with its Georgian doorcase and fanlight, faced to the north, down the hill towards the sea. On 6 July 1829, *Saunders's News-Letter* described the house as a 'most desirable country residence … delightfully situated … (with) a Lawn, most excellent Garden, well stocked with choice vegetables and fruit, large Field and very extensive Out Offices … and its own good supply of water'.

In view of Semple's extraordinary architectural work elsewhere, one could speculate on why his own home should be such a simple, almost austere building: perhaps because he had to support such a large family, Semple needed to be careful with money; perhaps he was a man of simple tastes in his personal life. Internally, the house has an essential Georgian feel in its decoration, with panelled doors, simple mouldings and sashed windows. Only the hallway gives a hint of the man's genius as a designer. Directly inside the centrally placed entrance, the hall is modest in size, wider than it is long, and symmetrically arranged with a door to a room on each side. However, the upper section is given a vaulted appearance by the inclusion of four corbelled fans rising from each corner to frame an octagonal plaster decoration at the centre of its ceiling. One could easily extrapolate that this hallway, which Semple must have seen every day, eventually provided the basis of his inspiration for the 'glorious extravaganza' that was to follow some twenty years later in the form of Monkstown Church.

A visit to Semple's home today (now called 'St Helen's') will reveal a house much altered by addition, with the main entrance now facing east to the road. However, many original features survive, including the layout of the gardens, the curved granite wall (which runs from just inside the entrance from the road towards the house) and the driveway (which still leads to the old, north-facing front door, now obscured behind the later addition of a porch).

'Fairyland' must have been an idyllic setting in which to raise a large family, very different to John Semple's own childhood in the crowded streets of Dublin's inner city, with their noxious vapours said to carry disease. Here, in the fresh sea air of their new home, the next generation of Semple children grew up. John and Mary had been married for sixteen years before the move and probably already had a large family. It has only been possible to

Could this entrance hall and ceiling in Semple's home of 'Fairyland', built in c. 1804, have been the prototype for what was to follow in Monkstown Church some 25 years later? The octagonal shape, the graceful arches, the corbelled fans at the corners, the delicate plasterwork — all are reminiscent, in embryonic form, of the spectacular vaulted ceiling of today's church.

identify six of their children: Edward (b. 1795) was nine when he moved to Dunleary, John (b. 1800) — our 'John Semple, Junior, Architect' — was four and James (1802–5) only a baby, while Mary and Kate were born in Dunleary in 1809 and 1810 respectively; another daughter, Isabella, married in 1817, when she was over 21, so she must have been eight or older at the time of the move.[5]

In the early 1800s, Monkstown Church was still the only church in the whole area and parishioners had to travel to services from as far afield as Dalkey and Killiney. The church of the day was the Georgian 'rectangular preaching box', completed in 1789 and with a seating capacity of about 340 (*see Chapter 4*). The Semples may have attended, but they were not pew-holders, the stamp then of church membership. It is also possible that they were 'dissenters', or Presbyterians, who were sometimes baptised in Church of Ireland churches. From Semple's own admission, he was not a regular attender of Monkstown Church; indeed, in 1823 when preparing plans and estimates for the new church he was to build, the Vestry minutes of 20 December record that Semple said, 'I have not of myself a local knowledge sufficient to judge of the numbers which would require accommodation in this church'.

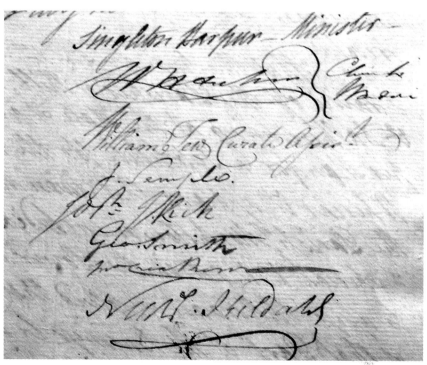

John Semple, Senior, who lived in the parish of Monkstown, signed the Vestry minutes on 23 May 1809 (possibly the only occasion he did this). His signature can be seen fourth on the list, directly below that of William Tew, the curate.

In 1808, at the Easter Vestry, 26 men were appointed as overseers of public houses in Monkstown. One of these was John Semple, Senior. Because he lived in Dunleary he was technically a Monkstown parishioner[6] and, as such, attended a Vestry meeting on 23 May 1809 and signed the minutes — the only time he ever did this, to our knowledge. The applotments of the Easter Vestry were confirmed at this meeting. (This was a system whereby people's taxes were calculated on the basis of the value of their property; *see Chapter 13*.) Semple would have been especially interested in these valuations because it is probable that he built or designed many of the houses in Dunleary — soon to be renamed 'Kingstown' in honour of George IV's 1821 visit. The 1809 applotments judged Semple's own house, 'Fairyland', as one of the best houses in the area and, as such, he had to pay £30 towards road repairs.

As mentioned earlier, there was often no distinction between builders and architects in those days. John Semple, Senior, probably did both. There are indications that he built houses in Monkstown, as well as in Dunleary. A satirical poem, written in 1832 by Nicholson Numskull in his *Essay on the rise and progress of architectural taste in Dublin*, slates Semple for his 'tasteless' houses 'all along the road' (probably Monkstown Road since these words come immediately after a mention of the church), going on to describe two of them as being 'back-to-back'. These houses may be 'Drayton Lodge' (No. 73), which is 'back-to-back' with 'Glenville' (No. 75), and 'Purbeck' (No. 77) with 'Heathfield' (No. 79) on Monkstown Road, which, since they first appear on an 1816 map, were probably built in *c.* 1810–16.[7] All these houses feature a full-height bowed wall to one side only, which was also a feature of 'Fairyland', Semple's own home in Dunleary, built in about 1804. (For Numskull's critique of Semple's Monkstown Church, *see p. xvii*.)

Thus, within a stone's throw of Monkstown Church, John Semple, Senior, may well have built residential houses. His son, too — John Junior — was to follow in his footsteps, building Belgrave Square, South, for example. But at this stage John Junior was still working with his father from their office at 21 Marlborough Street, close to St Thomas's Church, where John Senior and all his brothers and sisters had been baptised.

In 1821 the lord mayor of Dublin and his sheriffs were caught on the hop, as the newly crowned king, George IV, was due to arrive in Ireland in six weeks' time and nowhere was thought sufficiently grand for his royal entertainment, which was to consist of a banquet and ball in his honour. Tenders were sent out hastily for builders. The fact that he was a sheriff's peer must surely have influenced the choice of John Semple, Senior, to build a suitable structure beside the Mansion House in Dublin's Dawson Street. Incredibly, the 'King's Room' (the present Round Room) was completed in less than five weeks, just in time for the royal visitor.[8] The construction of its domed roof was unusual: it was a perfect circle, measuring 30 metres (100 feet) in diameter and consisting of 'canvas stretched over counter battens fixed to the roof sheeting boards and saturated with pitch'. The inside of the dome was painted to resemble a summer sky, so that the overall appearance was described by the secretary to the Admiralty, John Wilson Croker, as an 'interior circular court of a Moorish palace open to the sky' (www.theroundroom.ie).

But it is for their churches that John Semple & Son are principally known. In 1824 they were appointed architects to the Board of First Fruits for the province of Dublin (which, besides County Dublin, included counties Kildare, Carlow, Offaly, Laois and Wexford). This body was responsible for the building or enlarging of churches and glebe houses. John Semple, Senior, was now 61 and his son 24. In the ten years between 1824 and 1834 they built some seventeen churches. All went up one after the other, some even at the same time, and very much to the same blueprint — except Monkstown. As far as we know, Monkstown was the first to be designed (1823), but probably one of the last to be completed (1831). There was a long and fascinating saga as to why this was the case (*see Chapter 5*).

Towards the end of this busy church-building period, the Semples were appointed city architects in 1829 (*Pettigrew & Oulton Directory*, 1829). With the death of Archbishop Magee in 1831 (the prime mover in getting new churches built), followed by the wind-up of their employment by the Board of First Fruits, the Semples' ecclesiastical work was abruptly terminated.[9] John Semple, Senior, was now 71, but still very much in business. In 1833–4, Semple Junior moved out of the family office at 20 Marlborough Street[10] to his own premises at 34 Lower Baggot Street, while his brother-in-law, Sir William Lynar (married to his older sister, Isabella), moved in with his father. This arrangement lasted until Sir William moved to Kingstown in 1835, and Semple Senior followed the next year (*Watson's Almanack* of 1836 gave his address as 'Haddington terrace, Kingstown'), although he continued as a sheriff's peer and city architect until his death in 1840.

Then, on Monday 25 May 1840, *Saunders's News-Letter* carried the following notice: 'Died … At Kingstown, on the 21st instant, in his 78th year, John Semple, Esq.' No details are known of the cause of death (deaths were not registered until 1864). The funeral service was taken by the Rev. John Grant, the curate of Monkstown. Perhaps Archdeacon Charles Lindsay, whom Semple Senior had worked with closely during those eight long years of planning the new church, was away or otherwise engaged. Three years later, on 17 April 1843, Mary Semple (née Russell) died, aged 72. This time Archdeacon Lindsay officiated at the funeral, one of only three that he took over a fourteen-year period between 1841 and his own death in 1855. Mary Semple was presumably thus honoured as the wife of the church architect. Even the funerals of Lieutenant General Sir Joseph Hugh Carncross, KCB, and Rear Admiral Sir Thomas Ussher were delegated to Lindsay's two curates.

Less than three weeks after his mother's death, John Semple, Junior, advertised 'Fairyland' to be let, partly furnished (*Saunders's News-Letter*, 6 May 1843). Those interested were to apply at 'Mr. Semple's Office', now at 13 College Green.

John Semple, Junior (1800–82)

At the age of 40, John Semple, Junior, found himself suddenly independent of his father, no longer the junior partner. But even before his work as architect to the Board of First Fruits had officially finished in 1834, John Semple, Junior, had graduated to secular buildings, such as Carysfort Royal School in County Wicklow, built during 1829–31 (Quane 1961).

He must have been highly regarded because at Michaelmas 1830 he was admitted to the ancient Freedom of Dublin by 'Grace Especial'. This category was the equivalent of today's Honorary Freedom and was reserved for dignitaries and craftsmen who were not in a trade guild. Other members of the Semple family had already been admitted by 'Birth' to 'the Freedom' (including his father in 1792 and his clergyman brother, Edward, in 1831, both of whom were described as bricklayers); this was a right granted to the sons of 'Free Citizens'.[11]

In 1831 John Semple, Junior, received another honour: he was elected as one of the two junior high sheriffs of Dublin, a most prestigious — and expensive — post. (As we have seen with his father's appointment, sheriffs had to be worth '£2,000 above their just debts'.)

Semple's first official dinner as high sheriff was in October that year. One month later, he was sworn on to the Dublin City Grand Jury, on 7 November 1831. Like his father, he later became a sheriff's peer, although he only served for a few years, from 1838 to 1841, as the Pettigrew & Oulton Directories for those years record.

As high sheriff, Semple had to attend all kinds of functions. In December 1831 he was invited to be one of the collectors at St Luke's Charity Sermon in aid of the parochial schools. On Christmas Day 1831 the lord mayor, high sheriffs and city officers all attended church at St Werburgh's. (If Semple did attend, he might have missed the opening service at 'his' newly built Monkstown, held on the same day; records give no indication of his presence.) In January the following year, as a loyal Orangeman, he was present at Morrisson's Hotel at a dinner for 'Orangemen and Protestants professing Orange principles' and, as the 'senior sheriff', he gave a speech promising to uphold 'the principles of Protestantism'. Also during his year as high sheriff he accompanied Sir Thomas Whelan, the lord mayor of Dublin, to London to present an address to William IV; their expenses were covered by the Corporation — £100 for Semple and £300 for Sir Thomas (Lady Gilbert 1891–1944, Vol. XIX).

Meanwhile, there were less enjoyable duties for Semple. Among these was the organisation and execution of sheriff's sales, or bankruptcy auctions (particularly ironic in the light of events that were to affect Semple himself less than ten years later; *see below*). As sheriff, Semple was also involved in debates on the 'Wide Streets' and parliamentary reform. He seemed to have more of a social conscience than many of his peers when he said, in January 1831, that 'it was delightful to see 30,000 of the working classes so well clad, and able to go to the expense of a Christmas pageant' (*Saunders's News-Letter*, 4 January 1831). In addition, as city architect, he was responsible for road and wall repairs.

His fraught working life was paralleled by a busy home life. In 1832 he and Harriet Cuppaidge were married.[12] Over the following nineteen years, while living at 'Lilliput' and then 'Eglinton House', both in Seaview Terrace, Donnybrook, and later at 'Merrion Lodge', Merrion, at least eight children were born to the couple: Edward Arthur (1834), James (1836), George (1840), Charles William (1842), William (1843), Jane (*c.* 1844),[13] Harriet Isabella (1845) and James Charles (1851).[14] The first James and Charles William probably died as children, since it was the custom to call succeeding children after those who had died. After his first two sons were born, Semple, aged 37, took the responsible step of insuring his life for £1,000 (almost €1 million in today's terms).

He also became actively involved in Donnybrook parish. In 1838, the Easter Vestry minutes record on 17 April: 'Resolved unanimously that ... John Semple Jun. be elected churchwarden for the Ensuing year'. Semple had therefore to present the parish accounts the following Easter, when he was elected one of the four officers of health and also one of the fifteen 'overseers of public houses'.

In 1842 Semple's work as city architect ended, although he continued on as pipe water engineer (1832–43) and architect to the prisons (1839–42).[15] While pipe water engineer, Semple seems to have come under scrutiny in some way during 1833–4. It is not clear whether there was a complaint, but 'some unpleasant matters having been stated relative to your Engineer, Mr. John Semple, Junior, it was deemed advisable that the subject should be investigated by a committee'. Semple was interviewed in January 1834 and suspended without pay for four months, by which time his father had resigned from his position as Trustee, presumably in protest. Semple Junior was reinstated in May and his salary paid 'not as a matter of right, but as a matter of justice' (Lady Gilbert 1891–1944, Vol. XIX). One assumes that this means that Semple was cleared of all allegations.

After what must have been a mortifying experience for Semple, the matter was seemingly forgotten since he continued to serve as pipe water engineer for a further nine years, until 1843. (In 1838 he had also been appointed to the responsible position of sheriff's peer, which office he held for three years.) Indeed, on 18 April 1843 he was handsomely rewarded by the 'Lord Mayor, Aldermen and Burgesses of the City of Dublin', who presented him with a bond worth £3,000, or an annual sum of £153-16s-11d (*Dublin Evening Post*, 9 June 1849).

Meanwhile, he carried on with his building. He was clearly extremely active and the money was rolling in. He leased his Donnybrook house, 'Lilliput', its outbuildings and garden in 1838 for 30 years at an annual rent of £25-6s-7d. In 1841 he leased over ten acres of Simmonscourt land from the Hon. Sidney Herbert for 99 years for £64-12s-7d. On this land, between 1841 and 1844, Semple built the 'six houses' (actually three fine three-storey over-basement semi-detached houses) of Seaview Terrace, which were valued at an annual rent of £640 in 1844. Semple and his large family moved into one of them — 'Eglinton House'.

Then, in 1844, he leased over six acres at 'Temple Hill' in Monkstown for 500 years at an annual rent of £300. Here, over the next four or five years, he built the first eight houses of Belgrave Square, starting on the south side. Listed in the *Thom's Irish Almanac* of 1848, the entry read: 'Belgrave-square, Eight new houses, Mr. J. Semple, not yet valued'. (Williams, in his 1994 book, has described these houses as 'some of the finest of Dublin's neo-Classical suburban houses. In the style of George Papworth, with emphatically panelled double doors and shutters. Grecian friezes and frothy plasterwork …'.) Semple was all set to finish the Square. In June 1849 there was enough fire-brick there to make six million bricks. But then things went badly wrong.

The first bankruptcy notice was published in the *Dublin Gazette* on 17 April 1849. In a longer notice in the *Dublin Evening Post* on 9 June, Semple is described not as an architect but as a 'Builder, Dealer and Chapman'. (A 'chapman' was someone who bought and sold, i.e. a dealer.) What had happened? We may never know. Perhaps Semple had borrowed too much; he could have been a gambler, developed some chronic illness, become depressed, drunk all his money or been hit by some building slump (it was, after all, almost the end of the Great Famine and bankruptcy cases had soared during that time).

At any rate, the bankruptcy destroyed Semple, at the relatively early age of 49. The family had to leave 'Eglinton House' for the smaller 'Merrion Lodge' at Old Merrion, on the Blackrock Road. Several years later, they moved again — to Rathmines, near Holy Trinity, the church that Semple had built, with his father, 31 years before. There was another move after a year or two, to Adelaide Road and then to Pleasants Street and Heytesbury Street, all 'downward' moves. Semple's younger brother, James, who was a barrister and a bachelor, lived with the family and also shared his brother's office at College Green, using it as his chambers.[16]

WHO DESIGNED MONKSTOWN CHURCH?

Semple tried to start again, but the odds were against him. He was obviously *persona non grata*: after his bankruptcy, he was never allowed to work again as an architect. He was no longer listed in the Dublin directories under 'Architects and CEs' (civil engineers), although he still retained his 'job description' after his name in the Street Directory section. In 1857, a new chancel was mooted for Monkstown Church, but a Mr John F. Lynch was asked to measure the 'proposed addition' instead of its original architect; five years later, when the chancel was actually being built, John McCurdy was the chosen architect, with Semple, as far as we know, not even being consulted (*see Chapter 7*). In 1859 Donnybrook Church needed refurbishment, but Semple, not only its architect but also a former parishioner and churchwarden, was not chosen; Joseph Welland, the diocesan architect, was given the job instead. In 1860 a competition was announced for the rebuilding of St Andrew's, off Dublin's Suffolk Street, which had been destroyed in a fire. Semple entered a design, which was roundly criticised, as reported in the *Dublin Builder* of May and June 1860: 'Delta is not as happy in his design for this as in some of his previously executed works, many of his features being too much cut up. His style, however, has some merit, but requires an amount of care in the treatment certainly not apparent here.' ('Delta' here refers to Semple's pseudonym; apparently, all architects had fictitious names when entering such competitions.) Semple's design was rejected: it did not even make the first six, out of fourteen submitted.

All these rebuffs were too much and John Semple never worked again. His wife, Harriet, had died before 1864 (when death registration began), so he may have had to face much, or all, of this rejection alone. In 1869, the first of his brothers and sisters who were close to him died: James, his younger brother who had lived with him for over twenty years, died at their home, 78 Heytesbury Street, aged 67; Mary followed him in 1874, Edward in 1880 and Kate in 1882.[17]

Aged 76, John Semple moved, in 1876, to 6 Ontario Terrace in Rathmines to live with his son, John George. Six years later, after a bad fall which confined him to bed, he died from 'age and contusions' on 15 October 1882, with his son by his side.[18] On the death certificate his occupation was given as 'civil engineer'.

The mystery of the headstones

Now we come to the rather strange circumstances surrounding the Semple headstones. As we have seen, John Semple, Senior, had been buried, with his wife Mary, in Carrickbrennan Graveyard; four of their children (Edward, Mary, Kate and John Junior) were buried at Deansgrange and Mount Jerome. But, unaccountably, there is absolutely nothing to identify their graves in any of these three places.

It is possible that the headstone in Carrickbrennan belonging to John Semple, Senior (d. 1840), and his wife Mary (d. 1843), if indeed it existed, may have been broken or defaced. We know that the churchyard had been vandalised before, in 1826, as reported in *Saunders's News-Letter* of March that year. However, it is more difficult to understand the circumstances surrounding the other two cemeteries.

65

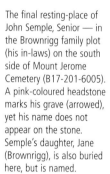

The final resting-place of John Semple, Senior — in the Brownrigg family plot (his in-laws) on the south side of Mount Jerome Cemetery (B17-201-6005). A pink-coloured headstone marks his grave (arrowed), yet his name does not appear on the stone. Semple's daughter, Jane (Brownrigg), is also buried here, but is named.

In 1874 Mary Semple (65) died and was buried in plot I/16/S in Deansgrange Cemetery; no name appears on the stone.[19] Strangely, this plot was already occupied by two members of the Bate family (Alexander, who had died in 1872, and Eliza, in 1871) of Longford Terrace, Monkstown, so why Mary Semple was allowed to be buried in this plot is not at all clear. The Bates had no obvious connection with the Semples. Two more Bates were interred after Mary's burial, in 1876 and 1878 respectively. Then Edward Semple (85), Mary's clergyman brother, died in 1880 and was buried in the same plot; again, there is no identifying name. In August 1882 Kate died and was buried there too. No Semple names appear on the gravestone, whereas all four Bate names are inscribed.

Two weeks later, her elderly brother, John Semple, Junior, aged 82, died. But instead of being buried with the rest of the family at Deansgrange or beside his wife Harriet (whose burial site is unknown), John Semple was buried at Mount Jerome Cemetery in a grave belonging to the Brownrigg family, whose red marble headstone stands against the south perimeter wall of the sprawling five-acre site. As at Deansgrange, the burial was registered in the cemetery register, but Semple's name does not appear on the headstone.[20] Two members of the Brownrigg family were already buried there: Dr Henry Brownrigg, who had died in 1873 at the age of 29, and his mother, Martha (d. 1877), as well as a Mary Jane Higginbotham (d. 1873).

There is no mystery here — John Semple, Junior, was buried in the same grave as his son-in-law, Dr Henry Brownrigg. Dr Brownrigg had married Jane Semple in 1870.[21] Their only son, Henry John, was born the following year. Two years later Dr Brownrigg died, aged only 29, after an illness of three days, and was buried at Mount Jerome.[22] When her father died in 1882, Jane Brownrigg buried him there too. The following year, in 1883, Jane paid the 'opening fee' for this plot, although the Brownrigg family had been using the grave for ten years. (Apparently, it was the custom in Mount Jerome for graves to be formally purchased only after two or three burials had already taken place.[20])

In 1906 Jane died and was buried in the same Brownrigg family plot at Mount Jerome. Her name was engraved on the headstone, presumably by her brother and executor, James Charles, who, inexplicably, did not add that of their father, John Semple. Then, in 1920, James Charles himself, the youngest son of John Semple, died.[23] He was buried in Deansgrange, with his two aunts (Mary and Kate) and uncle (Edward), but no name was engraved on the stone. (When his wife died in 1936, she was buried at Mount Jerome, in yet another plot.[24])

Rejected in death — and in life?

Why did the Semples' names not appear on the stones above their last resting-places? It seems almost deliberately selective. Did it derive from ineptitude, penury, penny-pinching or laziness, or could it have been intentional? Whatever the cause, the whereabouts of their graves was soon forgotten, which must have facilitated their rapid lapse into obscurity.

A satirical poem written by Nicholson Numskull in 1832, lambasting Dublin architects of the period, gives the first real inkling that the Semples may have been unpopular. Semple Senior was described in the poem as 'a Carpenter, a little red-faced tub of a man', and Semple Junior as a 'dandy'.

There are other indications that the Semples were not generally accepted by their peers, that they did not 'mix'. Professionally, they were highly regarded architects: for example, in November 1828 they were chosen out of the 'experienced architects' (William Farrell, Matthew Price, Edward Parke and the Semples) consulted by the Chapter of Christ Church Cathedral when the vaults seemed to be unsafe.[25] However, socially it may have been a different matter. It seems the Semples were not present at the founding meeting of the new Royal Institute of Architects of Ireland (RIAI) in 1839 (O'Dwyer 1989). If they — as the Dublin city architects — were not invited, it was a monumental oversight, when all of Dublin's other leading architects were present, including Papworth, Welland and Murray. On the other hand, unlikely though it may seem, they may have been asked but declined the invitation.

At the Masonic Hall in Molesworth Street, the Semples were conspicuous by their absence from the list of Freemasons involved in the building trade in their day. Because they were not Freemasons, as most architects were then, had they deliberately put themselves outside the 'old boy' network?

Most architects of nineteenth-century Dublin came from established middle-class families. But John Semple, Senior, came from a long line of masons and carpenters, plasterers and stuccodores. Even though he could claim that his uncle, George, had put the spire on St Patrick's Cathedral in 1749 and rebuilt Essex Bridge in 1752–4, his family had sprung from 'trade'. The 1832 poem cattily reminded him that he was only 'a carpenter'. Although, in the Protestant Dublin Corporation, both Semples were elected to positions of high office and brushed shoulders with knights and members of the landed gentry, were they considered 'upstarts'?

Daughters of both Semples had married well. Isabella, daughter of John Semple, Senior, married William Wainwright Lynar, who was knighted by the marquess of Anglesey for his services as high sheriff of Dublin in 1832–3 (*Pettigrew & Oulton Directory*, 1833); he was also a magistrate and commissioner in Kingstown, and one of 'the Irish RMs' (resident magistrates).[26] Sir William Lynar lived at 'Birchfield' on George's Street, Upper, Kingstown (Dublin directories, 1835–9). Jane Semple, the daughter of John Semple, Junior, married Dr Henry Brownrigg, physician, surgeon and apothecary, in 1870.

In the bankruptcy notice of 1849, John Semple, Junior — the former city and diocesan architect, sheriff's peer and senior high sheriff — was demoted to 'a Builder, Dealer and Chapman'. After his bankruptcy, there seems to have been a deliberate 'squeezing out' of John Semple, Junior. The final insult was that, when he died, there was no obituary in any of the main Dublin newspapers (*Saunders's News-Letter*, the *Evening Packet*, the *Freeman's Journal* or the *Dublin Evening Mail*). Furthermore, a letter published in *The Irish Builder* of 1 August 1872, asking for information about John Semple, was apparently not responded to by anyone. It was as if the whole architectural community had sent the Semples 'to Coventry'. And, after their deaths, the closest members of their own families seem to have done the same.

Some conclusions

In the light of all we know about John Semple, father and son, can we decide which of the two architects was ultimately responsible, as Maurice Craig (1992) describes it, for his 'own brand of Gothic, which can be identified at longer range than any style (he knew)'? I think we can, although my conclusions may differ, in some important respects, from current opinion.

In their lifetimes, the Semples apparently attracted little attention, except opprobrium, from the majority of people, and died almost unnoticed and unremarked by their contemporaries. It is only relatively recently that an interest in their work has resurfaced. Today, over a century later, John Semple, Junior, has been credited with the primary hand in the partnership.[27] Allen (1993) believes that the elder Semple was 'a building contractor rather than an architect with design ambitions' and that it was his son who was the 'innovative' influence. Because John Semple, Senior — well into middle age when the two were appointed as diocesan architects — was not known to have produced any previous work of importance, it has been assumed that it must have been his precocious son whose genius spawned these unusual churches, or that Semple Senior needed the catalytic stimulus of his son to produce his striking church designs. Thus John Semple, Junior, has been given the chief credit for Monkstown Church — and all the others.

Such a theory would appear reasonable until one does some research into how John Semple, Senior, related to others and, therefore, to his son. The relationship between the father and son is surely the crux of the matter.

As mentioned above, Christ Church Cathedral experienced structural problems in November 1828. The Cathedral Chapter consulted the Semples — as the diocesan architects — about the state of the cathedral's foundations. While the Chapter seemed to put the two on an equal footing ('Agreed and ordered … to employ two architects of acknowledged skill and celebrity'), John Semple, Senior, 63, obviously had different ideas. It is here that he demonstrated his patriarchal attitude towards his son, 28. It was he who wrote all the letters to the Chapter and signed them, without any reference to his son. Although he did refer initially to the partnership of 'my son and I', thereafter he expressed his own thoughts and opinions: '*I* submit that *I* ought to be further empowered … *I* have to request that a carpenter and a Mason … should meet *me* … *I* wish you to understand that *I* do not at present conclude …' [author's emphasis].[25]

This little interchange puts John Semple, Senior, firmly in the driving seat in 1828, which is right in the middle of the Semple church-building period. He comes across as a strong-minded, even pugnacious, individual, who does not suffer fools gladly. This self-made man, who was apparently looked down on because he had risen from 'trade', was patently not afraid to stand up to the revered Cathedral Chapter, headed by the titled Charles Lindsay, dean of Christ Church, bishop of Kildare and patron of Monkstown.

If he was behaving like this in 1828 towards his son, is it likely that he would have allowed him to design his first church, Monkstown (with so many similarities to the sixteen which followed it), five years earlier, in 1823, at the age of 23? It is certainly true that it was John Semple, Junior, who met the Monkstown Vestry for the first time in December 1823, but the Vestry clerk makes it clear that he is doing so on behalf of his father: '(He) produced on the part of Mr. Semple … estimates of two plans'.

A quote from the *Building News* of 1857 gives additional support to the fact that it was John Semple, Senior, rather than Junior, who was the creative partner. The writer had heard that Monkstown was planning an addition to the church (i.e. the chancel) and warned against tampering with the 'chef d'oeuvre of the late Mr. Semple'. Up to now, it has been assumed that this referred to John Semple, Junior, who had disappeared into architectural obscurity at this stage, and that the writer was mistaken in assuming that he was dead. However, 'the late Mr. Semple' referred to is actually John Semple, Senior, who had died in 1840 and whose *chef-d'oeuvre* was indeed Monkstown.

On these grounds, I believe that Monkstown and the other Semple churches were primarily the work of John Semple, Senior.

Semple Senior and his influences

> *The Architect [John Semple] has built for posterity; and this edifice and other similar*
> *structures, although cavilled at by superficial observers, may justly claim precedence over*
> *the many gimcrack structures of modern times miscalled Gothic.*
> *Dublin Penny Journal,* 14 September 1833, on Holy Trinity Church, Rathmines

Sir Christopher Wren (1632–1723) believed that the pointed arch had been brought back by the Crusaders from the east and was therefore barbaric and retrograde: 'The Goths and Vandals, having demolished the Greek and Roman architecture, introduced in its stead a certain fantastical and licentious manner of building which we have since called modern or

Gothic'. The word 'Gothic' still carried connotations of bad taste as late as the 1880s: 'The scenery of the place [Torquay] has been quite spoilt … by Gothish "improvements"', reported the *World* on 10 November 1880.

Until 1820, Gothic buildings were almost all non-ecclesiastical; they were seen as romantic and appealed to the wealthy for their homes. Few churches were being built in England at the time: in London, only twelve churches were built between 1760 and 1820. But after that date there was an explosion of activity in England. The Church Building Act of 1818 meant that £6 million was poured into 214 churches between 1818 and 1833. Of these, more than 80% (174) were built in the 'Gothic' style, which the Church Commissioners had recommended not for its aesthetic qualities but because they considered it 'the most economical mode of building churches, with a view to accommodating the greatest number of persons at the smallest expense' (Clark 1974).

Meanwhile, in Ireland, church-building and its fashions followed a similar pattern. Before 1820 new churches were few and far between. The appointment of the dynamic Archbishop William Magee to Dublin and, around the same time, the establishment of the Board of First Fruits together galvanised a sudden burst of activity. John Semple & Son, newly appointed as the diocesan architects for the province of Dublin in 1824, were in the happy position of being swamped by requests for their services. In their ten years in office, they built or extended at least seventeen churches and possibly several glebe houses.[28] (Interestingly, at the time the plans for the enlargement of Monkstown Church were presented to the Vestry, in December 1823, the Semples had not yet been officially appointed as diocesan architects. Their involvement may have been due to the personal initiative of Archbishop Magee, who had a deep interest in the development of the church.)

If it was indeed John Semple, Senior, who was the driving force in the father and son partnership, what were his influences? What made him deviate from the 'pure and correct architectural style' so zealously followed by the vast majority of his fellow architects?[29] Consider his personal history. Semples had rarely strayed from any occupation not associated with building for the past hundred years. They were considered reliable, 'safe' workmen. John Semple's great-uncle, George, had built Essex Bridge, St Patrick's Hospital and the spire on St Patrick's Cathedral. But, according to Craig (1990), John Semple, Senior, was a 'maverick'. From the evidence of his work, he did not want to produce more of the same: he wanted to develop an individual style, while keeping to the 'economical' ecclesiastical Gothic clothes-horse. Although his churches were certainly very different to others at the time, they were very similar, often almost identical, to each other.

Sir William Chambers (1726–96), the eminent architect (for example, of London's Somerset House and Dublin's Marino Casino), was convinced that architects should travel. He wrote: 'It seems almost superfluous to observe that an architect cannot aspire to superiority in his profession without having travelled; for, it must be obvious that an art founded upon reasoning and much observation is not to be learnt without it; books cannot avail; descriptions, even drawings or prints, are but weak substitutes for realities'.[30] Most drawings and prints fall into this category, but what if the artist has the gift of demonstrating what is called, in our computer age, 'virtual reality'? What if the seminal work, translated by a gifted hand onto paper, travelled to the architect, rather than the architect to the work?

Douglas Scott Richardson (1983) has suggested that John Semple, Senior, may well have spent some time in Spain (during the Peninsular War of 1808–14). He bases this on the similarity between Semple's diaphragm arches in several of his churches, such as Kilternan, and those in thirteenth-century churches of Catalonia, Valencia and especially Poblet, near Tarragona, where the arches of the main dormitory of this Cistercian monastery bear a striking resemblance to those of Kilternan.[27] A small British force was stationed near Tarragona in 1813 and Richardson suggests that Semple was among them. But from all that is known of Semple, the author feels that it is highly unlikely that Semple ever travelled outside Ireland for the following reasons: (1) Semple was of neither the right age nor background when the Peninsular War broke out in 1808; he was 45, the father of at least three young children and a busy, successful architect, living in his dream home of 'Fairyland' in Dunleary; (2) no source suggests that Semple had a military background: he had no military title and was always called plain 'Mr Semple'; (3) it is unlikely that he was in Spain in 1808–11 since his two daughters were conceived and born between 1808 and 1810, and he also attended the Monkstown Easter Vestry in 1809 *and* signed the minutes; (4) also between 1808 and 1814, he was listed in the Dublin directories as 'John Semple, Sheriff's Peer & Builder, 21 Marlborough St.'; (5) he was elected annually as 'sheriff's peer' from 1798 to his death in 1840; it is unlikely that an absentee would have been elected to this responsible position.

One of the most remarkable books of Semple's day was a posthumous work by a fellow Irish architect, James Cavanah Murphy (1760–1814).[31] His was a romantic story: the gifted boy from a deprived Cork background who was seen sketching by an altruistic patron of the arts (Sir James Chatterton), plucked from obscurity and sent to perfect his drawing at the Royal Dublin Society (Plunkett 1909). He confirmed his early genius and, by the age of 26, was said to be one of seven architects consulted about additions to the Irish House of Commons. Two years later, in 1788, his friend and benefactor, the Hon. William Burton Conyngham, sent Murphy to draw the church and monastery at Batalha in Portugal, so impressed had he been on seeing it first, in 1783. Murphy realised that some of the Dominican friars at Batalha were suspicious of his motives and, anxious to complete the task accurately, he worked day and night for 22 days, making himself ill in the process.

After returning home, he published, in 1795 in London, his *Plans, elevations, sections, and views of the church at Batalha … to which is prefixed an introductory discourse on the principles of Gothic architecture*. Murphy departed again in 1802, this time to Spain, and was soon immersed in Moorish architecture in Granada, Cordova and Seville, writing afterwards that 'Seven years were unremittingly devoted to these delightful pursuits'. In 1809 he returned to England to complete his notes and plates, based on about twelve years of continuous work: 98 large folio plates illustrated every minute detail, while ground-plans and inscriptions testified to his accuracy. His drawings 'were not merely easy sketches, but calculated with all the pains and accuracy which a man would use who desired to reproduce the originals from working drawings'. (J.F. Fuller, a Dublin architect, later used Murphy's drawings to reproduce an accurate Alhambra ceiling at 'St Ann's', the residence of Lord Ardilaun.) Murphy died in 1814, at the age of 54, before publication of his *Arabian antiquities of Spain*. This work contained the first accurate and detailed drawings of Moorish architecture ever seen in England or Ireland (Plunkett 1909).

While at Batalha, Murphy made a curious discovery. The original architect of Batalha was not Portuguese: he was believed to be an Irishman called David Hacket (probably also known as Master Ouguete or Huguete), who had lived there from 1402 to 1451 and had completed the building by 1416 (Plunkett 1909). The wheel seems, extraordinarily, to have come full circle. Someone who first studied Murphy's plates of Batalha and then looked at the skyline of Monkstown might feel a sense of *déjà vu*: indeed, Monkstown Church has been aptly described as 'a glorious extravaganza … less amazing if it were in Portugal than in alien majesty in the middle of genteel Monkstown' (De Breffny and Mott 1976). Is it too far-fetched to conclude that drawings — by an Irish architect (Murphy) of a Portuguese church (Batalha) designed by another Irish architect (Hacket) — may well have been the flame that ignited the enthusiasm of the Irish architect of Monkstown (Semple)? The timing of Murphy's publications on Batalha (1795) and on Moorish architecture (1813–16) and Semple's first Monkstown plans (1823) fit, allowing for a few years to give him time to see and study them. This idea was first suggested to the author by Maurice Craig in 1998.

Monkstown largely gets its Moorish flavour from its skyline. It is the upper section with minaret-like turrets and towers that lends a Portuguese flavour to the whole. Inside, too, it is the ceiling and upper half of the building that is particularly Arabic — the great segmental arches, the 'immense blocks' etched on the walls ('Perhaps the architect, as the whole inside is in the Arabesque style, wished, by the position of these ponderous blocks, to give the idea of the prophet's tomb suspended in the air', quipped the *Irish Ecclesiastical Gazette* of 20 March 1880) and the geometrical patterns, so basic to Islam, on the gallery fronts. No wonder 'genteel Monkstown' was scandalised, to find a 'heathen' building in such an ostentatious and commanding position. And the joke was that, as the building rose in their midst, no-one realised, until the last weeks or months, that its eventual style would not be thought 'suitable for a Christian place of worship'.

Semple even copied the Moors in his method of converting the plain Georgian 'preaching box' into his 'gorgeous edifice'. Typically, the conquering Moors tended to adapt surviving buildings and make them their own by adding on minarets and external embellishments — in much the same way as Semple did to the older church (Fletcher 1938). Inside, Semple kept the west end intact, but married it to his larger addition by extending his 'granite' blocks throughout and adding details, such as topping the Georgian windows with his characteristic drip-mouldings inside and out. (It is also interesting, in this context, that Semple's King's Room of 1821 was described as 'a Moorish palace'.)

Of course, the fanciful story of Cavanah Murphy's Batalha is only one of the hypotheses that might be advanced as to how Monkstown Church acquired its Moorish character. However, a curious combination of other themes is found in Monkstown, described by a contemporary as 'a mule between the Gothic and the Saracenic'. Semple would not have had to travel outside Ireland to find his ogee doors (as in the west doorway of Dunmore Friary, Galway, or the church on Devenish Island in Lough Erne, Co. Fermanagh) or his vaulted stone roofs (as in St Kevin's of Glendalough or Cormac's Chapel in Cashel). Buttresses, string-coursing, crocketed pinnacles and crenellations are strong features of the Chapel Royal in Dublin Castle, which, as Richardson (1983) points out, Semple would have known well since the First Fruits' office was also at Dublin Castle.

The characteristics of Semple churches

The Semples designed seven churches in County Dublin and at least another ten in counties Kildare, Laois, Offaly and Wexford. These were all in the original province of Dublin. They were all built within the space of ten years and all to the same blueprint. The following list of 'Semple Temples' has been compiled with the help of Patrick Farrell, Maurice Craig (1990) and Cormac Allen (1993):

> *Dublin and county:* Monkstown; Holy Trinity, Rathmines; Whitechurch; Simmonscourt (Donnybrook); Kilternan (Kilgobbin); St Mary's Chapel of Ease (the Black Church); Tallaght.
> *Co. Kildare:* Feighcullen; Ballysax; Thomastown; Newbridge; Rathangan.
> *Co. Laois:* Abbeyleix (west end).
> *Co. Laois/Co. Carlow:* Killeshin (Semple's west end in Laois; Welland's east end in Carlow).
> *Co. Offaly:* Cloneyhurke; Ballykeen (Killeighy), now demolished.
> *Co. Wexford:* Selskar, Wexford town (hitherto unidentified as Semple's work).[32]

On superficial inspection, Monkstown Parish Church appears to be completely different to all the rest. But even a rapid inventory will reveal a host of similarities. Semple had a particular vision of church architecture, which he worked as a formula. Once one is familiar with that formula, it is almost impossible to pass a Semple church without identifying it correctly. The illustration on pp 74–5 shows the main architectural characteristics of Monkstown Church. Additional Semple features demonstrated in his other churches, but not at Monkstown, include:

- Vaulted stone roofs, as in Rathmines, Abbeyleix and the Black Church; today, only the Black Church retains its vault, an unusual parabolic design.
- Diaphragm arches of timber, spanning the church and supported on stone corbels, as in Kilternan and Tallaght.
- Blank niches flanking the west door, usually framed by string-coursing, as in Holy Trinity, Rathmines, and Kilternan.
- Closely spaced buttresses at intervals along the external north and south walls, as in Tallaght and Donnybrook.
- Square narrow towers, topped by a parapet with corner pinnacles, often with a slender spire, as in Whitechurch and Kilternan.
- The Communion table stood at the east end, sometimes on a 'Communion platform'. The reading desk was on the north side and the pulpit on the south (this is the opposite arrangement to that of today).
- An extremely narrow, pointed-arched doorway at the west end, as in Whitechurch, Kilternan and Holy Trinity, Rathmines.
- A Greek cross carved into stone above the west door, as in Whitechurch, Kilternan and Holy Trinity, Rathmines.

Semple's Monkstown Church, completed in 1831 — built with local Dalkey granite and set in a commanding position facing down Monkstown Road. Semple & Son designed some seventeen churches in the original province of Dublin, including St Mary's (the Black Church), Whitechurch, Kilternan, Donnybrook and Holy Trinity, Rathmines. Monkstown was the largest, most elaborate and most expensive of all, combining many of the features used in other church designs but on a much grander scale, resulting in this unique architectural 'extravaganza'.

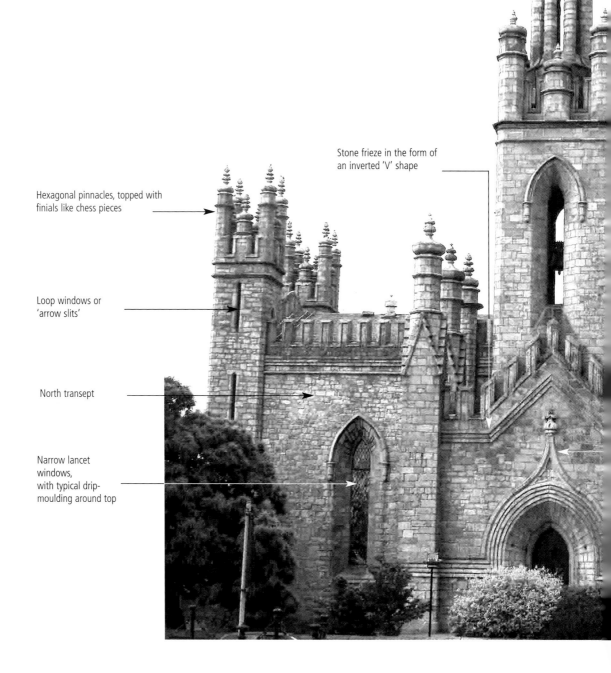

Stone frieze in the form of an inverted 'V' shape

Hexagonal pinnacles, topped with finials like chess pieces

Loop windows or 'arrow slits'

North transept

Narrow lancet windows, with typical drip-moulding around top

The inside of Monkstown Church is as unusual as the outside: the spectacular ceiling, with its scalloped plasterwork, is dominated by great corbelled fan vaulting and soaring segmental arches, the walls are 'uttered and jointed to represent granite stone', as per Semple's instructions, and the 'hairpin' decorations on the gallery fronts all lend an exotic, almost Moresque, air to this place of Christian worship.

Greek cross

Decorative ogee arches

Lantern

Crenellated parapet

Bell-tower

Tiled or slated effect on pinnacles

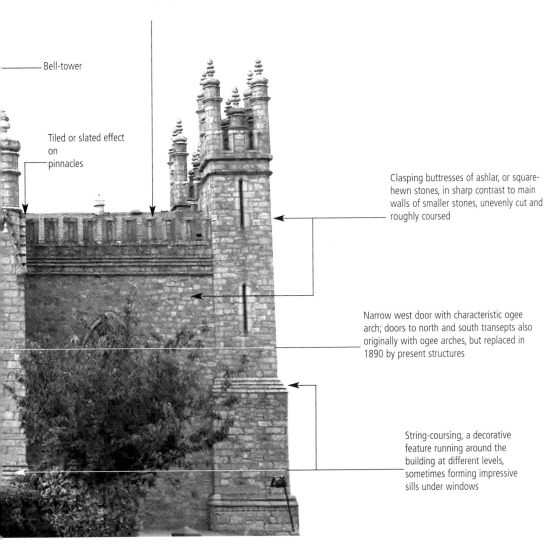

Clasping buttresses of ashlar, or square-hewn stones, in sharp contrast to main walls of smaller stones, unevenly cut and roughly coursed

Narrow west door with characteristic ogee arch; doors to north and south transepts also originally with ogee arches, but replaced in 1890 by present structures

String-coursing, a decorative feature running around the building at different levels, sometimes forming impressive sills under windows

In addition, most Semple churches were correctly orientated (i.e. towards the east) and were built of local stone. Several of the churches were built in a commanding position, often in the middle of the road (for example, Monkstown, the Black Church, Donnybrook and Holy Trinity, Rathmines). Most of the Semple drawings (for example, Monkstown, Rathmines and Donnybrook) show a small vestry or robing room behind the east end, with access through a door beneath the east window.

Semple insisted on the highest standards, as seen in this series of instructions: 'The painting to be done in the best manner and to get three coats including the priming. The windows to be put together in the most substantial manner, a compartment to open. The stone masonry in the foundation and superstructure to be done in the most solid and substantial manner; the bottom course of the foundations to be of large dimensions and well grouted. The works to be composed of river or sharp bank sand and good lime. None but the best North of Europe timber to be used in the Building. The trusses and other portions of the roof must be worked with great accuracy, and great care must be taken to place the sundry bolts of the trusses in position shown in the drawing of the roof at large.'[33]

Monkstown's differences

In Monkstown Church, Semple reproduced many features from his other churches but on a very different, often spectacularly grandiose, scale. For example, he used timber, lath and plaster to make his slender diaphragm arches, seen in Kilternan, Feighcullen and Tallaght. Using exactly the same materials, he created the magnificent ceiling of Monkstown — 'formed with lath and plaster on an elaborate timber framing', according to the 1985 architect's report of Wilson Guard. Feighcullen was Semple's only other church with ogee arches, found relatively inconspicuously on its narrow tower and inside on the west wall; in Monkstown, however, ogee arches framed all three entrance doors, while that at the west end was emphasised by a deeper string-coursing than that found in any of the other Semple churches.

Although Monkstown was similar in many ways to other Semple churches, there are also major differences.

- The most obvious difference is the roof-line. The 'spiky Gothic' of the other churches has been replaced by crenellations, towers and turrets with finials like chess pieces.
- Monkstown is at least two or three times larger than any of the other churches.
- Monkstown cost nearly twice as much as even the most expensive of the others — £8,665 compared to costs of between £830 and £4,843.
- Monkstown was the only one to be built on the actual site of a previous church and to incorporate its walls into the building. (Tallaght and Selskar were joined to the earlier building by a kind of porch.)
- Monkstown was the only church with transepts; these were to accommodate the huge numbers (a congregation of 1,200). Selskar had a

west gallery; Monkstown had three (one in each transept and at the west end).

- Monkstown was the only church with 'arrow slits' (loop windows).
- Monkstown was the only church with vaults under the building.
- As far as we know, Monkstown was the only church with a 'three-decker' pulpit, necessary for the sheer scale of the church.
- Monkstown took the longest to build (nine years from drawing-board to completed church).
- As far as we know, Archbishop Magee was more closely involved with Monkstown than any of the other churches, although the more one looks, the more his close interest is revealed.[34]

Monkstown somehow stands apart, similar in so many ways to Semple's other churches and yet so different — a 'one-off', 'an extraordinary architectural phenomenon', as the Parochial Register Society of Dublin called it (Guinness 1908), unparalleled in Ireland.

At the end of the day, we can only speculate as to why the parish church at Monkstown was transformed from a 'rectangular preaching box' into 'a glorious extravaganza' by 'a jobbing building contractor' — 'a little red-faced tub of a man', according to Numskull (1832) — and his 'dandy' son. Perhaps implicitly condescending views of the Semples such as these should be re-evaluated in the light of such obvious original genius.

CHAPTER 7

McCurdy's chancel
and other changes (1862–1947)

Nothing is permanent but change.
Heraclitus

E ven as Semple's enormous new church in Monkstown opened on Christmas Day 1831, with room for 1,200 people, it seems to have already been too small. Attendance was said to be 1,300, according to the 1st Report of the Commissioners of Public Instruction (1835). This seems to be supported by other sources. For example, a letter-writer to the *Dublin Evening Post* on 7 February 1832 (a month after the church opened) complained: 'Two additional Chapels, at least, are wanted for the celebration of Divine Service'. It must be remembered that Monkstown Church was 'the only church from Ringsend to Bray, the extremity of the county, an extent including eleven populous villages, and a very thickly inhabited country' (Warburton *et al.* 1818).

As more and more people moved into Dublin's new coastal suburbs, trees were felled and the patchwork of little fields taken over by houses. Reforms in the Church of Ireland during the 1820s and '30s had led to an evangelical revival and its members were enthusiastically attending church again after the arid Georgian period. But many of them could only find standing room in the vast new church of Monkstown. Obviously, a larger church was needed to cater for the immediate congregation, as well as more churches in the wider parish area.

The Protestant population of Monkstown and its united parishes increased by nearly 400% between 1806 and 1831, two dates for which we have some idea of the figures. According to the Vestry book of 1805–29, there were 195 households in 1806, with approximately 780 Protestants; by 1831 there were 3,137 Protestants, according to the 1st Report of the Commissioners of Public Instruction (1835). Thus, in 1806, the church built in 1789 could not have accommodated the estimated 780 Protestants in the Union, if they were all to attend church (it only had a capacity of 340 seated). Even Semple's vast church of 1831 could only seat 1,200, whereas there were three times that number in the Union. Churches had to be built, albeit somewhat retrospectively. Over a period of 35 years, between 1835 and 1870, eleven churches sprang up, and three 'rooms' were used for services, within the original Union of Monkstown (*see Appendix 1*).

Not only was Monkstown Church too small for the number of its parishioners, its interior design was also becoming redundant. This was because of radical ecclesiastical reforms being made in the Church of Ireland at the time, which affected the liturgy; this, in turn, affected the internal layout of churches (*see below*). When Semple enlarged the 'rectangular preaching box' church of 1789, he lengthened it and added huge transepts, a shallow extension and 'vestiary' at the east end. There was no chancel involved. They were simply not fashionable: churches then were designed to be 'auditory churches', where the sermon was the highlight of the service and to be heard by everyone. If the 'man in the pew' was to hear the preacher in the pulpit, strict guidelines had been laid down by Sir Christopher Wren (1632–1723). As the architect of over 50 churches, including St Paul's Cathedral, he had pronounced that a preacher's voice could best be heard 66 feet in front of him, 22 feet to each side and 11 feet behind.[1] This formula was to influence church building during the late seventeenth and eighteenth centuries, and is also evident in Semple's plan for Monkstown.

The interior of Monkstown has been totally transformed since Semple's day. His magnificent ceiling and gallery fronts remain, but his pulpit and seating have all been swept away. If we visualise Semple's church as a giant 'T', a huge 'three-decker' pulpit dominated the central aisle, at the crossing point. All the pews faced inwards, towards the pulpit, including those in the small extension at the east end containing the 'vestiary'. The 'three-

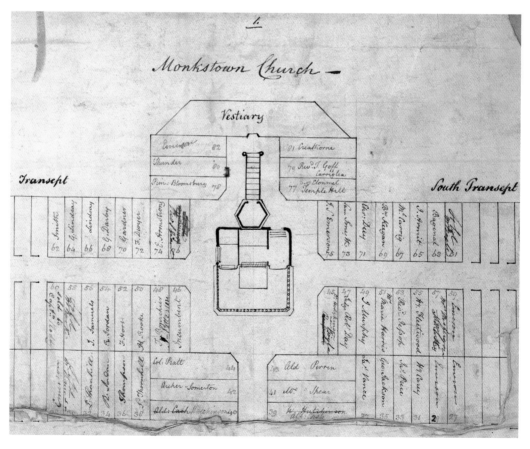

Seating plan of 1832, showing vestiary, wide transepts and great central pulpit, with many of the pews already allocated to private owners.

decker' pulpit was built on different levels: the pulpit itself at the top for the clergyman, the desk in the middle for the parish clerk, and Communion rails at ground level. Having the pulpit at such a height was useful for the clergyman to keep an eye on his often-inattentive congregation, hiding in their high box pews. The haphazard conduct prevalent in church in those days was dealt with by the parish beadle, whose duties included keeping order in church, waking the sleeping and chasing out stray dogs.

The necessity for church reform

Even as Semple was building Monkstown, a movement was growing within the Anglican Church to try and reform the abuses of the day, including pluralism, absenteeism and nepotism, to name but a few. Church services were generally poorly attended: for example, on Easter Day 1800 there were six communicants in London's St Paul's (unfortunately, we do not have the relevant preachers' books to tell us how many there were in Monkstown). Dean Swift delivered stinging sermons on 'Sleeping in Church' and on poor attendance, saying 'There is no excuse so trivial that will not pass upon some men's consciences to excuse their attendance at the public worship of God' (Davis 1948). Although in 1813 Monkstown was said to have had 'a more numerous population of the established religion than in any other part of Ireland' (Warburton *et al.* 1818), attendance was typically poor and the clergy of the parish were as guilty as others of abusing their position.

Fundamental church reform was necessary to stamp out these abuses. But there was such resistance to change in Ireland that the government appointed the English-born Richard Whately as archbishop of Dublin in 1831. Under him, the Church Temporalities Act of 1833 brought in some drastic changes. Ten bishoprics were suppressed and tithes (taxes of one-tenth of annual produce, taken to support clergy and church) were to be handled in future by the Ecclesiastical Commissioners. (It was in response to these changes in the Church of Ireland that John Keble gave his famous sermon, 'National Apostacy', in Oxford in 1833 and launched the Oxford Movement, which was to have such a huge influence in every part of church worship (Johnston *et al.* 1953). Keble argued that parliament could not suppress bishops, whose authority was by apostolic succession, and accused it of a 'direct disavowal of the sovereignty of God'.)

These adjustments in the Church of Ireland could not be achieved without upsetting a great many people and certainly not overnight. The conservatives associated Whately's innovations with 'Puseyism' (so called after Pusey of the Oxford Movement) and 'popery', both of which were anathema to them (Brooks and Saint 1995). So, although Whately began the reforms, it was not until the time of his successor, Richard Chenevix Trench, that the main ecclesiastical, or ecclesiological, changes to churches were made.

In 1865 Archbishop Trench, in his primary charge, criticised 'the extraordinary unsightliness of many of our churches, indeed of almost all that were built in the last century or during the first decades of the present; the unecclesiastical character of their arrangements; the huge wooden fortress rising up in the centre, blocking out all view of the chancel; the Communion table safely nestled behind the pulpit; all this is a legacy from past times, we must accept, labouring indeed to see it gradually remedied and removed' (Crawford 1996).

Trench's reference to 'the unecclesiastical character of their arrangements' was the nub of the matter. The huge changes in the church initiated by the Oxford Movement had led to changes in the liturgy, which meant that churches had to be altered accordingly. To emphasise the new importance given to the Eucharist, chancel extensions were built onto the oblong Georgian churches. The cumbersome three-decker pulpits (Trench's reference to the 'huge wooden fortress'), which stood at the east end of the nave in front of the Communion table, were done away with, so that worshippers could have an uninterrupted view. Music was to take a more central role in the new liturgy, so the organ was moved from the west gallery, at the 'back' of the church, to the new chancel at the 'front', where there was now room for a choir. These changes helped to create a more vigorous church, which drew larger congregations, and so galleries and transepts were often added to accommodate them. The pulpit was placed at the north side of the chancel, while the lectern or reading desk was set on the south (Yates 1991).

The peak years for Victorian church-building and restoration were in the 1860s and '70s, and Monkstown did not escape. It has been shown that a new incumbent — the proverbial 'new broom' — was the most influential factor in launching any major changes. An enthusiastic churchwarden could also swing the balance. Of 225 Victorian church restorations in England, 45% took place within three years of a new incumbent being appointed and 66% within five years (Brooks and Saint 1995). Events followed much the same pattern in Monkstown, as we shall see. All the relevant liturgical changes were made to the church, including the major structural addition of a new chancel, built in 1862, cleverly camouflaged both inside and out to blend with Semple's design.

Another church in Monkstown — or a new chancel?

Since the Vestry minutes covering the years 1829–71 are not extant, we have to glean the history of Monkstown Church from newspapers and other sources of the day. The first proposal was an ambitious one — to build a new church. This was suggested in 1856 (the year after Fitzgerald's appointment as incumbent), according to a letter in *Saunders's News-Letter* of 30 September 1857 from 'a parishioner'. It said, 'Last year, an effort was made to raise funds to build and endow a new church, but without success; so that no alternative remains but to enlarge the parish church'.

Since the idea of a new church failed to generate funds, an alternative suggestion was made — to add a chancel onto the existing building shortly after MacDonnell's appointment in 1857. The word 'chancel' comes from the Latin *cancelli*, meaning 'bars of lattice work', and was used to refer to that place, enclosed by a lattice-screen, originally in a basilica, where the judges and council sat apart from the ordinary people. From that, the word came to mean the eastern end of a church, separated from the main body by a screen (Burn 1809). Traditionally, the chancel was the responsibility of the incumbent, whereas the churchwardens looked after the rest of the building. Clergy were often buried in the chancel, as described in the Rev. George Crabbe's poem 'The Borough' — 'Where ends our chancel in a vaulted space, Sleep the departed Vicars of the place'. Allan Maddison (incumbent of Monkstown, 1691–1741), for example, was 'buried under the Communion Table' of Carrickbrennan Church on 29 January 1741/42. His curate, Matthew Gibson, had died a year earlier and was 'buried at the right side of the Holy Table, April 1740'. And when Mary, Maddison's widow, died in 1771, she too was 'interred in the chancel' (Guinness 1908).

Having decided to add a chancel, an estimate was sought from the builder John F. Lynch of 'Black Rock', whose reply, dated 23 June 1857, said: 'According to Mr. Betham's [Molyneux Betham, a churchwarden] wishes, I have measured the proposed addition to Monkstown Church, and find by the closest calculations that it cannot be executed for less than one thousand and thirty pounds'.[2]

The proposal was then introduced at a Vestry meeting on 22 September 1857, followed up quickly by an announcement in *Saunders's News-Letter* on 24 September: 'Monkstown Church. It is proposed to enlarge this church, according to plans prepared by Mr. Welland, architect to the Ecclesiastical Commissioners, the cost to be defrayed by public subscriptions.' A notice also appeared in that month's *Irish Ecclesiastical Gazette*, stating that 'collections are being made towards defraying the expenses of erecting a new church in this large and important parish'. (Note the disparity here between 'enlarging' the old and 'erecting' a new.)

Others were dismayed at this news. A letter appeared in the British *Building News* of 1857, warning that the 'chef d'oeuvre of the late Mr. Semple' should not be tampered with (Kilternan Parish Church 1976). (The 'late Mr. Semple' must refer to John Semple, Senior, who had died in 1840; *see Chapter 6*.) Several unhappy parishioners used the pages of *Saunders's News-Letter* to publicly air their dissatisfaction with the whole idea. One, on 28 September 1857, accused a 'zealous' few of forcing their wishes on the majority: 'The questionable proposal to enlarge our beautiful church … is viewed throughout the entire parish with the strongest disfavour'. The writer went on to criticise the system where 'a vestry, comprising about twenty people … should be quietly permitted to resolve upon an alteration to the church, and … adopt a plan about which they know no more either as to cost or merit than they do about the mountains of the moon'. Perhaps this vocal majority swayed the Vestry. At any rate, plans for the chancel went into hibernation for four years.

Since no Vestry minutes exist, we do not know what prompted the resurrection of the plans, but on 1 March 1862 the diocesan architects, Welland and Gillespie, drew up a 'specification of works necessary to be done in Enlarging the Church of Monkstown'; this was accompanied by a rough plan of the chancel.[3] (The 'Welland' mentioned here is Welland Junior; his father, Joseph, who had drawn up the original plans for the chancel in 1857, had died in 1860.) A couple of weeks later, these documents were sent to Archbishop Trench with a letter from the Rev. Ronald MacDonnell and the churchwardens, asking for authorisation of these 'alterations and improvements'. Trench wrote on the chancel plan, 'Approved, R. Dublin'.

As far as we know, John Semple, Junior — who, with his father (d. 1840), was the original architect of Monkstown Church — was never consulted about the design of the new chancel. He had been declared a bankrupt in 1849 and seems to have been shunned as an architect and builder from that day onward (*see Chapter 6*).

McCurdy's chancel of 1862

Work began immediately on the new chancel. Semple's east end of the church, with its small vestiary, was demolished. Thomas Lacy (1863) wrote that the church in 'June 1862 (was) undergoing extensive repairs and improvements, whereby it (would) be considerably enlarged'. However, the later date of October appears on another set of detailed plans for the chancel, bearing the stamp of 'John McCurdy, Architect and C.E., 1 Harcourt Place, Lower Merrion Street, Dublin', with the note 'Plan referred to in the Articles of Agreement this day Executed by me bearing date this 13th day of October 1862, present George Farrell, O Ball'.[4] (George Farrell was probably a builder.)

There are slight differences between the March 1862 drawings of Welland and Gillespie and these later, October ones: the five-light east window has become a large tripartite window and stairs have been placed behind the pulpit to the Vestry rooms below. For some reason, Welland and Gillespie were replaced by John McCurdy, perhaps because he was a parishioner of Monkstown and may have offered a cheaper estimate.

John McCurdy[5] (1823–85) was a pupil of Frederick Darley, the architect of Monkstown's chapel of ease at Killiney (the present St Matthias's), completed in 1835. McCurdy was responsible for some well-known buildings, including Dublin's Shelbourne Hotel in 1865 (a 'mid-Victorian masterpiece', Bowen 1951) and Dunleary's Marine Hotel, which made the company bankrupt in 1869 (Williams 1994). He worked in partnership

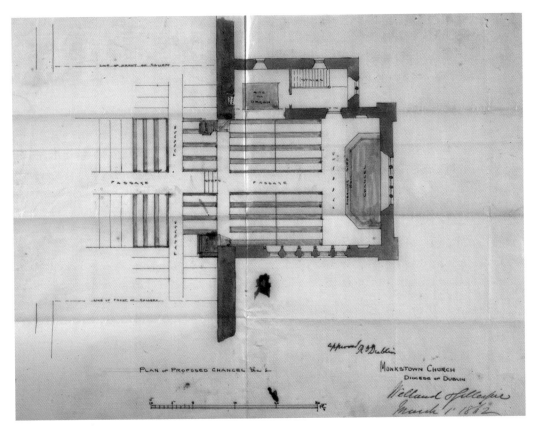

Welland and Gillespie's plan for the new chancel of Monkstown Church, dated 1 March 1862 and bearing Archbishop Trench's authorisation, 'Approved, R. Dublin'.

with William Mitchell from about 1873, building, for example, the Masonic Girls' School in Ballsbridge in 1882 (which now retains only its façade and has been developed into apartments and a hotel). In 1875, McCurdy and Mitchell lived almost next door to each other in Monkstown's Trafalgar Terrace, at Nos 11 and 14 respectively. McCurdy also rebuilt the Salthill Hotel in 1865, enlarging and refurbishing the original building, within a few hundred yards of Monkstown Church. (The hotel was demolished after a fire in 1972 and is now the site of the Salthill Apartments.)

McCurdy was one of those who had entered the competition for the rebuilding of the fire-damaged St Andrew's Church in Dublin with John Semple, Junior, in 1860. Semple's design was criticised severely and rejected. The judges thought McCurdy's entry was 'a most creditable and well-studied composition', although his drawings were 'somewhat too warmly tinted' (*Dublin Builder*, May and June 1860). One can imagine the 39-year-old McCurdy's rather awkward position in relation to John Semple. McCurdy had just finished building the second side (west) of Semple's Belgrave Square in Monkstown, the whole originally designed by him but abruptly terminated in 1849 after his bankruptcy, with only one side (south) complete. McCurdy was now about to make major modifications to 'Semple's church' by the addition of a chancel. It was like being asked to write another act of *Hamlet* while Shakespeare was still alive.

However, McCurdy was extraordinarily sensitive to Semple's design. Looking at it today, it is hard to imagine the church without the chancel, so well does it fit in, both inside and out. The pinnacled towers with their 'arrow slits', the lancet windows with characteristic drip-mouldings, the decorative string-coursing, the crenellated battlements, the very stone itself — all these features have been faithfully copied by McCurdy. Inside his new two-storey chancel, he copied Semple's unusual ceiling meticulously. For liturgical reasons, he had to change certain elements. His plans show that he removed Semple's old pulpit from the three-decker arrangement and placed it at the angle between the north transept and the chancel, with a lectern or reading desk in the corresponding position on the south side. He took the organ from the west gallery, over the main door, and reinstalled it in an 'organ room' on the north side of the chancel. Just behind the pulpit, a spiral staircase (now removed) led down to the large new Vestry rooms beneath, on the same level as Semple's vaults under the nave.

The nave aisle approached the chancel between two blocks of inward-facing pews at the bottom of the chancel steps and then up three wooden steps to the chancel level, where the narrow aisle approached the Communion table between four rows of choir pews. The space in the centre of the church, formerly occupied by Semple's three-decker pulpit, was filled with pews. One of the few complaints about McCurdy's design arose from this arrangement, when the *Irish Ecclesiastical Gazette* of 20 March 1880 protested that the chancel was 'too much closed in with pews. Surely a little more space between the Communion rails and the Lord's Table would not be amiss'.

McCurdy installed five lancet windows on the south side of the chancel and four on the north side, while he embellished the east end with three large lancet windows in a tripartite arrangement — all in plain glass. (The glass in the east window was replaced in 1870 with new stained-glass 'carpet' windows, so called for their resemblance to a Persian carpet; *see*

McCurdy's elevation of the chancel's north wall, showing Semple's 'old pulpit to be refixed' and the spiral staircase leading down to the large new Vestry rooms at vault level.

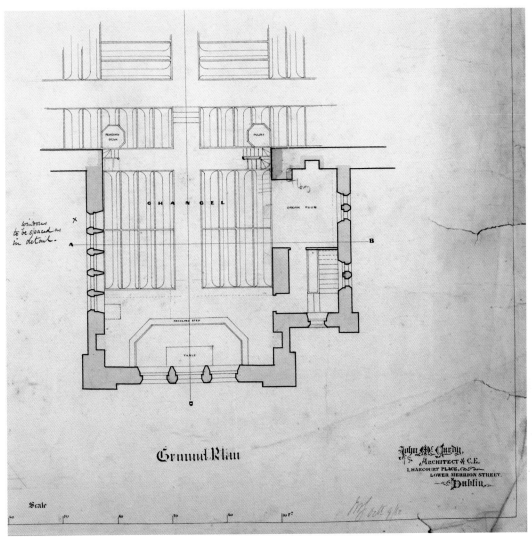

McCurdy's 1862 plan of the chancel, showing the pulpit on the north side and the spiral staircase to the Vestry rooms below, the reading desk on the south side and the 'organ room' with its fireplace. Choir stalls crowd the chancel; similarly, pews fill the available space in the nave.

Chapter 8.) A crenellated design ran under the east window, while a scripture text was painted on the east wall behind the Communion table (Harden 1911).[6] Also at the east end of the chancel was a 'trompe-l'oeil of oak wall paper, on which, by the art of the house painter, "Gothic" arches (were) boldly outlined and shadowed forth in the realistic fashion of the stage', reported the *Irish Ecclesiastical Gazette* of 5 January 1884. McCurdy's plans show nineteen trefoil-topped arches along the east wall of the church, with the Communion table in the centre.

McCurdy's new chancel cost between £2,000 and £3,000. Even though most people would not realise that it is an addition from the inside, close inspection on the outside will reveal, to quote Allen (1993), that some of the 'external details (are) untidy'. In the 1980s, vertical cracks appeared between the new and old work owing to settlement of the chancel.

A panorama of Monkstown today — from the two-storey curates' house 'Churchville' (left) to the Knox Memorial Hall (right), with the huge bulk of the parish church in between. This view shows how well McCurdy's chancel, added at the east end in 1862, fits in with Semple's earlier T-shaped building of 1831. McCurdy faithfully reproduced all of Semple's features — from the finials like chess pieces crowning the pinnacles to the crenellated parapet, string-coursing and drip-mouldings of the windows. Indeed, to most eyes, it is hard to imagine that the chancel is not part of the original design.

Later furnishings and fittings

During 1871, Mr F. Mitchell, Carpenter and Builder, of 63 York Street, was employed to make various improvements to the church. In March he built 'three flights of winding stairs to gallerys'. (Hand-rails were later fixed to the 'wallside' of all four flights of stairs in the two transepts, costing £11-10s in 1874.) It was decided to replace Semple's wooden pulpit with a new one of Bath stone (a type of oolitic limestone). A reading desk, of similar design and material to the pulpit, was installed on the south side of the chancel. In April Mr Mitchell sent this rather breathless — but exceedingly reasonable — estimate for this work and more:

'To taking down pulpit and Seats and Cutting flooring for foundation of pulpit and Making pertition for front of font and putting up said with Iron Stays to D(itt)o and Sundrie Cutting and fitting Seats and rea Setting said and making good Loss and flooring where required and putting up Stiles for oak door and hanging said with lock and hinges for said and putting Iron Stays to Communion Rail and Easing doors of Do and Easing pew doors and gallery doors and priming all New Work with two Coats of paint, furnishing all Materials £7-5s-0d.'

When Mr Mitchell had finished his work, the firm 'Church Upholsterers, Warerooms and Manufactory' of 27 Lincoln Place moved in. They upholstered everything possible in the chancel with crimson velvet, lined with silk, from the top of the pulpit ('curled hair and velvet, lining the inside with crimson cloth and silk simp') to the organist's seat, choir pews and kneeling stools. They made velvet pillows for the reading desk and the seat next to the pulpit, and carpeted the floor with the 'best yard wide crimson carpet'. The font was given an oak cover, with a 'medieval iron ring handle', and bookshelves were fitted in the pulpit and reading desk. To preserve all this finery, the pulpit, reading desk and font were each fitted with 'an overall cover of best Holland linen'.

Architects connected with Monkstown

It is interesting to note that architects were particularly thick on the ground in Monkstown, so that, with only one exception, all of the major changes to the church were made by people who lived in the parish.

- John Semple, Senior (enlargement of church, 1831), of 'Fairyland', Kingstown Hill (the present York Road), Kingstown (1804–*c.* 1829), and Haddington Terrace, Kingstown (1836–40).
- John McCurdy (chancel, 1862) of 'St Alban's', Albany Avenue (1862–9), 'The Cottage', Newtown Park (1870–2), 11 Trafalgar Terrace (1874–5) and 'Chesterfield House', Cross Avenue, Blackrock (1877–85).
- Thomas Drew (modifications to chancel, transept entrances and other refurbishments, 1883–90) of 'Gortnadrew', Alma Road, Monkstown (1878–1910); registered vestryman in, at least, 1886, 1898–9, 1900–1, 1906–8, 1910.
- William Mitchell (partner of McCurdy and of Drew) of 14 Trafalgar Terrace (1874–81), 'Glenart', Glenart Avenue, Blackrock (1882–6), 'Lota', Cross Avenue, Blackrock (1887–93), 'Fareham', Silchester Road, Glenageary (1894–1906) and 'Abbeylands', Killiney (1907–10); churchwarden in 1880.
- William Kaye Parry (amended design of organ case in 1898; Dockrell Memorial porch, 1901) of 1 Tivoli Parade, Kingstown (1881–8), and 6 Charlemont Terrace, Kingstown (1889–1905); Monkstown church architect, *c.* 1886–1901
- Richard Chaytor Millar (Knox Memorial Hall, 1904) of 'Clifton Villa', Monkstown (in childhood), 3 Eaton Place, Monkstown (1877–80), 'Brooklawn', 30 Mount Merrion Avenue, Blackrock (1881–1902), and 'Ervillagh', Foxrock (1904–8); his father, Adam, and brother, Fitzadam, were both churchwardens of Monkstown.
- Sir Thomas Deane of 26 Longford Terrace (1863–71): as a parishioner, he was on the committee for the east 'carpet' windows, but does not seem to have had any professional involvement.
- Richard Caulfeild Orpen, the one non-parishioner who did much work for the church, was a parishioner of Tullow in Foxrock.

Thomas Drew (1838–1910)

Halfway along Alma Road in Monkstown is an unusual, eclectic, semi-detached red-brick house. 'Gortnadrew', described by a contemporary as 'a noble residence', was built in 1878 by a Monkstown parishioner, Thomas Drew (1838–1910).[7] Like McCurdy and Semple Junior, Drew had entered the St Andrew's competition in 1860 and, although not placed, had been praised as 'a young architect [he was 22] evidently of ability' (*Dublin Builder*, May and June 1860). Later, with his partner and fellow parishioner William Mitchell (who lived around the corner, in Trafalgar Terrace), Drew was responsible for the Victorian refurbishment of Monkstown Church in 1883. Their main changes inside the church involved decorative stone arcading on the east wall of the chancel, the creation of an elaborate reredos, stone steps leading up to the chancel with a low curb wall on either side, and modification of the lancet windows on the south chancel wall. Outside, he remodelled the entrances to both transepts.

Drew's father, the Rev. Dr Thomas Drew, was a militant Orange clergyman in Belfast. His son, also called Thomas, went to school in Belfast and was then articled to Sir Charles Lanyon, in whose office he showed great promise in his architectural designs. When he was 24 he joined the office, in Dublin, of William Murray, whose sister, Adelaide, he later married.

In his obituary, published in the *Irish Builder and Engineer* on 19 March 1910, Drew was described paradoxically as 'the most distinguished of living Irish architects'. He became president of the Royal Hibernian Academy (1900–10), the Royal Institute of Architects of Ireland (1889–1901) and the Royal Society of Antiquaries (1895–7).[8] He was also editor of the *Irish Builder and Engineer* from about 1864. He was the diocesan architect for Down, Connor and Dromore. There are dozens of examples of his work throughout Ireland, but especially in Dublin — including, among others, the Ulster Bank, College Green; St Kevin's Church, South Circular Road; Trinity College Graduates' Memorial Building (GMB); the Law Library at the Four Courts; Clontarf Presbyterian Church; and Rathmines Town Hall. In 1900 the lord lieutenant, Earl Cadogan, knighted Drew and, only a few weeks before he died, he was asked to become professor of architecture at University College, Dublin.

Sir Thomas was one of those people who make you feel breathless when you read of their workload. He was energetic and hearty, throwing himself into everything he did with enthusiasm. He had an unaffected and passionate love of architecture and every St Stephen's Day gave a talk in Christ Church Cathedral at Strongbow's tomb. It was a popular occasion because 'a ready and witty speaker, he had the great gift of making himself interesting on almost any subject'.

He was a man of total integrity, as illustrated by the anecdote (again told in his obituary) of his being consulted about a church, designed by another architect, which was showing serious structural faults. Drew did not mince his words in his strongly critical report, but before despatching it he sent a copy to the architect concerned 'as a matter of professional courtesy'. Forgetting Drew's reputation, the architect called on him immediately and, 'with more courage than wisdom, desired to know for what pecuniary consideration the report might be modified. The exact text of Drew's reply are [*sic*] not recorded, but they had intimate reference to alternative modes of egress from the room'. Drew was not a 'brown envelope' devotee.

Although much of the work he was asked to do was secular, Drew delighted in ecclesiastical commissions. He was a curious mixture of stubbornness and flexibility: when he was asked to design the new cathedral in Belfast, he produced plans of a neo-Gothic building. After some discussion, these were felt to be unsuitable, so he went back to the drawing-board and drew the Byzantine design that we see today. On the other hand, he held strong views and was unafraid of speaking his mind, so it was not surprising that he did not always see eye to eye with everyone. In his obituary we read that 'he had imbued a little of what Whistler has called "the gentle art of making enemies" '.

When we see what Drew was capable of, Monkstown got off lightly. In St Brigid's Church, Stillorgan, he wanted to virtually remodel the church in 1876 by removing the tower, galleries and vestibule, but 'thankfully, the vestry proceeded no further', as Ingram (1997) comments in his history of that church. Before his work at Monkstown, Drew spent seven years on the restoration of Christ Church Cathedral. When Victorian architects said 'restoration', they usually meant 'reconstruction'. Between 1870 and 1877, Drew and Street knocked down the fourteenth-century Christ Church 'Long Choir' and built a new east end. Leaving little untouched, they swept through the medieval cathedral, 'improving and refurbishing'. Most of the wall monuments, including brand-new ones, were taken down and put in the crypt, with piles of medieval stonework. There was a public outcry about this at the time. We can imagine the fury of grieving relatives who had taken the trouble and expense to have an ostentatious memorial erected in the cathedral nave or transept, only to find it banished to oblivion, without even referring to them. When Caulfeild Orpen called Drew 'a robust and virile Gothic' in an article for the *Irish Builder and Engineer* on 2 April 1910, did he really mean 'Goth'?

To be fair to Drew, he does seem to have respected Semple's work at Monkstown more than he did that of the fourteenth-century builders of Christ Church. Although he did introduce the first elements of decoration into the church, restricted to the chancel, they marry reasonably unobtrusively into Semple's church. This was probably intentional: when he refurbished Hillsborough Church in County Down during 1898, an observer wrote in the *Irish Builder* of 1 July that year, 'After studious care, he has succeeded in … keeping in view the ideas of the first builder'. McCurdy's chancel had been in harmony with Semple's work; Drew and Mitchell followed his example.

William Mitchell (1843–1910)

William Mitchell was also involved in Monkstown Church as Thomas Drew's partner. He and Drew were lifelong friends, but it was a case of 'chalk and cheese'. According to the *Irish Builder and Engineer* of 2 April 1910, where Drew was outspoken, Mitchell was 'shy and retiring'; where Drew was irascible, Mitchell was 'one of those rare Christian characters who neither think nor speak evil of any man, it (could) be truly said of him that he had no enemies'. Drew's passion was ecclesiastical architecture, whereas Mitchell's was commercial. They lived around the corner from one another in Monkstown: Mitchell in Trafalgar Terrace and Drew in Alma Road. Incredibly, these two old friends died within a day of each other, both of heart failure: William Mitchell on Saturday 12 March 1910 and Sir Thomas Drew on Sunday 13 March 1910, three weeks after an operation.[9]

Modifications by Drew and Mitchell to McCurdy's chancel in 1883 are all essentially intact in the present church.

Mitchell was a pupil of Sir Thomas Deane. After leaving Deane's office, he went into partnership with John McCurdy, architect of the 1862 chancel in Monkstown. After McCurdy died in 1885, Mitchell worked alone or in partnership with Drew. Besides his work with McCurdy, he also designed many hotels, including Dublin's Hotel Metropole and the Grosvenor Hotel, and Lucan's Spa Hotel, as well as several houses in Grafton Street and an extension to Mercer's Hospital. In Monkstown, the gatelodge to 'Dalguise' on Monkstown Road is his work (this was the home of Mrs F. Hart, the benefactress of the 1883 improvements to Monkstown's chancel).[10]

Their mutual friend, Richard Caulfeild Orpen, wrote a moving tribute to Drew and Mitchell on the day after Drew's death, published in the *Evening Mail* of 14 March 1910:

> 'There are grey days in the spring of the year when the pulse of Nature seems to beat feebly. Such a day is this, when we know that two life-long friends … lie dead. We architects meet one another in the street, and there is real sorrow in our faces. Two of our leading men have stepped aside into the silence: men so intimately connected with our professional life in Dublin, members of our Council and past presidents of our Institute. We, their juniors, are filled with a sense of the insecurity of things and count our own accumulating years. Our loss is too recent to permit us to appraise the splendid qualities of each. We walk the streets, busy with the affairs of the moment, for life must go on and the day's work be done, though our hearts contract within us; and, here and there, through the grey city — scourged by the March wind — we see the memorials of these two men whose drawing boards are today idle, and whose T squares have been hung up.'

Changes by Drew and Mitchell (1883–4)

> *The Church's Restoration*
> *In eighteen-eighty-three*
> *Has left for contemplation*
> *Not what there used to be.*
> John Betjeman, A parody on *The Church's One Foundation*

During 1883–4, the architects Drew and Mitchell, both Monkstown parishioners, were employed to make changes internally and externally to the church. Their first embellishments were to the chancel. They replaced McCurdy's *trompe-l'oeil* arches on the east wall with 'handsome stone arcading about 8 feet high, the spandrels between the arches being exquisitely carved in foliage of varying design', enthused the *Irish Ecclesiastical Gazette* on 5 January 1884. *The Irish Builder* of 1 January 1884 also had high praise for the sculptors of the arcading:

> 'The design … has been carried out with much taste by C.W. Harrison of Great Brunswick Street, the various foliage of the spandrels being especially well carved and admirable.'

Six different species of plants were painted on the panels within the arches, each giving symbolic lessons: passion flowers (for the suffering and death of Christ), wheat, the vine and grapes (for the bread and wine of the Communion), olives (for peace and reconciliation), lilies (for purity and innocence, but also for surrendering oneself to God) and pomegranates (for resurrection and rebirth). There are eighteen panels, three of each design. They were apparently incomplete until 1894, when Canon Peacocke, as a parting gift, paid for the

Four of the painted panels on the east wall of the chancel, showing (from left to right) lilies, olives, pomegranates and passion flowers.

94

remaining ones to be painted.

Drew and Mitchell designed an elaborate reredos behind the Communion table, carved from cream-coloured limestone, known as Caen stone, from France. It was sculpted by the same firm who had done the stone arcading, C.W. Harrison & Sons. The *Irish Ecclesiastical Gazette* on 5 January 1884 described the whole: 'The portion behind the holy table is divided from the rest by panelled buttresses and elevated with three gablets surmounted with crocketed finials. The style is what is known as "decorated" Gothic [i.e. foliage copied faithfully from Nature] and is so far the introduction of some recognised consistent style into the church.' The four arches in the reredos once bore an inscription — a four-line verse from I Corinthians 11:26 ('As often as / Ye eat this bread and drink this cup / Ye do shew the Lord's death / till He come'), with the injunction beneath, 'This do in remembrance of Me'. The words were painted over in 1961 because of their 'adverse effect on the arrangement of the floral decorations' (recorded in the Vestry minutes of 10 May 1961), but their faint outline can still be discerned.

On the central medallion of the reredos are the intertwined letters 'IHS', the first three letters of the name Jesus in Greek. On the right-hand side, an angel with outstretched wings holds a shield bearing the date of the refurbishment — 1883. If we look closely at the shield held by the angel on the left, we see the initials 'F' and 'H'. These refer to the fact that the work in the chancel was due to 'the munificence of a lady, a resident of the parish'. The Select Vestry minutes of 18 January 1884 reveal her identity:

> 'That the best thanks of the Select Vestry … are hereby tendered to Mrs. Hart for the munificent gift in the improvements effected by her in the Chancel.'

The only Monkstown 'Mrs Hart' lived at 'Dalguise' on Monkstown Road between 1881 and 1888. (Interestingly, as mentioned above, Mitchell had designed the gatelodge to this house.)

Referring to the 'introduction of some recognised consistent style' mentioned by the *Irish Ecclesiastical Gazette* (*see above*), it would appear that Drew and Mitchell have subtly integrated elements of Semple's design in their reredos. For example, at either end there is a panel depicting a stylised ogee door in miniature with

The brass eagle lectern was presented in 1885 by John and Joseph Galloway, in memory of their parents, John (d. 1866) and Eliza (d. 1844).

a trefoil shape above it, surmounted by a fleur-de-lis finial. This almost mirrors Semple's design of the church's west door. In addition, there are several rows of scalloping above each panel, reminiscent of Semple's ceiling. The architects may also have been trying to include other features in their design, such as the Cork red marble columns in the reredos reflecting those in the 1871 pulpit.

Drew and Mitchell replaced McCurdy's carpeted wooden steps to the chancel with 'a flight of stone steps and a richly carved balustrade or curb wall to a higher level of the chancel floor, coped with polished marble'. The stone steps were voted 'an immense improvement upon the previous wooden steps' by the *Monkstown Herald* of January 1885. C.W. Harrison & Sons, the sculptors of the reredos, also built the curb wall, with its elaborate carvings of acorns and oak leaves, reflecting the patterns in the arcading's spandrels.

Craven Dunnill of Ironbridge, Shropshire, manufactured the rich encaustic tiles laid in the sanctuary, the area around the Communion table. (Their main Dublin agents were Thomas Dockrell & Sons, who were Monkstown parishioners.) The tiles were copied, not always faithfully, from some of the famous ancient examples in Christ Church and used not only for Monkstown Parish Church but also for St John's of Mounttown and several other Dublin churches. The popular motifs of the day were stylised leaves and flowers, like the trefoil, quatrefoil or fleur-de-lis, with the tiles laid in blocks of four to make an overall pattern, such as the lions' heads facing each other in a circle with their tongues almost touching.

The London firm of Messrs Potter & Co. installed the brass Communion rails. (In 1897, the brass hand-rails on each side of the chancel steps were fitted.) It is probable that McCurdy's spiral staircase behind the pulpit, leading down to the Vestry rooms, was removed at this point. Until this area of the Vestry was decorated recently, a faint outline of the staircase could be seen on the walls. Miss Edith Dowse, born in 1899 and daughter of the rector, Chancellor Dowse (1894–1929), is adamant that the stairs were not there in her childhood.

At the request of the Select Vestry, Drew and Mitchell blocked off two of McCurdy's five lancet windows on the internal south wall of the chancel, leaving only three visible on the inside, while outside there still appear to be five. Stained 'cathedral glass' was then installed in the three remaining windows (*see Chapter 8*). New furniture was placed in the chancel: an oak prayer desk (currently on the north side) was presented in 1885 by the Young Ladies' Bible Class and a matching seat was given by the Young Men's Christian Association. John and Joseph Galloway presented the brass eagle lectern in memory of their parents (*see Appendix 7*).

Besides their work on the chancel, Drew and Mitchell were also asked to revise the seating in the church. The *Irish Ecclesiastical Gazette* on 5 January 1884 reported the architects' plans: 'The old and ill constructed painted pews on the ground floor will be entirely swept away [this sounds like Drew], the passages re-arranged, and the whole area seated with new open benches of pitch pine of the modern and improved type'. At last those cramped pews of Semple's design were to be replaced; to ensure the maximum number of worshippers, he had made the pews narrow, with little leg room, and had managed to squeeze in 188 pews. The *Gazette* on 20 March 1880 quoted one worshiper who had complained that the pews were 'so narrow that it (was) impossible in some of them to kneel, and once, when one of the clergy preached on the subject of kneeling, he received

Drew modified the entrances to both transepts at the request of the Select Vestry in 1890 (south transept shown here). This photograph shows the results of his work.

an anonymous letter, asking him had he tried to kneel in them!' The parishioners seem to have approved of the changes, as reported in the *Monkstown Herald* of January 1885: 'We must particularly notice the seating of the congregation all facing towards the Chancel as a most desirable change.'

To ease congestion in 1884 the two original arched openings were blocked up (with panelling and glass) between Semple's narrow porches and the main body of the church; a central entrance was made instead. (See plan of church on page 102.) Several years later, Drew also made external changes to Semple's entrances to the north and south transepts. Originally these doorways, like the present door at the west end, had ogee-shaped arches, as can be seen in an engraving of 1834 (*see p. 52*). However, in the eyes of the Select Vestry of 1887, Semple's narrow doors were a major design fault, acting as a bottleneck to the huge

The Children's Church, under the north gallery, was dedicated in June 1951. Various gifts were donated by parishioners to furnish it.

congregations of the day as they flowed in and out of the church. The Vestry therefore asked the Fabric Committee on 10 October 1887 to prepare a report on widening the doors and also to explore 'the possibility of providing additional exits'. It took another two years before the entrances were actually widened, after modifications had been made in order to reduce the cost.

In June 1890, for the cost of £210, Semple's ogee doorways were removed and the present wider entrances were constructed to Drew's plans. The consequence of widening the doors in this manner impacted negatively on Semple's design because of the necessity to insert the weight-bearing lintels and the stonework contained above each door (in the tympanum). To cap it all, the stepped arrangements over each door (presumably an attempt to emulate Semple's embattled roof-line) project above the base of the lancet windows, interfering with the clean lines of the original string-coursing. All that remains of Semple's original doorways are the cut-granite semicircular steps leading up to them and parts of the string-coursing on either side.

Later modifications to the church included the widening of the stone steps on the north transept side leading down to the Vestry and vault level, and the heavy outer doors of both transepts were repositioned several feet in from the entrance to each porch. (The original iron fittings for Drew's doors can still be seen on either side.) A new door was added (date unknown) on the north wall of the west end, below the lancet window; it opens into the

The poisoned chalice is the symbol of St John the Evangelist, seen in the left panel of this finely carved Communion table, which came to Monkstown in 1985 from St John's in Mounttown. The story goes that St John was challenged to drink from a poisoned chalice from which two condemned men had already drunk and died. His prayer drew out the poison in the form of a serpent and he drank from the chalice unscathed.

little storeroom to the left of the main entrance porch and has been integrated in a fairly sympathetic manner. A further addition in 1992 involved the building of a ramp up to this door, for wheelchair accessibility; it was constructed from granite stones taken from the old Carrickbrennan Graveyard.

Richard Caulfeild Orpen (1863–1938)

Although not a Monkstown parishioner, another architect who did much work for the church was Richard Caulfeild Orpen, the older brother of the artist Sir William Orpen (1878–1931). He designed Monkstown's World War I memorial on the south wall of the chancel, as well as the simple yet elegant Communion table of carved oak, in memory of Chancellor Dowse, and the matching credence table. The trefoil arches of his Communion table echo those in Drew's stone arcading and reredos, and also the patterns in the 'carpet' windows above.

Orpen was described as 'probably the cleverest and most able draughtsman in Ireland' (*Irish Builder*, 26 November 1910). He was president of the Royal Institute of Architects of

99

Ireland from 1914 to 1917, the youngest since its foundation in 1839. He had worked with Drew for eleven years and was appointed as the architect to Christ Church Cathedral on Drew's death in 1910; he was also the architect to St Patrick's, Trinity College and St Columba's College in Dublin (where he had been a pupil) and to St Canice's in Kilkenny. (He designed the brass memorial plaque to Drew in Christ Church.) His work includes the red-brick Dental Hospital in Lincoln Place and Alexandra College, Earlsfort Terrace (now demolished). He was also said to be 'the originator of the bungalow in Ireland, and has built quite a colony of pretty red tiled gabled houses in the fashionable residential district of Foxrock' (*Irish Builder*, 27 August 1904).

Further changes to the church (1946–53)

Old photographs show that before 1946 the brass eagle lectern stood in the middle of the aisle, at the top of the stone steps, obstructing access to the chancel. In 1946–7 it was moved to its present position in the south transept, beside the font. At the same time, the reading desk of Bath stone, dating from 1871 and matching the pulpit, was removed from the south side of the chancel. The existing curb wall was extended to fill the gap with the addition of six new panels, probably by the original sculptors, C.W. Harrison & Sons of 178 Pearse Street (formerly Great Brunswick Street). They also made a new reading desk of oak, which was an exact copy of the 1885 desk presented by the Young Ladies' Bible Class. It was made in memory of the Rev. Harold Forde (1931–45) and was dedicated on 22 June 1947, the second anniversary of his death.[11]

During 1951–3 the Children's Church was set up in the north transept. Various gifts for it were presented in 1951, including Holy Communion rails (in memory of Mr and Mrs J.A. Miller), a platform for the Communion table (presented by Mr E. Gray), a carpet of red felt for the sanctuary (from the Mothers' Union in memory of Mrs Miller) and the stained-glass for the window behind the Communion table (presented by Mr Gorsuch).

This side chapel is now used for early morning Communion services. Its Communion table came from St John's in Mounttown when it was sold in 1985.

CHAPTER 8

Stained-glass windows

The eye can easily find many points of beauty to rest on,
whether in … the numerous stained glass windows,
which are excellent alike in both colouring and design …
Irish Ecclesiastical Gazette, 14 January 1898, referring to Monkstown Church

The windows in Monkstown Church tell much about the values and tastes of their contemporaries. Apart from the 1789 west end, which retains its plain glass, all the windows are of stained glass. They date from the early and mid-Victorian period to just after World War I. Their names and locations are as follows:

Early Victorian
East side of north and south transepts: 'Bishop' window and its twin (1843). Artist unknown.

Mid-Victorian
East end: 'Carpet' windows (1870) by Mayer & Co., Munich and London.
South transept, south side: Betham Memorial Window (1866) by M. & R. Sillery, Dublin, and Jordan Memorial Windows (*c.* 1875).
North transept, north side: Garner Memorial Windows (1879).
Chancel, south side: 'Cathedral glass' windows (1884).

Twentieth century
West side of north and south transepts: War Memorial windows (1920) by Douglas Sons & Co., Belfast.

The Georgian church of 1789 originally had sliding sash windows, with plain glass and linen blinds. The Vestry minutes of 20 March 1815 record that the 'window blinds' and 'skirts for pulpit' cost £25-1-1 in 1814. The blinds were renewed in 1828, when the minutes of 7 April note: 'Resolved that ten pounds be the rate for repairing the sashes and sash cordes and procuring white linen blinds for the church windows'. Even with linen blinds, the Georgian church would have been much brighter inside than it is today. The building was only 70 feet long and had fifteen windows in all (six large lancet windows each side, north and south; two lancet windows at the west end; and probably one larger window at the east

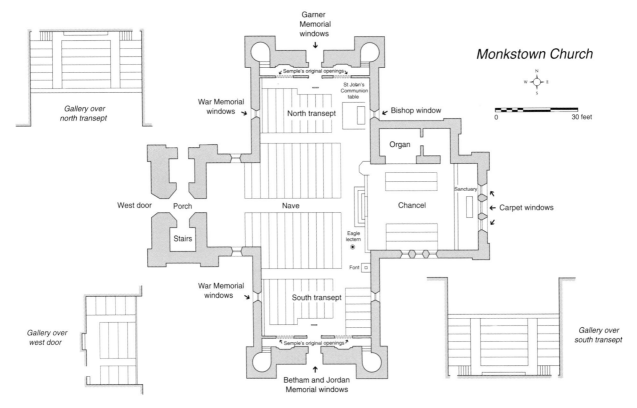

Plan of present church, showing position of windows.

end). Today's church is three times the size, but has only eighteen windows in total (if one counts each tripartite window as three windows).

Semple's church of 1831 would also have been bright, with leaded windows containing diamond-shaped panes of plain glass. (In his specifications for Kilternan Church, he stipulated that 'the windows (should) be put together in the most substantial manner, a compartment to open'.) As the preacher stood in his elevated pulpit, at the top of the three-decker, half-way between the transepts, the light streaming through the large east window behind him would dazzle the congregation. As a writer in the *Dublin Penny Journal* of 12 July 1834 complained, 'From the cross-lights behind the pulpit, where there should be no light, is a large window of three divisions, so that it is impossible to see the preacher'. This reproach makes sense when we remember that Semple's church had no chancel; instead, there was a kind of shallow extension at the east end, with three box pews on each side, and the east window was above the door to the small 'vestiary' (*see Chapter 5*). Perhaps this public criticism goaded the Vestry into action. At any rate, a large 'window blind … £2-3-4' was purchased the following year to cover the east window.

When stained glass was later installed, it was added from the inside, so that all of Semple's original diamond-paned plain glass still remains on the outside of the window openings except, unfortunately, the tripartite window in the south transept (memorials to Betham and Jordans).

Early Victorian (1843)

Some twelve years after Semple completed the church, stained-glass windows were installed on the east side of each transept. There is a mystery here. The window in the north transept seems to have some connection with a bishop: a mitre and two initials, which appear to be 'G.H.', are painted at the top of the window, as well as the date '1843'. The stained-glass pattern is reminiscent of the etched glass in the doors of the west gallery. The twin window in the south transept is similar in structure, the top diamond-shaped part being identical.

The only bishop connected with Monkstown around this time — and the obvious candidate — was Bishop Charles Lindsay, dean of Christ Church Cathedral, bishop of Kildare, patron of Monkstown and father of the incumbent at the time (of the same name). But Bishop Lindsay died in 1846, not 1843. A thorough search has uncovered no bishop with the initials 'G.H.' (or even a diocese beginning with 'H', as in 'George Dublin') of the

The 'Bishop' window on the east wall of the north transept. Note that in the pane above the bishop's mitre in the left panel the initials 'G.H.' and the date of 1843 are reversed.

Anglican Church (whether Church of Ireland, Scotland or Wales, or as far afield as Calcutta) who died, or was consecrated, in 1843.

At some point, this so-called 'Bishop' window has been reversed since the initials 'G.H.' are back to front, which suggests that it was moved from another site — or, possibly, even another church.

Few nineteenth-century windows were signed, so, without documentary evidence, it is difficult or impossible to discover the identity of their makers, compounded by the fact that there were over 50 small stained-glass studios in Dublin at the time (Wynne 1975).

The Betham Memorial Window, installed in 1866 in the south transept.

Mid-Victorian

Betham Memorial Window (1866)

It is appropriate that an armorial achievement should take pride of place in the memorial window of Sir William Betham (1779–1853), the Ulster king of arms, whose whole life revolved around heraldry (*see also Chapter 14*). The window was probably designed by his two sons, Molyneux and Sheffield, who were the Dublin and Cork heralds and also, like their father, churchwardens at Monkstown. The stained-glass window was installed in 1866 on the south wall of the south transept, as the centrepiece in the large tripartite plain glass window. (Some nine years later the whole window would be converted to stained glass with the addition of the two Jordan windows, flanking Betham; *see below*.)

The crest at the top of the Betham window is an elephant's head emerging from a crown. The elephant's head had been granted to another branch of the Betham family in 1566; when that branch died out, William Betham adopted the elephant crest himself and changed the colour (Betham *c.* 1905). Betham's coat of arms is an 'instant' family tree. The left half is his; the right half belongs to his wife, Elizabeth, who was a

Crampton. Betham's half is quartered or divided into smaller compartments, each belonging to Betham's immediate ancestors — the FitzRogers, Banisters, Burtons and Damants. A white turnip on a black background can be seen on the bottom left. Betham inherited this unusual coat of arms from his mother, who belonged to the Huguenot family of Damant. The Betham portion consists of two identical sections repeated in the left half: three blue fleurs-de-lis on a gold background (Walker 1993).

Immediately under the coat of arms is the motto *Per Ardua Surgam* ('Through hardship, I will overcome'), and lower down again a blue and white scroll, *Quis Seperabit? MDCCLXXXIII* ('Who will separate us? 1783'). (Betham's sons must have been upset when they saw the misprint — 'Seperabit' should be spelt as 'Separabit'.) This is the motto of the Most Illustrious Order of St Patrick, founded in 1783. Betham, as Ulster king of arms, was the king of arms of the order and was responsible for its organisation and ceremonial (Galloway 1983). He organised the installation of new knights of St Patrick in 1819 and also in 1821, on the occasion of the visit of George IV to Ireland. In 1831 he travelled to London for the 'investiture of extra knights of St Patrick' there, as reported in *Saunders's News-Letter* of 15 October that year.

The inscription towards the bottom of the window reads:

In Memory of
Sir William Betham Knight
Ulster King of Arms
of all Ireland,
of Stradbrook House
Born XXII May MDCCLXXIX
Died XXVI October MDCCCLIII
and Elizabeth his Wife
Died XXX December MDCCCLVI.

The window is signed at the bottom, with the words 'Executed by M. & R. Sillery, Abbey St, Dublin'. There is a bill in the Vestry archives from the Sillery firm:

'To furnishing 2 Timber Frames, Altering and Aditions to Stained Glass Windows for Monkstown Church, pr agreement £17-0s-0d. Received same … M. Sillery … 2/2/66.'

In the churchwardens' accounts of 4 April 1866, the entry for the same item reads, 'Sillery. Stained Glass Windows replaced, £17-0-0'. The word 'replaced' indicates that existing windows had been removed.

Jordan Memorial Windows (c. 1875)

This memorial to Richard and Ellen Jordan consists of two heraldic windows, set on either side of the Betham Memorial Window in the south transept in about 1875. The windows were probably installed by the Jordans' son-in-law, William Garner, who had married their only child in 1847, named Ellen after her mother. When she married, her father settled £300 a year on her, a substantial sum in those days.[1]

105

Richard Jordan and Ellen Dwyer were married in 1810 and lived at 'Richview' on the Monkstown Road.[2] He was a wealthy attorney[3] who owned hundreds of acres in Tipperary. He died in 1854, having survived his wife by over 40 years. Sadly, she died two years after their marriage, aged 28, having given birth to a daughter in 1812 and so most likely died in childbirth. Because she was a woman, Ellen Jordan's coat of arms was lozenge- or diamond-shaped. The inscriptions on the windows read:

<table>
<tr><td align="center">Sacred
to the Memory of
Richard Jordan Esqr.
Late of Rich View
Monkstown
and formerly of the
City of Cashel
Who Died Novbr XVth
MDCCCLIV
Aged LXXXII
years</td><td align="center">Sacred
to the Memory of
Ellen Jordan
Wife of
Richard Jordan Esqr.
Late of the
City of Cashel
Who Died July III
MDCCCXII
Aged XXVIII
years</td></tr>
</table>

Garner Memorial Window (1879)

Sacred to the memory of
William Cathcart Garner Esq.
who died on the 3rd day
of October 1875 aged 57 years

A tripartite window in memory of William Garner in the north transept faces, across the width of the church, the memorial windows he had erected for his parents-in-law, Richard and Ellen Jordan. When Richard died in 1854, William and Ellen Garner moved into the Jordan family home of 'Richview' on the Monkstown Road.[4] They had one son, born in 1850 and named Richard after his grandfather.[5] When he was twelve, his mother died (aged 50) and William had a simple white marble wall memorial to her memory installed on the north side of the new chancel, just completed by John McCurdy in 1862. Ellen Garner's memorial is one of the few to women in the church.

An interesting aside is that 'Richview' was renamed 'St Grellan's' in 1880. It became the home of the Vaughan School (founded in 1872 by the Vaughan sisters) in 1925 — later to be renamed The Hall School. The school had originally been located at 32–3 Belgrave Square (now Comhaltas Ceoltóirí Éireann), built, coincidentally, by John Semple, Junior (joint architect of Monkstown Church in 1831). In the 1970s, the three schools of The Hall, Park House and Hillcourt were amalgamated to form Rathdown School, and the Monkstown premises, with their seven acres of playing fields and tennis courts, were sold to a housing development (the present 'Monkstown Valley'). The only part that remains of the Georgian house of 'St Grellan's', demolished in 1982, is its granite portico, which was re-erected near the entrance to the new estate (O'Rafferty 1999).

'Carpet' windows (1870)

When John McCurdy added the chancel in 1862, his large tripartite east window was of plain glass. In September 1869, a meeting in Monkstown about the forthcoming Lay Conference drew a 'large … number of the most influential gentlemen in the parish'. Seeing this, Thomas Dockrell, justice of the peace and churchwarden, moved a resolution that stained glass should be installed in McCurdy's east windows 'to complete the recent improvements of Monkstown Church'. The resolution was passed unanimously and a committee of ten was appointed, including the architect Sir Thomas Deane (then living at 26 Longford Terrace) and Thomas Dockrell himself.

The windows were installed in 1870. They cost £244-15-2 and were designed by Messrs Mayer and Co. of Munich, whose London branch had opened in 1865. The glass was transported to Monkstown in a cart (probably from Kingstown) and some men co-opted into carrying it into the church; the receipt, dated December 1870, shows 'Allowance to men for assisting the carter of stained glass, 3/-'. However, in spite of the new stained glass, which cut down on the light considerably, the new Select Vestry of Disestablishment thought the chancel was too bright and thus the inevitable linen blinds were installed ('To repairing and putting new pulley and cords to 3 blinds on large gothic stained glass window', from receipt dated 27 August 1870).

The east windows are called 'carpet' windows from their resemblance to the patterns and

'Carpet' windows were installed in 1870 on the east wall of McCurdy's chancel. So called for the Persian-carpet effect of the stained glass: ivy leaves, stylised flowers and sheaves of wheat fill every inch of space in profusion.

colours of a Persian carpet. A rich red background highlights an intertwined pattern of ivy leaves and stylised flowers. The *Irish Ecclesiastical Gazette* (forerunner of the *Church of Ireland Gazette*) explained their choice in an article on 20 March 1880:

> 'It is said that the subscribers wished for Raphael windows, but that the present kaleidoscopic designs were chosen in preference from the dread of a cry of Ritualism being raised!'

The writer is referring to the fact that, during the eighteenth century, paintings by well-known artists like Raphael and Reynolds were copied onto stained glass. They were sometimes reversed to suit the window or one figure alone plucked out of a painting (Harrison 1980).

Later, during the 1850s and '60s in Ireland, there were some very strong feelings against the representation of people in windows. This was partly a reaction against anything that smacked of 'popery', the association of ritual with Rome. In the eyes of Church of Ireland parishioners then, 'ritualism' included turning to the east in prayer, bowing during the Creed, calling the Communion table the 'altar', wearing vestments for the different festivals of the church, and having altar-coverings, flowers and candles on the Communion table. (A derogatory term for 'Puseyites' was 'posyites' because of their liking for flowers on the Communion table.) Ritualism also included the portrayal of the Holy Family, saints or angels in stained-glass windows. Most Church of Ireland parishioners today would be perfectly happy with most of these practices, but the Church of Ireland then was much 'lower' than it is now.

These strong feelings against depicting images in churches erupted in 1856, when the local newspapers berated the windows in Down Cathedral because they portrayed St Patrick, St Columba and St Brigid. The windows were deliberately broken on two occasions and eventually removed some months later, with the approval of the *Irish Ecclesiastical Gazette*, as written up in its November issue that year. They were not replaced for 40 years (Rankin 1997). Again, in 1863, three similar windows in the new church at Enniskerry, Co. Wicklow, were smashed in protest and a card, accompanied by a piece of orange peel and a daub of blue paint, was attached to the churchyard gate. It read (Brooks and Saint 1995):

> IF THE PARISH WISHES TO SAVE EXPENSE AND MORE OF TROUBLE
> THEY WILL KEEP DOWN WHAT IMAGES ARE BROKE AND TAKE
> DOWN THE REST AS SOON AS CONVENIENT.
> NO SURRENDER

In the Rev. Ralph Harden's book (1911) on *St John's, Monkstown*, he tells of a parishioner there, Thomas Hone, who wanted 'to erect three stained glass windows without figures of any kind, in the chancel' in 1868.

With attitudes like this prevalent, it was courageous for some of the donors at Monkstown to request representational windows (with figures). But, not unexpectedly, they were overruled by the 'safe' vote and the 'carpet' windows were the inevitable result. There are indications that the 'carpet' windows were never popular: there were two attempts to replace them. When the Select Vestry was discussing a fitting memorial to the soldiers who died during World War I, new east windows were proposed ('to a better style of architecture', as the Vestry minutes of January 1919 state), but the idea was turned down as being too expensive (the same minutes note that 'a memorial East window (with brass tablets annexed)' would cost £900–£1,000, plus £600 for alterations to frame). In 1931 the idea arose again, this time as a memorial to Canon Dowse, but his widow insisted that the 'money should not be spent except for a useful purpose', so a new Communion table was installed instead (the present one).

'Cathedral glass' windows (1884)

In 1862 John McCurdy installed five lancet windows of plain glass on the south wall of his new chancel, through which the sun streamed. But, as we have seen, the Victorians disapproved of bright churches and so the Vestry moved into action in its customary manner: its receipt of March 1864 details '5 shaped gothic frames fitted to upper parts of south window in chancel and covered in buff holland at 11s. each … £2-15s'. ('Holland' was a type of unbleached linen, originally from the Netherlands.) 'Buff blinds on the sanctuary windows' were popular at the time in Church of Ireland churches; the church in Boyle was criticised in 1883 because of them (McFarlan 1990).

In 1879 the Select Vestry felt strongly that the five plain glass windows on the south side of the chancel should be replaced by stained glass. It was said that 'in their present condition they are not in keeping with the rest of the church, and the strong light which comes through them spoils the effect of the large East window' (which had, for nine years now, been fitted with the stained 'carpet' glass). In response to this appeal, in March 1882, Mrs Alphonso Busby was given permission for a 'memorial window', provided that the rector and Select Vestry approved. They considered a design by Heaton, Butler and Bayne, but 'the geometrical portion at the top and bottom was not approved of, and the churchwardens were directed to return the design'. However, 'the churchwardens announced that Mrs Busby was unwilling to modify the design', as recorded in the Select Vestry minutes of January 1883.

Two months later, Thomas Drew attended the Select Vestry to explain his plans for alterations to the chancel (*see Chapter 7*). When the work was finished, in 1884, the Vestry was still unhappy: presumably they still thought the chancel was too bright. They had decided, according to the minutes of 5 December 1883, that 'the windows at each end of the five at the side of the Chancel (should) be built up with brickwork and the three centres glazed with Cathedral glass'. At the same time, the three window-sills were to be raised to the level of the chancel stonework. Thus, today, only three windows are evident on the interior south wall of the chancel, while five are seen on the exterior of the building.

By January 1884, the Select Vestry had studied a book of standard 'Cathedral glass' patterns and approved of 'the design marked V.[2] by Mr. Barnett (costing 6/6)'. This type of stained glass was described by Sir John Betjeman as 'that odious invention in green and pink' in his address, entitled *Fabrics of the Church of Ireland*, given in 1943 to the clergymen

War Memorial windows: north transept (right); south transept (far right). They were originally a two-light window in St John's of Mounttown, dating from 1920. When that church closed in 1985, the window was divided in two and installed in the north and south galleries of Monkstown Church.

of the Church of Ireland (Lycett-Green 1997). It would be interesting to have seen the Heaton, Butler and Bayne design, chosen by Mrs Busby.

In 1899 Maurice Dockrell wanted to erect a stained-glass window in memory of his father, Thomas. He suggested the middle of the three Cathedral glass windows. The Select Vestry turned down the design submitted (which again included one by Heaton, Butler and Bayne) and asked Mr Dockrell 'to allow the memorial to take another form'. Instead, he built the Dockrell Memorial Porch in 1901 in the north-east corner of the church, as the entrance to the Vestry rooms at ground level. This small addition fits in quite well, picking up several of Semple's design features, such as the narrow lancet windows, the crenellated gable and the fine granite stonework.

Twentieth-century windows

The two War Memorial windows, today on the west walls of the galleries in the north and south transepts of Monkstown Church, date from 1920. They were originally a single two-light window in St John's of Mounttown, in memory of the fifteen young men of that parish who had died in World War I. Their names were listed 'in the order in which they fell' on a large brass plaque. The dedication took place during morning service on Sunday 31 October 1920, with the archbishop of Dublin, the Most Rev. Charles Frederick D'Arcy, taking the service. The event was covered in the *Church of Ireland Gazette* on 19 November 1920. When St John's was sold to the Order of St Pius X in 1985, the window was moved to Monkstown, divided in two and reinstalled. The brass plaque too was re-erected, to the left of the window in the south transept.

The window in the north transept is signed 'Douglas Sons & Co.' at the base, which is almost hidden by a diagonal partition. The families of the young war dead chose William Douglas of Belfast to design the memorial windows. As a young man, Douglas had been noticed at the second Irish Arts and Crafts Exhibition in 1899, when he demonstrated his versatility in stencil-work, carved mahogany panels and especially in his stained-glass designs (Rathbone 1901). The *Belfast Newsletter* of 21 November 1899 wrote:

> 'This industry, so far as Ireland is concerned … has reached its highest development in Belfast. Some of the best specimens of this kind of work we have seen are on view, and the designer, Mr. W.J. Douglas, is an artist of original conceptions and a bold and skilful draughtsman. Messrs. Ward and Partners are the pioneers in this kind of decorative work'.

In 1918 Douglas decided to set up his own company with his sons. He worked for a further twenty years until his death in November 1938. There was a thriving stained-glass studio — *An Túr Gloine* (the Tower of Glass) — in Dublin, so work from a Belfast firm is an unexpected find in Dublin.

These two windows, typical of the Arts and Crafts Movement, show pre-Raphaelite and Celtic influences, and are full of symbolism (Larmour 1992). As one would expect, they romanticise war. (The design is very similar to another war memorial window in St John's Church, Malone, Belfast, by William McBride.) The window in the south transept depicts a young soldier in armour. In his right hand he grasps a spear, from which a red flag, displaying a white cross, unfurls. His left hand rests on a white shield with a red cross. The identity of the soldier is suggested by the sun emblazoned on his chest and the gold halo encircling his head. These two clues ('For the Lord God is a sun and shield', Psalm 84:11), together with the lines underneath (from Hymn 195 in the *Church Hymnal*) written by Bishop Reginald Heber (1783–1826), confirm the answer:

> *The Son of God goes forth to war,*
> *A Kingly crown to gain;*
> *His Blood-red banner streams afar,*
> *Who follows in His train?*

In the corresponding window in the north transept, the same young soldier stands, holding a huge sword like a cross in front of him. Hanging on his left arm is a shield, proclaiming 'Pro Patria'. This is taken from a quotation by Horace (one with which most parishioners would have been familiar, and which many believed, during the Great War) — *Dulce et decorum est pro patria mori* ('Lovely and honourable it is to die for one's country'). Over the soldier's head are the linked shields of St George of England and St Patrick of Ireland. The last verse of the same hymn is written underneath:

> *They climbed the steep ascent of Heaven,*
> *Through peril, toil, and pain;*
> *O God, to us may grace be given*
> *To follow in their train.*

The figure of Jesus occupies a central position in both windows. To complete the Trinity, symbols for God the Father (a crown) and God the Spirit (a dove) are depicted at the apices of both windows. Near the base of each window there are four shields representing the Allies: Britain, France, Belgium and Japan in the south transept, and Italy, Serbia, the USA and Russia in the north transept. In the midst of the shields are symbols of peace and reconciliation: the Lamb with the flag (the sacrificial lamb) and a reclining lion.

A Roll of Honour listing all the men from St John's who survived the Great War now hangs in the north porch of Monkstown. The names are framed by an intricate Celtic design, based on the illuminated manuscripts of early Irish art, the work of Theodora Lawrenson of Glasnevin.

CHAPTER 9

The Monkstown organs

There let the pealing organ blow,
To the full voic'd Quire below,
In Service high, and Anthems clear,
As may with sweetness, through mine ear,
Dissolve me into extasies,
And bring all Heav'n before mine eyes.
John Milton, *Il Penseroso*

The first organ (*c.* 1789)

Monkstown's present organ was built in 1898 and is the fourth organ to be installed in Monkstown Church. (For specifications of all four organs, *see Appendix 2.*) The first organ was probably installed when the Georgian church was built in 1789. Like many organs at the time, it was positioned in the organ gallery at the west end, over the main door. It was first mentioned eleven years later, in the *Hibernian Magazine* of 5 September 1800: 'Monkstown can boast the fairest country church in Ireland, containing a good organ …'. A later Monkstown organist, B. Warburton Rooke, gave some indication of its size when he wrote that 'though greatly praised at the time, it was evidently a small instrument. My father in his boyhood often amused himself playing on it when … it stood in the west gallery' (from Rooke's 1923 lecture).

Saunders's News-Letter of 27 March 1832 described the organ as consisting 'of a Principal, Twelfth, Fifteenth, Open and Stopt Diapasons, Flute, Cornet and Sequealtra [*sic*; should read 'Sesquialtera']. It stands twelve feet high and nine feet broad, in a handsome mahogany case'. It was tuned by 'Mr Woffington, organ builder', with yearly amounts listed (£3-8-3 in April 1806 and in April 1813). The tuner was probably Robert Woffington, described by Holmes (1984) as '*The* organ builder in Dublin' from about 1784 until some time before his death in 1819. By 1817 Woffington had been replaced by John Hall at the cheaper rate for tuning of £2-5-6.

The first organist that we can identify, from the Vestry book of 1805–29, was Peter Alma, who filled the post for about 36 years. (For a full list of Monkstown's organists, *see Appendix 2.*) Bartholomew Warburton Rooke (organist, 1882–1937) wrote of him:

'We find Peter Alma, like Johnnie Walker, still going strong. He not only acts in the capacity of organist but continues with it the offices of High Constable of the Barony and Assistant Valuator. What a blessing it is that these offices are not continued now-a-days!' (from Rooke's 1923 lecture).

In 1819 the Select Vestry asked Mr Alma to train three 'singing girls ... in the singing service of the Church', paying them about £4 each a year. When Alma died suddenly in 1825, advertisements were put in *Saunders's News-Letter* and the *Evening Mail*:

> ORGANIST
> Such persons as wish to become candidates for the situation of organist to the Parish of Monkstown are requested to send their applications on or before the 14th day of this present month directed to the church wardens of Monkstown, 34 College Green. Salary £40 a year.

There were two applicants, who were asked to play the organ for the Vestry and were marked accordingly: 'Mr. Crofton 12; Mr. Robinson 10'. Ernest Crofton was appointed, although he did not take up the post for another eighteen months and resigned after another twelve. In 1828 the Vestry was so dazzled by one applicant's qualifications that he was immediately appointed: the minutes of 27 April record that '... the pretensions and certificates of Mr. Henry Hooper were such as to induce the vestry to prefer him to any other'. This marvellous gentleman was simply too good to be true — he lasted less than two months and was replaced by a Mr Jephson.

Entries in the Vestry minutes refer to the organ's maintenance over the years: 'The church wardens (were) directed to have the organ put into perfect repair. Expense not to exceed 30 guineas' (24 March 1818). There were further expenses noted, 'for erecting iron railing with brass knobs round the organ, £3-15-7½' and 'for repairing organ, £2-5-6' (8 April 1822). In 1831 the organist collected a salary of £40 a year and the organ blower 6 guineas. These were princely salaries — 100 years later, in 1941, Mr William G. Ebbs was engaged on a salary of £60 a year.

When Semple & Son rebuilt the church in 1831, they left the inside of the west end, including the organ gallery, virtually untouched. But the Vestry had decided on a new organ, so the old 1789 instrument was advertised for sale in *Saunders's News-Letter* on 27 March 1832, saying that it had 'recently undergone a thorough repair'. They asked for 'proposals [offers] in writing' to be sent to the churchwardens.

Second organ (1832)

Meanwhile work was progressing on its replacement, which was 'nearly completed'. The builder of this new organ is unknown, but the cost was noted as £392. At the dedication service held in September 1832, Charles Lindsay, bishop of Kildare and patron of Monkstown, preached the sermon. Being also dean of Christ Church, he brought with him 'the young gentlemen' of the choir. The organ was described by *Saunders's News-Letter* of 12 September 'as an instrument of great power and sweetness'. It had two manuals and eighteen stops (*for abridged specification, see Appendix 2*).

Less than ten years after its installation, the rural dean reported, during his Visitation of 1840, that 'the organ appear(ed) to be suffering considerably from the damp in that part of the building' (the organ gallery) and suggested that 'the Provincial Architect should inspect the roof' since the lead seemed to be 'defective'. (This was a recurring problem; some 23 years before, the Vestry minutes record on 8 April 1817 that a 'carpenter (was paid) for repairing the ceiling of church over the organ'.) The organ-builder who came along to repair the damage to the instrument was a young man called William Telford, who was paid £10 for his work.

During the 1850s, the internal layout of churches gradually changed in parallel with new ideas about worship (*see Chapter 7*). Chancels were built to emphasise the central role of the Eucharist and music became more important in the liturgy. Thus the church organ, which had up to now always been at the back of the building, was moved right up into the chancel, and a choir was often installed there too. Monkstown followed the trend, with John McCurdy's new chancel being added in 1862. The 1832 organ was removed from the organ gallery at the west end and reinstalled in a new 'organ room', tucked away on the north side of the chancel, behind the pulpit. Unusually, a fireplace had been included nearby, most thoughtfully for the organist at least and his bellows-blower, since this may have been the only heating in the church at the time, but detrimental to the organ itself.[1]

In fact, it would probably have been far better to have left the organ where it was. Acoustically, the west gallery is the ideal position for an organ since, from there, members of the congregation in the body of the church can hear it more or less equally. On the other hand, an organ in the chancel tends to deafen the choristers sitting beside it and may not be heard at its best from the west end or in the transepts around the corner. The organ sounds better when it is in an open position rather than in a constricted chamber and also when it is on a higher level (Addleshaw and Etchells 1958). So it would seem that, in its attempts to modernise the church, the Vestry took a retrograde step in 1862. When the organ was reassembled in its new position, it was 'boxed in' on three sides and, on the remaining side, the solid chancel pews (four rows on each side, for the choristers) tended to absorb and muffle the music. This situation continued up until the 1890s, when some pews were removed. (Today, there are fewer pews in the chancel to interfere with the sound, which is much improved.)

The organ was to survive only ten years after its move. Ironically, the older part of the church was sounder than the most recent. In the winter of 1870–1, a leak in the chancel's roof seems to have damaged the organ irretrievably. A receipt of 17 December 1870 records: 'Slater & assistant 1½ day staunching roof over organ chamber, taking down pipes, letting in lead slips, flashing on top of embraisure, putting zinc under cracked slates, etc., 12/9; Slates, cement, zinc, etc. used, 17/-'.

This can only have been a patch-up job since, one month later, the roof leaked again: 'Jan. 21 1871, slater and assistant 1 day staunching leak over organ and down pipe to chancel south side, 8/6'.

Coincidentally — or perhaps this leak was the last straw — the long-serving organist, Henry Toole, resigned in January 1871 and a temporary organist was employed until someone permanent could be appointed. Toole's successor was Francis Quin, the organist (1861–70) of the Mariners' Church in Kingstown, which had had a Telford organ installed in 1860.[2] Perhaps he made his appointment conditional on the purchase of a new Telford. At any rate, he was officially appointed in January 1871; a new organ by Telford & Telford was ordered on 14 August that year and was officially inaugurated in March 1872.[3] The old 1832 organ was sold to the Free Church in Cork some months later.

Third organ (1872, Telford & Telford)

An anonymous donor presented this organ to the church. Even the Select Vestry minutes were discreet as to his identity; it was recorded on 23 August 1871 (about a week after the organ was ordered from Telford & Telford) 'that the thanks of the Select Vestry be conveyed to the donor of the New organ for his noble gift & for the handsome manner in which the offer has been made'. In 1875 Monkstown's generous sponsor died, confident that his secret was safe. Five years later, a writer in the *Irish Ecclesiastical Gazette* of 20 March 1880 publicly unmasked him: 'It ... was the anonymous gift of, it is believed, the late Mr. Hone ... It cost a large sum of money, over £700 we have been informed.' (An equivalent organ today would apparently cost in the region of €350,000 to €450,000.)

Thomas Hone of 'Yapton', Monkstown, was a stockbroker, a freeman of the City of Dublin and a director of the Bank of Ireland. He had recently (1868) offered to erect stained glass in the new church of St John's at Mounttown. Apparently his son had survived a train crash and his daughter a 'fever', and Hone wanted to donate the windows 'as a thank-offering for mercies received' (Harden 1911). Presumably the same motivation led to his giving an organ to the parish church. But why the secrecy? Because he was officially a Quaker, Hone may not have wished his gift to be public knowledge. Quaker services are simple and austere; organ music and stained glass, however plain, would have been considered 'extravagant'. Two years after Hone's death, the Vestry thanked his son, William, who had donated £1,000 to charities in the Monkstown area 'in fulfilment of the generous desire expressed by his late father' (Select Vestry minutes of 2 April 1877). William played cricket for Ireland and was one of the five Hones on the 'Gentlemen of Ireland' team who first toured America in 1879.

Extraordinarily, this latest organ of 1872, the most modern and expensive to date, only lasted 26 years. (The 1789 organ had lasted 43 years, while the 1832 organ had managed 39 years.) The builder of the new 1872 organ was William Telford. Telford's first known commission was the rebuilding of St Catherine's organ in 1830, originally built by Ferdinand Weber in 1767. At this time Telford was only 21 and still working from home; four years later he set up his own business at 45 Bride Street in Dublin city. He had been to Monkstown Church before, in October 1840, when he had repaired the previous organ, damaged by damp. In 1848 his brother, Henry, joined him as partner and the firm Telford & Telford was born (Holmes 1984).

Besides Telford's obvious business acumen and ability, his timing was auspicious: churches were springing up all over Ireland and they all needed organs. The *Irish Ecclesiastical Gazette* reported in 1826 that 'His Majesty's Commission for Building New Churches (had) determined upon and made promise for the erection of 165 additional churches and chapels, and 64 of that number either have been, or are ready for consecration'. Telford organs were soon scattered all over Ireland and England, and even as far afield as Wellington

The Telford & Telford organ, installed in 1872 and donated by a parishioner, Thomas Hone, cost over £700 but only lasted for 26 years. It was a large instrument, with three keyboards, pedals and 28 stops, and projected beyond the 'organ room' built by McCurdy to accommodate its smaller 1832 predecessor.

Church in New Zealand and Port Stanley in the Falkland Islands. According to *The Dublin Builder* of 1 April 1860, they were found in nine cathedrals (including Dublin's Christ Church), six collegiate halls or churches (including Trinity College and Maynooth), 22 monasteries, convents and asylums, and nearly 100 churches throughout Ireland. In England he built the organs at, among others, St Peter's, Radley, Oxford; Padstow, Penzance and St Ives in Cornwall; and for the earl of Harewood.

Telford's early work is now considered much better than his later output. By the 1860s, his individually handcrafted organs (*see description, Appendix 2*) had given way to more stereotyped factory-made pieces, churned out in response to the huge demand. His organ in Christ Church Cathedral, Dublin, proved troublesome and was described in a letter by its increasingly exasperated organist, Sir Robert Prescott Stewart, to the Rev. Edward Seymour as 'a saw sharpener … I despise and detest our own organ daily more and more' (Grindle 1989).

The new Monkstown organ was much larger than the old 1832 organ (which Telford has taken away in part exchange and sold to the Free Church in Cork in 1872). It had three keyboards, pedals and 28 stops (*for full specification, see Appendix 2*) and now emerged partly in front of the archway which had originally framed its predecessor. On 1 March 1872 it was officially 'opened' by Sir Robert Prescott Stewart, ex-organist of Christ Church, organist of St Patrick's and professor of music in Trinity College, Dublin. (He also edited

117

the *Irish Church Hymnal* (1876) and was the leading composer of church music of his day.) But, like the Christ Church organ, no one was ever very happy with the new Monkstown organ. Whatever about its quality, the problem of its hemmed-in site (in the 'organ room', designed by McCurdy on the north side of the chancel) still existed. However much Telford tried, he could not make the organ more powerful since the fundamental problem was its poor location. In December 1872, the Vestry minutes observed that the organ was 'not … yet perfect' and the organist, Francis Quin, was requested 'to state in writing whether the organ (was) now in perfect order and if any defects exist to specify them'. Telford recommended that water should be used for 'blowing' the organ, instead of Charles Riggs, who was doing it manually for £6-10s a year. The alterations would cost £50-10s. The choir committee delegated Captain Betham to ask the 'Black Rock Commissioners' about the supply of water necessary.

Then, presumably in desperation, in 1878 the Vestry approached another organ-builder, Richard Benson of Cuffe Street, and asked him to put the organ 'in thorough repair'. For £100, Benson cleaned the 'entire organ … and left (it) in perfect order'.[4]

The organist Francis Quin died in 1882 and B. Warburton Rooke was chosen in his stead, out of twenty applicants. (Rooke's father was archdeacon of Wicklow and his uncle Thomas had been a curate at Monkstown.) Rooke was only eighteen years of age when he was appointed but, like the experienced Quin before him, he was unhappy with the organ. He wrote glumly: 'This organ, always a harsh one, became almost unplayable owing to the action in the course of time becoming defective. It was no uncommon thing for me to have to spend part of Saturday afternoon lying flat on a very dirty bellows … trying to tie up the action with string so that I could use it on Sunday' (from Rooke's 1923 lecture).

Rooke continued Quin's practice of teaching 'the theory and practise of music' to schoolchildren and he also continued the 'weekly evening congregational practise of church music' for the whole congregation, 'with a view to the improvement of the singing in church which … (had) greatly fallen off lately'. The children were joined in 1891 by '2 paid male voices, tenor and bass … to strengthen the choir, at a cost not exceeding £30 per annum' (Vestry minutes, 26 January 1891).

William Telford died in 1885 and his two sons, William Hodgson and Edward, took over the family business.[5] In 1891 William Telford, Junior, was the organist at the Mariners' Church in Kingstown, playing on the organ his father had built.[2] But, although the brothers were competent organ-builders, the business continued to go downhill. Monkstown renewed its contract for organ maintenance with them in 1885, but were unhappy with their work and terminated the agreement in 1890.

Fourth organ (1898, Gray & Davison)

Praise Him with the timbrel and dance:
Praise Him with stringed instruments and organs.
Psalm 150:4, sung at the dedication of the Monkstown organs in 1898 and 1966

One evening in 1897, after a meeting, some members of the Vestry went up to the chancel

The Gray & Davison organ of 1898 with its handsome organ case, designed in part by William Kaye Parry, was installed in 1898. It has undergone several major restorations, the latest in 1965–6. The interior decoration of the church has also changed radically, from the typical late Victorian treatment (above), with dado and decorative fleurs-de-lis, to the striking decor of today (left), with Semple's 'granite blocks' picked out in subtle shades and bold terracotta bands encircling the whole church.

to talk to Mr Rooke, who spoke to them 'from his customary position on the bellows'. As Mr Rooke added in his lecture notes (1932), 'It proved a fortunate, if unexpected meeting, as directly afterwards the Vestry decided to relieve me of my activities [lying on the bellows] and purchase a new organ'. Monkstown's fourth organ was by Gray & Davison; it cost £1,036-10s, with '£5 additional for connecting with the present blowing apparatus'.[6] The Vestry refused an offer of £100 for the old Telford & Telford organ, which was said to be worth £250. Its present whereabouts are unknown.

The Choir Committee was unhappy with the Gray & Davison design of the organ case, so it sent an 'amended design' by the church architect, Mr William Kaye Parry, to the organ-builders on 15 June 1898 'with an intimation that our Architect thinks it ought not to be more expensive than the original design'. Parry may well have tried to emulate elements of the church architecture, as Drew had before him (*see Chapter 7*): on each side of the organ case are great carved 'shuttlecocks', almost identical to Semple's vast fan vaulting above them.

One would have imagined that the purchase of a new organ would have delighted Rooke, but there is a distinct lack of enthusiasm in his statement, 'And so in 1898, (the 1872 organ) was superseded by the present instrument, the work of Messrs Gray & Davison of London' (from Rooke's 1923 lecture). This muted response could be explained by the fact that Rooke had probably campaigned long and hard for a new organ; earlier that year, he had travelled as far afield as Birkenhead 'to inspect an electric organ', as reported in the Choir Committee minutes of 10 March 1898.

When the new Gray & Davison organ was installed in Monkstown, Rooke seemed disappointed with its performance (*for full specification, see Appendix 2*). Clearly, the problem of siting still existed: changing the organ was not going to remedy that. In his notes for a lecture delivered in 1923, he wrote that 'a deep carpeted chancel with no opening from the organ chamber into the transept is ruinous from the musical point of view', but then changed his mind about making such a negative observation and crossed out the sentence. Years later, Rooke was still considering the possibility of making an opening from the organ chamber into the north transept and an architect was consulted. But the Select Vestry minutes of June 1911 record 'that having obtained architect's report and contractor's estimate amounting to £77 … we are unanimous of opinion, having regard to possible risks and doubtful results in securing additional sound, that the matter be not further proceeded with'.

The dedication of the new organ by the archbishop of Dublin, Dr Joseph Peacocke, took place on Thursday evening, 17 November 1898, with 23 other clergy in attendance. He was a former curate (1863–73) and incumbent (1878–94) of Monkstown, who 'considered it … a mistake to provide anything grand or elaborate except on very special occasions. All the ordinary parish church required was simple music well rendered', as reported in *The Irish Times* of 18 November 1898. The organ fund still needed £300 and the Service Sheet reminded the congregation that 'further subscriptions (were) earnestly solicited'. To encourage generous donations, '14 gentlemen (were asked) to act as collectors & stewards, and others to act as stewards' at the dedication service.

There is a strange twist of events here. Nearly 30 years earlier, Monkstown had purchased a Telford organ, almost certainly recommended by their new organist, Francis Quin, ex-organist to the Mariners' Church in Kingstown. Now the situation was reversed: in 1900 the Mariners' Church bought a Gray & Davison organ and asked Mr Rooke, the serving Monkstown organist, to oversee the whole installation.

Monkstown seems to have made a habit of falling out with its organ-tuners. After dispensing with the services of Telford & Telford in 1890, Gray & Davison had been taken on as tuners. But this arrangement did not last long: on 12 January 1909, the Choir Committee was 'of opinion that the agreement with Gray & Davison should be cancelled and that Conacher & Co. should be appointed'.

Restorations of 1898 organ

The present organ in Monkstown Church is the old 1898 Gray & Davison model restored. Work was undertaken many times over the years, with a further rebuild in 1965–6. The first major overhaul was in 1911, when the firm of Abbott & Smith was called in and the organ was 'taken to pieces, cleaned and improved' for the first time since its installation thirteen years before. In 1928, further work on the organ was necessary owing to a leakage in the roof. Then, in 1941, the 'splendid organ was completely overhauled and restored' for £95 by Evans & Barr of Belfast and Dublin. They suggested a way to save money: 'We have just salvaged parts of a large organ destroyed by enemy action, and one of the few parts which has not suffered is the pedal board, this was quite recently installed and is of exactly the same scale and dimensions as the new one we should make. We could clean up the pedal board to make it quite new in appearance and could reduce our estimate to you by three pounds.'

The great organ pipes of the 1898 Gray & Davison instrument are beautifully painted with stylised floral motifs in complementary colours, sympathetic to the overall scheme of the interior.

A note on the letter says, 'Telephoned and said "yes" '.

Evans & Barr restored the organ again in 1953 at a cost of about £152, this time under the watchful eye of Mr E.G. Barton, an amateur organ enthusiast. He had already supervised several organ restorations, including those at St Michan's and Bray Methodist churches, and would, in the future, supervise those at St Paul's of Bray and Kingstown Presbyterian Church.[7] From his letters, it appears that Barton was present throughout the work, supervising every step minutely. He described working with the tuner for three full days, dealing with almost 2,000 pipes in the organ, many more than once. He kept the Select Vestry fully informed of progress and sent frequent updates to Mr Lidstone, the honorary secretary, submitting his 'Final Report on Organ' on 18 July 1953.

Barton's conscientiousness, attention to detail and humour are captured in his letters. For example, on 25 October 1954 he wrote: 'The V[ox] H[umana] never approximates to the human voice, it is a fair copy of a goat. It is useless, difficult to keep in tune, and seldom used by Mr. Ebbs or any artistic player. Just a relic of Victorian vulgarity.'[8] He certainly did not suffer fools gladly, as one organ-builder found out on submitting his estimate on 31 March 1953; he had ended his quote with the phrase, 'Trusting this will cover your requirements'. Barton, who had gone through the letter underlining and writing caustic comments, made the retort, 'It most certainly does nothing of the kind'. Needless to say, the organ-builder's estimate was not accepted.

Disaster struck after this restoration of the organ in 1953. In November the following year the organ suffered damage, partly, it seems, from glue melting within its works owing to overheating of the church (which had been 'like the tropical house at Glasnevin', according to Barton). Also, the chancel's roof was leaking again (as had occurred in 1870–1 and in 1928). More restoration work had to be carried out, costing £145.

Finally, in 1964, it was decided that the organ needed a major overhaul and the estimate for the work involved was £4,000. An expert from Rushworth & Dreaper, a Liverpool firm of organ-builders, had been brought in to inspect it and he was 'agreeably surprised and pleased with the organ … Although the mechanism (was) obsolete by modern standards, (it had) stood the test of time'.[9] A leaflet was published by Monkstown Parish Church in 1964, entitled *Why we need to spend £4,000 on the organ, and how you can help*, appealing to parishioners for subscriptions.

The Dublin firm of R.E. Meates & Son, Organ Builders, carried out most of the restoration work during 1965 and 1966, although some of the reeds had to be sent to England for specialist attention. According to Barton, 'the Gray and Davidson [*sic*] pipe work proved to be in such excellent condition that all was retained, excepting the Vox Humana stop replaced by a more useful one'. The Meates family had been in the business for generations, having been connected, since 1830, with Telford & Telford, the makers of dozens of organs, including the Monkstown 1872 instrument. The grandfather, father (William) and three uncles of Richard Meates (the owner in 1965) had all worked with the Telfords. After William Telford's death in 1885, his two sons continued to run the business, but it was not going well. Eventually, William Meates took over Telford & Telford in 1917. It closed as a company in 1950, but was re-established by William and his son Richard as Meates & Son.[10]

The restored and augmented organ was ready on Thursday 13 October 1966, when the archbishop of Dublin, Dr George Otto Simms, rededicated it at a special service. The organist, Mr W.G. Ebbs, in his concluding recital played, among other pieces, *Pastorale* by A. Guilmant, which Mr B.W. Rooke had played almost 70 years before at the original dedication service on 17 November 1898.

On 8 July 1967, Monkstown Parish Fête was held at The Hall School on Monkstown Road. One of the objectives was to try and raise £1,000 in aid of the Organ Repair Fund. The taoiseach, Jack Lynch, opened the festivities, drawing such crowds that the rector, Mr. Billy Wynne, was able to tell him in a letter afterwards that £1,370 had been raised and the 'great debt' was wiped out.

Organists, the Choir and other musical matters

In 1932 Monkstown celebrated the centenary of the rebuilding of the church by Semple. On 26 October the remarkable organist, Mr B.W. Rooke — described by Canon Albert Stokes as 'a tiny little man with a big moustache' — gave 'a most interesting lantern lecture' on the history of Monkstown, apparently a repeat of one he had originally prepared in 1923. (His dark blue notebook still survives, with the 'Draft and Notes' of his lecture, held in the Representative Church Body Library today.) Later, at the parish centenary social, Rooke was presented with 'a silver salver bearing a suitable inscription' to mark his outstanding achievement of 50 years as organist and choirmaster. The event was reported in the *Church of Ireland Gazette* on 11 November 1932. He was to serve another five years, retiring at the age of 73.

Bartholomew Warburton Rooke, organist and choirmaster at Monkstown for 55 years (1882–1937), pictured in 1912 playing on the Gray & Davison organ of 1898.

Bartholomew Warburton Rooke, Monkstown's organist and choirmaster for 55 years, died on 10 February 1942. Appointed at the tender age of eighteen, Rooke was a talented and dedicated musician, a bachelor of music (TCD), a professor at the Royal Irish Academy of Music and writer of a book on harmony, as well as being a keen amateur local historian. His memorial is placed appropriately on the wall beside the organ in the chancel and reads:

TO THE GLORY OF GOD
AND IN LOVING MEMORY OF
BARTHOLOMEW WARBURTON ROOKE
MUS.BAC. UNIVERSITY OF DUBLIN
FELLOW ROYAL IRISH ACADEMY OF MUSIC
ORGANIST AND CHOIRMASTER OF
MONKSTOWN PARISH CHURCH FROM 1882 TO 1937
SON OF ARCHDEACON ROOKE OF WICKLOW
BORN DEC. 2 1864 — DIED FEB. 10 1942
'I know that my Redeemer liveth'

Rooke was a hard act to follow. His successor was George Rothwell, appointed in 1937 as organist. He and the other candidate for the post were invited to take a morning and evening service, and to give a short recital after each. The unsuccessful aspirant was paid two guineas for her trouble and Mr Rothwell was offered the position at £60 a year. His tenure only lasted four years — he resigned in September 1941, giving less than a week's notice, to become musical director of the Cork Opera House. Mr William Gabriel Ebbs, former organist at Raheny, was appointed in his place. He was to serve for 49 years (1941–90), almost equalling Mr B. Warburton Rooke's record of 55 years. (For a complete list of Monkstown's organists from *c.* 1789 to the present, *see Appendix 2.*)

Other events involving the musical side of the church were moving apace. For example, the members of the Choir were robed in 1949 and gently satirised in the words of G.A. Mackay in his 1958 poem *Monkstown memories* (the 'Arthur' referred to is, of course, the Rev. Arthur Butler, rector during 1945–58):

The Choir was good and sang with zest —
All dressed up in their Sunday Best.
But Arthur, always on the go,
Soon robed them all from top to toe.
The ladies lost a source of chat —
'Did you see Mrs. So-and-So's ghastly hat?'
But men — when cassock low descends
Find it hides frayed trouser ends.
Now that they all looked so serene
It was essential that they be seen
So the Reading Desk — that stood in the way —
Vanished, without regret, one day.

In 1964 the Rev. Billy Wynne wrote in the Annual Review:

'We owe a special word of thanks to our Organist and Choirmaster, Mr. W.G. Ebbs, for all he has done to build up the choir to its present high standard and he holds the affection and respect of all of us. An average choir attendance at Morning Service of 22 and at Evening Service of 21 speaks for itself. Anthems were sung on Whit Sunday and at Harvest. On Good Friday we sang Shaw's "The Redeemer", which was first sung in Ireland by our choir nearly 20 years ago.'

Two music scholarships were established in the 1990s. The Monkstown Organ Scholarship was set up to encourage young people to learn the instrument. It provides free organ lessons for one year and €130. It is supported by the 'Music in Monkstown' Fund, which also helps finance the Junior Choir and seeks to encourage the participation of young people in music in the parish. In addition, instrumental scholarships, covering tuition for one year, are funded by the Joan McWilliams Scholarship Fund. Joan McWilliams (née Aplin) was Choir Leader from about 1956 (at a salary of £30 per year) until 1993.

The Adult Choir is a mixed four-part choir, with a membership of about 22. It sings anthems regularly at the Communion services twice a month and makes a major musical contribution to all the church festivals — the Nine Lessons, Carols at Christmas, and Easter and Harvest festive music. In recent years the choir has sung at Harvest festivals in Mountmellick, Castledermot and Inch, and travelled to Tewkesbury Abbey, Gloucester, in August 2003.

Drawing, probably by Mrs Nancy Pollard, Choir Leader during the 1950s, to mark her increase in salary by £5 per year.

The Junior Choir was restarted in 1992, shortly after the arrival of Siobhán Kilkelly, the present organist. There are about fifteen young people, aged between eight and seventeen, who sing at the 11.15 family service every month and at all the major church festivals. The choir is affiliated to the Royal School of Church Music, which runs a scheme for junior choirs. Medals with different coloured ribbons are awarded and the children receive payments based on their levels of achievement, ability and effort. The choir has its own annual concert and has sung in many other parish churches in Dublin and further afield: in 2001 the choir travelled to St David's Cathedral in Wales to sing at Evensong and in 2002 to Lismore Cathedral, Co. Waterford. Both choirs, Junior and Adult, were kitted out in burgundy red robes in 1998.

CHAPTER 10

The Knox Memorial Hall

The Knox Memorial Hall opened its doors in June 1904, thanks to the generosity of Alice Chaloner Knox, who wished for a suitable memorial to her beloved husband, Captain Edward, and their favourite nephew, Eustace. Monkstown was badly in need of such a facility, as the *Church of Ireland Gazette* of 14 March 1902 reported: 'The parish of Monkstown has for some time felt the want of a parish hall. A generous donor — Mrs Challoner [*sic*] Knox — has recently offered the large sum of £2,000 for this purpose. We believe an excellent site has already been secured close to the parish church.'

Two years later the Monkstown Select Vestry, in its Annual Report of 1904, stated: 'It would be difficult to exaggerate the importance of the Hall to the Parish, which now provides a common meeting place for all parochial purposes … It may well be hoped that the possession of it by the Parish will bring its members into more frequent intercommunication, with the certain result that they will stimulate each other to increased zeal and effort for Christ's work on earth.' Years later, it was still being described as 'the largest parochial hall in the diocese of Dublin', according to the rector, the Rev. Arthur Butler, in the *Monkstown Review* of 1956.

The Knox family

Few of us can claim to be related to such conflicting characters as Queen Victoria, who famously said 'I will be good', *and* to Macbeth, of whom it was said 'Not in the legions of horrid hell can come a devil more damn'd in evils to top Macbeth'.

One who could claim these wildly contrasting relations was Captain Edward Chaloner Knox. It is unclear whether he even knew of his distinguished ancestry.[1] Like Queen Victoria, he was said to be a direct descendant of Kenneth McAlpin, the first king of Scotland, who ruled for about ten years, from AD 850 to 860. Captain Knox and Victoria were 23rd cousins, once removed. His relationship to Macbeth McFinlay, on whom

Shakespeare's Macbeth was based, was through a great aunt (to the power of 23).

The Knox family tended to make astute marriages and even owed its surname to one of these alliances. Adamus, who was the great (x 9) grandson of Kenneth McAlpin (the first king of Scotland), as well as the great (x 14) grandfather of Captain Knox, married the niece of Walter, the lord high steward of Scotland. Walter owned vast estates in Renfrewshire and gave Adamus the lands of Knock Ranfurlie and Griffe Castle. Thus Adamus became known as Adamus Knock, or Knox (the word *knock* comes from *cnoc*, which, as in Irish, means 'hill').

The Knoxs continued to intermarry with other branches of the family[2] and also with daughters of the titled. Captain Knox was distantly related by marriage to the De Vesci family, the ground landlords ('lords of the soil') of Monkstown. (Captain Knox's grandfather, John Knox of Castlerea, had a fourth cousin, Thomas Knox, Viscount Northland, who married Anne, daughter of Lord Knapton and sister of Viscount de Vesci.) Another descendant of John Knox was Alberic Edward Knox, who married Emily Adela, the granddaughter of Sir William Betham, the Ulster king of arms, in 1868.

To return to Captain Edward Chaloner Knox, he was born in Sligo on 20 January 1815 to Major John Knox and Catherine (née Chaloner) of Dominick Street, Dublin. The family had strong military connections. Edward's elder brother, Lieutenant General Richard Knox, raised a cavalry regiment, the 18th Hussars, which he commanded for fifteen years. One of Richard's six sons, Eustace, became lieutenant colonel and brevet colonel of the same regiment; another four of his sons also joined the army.

Edward graduated from Trinity College, Dublin, in 1837 (Burtchaell and Sadleir 1935) and two years later was called to the Irish Bar.[3] He then moved to Tyrone, where he became a captain in the Tyrone Militia. He continued the family tradition of making advantageous marriages when, in 1856, at the age of 41, he married 25-year-old Alice Hewitt Caroline St George, daughter of Acheson St George, of 'Wood Park', Co. Armagh, and granddaughter of the Hon. John Hewitt, dean of Cloyne.[4] Because Edward and Alice had no children of their own, it seems that they were particularly close to their nephew, Eustace (born on 19 March 1860), who had also been given the name 'Chaloner' (like his uncle Edward), after his grandmother, Catherine Chaloner.

The Knoxs lived initially at 'Desertcreat' in County Tyrone, where Edward became a justice of the peace (JP) and deputy lieutenant for the county. In 1875 they moved to Dublin to live at 'Belgrave Hall' in Queen's Park, Monkstown. Then, in 1885, they bought 'Silverton', 4, The Hill, Monkstown. Edward became a JP for County Dublin and a registered vestryman for Monkstown; he was appointed churchwarden in 1883 and 1884. Four days after his death (on 4 April 1896, aged 81), the parishioners passed a resolution at the Easter Vestry recording the 'deep sense of the loss' the parish had sustained by the death of Captain Knox. They remembered his 'diligent discharge of (his) duties' as churchwarden and vestryman, his 'great interest' in parish affairs and his generosity — he had been 'ever ready by ungrudging labour and large-hearted liberality to further every good cause ... The Church and the world (were) the poorer by his death', as reported in the *Irish Ecclesiastical Gazette* on 17 April 1896.

Captain Knox was buried on 9 April 1896 in Deansgrange Cemetery. *The Irish Times* of the day reported: 'On arrival at the cemetery, the massive oak coffin, mounted in brass, was placed on the mortuary carriage, which was preceded by the Lord Bishop of Meath and the Rev. J.C. Dowse [incumbent of Monkstown] reading the opening passages of the burial service'. At the private funeral, Bishop Peacocke, who had been incumbent of Monkstown (1878–94) during Captain Knox's time in the parish, gave 'an impressive address'. Listed as the chief mourners were Captain Knox's brother (Captain Richard J. Knox), his three nephews (Captain Eustace Knox, Colonel Richard Knox and 'Captain L. Knox' [*sic*; this should be either Captain Charles Knox or Captain Francis Knox] and his brother-in-law (Acheson St George).

Three years later, the Boer War began (1899–1901). Edward's favourite nephew, Eustace, had enlisted, at the age of twenty, in the 18th Hussars (commanded by his father, Richard). Eustace received a commission after serving as a trooper for three and a half years and fought in the Nile Campaign of 1884–5. With the 18th Hussars when war broke out in South Africa, Eustace was 'frequently' mentioned in dispatches and was made lieutenant colonel of the regiment in 1900, commanding it until the end of the war in 1901 (*Annual Register*, 1902).

While Eustace was stationed at the garrison of Ladysmith, the Boers besieged it. The siege lasted 118 days. Two thousand horses, including those of Eustace's cavalry regiment, were slaughtered to feed the 19,000 starving men, women and children inside. Although the Boers' famous gun 'Long Tom' bombarded the town with 3,000 shells, typhoid killed over 550 in those four months, ten times more than the enemy action. Richard Harding Davis, an English journalist and one of the first to enter Ladysmith after its relief by General White, gives a moving account of what they found there in his 1901 book, *With both armies in South Africa*.

It is not surprising perhaps that, after the deprivations of Ladysmith, Colonel Eustace Knox died the following year, on 18 February 1902, aged only 41 years. (Many of the soldiers were so hungry that, when the siege was lifted, they overindulged; weakened by starvation and fever, some 60 of these men died within the following week.) The official cause of Eustace's death, as reported in *The Irish Times* of 22 February 1902, was 'acute pneumonia', but it is likely that Ladysmith was ultimately responsible.

Building a memorial

Alice, the widow of Captain Edward Chaloner Knox, now aged 71, immediately began to organise a practical project in memory of her beloved husband and her nephew, Eustace. (Her husband had left her £35,000 in his will, making her a very wealthy woman.[5]) The Knox Hall was her brainchild.

Monkstown had been in need of a parochial hall for some time. A 'Diamond Jubilee Memorial Hall', to commemorate Queen Victoria's 60 years on the throne, had been mooted at the Easter Vestry of 1897, but the project was apparently dropped, presumably through lack of funding, according to the minutes of the Select Vestry on 23 April.[6] It was difficult to run parish events without a suitable venue. In 1902, Monkstown table tennis and cricket tournaments and the Cricket Club AGM were all held in the Town Hall, Kingstown, within a two-month period.

The Knox Memorial Hall, on Monkstown Road, was built through the generosity of Alice Chaloner Knox in memory of her husband Edward and nephew Eustace. It was designed by Richard Chaytor Millar, a parishioner, and opened in 1904.

On 18 April 1902, exactly two months after the death of Eustace Knox, 'Mr. R. Millar submitted a rough sketch of the proposed parochial hall' at a meeting of the Monkstown Fabric Committee. After some discussion, Mr Millar was asked 'to prepare plans, etc. on the basis of his sketch'. The 'Mr R. Millar' in question was Richard Chaytor Millar (1844–1915) of the firm Millar and Symes of 186 Great Brunswick Street — honorary architect of the Bank of Ireland in College Green during the years 1879–1907 (Curran 1977) and of many Edwardian houses in Foxrock.

Richard Chaytor Millar had been born in 'Clifton Villa', Monkstown, the son of Adam Millar, a tea, wine and spirit merchant, and a churchwarden (1855) of Monkstown.[7] (Richard's younger brother, Fitzadam (1893–1921), of 'Windsor House', Monkstown Avenue, was also prominent in the parish, being appointed churchwarden seven times over the years; *see Appendix 4*.) Richard later lived in Blackrock, at 'Brooklawn', 30 Mount Merrion Avenue. William Symes, the son of Sandham Symes (the architect of Holy Trinity, Killiney, in 1859), was his partner from 1874 until his death in 1892. Then Richard's son, Adam Gerald Chaytor Millar, became his partner from 1898 (Curran 1977). The firm (still called 'Millar and Symes' even after Symes's death) continued for some years to do work for Monkstown Church. In 1905, for example, it carried out some refurbishment of 'Churchville', the curates' house (as recorded in the minutes of the Fabric Committee on 13 December), and in a letter dated 13 October 1926 A.G.C. Millar, on behalf of the firm, recommended that the church roof timbers should be 'dressed down and treated with carbolinium' owing to their being attacked by 'the boring beetle'.

130

Advertisements for builders of the Knox Memorial Hall were inserted in the papers, but by July 1902 only one firm (Messrs John Lowry & Son) had submitted a tender. The Vestry told them that, since they did not belong to the Dublin Master Builders' Association, they could not be considered; however, they were advised that their tender would be considered if they were to join the Association. The work was advertised again. This time eight contractors submitted tenders, ranging from £2,691 to £3,090. That of Mr Christopher Jolley (or Joly) was the lowest and was accepted on condition that he reduce it further, to £2,500. This drop (of nearly £200) would have been a significant amount for Mr Jolley, but he was obviously keen to take on the work, especially with the current slump in the building trade, partly owing to the recent Boer War in South Africa. The contract was signed on 19 December 1902, with the work agreed to start in May 1903 (Walker 1992).

Building progressed on schedule and the Knox Memorial Hall was completed by June of the following year. The property was secured by a 5½-foot wall and railings built in front of the hall, costing £138-14s-6d. The Fabric Committee saved three guineas by reducing the height by six inches. The architect, Richard Millar, advertised for estimates for 'a suitable unclimable fence of an inexpensive description' for the side and rear boundaries. Three estimates were received: the cheapest was £21-16s-4d and the dearest £72-7s-8d. The Fabric Committee, as usual, chose the cheapest option, but decided on a 'bow-topped' pattern rather than a 'pointed' one, as recorded in the minutes of 10 March 1904.

The bishop of Meath, Dr Joseph Peacocke, had been elected archbishop of Dublin in 1897. As incumbent of Monkstown up to 1894, he was invited back to the parish to open the Knox Memorial Hall on 28 June 1904. Alice Knox had hoped to hold a sort of private tea party to mark the occasion, but was instructed by the Vestry that 'special invitations for

Progress of George V and Queen Mary along Monkstown Road during their visit in 1911, with the Knox Memorial Hall seen in the background.

The Knox coat of arms is proudly displayed in the great window of the Knox Memorial Hall, opened in 1904. The crest of the family was a falcon and their motto was *Moveo et proficio* ('I move and prosper').

tea would be inadvisable and that the proposal be abandoned'.

The hall's great neo-Tudor window, facing onto Monkstown Road, celebrates the Knox family. It displays a colourful coat of arms, divided into six compartments showing the ancestry of Edward and Eustace Knox. The Knox arms (on the upper left, the most important position on the shield) show a falcon on a red background, while the Chaloner arms (upper central) show a chevron and three cherub heads.[8] Below is the Knox family motto — *Moveo et proficio* ('I move and prosper'). Beneath the window is a brass plaque, with the dedication:

THIS HALL
WAS ERECTED AND PRESENTED TO THE PARISH OF MONKSTOWN
BY MRS. E.C. KNOX, IN MEMORY OF HER HUSBAND,
EDWARD CHALONER KNOX OF SILVERTON, MONKSTOWN
WHO DIED APRIL 4TH 1896, AND OF THEIR BELOVED NEPHEW
LIEUT-COLONEL & BREVET COLONEL EUSTACE CHALONER KNOX
OF THE 18TH HUSSARS, WHO COMMANDED HIS REGIMENT
THROUGHOUT THE SOUTH AFRICAN WAR, 1899-1901,
INCLUDING THE DEFENSE OF LADYSMITH, AND DIED
IN LONDON, FEBRUARY 18th 1902, AGED 41

In 1911 Alice Knox was still living in some style at 'Silverton', with the help of a butler, cook, housemaid and two nurses. Hers was the only house in Monkstown with a butler, according to Miss Edith Dowse. On 1 October 1913, she died and was buried with her husband in Deansgrange (Dun Laoghaire Genealogical Society 1994).[9]

132

Parish activities

A Parochial Hall Committee was set up to deal with bookings for the Knox Memorial Hall. Its minutes of 18 October 1904 give some details: the charge for using the building ('if collections were taken up') was 1/- per hour without gas (lighting) and 2/6 per hour with gas; a whole day, including the evening with gas, cost £1; heating and the use of the gas stove cost 5/- extra; all church meetings without collections were free.

In October 1904 there were a couple of minor disputes with the Badminton Club, which apparently was not under the auspices of the parish. The Parochial Hall Committee was unhappy about 'the letting being made to ladies'. When the offending female names were replaced by the names of two gentlemen, the committee conceded. But it refused to allow smoking in the gentlemen's dressing room. However, this rule, too, was eventually relaxed: 'The representatives of the Clarence Badminton Club having conveyed to (the secretary) that they would regard a refusal of their request for permission to smoke cigarettes in the gentlemen's dressing room as exceedingly stringent and harsh, he had consulted the members of the Committee, and it was decided to concede the point, provided the Secretary of the Clarence Club gave a written undertaking that no smoking would take place outside the dressing room'. (Miss Edith Dowse, the rector's daughter, remembers 'a grand notice' saying 'NO SMOKING HERE' posted up in the Knox Hall by the 'dictatorial' sexton, Mr Lewis, an ex-policeman.)

All kinds of activities went on in the hall, such as meetings of the Monkstown Lawn Tennis Club, illustrated lantern lectures and the annual sale of the Church Missionary Society (CMS). The latter would last for two days and finish with a supper in the Minor Hall (the present Friendly Room), with a total of £300–£400 in sales being considered 'excellent'. According to the librarian at the Quaker Reading Room, after a fire at the Friends' Meeting House the Knox Memorial Hall was even used for a Quaker wedding around this time.

In 1907 the charges for using the hall rose sharply. Parish meetings cost at least 10/- for two hours or less; heating and lighting cost an extra 5/-. 'Extra-parochial' meetings were charged £1-2s-6d for two hours, inclusive. 'Entertainment' for the parish or for the 'Dublin Poor' cost £1 per day; the CMS sale paid £3 for two days; and concerts were £2. 'Private entertainments' held in the evenings cost £3, while during the afternoons, up to 7pm, the charge was £1.

The Knox Memorial Hall was an ideal venue for the 'Entertainment for the Dublin Poor', which was an annual feature by 1913. War shortages nearly cancelled the event in 1917 when, at a meeting of the Finance Committee, 'the Rector ... mentioned that he was afraid owing to the difficulty of obtaining sugar and potatoes that it would not be possible this year to have the usual Entertainment for the Dublin Poor'. However, a Mr Millar promised to supply potatoes so that the function could go ahead as planned (this could have been Fitzadam Millar, so active in parish affairs).

Now that there was a venue, gradually more clubs and societies were founded in Monkstown (*see also Chapter 19*). The parish formed its own Badminton Club in 1920, which was first known as the 'P & P' because it consisted of 'Past and Present' members of a Bible class; then it became known as the Albany Club until 1957, when it became the Monkstown Parish Badminton Club (Albany). The Table Tennis Club was founded in 1934. In 1944 the Claremont Institution (for Deaf and Dumb Children), which had moved to Carrickbrennan Road (the present 'Carrick Manor') from Glasnevin in 1943, ran a 'gymnasium class' in the Minor Hall on Wednesday evenings, from 7pm to 8pm.

During the 1950s and '60s, garden fêtes to raise money for the Knox Memorial Hall were held in the grounds of the Claremont Institution. In 1950, for example, the Annual Report of the Select Vestry recorded that 'the outstanding event ... in the Parish was the Knox Hall Fête held in August ... (which), were it not for the somewhat uncooperative assistance of the Clerk of the Weather, might have surpassed even our wildest aspirations'. Costs of £300 had to be met in 1952 when dry rot and 'boring beetles' were treated in the roof of the hall.

In the 1960s the hall was used for livelier functions — 'record hops', Guild of Youth dances, the Brook House School Old Boys' Dance (April 1964), the Dramatic Society, the YWCA Turkey Drive and a series of 'You're Welcome' parish get-togethers (consisting of parish suppers, sales, whist drives, brains' trusts and a film on 'The Holy Land'). The Missions to Seamen held coffee mornings, Monkstown Hospital held sales of work (known as the 'Pound Day'), jumble sales were organised and The Hall School had its prize distributions. In May 1966 the 'Over 25' Indoor Bowling Club was started. A fashion show was held in aid of Mrs Smyly's Homes and the Brook House Carol Service took place (December 1967). In April 1968 the Dublin Battalion of the Boys' Brigade were organising a table tennis match against the Glasgow Boys' Brigade and wrote to the Parochial Hall Committee: 'As we wish that the match should be played in the best possible venue, we would therefore like to ask permission to stage the match in the Knox Hall'. Flattery worked — permission was granted. At the Brook House prize-giving of 1968, contemporary fashion reared its head: 'I put a note on the invitations asking the ladies not to use stiletto heels, and it seems to have been observed'.

In 1967 the main hall and Minor Hall (which was to become the Friendly Room the following year) were redecorated and a new floor laid ('Iroko hardwood strip flooring secretly nailed on existing joists') for £1,500.

The Friendly Room

The Friendly Room of the Knox Memorial Hall was officially opened by Norman Ingram-Smith on 14 January 1968. The concept for such a meeting room had come from the incumbent, the Rev. Billy Wynne, and turned out to be of historic importance, for from it developed the beginnings of the Samaritan Movement in the south of Ireland (*see Chapter 11*).

Mr Wynne had written an open letter to his parishioners, outlining his ideas and asking for prayer and support. His original idea was that the parishioners would meet together in the Friendly Room on occasions other than church services, as part of a 'Daily Church Movement'. The room was manned for two hours every morning, including Sundays (10.30 to 12.30), and again on weekday evenings (8pm to 10.30pm), after the 7.30pm service.[10] It

The Friendly Room in the Knox Memorial Hall was the brainchild of the Rev. Billy Wynne and was officially opened on 14 January 1968 by Norman Ingram-Smith of St Martin's-in-the-Fields, London. Present at the opening were (from left to right, back row) Arthur Lawrence, Brian Taylor, Tom Aplin, J. Reeves, David Mitchell, Bill McClatchie and George Dyke; (front row) Billy Wynne, Dorrie Martin, Norman Ingram-Smith, Dolly Blakeley and Elsie Jones.

also opened on Wednesday and Friday afternoons, from 3pm to 5pm. Volunteers supplied tea or coffee and welcomed anyone who dropped in. The idea was that people should feel welcome to come in for a cup of tea, a chat or advice, whether spiritual or practical. A private room for quiet interviews was equipped with a telephone and was set up on the stage, then at the end of the Friendly Room.

At the Easter Vestry of 1968, Mr Wynne reminded parishioners that, although 'the Friendly Room ... was helping many people already, (it) would not achieve its full objectives until it was being run by all, for all'. He stressed the fact that 'the greatest need in the world today (is) to improve human relationships and give spiritual guidance'. A year later, on 9 April 1969, he reported that there had been 12,000 attendances in the first year and then, in March 1970, came the announcement of 'the long-awaited launching of the Samaritan Organisation' in Dublin (Samaritans 1995).

In the 1970s activities in the Knox Memorial Hall included an ecumenical crèche, sales of work for Mrs Smyly's Homes and Monkstown Hospital, Guild of Youth dances, a fashion show, the Indoor Bowling Club Bring & Buy, antique auctions and the Table Tennis Club's jumble sale. During the '80s the hall was used for table tennis, badminton and bowling, the Brownies, the Missionary Union Sale, the Parish Harvest Supper, sales for Mrs Smyly's Homes, the parish Dramatic Society, an art auction and St John's Musical Society.

Another innovation took place in the hall in 1984 with the establishment of the Diocesan Employment Bureau. This was founded by Mr Frank Luce during a period of great unemployment. As reported in the *Monkstown Parish Newsletter* of April 2003, 'Mr Frank Luce ... at the Diocesan Synod challenged the diocese to show concern for those

135

without work … He approached (the Rev. Kevin Dalton) with a view to obtaining an office (in Monkstown) … For the next 19 years, the office in the Knox Hall was manned voluntarily by Mr Ronnie Osbourne and during those years … managed to place nearly 500 people in permanent jobs and another 400–500 people in part-time employment … The same group of committed men and women (were involved in the setting up of) SPADE,[11] which involved the conversion of the redundant St Paul's Church in North King Street to provide enterprise centres for people starting small businesses. This daughter project of the Diocesan Employment Bureau continues in business and provides 44 enterprise units for budding entrepreneurs' (Dalton 2003b). As the country's economic situation improved, the role of the Monkstown office became redundant and it closed down in 2003. The room has now been adapted to serve as the Parish Office (which used to be run from the Rectory).

Today, the Knox Memorial Hall still proves indispensable. Typical activities in 2001 included bridge, ballet classes, indoor bowling, table tennis, the Monkstown Missionary Sale, the Irish Guide Dogs' Sale, Bring & Buy Coffee Mornings in aid of the Dun Laoghaire Lifeboats, an Edwardian evening, art exhibitions, the Claremont Institution Exhibition and a Christmas party for the homeless. The hall has also been used as a polling station for general elections and referenda for many years. In the past few years, the College of Dance has run a two-year full-time foundation course for young adults in the hall, teaching ballet, jazz, tap and dance history.

Mrs Dorrie Martin looked after the Friendly Room from its opening in 1968 until her death in 2001. Billy Wynne knew the importance of choosing the right person for this responsibility and, after praying about it long and hard, he set off to visit his parishioners. A friend had asked Dorrie Martin to look after her house while she was away, so Billy was surprised to find someone else (Dorrie) in the house. When she answered the door to him, he said, 'The very person! Will you look after the Friendly Room for me?' To this unusual request Dorrie replied 'Of course I will!' and continued to look after the room for the next 35 years.[12] Today, a watercolour of Monkstown Church, by Esme McDowell, hangs in the Friendly Room, dedicated to the memory of Dorrie Martin in October 2001.

CHAPTER 11

Incumbents and curates

As the French say, there are three sexes—men, women and clergymen.
The Rev. Sydney Smith

Monkstown has been blessed with a series of outstanding clergy, all of whom have enriched the parish during their ministry. A complete list of the district and perpetual curates and incumbents from 1615 to the present day is included in Appendix 3, as well as the curates from 1699 to 2001. In compiling these, I am indebted to W.J.R. Wallace for his monumental *Clergy of Dublin and Glendalough* (2001), from which I have unashamedly pirated biographies of some of the Monkstown clergy.

But first a few definitions may be needed (Acheson 1997).

- A 'perpetual curate' was a post that came into being after the Reformation. Whereas the monks had been temporary curates, their successors' posts were described as 'perpetual' because their appointments were permanent; their licences could only be revoked by the bishop, and not by his lay rector (or patron of a parish), and the position could be endowed.
- An 'incumbent' was the holder of an ecclesiastical benefice or parish, a term mainly used after Disestablishment.
- A 'curate' was originally nominated by the incumbent of a parish, who paid his stipend. He was licensed for duty by the bishop and his employment terminated if the incumbent changed. He often bore the main brunt of the work for pluralist or absentee incumbents. Today, curates are only found in large parishes as assistants to busy incumbents.
- A 'prebendary' was a canon of a cathedral or collegiate church who held a prebend, the revenues of which estate served as his stipend. Today, it is an honorary title.
- A 'rector', in the modern sense of the word, is the incumbent, vicar or minister of a parish. In the original sense it meant the 'patron' of the parish, often a powerful, land-owning layman, of any denomination, who owned the advowson or right to appoint the perpetual curate.

A short biography of each of the incumbents over the past 150 years is given below. Earlier incumbents are referred to throughout the text, while a separate biography of Archdeacon Charles Lindsay is provided in Chapter 22.

William Fitzgerald, perpetual curate of Monkstown (1855–7)

William Fitzgerald (1814–83) was made a deacon at the age of 24. He decided to delay his ordination as a priest for some nine years since he was having difficulties with some of the basic foundations of his faith. He spent these years 'thoroughly (sifting) the grounds of belief' (Webster 1920) and was eventually ordained in 1847, after serving as a curate in Clontarf. He was appointed prebendary of Donoughmore, St Patrick's Cathedral (1848–51) and vicar of St Ann's, Dublin (1851–5). An academic, he held the chair of moral philosophy in Trinity College, Dublin, from 1847 to 1852 and wrote a series of papers called *Cautions for the times* between 1851 and 1853. (These were intended as a rebuttal to the *Tracts for the times* of the Tractarians, or Oxford Movement.) He was appointed Berrisford professor of ecclesiastical history (1852–7) in Trinity College and was joint editor of the *Irish Church Journal* in 1857. 'An active and original thinker' (*Irish Ecclesiastical Gazette*, 20 February 1886), he was the author of a great many scholarly works, mainly on theological subjects. In a letter to a friend, Archbishop Whately recommended one of his books, adding that Fitzgerald's preface 'deserved letters of gold'.

Fitzgerald had an intransigent streak. He said of himself, 'For my part, I would tear the lawn from my shoulders and sink my seal "deeper than ever plummet sounded", before I would consent to hold rank or wealth on the disgraceful tenure of always "swimming with the stream", and never contradicting "public opinion" ' (Webster 1920). This approach made him unpopular.

During his two years at Monkstown (1855–7), when he was also the archdeacon of Kildare and prebendary of Tymothan (St Patrick's Cathedral), his refusal to yield to popular feelings on the burial of 'dissenters', or Presbyterians, led to a discussion in parliament and the lord lieutenant had to intervene to avoid trouble (Hansard 1856). He continued to make ripples, even when elected bishop of Cork, Cloyne and Ross (1857–62) and then bishop of Killaloe (1862–83). While in Cork, he made himself unpopular by speaking out against, among other things, the common custom of baptising children privately and large public prayer meetings, which senior clergy of the Church of Ireland had attended. Webster (1920) wrote: 'It cannot be said that Dr. Fitzgerald was a popular bishop, and he had not popular gifts'; he had to 'judge and to guide … unless he was satisfied to be a nonentity … This he did with impartiality and fearlessness'.

In 1840 Fitzgerald married Anne Stoney and they had six children: Anne (b. 1847), Maurice (b. 1850), George (b. 1851), William (b. 1852), Edith (b. 1856) and Beatrice (b. 1859). Sadly, Fitzgerald was widowed in 1859, his wife dying of 'a rapid consumption' after the birth of their last child.

His second son, George Francis Fitzgerald (1851–1901), lived at Monkstown glebe house in Kill-of-the-Grange for two years as a child, between the ages of four and six. He entered Trinity College, Dublin, at the age of sixteen and, apart from visits home to Killaloe, where his father was now bishop, he remained at Trinity for the rest of his life. He has been described as 'the most distinguished Irish scientist of his age' (Coey 2000). In 1881 he was appointed Erasmus Smith's professor of natural and experimental philosophy. In 1895 he made the first attempts at flight (in Britain and Ireland) in College Park, reaching a height of a couple of metres (about 6 feet), which earned him the nickname of 'Flightless Fitzgerald' (Mollan *et al.* 2002). He was the first to suggest a method of producing radio frequency waves, widely used today for radio and television, navigational aids, mobile phones, satellite communication and radio astronomy. But he is chiefly remembered for the Fitzgerald–Lorentz Contraction (1889), a crucial element in Einstein's 1905 Theory of Relativity. His paper in the *American Journal of Science* went unnoticed at the time, but was rediscovered in 1967. In 1901 George Fitzgerald died of peritonitis, aged 49, and is buried in Mount Jerome.[1]

In 1917, Second Lieutenant William Wilks Fitzgerald, grandson of Bishop Fitzgerald, was killed in action in France, aged 22 (University of Dublin War List 1922). A brass plaque was erected to his memory behind the font in Monkstown Church.

Ronald MacDonnell, last perpetual curate of Monkstown (1857–78)

Ronald MacDonnell (1825–89) was the sixth son of Dr Richard MacDonnell, provost of Trinity College, Dublin, and his wife Jane, the daughter of Dr Richard Graves, dean of Ardagh. (It had been Richard Graves, just ordained two years and a junior fellow of Trinity, who had given the sermon at the consecration of the new Georgian church in 1789; *see Chapter 4.*)

MacDonnell was licensed to Monkstown on 8 April 1857; on 26 August he and Jane Rotheram were married in Monkstown Church (MacDonnell 1889). They had four children: Barbara (b. 19 August 1858), Ronald (b. 1862, later curate at St John's, Mounttown, 1886–8), Edward (b. 19 October 1866,[2] d. 29 September 1867) and Richard Graves. In August 1874 Dr MacDonnell became ill and was advised by his doctor 'to abstain from public work or preaching' for a year (Vestry minutes, 24 August 1874). (His illness was probably partly caused by the ongoing row with Kill Parish over the glebe house; *see below.*) He recommended that the Rev. Alured Alcock be appointed as his locum for the year and the Vestry agreed, 'provided that (he could) be heard at the extreme parts of the church'. Parishioners subscribed £300 so that Dr MacDonnell could take leave of absence. Then, in 1878, in a letter to Mr R.H.M. Orpen, rector's churchwarden, Dr MacDonnell had to admit that 'nothing but the decided consciousness that (he) was becoming more and more unequal to the responsibilities of (his) position would have induced him to sever the bond that, for 22½ years, connected (him) with the people of Monkstown' (Simms 1983). He resigned that year and went to the less arduous parish of Tullow, where he served for a further six years. When his wife, Jane, died in 1885, Dr MacDonnell retired. He died on 22 December 1889 at 5 Vesey Place, Monkstown.

Two of Dr MacDonnell's brothers died as a result of the Indian War. On his appointment, Monkstown's parishioners would have known of the death of their new rector's young brother, Charles, in 1853 and that another brother, Frederick, was still in India (only to be killed in 1858). And so Monkstown raised more for this cause in October 1857 than for any of the 'home-grown' charities, such as Monkstown Hospital or the Parochial Schools (which usually raised the most). The Vestry minutes record, 'Service of Humiliation for Indian Insurrection: Collection for Sufferers, £73-6-0'.

Joseph Ferguson Peacocke, first incumbent of Monkstown (1878–94)

Joseph Peacocke, curate (1863–73) and incumbent (1878–94) of Monkstown. Since Dr Peacocke is wearing a rochet, the wide-sleeved surplice worn by bishops, and from his apparent age of about 70, this photograph was probably taken after he became archbishop of Dublin (1897–1915).

Joseph Peacocke (1835–1916) was born in Abbeyleix. After a distinguished undergraduate career in Trinity College, he was ordained for the curacy of St Mary's, Kilkenny (1858–61). He was secretary to the Hibernian Church Missionary Society (1861–3) and then came to Monkstown as curate (1863–73). He left Monkstown to become incumbent of St George's, Dublin (1873–8). On the resignation of Dr Ronald MacDonnell, Monkstown parishioners asked Peacocke to return as their rector. He did and stayed for sixteen years. He was extremely popular: he was good at pastoral work, a born teacher, an excellent and clear preacher, a conscientious visitor and a good organiser. He was appointed prebendary of Dunlavin, St Patrick's Cathedral (1875–94); professor of pastoral theology at TCD in 1894; select preacher at TCD in 1877–8, 1883–4 and 1888; select preacher of Cambridge Union in 1899; and chaplain to the

lord lieutenant (1886–94). He left Monkstown in 1894, having been elected bishop of Meath (1894–7) and then archbishop of Dublin, primate of Ireland and bishop of Glendalough and Kildare (1897–1915).

While curate of Monkstown, Peacocke married Caroline Irvine in 1865. They had five children: Joseph (b. 1866), George (b. 1868), Gerald (b. 1869), Percival (b. 1871) and Sarah (b. 1872). Joseph became bishop of Derry and Raphoe, and Gerald was appointed archdeacon of Kildare.

The refurbishment of McCurdy's chancel by Drew and Mitchell took place during Peacocke's time at Monkstown (*see Chapter 7*). He was a plain-speaking man. When asked to dedicate a reredos but to call it a 'panelling' because Irish congregations were still suspicious of anything that might smack of 'popery', he replied, 'If it is a reredos, I will call it so'. After 1894 he often returned to Monkstown, sometimes to attend services, when he would sit in the west gallery (which became known as the 'Bishop's gallery'), and sometimes to conduct them, as when he returned in 1896 to take the burial service of Edward Chaloner Knox and again in 1904 to dedicate the Knox Memorial Hall. He retired in 1915 and died a year later, at the age of 82. A resolution passed at the Monkstown Select Vestry meeting on 1 June 1916 noted: 'He faithfully served his generation, and he has left an example as Pastor, Friend and Bishop which cannot but serve as an inspiration to us all, in whatever position God has placed us'.

Bishop Peacocke's memorial window in Kildare Cathedral calls him a *Pastor Fidelis humilis et sanctus corde* ('A faithful, humble and holy pastor'). His memorial in Christ Church is a rare Arts and Crafts monument, designed by the cathedral's architect, Richard Caulfeild Orpen — 'a beautiful memorial in stone, brass and enamel work, to be placed in the N aisle of the Cathedral', noted the *Church of Ireland Gazette* on 12 October 1917.

John Clarence Dowse, incumbent of Monkstown (1894–1929)

John Clarence Dowse (1856–1930) came from a strongly clerical family. He was the son of John Robert Dowse, dean of Ferns; the twin brother of William Dowse, dean of Connor (formerly curate of Monkstown, 1886–92); the brother of Charles, bishop of Killaloe; and the nephew of Richard, dean of Clonmacnoise. His second cousin, Charles Dowse, was the incumbent of St John's, Mounttown, from 1910 to 1945.

John Clarence Dowse, incumbent of Monkstown (1894–1929).

After curacies in Wexford (1879–86) and Zion, Rathgar (1887–9), he became rector of St Paul's in Glenageary (1889–94). Then, on 9 July 1894, Mr Dowse was instituted to Monkstown and served the parish for 35 years. During his incumbency he was appointed to three honorary positions in Christ Church Cathedral: prebendary of St John's (1913–14), prebendary of St Michan's (1914–16) and prebendary of St Michael's (1916–21). In 1921 he was made chancellor of Christ Church.

In 1889 he married Jane Boxwell and they had five children: John (b. 1891), Henry (b. 1893), Charles (b. 1895), Richard (b. 1897) and Edith (b. 1899). Three of his four sons fought in the Great War; two of them, Charles and Henry, were killed (*see Chapter 22*). His eldest son, Major-General John Cecil Alexander Dowse, was inspector of medical services, Middle East Forces. In 2003 his daughter Edith was in good health and still living in the area; she has provided the author with many interesting, usually humorous, recollections of life in the parish over the past 100 years. Chancellor Dowse retired from Monkstown on medical grounds in 1929 and died the following year, aged 73.

John Ernest Leonard Oulton, incumbent of Monkstown (1929–31)

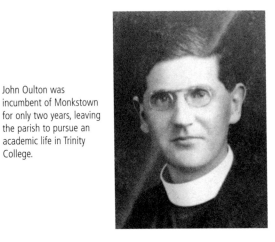

John Oulton was incumbent of Monkstown for only two years, leaving the parish to pursue an academic life in Trinity College.

John Oulton (*c.* 1887–1957) followed a brilliant career as a student at Trinity College (including the Vice-Chancellor's Latin Medal 1907 and the Bishop Berkeley Gold Medal 1909) with curacies at Harold's Cross and St Stephen's. While still a student, he was the organist at Christ Church, Dun Laoghaire, until May 1907. During his curacies he became assistant lecturer in divinity at TCD and lecturer on the Bible. He was appointed as incumbent to Chapelizod (1927–9) and then to Monkstown. In 1931 he left to devote himself entirely to an academic life, becoming Archbishop King's professor of divinity at TCD (1930–5) and subsequently Regius professor of divinity from 1935 until his death in 1957. He was made prebendary of Swords, St Patrick's Cathedral (1930–49), treasurer of St Patrick's Cathedral (1949–52) and chancellor of St Patrick's Cathedral (1952–7).

Dr George Otto Simms wrote after his death:

> 'The spare, begowned, unmistakably clerical figure, treading its way in a self-chosen meander across the cobbles of the Front Square, is acutely missed … In all his writings — the full list is quite considerable — he never published rashly, he never had to eat his words. Every point was verified, references were fully provided, evidence was never strained … (He) made his name as the distinguished translator of the intractable historian Eusebius … (His version) was accepted in the famous Loeb series of translations from Greek and Latin authors' (Simms 1957).

Harold Giles Forde, incumbent of Monkstown (1931–45)

Harold Forde, incumbent of Monkstown during 1931–45.

Harold Forde (*c.* 1890–1945) was the son of a Methodist minister, the Rev. Thomas Forde of Manorhamilton. After graduating from Trinity College, Forde became curate of Rathmines, followed by an incumbency of Clondalkin Union and St George's. In 1931 he was appointed incumbent to Monkstown. He married Adrienne Jackson in 1921 and they had two children: Harold (b. 1922) and Adrienne (b. 1926).

He was president of the Dublin Battalion of the Boys' Brigade and chairman of the Dublin Diocesan Committee for Temperance and Social Welfare. He had a keen interest in missionary work and started the Guild of Youth in Monkstown (Annual Report of Monkstown Vestry 1945). He died on 22 June 1945, while still incumbent of Monkstown.

Arthur Hamilton Butler, incumbent of Monkstown (1945–58)

Arthur Butler (1912–91) was appointed curate to Monkstown from 1935 to 1937 and then served two curacies in London. When war broke out in 1939, he enlisted as chaplain to the 2nd Battalion of the Duke of Cornwall's Light Infantry. He served with the battalion in France and was evacuated from Dunkirk. He then became senior chaplain to the 1st British Division serving in North Africa, Italy and Palestine. After the war, he was awarded an MBE. He returned to Monkstown in 1945 and was instituted as incumbent on 28 November.

Arthur Butler, incumbent of Monkstown during 1945–58.

Mr Butler proved a popular rector during his incumbency. Among the innovations he made was the setting up of the Men's Meetings in 1944. Held in the Knox Memorial Hall over the winter months, they were intended to be informal discussions on 'subjects of general interest'. They proved to be an outstanding success. Mr G.A. Mackay wrote a humorous poem called *Monkstown memories*, written on the departure of Mr Butler in 1958 and celebrating the achievements and highlights of his twelve years in Monkstown. The poem begins with the lines:

> *This tale is as simple as A.B.C.*
> *Arthur Butler's initials are A.B.,*
> *If simple conundrums — you can do 'em,*
> *You'll know the 'See' refers to Tuam.*

In 1938 Arthur Butler married Elizabeth Pringle and they had one child — David (b. 1940). In 1958 he was elected bishop of Tuam, Killala and Achonry (1958–69) and then bishop of Connor (1969–81). Elizabeth had died in 1976 and Butler married again in 1979, his new wife being Dr Elizabeth Mayne. He retired in 1981 and died ten years later.

At his funeral, Archbishop Eames said that Bishop Butler was a man who 'instilled confidence and respect, not just because of what he said but because of what he was'. He told the story of how, during World War II, Field Marshal Sir Gerald Templar would summon Butler, an old friend, to his divisional headquarters — a difficult and dangerous journey. They would spend several hours together, talking over a meal while Templar 'unburdened his heart'.

Richard William (Billy) Maurice Wynne, incumbent of Monkstown (1958–78)

Soon after his arrival in Monkstown, Billy Wynne (1919–2000) was phoned by a lady parishioner who said, 'You know, we worshipped our last rector, Arthur Butler'. In characteristic style, Billy Wynne retorted, 'Well, from now on, I hope you'll worship Almighty God'.[3] His stated philosophy was summed up in the 1925 operetta *No, No,*

Billy Wynne, incumbent of Monkstown during 1958–78 and founder of the Samaritans in the south of Ireland.

Nanette — 'I want to be happy, But I won't be happy, 'Till I make you happy, too!'[4]

Billy Wynne graduated from Trinity College in 1944 and was ordained the following year. He served curacies at Clontarf and Rathmines, and was then appointed incumbent of Delgany (1952–8), followed by Monkstown. He became the Samaritan contact in the south of Ireland in 1959, established the 'Friendly Room' in the Knox Memorial Hall in 1968 and opened the Dublin Samaritan branch on 2 March 1970 (*see below*). He started the popular annual event of the 'Messiah for All' in Monkstown (and was thereafter dubbed 'the Rector who made a Mess of the Messiah' by a fellow-clergyman[5]). The first performance was introduced by Gay Byrne, who waived his usual fee, and the proceeds went to the Samaritans. Mr Wynne also initiated 'May in Monkstown', a fortnight of music with well-known artists performing, such as Bernadette Greevy. Another of his projects was the foundation of the 'Friends of Monkstown', inaugurated in 1974 with Sir John Betjeman as patron. (Monkstown Church was one of Betjeman's 'first favourites for its originality of detail and proportion'; *see p. xx.*) The purpose of the Friends was to raise funds for the upkeep, repair, improvement and maintenance of the parish buildings. Unfortunately, the group was disbanded in about 1978, the year Mr Wynne left Monkstown.

In 1949 Billy Wynne married Cecil Collins and they had three sons: John (b. 1950), Peter (b. 1955) and Stephen (b. 1958). He was appointed prebendary of Dunlavin, St Patrick's Cathedral (1976–87). After leaving Monkstown in 1978 he became the incumbent of St Ann's Group until his retirement in 1987. He was the chairman of the Missions to Seamen (1985–96). He received a 'People of the Year Award' in 1983, an honorary doctorate in law from TCD and the lord mayor's 'Millennium Award' in 1988. He died on 17 January 2000.

At his funeral, Canon Cecil Hyland, who had been his curate in Monkstown (1966–8), gave the address. He said that Billy often reminded his curates of the phrase in the Book of Common Prayer asking God to 'cheer, heal and sanctify the sick'; he would always point out that the word 'cheer' came first. Canon Hyland described the visual aids used by Billy in worship: 'Toy aeroplanes flew around Monkstown Church. Table tennis balls were thrown at the congregation. He always wanted to ride a bicycle up the aisle, but he couldn't find a message to fit this action.' However, he told Canon Hyland that he would come up with an idea and promised to let him know in advance. 'Some ten years later, the 'phone rang at 11.30 one Saturday night. "I'm doing it in the morning", said the voice and the 'phone went dead.' And indeed he did: his text was Romans 8:28 — 'All things work together for good to them that love God'.

Over the years 1992 to 1999, with Fr Francis MacNamara, OP, Canon Billy Wynne wrote the fortnightly *Irish Times* column 'Thinking Anew', selections of which were published in the book *Called to think anew* in 2000.

In June 1959 Chad Varah, founder of the Samaritans in London in 1954, wrote to Billy Wynne, asking him to act as the Southern Irish contact for the Samaritans. He had seen a letter Billy had written to someone who subsequently contacted the London Samaritans. As a result of Chad Varah's request, Billy became increasingly busy over the next ten years. He travelled all over the country to give talks on the Samaritans to different groups and appeared on the *Late Late Show*. It was an uphill battle; he was told that such an organisation was unnecessary in a small country like Ireland where people could contact their church or their doctor if they needed help. Others thought that it was wrong to talk openly about suicide or that the clergy should not become involved in this sort of social work.

But Billy Wynne was undeterred: he gradually became known as the main Samaritan contact south of the border and was snowed under with work. 'It was a hell of a time and I took a hell of a risk. I risked the peace of my own mind, the peace of my marriage, my finances, my health, you name it … but I am none the worse for it and it was all worth it in the end' (taken from the first chapter of an unfinished autobiography, written in 1980–1). One morning he had to set off at 5am for Tralee to meet 'a client' (one of his Samaritan contacts) and then drive home the same day for a meeting of the Mission to Lepers at which Geoffrey Fisher, the archbishop of Canterbury, was speaking. Sitting in his chair on the platform, Billy Wynne fell fast asleep from sheer exhaustion.

Throughout this hectic time, he found Archbishop George Simms 'a tremendous friend and advisor'. Meetings about the Samaritans were held in Monkstown, at which Chad Varah and other London Samaritans spoke. The Friendly Room in the Knox Memorial Hall opened in January 1968, 'offering coffee and friendliness … during the hours it was open … as a safety valve for a person who (was) lonely or in need of such a place or such a welcome'. Although the room was never used for Samaritan work as such, Billy Wynne had a telephone installed and a small room set aside for private conversations, in case he needed an emergency venue before the official branch was established. By 9 April 1969 there had been an astonishing 12,000 attendances. However, he realised that it was important that 'we (should) say goodbye to the heavy emphasis of denominational competition. It was far better to put it in a neutral spot, like Kildare Street, than to link it with a parish hall in this wretched country where we emphasise denominations to such a bitter extent'.

A meeting was held in the Hibernian Hotel on 18 July 1969, chaired by Vincent Grogan. About 100 people of all denominations attended. Billy Wynne recalled his feelings on the occasion: 'I knew when that happened that we had succeeded after all the years and I could hardly speak as I knew that my part was really over'. A steering committee was appointed that night and the following year, on 2 March 1970, the Dublin Samaritan Branch opened, with 600 people turning up to the inaugural meeting at the Royal Dublin Society. When the Samaritans opened in temporary rent-free premises at 39 Kildare Street (due for demolition), there was only a limited service from 2.30pm to 11pm. By 1 November that year, the goal was reached of a fully manned, 24-hour service, seven days a week. In 1970 there were 200 volunteers and 1,048 contacts by phone, visit or letter; expenses were £2,114. By 1994, 340 volunteers coped with 83,060 contacts and expenses had risen to £104,000 (Samaritans 1995).

Kevin Dalton, incumbent of Monkstown (1979 to present)

Kevin Dalton, present incumbent of Monkstown since 1979.

Kevin Dalton likes to tackle huge projects — as illustrated by his own story in the recent book *That could never be*, describing his difficult childhood and early adolescence (Dalton 2003a). Born in 1932 and brought up in orphanages, he worked in a variety of different jobs, eventually becoming a qualified miller. Most young men in his situation would have accepted that it was virtually impossible to enter the ordained ministry of the Church of Ireland in the 1960s without secondary school education or financial means. But to Kevin Dalton obstacles are challenges rather than obstructions. He sat Latin nine times in all, three times a year for three years, until finally passing the subject and matriculating into Trinity College, Dublin. While there, he was elected auditor of the 'Theo' (Theological Society); at the inaugural meeting he read a paper entitled 'The Oracles are dumb', about how the church could not communicate the Gospel meaningfully to the modern world.

He was ordained as a deacon in 1966. He won a scholarship to the Church Divinity School of the Pacific, Berkeley, California, where he got his bachelor of divinity in 1967. He returned to Ireland and was ordained as a priest, serving for six years as curate in Stillorgan. He then became the incumbent of Drumcondra and North Strand (1972–9), before being appointed as the 27th incumbent of Monkstown in 1979, in which parish he serves to the present day. He married Jennifer Dickie in 1967 and they have two daughters — Tara and Sally-Ann. He was appointed rural dean of Monkstown in 1992.

During his incumbency in Monkstown, he organised the celebration of three important milestones in the history of the church — 1981, 1989 and 1998. The first event marked 150 years since the opening of Semple's Monkstown Church on Christmas Day 1831; the service was broadcast on that day in 1981. The 1989 celebrations marked the bicentenary of the Georgian church, consecrated in 1789; again, a television broadcast was made of the bicentenary service. Fund-raising events took place throughout the year, including a garden fête, 'All Priests' show, a team quiz, an antique and art auction, and a splendid Bicentenary Ball; the Village Day in September was the highlight of the year, with the area around the church thronged with revellers, many in period costume. All money was divided between Our Lady's Hospice in Harold's Cross and restoration work on the church. The third major event was 'Monkstown 1200', celebrated on 26 September 1998 as a Village Day to commemorate the coming of the monks to Monkstown (*see Chapter 1*).

Mr Dalton has also supported and organised other important ventures in the parish to help those marginalised by society, including the Diocesan Employment Bureau, which helped find jobs for almost 1,000 people (*see pp 135–6*), and the Interchurch Care Group, which provided midday meals to the homeless in the adapted vaults of Monkstown Church, starting in December 1999; in the first fifteen months 6,000 meals were served. In 2004 he will launch a major fund-raising programme for the refurbishment of the church, with a target of *c.* €2 million.

Curates

'Of late years, an abundant shower of curates has fallen upon the north of England: they lie very thick on the hills; every parish has one or more of them; they are young enough to be very active, and ought to be doing a great deal of good' — the opening lines of Charlotte Brontë's novel *Shirley* sum up the situation well in the England of the mid-1800s — and probably Ireland, too.

Years earlier, in 1709, William King, archbishop of Dublin, had written to an incumbent searching for a curate: 'I do hope … that you will not offer him less than 40 lb per ann. which is the least any clergyman ought to have' (Kennedy 1968). Over 100 years later, according to the Rev. James Hurdis, English curates were only getting 'forty pounds, carpenter's wages'.

There were often two curates at the same time. They did comparatively well in Monkstown. For example, in 1800 James Dunn received £50; by 1818 Charles Galwey was getting £75, William Mulloy £80 in 1854 and Thomas Hobson £100 in 1860.[6] A few years later the two curates were getting, on average, the fifth highest salary in the diocese (in 1872 Joseph Peacocke received £203 and Abraham Palmer £150). Sometimes the stipend fluctuated wildly: in 1863 Joseph Peacocke's was £120, whereas the following year Henry Johnson's had dropped to £80.

Curates often began to officiate in the parish months before they were officially licensed. For example, Edward Beatty (1775–85) served for five years before being licensed on 28 March 1780. Because the patron of Monkstown was also the bishop of Kildare, dual or consecutive appointments in the diocese of Kildare were common.

The parish generally looked after its curates well, usually presenting them with generous presents on their departure or financing their holidays. When the Rev. Thomas Rooke, curate during 1850–9 (uncle of the organist, B. Warburton Rooke), left Monkstown, he was showered with gifts — the *Irish Ecclesiastical Gazette* of March and April 1859 reported a purse containing 300 guineas and a silver salver from the parishioners, a 'very handsome silver inkstand, with an appropriate address' from his 'adult class' (probably a Bible class), an address and 'a handsome Silver Tea and Coffee Service' from the Sunday School children and their 38 teachers, an 'address and Tea kettle to match the above service' from the Saturday Class, an address from 'the pupils of the Kingstown Night School' and 'an address and very beautiful vase' from the teachers and children of the Infants' School. In 1856 the parish had already given Rooke 'a purse containing £50, for the purpose of defraying his expenses on a tour of recreation', reported the ever-vigilant *Irish Ecclesiastical Gazette* in October of that year.

'The parish is full of money,' noted the same newspaper on 20 March 1880. 'Witness the three testimonials [presentations] simultaneously given lately to the retiring clergy making in the aggregate a sum over £500 [Dr MacDonnell and his two curates, the Revs Abraham Palmer and James Kennedy, all left the parish in 1878]; and, two years before, a sum of £300 was subscribed for Dr Macdonnell [*sic*] to enable him to take leave of absence for the benefit of his health. This is but a small portion of what the parishioners give to all good causes that come before them' (*see also* Chapter 17).

Nathaniel Mahaffy — one curate's tragedy

Figures alone cannot bring home the appalling mortality rate among young children before the days of better hygiene, antibiotics and effective medicine in the twentieth century. In most Irish families, two or three children, at least, 'died young'. This was not confined to the poor. In the pages of one Monkstown register of baptisms, marriages and burials (1827-35), the fate of one family in the parish is tragically told.

The family in question was that of Monkstown's young curate, Nathaniel Brindley Mahaffy (1799–1855). He was the grandson of Brindley Hone and cousin of Nathaniel Hone, the artist (Stanford and McDowell 1971). After graduating from Trinity College, Dublin, he became curate of Monkstown in 1824. On 13 September 1827 he married Elizabeth Pentland, only child of Dr John Pentland, former master of the Rotunda Hospital, in Monkstown Church. The couple stayed at home while Nathaniel continued with his duties, until a late 'honeymoon' in Italy two years later, where their first child was born.

'Venice, June 16, 1829, I certify that according to the due and proscribed order of the Church, on Sunday the Seventh day of June 1829, and at Florence, I baptised Robert Ninian ... [signed] Nathaniel Brindley Mahaffy' — so reads Mahaffy's hand-written note pasted into the Monkstown Baptismal Register. The child was called after his paternal grandfather, the Rev. Robert Mahaffy, and great-grandfather, Ninian Mahaffy. Nathaniel and Elizabeth returned home, to their house in Montpelier Parade, where, over the following five years, three more children were born: John Pentland (baptised 3 October 1830), Annette (baptised 15 May 1832) and Philip Henry (baptised 5 May 1834).

Then came the dreadful week in November 1834 when scarlet fever entered the Mahaffy home:

> November 18: burial of Robert Mahaffy, aged 5;
> November 22: burial of John Mahaffy, aged 4;
> November 23: burial of Annette Mahaffy, aged 2.

Although six-month-old Philip and his nurse also contracted the disease, they were pulled through 'with great difficulty' (Stanford and McDowell 1971).

It was the custom then to call children after earlier siblings who had died. Nathaniel and Elizabeth had another baby the following year and they called her Annette ('Annette Mahaffy baptised October 2, 1835'). However, it seems that little Annette died too, as she is not mentioned in Mahaffy's biography.

During this time, although not officially licensed for Monkstown, Mahaffy took services and worked with the poor (Poor Fund Book, 29 April 1836). After a couple of years as chaplain at Christ Church, Carysfort (1835–7), the Mahaffys decided to turn their backs on the scene of their appalling tragedy and with Philip, their only surviving child, moved to the Continent, to settle near Vevay on the lake of Geneva. There two more sons were born (Robert in 1837 and John Pentland in 1839). The family moved on to Lucerne, where Nathaniel acted as British chaplain from 1840 to 1843, and then to another chaplaincy at Bad Kissingen in Germany. In 1848 revolution broke out in Germany and the Mahaffys returned to Ireland to their estate in Donegal. It would appear that Nathaniel Mahaffy never worked again in his capacity as a clergyman. Although the estate was small, it brought in enough to support the family. Mahaffy taught his sons at home rather than sending them away to school.

When Nathaniel Mahaffy died in October 1855, aged 57, his funeral service was held at Monkstown. It was the same year in which his son, John Pentland (1839–1919), entered Trinity College, to carve out a brilliant academic career. He was ordained in 1864 and stayed on at Trinity for another 55 years, serving as tutor, professor, vice-provost and eventually provost (1914–19) at the age of 75. He was knighted in 1918, the year before he died. A man of many talents, his main passion was for Greek literature and history, but he also spoke French and German fluently and was a learned and witty conversationalist, not least in his sermons. Indeed, he wrote *The principles of the art of conversation* in 1887 and was probably a great influence on Oscar Wilde, a young student at Trinity during the years 1871–4. A typical epigram of Mahaffy's was 'Ireland is a place where the inevitable never happens, and the unexpected always occurs'.

Monkstown glebe house

In 1691, when Allan Maddison arrived in Monkstown as the new perpetual curate (1691–1741), nobody in the parish could tell him where its glebe, or church land, was situated. Over 30 years later he was still in the dark. He knew, as he stated in the Visitation of May 1723, that 'there (were) two Acres of Glebe land in ye parish of ye Kill, but in wh(ich) part of ye lands of ye Kill of ye Grange they lie I could never find out'.[7]

If Maddison had asked the person who owned that land — William Moreton, the patron or 'rector' of Monkstown, the dean of Christ Church (1677–1705) and owner of all the 160 acres of 'Kill of the Grange of Clonkeene, commonly called the Dean's Grange' — he might have been told where his glebe lay ('reserving to the curate there the house, place, garden, etc., formerly reputed as 2 acres'). Dean Moreton had leased the land himself in 1686 and should have been able to tell Maddison the details (McEnery and Refaussé 2001).

Although he may have been hesitant in asking his 'rector' a perfectly reasonable question, Maddison had no such compunction with his archbishop, William King. Dismissing the glebe land at Kill as 'inconvenient by their situation', he made a rather daring suggestion to the archbishop during his Visitation in June 1723: 'There are Glebes wanting in ye parish of

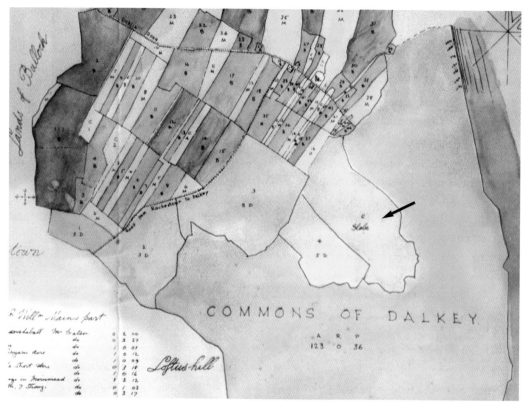

Map of Dalkey in 1765 by Thomas Reading, showing the 'Glebe of the Minister of Monkstown', with an area of 14 acres 1 rood 14 perches (the plot of land labelled 'Glebe', arrowed).

Monkstown & his Grace ye Lord Archbishop of Dublin has in right of ye Church fifty-five Acres of land in ye parish of Dalkey (which) would be convenient for Glebes for ye said parish of Monkstown'. Maddison must have preferred the sea view at Dalkey to the inland Kill-of-the-Grange. The archbishop responded positively to Maddison's forthrightness and on 8 November 1728 sold 'the Twelve Acres, part of the Furlongs in Dalkey' to him for the nominal fee of 'five shillings sterling'. It seems that Maddison was already living in Dalkey and the archbishop presented him with a bargain, allowing him to stay there at the 'rent of one pepper-corn only', to be paid every Easter.[8] This land (in fact measuring over fourteen acres) was labelled 'Glebe of the Minister of Monkstown' on Thomas Reading's 1765 map of Dalkey, but there is no mention of a glebe house on the land.

That innocuous two-acre plot of land in Kill, whose whereabouts was not even known by its rightful holder (Maddison), was to cause repercussions right down to the 1870s, when the parishes of Monkstown and Kill fought bitterly over its ownership (*see below*). After the Dissolution of the Monasteries in 1539 the parish of Kill came under the ownership of the dean of Christ Church and thereafter was known as the Dean's Grange (*see Chapter 3*). The lands at Kill were leased in 1542 to the curate or 'chaplain', John Callan, including a two-acre plot of land to the east of the church on which stood a house and a flax yard, and in 1561 to John Hore, who succeeded him. According to the local historian Francis Elrington Ball (1902), this plot lay in the farm of Clonkeen (or Kill); when the farm was leased in 1592, 'the "curate's" house, with its curtilage … was excepted, and besides a money rent it was agreed that there should be annual offerings of corn and hens, and the best beast on the death of the lessee'. Thus the curate of Kill lived for 100 years beside the church of Clonkeen, dedicated to St Fintain, originally the 'mother-church' in the area for the chapels of Carrickbrennan and Dalkey. At this point Carrickbrennan was subservient to Kill.

But this was to change. Although St Fintain's Church was still 'in good repair' in 1615 and had a congregation of 24 in 1630 (in spite of recent storms having blown off its roof),[9] it became ruinous during the Cromwellian period of 1649–58 and was never again used for services. When Carrickbrennan Church was rebuilt in 1668, it was the only church 'in repair' (meaning suitable for use) in the neighbourhood, and so Monkstown took over from Kill as the mother-church of the area. Thus was the Union of Monkstown set up, consisting of Monkstown, Kill (which included Stillorgan and Kilmacud), Killiney, Tullow and Dalkey. (It may be significant that the name of 'Kill' always followed immediately after 'Monkstown' in the list, indicating that Kill was second in order of precedence in the Union.[10]) Since Monkstown had no glebe land, the glebe land in Kill became the glebe land of the Union of Monkstown. As we shall see, this was to prove a contentious point more than 200 years later.

Even though the glebe house and land in Kill were available to Monkstown from 1668 onwards, it seems that they were never used by the perpetual curates Thomas Ward (1670–85) or William Dean (1685–91). When Maddison took over in 1691 the house was apparently derelict and the whereabouts of the glebe forgotten. Ward and Dean were both pluralists, who almost certainly (like most clergy at the time) were not resident in the parish. (Non-resident clergy led to all sorts of problems: the clergyman often neglected his Sunday services or paid some poor curate a pittance to take them for him. He might have to ride for miles to get to his church or alternatively rent lodgings in the parish. The parish invariably suffered.) But although Ward and Dean may have been absentees, Maddison seems to have been faithful to his flock and lived in the parish during the whole 50 years

Originally the mother-church of the area, St Fintain's in Kill-of-the-Grange, dating from the eleventh or twelfth century, has been in ruins since the 1650s.

of his incumbency (1691–1741). In the 1723 Visitation he stated categorically that he '(resided) in ye parish & ye Cure (was) served by himself in person'.

Robert Fowler became archbishop of Dublin in 1778 and almost immediately began to campaign for glebes to be bought and glebe houses built. Monkstown came to his attention when an Act of Council for the Perpetual Union of Monkstown was signed by the lord lieutenant on 9 December 1780.[6] In the act it was stated that 'there is no Glebe House in any of the said parishes [Monkstown, Kill, Dalkey, Killeeny otherwise Killeen, Bullock and Carrickbrennan], but there is a Glebe of fourteen Acres in the said parish of Monkstown'. (These fourteen acres refer to the glebe in Dalkey, which was in the parish of Monkstown, where Maddison was already living in 1728.)

Archbishop Fowler extracted a promise from the perpetual curate, John Forsayeth (1780–2), 'to build a Glebe House and make other improvements fit and convenient for the residence of himself and his Successors'. In fact Forsayeth only stayed in Monkstown for two years and certainly did not fulfil his pledge. His short stay may be explained by the archbishop's reminder in May 1781 that 'All Gentlemen who have been 3 years in poss/on of Benefices were ordered at the last Visitation to present Memorials for building Glebe houses within 3 months from thence'. Obviously the archbishop was determined to implement his order.

The Irish government felt the same way. In March 1782, in the Irish House of Commons, Sir Henry Cavendish warned non-resident clergy that they had better mend their ways. He said that all clergy would be 'scrutinised' during the coming year, from June 1782 to June 1783, to discover if they were resident or non-resident, and if they were taking 'Divine Service'. Cavendish optimistically believed that a return of the resident and non-resident clergy would 'produce residence where there is no residence; divine service will be performed where no divine service has been performed; the sick man will find the comforts of religion which are now sometimes sought for in vain; and the public mind will be satisfied that this House expects attention to his duty from every clergyman' (Kennedy 1968).

Archbishop Fowler carried out another of his Visitations that year. The clergy must have dreaded them. He came to Monkstown again, but Forsayeth had flown. The perpetual curate was now Dr William Jephson (1782–91); he was not resident in Monkstown (spending most of the time at his living in the diocese of Raphoe) and there was still no glebe house. According to the Visitation book of 1782,[11] Jephson gave two addresses at which he could be found: 'at Mr David's, Blackrock' (probably the parish clerk) or at 'Major Butler's, Molesworth Street'. Dr Jephson was reprimanded and instructed 'to shew cause why he does not reside immediately'.

Fowler reissued his orders, again directing that 'all Clergymen 3 years in possession of a Benefice who have a Glebe and no Glebe-house (must) … give in a Mem/l [memorial or particulars] for Building on or before Michaelmas next'. This time he added a threat — 'otherwise their livings to be sequestered' (in other words, their parishes to be confiscated). When he descended on Monkstown for his 1788 Visitation, however, he let Jephson off with another warning. Perhaps he was mollified to see the new church on its splendid new site (the present location) nearly completed (it would open the following year, 1789; *see*

Chapter 4), even if no glebe house had yet appeared. Jephson was again told 'to present a Memorial for Building a Glebe House'.

Jephson's failure to build a glebe house may be partially explained by an entry in the Visitation book of 1788–91, which records that a letter had been posted on 15 August 1789 on behalf of Archbishop Fowler 'to the Rev. Dr Jephson (in) Raphoe desiring the Dr.'s attendance at Monkstown on the 30th Inst. when his Grace of Dublin means to consecrate the Church of Monkstown'. A further note adds: 'Dr. Jephson order'd to attend … and to present a Memorial for Building a Glebe House & to Reside'. It sounds as if Fowler was losing patience. Not only had Dr Jephson repeatedly ignored his orders to build the glebe house but he actually had to be 'ordered' to attend the consecration of his own brand-new church in Monkstown.[11]

Jephson was a flagrant pluralist. In 1782 he had taken on four positions which were geographically poles apart: as perpetual curate of Monkstown in Dublin, rector of Raymochy (in Raphoe, Co. Donegal), vicar choral of Cashel, Co. Tipperary, and the prebendary of Kilbrittain and rector of Rathclaren, Co. Cork. Since he could only be in one place at a time, as far as Monkstown was concerned, he paid his curates (Edward Beatty and then John Burrowes; *see Appendix 3*) to look after his clerical duties for him. (In fact, on the auspicious occasion of the consecration of the new Monkstown Church in August 1789 it was Burrowes who took the service.) Jephson died in office two years later, still without building the glebe house.

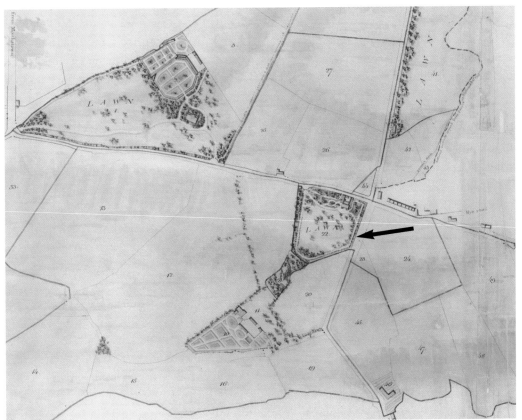

Monkstown's glebe house in Kill stood on a two-acre site diagonally opposite the Baker's Corner of today. The site of the glebe land is shown in this 'Survey of Kill of the Grange, Co. Dublin, the estate of the Dean of Christ Church, by John Longfield, 1814' (indicated by arrow).

Monkstown glebe house, built in 1797, used to be in Kill-of-the-Grange — at today's 'Fairholme', opposite Baker's Corner — up until the 1870s, when the property was claimed by Kill, made an independent parish in 1860. A 'land war' followed between the two parishes until *c.* 1876, when the property was sold.

Monkstown glebe house was not built until 1797, six years after the appointment of Jephson's successor, John William Dudley Ryves (1791–9). The Board of First Fruits gave a grant of about £138 towards it. The original construction was apparently substandard. When the well-heeled Charles Lindsay arrived as perpetual curate in 1815, he found the house 'in very bad order' and related that he had 'expended £2,400 British in rebuilding it, out of his private funds, without having any charge on his successor for the repayment of any portion thereof', to which he was entitled. Lindsay lived in the glebe house for 40 years until his death in 1855 and apparently looked after it well. When the rural dean visited the parish in 1840, he reported that the 'Glebe House and offices (were) in beautiful order'. The house still stands today, but no longer in its original two acres: called 'Fairholme', it is a large Georgian house, partly hidden by trees and behind a high wall, at the crossroads of Kill-of-the-Grange (diagonally opposite Baker's Corner). It is a protected structure since 2000.

In 1820 Archdeacon Lindsay affirmed that he had 'lodged (a map of the glebe lands) in the Registry of the Consistorial Court of Dublin, pursuant to order at the Archbishop's primary visitation of the diocese in the year 1820'. This map confirmed that there were over fourteen acres of glebe land in Dalkey and over two acres in Kill. At the time of Disestablishment the total annual value of the house and land at Kill was £105 and the 'purchase money of house, garden and curtilage and additional land' was £260 (Commissioners of Church Temporalities in Ireland 1875).

When the Rev. Ronald MacDonnell became incumbent of Monkstown (1857–78), he immediately complained about the state in which his predecessor, William Fitzgerald (1855–7) — who was now bishop of Cork, Cloyne and Ross — had left the glebe house. A commission was set up to assess the 'dilapidations' suffered by the house; a detailed 21-page inventory survives, describing the property and the repairs needed.[6] The rambling glebe house had six main bedrooms, a dressing-room, water closet (toilet) and storeroom, small parlour, drawing-room, hall, study, dining parlour, pantry, back porch and larder, attic room over the kitchen, west and east bedchambers over the kitchen, slop closet over the kitchen, scullery, kitchen and servants' room. Outside, there was a shed containing a storeroom, dairy, knife and shoe room, and privy (outside toilet); there was another privy in the garden, a stable, coach-house, harness room, coal-hole and ash-pit. Another building contained a car (carriage) house and tool house, with lofts over each. A gatelodge and greenhouse completed the list.

The Commissioners recommended that the Right Rev. William Fitzgerald should pay for all the necessary repairs, amounting to £189-3s-1d (equivalent to about €17,000 today). The archbishop of Dublin, Richard Whately, confirmed their decision. This settlement seems hardly fair considering that Fitzgerald had only occupied the glebe house for two years while his predecessor, Lindsay, had lived there for 40 years. It beggars belief that Fitzgerald could have caused such 'dilapidations' in such a short time. According to statutory law, a predecessor was 'chargeable only for the dilapidations which occurred during his own incumbency, by his own neglect and permission and sufferance, and from the want of the annual and necessary repairs' (Burn 1809).

Land war between Monkstown and Kill

In 1860 Kill was made a parish in its own right, independent of Monkstown. In 1872 the Diocesan Council wrote to Dr MacDonnell, incumbent of Monkstown, saying that the parish of Kill was claiming Monkstown glebe house since it was within their parish boundary. When MacDonnell read this letter to the Select Vestry on 4 December 1872 there must have been sparks flying, but the minutes are deliberately low-key, simply recording that 'the Rector was asked to reply … claim to be distinctly negatived'. MacDonnell's letter of 20 January 1873 was certainly not low-key (it was obviously not the first to the Diocesan Council). With words heavily underlined several times, MacDonnell claimed that he 'seldom had the pain of perusing a more recklessly inaccurate document' than that which he was returning, that he was 'not (stigmatising them) with the severity they deserve', that any competent 'ecclesiastical lawyer … would simply laugh at the preposterous' claims that the Council was making on behalf of Kill, and that 'but for the Irish Church Act, (the glebe house) would have remained for hundreds of years (in the hands of) the Incumbents of Monkstown'. (The Irish Church Act of 1869 took away the rent charge of Monkstown and therefore, apparently, also the right to the glebe house.) He finished by washing his hands of the whole affair and asking that any further communication from the Glebe's Committee should be addressed not to him but to the Select Vestry of Monkstown.

However, MacDonnell could not abdicate that easily. In March 1873 a delegation from Monkstown (consisting of MacDonnell, the churchwardens and members of the Vestry) met the secretary of the Representative Church Body in order to 'take immediate steps for the protection of the rights of this parish to said Glebe House' (Vestry minutes, 3 March 1873). A month later this group reported back to the Select Vestry that it had 'made a full statement of circumstances relative to (the) claim of this parish to said Glebe House and land' (Vestry minutes, 7 April 1873).

Shortly after this, in August 1784, Dr MacDonnell became quite ill and was advised to take a year off from parish work. The stress caused by the ongoing 'tug-of-war' over the glebe house must surely have contributed to his illness: he was out of action from 1 October 1874 for a full year. In the meantime, the Rev. Alured Alcock acted as locum and took over MacDonnell's parish duties, while the Select Vestry took on the mantle of responsibility for the glebe house. In November that year it appointed one of its most stalwart members, the solicitor John Galloway, to represent the parish's claim to the glebe house and gave him 'full power to prepare cases and engage counsel to advise and if necessary to argue the claim before the legal committee of the Representative Body'.

But in December 1874 the Select Vestry realised that it was not going to win, and the following summer it accepted the outcome of the court case in Kill's favour (Select Vestry minutes, 5 July 1875). At this point, determined to make the best of the situation, the Select Vestry recommended that when the glebe house and land were sold the 'highest market price' should be sought. Kill did not intend to use the glebe house or land for its rectory; the property was to be sold and the profits divided among the parishes in the Union of Monkstown. Then the Union would be formally dissolved. Thus, in 1875, 'Messrs. Battersby and Co. of Westmoreland Street and Mr. Downes of Monkstown … (were) directed to put the Glebe of Monkstown on their books'. In 1876 the house was valued at about £2,000 (possibly worth well over €1 million today). Dr MacDonnell and his family moved out, to a house he had bought at 5 Vesey Place in Monkstown.

Monkstown now had no rectory. The minutes of the Select Vestry of 9 November 1875 record that the Monkstown Glebe Committee was formed to 'consider the general question of providing a suitable glebe house for this parish and the means at the disposal of the vestry'. A Glebe Purchase Fund was set up. Tentative steps were taken towards finding a site on which to build a new rectory, but nothing happened. For the next 61 years the incumbent of Monkstown had to purchase or rent his own house.

Homes of the rectors

> *Let's all move one place on.*
> Lewis Carroll, *Alice in Wonderland*

The Rev. Joseph Peacocke (1878–94) moved in practically next door to his predecessor, the now-retired Dr MacDonnell, at 3 Vesey Place. He was given an annual allowance of £100 in lieu of a rectory. In 1885 he moved to 6 Belgrave Square, South, next door to one of his churchwardens, Fitzadam Millar. (The architect of this fine terrace of houses, built during 1845–8, was John Semple, Junior, who, with his father, had been joint architect of Monkstown Church; *see Chapter 6.*)

The Rev. John Clarence Dowse (1894–1929) succeeded Peacocke and lived at No. 2 'Uplands' on The Hill, Monkstown. In 1900 he moved to 'Seafield Lodge' on Seafield

Avenue. Then the Rev. John E.L. Oulton (1929–31) became rector and lived at 'Cliftonville', 60 Monkstown Road. He was succeeded by the Rev. Harold G. Forde (1931–45), who moved into 'Revagh' in 1932, at 17 Alma Road. A year later he moved to 'Seapoint Lodge', 31 Seapoint Avenue, where he stayed until 1937.

In the meantime, the Select Vestry had decided to purchase a rectory during 1932, in memory of Chancellor Dowse (who had died

Monkstown rectory, at 62 Monkstown Road, as it was in 1991. The house was acquired in 1945 and cost the parish 'the very high figure of £5,250'.

in 1930, having served the parish for 35 years) and to commemorate the centenary of Semple's church. A property was not secured, however, until 1937. No. 5 Brighton Terrace was a terraced house on the seafront which was eventually purchased for £1,467 (£700 from the Glebe Purchase Fund and a loan of £767 from the Representative Church Body). The incumbent, the Rev. Harold Forde, was the first occupant of the new rectory and lived there from 1938 until his death in 1945. Then, 'after careful consideration, the vestry decided to sell the Rectory, 5 Brighton Terrace … Considering the general disrepair of the premises, the price of £2,450 must be considered a good one', stated the Annual Report of 1945. The house next door, 4 Brighton Terrace, was rented for several months (at £150 per annum) until the new rectory was ready.

'The new Rectory, "Winton Lodge" [62 Monkstown Road], is very well situated and in very good general repair and decorative order and has central heating installed, but it has cost the parish the very high figure of £5,250', said the 1945 Annual Report. (Canon Oulton had lived just next door, at 'Cliftonville', during the years 1929–31.) A letter from William B. Conyngham, a senior member of the Select Vestry, to Mr Lidstone, its honorary secretary, described his meeting with the owners of 'Winton Lodge' and settling on the price of £5,000 plus fees; he wrote: 'May what we have done be for many years a blessing under God's gracious hand, to that dear parish of Monkstown'.

That same year, 1945, the Rev. Arthur Butler was appointed incumbent to the parish and became the first occupant of the new rectory. G.A. Mackay records the events in his humorous poem, *Monkstown memories*, written in 1958 (the reference to CIE was to the tram lines that ran along Monkstown Road at the time, past the rectory):

A nice new Rectory, then, we got,
The old one suffered from dry rot.
Tho' losing vistas of the sea
The Rector could study C.I.E.
At the change he did not baulk,
'Twas nice he hadn't far to walk.

157

Mr Butler lived in 'Winton Lodge' until he left the parish in 1958 to take up his duties as bishop of Tuam, Killala and Achonry. Since then it has been the home of Canon Billy Wynne (1958–78) and the Rev. Kevin Dalton (1979 to the present).

The curates' house

'Churchville' at No. 16 The Crescent, Monkstown, came into the hands of the parish through the will of Mary Anne Battersby in 1905. This two-storey house had been built in about 1866 at the end of The Crescent, next door to the church grounds (*see picture on p. 88*). (Thom's Dublin Directories tell us that there were thirteen houses in Monkstown Crescent in 1865 and sixteen in 1866.)

The Vestry carried out repairs and redecoration, added a bathroom (all for £270) and then let 'Churchville' for £40 per year, with 'the tenant paying all taxes and keeping the interior of the premises in good repair and condition'. Then it was used as the curates' house from 1906 until the 1940s. Mr and Mrs Frank Hartigan leased it from 1957 until Frank Hartigan died in 1978. With his brother, he had carried out valuable maintenance work and repairs to the church roof during 1959–66. His wife, Maisie, remained in the house until her death. It was eventually sold in 1988 for £20,400. In about 1995 another curates' house was purchased (the present 2 Grange Crescent) — ironically in Kill-of-the-Grange, where the original Monkstown glebe had been more than 300 years before, where the first Monkstown Glebe House had been built almost 200 years before, and from which area Monkstown had been ejected by the parish of Kill, more than 100 years before.

CHAPTER 12

The outside world encroaches

TO BE LET, three Windows, to view Royal Procession, near Monkstown Church;
best position along route. Apply G.L. McCormack, The Pharmacy, Monkstown.
Advertisement in *The Irish Times*, 2 April 1900

O ver the years Monkstown was involved, in one way or another, with great events of the time. Some of these had a direct impact on the parish, such as the visits by three ruling monarchs (George IV, Victoria and George V), while others seemed not to concern it to any great extent, such as the 1916 Rising. How some of these events affected the parish, and the Vestry in particular, is described below.

Following the death of his father, 'the mad King George', George IV came to the throne and was crowned in July 1821. He came to Ireland on a State visit, arriving in Howth on 12 August and departing from the new, almost completed, east pier in Dunleary on 3 September. Dunleary was renamed Kingstown at this time in his honour. For a month before his visit the country erupted in a flurry of activity. The Harbour Commissioners employed 'upwards of 500 men … in repairing the roads in the vicinity' of the new harbour, reported the *Freeman's Journal* of 21 July 1821. John Semple & Son, the future architects of Monkstown Church, built 'the King's Room' (the present Round Room) next to the Mansion House for a banquet and ball; incredibly, the building was completed in less than five weeks.

In Monkstown, the Vestry purchased a flag. The minutes of 8 April 1822 record, 'Expense of Flag and erecting do on Steeple in honor of His Most Gracious Majesty's Visit to Ireland — Geo 4th, £6-11-6½'; a note added, 'Flag, value about £3'. Archdeacon Lindsay, the perpetual curate of Monkstown, organised a party for the schoolchildren in the church grounds. The event was described in the *Freeman's Journal* of 25 July 1821:

'Amongst the numerous scenes of festivities produced by his Majesty's visit to Ireland, perhaps few can equal, in point of rural simplicity, one which occurred at Monkstown Church on the 23rd instant, in honour of the present happy occasion. The Rev. Charles Lindsay, Archdeacon of Kildare, had a most excellent hot dinner, provided for upwards of two hundred children belonging to the Schools of the Union of Monkstown; for which purpose tables were laid out in the beautifully improved piece of ground surrounding the church, with a large Arch, composed of evergreens and flowers placed across the centre, with the words, "God save the King", formed of green leaves by one of the children. The Archdeacon himself presided and it must have afforded to him, as well as to the numerous spectators, a gratifying sight, to witness so many poor children partaking of his bounty with warm and grateful hearts. The evening was spent in dancing to the merry notes of a fiddle and bagpipes provided for the occasion.'

In 1886 Gladstone introduced a Home Rule Bill. The Monkstown Vestry promptly made representations to the government, opposing it. The text of the message read: 'The Humble petition of the Registered Vestry of the Parish of Monkstown in the County of Dublin in Easter Vestry assembled sheweth that your Petitioners, in common, as they believe with almost all the Protestants of every denomination in Ireland and a large number of Roman Catholics, view with alarm the proposals contained in the Bill introduced into the House of Commons to establish a legislative Body in Dublin. They conceive that such a measure would seriously endanger the safety of the loyal subjects of the Queen in Ireland, impoverish the country, both by causing capital to leave it and by the depreciation of property and would they really fear lead to civil and religious strife. Your petitioners therefore pray this Honourable House to reject the Bill.' It was signed by the rector himself, 'J.F. Peacocke, Chairman, 26 April, 1886'. The Bill was defeated and Gladstone resigned.

When Queen Victoria visited Dublin in April 1900, *The Irish Times* reported that 'everywhere was an unanimous manifestation of fervid and most convincing enthusiasm. All

The Select Vestry of 8 June 1896 resolved that a letter be sent to the manager of the Electric Tramway Company, complaining about the 'ringing of Bells during service when passing church'.

classes shared in it; and there could be no mistaking the intensity of the people's feeling'. Not everyone felt this way, however, particularly the Nationalist majority sitting on Blackrock Urban Council for the first time that year. The address of welcome to the queen was not passed without some controversy. Mr T.A. Byrne wanted an amendment to be added, noting that 'we ... consider the action of the loyal minority and their national associates in presenting such addresses as unwarrantable and uncalled for, inasmuch as Her Majesty, through the Lord Lieutenant, expressed her wish ... that her visit should bear no political significance whatever, and we are convinced that such exhibitions ... but tend to mislead Her Majesty and her Ministers as to the real feeling that animates the majority of the Irish people, that will never be either loyal, prosperous, nor happy so long as the right to govern themselves is denied'. After some heated discussion, the amendment was not included.

Even before Victoria arrived, the newspapers were full of notices advertising 'flags, not rags', 'Kodaks ... and opera glasses', 'welcome mottoes, painted in oil on sateen, 4s. 6d. each', flag-staffs, 'three colour wool bunting, on sticks, with turned knobs. Complete, for 1s. 6d. each', 'illumination devices, shields, banners and decorations' and even 'windows to let, commanding good view of procession'. On the front page of *The Irish Times* on 2 April 1900, the following advertisements appeared:

> QUEEN'S VISIT — The best 5s. Seat to witness Her Majesty's drive to
> Dublin is at Monkstown Crescent.

> ROYAL VISIT, MONKSTOWN.
> TO BE LET, three Windows, to view Royal Procession, near Monkstown
> Church; best position along route. Apply G.L. McCormack, The Pharmacy,
> Monkstown.

On arrival at Kingstown, the queen was greeted by a huge display of fireworks and then her procession made its way to the Viceregal Lodge (the present Áras an Uachtaráin) in the Phoenix Park. *En route*, it wound its way through Monkstown, Blackrock, along the Rock Road, past the Royal Dublin Society to Leeson Street Bridge. Here, as one of the old boundaries of Dublin City and near the original site of Baggotrath Castle, one of the ancient city gates, Victoria was presented with the Freedom of the City by the lord mayor, amidst all the trappings of medieval heraldry. Sir Thomas Drew, a Monkstown parishioner and the architect who refurbished the church's chancel in 1883, built a triumphal arch at the bridge for the ceremony. Made of wood and canvas and based on a print of Baggotrath Castle, it turned out to be 'one of the most successful efforts of the Decoration Committee', reported *The Irish Times* on 10 April 1900. (After her death in 1901, Drew was the only Irish architect invited to submit a design for the Queen Victoria Memorial in London; not only did he do so, but he also sent a detailed proposal for a face-lift of the façade of Buckingham Palace, as reported by *The Irish Builder and Engineer* in an article on 19 March 1910.)

When Victoria's procession reached Monkstown, she would have seen the church, in its 'prominent position on the Monkstown road ... handsomely decorated with numerous flags'. Here, at the 'cross roads', she passed under a 'glowing triumphal arch'. Naval bands

The visit of George V and Queen Mary on 8 July 1911 brought huge crowds to Monkstown, which was festooned with streamers and bunting, while tiered stands gave spectators a good view. Flags hung from the church tower in honour of the occasion.

were stationed along the route and stands positioned all along Monkstown Road (including three enormous stands erected by Sir Maurice Dockrell), 'decked in gay colours, and gorgeously decorated with festoons and streamers of varying hues' for 1,800 of 'the inhabitants of this fashionable quarter'. The stand nearest the church had four tiers of seats and was 15 feet above the road. It was 'a most substantial structure, secured with bolts, screws and braces, and (was) … approached from the rear by four flights of steps, so that there (was) … no inconvenience or crush'. A smaller stand accommodated the schoolchildren, including those from the Meath Protestant Industrial School whose 'boys' band … enliven(ed) the wait with a musical programme' and played the National Anthem as Victoria passed by. All along the route, people thronged to cheer the queen. The 'demand for window accommodation … (was) excessively keen' and windows were hired for 'smart figures'.

On the death of Edward VII on 20 April 1910 a special memorial service was held. The Select Vestry met at 12.15pm to compose a letter of condolence. It said: 'The Select Vestry on behalf of the Parish of Monkstown, Co. Dublin desire most respectfully to express to His Majesty King George V their profound sorrow at the death of His Majesty King Edward VII and their deep sense of the loss sustained by Ireland and the Empire at large. They beg most dutifully to assure His Majesty King George of their unswerving loyalty and unalterable devotion to His Person and Throne.' This letter was acknowledged by the Home Office in a reply dated 2 August.

Another State visit occurred in 1911. George V and Queen Mary visited Ireland, progressing along the Monkstown Road on 8 July in open carriages on their way into Dublin. The street was densely packed with cheering crowds. The party passed Monkstown Church and the Knox Memorial Hall, and was witnessed by Edith Dowse, daughter of the rector and then twelve years old, who viewed the parade from Dr Heard's garden, next door to the Knox Hall.

The Easter Rising of 1916 in Dublin had little apparent impact in Monkstown, only causing postponement of the Easter Vestry for a couple of months. The following understated entry appears in the minutes of 1 June:

> 'The Chairman read the Requisition of His Grace the Archbishop of Dublin authorizing the holding of the Easter Vestry and election of officers which could not be held at the usual time owing to the Rebellion.'

In the Preachers' book for 16 April 1916, in the column marked 'Observations', Canon Dowse wrote, 'Sinn Fein Rebellion'. During the month of May that year he changed the time of the Sunday evening service from 7pm to 6pm, with the comment 'Hour changed in consequence of Rebellion'. In June the service time reverted to 7pm.

The Civil War broke out in Ireland in June 1922 and was the cause of 'a general exodus' of several families from the parish. The Annual Report of 1922 stated:

> 'The Select Vestry desire to express their gratitude to Almighty God for His continued presence and help, and for the comparative immunity which the Parish continues to enjoy from those acts of violence and lawlessness so prevalent in the country. They have to report the departure of several families who have thought it prudent to remove to places where the security of life and property is assured, with the result that the onus of adequately maintaining the Church and its Services is thrown upon a smaller number.'

Among those who left were Dr Robert Lynn Heard (churchwarden, 1903–4) of 'Carnsore' (today's 'Glensilva') with his wife and family of six sons and two daughters. The names of Dr Heard's four sons who fought in the Great War are included on the Monkstown Rolls of Honour (1914–18) in the transept porches today. A farewell present in the form of a large illuminated book, intricately hand-painted, was presented by the parishioners to Dr Heard on his leaving the parish. (This book has since been given back to Monkstown Parish by Dr Heard's family for safe-keeping.) Others who left Monkstown at this time were Captain R. Magill and the Misses Galloway.

During World War II there were restrictions and shortages of various kinds that affected the church and parish, some more serious than others. For example, at a meeting of the Select Vestry on 10 December 1941 it was agreed that 'the Rector should ask the congregation to sit in the main Isle [*sic*] at the 7 o'clock Sunday Evening Services in order to comply with National requirements for Conserving Electricity'. In the event, the rector changed his mind, as 'the amount of current saved … would be very small'.

In January 1943 the secretary of the Select Vestry wrote to the Department of Supplies

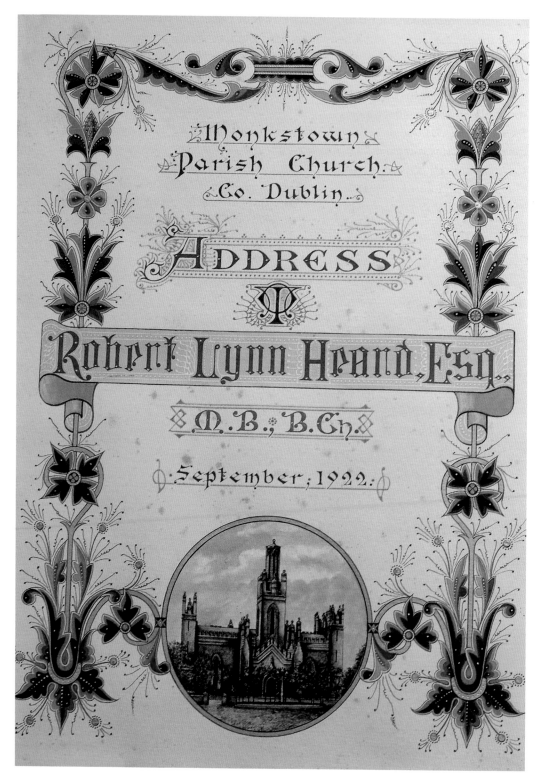

The beautiful hand-painted farewell address designed by the Misses McConnell of Lincoln Place and presented to Dr Heard in 1922 by the parishioners.

in Kildare Street, asking for a permit to buy about 7lb of 'hard soap' monthly, in order to clean the church, school and Knox Hall. An official typewritten letter was returned, stating that it was 'regretted that the application (could not) be granted, as the supply position (did) not permit of soap being made available under license for the purpose mentioned in your letter'. At the bottom of the letter was written, 'Abrasive and scouring powders, which are suitable for washing floors, are not rationed'. Again, on 22 August 1944 the Vestry minutes record that 'it was noted that the stonework of the reading desk had been cleaned, but not the pulpit. This was apparently due to the difficulty in obtaining sufficient "Monkey Brand" soap, and it was suggested that a supply of this soap could be made available for cleaning the pulpit, by temporarily suspending cleaning of other parts of the church'. The entry ends with the rather withering comment, 'The use of "Elbowese" was also suggested as an alternative'.

The Badminton Club was also affected — there was a shortage of shuttles during October 1944. The honorary secretary of the club wrote to Mr Lidstone, secretary of the Select Vestry, on 14 October that year to say that the members '... think it better to give up the Hall [the Knox Memorial Hall] for the present, but would like to start again if they can secure the shuttles'.

When the Republic of Ireland left the British Commonwealth in 1948, the Easter Vestry minutes of 20 April 1949 record that the incumbent, the Rev. Arthur Butler, 'referred to the new situation created by the coming into being of the Republic which would mean that there would be no future reference in the Church prayers to the Royal family except on rare and special occasions when a Commonwealth of Nations would be prayed for and the name of King George VI would then be used'.

PART 3:
PARISH BUSINESS

CHAPTER 13

The role of the Vestry

The small room usually built onto the east end of a church became known as the vestry because the clergy robed or 'vested' themselves there. Then, because they usually met in the vestry room, the word 'vestry' also came to mean the group of laymen (and laywomen, nowadays) who help to run the parish.

Before Disestablishment in 1871, Vestries had civil as well as religious duties, acting like local authorities, answerable to the Grand Jury of the county. These duties varied from parish to parish, depending on the clergy in charge and on the social awareness of the local gentry. Every Vestry was a law unto itself, to some extent. A good Vestry would do what it needed to do in the situation in which it found itself. A city Vestry might run a fire-engine, organise the collection of rubbish or set up a parish watch to deter crime, whereas a seaside one might be responsible for shipwrecks and their victims.

Monkstown had an active philanthropic Vestry, apparent from the detailed records kept in its Vestry minute books from the eighteenth century onwards. Those attending the early Vestry meetings, according to the earliest book that has survived (1744–77), included many native Irish (with names such as Connors, Maguire, Gilligan, Doyle, Byrne, McCarthy, Mooney and Murphy) and also 'marksmen' (those who signed themselves with an 'X'). This would seem to suggest that residents of the parish of all classes and denominations attended Vestries, not just the élite. By the early 1800s this situation had changed — the small number of people who signed the Vestry minutes had almost exclusively Anglo-Irish names, such as Armit and Browne.

The Easter Vestry originally met on Easter Monday every year. (The timing of this custom has gradually become less rigid, so that now it can be held within 21 days before or after Easter Sunday, apart from Holy Week.) The purpose of the meeting was to discuss the election or reappointment of churchwardens and other parish officers (such as applotters and appraisers, overseers of the roads, parish and Vestry clerks, beadles and constables, pound-keepers and sextons). At the same time, the churchwardens presented the accounts for the previous year. Annual salaries were also discussed.

The tools of the Vestry clerk — large walnut inkstand with two glass bottles, cost £1.15s. Brass plate engraved 'Monkstown Church Vestry 1872' and mounted on stand, cost 6s. By Thos. K. Austin & Co., Dressing Case and Despatch Box Manufacturers, Dublin.

Only church members were supposed to attend Vestries called specifically for church matters. However, for general secular matters Roman Catholic and Presbyterian ratepayers of the parish could also attend and vote. An act of 1826 stated that 'Every parishioner, of whatever religious persuasion he may be, who shall be chargeable to the Church Rates or Cess in such parish … and not disabled by Law (is) to vote'.[1] Notification of general Vestry meetings had to be advertised in advance in the appropriate places, with copies posted on the door of the parish church, as well as on the doors of the 'Roman Catholic Chapel and Presbyterian Meeting House in the Parish'.

Occasionally Catholics were appointed as churchwardens. For example, the Catholic John Mapas of 'Rochestown House' was elected churchwarden of Monkstown in 1768 (*see Appendix 4*). This practice officially came to an end in October 1805, when 'Papists (were) disabled to vote on the election or choice of church wardens'.[2] But this rule was often flouted: when Bishop Charles Lindsay, the patron of Monkstown and bishop of Kildare, made his Primary Visitation around his new diocese of Kildare, he found four churches (including Naas on 6 August 1806) with one Protestant and one 'papist' churchwarden.[3]

Functions of the Vestry

In Monkstown, the Vestry took the following upon itself:

- **To elect overseers**, who kept the parish roads in good order and repaired them when necessary (*see below*).

170

- **To elect appraisers**, who assessed the amount of cess (a church tax) that had to be paid by everyone in the parish, irrespective of their denomination.
- **To elect applotters**, who valued all the houses and land in Monkstown Union in order to levy a cess on householders, according to the value of their properties (*see below*).
- **To erect and maintain stocks**. These punitive devices were erected at Monkstown in 1747, 1753 and 1764.
- **To finance coffins and burial of the destitute**, and conduct inquests where necessary. Examples of costs were:
  1748: Inquest on a child, 13s-4d.
  1827: 'For burying a child supposed to be murdered, 2s-8½d. Doctor Duffey for attending the inquest of said child, £1-2-9'.
- **To supervise public houses**. In 1808, 27 men were appointed as 'overseers of Houses licensed for sale of spirituous and other liquors' and nineteen (including one doctor and six clergy) in 1829.
- **To maintain the parish cattle pound**. The earliest mention of a pound in Monkstown was in 1747 and the latest in 1853.
- **To run a school**. There were charity schools operating in Monkstown from 1723; the Parish School beside the church was built in 1791 and finally closed down in 1986.
- **To be responsible for any foundlings** found in the parish. Each parish was responsible for its foundlings, which were either looked after by women in the parish or left at the Foundling Hospital, closed down in 1830.
- **To organise poor relief**. In 1773 a committee was elected for this purpose.
- **To check weights and measures**. In 1762 the Vestry minutes record that 'Edward Lansdell (to) be appointed sworn measurer of coals in the Parish of Dunleary with an allowance of two pence per tun, one half to be paid by the buyer and the other half by the captain of the coal ship'. According to John Lodge, the antiquarian, in 1768 sea-coal from Whitehaven was imported into the Dunleary/Dalkey area, where it was the primary fuel, and was sold for 15 shillings a ton during the summer at Dunleary.
- **To appoint constables**, who would administer law and order in the parish.
- **To raise a militia** if and when necessary. In 1807 the Union of Monkstown was responsible for raising sixteen men for the Dublin Militia.
- **To look after public health**. The Vestry minutes of 4 April 1820 note that it was 'Resolved that the sum of ten pounds be levied off the Union … this present year for the purpose of white washing and cleansing the houses of the poor in which fever prevails'. Dr Arthure and four laymen were appointed to make sure this was done.

Applotments

Applotments were a means-tested system of raising money. In 1807 Monkstown was responsible for financing sixteen militia men for County Dublin. To do this, the Vestry decided to value all the houses and land in the Union and collect a 'cess', or tax, from each householder, according to the value of his property. But before embarking on this, the opinion of the attorney general, William Saurin, who lived within the parish at Carysfort, was sought to make sure that the Vestry was legally entitled to take such a step.

When Mr Saurin gave his approval, the Vestry appointed five 'valuators'. They were given guidelines: 'the cabins of the poor' were to be omitted, but all other houses were to be valued between £2 and £20. The Vestry stipulated 'that comfortable cottages such as Mr Abbott's near the Church (should) be valued at £2 … that small Houses two stories high such as Mr Grant's … at £5 … that good Family Houses such as those on Mt Pelier Parade … at £10, that in gentlemen's seats where the Houses are large and good such as Colonel Sankey's, Mr Ashworth's, etc … £15, that spacious mansions such as Lord Clonmell's, the Attorney General's and Mr Armit's … £20'. The land, too, was valued — at £1 per acre. Although the churchwardens were actually responsible for collecting the parish cess, they were allowed to hire a 'collector'. The schoolmaster, John Abbott (who lived in one of those 'comfortable cottages near the Church'), was appointed Vestry clerk and instructed to enter the appropriate sum opposite each name in an Applotment book, as well as to 'do all such duties incident to said office so as that said Applotments be regular and legal and so that the same can be supported on any dispute or trial at law' (Vestry minutes, 6 November 1807).

Repairing the parish roads

As vehicular traffic increased, it was essential that some efficient means should be found of keeping the public roads in repair. An act of 1613 stipulated that each parish was responsible for its roads, under the Grand Jury for the county. Various systems were tried and abandoned. One of the earliest was 'the six days labour' scheme, which meant that everyone in the parish who had the means had to repair local roads for six days in the year. The Vestry book of 20 April 1747 recorded 'Mr Edmond Shanly of Newtown & Lewis Roberts Esq. overseers for the parish of Monkstown & praisers [appraisers] for the same for the six Days Labour…'

This six-day system was never popular in Ireland. It was thought to be unfair that parishes should have to maintain roads carrying through traffic rather than local. So the 'turnpike' or toll-road system evolved. Access to each section of the turnpike was controlled by a gate and a toll house at which a toll had to be paid, so that only those who used the road paid. In 1729 the first Irish turnpike was established from Dublin to Dunleer in County Louth (Broderick 1996). The system spread throughout Ireland but was beset by financial problems, and within 30 years most turnpikes were heavily in debt. In the 1760s they were replaced by a local taxation system. This used the applotment system and was relatively fair: part of the parish cess paid by each householder, depending on the value of his property, went towards financing road repairs.

In July 1811 the 'County Treasurer' sent a warrant to the churchwardens of Monkstown, instructing the Vestry to appoint two 'valuators' for all the houses in Dalkey within a month. (Dalkey was within the Union of Monkstown at that time, as were Kill, Killiney and Tullow.) The purpose of the valuation was to collect taxes for the repair of the Grand Turnpike Road (the main Dublin to Cork road, starting near the Tallaght of today). Even though Dalkey was miles away from the Grand Turnpike Road it had to pay its share because it lay in the Barony of Uppercross. The majority of Dalkey residents would hardly have heard of this road, let alone use it. Still, the official position was that the 'Barony Cess' levied was to repair 'the Road within the Barony of Uppercross and Newcastle in which are situate on the south side of the Grand Turnpike Road leading from Dublin to Cork by Rathcoole and Naas'.

The Dalkey houses to be valued had to be more than 'the yearly value of £5 Irish' and less than £50 rent per annum. Even allowing for the absence of 'the cabins of the poor', the resulting list of seventeen householders shows how small Dalkey was in 1811:

Joseph Sandwith	£30	Richd. Atkinson	£10
Robt. Henry	£30	John Keogh	£10
Michl. Legge	£30	Peters	£10
John Risk	£30	Daniel Maguinis	£5
Gaw Lane	£25	Cathn. Shurman	£5
Thomas Carter	£25	Michael Ward	£5
Chas. McCarthy	£25	Mrs. Hasler	£5
Benedict Hamilton	£15	Henry G. Maloney	£15
do small house	£5		

Michael Legge and Joseph Sandwith, two of the Dalkey householders, were the two 'valuators' appointed by Monkstown Vestry. They had to swear that they had 'made the ... valuation ... fairly and justly according to the best of their skill and judgement without favour, affection or malice to any person'. Because Sandwith was 'one of the people called Quakers', he would not swear an oath and so was 'duly affirmed' instead. The Vestry had to meet within fourteen days of receiving the valuation, 'for the purpose of confirming, altering or amending' it, and it then had to be returned to the treasurer's office in North Great George's Street (Vestry minutes, 3 September 1811). When the Dalkey valuations were completed, the Vestry appointed two other 'valuators' to assess the houses in the rest of the Union of Monkstown. When this list was returned to the Vestry for confirmation there was obviously some difference of opinion, since the perpetual curate, Singleton Harpur, wrote 'The Vestry divided — the Ayes were seventeen — the Noes were eight' (Vestry minutes, 23 October 1811).

Valuations of houses were supposed to be carried out at regular intervals so that, as new houses were built, their owners would start paying towards the upkeep of the local roads. But after 1811 no further valuations took place in the Union of Monkstown for over 30 years. It seems that during this period the treasurer of County Dublin sent requests 'many times' for valuation of all the houses in the Union. Nothing happened. The churchwardens, who were also house-owners, not altogether unexpectedly, apparently ignored the letters. Because no valuations had been carried out, any houses built between 1811 and 1842 were not recorded and therefore their occupiers avoided paying their fair share towards the upkeep of the roads. This was the 'boom' period, when Monkstown and its environs experienced a 'great encrease of houses and population', with a corresponding 'encreased number of Roads, Bridges and other public works'.

Matters came to a head in November 1843, when Queen Victoria took the churchwardens of Monkstown to court.[4] Two valuators, James Nugent and William Frost, had actually been appointed but had done nothing — '… under various pretences, evasions and delays absolutely neglected … to value the houses in said Union and to make out and certify a list'. The queen censored the churchwardens and Vestry: 'And you, the said churchwardens and Inhabitants, refuse or neglect to carry into effect on your part the provisions of said Statute … in contempt of us, and to the great damage and grievance of the Inhabitants of said Union'. The court ordered that there should be no further 'unnecessary delays'; the valuators were 'peremptorily (commanded) immediately upon receipt of this … writ' to value the houses 'according to the fair, just and reasonable value thereof'. They were to swear on 'oath before any Justice of the Peace … that they had made the … applotment fully and justly according to the best of their skill and judgement without any favour, affection or malice to any person'. Within fourteen days of receiving the valuation the churchwardens were to call a Vestry, which was 'empowered to hear all parties who should object to said applotment and … to make such alterations or amendments as to them should seem just and reasonable, and then finally to settle … the same'. The churchwardens were to return the final valuation to the treasurer by 11 January 1844.

Edmond Atkinson and Horatio Nelson Wallace, the two churchwardens, recklessly ignored the queen's command, leading inevitably to their summons to the Queen's Bench in November 1843. Here the story goes cold — unfortunately, there is no record of subsequent events.

Church tithes or taxes

> *That a rector, being a big sort of a parson, owned the tithes of his parish in full …*
> *and that a vicar was somebody's deputy, and therefore entitled only to little tithes,*
> *as being a little body: of so much we that are simple in such matters have a general idea.*
> Anthony Trollope, *Framley Parsonage*

It is easy to see why people, the vast majority of whom were Roman Catholic, felt resentful about having to support the minority church in their midst. Before 1825 tithes were only levied on tillage land. This meant that the bulk of the tithes was paid by the poor: the owners of small tillage plots, who were mainly Roman Catholic, had to pay, while the wealthier landowners, who were mainly Protestant, were exempt because their vast estates were in pasturage.

The people also objected to the payment of their own priests. In 1825 Oliver Kelly, the Roman Catholic archbishop of Tuam, said that the people resented 'tithes, taxes, Grand Jury cesses, vestry cesses, the payment of the Catholic clergy, the high price of land, all those things together'.

The first of these unpopular taxes had come into being in 1698 with the 'Minister's Money' tax, levied on all urban ratepayers, for the payment of the incumbent's stipend. Like most taxes, it was based on house valuation. As the majority of householders in the parish were Roman Catholics, the brunt of this unfair tax fell on them. The tax was abolished in 1857, when the Ecclesiastical Commissioners took over handling church finances.

By the mid-nineteenth century the ordinary householder had to dig deep into his pocket for all kinds of taxes, which were 'levied' in Vestry meetings on those not belonging to the Established Church. (The word 'levy' comes from 'eleven pence', and so came to mean the raising of money.) Besides the 'Minister's Money', the unfortunate householder, according to the Vestry minutes of Donnybrook, might have to pay 'land tax', 'parish cess', 'Barony cess', 'militia cess', 'foundling tax', 'Grand Jury cess' and even 'cholera tax'.

The parish, or church, cess was for cleaning the church, ringing the bell, washing the minister's surplice and other linen, buying bread and wine for Communion and paying the parish clerk's salary. It was naturally extremely unpopular among those who did not attend the parish church and there were often noisy protests outside the church on Easter Monday, when the main Easter Vestry was held. Unlike applotments, the cess was not means-tested: in 1753 it was agreed that £10 was to be cessed for the salary of a parish clerk 'in the proportion of nine pence by the house'. (This would have meant tax collections from at least 111 households.)

On Easter Monday 1772 the Monkstown Vestry was 'called and assembled … for examining and confirming the several applotments of the parish cess', but the meeting had to be adjourned until June because the Tullow parishioners disagreed with the amount. In June it was resolved that the cess decided upon by Luke Mercer and John Davis, the Tullow applotters, should 'stand good'. Other groups simply refused to pay. In 1804 the 'dissenters' (non-conformist Protestants, such as Presbyterians, Baptists and Quakers) strongly objected to payment of the church cess. The Vestry minutes of Easter Tuesday 1805 record 'that the Dissenters who have refused shall be compelled to pay their parts of the Parish Cess for the year 1804'. The refusal of the Monkstown dissenters to pay the tax that year was not an isolated incident. A representative selection of entries from the Vestry minutes tell the same story: on 24 April 1810, 'Resolved that the churchwardens are … requested forthwith to collect and wherever necessary to enforce the payment of the cess for the ensuing year and also the arrears due', and again, on 8 June 1812, 'Resolved that it appears to this vestry that a sum of £41-12-5 of the cess of the year ended the 25th March 1812 remains uncollected'.

The tithe collectors, or proctors, were especially resented. Their methods were often questionable and they could confiscate the property of defaulters. But they were well paid for their trouble. The Vestry minutes of 28 March 1815 record, 'Resolved in consequence of the great difficulty and trouble in collecting the Parish Cess, that the churchwardens be directed to pay the collector the sum of four pounds as a gratuity out of the balance of £43-3-5 remaining in their hands'. By 16 May 1816 the sum had increased: 'Proctor's costs by order of vestry, £2-8-6; Collector of cess per vote of vestry, £4-0-0; Collector on receipt of £169-19-4½, £12-19-1½'.

The Tithe Wars

Trouble was brewing owing to the unpopular nature of the taxes. In 1823 the beginnings of reform were introduced in the form of a Tithe Composition Act. This meant that tithes could be replaced by a tithe composition or fixed tax. Special Vestries were to be set up in each parish, with those who paid the largest amount of tithes attending. These Vestries were to vote as to whether or not they wanted a tithe composition. If the Vestry or incumbent refused to accept the principle of composition, the matter had to be abandoned and the Vestry adjourned. In other words, the composition was voluntary.

In Monkstown, between 8 July and 16 November 1825, twenty special Vestries were held to determine the tithe composition for each parish in the Union. Again and again the exasperated comment was entered in the minutes, 'A sufficient number of special vestry men not having attended, no Business was done', and the Vestry had to be adjourned. In fact, over one-third of all special Vestries meeting for this purpose throughout the country were adjourned. In 1824 the government therefore introduced a Tithe Composition Amending Act, which meant that tithe composition could be made compulsory. The overall effect of these 1823 and 1824 statutes was that tithe payments were rationalised; by 1832 tithe composition was achieved in over half the parishes of Ireland.

Among the Minutes and Correspondence (1815–36) of Kingstown Harbour Commissioners is a small slip of paper. This is the only known surviving form that shows how applotters in Monkstown carried out their unpopular job. It dates from the middle of the so-called 'Tithe Wars' and is printed on one side, as follows:

NOTICE

UNION OF MONKSTOWN

Parish and Church Cess, ... £

The Collector has called for the above Sum, and requests that the amount may be paid, or left out for him, on his next application, on .... next, to prevent the necessity of taking the necessary legal proceedings.

Dated this............ day of 1831

.... Collector

On this rather threatening note the collector, George Darby, had filled in the date (23 June 1831), the amount that the Harbour Commissioners had to pay (£2-14s) and had signed his name. On the other side of the paper were the words:

I have, Sir, the Applotment Book dated the 14th of May 1831 —
The Parish & Church Cess — £2-14-0

Signed John Murphy)   Church
Fenton Hort   )   wardens

James Nugent   )
John Abbott   )   Applotters
James Tully   )
Richd. Walnutt)

Kingstown, July 4th 1831   Rich Toutchier

In 1831 there was organised resistance to tithe collection throughout Ireland. Many clergy, police and proctors were injured or murdered. Bailiffs, constables and the military confiscated cattle, sheep and pigs if tithes were not paid, so to prevent animals being impounded the people moved them from farm to farm during the night. No tithes were paid that year and many clergy whose only income came from this source suddenly found themselves destitute.

In May 1832 a bill was brought in to advance £60,000 to pay the clergy. The government undertook to collect the tithes owing, as Edward Stanley, the chief secretary (1830–3), said that the people must be made to respect the law. The Tithe Arrears Act became law on 1 June 1832. This was the signal for war as the authorities tried to collect unpaid tithes. Bonfires burned on the hills, more clergy and police were murdered, and people became ever more embittered against the Established Church and the government. In that year alone there were 242 murders, 1,179 robberies, 401 burglaries, 568 burnings, 280 cattle maimings, 161 assaults, 203 riots and 723 attacks on houses — all said by Lord Gort to be due to tithe enforcement.

By 1833, with tithes still unpaid, the government again advanced money for the relief of the clergy — this time a staggering £1 million. But some clergy never recovered from these years of financial hardship. Other sources of money were also forthcoming: *Saunders's News-Letter* of 2 December 1836 reported that 'a large sum for the relief of the Irish clergy is expected next month from Madras'. Archbishop Beresford of Armagh sent Charles Lindsay, patron of Monkstown and bishop of Kildare, a draft for £500, 'which (he had that) day … lodged at the Bank's House of Messrs. La Touche, to be used as occasion may be for the relief of the clergy of the Diocese of Kildare suffering from nonpayment of tithes'.

In 1833 major reforms, long overdue, took place within the Church of Ireland with the passing of the Church Temporalities Act. Among these measures the contentious parish cess was thrown out at last. Effectively, from this date the minority Church of Ireland parish was no longer able to tax the whole population for its benefit and was now solely a religious unit. After 1833 the Grand Jury of each county was supposed to take over from the Vestry the sole responsibility for the roads, public health and all other secular concerns. Instead of enforcing its own applotments for road repairs, ironically we now find the Donnybrook Vestry protesting in 1835 'against the Injustice of the Grand Jury demanding Tax for that part of Donnybrook called Church Lane' because the road was 'in a scandalously ruinous state and (had) not been repaired for many years'.

In 1838 another major tithe reform was effected with the Tithe Commutation Act. Tithes and compositions were replaced by a rent charge, which meant that church tithes had to be incorporated in the rents of Irish landlords instead of being paid to the church. The rent charge amounted to about three-quarters of the old composition and the arrears of the three previous years were written off. The immediate source of discontent — the tithe proctors — was also removed.

A new role after Disestablishment

After the Disestablishment of the Church of Ireland on 1 January 1871, the Vestry lost its local government role and became responsible for the famous '3 Fs' — the Finance, Fabric and Furnishings of the church — as well as the appointment of salaried church officers. As a result, in Monkstown, from 1875, committees were set up to supervise the School, Charity, Fabric, Vaults, Choir, Finance and Legal, which covered just about everything apart from the spiritual side of the parish. After the building of the Knox Memorial Hall in 1904, the Parochial Hall Committee joined the other committees.

In 1953 the incumbent, Mr Arthur Butler, gave the new Select Vestry a 'pep talk' on 'some of the duties of vestrymen'. The minutes of 13 May record how 'he spoke of the responsibilities of vestrymen in the temporal welfare of the parish and their help in Christian activities pertaining to the parish. The value of teamwork by vestrymen on all matters was stressed; and a reminder that confidential problems often came before the vestry and were to be treated as such. Vestrymen will set the example to parishioners by their own regular attendance in church, and assisting the congregation in every possible manner to take their full part in the services.'

Monkstown's Vestry records

Monkstown's earliest Vestry book dates back to 1744 and covers the years until 1777. It is bound in white vellum and bears the following inscription inside the cover, in the hand of Sir William Betham: 'This book was rebound 1817. W. Betham, G. Waller, Churchwardens.' (Betham, practically single-handedly, set up the Public Record Office in Ireland and would have been very aware of the value of preserving such an old volume; *see Chapter 14*.) According to the churchwardens' accounts, the binding cost 16s 3d (recorded in the Vestry minutes of 12 April 1819). On opening the book, the first page reads as follows:

Parish of Monkstown with the United Parishes

At a Vestry Called and held in the Parish Church of Monkstown on Thursday the 19th Day of April 1744 Proper Notice being given thereof the Sunday before

Proper Voucher being produced for the Expending the Sum of	£8-11-2
For Bread and Wine for the Sacrament	0-16-8
For Elioner Hall paid her Sallery	1-0-0
For Whitewashing and painting the Church pd	0-11-4½
For Margery Cabe paid her for Nursing the Parish Foundling for half a year due ye 1 of Janry 1743	1-0-0
For Richd. Handberry for being Vestry Clerk	2-0-0
For Glazing ye Church Windows paid Thos. Seymor	1-2-8
For Defraying the Church wardens Expences	0-13-4
For Visitation Articles of presentment	0-3-4
For flooring 2 Seats and Sceiling ye Church paid Joseph Smith	1-0-3
By Ld. Allen v Sess unpaid	0-9-4
Expended at the Vestry	0-3-4½
Paid the former Church Wardens	0-4-10½
	9-05-0½
	8-11-2
Discharge of Samuel Gravel and Jas. Byrne	0-13-10½
Due to ym	

We the Minister, Church Wards & parishioners of ye above sd Parishes have Examin'd ye above Accompt and do find ym to be Just & rite and find ye Sum of 13-10½ Due to ym which we desire ye Ensuing Church Wards to pay ym as Witness our hands the Day & Year first above Written.

Thos. Heany	Minister
Thos. Maguire)	Church
Michael Gilligan)	Wardens
Christr. Smalley	
Thos. Fisher	
John Graville	
Thomas Connor	

The number '21' is written at the top of this page, so one assumes that the first twenty pages are missing (probably covering at least ten years before 19 April 1744, the date of this first surviving entry). Page '21' is also grubbier than any of those that follow it, perhaps indicating that there was no cover on the book for some time. Also, throughout the book, there are several missing years (1745, 1754, 1756 and 1758). As mentioned above, the book was rebound in 1817. These factors would support the probability that the book was literally falling apart by then; its pages were loose and sections had already been lost. A letter written by the previous incumbent, Thomas Robinson, who had resigned in 1775, was said (on 31 March 1777) to be 'annexed to this Book', but it is missing. The succeeding Vestry book (covering the years 1777–1805) was probably missing by 1817, since Betham, as churchwarden, would most likely have re-bound this one also.

Since the Vestry minutes began, there have been three noteworthy periods in the history of Monkstown Church — 1785–9, 1831 and 1862. These are the dates, respectively, when the Georgian church was built, when Semple's church was completed and when McCurdy's Victorian chancel was added. The Vestry minutes containing these three periods are no longer extant: the records are missing or lost. This cannot be a coincidence.

Sometimes Vestry minutes refer to earlier Vestry books which are now missing. For example, at the beginning of the book now used for the Easter Vestry minutes are the following words, dated 21 June 1858: 'From the Vestry books which have come into the possession of the present Church Wardens … it would appear that Vestrys were … held from 1805 to the present'. Nine pages follow of extracts transcribed from two Vestry books — 1805–29 (which is extant) and 1830–58 (which is sadly missing).

It is easy to imagine the circumstances in which Vestry books could be mislaid and then permanently lost: the Vestry clerk could have fallen ill or died while in possession of one or several of such books, or they could have been borrowed by a local historian: there was a huge interest in local history during Victorian times. We all know the problem of trying to retrieve borrowed books; like the needle in the haystack, they get 'lost' and forgotten on someone's bookshelf.

When the Church of Ireland was disestablished on 1 January 1871 its registers became 'public property' and, as such, were ordered to be housed in the Four Courts, which was then the Public Record Office: 'All and singular, the records, books, accounts, deeds, maps, documents and papers … shall, within three months … be delivered up to the Commissioners by the respective registrars … Provided that the … Commissioners shall preserve (them) … and shall permit reasonable access … and shall hand over to the same Representative Body such of the said books, accounts, etc … and at the close of the Commission shall lodge the residue thereof in the Public Record Office of Ireland.' Later, this directive was relaxed somewhat and church registers were allowed to be kept by the church in 'local custody', provided that they were kept securely.

During the Civil War of 1922, the Four Courts was used to store ammunition and was subsequently blown up, destroying a huge amount of its records. *The Irish Times* of 3 July 1922 reported that of the 1,006 church registers only four survived. Fortunately, many clergy had opted to keep their registers in 'local custody', as permitted. Thus these 637 registers were, and are, all safe, including those of Monkstown.

Today, the Monkstown Vestry Archives are held in the Representative Church Body Library (RCBL) in Dublin.

CHAPTER 14

Monkstown's churchwardens

Glass globes to be cleaned by sextonesses or their salary to be stopped …
The church bell not having been rung in proper time last Sunday evening …
stated to be a quarter of an hour late: Bell ringer to be fined 1/-
to be deducted from next week's pay.
John Galloway, Churchwardens' Order Book, 6 June 1865

Since at least 1706, two churchwardens have been elected annually at Monkstown's Easter Vestry, one by the rector and the other by the parishioners. A list of Monkstown's churchwardens from 1706 to the present day is included in Appendix 4. As we can see from the extracts above, nineteenth-century churchwardens, like John Galloway, were autocratic compared to those of today. A little book, *The churchwarden's guide*, must have been owned by many of them; edited by W.G. Brooke, it is now in its tenth edition (a copy can be seen in Dublin's Representative Church Body Library). It goes into great detail listing all their duties, 'ecclesiastical' and 'temporal'.

Ecclesiastical duties encompassed looking after the church and its fabric. The list was interminable: the churchwardens had to make sure, among other things, that there were appropriate Communion vessels, a font, a pulpit, a bell, a surplice for the clergyman, a Bible, a Book of Common Prayer, a table of the Ten Commandments at the east end, registers and preachers' books. They had to ensure that the church building was maintained properly, that it and the churchyard were kept clean, that services were orderly and decent, that bread and wine were provided for communicants, that alms were collected and — a very time-consuming and important duty — that parishioners were seated 'according to their rank and state'.

Their temporal duties included the organising of Vestry meetings, looking after the parish if the minister was absent or dead, providing adequate burial ground and — an obsolete duty now — the annual 'perambulation of the parish'. This was necessary when the boundary line of the parish was crucial, since the payment of parish cess depended upon the parish in which a house was located. (This contentious tax was abolished in 1833; *see Chapter 13.*) *The churchwarden's guide* urged the churchwardens that they 'may and ought to enter and pass through houses standing upon the boundary line' of adjoining parishes.

Churchwardens were given a relatively free hand as long as they could account for the expenses incurred. On Easter Monday 1760 the Monkstown Vestry 'ordered that the churchwardens … shall repair whatsoever both within and without side the church, shall be

181

by them thought necessary, and the parishioners do by this act of vestry oblige themselves to repay them, whatsoever sum, or sums of money, shall be by them expended for that purpose'.

Outgoing churchwardens had to present their accounts at the Easter Vestry and there was usually an effusive entry in the minutes, thanking them for their services over the previous year. For example, in the Vestry minutes of 14 May 1827 it was 'Resolved unanimously that the particular thanks of this vestry be given to the late Ch:Wardens for their active, diligent and correct discharge of the duties of their office'.

Two scraps of paper among the 1864 'Economic Vouchers' (receipts for items bought or work done for the church) demonstrate how closely the churchwardens supervised the upkeep of the church. The first note reads: 'Mr. Williamson to Patrick Callanan: Dn to making A whells Barrow for the use of Monkstown church, £0-13-0 … Oct 21 64' and 'Mr. Hackett, please examine wheel and if all right pay this bill … John Mallet Williamson … 21 Oct 1864'. The second note reads: 'Delivered to J. Williamson Esq. of Monkstown Church 42 loads of Killiney Gravel at 2s. 6d: per Load: P. Goggins … Amount £5-5-0' and 'Mr. Hackett, please pay this Bill, when Davis certifies to you that the number of loads of gravel charged for were delivered … 25 Oct 1864 … John Mallet Williamson'. John Mallet Williamson was the churchwarden who ordered the gravel and wheelbarrow, Peter Hackett was the parish clerk who paid the bills, Patrick Callanan made the wheelbarrow and Christopher Davis was the sexton and general caretaker.

On at least two occasions in Monkstown an embarrassing infringement occurred, when the churchwardens failed to present their accounts. The first occasion was on Easter Monday, 8 April 1765, when neither churchwarden turned up in spite of 'several applications'. In 1812 history repeated itself. The outgoing churchwardens failed to attend the Easter Vestry to present their accounts. (They had already spoiled their copybook at least once: the previous year, in the minutes of 15 October 1811, Singleton Harpur wrote in his characteristic scrawl, 'The churchwardens not having attended — there could be no vestry held'.) The Vestry was reconvened for the following Monday, when only one churchwarden turned up and no accounts were presented. A week later the Vestry assembled again only to find exactly the same state of affairs. They gave the offenders two weeks' grace and 'the said late churchwardens pledge(d) themselves finally to close their Accounts'. In spite of this promise, a fortnight later the Vestry gathered to find nothing done. This was the last straw; the Vestry clerk was directed to write: 'Resolved that this vestry be now adjourned to this Day Fortnight Monday 8th June half past eleven o'clock to be here held and that if the late churchwardens shall not then deliver in their Accounts and pay the Balance due by them for the Cess laid upon the Parish for the year ended at last Easter, they shall be proceeded against as the Law directs'. The Vestry did take proceedings against the two culprits in the ecclesiastical court: John Creathorne, one of the wayward churchwardens, was instructed to pay the attorney's fees.[1]

As the list in Appendix 4 shows, the same person was often re-elected as churchwarden again and again. John Lees, for example, was churchwarden eleven times in the thirteen-year period between 1784 and 1796. In 1826 an 'Act to … amend the Laws which regulate … the Election of Churchwardens' stipulated that 'no person shall serve as churchwarden for two successive years if any other qualified person can be found'. The Vestry was careful to keep to this directive until the 1860s, when the old system crept in again and continues to the present day.

Prior to Disestablishment, women were entitled to attend and vote at Vestries and even to be appointed as churchwardens. However, this was virtually unknown and certainly did not happen in Monkstown. This right was taken from women in 1870 until 1920, when they again became eligible for parochial office, including that of churchwarden but not synodsman. At the Easter Vestry of 1921 Chancellor John Dowse 'cordially welcomed the Ladies for their attendance in pursuance of their rights under the new law of the Church of Ireland as Registered Vestrywomen'. At that meeting Miss Mabel Kough became the first woman on Monkstown Select Vestry.[2] It took another 60 years before Mrs Louise Lowe became the first female Monkstown churchwarden, elected by the parishioners in 1982.[3]

Monkstown's churchwardens have been a mixed bunch of villains and saintly men, hotheads and philanthropists, peers and commoners, the depressed and the cheerful. Some of them played an important, indeed a crucial, part in the history of Ireland. Even in their own day some of these men were unusual. A selection of their stories is included below.

Captain Luke Mercer

The churchwarden (1766 and 1767) who foretold the French invasion of Ireland

In December 1796, 43 French ships left Brest bound for Bantry Bay, carrying General Hoche and 'Citoyen Wolfe Tone, Chef de Brigade', with 15,000 soldiers. Poor weather sank one large ship with over 1,000 men and the French fleet soon became dispersed. When they did arrive in the bay, storms and poor visibility made it impossible to land, although they were 'near enough to toss a biscuit ashore', according to Wolfe Tone. The invasion never happened, but it was a close call. As Wolfe Tone said, 'England has not had such an escape since the Spanish Armada'. If the weather had not been so atrocious, if the French sailors had been more experienced and if the English had heeded all the warnings, the French invasion at Bantry Bay would have succeeded.

In the light of what we know actually happened at Bantry, these words of the churchwarden Captain Luke Mercer in 1768, nearly 30 years earlier, are eerily prophetic: 'This Bay [Bantry Bay] is also open & convenient for a Landing and a very probable place for the French to attempt an Invasion as they carry on a Fishery every year in that Bay for Mackerel, by which means all the hands in their fishery Boats become Pilots and is within 48 hours sail of Brest or any part of the Bay of Biscay'.

Lord Townshend, the first resident English lord lieutenant of the eighteenth century (1767–72), arrived in Ireland in August 1767. With him was his private secretary, John Lees (later churchwarden of Monkstown during the 1780s and '90s; *see below*). Townshend had been an army commander and was particularly concerned about the defence of Ireland, adding 3,000 extra soldiers to the 12,000 already there (Dickson 2000). In 1768 he made contact with Captain Mercer, one of a handful of those who knew the coast of Ireland intimately.

183

Luke Mercer was a dashing revenue officer who had since retired to Brennanstown Castle and owned much of the land now occupied by Cabinteely. He was renowned for chasing smugglers along the coast in his heyday, as commander of the *Thompson* galley and then of the *Bessborough*. On one occasion he had a narrow escape, reported in *Pue's Occurrences* of 22–26 November 1743: 'Saturday last the Bessborough Galley, Capt. Mercer, was drove on the Rocks near Wexford, but happily got off without any Damage but losing a false Keel she had on; at the same Time a Ship at a small Distance from her, was dash'd to Pieces and the whole Crew lost'. Mercer seized so much contraband that he was promoted to escorting previous lord lieutenants (Townshend's predecessors) to and from Ireland. On these journeys a hundred soldiers accompanied him, as well as food and wine in abundance in case of delays.

Townshend hauled Mercer out of retirement and asked him to write 'A description of the Sea Coast of the Kingdom of Ireland with all the Principal Harbours, Creeks and Rivers adjoining to Sea Ports'. Mercer produced a fourteen-page booklet under this title in about 1768, written in his own sloping copperplate hand. Townshend obviously went through it with a fine-tooth comb, making notes in the margins at strategic points. (The manuscript can be seen today in the National Library.)

The objective of the book was to assess the vulnerability of each point along the Irish coast to access by enemy ships. Townshend recognised Mercer's expertise and wrote that Mercer was 'esteem'd to know (the coast of Ireland) … as well as any Man in the Kingdom' owing to knowledge gleaned from a lifetime spent playing 'hide-and-seek' with smugglers in his job as a coastguard. In hindsight, Mercer's foresight was astonishing. He considered that it was 'not probable that an Enemy will ever think of Landing between Waterford and Belfast or nearer than Derry to the Northwards and Waterford to the Southwards from the many Difficultys that attends the Navigation between these parts of the Coast'. The Martello towers built along the east coast, specifically to protect against a French invasion, would therefore have been deemed unnecessary by Mercer. Time has proved him right here, as with the potential dangers of Bantry Bay.

Mercer had served under Lord Townshend's predecessor and, as Monkstown churchwarden in 1766 and 1767, would undoubtedly have known John Lees of 'Blackrock House', Townshend's private secretary (who may well have introduced him to Townshend). During the summer Townshend lived at 'Rockfield' (today's 'Cluain Mhuire' on Newtown Park Avenue), a huge estate stretching as far as Blackrock and within the parish of Monkstown. Mercer lived a few miles away, at Brennanstown, where he turned the unproductive moorland into formal gardens; in December 1763, according to *Pue's Occurrences*, strawberries ripened and apple trees blossomed in his garden.

When Lord Townshend was leaving Ireland in 1772 he gave Thomas Robinson, the perpetual curate of Monkstown, £40 for the poor. Luke Mercer died in 1781, leaving everything to his niece and her husband, the later Viscount Carleton, chief justice of the common pleas.

Charles Jones, Lord Ranelagh

The churchwarden (1766, 1767, 1782 and 1788) who set up one of the first 'neighbourhood watch' schemes

One of Lord Ranelagh's residences was beside the 'old' Monkstown church (on the north of the present Carrickbrennan Graveyard, opposite Monkstown Castle). He attended church there every Sunday, brought his children to be baptised and was an active member of the Vestry. His scrawling signature appears frequently in the pages of the first Vestry book (1744–77).

Before the days of a regular police force, Dublin's city parishes had to organise their own parish watch. They were so efficient that it became more difficult for the numerous footpads and burglars to earn their livelihood through crime. Some decided that the suburbs might be an easier option and, accordingly, decamped from the city centre. Journeys along the Rock Road became dangerous, with highwaymen frequently holding up coaches and robbing their well-heeled occupants.

But the residents of Blackrock were not prepared to put up with this situation for long. In 1787 Lord Ranelagh chaired a special meeting of the Blackrock Association in Jannett's Tavern in Blackrock.[4] The members decided to organise a nightly patrol from Blackrock to Baggot Street and offered a reward of £20 (a huge amount then, maybe to some two years' salary) to anyone who supplied any information leading to conviction.

Thomas Dixon

The knife-wielding churchwarden (1844)

'Mr. Thomas Dixon, of Monkstown, was attacked by a gentleman of the pad [footpad or robber] on Wednesday night last, on his road homeward through the Black rock. The assailant tripped up Mr. Dixon, and having succeeded in leaving him prostrate, displayed every intent to keep him in that situation, by throwing himself on his person. Mr. Dixon, however, happened to be armed with a dirk, which he drew from his pocket, and having given a few convincing proofs that the party with which he was engaged had met with an awkward customer, the attacker made off.'

This incident was reported in *Saunders's News-Letter* of 10 February 1826. It continued: 'It is supposed, from the state of Mr. Dixon's clothes and person, that the assailant must have been severely wounded. The police have been actively employed in an endeavour to secure him, but he has as yet eluded their vigilance.'

Sir John Lees

The unscrupulous churchwarden (1784–5, 1787–9 and 1791–6)

In Carrickbrennan Graveyard there is a damaged neglected stone to the memory of Sir John Lees (1737–1811). Inside Monkstown Church an intact wall memorial extols his virtues, in particular 'his great public and private character' and the fact that 'he died universally lamented' (for the complete inscription, *see Chapter 22*). This accolade to John Lees is a figment of its author's imagination. Lees was actually an unscrupulous self-motivated swindler. Today, he would most probably have finished up in gaol for fraud and embezzlement, or in a tribunal. But because of his friendships in high places he could pull all the right strings and manage to evade further scrutiny.

As a churchwarden of Monkstown for at least eleven years (between 1784 and 1796) Lees was one of the prime movers in the building of the 1789 church on the new site (the present location) acquired from Lords Longford and de Vesci (*see Chapter 4*).

Although not a paragon of virtue, Lees was undoubtedly very able. Born in Scotland in 1737, he distinguished himself in Germany as a young officer under the dashing marquis of Granby — father of the duke of Rutland, who laid the foundation stone of Monkstown Church in 1785. Lees then came to Ireland in 1767, as the private secretary of Lord Townshend, the lord lieutenant, and subsequently secretary to his successor, Lord Harcourt. Lees became secretary of the Post Office in 1774, usher of the Black Rod in the Irish House of Commons in 1780 and under-secretary of the War Department in Ireland in 1781. Two years later he was offered the position of under-secretary of state for England but turned down this considerable honour, pleading poor health and his unsuitability for the post (Butler 1953).

The real reason may have been that Lees saw more scope for his talents in Ireland. In 1783 he helped to separate the Irish and British Post Offices and gradually became more powerful in his position as secretary of the Irish Post Office, which had originally been little more than a sinecure. John Lees's annual salary was £2,000; he left £250,000 in his will (Butler 1953).

Confidant of the titled and distinguished, Lees held 'court' at his home, 'Blackrock House' on Newtown Avenue, which became the mecca of fashionable society and the summer residence of a string of lord lieutenants, including Rutland and Townshend. According to an anonymous poem published in the *Hibernian Magazine* on 5 September 1800:

> *Here, Rutland, whose decease we all lament,*
> *Quaff'd the full cup of pleasures innocent …*
> *Here Temple, Camden, Westmoreland deplor'd,*
> *That England could not such a spot afford;*
> *Here Castlereagh and Cooke unbent their minds,*
> *And Elliott threw his sorrows to the winds!*

The poet extolled 'Blackrock House', saying that this 'handsome building rises in the air; With just agreement framed in every part, Polished with elegance, and nicest art'. Like Lees's memorial, there is some hyperbole here: 'Blackrock House' is a fine residence, a little unusual in that it was one of the last brick-built Georgian houses, but it is not outstanding architecturally. (It is now in flats and its fine cut-granite wall fronts onto Newtown Avenue.)

In 1790, as secretary of the Irish Post Office, Lees set up a very efficient system of post roads throughout Ireland, carrying mail coaches — a clever way of government control. It was, according to Pakenham (1972), 'much more than a postal service. It was a finely spun web of communications that held the country together. Apart from the odd military express, all Government messages went by mail coach: an SOS from a beleaguered magistrate, a reassuring reply from the Castle, a peppery general order from military headquarters, a spy report from Wexford … Destroy the mail coaches, and you would not only spread panic in the garrison towns; you would paralyse the Government of Ireland.' Under Lees the number of post offices increased from 145 in 1784 to 266 in 1800 (Dickson 2000). He was knighted for his services in 1804.

Besides organising the whole mail network, including the mail boats, Lees conveniently created highly paid positions and sinecures for an amazing number of his relatives. Two of his sons, Townshend and Thomas Orde, were made 'Searchers of the port of Wexford' in 1798, earning £500 a year jointly. Another son, Edward, was appointed, with his father, as joint secretary of the Irish Post Office in 1801. When in 1809 investigation of fraud led to the dismissal of the clerks of the roads, Sir John and his son Edward survived (Butler 1953).

Portrait of Sir John Lees by Gilbert Charles Stuart, on exhibit in the Georgian House Museum (ESB) at 29 Lower Fitzwilliam Street. (Courtesy of An Post.)

(Edward was finally dismissed from his post in 1831, but managed, through his connections, to secure a well-paid job in Edinburgh — with £600 a year, a house, coal, candles and £200 a year for expenses.) Yet another son, the Rev. Harcourt Lees, was a prolific correspondent and pamphleteer who took advantage of his brother's position in the Post Office to escape mail charges and to get free secretarial services and stationery (*see Chapter 22*). Both Lees and his relatives found all sorts of ingenious ways to bleed the system: impossibly high expense accounts, embezzlement of private property, fraudulent claims, the use of free postage, and probably the misappropriation of charity funds that passed through their hands. They were careful to destroy the evidence so that, in spite of several inquiries, they never got the come-uppance they deserved.

John Lees does not even come across as a likeable rogue. When Lord Edward Fitzgerald was wounded during his arrest, Lees's aspirations for him are chilling. He wrote in a letter to Lord Auckland on 22 May 1798:

> 'Lord Edward — damn him — continues in great pain — the ball's not extracted — his life was not considered in danger from his wounds — the rope, I hope, however, will soon dispose of it' (Pakenham 1972).

The confident prediction on his wall memorial that 'his great public and private character will remain long after this frail monument shall perish and be forgotten' has not been realised. Instead, when Lees and his clan arise in conversation nowadays, they are likely to be described as 'an intriguing shower of gangsters' (Mac Cóil 1977). There is an unexpected twist in Sir John Lees's story: his great-great-great-grandson was Canon Richard William Maurice Wynne, better known as Billy Wynne, incumbent of Monkstown during 1958–78.[5] *His* memory, unlike that of Lees, will never perish or be forgotten.

William Digges La Touche

The philanthropic churchwarden (1790)

> In the East ... I suppose he never saw such a thing as public worship, or ever heard the voice of Christian instruction ... Yet in his letters, there is the ... recognition of the existence and goodness of providence — his books all have at the head of every page, the title "Laus Deo" – Glory to God — and you know far better than I do the warmth with which his ... mind glowed in gratitude to God for every benefit ...'

This tribute to William Digges La Touche (1747–1803) was written by James, his eldest son, to his mother Grace about the eighteen years his father had spent in the Persian Gulf.

We think of William Digges La Touche perhaps as a predictable, stay-at-home, Dublin-born Huguenot banker. But, in keeping with his family history, he had a colourful youth. He was the grandson of David Digues La Touche, the founder of the Irish La Touches (*Burke's Irish Family Records* 1976). David was born in the Château de la Touche on the

Loire. When the Edict of Nantes was revoked in 1685 and the Huguenots lost their religious freedom, he escaped from France along with 200,000 others. He fled to his uncle in Amsterdam and joined the Huguenot regiment of King William's army. Aged nineteen, he fought at the Battle of the Boyne in 1690 and, with many other Huguenots, settled in Ireland when the regiment was disbanded. He moved to the Liberties of Dublin, where he started a small weaving business and, later, the first bank in Ireland. Business flourished, and by the time he died the La Touche bank had contacts in cities throughout Europe and was the agent for several banks in London.

David left the banking business to his elder son, also David, who was now his partner. The bank remained within the family for five generations. (In 1870 it was absorbed by the Munster Bank.) James, the younger son, inherited the weaving business (Bradley 1996). He had three sons, the youngest of whom was William, born in 1747 in Dublin. (At this point David decided to drop the 'Digues' (or Digges) from the family name, as did most of his ten children, except his eldest son, David of Marley Park, and his youngest, James, who retained it.) William was educated at St Paul's School in London and, after leaving, at the age of eighteen, he accompanied Henry Moore, the British resident, or diplomatic representative, to Bassora (or Bussora, present-day Basra, now in Iraq), situated at the head of the Persian Gulf and on the trade route between the East Indies and Europe. William's official post was that of a 'writer'.

When Henry Moore died, William succeeded him as British resident and became very popular among the people of Basra. Instead of patronising them like most Europeans at the time, he regarded them as friends and equals. He kept the British government informed, by letter, about the political situation in India and Ceylon, as well as in the Gulf (Historical Manuscripts Commission 1876). He stayed in Basra for eighteen years, keeping in touch with his family in Ireland by writing home regularly. Then, in 1784, at the age of 37, with his fortune made, William returned home via London. There he met the Pugets, another Huguenot banking family (whose bank dealt with monetary transactions between Ireland and England), and fell in love with their daughter, Grace. They were married that same year, 1784.

William brought home to Ireland his collection of valuable Persian manuscripts dating from the sixteenth century, which he later gave to Trinity College, Dublin. In 1786 he presented the manuscript of a 'poem in eulogy of Shah Tahmasp AH 1144 from the Royal Library at Shiraz. A fine specimen of Persian calligraphy and binding'.[6] On 24 February 1787 the librarian at Trinity wrote: 'This day were recd. by the hands of the Revd. Mr. Moore two very elegant Persic mss. which with three others recd... . a few days since are the gift of William Digges Latouche to the College. Placed same time in the mss. room.'[7]

From 1784 William settled down to a less exotic life in Dublin. He became a partner in the La Touche family bank and built a town house on St Stephen's Green. He also bought a country mansion at Booterstown, called 'Sans Souci' (now the site of a housing estate of the same name). The La Touche family attended Monkstown Church. William was appointed churchwarden in 1790. At that time the perpetual curate was Dr William Jephson (1782–91), who lived elsewhere and was apparently totally disinterested in any building programme in Monkstown (*see Chapter 11*). And yet it was during Jephson's incumbency that the church (1785–9) and the school (1791) were built. William was definitely one of the main influences in the building of the school; he was treasurer of its fund-raising campaign and also contributed a substantial amount himself (about 25%). The school was opened within one year of his becoming churchwarden (*see Chapter 16*).

William's wife, Grace, did a great deal of charitable work. She was vice-patroness of the Magdalen Asylum in Leeson Street, where she worked with the founder, Lady Arabella Denny; its objects were 'the protection and subsequent reformation of deserted females, who having at first departed from the paths of virtue, have become disgusted with vice, and seek the means of qualifying themselves once more to associate with moral society'. She often visited the little Parish School in Monkstown church yard, where over 100 children were taught. (Grace is 'the children's friend' in the anonymous poem published in the *Hibernian Magazine* of 5 September 1800: 'If we desire to see the children's friend, To Monkstown School our willing steps we bend.')

William vehemently opposed the Union and in 1798 chaired a huge meeting of Dublin merchants to mobilise the city against it. He prophetically believed that 'instead of strengthening the two countries … (it) would eventually cause their separation'. He thought absentee landlords had helped to cause the country's political problems. Lecky, in his *History of Ireland* (Vol. III, 1913), noted that five La Touches had 'sat together in the [Irish] House of Commons, and (the) family may claim what is, in truth, the highest honour of which an Irish family can boast — that during many successive Governments and in a period of the most lavish corruption, it possessed great parliamentary influence, and yet passed through political life untitled and unstained'.

In Dublin's Civic Museum in South William Street there is a large granite stone. Engraved on it are the words 'LATOUCHE BRIDGE 1791'. This stone graced what is now called Portobello Bridge but was originally called after William La Touche, as one of the directors of the Grand Canal Company.[8]

William's grandfather, David, had died suddenly while on his knees at prayer in the Viceregal Chapel, around the corner from his Castle Street bank. William's own demise was equally unexpected. On Monday 7 November 1803, at a meeting in the Exchequer, he was just about to stand up to speak when he had an attack of apoplexy (a stroke). He was carried home unconscious to his St Stephen's Green house and 'the best medical aid obtained', but he died the following morning. He was only 56. An imposing wall memorial was erected by his wife, Grace, in Monkstown Church (*see Chapter 22*).

On the Sunday after his death, 13 November 1803, the perpetual curate, the Rev. James Dunn, a close friend of the family, eulogised William La Touche in a moving sermon in Monkstown Church and spoke directly to his young family. William's eldest son, James, was said to be so affected by the sermon that he gathered his brothers and sisters around afterwards and read it to them again (Urwick 1868).[9] He was now the head of the La Touche family and took his responsibilities seriously, delaying his commencements at Trinity College for about a year until his father's affairs were in order. A lover of the Irish language, when James would return home to 'Sans Souci' each evening he would hear his own children's Irish and French lessons. He became one of the founders of the Sunday School Society in Ireland in 1809 and was its secretary until his death 'of a fever' at the early age of 39 in 1827.

William Betham

The 'Ulster king' churchwarden (1816–18)

William Betham (1779–1853) wrote, 'I have not the honour to be an Irishman except by adoption' (Phair 1972). Although he did not come to Ireland until he was 26, Betham grew to love the country, its ancient records and antiquities — even the language, which he tried to learn as an adult. Perhaps more than anyone else, this Englishman was responsible for preserving, single-handedly, a huge volume of Irish heraldic and genealogical material which would otherwise have been destroyed. He battled for years with the authorities to set up a Public Record Office for Ireland, which was eventually opened in 1867, fourteen years after his death.

On one occasion Betham accidentally found himself caught up in the middle of one of Daniel O'Connell's 'monster meetings' or political demonstrations, a potentially dangerous situation for one such as Betham. Suddenly, one of the mob recognised him and shouted, 'That's Sir William Betham, the poor man's friend!' Betham was able to extricate himself and drive off safely in his carriage, 'amid cheers' (Betham *c*. 1905).

William Betham was born in Stradbrooke in Suffolk, the eldest son in a large family of fourteen children. His father, the Rev. William Betham, was headmaster for nearly 50 years of the Endowed School at Stonham Aspall. William imbibed his father's love of genealogy and helped him as a teenager with his 'Genealogical Tables of the Sovereigns of the World' and five volumes on English and Scottish baronetages. Betham's older sister, Matilda, was a writer and painter of miniatures, and a member of the literary circle that included Charles and Mary Lamb, Coleridge and Southey (Phair 1972).

William married Martha Norton in 1802 when he was 23 years of age. Sadly, a year later she and their baby daughter both died, a week after the birth. Around this time William had a violent argument with his father (the subject of which is not known) and the subsequent estrangement meant that he was almost penniless. He went to work in London with a legal firm and, around 1805, came to Ireland on business to look for some documents. When he visited the Bermingham Tower at Dublin Castle, where the public records

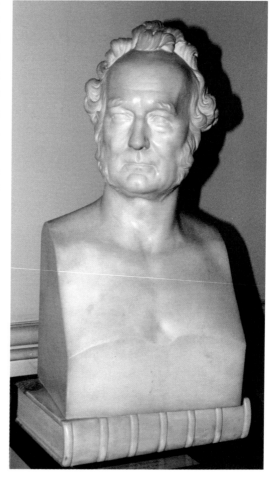

Bust of Sir William Betham by J.E. Jones of London, sculpted in 1846 and on display today in the Heraldic Museum on Kildare Street. Under the Ulster king of arms is the volume *Etruria Celtica* (1842), Betham's last published work. (Courtesy of the manager of the Heraldic Museum, National Library of Ireland.)

were housed, he was appalled to find such disorder. He realised that the office needed a radical overhaul, that the records had to be indexed and organised, and that he would dearly love to do this work. Two years later he became deputy Ulster in the Office of Arms. (The Office of Arms granted and confirmed coats of arms, compiled and registered pedigrees and was involved in ceremonial duties, such as the processional order at the laying of the foundation stone of Nelson's Pillar, which Betham was to organise in 1808.)

At the time of his appointment, the 'Ulster King of Arms and Principal Herald of all the Kingdom of Ireland' was Rear-Admiral Sir Chichester Fortescue. This was really just a sinecure since there was virtually no work going on in the Office of Arms, which was simply a room in the house of Theobald Richard O'Flaherty, the registrar and book-keeper. The office had no permanent address and was usually in the king of arms's house, so books and records became dispersed over the years. The title 'Ulster', which dated back to 1552, had no territorial significance. But because there was already an 'Ireland' king of arms in the Heralds' College in London, the Irish king of arms was given the title 'Ulster king of arms of all Ireland'. (The title nowadays is the chief herald of Ireland.) Some 'Ulsters' considered heraldic manuscripts as their own private property, so many early records were lost or ended up in other archives, especially in Trinity College, Dublin, and the British Museum in London. For example, Betham discovered that James Terry, the Athlone pursuivant, or herald, took many books and manuscripts with him when he fled to France with James II in 1688, as well as the official seal (Barry 1970).

Betham's arrival on the Dublin scene in 1807 revolutionised the Office of Arms. The Irish records were scattered, unindexed and neglected. Before Betham, only one letter-book, containing copies of letters from the office, existed for the period 1789 to 1812, whereas, after Betham, for the period from 1810 to 1850 there are eighteen bound volumes. Betham actually paid Sir Chichester a quarterly sum to keep away from the office so that he could have a free hand. At first the office was operated from Betham's own home, but since he moved house six times this was an unsatisfactory arrangement; eventually he secured a room in Dublin Castle, which then became called the Record Tower (Phair 1972). He immediately started to increase the amount of heraldic and genealogical material in the office. He made abstracts of wills, most of which were later destroyed in the Four Courts during 1922, so his copies or compilations from old documents are all that now survive. His work was meticulous and accurate. When Sir Chichester died in 1820 Betham became Ulster king of arms. The lord lieutenant had knighted him in 1812 to stress the importance the government now attached to the work he was doing.

Besides being deputy Ulster of arms, Betham was also appointed sub-commissioner of the Irish Records Commission in 1812. The official keeper of the records was Lord Stanhope, whose salary was £500 a year — a generous sum for a position that was in name only. Stanhope simply paid his two sub-commissioners twelve guineas each a year to do all the work. Betham often worked eight to ten hours a day, not for the miserly salary but for the enormous satisfaction he got from being immersed in old records. In 1837 Betham referred to his fees: 'The fees for searches ... have not, I verily believe, netted me £10 a year ... so that my emoluments in that respect would scarcely tempt the jealous avidity of anyone. My emoluments arise from my private collections of references to records, which I have collected and compiled for the last thirty years, with almost incredible labour and application; which now consist of many hundred volumes, all methodized, indexed, and rendered easy of reference ... by which I am enabled to assist a solicitor, or other inquirer, on any given subject, genealogical, topographical, legal, or any other question ... I can generally make out the descent of property, or heirship of law ... to establish the necessary facts, in a few days, or perhaps hours, and for a few pounds (or even shillings) fee; which, without my books, would occupy weeks, months, and even years to accomplish; and in some cases could not otherwise be done at all.' (This extract is from the obituary of Sir William Betham, published in the *Gentleman's Magazine* of December 1853.)

With William Warburton, his fellow sub-commissioner, Betham's job was to 'methodize, regulate and digest the records in their care, mainly pipe rolls, patent and plea rolls'. This often involved deciphering antiquated writing and language, which, he claimed, only one or two people in Ireland were qualified to do. His eyes were 'much fatigued and exhausted by three or four hours close attention to the black letter' and he asked for increased pay. When he was offered a halfpenny an hour extra, he resigned. He had a row with the secretary of the Commission, whom he dubbed his 'Arch Enemy' (Phair 1972). This was to be a trend in Betham's dealings with people; unfortunately, he never learned to curb his tongue or his temper with his peers and he would often become embroiled in rows.

On one occasion Betham had three priceless antiquities in his possession: he purchased the Book of Dimma and the Shrine of the Misach, and was lent the shrine of the Cathach of St Columba (Colmcille) by Lady O'Donnell. In 1826 he brought all three to London and wrote triumphantly to a friend: 'I returned this morning. I exhibited my precious relicts in London to many of the learned who have unanimously surrendered the palm of honourable antiquity to Ireland.'

Betham's insatiable curiosity for antiquities led him to explore the wooden box within the shrine of St Columba. This was faced with patterned bronze and silver plates, dating back to the eleventh century. On poking a wire inside the box, Betham found not the bones of the saint but an ancient manuscript. Lady O'Donnell, the owner of the shrine (which had belonged to the O'Donnells of Donegal for centuries), threatened Betham with legal proceedings for his tampering with the relic, but she eventually allowed him to open it in the presence of her son (O'Byrne 1996). Then Betham discovered what is probably the earliest known Irish manuscript. It is a copy of the Psalms, measuring 9 inches by 6 inches, and has been dated by modern scholars to the late sixth or early seventh century. Traditionally it is attributed to St Columba (which is possible, according to its dating) and is supposed to be the famous manuscript responsible for a battle, a flight and an aphorism. Columba is said to have copied it secretly at night from a psalter belonging to St Finnian. When discovered, he claimed the copy, but the king, Diarmuid Mac Cerbhaill, decided in favour of Finnian, announcing 'To every cow its calf; to every book its copy' — the first copyright judgment. The resulting dispute led to a great battle, followed by Columba's 'flight' and self-exile in Iona. Whether the manuscript found by Betham was in Columba's own hand is doubtful, but it was a historic find and had special significance for Monkstown (where Sir William was a parishioner), with its links to Mochonna and therefore possibly to Columba. (The ancient church in Carrickbrennan Graveyard was dedicated to Mochonna; *see Chapter 1*.)

Betham's passion lay in ancient manuscripts and during his lifetime he collected over 21,000 volumes. In 1849 he sold most of his Irish manuscripts to the Royal Irish Academy and Sotheby's auctioned the rest after he died (*Gentleman's Magazine*, August 1854). The total value was said to be £10,000 (almost €1 million today). They included original thirteenth-, fourteenth- and fifteenth-century vellum manuscripts in Latin (sold for between £3-10s and £27), a letter from Oliver Cromwell to his son (sold for £17) and unpublished poems in Jonathan Swift's hand (sold for 10 guineas). Some of these manuscripts were purchased by private individuals, as well as by Trinity College, the Public Record Office, the Office of Arms and the British Museum. The whereabouts of others are unknown.

In 1807 William Betham had married for the second time. Elizabeth Crampton was the daughter of the Rev. Cecil Crampton, sister of the Hon. Philip Crampton, a justice of the Queen's Bench, and cousin of Sir Philip Crampton, the well-known flamboyant Dublin doctor. William and Elizabeth had six children. Two of their sons, Molyneux (b. 1813) and Sheffield (b. 1817), followed their father into the Office of Arms — Sheffield as the Dublin herald and Molyneux as the Cork and deputy Ulster. They both also became churchwardens of Monkstown, like their father (*see Appendix 4*). And they put Monkstown on the map for sports. For about 30 years (1846–77) the County Dublin (Monkstown) Archers had a golden era, largely thanks to the Betham family. There were only three archery clubs in Ireland at that time — Monkstown, Armagh and Derry. Molyneux Betham was the Irish champion twelve times, while his daughter was the Irish lady champion for two years and the English for three (Kenny 1978).

In 1825 Sir William was living at 'Montpelier Castle', now demolished. Brewer (1825) in his *Beauties of Ireland* described the estate: 'The grounds attached to this agreeable residence have been improved by Sir William Betham, with exquisite taste, and command views almost unrivalled in beauty, reaching over a rich expanse of varied scenery, and bounded by the Wicklow mountains, a limit at once lovely and sublime'. His next home was 'Stradbrook House' (called after his birthplace, Stradbrooke in Suffolk), after which Stradbrook Road was named. While living there in 1834 Sir William, together with his sister Elizabeth and his son Sheffield, became ill with typhus. Sheffield recovered, but Elizabeth died (6 January 1835), aged 35, and was buried in Carrickbrennan Graveyard. Sir William took seven months to recover and became lame as a result of the illness (Phair 1972).

For the last seven years of his life Betham laboured to get a Public Record Office for Ireland. He made detailed reports, wrote letters and badgered the authorities to achieve this end. It was his suggestion that the records could be housed in the Four Courts. It was to take fourteen years after Betham's death, in 1853, for the Public Record Office to open, in a building beside the Four Courts (Phair 1972). Fortunately, Betham was spared the knowledge that a huge proportion of the priceless documents stored there were destroyed in an explosion on 30 June 1922 during the bitter fighting of the Civil War.

Sir William worked right up to the time of his death, at the age of 74. His daughter, Harriette, had died about two weeks earlier, which may have been a precipitating factor in his death. (She was only 32 years of age.[10]) At the time Sir William was living in 'Rockford House', Blackrock.[11] After passing through various private owners, the house became a school in 1959, run by the Presentation Sisters and called 'Rockford Manor', until the mid-1990s. The property developer who then bought it has built houses and apartments on the seven acres of land, with the old house incorporated into the development.

Sir William wrote in his will that he wanted 'to be buried in the church yard of Monkstown in the most private way possible without expense, at least with as little expense as possible'. This was an unusual request in Victorian days, when funerals and mourning, particularly of the affluent, were elaborate and public occasions (*see Chapter 21*). However, Sir William's wishes were fulfilled and he lies today in Carrickbrennan Graveyard, marked with a simple headstone and with his sister Elizabeth and daughter Harriette nearby. The only extravagance expended in his memory was the installation by his sons, Molyneux and Sheffield, of a large stained-glass window in 1866 in the south transept of his beloved Monkstown Church (*see Chapter 8*).

In spite of his busy workload, Sir William was always deeply concerned with Monkstown: he attended the church and was appointed churchwarden during the years 1816–18. He was also on the Building Committee that asked John Semple to draw up plans for the enlargement of the church and would no doubt have been present at its consecration on Christmas Day 1831. Entirely in keeping with his life's work of preserving old records and manuscripts, Sir William probably saved Monkstown's oldest Vestry book (1744–77) from destruction: inside the white vellum cover of the book, in Betham's hand-writing, is the inscription 'This book was rebound 1817', signed by him and his fellow churchwarden, George Waller (*see Chapter 13*).

Ralph Ward

The suicidal churchwarden (1768 and 1784–5)
In the column on 'Obituaries of Considerable Persons, with Biographical anecdotes' in the *Gentleman's Magazine* of July–December 1788, the following piece was included: 'Sept. 6, Mr. Ralph Ward ... put an end to his life in the Castle Garden, by opening the arteries of his neck with a penknife ...'

The lead-up to this tragic event started on Saturday 31 August 1788. Ralph Ward (?–1788), surveyor general of the Ordnance, was staying at his country seat in 'Newtown House', Blackrock, when a visitor called with disturbing news. A small group of men had arrived at Ward's department in Dublin Castle. They were Isaac Corry, Captain Pakenham and the captain of the guard. They had instructions from the new lord lieutenant, the marquis of Buckingham, to suspend all the Ordnance staff, lock up the whole department and give the keys to him. Buckingham, who had arrived the previous November, had decided to do something about the widespread fraud and corruption endemic in the administration of his predecessor, the duke of Rutland. He noticed a discrepancy in the accounts and ordered that every office and store in the Ordnance should be sealed up while all the books were checked. The story was covered in the *Gentleman's Magazine* of 2 September 1788 and in the *Dublin Chronicle* of 2–4 and 6 September 1788.

This must have been a disquieting experience for Ward, the trusted surveyor general of the Ordnance for the previous 26 years. He was summarily dismissed and Isaac Corry (later chancellor of the Exchequer, who fought a duel with Henry Grattan in 1800) was appointed instead. There was to be a thorough investigation into the accounts and 'the doors (of the Ordnance were locked) to prevent any arrangements … to puzzle and perplex a business which must now be probed to the bottom'.

Ralph Ward was in sole charge of the Department of the Ordnance, which controlled military supplies, and vast amounts of money passed through his hands daily. It was immediately obvious to everyone that he was suspected of embezzlement. According to the *Gentleman's Magazine*, initially 'he seemed somewhat affected but not alarmed, expressing his wish that every matter might be scrutinised, not doubting but his character would be found altogether founded on the firm basis of honour and strict integrity'. The following day he still insisted on 'his innocence, disclaimed all knowledge of fraud, embezzlement , or any (of) the slightest peculation' to some friends who visited him, reiterating his belief that the only way to clear his name was by a thorough investigation.

Then on Tuesday 2 September, to everyone's horror, Ralph Ward was found by one of his servants, slumped at his desk, covered in blood. He had cut his own throat, apparently with a paper-knife. In spite of being seen almost immediately by the surgeons, Ward died several days later. He left a note saying that he was blameless and that he had had 'an unblemished character, revered and respected' in Ireland. But he could not face life with a ruined reputation.

What had he done that was so dreadful? Everything came out into the open after his death. A close colleague at the same Ordnance department (in charge of small arms) obviously felt partially responsible and told of his own involvement. He had called on Ward on the evening of his attempted suicide and reminded him of a transaction between them — one that had taken place eight years earlier and which Ward had apparently totally forgotten. On that occasion Ward had approached him 'in distress … occasioned by some play-debts', saying that 'his character would be ruined' if they were not discharged. His friend had refused, but for two months Ward pleaded with him to sign a 'fabricated order for … a thousand stand [sets] of arms', promising that the money would be 'soon and properly replaced'. He had eventually signed the warrant but had never been repaid. When he called on Ward on 2 September to remind him about this incident, Ward had become 'extremely agitated' and, soon after his departure, had cut his own throat.

After his suicide attempt Ward initially refused any treatment, but 'his distracted family' eventually persuaded him to agree to medical care. He also saw a clergyman (possibly the Rev. John Burrowes, headmaster of the nearby Prospect School in Blackrock and also curate of Monkstown) and received Communion when he realised he was dying. One of his chief concerns was that his only grandson, 'a fine youth who was just preparing to enter the College, should not know that he had died by his own hand'. The *Gentleman's Magazine* noted approvingly that he 'prayed fervently with every apparent sign of repentance, and died with his family about his bed' on Saturday afternoon, 6 September 1788. Instead of being buried at his own parish of Monkstown, he was privately interred at 8am the following Monday in St Ann's Cemetery in Dawson Street, as reported in the *Dublin Chronicle* of 6–9 September 1788. If a tablet was inscribed to his memory it has not survived.

It is ironic that we should know more about the death of Ralph Ward than about his life. He was English and had come to Ireland in the late 1850s, having previously worked as second architect in the Tower of London. He was probably a widower, who had remarried but who seems to have been living apart from his second wife. There was a grandson, 'Master Read', of whom he was very fond, the son of his only daughter. He also seems to have suffered from 'a dreadful disorder (for which he had visited all the English watering places for relief without any effect)'.

In the eyes of his contemporaries Ward committed two serious crimes — embezzlement[12] and attempted suicide. About two weeks after his death there were further suicides by two other men in positions of authority, one a member of parliament who was also 'a commissioner of the Imprest-office' (Edward Bellingham Swan), and the other in the Bullion Office (Mr Warren), reported in the *Gentleman's Magazine* of 21 and 22 September 1788 respectively. One shot himself and the other cut his throat (as Ward had done). These two suicides were probably no coincidence: it is possible that, like Ward, these unfortunate men, former pillars of the Establishment, were afraid that their past indiscretions might also be uncovered by the lord lieutenant's detectives.

Besides his position in the Department of Ordnance, Ward was also a prolific builder and architect. He built his own home in Blackrock, 'Newtown House', as well as houses in Merrion Square, North — No. 15 and Nos 23–27, with No. 26 designed for Viscount de Vesci of Monkstown (Georgian Society of Ireland 1912). He also built 'the whole range in Capel-street, connected with Little Britain & Green-street' (*Dublin Chronicle*, 6–9 September 1788). In addition he oversaw other work, such as a kitchen extension to 'Frescati House' in Blackrock, home of Emily, duchess of Leinster (Fitzgerald 1953). ('Frescati' is now sadly demolished and the present location of Roches Stores.) Lady Louisa Connolly in her letters to her sister, the duchess, mentioned Ward frequently, obviously regarding him as 'the oracle'; she wrote that 'Mr. Ward's approving of the work is my only comfort, and he did seem to think you had the worth of your money' (22 October 1775). She wrote to William Ogilvie (the former family tutor who was now Lady Emily's second husband), saying that 'Mr. Ward will take care not to have the windows out of proportion' (6 August 1775). The following year, when Frescati was being sold, Lady Sarah Bunbury passed on Ward's recommendations to the duchess: 'Mr. Ward says it will sell better unfurnished' (29 January 1776).

Ralph Ward also took an active role in Monkstown Church, as churchwarden for three years — 1768 (when he purchased some 'books for the church (costing) … £1-10-0') and again in 1784 and 1785, when his fellow churchwarden (and next-door neighbour in 'Blackrock House') was the unscrupulous Sir John Lees (*see above*). As the incumbent, Dr Jephson, took no interest whatsoever in Monkstown, it was Ward and Lees who did all the groundwork for the new church. It was they who approached Monkstown's 'lords of the soil', Longford and de Vesci, in 1785 for 'a convenient and suitable piece of ground for a new church and churchyard'; the request was granted and building began that same year on the new site 'adjoining the Road of Monkstown', the present location (*see Chapter 4*). Ward had built Viscount de Vesci's house at 26 Merrion Square, North, about twenty years earlier. Since the Vestry minutes for this period are missing, there are no surviving documents to identify the architect of this Georgian church — 'the fairest country church in Ireland', according to the *Hibernian Magazine* of 5 September 1800. However, it is possible that Ralph Ward was responsible. His suicide in 1788 may well have delayed the completion of the building or its consecration until the following year, 1789.

Ward had been for 26 years surveyor general of the Ordnance, at a salary of £400 a year. Interestingly, his will shows that he was worth 'upwards of £18,000' at his death, most of which he left to his only daughter. She had married Mr Read, 'a bricklayer', whose job as a surveyor at Ringsend, earning £200–300 a year, had been obtained for him by Ward. Read was also bequeathed £700 a year, as well as Ward's town and country houses. Ward left his grandson, 'Master Read', £200 a year. He left his wife a mere £300 a year.

CHAPTER 15

Parish officers

Parish and Vestry clerks

> *There goes the parson, oh! illustrious spark,*
> *And there, scarce less illustrious, goes the clerk!*
> William Cowper

The parish clerk — as one of the few literate people in the parish, apart from the clergy and gentry — was a person of importance in most parishes of the eighteenth century. He was often also the Vestry clerk and sometimes the schoolmaster, as in Monkstown. His responsibilities are spelt out handily in this seventeenth-century poem by Christopher Harvey, called 'The Synagogue' (Grosart 1874):

> *The Churche's Bible-Cleark attends*
> *Her utensils, and ends*
> *Her prayers with Amen;*
> *Tunes Psalms, and to the Sacraments*
> *Brings in the elements,*
> *And takes them out again.*

At a time of widespread illiteracy and few prayer books, the parish clerk's role was pivotal. During services he sat in the clerk's desk in the ubiquitous 'three-decker' pulpit and led the responses 'with a loud voice' (Book of Common Prayer, 1662). As one of John Betjeman's 'Church Poems' says:

> *And firmly at the end of prayers*
> *The clerk below the pulpit stairs*
> *Would thunder out, 'Amen'.*

The congregation took their cue from the parish clerk as he steered them through the service, kneeling during the prayers and standing during the Creed and Gospel. He chose the psalms each Sunday and had to intone them, not always very musically. Samuel Pepys was entertained by his trainee parish clerk: 'This day to church where mighty sport to hear our clerk sing out of tune, though his master sit by him and keep tune aloud for the parish' (diary entry, 13 November 1664). The parish clerk was also responsible for the bread and wine for Communion and the vestments.

The parish clerk's guide by Benjamin Payne was first published in London in 1709 and reprinted several times during the eighteenth century. It stressed that, besides being able to read, write and possess some musical skills, the clerk should live an upright life and set a good example, 'otherwise the ignorance and impiety of the clerk may bring an unavoidable scandal …'. Perhaps the author was thinking uneasily of the philandering 'amorous Absolon' in Chaucer's *Miller's Tale*, who travelled around 'sensynge [censing] the wyves of the parisshe faste' and developed 'in his herte swich a love-longynge' for Alison, the miller's young wife (Benson 1988).

The duties of the Vestry clerk were more clerical in nature. Daniel Kinehan, barrister and churchwarden of Taney (and, incidentally, in 1847 the next-door neighbour of John Semple, Junior), defined the Vestry clerk's role: 'To receive instruction from the clergymen and churchwardens for serving notices of vestries, to prepare same, and have them served by Beadle of the parish, to keep up the minutes of the Vestry, and to write out copies of the Parish and Grand Jury Cess' (Ball and Hamilton 1895).

A complete list of the Monkstown parish and Vestry clerks from 1702 to 1872 is given in Appendix 5. The Vestry minutes of 1747–73 illustrate the life of one eighteenth-century parish and Vestry clerk: Edward Lansdale (1747–72). He had five different roles — parish clerk, Vestry clerk, bell-ringer ('towling the bell'), measurer of coal in Dunleary and parish pound-keeper. His starting salary in 1747 was £3 a year, but this jumped dramatically in 1753 following an 'Act of Parliament for the Maintainance of Parish Clerks', which recommended that £10 should be assessed from each parish for its Vestry clerk. The Vestry had to find the extra money by taxing 'the several families in the proportion of ninepence by the house'.

In 1762 Lansdale was appointed parish pound-keeper and also 'sworn mesurer of coals in the port of Dunleary with an allowance of two pence per tun, one half to be paid by the buyer and the other half by the captain of the coal ship'. In 1766 Lansdale was the head of his household with two dependants, according to a census taken by the Rev. Thomas Heany.[1] Two years later he married, possibly for the second time; he wrote the entry in the parish register as 'Edward Lansdall, Clark of the Union of Monkstown, and Elizabeth Smith of the Cyti of Dublin, were married by vertue of a lycense from the Consistory Court of Dublin on the 11th of February 1768, by the Rev. Mr. Thomas Heany, Parish Minister'. This entry was typical of Lansdale's idiosyncratic spelling. Even his own name was spelt incorrectly. Somehow he managed to spell 'licence' nine different ways in the parish register, none of them correct (license, lissons, lycense, lysons, lycenen, lycense, lycens, lycencs, and lycences). Another of his entries reads, 'Charllot Gray, a natef of Jamace, was baptiezed the 10th of Novenbr 1765'.

Edward Lansdale died, apparently unexpectedly, in 1772 after 25 years of service. He was buried in Monkstown on 24 July. After his death there was consternation among the Vestry.

The following May, Thomas Parry presented the parish accounts for the previous four years, during which Lansdale, as parish clerk, had collected and dispensed money on behalf of the churchwardens. The Poor Fund account was short by £18-5-9¾; Lansdale had 'cooked the books' by borrowing from the parish cess to cover up the shortfall. In a contemporary poem, 'The Borough', the Rev. George Crabbe had parodied a supposedly incorruptible parish clerk who had yielded to temptation and siphoned off money from alms dishes (Crabbe 1840). When a clerk who was unaccustomed to handling money suddenly found himself with access to relatively large amounts of money, with little supervision and little chance of detection, it is surprising that it did not happen more often.

The Vestry remained uneasy after this experience and Lansdale's successor, Robert David (1773–82), suffered unfairly from the consequences. There were suggestions that he, too, was 'dipping his hand in the till'. In May 1776 seven of the most influential parishioners (including Lord Ranelagh, Luke Mercer, John Mapas and Isaac Espinasse) were appointed to a special committee 'to inspect into the Poor List and Acc(ounts)'. They met with David at the school, to examine all his vouchers and ledgers. Their judgement cleared David's reputation: they confirmed that 'Robert David has given in a Satisfactory account, both of the Receipts and Disimbursements of the poor Money'. They said that he had been 'faithfull in the same, & that the Report of his having Embazled the money and having Defrauded the poor was a Malicious and groundless Slander'.

In 1826, according to the Parliamentary Debates, a parish clerk in England was supposed to get £10 a year if he attended only one day a week. In Ireland many parish clerks — like John Abbott (parish and Vestry clerk, 1797–1834) — were earning two or three times the English rate, an abuse of the system of church rates. When the 'new' church was proposed in 1823, Monkstown parish found itself in difficulties trying to raise enough money. Archdeacon Lindsay sought the professional opinion of the Right Hon. John Radcliffe (judge of the prerogative court and vicar general) to see whether the parish outgoings could be reduced in any way, saying that 'a careful regulation of our parish affairs is necessary before we enter such difficult undertaking'. Radcliffe wrote back to say that 'as there was no service on common days, the clerk's salary should be 10£'. He added that he did not 'see … why fees should be paid for applotting the cess'. He reminded Lindsay that 'the maximum and minimum thereof [salary of the clerk] is regulated by Act of Parliament'. In spite of obtaining Radcliffe's opinion apparently to the contrary, Abbott's annual salary of £33-5-0 (since 1808) remained the same.

Parish beadles

> *Mr Bumble … was in the full bloom and pride of beadlehood;*
> *his cocked hat and coat were dazzling in the morning sun.*
> Charles Dickens, *Oliver Twist*

The word 'beadle' comes from the Old English *bydel*, meaning 'to bid'. The parish beadle was elected by the Vestry, which he had to attend, and acted as its messenger and servant.

He had to let parishioners know when and where Vestry meetings were to be held. Sometimes, as in Monkstown, he was also the bell-ringer, the grave-digger and the parish constable. (For a list of Monkstown's parish beadles for the years 1806 to *c.* 1875, *see Appendix 5.*)

The duties of the beadle at St John the Evangelist's in Dublin city were spelt out precisely in its Vestry minutes of 20 March 1823 (Hughes 1889) — and those of the Monkstown beadle would have been similar:

> 'He is obliged to be in attendance at the outer door, whenever the same shall be opened for Divine Service; and he is to preserve strict order in the porch of the Church during the continuance of Divine Service.
>
> He is obliged to keep the space opposite the Church and the avenue leading thereto cleanly swept.
>
> He is obliged to serve the Parishioners with all notices of Vestry.
>
> He is to hold himself in readiness to attend the Churchwardens on all lawful occasions.
>
> He is required to attend the Parishioners in making lawful seizures or distresses for Rent on being pd the customary fees.
>
> He is required to keep a Bell for the purpose of notifying throughout the Parish all casualties, such as articles lost, stolen or strayed.
>
> He is obliged to appear on all Parochial occasions in the Parish costume, in a large brown livery coat and cocked hat.'

A beadle's livery or uniform was most important since it gave authority to the wearer. St John's beadles wore a brown livery, while the beadles of Donnybrook wore 'a long blue coat with brass buttons', matching 'trowsers' and hat. Monkstown's beadles also wore distinctive livery. They were supplied with a greatcoat and cocked hat, which were extremely expensive and rather splendid affairs (costing several hundred euro in today's money), needing frequent replacement. The cocked hat was three-cornered, with its brim permanently turned up. Unfortunately there is no record of the colour of either item.

James McDonald, parish beadle during 1806–19, was supplied with a new coat every year between 1806 and 1809, and a new cocked hat in 1810. His coats seemed to vary markedly in price, costing between £4-11s and £2-3s, while the cocked hat was even more exorbitant, at £3-7s-7d — more than half his annual salary of £5. McDonald was also the grave-digger from 1803 to 1809. In 1815 the cost of his official outfit was as follows: the material for the greatcoat cost £1-16s-5½, while the tailor who made it charged 11s-3d. McDonald's salary by now, as beadle and bell-ringer, was £9-2s a year. He also earned generous tips for delivering letters (for example, 'Paid for distributing letters etc. relative to the Charity Sermon, 16/3').

By 1818 McDonald — who was either elderly or ill — was unable to cope alone, so Samuel Overin was appointed as an assistant beadle, at an annual salary of four guineas, until the death of McDonald the following year. Then Samuel Overin was appointed in his place and served for the next seven years until 1826, kitted out appropriately: as the Vestry minutes of 12 April 1819 note, 'Resolved … that a cocked hat and coat be provided for the use of the beadle during his attendance at Divine Service'. On 3 July 1821 Lord John George

Beresford, archbishop of Dublin, confirmed 51 candidates at Monkstown; among them was Samuel Overin 'Sen' [Senior], the beadle, and his fifteen-year-old son, Samuel 'Junr', both of 'Black Rock'.

Grave-diggers sometimes worked covertly with body-snatchers or 'resurrection men', such as the two grave-diggers of St Andrew's in Suffolk Street, one of whom was sent to prison in 1732 for allowing graves to be robbed under his very nose (Fleetwood 1988). In 1826, when George Hughes was appointed Monkstown beadle and grave-digger, he was specifically instructed to 'dig the graves himself — and do not allow any person to dig for him, except it be in his own presence and under his own eye'. Hughes was supplied with the tools of his two trades — his beadle's greatcoat and 'a spade, shovel and pick, 13/11' for his grave-digging duties.

Often the beadle also doubled up as the parish constable since the duties of the two positions tended to overlap. This first happened in 1854, when William Martin, the parish constable (1854–63), was also employed as the beadle and dressed appropriately: 'Wm. Martin, Clothing by order Revd. Mr. Rooke, £5-11s-7d'. At this time the bell-ringer (Charles Riggs) and grave-digger (George Argue) had separate posts, earning 10/– each a month, while Martin was given 16/– for four Sundays' attendance as parish constable.

In 1862 the parish of Taney dispensed with the services of their beadle (Ball and Hamilton 1895). However, Monkstown continued with the post, although it seems to have stopped employing the constable in around 1864. (Parish constables were discontinued in England in 1872.) In 1864 a new beadle, Christopher Davis, was appointed, apparently dressed as splendidly as ever: 'Hat and goldband for Beadle, 16/–' (25 August 1864) and 'Coat and vest for Beadle, £3-15-6' (3 September 1864). He was fulfilling the traditional duties: 'Posting notices of Vestry meeting, 1/–' and 'Posting notices of Fem(ale) Education Meeting, 6d' (19 March 1864), 'Davis for posting notices, 2/–' (19 November 1864). He was also acting as the grave-digger and general factotum: 'A hoe for the use of beadle, 1/10' (8 December 1865), 'Davis removing rubbish, 3/–' (1868), 'Davis for sowing grass seeds, 5/–' (26 June 1870) and 'Davis digging ground etc, 15/–' (April 1871). Christopher Davis, the last of the Monkstown beadles, died, probably of overwork, in about 1875.

Parish constables

Before there was an organised police force each parish was responsible for law and order within its boundaries. To do this it employed parish constables, whose duties included supervising the parish stocks, whipping vagrants where necessary, making sure that the ale houses were orderly and that beggars were not a nuisance, and collecting fines. Another important function in seaside parishes was helping with shipwrecks, although this has not been documented in Monkstown. (For a list of Monkstown parish constables for the years 1807 to 1863, *see Appendix 5*.)

Ironically, the dictates of the Monkstown Vestry could sound very authoritarian towards their own constables, who were themselves supposed to uphold law and order. For example, the Vestry minutes of 30 March 1807 state 'That Thomas Connors, Alexander Watson and

George Hanlon, Master Porters, be appointed Parish Constables to act on Dunleary Quay without salary — and that it be notified to them that if they suffer pilfering of coals on said Quay, the Parish will take the proper steps to have them removed'. Again, on 12 April 1819 the minutes record, 'Resolved that the Non-attendance at Church of Richard Martin, Parish Constable, be taken into consideration on Whit Monday next, and that he be informed of this Resolution'. It seems that the constable was in trouble again on 30 May that year, when the minutes state, 'Resolved that it be intimated to Rd. Martin, the Parish constable, that if he do not discharge his duty as Parish constable more to the satisfaction of the parishioners that they will appoint another in his place at the next Easter Monday'. Despite these reprimands, Constable Richard Martin served the parish for 21 years, from 1808 to 1829. William Martin, possibly his son or grandson, later served as parish constable, from 1854 to 1863, and was the last identifiable person in that position; he also acted as beadle for the same period.

Parish stocks

The only surviving stocks in Ireland — in the crypt of Christ Church Cathedral.

Stocks have a very ancient history, stretching back to Old Testament times. For example, Jeremiah 20:2 says, 'Then Pashur smote Jeremiah the prophet, and put him in the stocks that were in the high gate of Benjamin, which was by the house of the Lord'. Again, Proverbs 7:22 states, 'He goeth after her straightway, as an ox goeth to the slaughter, or as a fool to the correction of the stocks'. Acts 16:19–24 relates how 'they caught Paul and Silas … and brought them to the magistrates … and the magistrates rent off their clothes, and commanded to beat them. And when they had laid many stripes upon them, they cast them into prison … and made their feet fast in the stocks'.

Stocks were still being used in Ireland up until about 1813. Each parish had 'a pair of stocks' (one set) to punish minor offenders, such as beggars and vagrants, drunkards and prostitutes. The stocks consisted of a wooden seat, where the culprit sat, with his or her ankles confined by holes in a pair of planks, held rigid by upright posts. Sometimes there were corresponding holes for the wrists. Pillories were similar except that the person had to stand, with his neck and hands secured. Since offenders in the stocks or pillory were exposed to public derision and abuse, the word 'pillory' came to mean 'expose to public ridicule'. The set of stocks in the crypt of Christ Church Cathedral is the only surviving specimen in Ireland. It has three pairs of holes to suit offenders of all sizes, from 4 inches for a grown man to 2½ inches for a child.

In Ireland, according to a paper read at the Royal Irish Academy in 1886 (Frazer 1888), stocks were said to have fallen into disuse from around the 1770s and pillories later. However, Taney parish, Dundrum, built new stocks in 1797 and the Vestry accounts of 1796–7 list the various expenses incurred (Ball and Hamilton 1895).

B. McClune for Timber	£1-17-3	
L. Kearney for Smith's Work	4-4	
Carriage of Timber	2-2	
Padlock and 3 Key	7-0½	
Carpenter's Work and Painting	£1-14-1½	
	£4-4-11	
John Wright for Masonry	£1-0-0	
	£5-4-11	

The earliest Monkstown Vestry book, covering the years 1744–77, records that three pairs of stocks were built in the parish, presumably at a similar cost to those at Taney — in 1747, 1753 and 1764 — indicating a 'life' of only between six and ten years. Perhaps this is because they were understandably vandalised by their potential victims. Since the next Vestry book for the years 1777–1805 is missing, it is not known whether the stocks of 1764 was the last set built. None are mentioned in the Vestry book of 1805–29. The minutes of the period show the following entries:

Monday 20th April, 1747: For a pair of stocks at Monkstown to be cess'd on the parish of Monkstown singly, £1-10s-0d.

Monday, 23rd April, 1753: And whereas a stocks is wanted in the Parish of Monkstown, it is agreed that the sum of £2-10s sterling be cessed on the Parish of Monkstown only for that purpose.

Monday 23rd April, 1764: For a pair of stocks to be erected at the churchyard gate, £3-0-0.

Monday 25th June, 1764: That £3 sterling be expended by the church wardens of said parish for the erecting of stocks in the town of Dunleary.

In Britain the use of the pillory was abolished, except for perjury, in 1815 and totally in 1837, the first year of Queen Victoria's reign. Ireland seems to have given up the use of pillories and stocks sooner; there are newspaper accounts of both being still in use up to 1813, for offences other than perjury. For example, *The Times* of London on 27 October 1813 reported that a man in Dublin, found guilty of indecent assault in Merrion Square, was 'sentenced to be publicly pilloried, between the hours of 12 and 1; to be imprisoned in the common gaol for 12 months, and not to be discharged until he gave security for future good behaviour, himself in 200 lb [£200] and 2 sureties in 100 lb [£100] each'. Meanwhile, in Limerick, the same newspaper, quoting *The Connaught Journal*, described how 'two females were exhibited for an hour in the stocks, nr the Exchange … as a punishment for forestalling. The Mayor is determined in the most exemplary manner, to punish regrators, by whose practises the price of provisions is enhanced on the poor; and on Friday, a noted forestaller of turf and potatoes, named Piers, was pilloried'. ('Forestalling' was the buying up of goods by 'regrators' and reselling them at a higher price, originally an indictable offence.) Interestingly, the pillory was still in use in Delaware, USA, until 1905.

Parish pound-keepers

A pound was a rectangular, walled-in enclosure where cattle or other animals were impounded or shut up. Pounds date from medieval times in England but have a far older history in Ireland where, owing to the importance of cattle in Irish culture, they pre-date St Patrick and are mentioned in the Brehon Laws. In the eighteenth century most parishes had a pound, with its resident pound-keeper, who usually lived 'over the shop'.

From the evidence of the Monkstown Vestry books, the pound at Monkstown (whose location is unknown) is first mentioned in the minutes of 20 April 1747 ('For gate lock and post for the pound of Monkstown to be cess'd on Monkstown Parish singly, 9/6'). It is mentioned again in 1772: 'For rebuilding the Parish Pound of Monkstown, £4-13'. There were several other pounds in the Union. There was one at Dalkey, the 'Killyny' [Killiney]

The well-preserved pound at Stepaside, used up until at least 1986.

pound was at 'Laughlin's Town' [Loughlinstown] and the 'Tullough' [Tullow] pound was at Carrickmines. (For a list of the Monkstown pound-keepers for the years 1759 to 1818, *see Appendix 5.*)

Each parish was responsible for the building and maintenance of its own pound and raised money for this by applotments (*see Chapter 13*). In the Union of Monkstown, between 1749 and 1810, pounds cost between £5 and £10 to build, while most repairs cost less than £1. Meanwhile, the pound was bringing in money for the parish: the owner of each impounded animal had to pay a fine of 2d per day, as well as the 'poundage' or payment for the animal's release. Monkstown's pound alone brought in £9 between Easter 1805 and Easter 1806.

The pound-keeper had to report regularly to the minister and churchwardens, so that the animals could be advertised, if necessary. Animals found straying would be brought to the nearest pound (which should be within three miles) and kept there, or animals could be confined temporarily to ensure a person's good behaviour or the payment of rent. Animals could also be 'distrained' or confiscated, in lieu of unpaid tithes. Animals found together had to be kept together in the same pound and not split up.

The size of pounds varied. In 1615 a pound was built outside Cork city, measuring 40 feet by 30 feet (Healy 1914). The existence of the old animal pound at Stepaside was identified by Rob Goodbody (1993); it is still well preserved today and measures 35½ feet deep by 25½ feet wide, with an entrance of 41 inches; the walls are 19 inches thick and nearly 8 feet high.[2] This pound was used for straying horses until at least 1986.[3]

In 1805 John Dunbar was appointed the Monkstown parish pound-keeper, at a salary of £5-13-9. He was also parish applotter and appraiser. Lords Longford and de Vesci, as 'lords of the soil', charged a ground rent of five guineas a year for the pound, paid by the Vestry while Dunbar was pound-keeper, as recorded in the Vestry minutes of 31 April 1805. In 1807 Dunbar was also appointed as one of the two parish constables for the Union of Monkstown (salary £10). In 1807 and 1808 he was again appointed the applotter of the parish and county cess, and appraiser for Monkstown and its united parishes.

In 1822 Sir William Betham offered to build the parish pound 'on His Ground on the Bray Road at Stradbrook' (he lived in 'Stradbrook House'). The Vestry decided to accept his offer. Betham was to appoint the pound-keeper himself, while the parish reimbursed him the salary of six guineas a year (Vestry minutes of 8 April 1822).

Most pounds fell into ruin owing to disuse since it became no longer a legal requirement to impound stray animals when the owner was known. The last mention of the Monkstown pound was recorded in the Poor Fund book on 14 December 1853: 'By Cash, Davis poor Prot. to release cow out of pound, 13/-.' ('Poor Prot.' was short for 'poor Protestant'.)

Officers of health

The Great Famine began in late 1845, after potato blight had struck in the early summer of that year, and lasted officially until 1849, although its effects were felt right though 1850. Although the Vestry minutes for this period are not extant, other documents offer a glimpse of what it was like in Monkstown at that time. The twin spectres of famine and fever visited even this parish, one of the wealthiest in Dublin. Fever killed probably ten times more than hunger. In the maligned 'eastern' end of the parish, the crowded and poverty-stricken courts of Kingstown provided ideal conditions for the spread of disease. The main infectious diseases, besides cholera, were typhoid ('black fever') and relapsing fever ('yellow fever'), both spread by lice. Those who had, as children, been exposed to endemic typhoid built up some immunity to the disease, whereas relief workers (particularly the middle-aged and middle class) were particularly vulnerable. Many clergy and doctors died in their efforts to help. Dr John Houston (aged 43), for example, died on 2 August 1845 and Dr Clement Taylor (28), surgeon to Dalkey Dispensary, on 26 October 1845.[4]

Many of the gentry in Monkstown worked extremely hard to help the poor, among them Lord Cloncurry of 'Maretimo', who chaired the Famine Relief Committee of 1845. Although the majority were Roman Catholic, a substantial number of the poor and starving were described as 'P. Prots', meaning 'Poor Protestants'. The term frequently appeared in the Poor Fund books and vouchers of the day. One entry, dated 22 September 1849, read, 'A Distressed Prot. family, 5 of whom have been taken away by cholera, £1'. Even the local grave-digger, George Argue (paid 2/6 for digging a grave for 'P. Prot.'), needed assistance; on 11 August 1846, 5/- was issued to him, recording that he was 'in great distress'. (For Argue's biography, *see below*.)

Each year the Monkstown Easter Vestry appointed five officers of health, who were like

The church's officer of health could authorise free coffins for the poor and destitute of Monkstown parish during the Great Famine and afterwards.

FORM OF OBTAINING COFFINS,

At the Expense of the Parish of MONKSTOWN, *sanctioned by the Church-Wardens.*

In cases of extreme destitution or where it has been satisfactorily ascertained that the surviving Relatives of deceased have not means for providing them.

NAME OF DECEASED.	AGE.	RESIDENCE.	DATE OF DEMISE.
Polly Keating	82	Collins Court Black Rock	7 March 1857

ORDER,

Supply the Coffin required as above, which charge to account of the Church-Wardens of Monkstown.

W Walmitt *Officer of Health.*

To Mr. *Hilton*
Contractor for supplying Coffins for the Parish of Monkstown.

the public health managers of today. These men included the rector, two churchwardens and two parishioners, who were often doctors; in 1828, for example, Dr Farrell and Dr William Plant were appointed. Other parishes were also active in these matters. In *Saunders's News-Letter* of 8 October 1858, the officers of health of St Peter's parish, Dublin, reported 'the following return of nuisances abated in the parish … privies cleansed, 228; ashpits do [ditto], 222; yards do, 133; sewers do, 9; premises whitewashed, 309. Total: 901'.

Whitewashing houses hit by epidemic fever was thought to slow down the spread of infection. During an epidemic in 1819–20 the Monkstown Vestry 'resolved that the sum of ten pounds be levied off the (Monkstown) Union (of parishes) … this present year for the purpose of white washing and cleansing the houses of the poor in which fever prevails' (Vestry minutes, 4 April 1820). Dr Arthure and four laymen were appointed as officers of health to ensure that this task was carried out. Some receipts survive to illustrate the procedure: on 27 October 1845 the officers of health bought whitewash and brushes, costing 15/8, for a house in Albert Road, Kingstown, while on 9 May 1849 the officers, Richard Walnutt and Samuel Whitely, purchased two lime buckets and some brushes.

It was also the responsibility of the officers of health to authorise the 'contractor for supplying coffins' to provide them 'at the Expense of the Parish of Monkstown, sanctioned by the Church-Wardens. In cases of extreme destitution or where it has been satisfactorily ascertained that the surviving Relatives of deceased have not means for providing them'. There are several bundles of these 'Forms of obtaining Coffins' among the Vestry archives. An officer of health filled in the personal details of the deceased on the form, which he gave to the bereaved family who had to get it countersigned by the clergy or churchwardens. Usually the fee (2/6) for opening the grave was waived and money given from the Poor Fund to cover the funeral expenses.

In December 1845 Mr A. Hilton, the contractor for supplying coffins, was reimbursed for five small (3/6) and five large (8/6) coffins. In 1849 his bill to the parish listed the names of fourteen destitute people who had died between 10 July and 28 August that year. It was the youngest and the oldest who were most at risk — seven of the dead listed were less than 4 years old, four were over 64, and the other three were aged 14, 43 and 46. Inquests were not generally held: none of these names was entered in the relevant coroner's inquest book, which listed three other names for this seven-week period.

The church's officers of health could sanction money for anything to do with public health that they felt was reasonable. Richard Walnutt, for example, sent a Poor Fund voucher, dated 3 September 1849, to Mr Elias Arnold, the churchwarden (1848–9), asking him 'Please to give bearer ten pence for the use of his Ass & Dray in carrying a poor Woman home that took ill in the street'. Another voucher said, 'Mr. Arnold, please pay bearer Laurence Byrne the sum of 12/6d for Tying and delivering to poor, 8 Tons of straw during the years 1849 and 1850. R. Walnutt. Sam C. Whitely'. (Straw was used for bedding and insulation over the terrible winter of 1849–50, when so many died of cholera.)

One short angry letter among the Vestry papers gives a good idea of how much the parish actually helped. The letter is undated but is addressed to Mr Arnold, churchwarden (so it must have been during the year 1848 or 1849): 'My D...r Sir, As I understand that a sum of £33 has been assessed for coffins for this parish, and a further sum of £50 for whitewashing, straw, etc, etc, I trust you will take care of us in this district, so that we may get our proper proportion of the funds, as the Kingstown district would swallow up double these sums, unless closely watched. [Unreadable signature], Black Rock, Tuesday.'

The writer obviously thought that the 'eastern' end of Monkstown parish (Kingstown) was depriving the western end (Blackrock) of its fair share of available funds. If coffins cost between 2/6 (for infants) and 8/6, £33 would have bought somewhere between 100 and 200 coffins, depending on their size. Although £50 seemed a huge sum for straw and whitewashing, it would not actually have gone very far: referring to costs mentioned above, it might buy a lot of straw (if 12/6 bought 8 tons) but would not whitewash many houses (if it cost 15/8 for whitewash and brushes for one house alone).

In the summer of 1849 one Monkstown parishioner decided to organise a 'bazaar' in the 'Harbour Yard' at Kingstown in aid of 'the distressed poor', regardless of denomination. The notice in *Saunders's News-Letter* of 6 June read:

> The Bazaar will be held by a few benevolent ladies of Kingstown and its immediate neighbours and the proceedings arising therefrom will be distributed amongst the distressed poor, who will be recommended by their respective clergy, without distinction of religion, as was the case during the past years of distress; and also to the different charities on the same principle. The few individuals who have exerted themselves, attended with considerable expense and trouble, for so desirable an object, most earnestly hope that the humane and benevolent inhabitants of this rising locality, both ladies and gentlemen, will contribute some trifles, in any manner most convenient, either in clothes suitable for the poor, fancy needlework, toys or sweetmeats for refreshment, as a table for the latter will be kept. All such contributions will be thankfully received by Mrs. Edward Ward Drewe, Valetta House, Kingstown. [Mrs Drewe was the wife of Colonel Edward Drewe, awarded the prized Waterloo medal for his bravery at that battle, and a town commissioner of Kingstown in 1845; *see Chapter 22*.]

Even though the Famine was officially over by the end of 1849, dire poverty still existed in Monkstown the following year. A voucher issued on Christmas Eve, 24 December 1850, recorded 'Four special objects of distress, £1-0-0'. The problem of poverty was not solved overnight. The poor continued to live in squalid hovels and to die of infectious disease. The Monkstown Parochial Union Benefit Society was founded in 1816 as a form of voluntary health insurance (*see Chapter 17*). Even in 1869 the 'Third Class', the very poor, had a high rate of sickness and death, compared to one death in the 'Second Class' and none in the 'First'.

Parish sextons

The title 'sexton' has been used since the sixteenth century to mean the church officer who looked after the fabric of the church and was usually also the bell-ringer and grave-digger (sometimes the parish beadle, too). Sextonesses, like Rachel Monks (née Dunn, 1761–87), cleaned the church and washed the linen. (For a list of Monkstown's sextons for the years

1744 to 1997, *see Appendix 5*.)

Several of Monkstown's sextons have served for lengthy periods. A recent sexton, Mr Ronnie Blay (1975–97), who died in office, served until his death at the age of 88. One Sunday morning in 1997 he was found lying beside the Communion table: he had died suddenly while preparing for the 8am service, a task he had carried out faithfully for the previous 22 years (Cullen 1997). But the record must be held by George Argue, sexton and grave-digger for Monkstown from *c.* 1810 to 1864, a term of over 50 years. The following is his story.

In February 1861 a keen local historian stood by the wall of Carrickbrennan Graveyard, idly watching the elderly grave-digger at his work. As he shovelled the earth out of the ground, an 'old-fashioned' shoe was uncovered (Stokes 1895). The bystander remarked jokingly that it must have belonged to one of the monks of Monkstown. He was totally taken aback when he heard the old man's reply, to the effect that it more likely belonged to one of his drowned shipmates from the 1807 *Rochdale* disaster. His name was George Argue, and he said that he had been the grave-digger at Monkstown for the past 50 years. At this point he was a fit 83 and carried on working for another three years. The year before, he had cleared the snow around the church for 3/-, as the Vestry minutes record on 23 December 1860.

As a young man George Argue had a very different occupation — that of soldier. In November 1807 he and his friends of the 97th Regiment embarked at the Pidgeon House in the troop-carrier the *Rochdale*. Just as the ship was weighing anchor, the officer in command realised that a 'box of valuables' had been forgotten and sent George back to Holles Street to fetch it. He returned only to find that the ship had sailed without him.

After the *Rochdale* left harbour, a snowstorm blew up during the evening and night, driving the ship helplessly along the coast. The ship passed so close to Dunleary that people there could hear the soldiers shouting and firing their muskets, but the snow was so thick that they could not see them. The sailors threw out several anchors, but the cables snapped with the momentum of the ship. A crowd of people — perhaps George Argue was among them — raced along the shore, trying to keep up with the ship, which was being driven towards Seapoint. They had to dive for cover as the soldiers shot towards land, but were unaware, owing to the thick snowstorm and the darkness, of how close they actually were. The doomed ship was wrecked on the rocks beneath the Martello tower at Seapoint and everyone on board drowned. The Embarkation Return listed '265 souls, not one individual of whom is known to have escaped', including 42 women and 29 children, as reported in the *Freeman's Journal* of 21 November 1807.

The *Prince of Wales* was wrecked at Blackrock in the same storm, with the loss of another 120 lives. The loss of the two ships and their 385 passengers led directly to the building of the 'asylum' harbour at Kingstown, which began ten years later with the laying of the first stone of the east pier on 31 May 1817.

One can imagine Argue's mixed feelings at his lucky escape. Instead of continuing as a soldier he became the sexton at Monkstown: he cleaned the church windows for £2, he removed the ventilators for 4/4, he mowed the churchyard for 5/-. He also dug graves, at 2/6 a burial. One sombre St Stephen's Day in 1838 he shovelled out the hard earth in

211

Carrickbrennan Graveyard for the grave of two children who had died on the sea-passage from Gibraltar, where their father served as a soldier. During the terrible years of the Great Famine he would have dug hundreds more. The graveyard of Carrickbrennan was the burial ground for the whole area — for Protestants, Catholics and 'dissenters' alike. During the 1840s Argue found himself on the breadline: he was given 12/6 in August 1843 by order of the churchwardens, when he was described as a 'poor Protestant'. The Poor Fund frequently paid for his clothes and boots, and a voucher of 11 August 1846 records, 'Argue in great distress, 5/-'.

Years later, on that day in 1861, he found himself digging yet another grave that must have brought back poignant memories of his narrow escape 54 years earlier. The grave was for three young seamen of the *Ajax* who had drowned while helping their captain in a rescue operation. The 'old-fashioned' shoe Argue had uncovered belonged, he thought, to one of his *Rochdale* shipmates. From the two ships, the *Rochdale* and the *Prince of Wales*, wrecked in 1807, 104 bodies had been buried in that very spot.[5]

George Argue and Phoebe, his wife, lived at 8 Albert Place, one of the courts of Kingstown, where they raised their family of boys: George (b. 1828), Robert (b. 1829; d. 1831), Henry (b. 1831) and Robert (b. 1834). Phoebe, eleven years younger than George, died before him, in October 1861, aged 72, and was buried in Carrickbrennan Graveyard. George was now living in 3 Alma Place, Monkstown, beside Mrs Mary Arnett, the sextoness. By this time Nos 1 to 3 Alma Place had become known as 'the Sextons' Cottages'. Argues were still living there in 1889 (when William and Thomas Argue of 'Sextons' Cottages' were confirmed).

One of Argue's last claims to the Poor Fund was on a scrap of paper, in shaky handwriting, dated 19 April 1864: 'Opening and closeing a Grave for the Remains of J. Blackmor. George Argue, 2s 6d.' He died nine years later, in December 1870. Beside his entry in the Monkstown Burial Register his age was given as '90', with the comment, 'For 40 years Grave Digger in this parish'. Who was right? According to George himself, it was closer to 50 years.

CHAPTER 16

Schools of the parish

That the Secretary of the Select Vestry do inform Mr. Hackett [the schoolmaster]
that it having come under their knowledge that he is keeping poultry etc.
in the playground of the children and that such poultry frequently trespass
on the ground surrounding the church, Mr. Hackett be requested forthwith
to discontinue keeping them as being unsuitable to such a confined space.
Select Vestry minutes, 10 September 1877

The doors of Monkstown Parish School opened in 1791 and closed on 31 December 1986. The schoolhouse in the church grounds, although over 200 years old, was not the first school in Monkstown. Children were receiving education in the parish in 1723 and possibly even earlier.

The genesis of English education in Ireland dates back two centuries before this time, to the troubled year of 1536 — two years after Henry VIII had finalised his break with the Roman Catholic Church. Under Lord Leonard Gray, the new Dublin parliament, consisting largely of Catholic nobility from the Pale, passed the Act of Supremacy, acknowledging Henry as 'the only supreme head on earth of the whole Church of Ireland called Hibernia Ecclesia'. It also stipulated 'that parochial English schools should be established in the country, and that all clergymen should be bound by oath to endeavour to learn and teach the English tongue to all and every being under his rule, and to bid the beads in the English tongue, and preach the Word of God in English, if he can preach'.

Monkstown's charity school

In May 1723 Monkstown's perpetual curate, Allan Maddison, wrote, 'There is no Free School-master in my parishes [of Monkstown and Stillorgan], but there are three school-masters Licensed, viz. Manassah Evans, Thomas Perry & Matthew Roch'.[1] Manassah Evans, one of the first teachers in Monkstown, must surely have been a Welshman, and possibly Perry (or Parry) too, suggesting close links between Dunleary and Wales. Teachers were offered derisory salaries then. The Vestry minutes of 7 April 1760 record the money received by the church cleaner and teacher of the day: Mrs Elizabeth Range received £2 'for washing the Linnen and Cleaning the Church' and 'For a schoolmaster for the parish of Monkstown, £2-0-0'.

Although the whereabouts of the school referred to above is unknown, it was financed by annual charity sermons, the big money-spinners of the day (*see Chapter 17*). In 1767 the patron of Monkstown, Dr Charles Jackson (also bishop of Kildare, 1765–90), preached on the school's behalf and a collection of £70 was made; the following year Dr Young, bishop of Leighlin, raised £60 from his sermon (Ball 1902). At the Easter Vestry of 1768 the most influential parishioners — Lord Ranelagh (the treasurer), Luke Mercer, Robert Lanford, George Glover, Dr Benjamin Domvile, Isaac Espinasse, the two churchwardens (Ralph Ward and John Malpas) and Thomas Heany, the perpetual curate — were elected governors of the new charity school. The Vestry minutes of 4 April 1768 record: 'Resolved at the same time, that the schoolmaster of the parish shall be entitled to the following prices and no more for teaching: To speel [*sic*] by the quarter, £0-2-2; To read, 3/3; To write and arithmatick, 4/4'. This came to the lordly salary of £1-19s a year. This apparent pittance was actually double that of Carysfort Royal School in Wicklow, where the teacher in 1784 was paid 1/1 for spelling per quarter, 1/6 for reading and writing, and 2/6 for reading, writing and 'cyphering' (Quane 1961).

Apart from the clergy and gentry, most of the parishioners were illiterate. The notable exceptions to this were the parish clerk and the Vestry clerk (often the same person), who had to be literate in order to write up the Vestry minutes and parish notices, make copies of applotments and read the responses to the congregation at Sunday services (*see Chapter 15*). As a result, the two posts of clerk and teacher were often combined. This practice seems to have started in 1787 with David Christian, who, besides being the parish clerk, was also the 'English school-master', teaching the children of the parish the '3 Rs' (*see Appendix 5*).

An advertisement in *Saunders's News-Letter* on 26 July 1779 tells us more about the aims and activities of the 'charity working school' in Monkstown. It was announced that the annual charity sermon would be preached by the Rev. Joseph Stack. The children were said to be 'the distressed offspring of Protestant Parents (who were) instructed in useful work, and in the Principles of the Christian Religion ... To guard them from an early engagement to a vagrant or vicious Course of life, and to preserve them from the influence of bad company and bad example, they (were) dieted, clothed, and lodged in a convenient house provided for the Purpose, and when qualified, (were) apprenticed to some useful Trade'. The advertisement also mentioned that 'a large quantity of choice herring nets (were to) be sold at same school'. Perhaps making nets was an example of the 'useful work' done by the children, or maybe the nets were surplus fishing nets that were sometimes sold for covering fruit trees.

Monkstown Parish School (1791–1986)

As soon as Monkstown's Georgian church was completed (1789), the parishioners began to plan a parish school for 'the Children of the Parish of every Denomination'. (The charity school may have actually closed by this time since the foundation of the new school was described as a 're-establishment'.)

The first step was a charity sermon on 26 September 1790, which raised £100-1-6, showing that the parishioners strongly supported the foundation of a school. Between

November 1790 and March 1791 a house was rented in Blackrock (for £6-16-6) where 40 to 50 boys were 'instructed in Reading, Writing, Arithmetic, and Netting, and from 30 to 40 Girls in the same, as also in Spinning, Knitting, and Plain-work, most of whom are provided with a comfortable Breakfast'.

In the meantime, the parishioners 'erected a Parish School House on part of said Ground near the Church'. Nowadays, the church dwarfs the school, but when the church and school were originally built beside each other they were much further apart: Semple still had not built his huge transepts nor McCurdy his chancel (*see Chapters 5 and 7*). There were also another 18 square yards inside the church grounds (taken in 1965 with the widening of Carrickbrennan Road) and the 1962 extension at the back of the building did not exist, so there was more room for the children to play around the school.[2]

Monkstown Parish School opened in April 1791, with 47 boys and 33 girls on the roll. According to the 1826 report of the Commissioners of the Irish Education Inquiry, the money for this schoolhouse was raised by 'public subscription'. There were 30 subscribers on the list, headed by the lord chancellor (who donated £34-2-6 'for Building', as well as an annual £5-13-9). The two largest donations, of £50 each, came from John Lees and William Digges La Touche, who, as the treasurer, accepted subscriptions at his bank in Castle Street. A staggering £395-8-9 was raised in this way by 15 June 1791 and £61-3-3 promised annually.

Written into the licence of the Rev. James Dunn, the perpetual curate during 1802–4, was his obligation, among others, to 'teach, or cause to be taught, an English school within the same United Parishes as the Laws in that case require'.

Monkstown schoolhouse, as it looks today. The notice below one of the windows on the front of the building reads, 'MONKSTOWN PRIMARY SCHOOL, built 1791' (this was written in September 1959, probably replacing an earlier notice).

The teachers' salaries had improved markedly since 1768; now the master and mistress earned £38 between them for nine months (1 November 1790 to 31 July 1791). The school was kitted out with new desks (£8-8-6½), books and stationery (£10-10-6½) and 'utensils' (£4-17-6), probably for the children's breakfasts for the nine-month period (7,942 meals served, costing £31-2-3) and Sunday dinners (118 meals, costing £1-13-6). Donations of clothes flooded in; these were awarded as 'premiums', or prizes, to the schoolchildren for good work and behaviour. Grace, wife of William Digges La Touche, was a great supporter and presented eight spinning wheels and two 'twisting wheels' to the school, as well as eight pairs of shoes, three gowns, 21 petticoats, 22 caps, eight bibs and aprons, and nine pairs of stockings.

By August 1791 the children had completed so much handiwork that it is difficult to see how they would have had much time for the all-important '3 Rs'. The notice for the charity sermon on 21 August that year listed their achievements: 'work done by the girls' consisted of 40 shirts, ten handkerchiefs, eighteen bibs and aprons, 21 petticoats, 22 caps, nine pairs of stockings, 54 dozen letters marked, 72lb of hemp spun and 3lb of flax spun. Meanwhile, the boys had made ten fishing nets and one garden net.

By 1800, the school was thriving, with over 100 boys and girls attending. It was described that year in idyllic terms in a poem (printed in the *Hibernian Magazine* on 5 September) dedicated to Sir John Lees, secretary of the Irish Post Office, parishioner and churchwarden of Monkstown:

> *If we desire to see the children's friend*
> *To Monkstown School our willing steps we bend:*
> *There decency and industry prevail,*
> *Saving the poor from hospital and jail;*
> *There godlike charity has fix'd her reign,*
> *Her blest abode; nor can we ask in vain;*
> *The terms of charity are never hard,*
> *Love and compassion are their own reward;*
> *The soul which succours modest worth distrest,*
> *Can with itself enjoy a noble feast!*

The 'children's friend' referred to in this poem was Grace Digges La Touche, who visited the school often. A footnote to the poem further eulogised this virtuous hive of activity: 'The school also is well worthy of the traveller's notice. It is perfectly clean and healthy, removed from the infection and bad example of the city. Eight females are boarded, and 100 poor children of both sexes are breakfasted, and instructed in spinning, knitting, needle-work, basket-making, reading, writing, which contributes so essentially to the relief of the neighbouring poor, to the welfare of society, to the peace of the neighbourhood, to promote morality and industry; that the author strongly recommends this school to the more serious care and visitation of the ladies in the vicinity of Monkstown.' The school had other 'friends' too. For example, the Easter Vestry minutes of 20 September 1835 record that Mr J.G. Emmerson donated eight pews in Monkstown Church to the schoolchildren, both day and Sunday schools. (This gift would have cost Mr Emmerson almost €20,000 in today's money.)

A rather different picture was given in an advertisement printed in *Saunders's News-Letter* on 29 December 1831 and 1 January 1832. The announcement was for a charity sermon for Monkstown school (also for Clonkeen, *see below*), to be preached on New Year's Day, one week after the opening of Semple's new church (on Christmas Day 1831). It painted the average inhabitant of Monkstown in rather unflattering terms, reminding its readers that:

> 'All who know anything of the Parish of Monkstown are aware that it abounds with temptations to Idleness and Vice of every description. There is therefore no need of any stronger argument in favour of the Institutions, which are the subject of this appeal. In these Schools the Children of the Poor are not only kept out of the way of that contamination, which, if suffered to taint the ears of their *Childhood*, generally leads to misconduct in their *Manhood*, but they are also fitted by a religious and useful education, and by the forming of orderly industrious habits, to fill a place in the community, not less important because an humble one.
>
> (The governors and governesses) earnestly request those who would not that the poor should be left a prey to ignorance, to visit the schools, and become themselves eyewitnesses (of) a combination of useful Education, good Discipline, and strict Economy, seldom if ever surpassed.
>
> It is particularly submitted to the consideration of Protestant parishioners that if these schools should be abandoned many Protestant children who now by means of their liberality and carefully brought up in the doctrine and discipline of the Established Church would be left entirely without the means of acquiring any useful knowledge.'

Schoolmasters over the years

The school building — 'a good house, with slated roof' — was better than most and in September 1826 was valued at £1,000 (Commissioners of the Irish Education Inquiry 1826).[3] In September 1808 the Rev. Singleton Harpur (perpetual curate, 1804–15) had nominated John Abbott 'as a fit person to be clerk and schoolmaster to the parish of the Union of Monkstown'. (For a complete list of Monkstown's school principals, *see Appendix 5*.) Abbott had actually taught at Monkstown since 1797 but was apparently still not licensed; he would continue to teach there until 1834, as well as performing his duties as parish *and* Vestry clerk. His wife, Mary, was the church sextoness during the years 1809–35, at an annual salary of £9-15s in 1834; she also taught in the school, earning an extra £30 a year. Abbott, as school principal, earned £46 a year, £30 of which came from 'the school funds, which (were) obtained from local subscriptions and an annual charity sermon'. The school was also supported by the Association for Discountenancing Vice (later the Association for the Propagation of Christian Knowledge or APCK). This organisation had been founded in 1792 by three Dublin men, one of whom was Singleton Harpur. It advocated the Bible and church catechism, and only Protestant children were supposed to attend their schools. But in their 226 schools around the country in 1824 there were 7,803

Protestants and 4,804 Roman Catholics, so it seems that a blind eye was usually turned to the situation. Indeed, in Monkstown Parish School in 1826, 75% of the schoolchildren were Roman Catholics (*see p. 223*).

John Abbott died on 8 November 1863 after 37 years of service to the parish. He left his half-share of 'Abbot's Cottage' (adjoining the entrance gate of Richmond Park, diagonally opposite the parish church) to his brother, Benjamin, for life and after his death to the parish of Monkstown (Vestry minutes, January 1877).

Thomas Eustace succeeded John Abbott as Monkstown's schoolmaster (1834–40) and also as parish clerk. By 1847 he was performing the duties of Vestry clerk too, earning £35 a year until 1855, when he died, apparently unexpectedly, while in Ballincollig, Co. Cork. He was buried in Carrickbrennan Graveyard. Previously, he had been the schoolteacher at Stradbally in 1824 and Vestry clerk in Donnybrook in 1825–6. His wife, Matilda, also taught in Monkstown school and they both took Sunday school. They had two sons, John (b. 1832) and Thomas Fox (b. 1837). Matilda died, aged 49, in February 1851.

When Eustace resigned as schoolmaster in 1840, William Campbell Clarke was appointed to the position. An entry in the rural dean's Visitation book of 1840 states, 'Schoolmaster not licenced, is properly qualified, 60 boys and 45 girls in daily attendance at the school. Another school [Clonkeen] in which there are 100 children'. Clarke was licensed in 1843 and a Miss C. Carty joined the school as mistress by 1847. Between 1838 and 1846 five children were born to William and Mary Clarke, who lived over the school: Hamilton McGrevy (b. 1838), John (b. 1840, d. 1847), Caroline (b. 1842), Charles (b. 1844) and Mary Jane (b. 1846). All were baptised at Monkstown Church.

Many of the children who attended the school were destitute. During the lean years of the Great Famine some may have attended school more for the food, clothes and warmth than for the lessons they received. In the years before and after, the children were given bread, milk, soup, clothing, shoes and coal. As the Poor Fund books record: 'Mr. Clarke to provide Bread and Soup for poor children of Monkstown School, £1-9-9' (17 May 1847); 'Mr. Clarke, for Fanny Henry's Breakfast, 5/2' (7 September 1842); 'James Cain (the tailor), for making clothes for the children of Monkstown School, 17/6' (13 February 1843); and 'Half Ton of coal for Clonkeen School by order cw [churchwarden], 7/6' (7 March 1853).

Peter Hackett succeeded William Clarke as schoolmaster at Monkstown in about 1853. On the death of Thomas Eustace in 1855, he also took on the role of parish clerk. He and his wife, Elizabeth, like their predecessors, the Clarkes, lived over the schoolhouse with their family: Alfred (b. 1853), Charles Arthur (b. 1856) and William Montague (b. 1857), all baptised in Monkstown. In July 1862 the schoolchildren were given practical items as prizes for their school work — 'clothes, socks, boots, dresses (4 for 10/-), Bibles, writing cases (4/6), work boxes, corduroy and flannel'. In 1868 there were 20 boys and 21 girls attending the school.

Hackett's dual responsibilities as clerk and schoolmaster sometimes clashed. The Select Vestry minutes of 4 March 1872 record: 'That inasmuch as Mr. Hackett's duties as parish clerk, requiring his attendance, at marriages, during school hours, are incompatible with the due discharge of his duties, as schoolmaster, it be referred to the Select Vestry, to consider whether any better arrangement can be made on their part for the proper performance of the duties of these two offices'. The problem was solved, to the satisfaction of the Select

Vestry, with Mr Hackett's offer to find a 'suitable substitute as parish clerk during school hours'. Again, in 1877 'Peter Hackett, master' once more attracted the attention of the Select Vestry, whose minutes of 10 September state: 'That the Secretary of the Select Vestry do inform Mr. Hackett that it having come under their knowledge that he is keeping poultry etc. in the playground of the children and that such poultry frequently trespass on the ground surrounding the church, Mr. Hackettt be requested forthwith to discontinue keeping them as being unsuitable to such a confined space'. Peter Hackett resigned in 1880 as schoolmaster. (In 1876 Amelia Harrison, schoolmistress of the Monkstown Female School, had also resigned, 'being about to go to Australia'.)

Monkstown under the National Board

In 1831 the National Board for the Education of the Poor and Working Classes was established. It was incorporated in 1845 under the name 'the Commissioners of National Education in Ireland'. The principle of this system was that poor children of all denominations were taught together, with separate religious instruction. In reality, what usually happened was that, if the teachers were Protestant, mainly Protestant children attended, and vice versa, particularly if, as in Monkstown, the school was beside the church and historically connected. But at least the rules did set out to maintain the principle of religious freedom.

In 1878 the Select Vestry decided to place Monkstown Parish School under the National Board because of 'difficulties in (their) management' and 'the want of funds to carry them on in an efficient state'. It was confident that the 'efficient system of inspection' would 'guarantee … a thoroughly sound education'. The religious education of the children would still be in the hands of the rector, for at least 45 minutes every day.

In spite of their obvious financial difficulties with their own parish school, the parishioners gave generously outside the parish. On 'Education Sunday' each year the offertory collections went towards the Board of Religious Education in the diocese of Dublin, Glendalough and Kildare. In 1881, 72 parishes contributed, reported the *Irish Ecclesiastical Gazette* of 9 July; of these, 63% gave under £10. Monkstown heads the list of the five largest collections:

Monkstown	£28-5-0
Harold's Cross	£25-0-0
St George's, Dublin	£18-15-0
Clane	£13-3-0
Christ Church Cathedral	£13-0-0

In 1881 John Morrison succeeded Peter Hackett as principal of the Boys' School, serving in that position until 1915. By now there were 85 pupils on the school rolls (50 boys and 35 girls) and some 'Ladies of the Parish' were asked to come in and help the teachers. (There were a further 70 pupils at the Cumberland Street Infants' School, also run by Monkstown parish; *see below.*)

In 1883, when the Inspector of the Diocesan Board of Religious Education examined the children, he found that the Boys' National School was the 'most efficient ... in the Diocese', and in his report to the Synod he held Monkstown School up as an example of 'some of the very best answering (he had) ever received'. In 1884 the Boys' School was still 'the best ... both in the average of passes and the quality of the answering. The whole tone of the School (was) beyond praise'. By 1888 John Morrison had married one of the schoolmistresses (sadly, she died in about 1902), who was replaced by Miss Annie St Lawrence.

Attendance figures at the school were, however, generally poor. For example, in 1890 of the 70 boys enrolled only 42 on average attended classes; similarly, only 39 of the 74 girls and 68 of the 120 infants. By 1903 the school numbers (121 children: 38 boys, 35 girls and 48 infants) were dropping owing to a 'decrease in the Church population in the neighbourhood'. This was blamed on 'the fact that no inducement is offered to members of our Church to settle in Kingstown or the neighbourhood for lack of suitable house accommodation', according to the Vestry's Annual Report of 1901. The report added that 'practically every child' in the parish 'between the ages of three and fourteen' was 'under instruction'. In 1904 the standard of teaching was still excellent, with five of the boys and seven of the girls obtaining 100% in Religious Knowledge. Miss St Laurence's salary was increased from £10 to £15 a year. Miss Edith Dowse remembers her as 'a little bit of a person, (but) a great disciplinarian'.

In 1911 numbers were still dropping (102 children: 27 boys, 32 girls and 43 infants). Two years later Miss St Lawrence left for Tandragee, Co. Armagh. The school roll had dropped to 78, made up of 22 boys, 21 girls and 35 infants. Canon Dowse wrote, 'I confess I am apprehensive as to the future of the school'.[4] Amalgamation seemed to be the only answer. Both principals were leaving in 1915 — Miss Mary Gilmore, principal of the Girls' School, was getting married and John Morrison, principal of the Boys' School, was retiring, so it was decided to delay the amalgamation until after that date. Then, on 1 October 1915, Monkstown Boys' and Girls' were amalgamated under the new principal, John McAdoo, aged 31 and former principal of Tralee Mixed School. (He was the uncle of Bishop McAdoo, primate of Ireland, 1977–85.) Miss Constance Brennan was appointed as junior assistant mistress.

As with all schools, teachers came and went. In 1917 Miss Brennan was replaced by the exotically named Miss Whelan-Pettigo. Mr McAdoo resigned in 1926 and was succeeded by Mr W.J. Whittaker, who only stayed a year. In 1927 Mr S.W. Power was appointed as principal and lived initially on the top floor of the Infants' School on Cumberland Street, Dun Laoghaire; in 1928 he married and had the use of the whole building, which had been previously occupied by caretakers. (By now, the infants were being taught in Monkstown schoolhouse.) In 1935 Miss F. Murphy was appointed as principal of the Infants. Then, in 1936, Mr Power was replaced by George Armstrong, who took over a school with only 47 pupils in total. Armstrong resigned, in December 1948, for a post in the government of Southern Rhodesia (now Zimbabwe).

Recovery with the Rountrees

When Mr Richard (Fred) Rountree was appointed school principal in 1948, the school was going through a difficult period, with only 46 pupils on the roll and two teachers. Mr Rountree's wife, Kathleen, became vice-principal in 1951, when Miss F. Murphy left. In 1951 Canon Dowse invited all 42 parents to a Parents' Meeting, in order to discuss the financial difficulties of the school. A Parents' Committee was formed as a result and the parents agreed to become voluntary subscribers.

Under the Rountrees, numbers grew rapidly so that by 1956 there were 81 children on the roll. That year children from Monkstown won 1st place in the Alexandra School Scholarship, 4th in High School, 1st at King's Hospital, 2nd in Mountjoy and 1st and 4th in the Avoca School Scholarship exams. The 1957 *Monkstown Review* printed a glowing report about Monkstown Primary School. The curriculum included English, Irish, French, arithmetic, geometry, history, geography, singing, needlework and physical training. In the Kindergarten, 'the little ones (made) rapid progress in Reading, Writing and Number Work'. Holy Scripture was taught daily by the teachers and clergy. The 'chief innovation' in 1957 was the introduction of a school uniform with a 'distinctive headgear … caps for boys and berets for girls of plain brown, with the letters "M.S." (intertwined) at front'.

The 1960s saw an even greater renewal in the school's fortunes. In 1960 there were 90 children on the roll and a third teacher (Miss Audrey Wilkinson) had been appointed to the Infants. Between 1957 and 1960 twelve scholarships were won, including four 'firsts'. Then in 1962 a complete refurbishment — 'a new milestone in the progress of our school' — resulted in 'what amounts practically to a new schoolhouse, with an additional classroom,

Senior School, Monkstown, Class of 1959, in their smart new school uniforms.
From left to right:
(*back row*) (unknown), Patricia Dalton, Winifred Murphy, Sasha Hermann, Sylvia Raby, Brian Carnegie and David Cashel;
(*third row*) David Harris, Alan Rountree, (unknown), (unknown), Brian Murray, (unknown) and Mervyn Smyth;
(*second row*) Herbert Pierce, Eddie Hartigan, Herbert Argue, Spencer Hartigan, June Carnegie, Joy Bailey, Mary O'Brien and Barbara Snow;
(*front row*) (unknown), Janet Cooke, Robin Wright, Fred Rountree, Arleen Hartigan, John Cooke, Pauline Reid and Robert Argue.

modern furniture and equipment, indoor toilet accommodation, bright airy classrooms (and) improved playing space for the children'. All this cost £7,500, of which £5,700 was a government grant. At a special service on 29 September 1962 the school was reopened by the archbishop of Dublin, Dr George O. Simms, with 'representatives from Church and State, the teaching, legal, medical, architectural professions, members of Dáil and Seanad Éireann, the Garda Siochána and Dun Laoghaire Corporation', as reported in *The Irish Times* on 1 October 1962. Inclement weather meant that the speeches afterwards had to be delivered in the doorway of the south transept, with the whole occasion captured on film by RTÉ. That year scholarships were won to Avoca, Alexandra and Diocesan schools.

In 1962 Mrs Rountree was appointed as principal to the new primary school at Kill, and two years later her husband replaced her in that position. A debt of gratitude is owed to the Rountrees, who had between the years of 1948 and 1964 built Monkstown school up from a dwindling 46-pupil school with two teachers to a scholarship-winning, three-teacher school with over 100 pupils.

The beginning of the end

Such high standards were difficult to maintain. In 1964 Mr John C. Kearon, ex-principal at Irishtown, was appointed and 'his understanding and friendly approach to both children and parents, coupled with great ability as a teacher, enabled the transition … with the goodwill of all concerned'. But the school was unsettled and there was a high turnover of teachers around this time: Miss Hannigan was appointed in 1964 as assistant teacher until her engagement in 1966; Miss Millar from Bailieboro' was appointed as junior mistress in 1964 in place of Miss Joan Taylor, who was leaving for the Diocesan School. In 1968 Miss Eileen Adair left to be married and Miss Patricia Hadnett and Mr D. Kenny joined the school staff.

In 1967 it was 'noted with pleasure that French, Art and Elocution (were) added to the curriculum as extras'. In 1968 the children of the Smyly's Boys' Home joined the school, so a new classroom was necessary. In 1972 Mr Kearon started a 'Song School' (Schola Cantorum) 'to provide specially trained young choristers' for the church; it was inaugurated on Sunday 14 May, when the first choristers were presented, as announced in the *Church of Ireland Gazette* on 12 May 1972. In 1973 Mr Kearon resigned and the first female principal, Miss Patricia Hadnett, was appointed.

In 1976 the Monkstown School Management Committee was formed, 'as directed by government and diocesan decree', taking the school management out of the hands of the rector and Select Vestry. The Parent–Teacher Association (PTA) was founded in about 1979. But by 1982 there were only 73 pupils attending the school, of which 33 were Church of Ireland (20 of these were parishioners), and the schoolhouse itself was riddled with dry rot. The Department of Education gave a grant of £33,118 towards the eradication of this problem and the parish raised a further £4,802. Miss Hadnett resigned in 1985 and was succeeded by Mrs Meta Morton as acting principal. In September 1986 only 42 children were on the school roll, with two teachers. The difficult decision had to be made — the school closed down on 31 December 1986.

Other schools in Monkstown parish

In 1808 there were three parish schools, according to the Poor Fund accounts. 'The expense of schooling poor children in Monkstown, Dalkey and Cornelscourt Schools' varied from month to month, possibly reflecting school holidays: April 17/6, May £1-12-9, June £2-2-6, July and August £4-13-0, September £1-18-6.

By 1826 there were twelve schools in the parish, where 509 children were taught — 385 Roman Catholic and 124 Protestant — according to the Second Report (1826) of the Commissioners of the Irish Education Inquiry.[3] Eight of these schools were Protestant-run and all except two took children from both denominations. Although the schools catered for all classes of society, the children attending them could still be described as 'privileged' since the vast majority of children in those days simply did not go to school. The twelve schools in the parish ranged from a small, all-Protestant boarding school in Newtown Avenue (with five boys and one girl) to the Mount Carmel Convent for girls, where one Protestant child found herself with 54 Catholics, or the school at Newtown, which was apparently housed in 'the chapel' and taught 60 Catholic children and five Protestants. The most egalitarian school was the Protestant-run school at Blackrock, where exactly half of the 20 boys and 20 girls belonged to each denomination.

The stated object of Monkstown parish schools, according to the 1865 Annual Report of Monkstown School, was 'to provide, free of expense, a sound Scriptural and useful secular education for the children of the poorer classes in the parish'. The schools set a high standard, especially the girls, who achieved the dizzy heights of coming second in the Dublin diocese that year, according to the Schools' Inspector.

The largest of the twelve schools was Monkstown Parish School, where there were twice as many girls (97) as boys (48). It had originally opened to children of all denominations; now, in 1826, 75% (109) were Roman Catholic and the rest (36) Protestant. Those who could afford it paid a nominal fee, while the Poor Fund subsidised the 'schooling of Boys (and Girls) whose Parents (were) unable to pay' to the tune of six shillings every month. By 1832 the proportions seem to have been reversed, with 120 Protestant and twelve Roman Catholic children attending Monkstown school.

By 1832 there was another school in the Union of Monkstown under church auspices. This was Clonkeen School (or Kill-of-the-Grange), where 60 Roman Catholic children were taught by Richard Dixon (or Dickson). The foundation of this all-Catholic school may have been prompted by the 1826 inquiry set up by the Commissioners of Irish Education into schools around the country. By 1837 Clonkeen and another school in Monkstown, apparently also for Roman Catholic children, were both under the National Board of Education and also 'aided by an annual donation from the RC clergyman' (D'Alton 1838b).[5]

On 11 March 1843 Charles Lindsay, bishop of Kildare, nominated Thomas Halpin as 'Literate English Schoolmaster of the School of Clonkeen situate in the Union of Monkstown' and his licence was duly sealed on 14 March. Tragically, Halpin's wife, Anne, died in October that year, aged 32, and Thomas died the following year, in February 1844, aged 36. The death rate in Monkstown, from the evidence of the burial registers, jumped almost 50% during 1843 to 1845, the years before the Great Famine, and the Clonkeen schoolmaster and his wife may have been victims of typhoid, probably caught from their pupils. Halpin was succeeded by Matthew Cranston, who, with his wife Henrietta, had two children, John and Elizabeth, born in 1846 and 1848 respectively.

In 1834 Lords Longford and de Vesci leased ground to Monkstown Church for a school at Cumberland Street, Kingstown, for 99 years, charging a yearly rent of one shilling. This was the Cumberland Street Infants' School, described as 'a spacious and airy building' (Brooke 1877). It was used by the Mariners in about 1837 while their church was being built. There was no water supply to the building for years: in 1863 the school accounts list 'water for cleaning, 6d' and a further shilling a week was spent on water, presumably for drinking. Other school expenses in September 1862 included 'Soda, 2d for cleaning; Paste to kill rats, 4d; Cane 1d; Riggs for cleaning Ashpit, washing Infant school, 11/-' and in January 1864 'Floorcloth and skipping ropes, 2/-'.

The school was appropriately named: in 1865 it admitted 125 infants, ranging from two to nine years of age. The school staff must have been thankful that usually only about 70 turned up, in spite of prizes of warm clothing every winter for 'regularity of attendance and good conduct'. Essentially the school seemed to function as a baby-sitting service, as well as performing its educational role. The School Committee stressed in the Annual Report of 1865 that it was important that mothers should be 'relieved from the care of their younger children during some hours each day' so that they would be 'enabled to devote more time to their household duties, and, in many cases, by their industry, to contribute to the support of their families' (Monkstown Parochial Schools 1866).

In 1879 the sisters Elizabeth and Jane Bradley were appointed principal and assistant teacher of the Infants' School. By 1881 there were 70 infants on the school rolls. In August 1882 the teachers of the Infants' School had to sit an exam 'for classification' by the National Board; unfortunately Elizabeth Bradley, the principal, failed and her sister, Jane, only achieved a 'second division of third class'. Jane was therefore promoted to principal and Elizabeth's salary as principal was withdrawn; she was demoted to assistant teacher in the Infants while she studied for the repeat exam. A year later, in September 1884, she passed and swapped places again with Jane.[6] In 1905, after 36 years at Monkstown, Elizabeth Bradley retired at the age of 61.[7] (Her sister Jane had already retired in 1901.) Canon Dowse wrote of Elizabeth that he did 'not think it would have been possible … to have had a more faithful, painstaking or conscientious servant. She loved her work and to it her entire thoughts and efforts were devoted'. Miss Bradley was succeeded by Miss Lily Ross.

Lectures were held in the school on Cumberland Street on Wednesday evenings (c. 1836–8). The building was also used as a savings bank, called the Monkstown Penny Bank, from 1877 until after 1912; it opened on Saturdays from 12 noon to 2pm 'for the benefit of the Poor of the Parish of Monkstown'. (Eventually, in 1938, the Cumberland Street Infants' School closed and the premises were surrendered by the Diocesan Board of Education to Lords Longford and de Vesci for £250.)

During the nineteenth century many children worked for long hours. If these working children or young adults wanted schooling, they had to attend during the evenings. Monkstown parish financed Kingstown Night School between 1856 and 1865, at least. Its stated object was 'to provide secular instruction for young men who are desirous of advancing themselves in life, but whose employment do not allow of their obtaining it during the day'. Some of the expenses involved are recorded in the Monkstown Church Funds book of 1855–8: 'Rent for Night school, £10-8-0; Coals for Night school, £2-8-0; Candles for Night school, £1-8-3; Master's salary, £15'. When the curate, the Rev. Thomas Rooke, left Monkstown in 1859, the grateful pupils of Kingstown Night School presented him with a farewell address (*see Chapter 11*). In 1865 the School Committee tried various strategies to reduce expenses for the Night School, such as closing it during the three summer months, students providing their own stationery and making small voluntary contributions from their wages. The Night School also saved on its rent (of £12 annually in 1865) by moving into the premises of the Cumberland Street Infants' School (Monkstown Parochial Schools 1866).

Another school in the parish at the time was the Golden Ball School at Kilternan, open during the years *c.* 1856 to 1862. The premises were rented for £10 a year. The curates of Monkstown had to hire a horse-drawn jaunting car (£1-4-0 in August 1856) for their weekly visits to the school, which was almost certainly Kingston School on Ballycorus Road, in part of a house owned by Samuel Stevenson (today called 'Kingston Grove'; note 'Kingston', not 'Kingstown'). Kingston School House ('the school-house near Ballycorus Mills') was licensed for Divine Service while Tullow Church was being built, from 1860 to 1864.[8] Records relating to the Monkstown Parochial Schools list expenses for the school: 'Reward books for Kingston School, 4/6' (December 1858) and 'Bibles for Golden Ball, 15/-' (December 1859). In 1862 we read the last 'Golden Ball' entry and the first for Cabinteely School House, for which Monkstown was paying the annual rent of £8.

The Claremont Institution for the Education of the Deaf and Dumb was originally run in a house called 'Carrick Manor' in Glasnevin. In 1943 the institution moved to a house called 'Mount Ussher' on Monkstown's Carrickbrennan Road and changed the name of the house to 'Carrick Manor' to retain continuity. The children attended the Parish School from 1975 until the Claremont closed down in 1978.

On 1 September 1997 a new school, Monkstown 'Educate Together' National School, opened in the grounds of Monkstown Community Centre, with Mrs Mary Stuart as its new principal. It 'welcomes children from all denominations and none, is co-educational and promotes a child-centred curriculum', and also caters for children with special needs. The school opened with 72 children and three teachers; by September 1998 there were 130 children and two additional teachers. In 2003, 240 children were taught by eight full-time teachers; in addition, there is a strong complement of full- and part-time staff dealing specifically with special resources and needs. The children come from a wide area — Sandycove, Dalkey, Sallynoggin, Glenageary and even as far away as Bray.

CHAPTER 17

A wealthy and generous parish

There are but two families in the world, as my grandmother
used to say, the Haves and the Havenots.
Miguel de Cervantes, *Don Quixote*

In the Book of Common Prayer of 1604, the rubric directed the curate 'earnestly to exhort the people to remember the poore'. After the Nicene Creed the priest would say 'Pray remember the poor' and then a collection was taken up, followed by the sermon. An Irish canon of 1634 required the churchwardens to provide an alms chest in the church. This usually stood at the west door and had three locks (the rector and two churchwardens each owning a key, so that it could only be opened in the presence of all three). The old church in Carrickbrennan Graveyard had such 'a Chest for ye Alms of ye poor'.

Thus a tremendous tradition grew up in Ireland of helping the poor — especially the Roman Catholic poor — which continued in Ireland long after it had died out in England. Bishop Jebb described this practice in the English House of Lords in 1824:

'In Ireland, we have no legal fund for the poor, but in all our churches, on the first day of the week, after the manner of primitive times, a collection is made for the relief of the poor.'

In Monkstown, this 'Parish Church Collection Fund' was also used to help 'Poor Protestants, who, from age and infirmity, are unable to procure their own liveliehood. It also maintains and educates, in the Protestant Faith, many destitute Orphan children belonging to this Parish, who are not provided for by the Monkstown Protestant Orphan Society, or by Vestry Assessment.'

Monkstown's Poor Fund established

Until the State took over, the whole system of poor relief, from the cradle to the grave, revolved around the parish: abandoned babies found within the parish boundaries were its responsibility, 'the children of the poor' were taught in the parish schools, and the poor were supplied with food, clothes, fuel, money and medical attention, as well as coffins and free burial. In addition to relieving their bodily needs, the Poor Fund also supplied 'food for the soul': we read of a large number of Bibles and prayer books being distributed in 1816 (£3-5s) and 1852 (£3).

In this context, we must remember that the 'Monkstown Parish' of the past covered a very large area. It stretched from Blackrock to Dalkey and inland to Cabinteely, Kill-of-the-Grange and Kilternan. Although it was largely the wealthy and titled members of the Established Church who lived in their seaside villas and imposing terraces near the church, further afield, in the courts and alleyways of Kingstown and Blackrock, destitute people lived in mud cabins. Epidemics of typhoid and cholera spread like wildfire in these crowded and filthy conditions, without running water or drains. Although the majority of these poor people were Roman Catholics, the Monkstown Parish Registers reveal that many were 'poor Prots'. And it was these 'poor Protestants' who formed the bulk of the Sunday congregation.

By 1767 a charity school and Poor Fund had been established in Monkstown. In 1772 the departing lord lieutenant, Lord Townshend, who had lived in the parish at 'Rockfield' on Newtown Park Avenue, gave the curate of Monkstown the huge sum of £40 for the poor. The churchwardens' accounts of Easter 1772 show that the parish paid for burials of the poor: 'To the Interment of Several poor persons, 15-8½'. The following year, in 1773, the Monkstown Vestry, in accordance with 'the Instructions of the Corporation Instituted for the Relief of the poor of the County of Dublin', appointed a committee for the Union of Monkstown, consisting of the perpetual curate, curate, two churchwardens and nine parishioners. In the early 1800s about £2–£7 was collected every week in the church's Sunday collection for the poor, with over £9 on Easter Sunday with a larger congregation. This was not enough to support the huge demands on the Poor Fund, so an annual 'Charity Sermon' was essential.

Charity sermons

Charity sermons were the most popular method of raising money for charities and this, supported by the generous weekly church collections, was how Monkstown raised the enormous amount of money it needed every year. Sometimes even this was not enough and special appeals had to be made. The enthusiasm surrounding charity sermons was unique to Dublin. Each charity or church had a set time of the year for its particular appeal, so popular preachers, such as Walter Blake Kirwan, were booked up months in advance and advertisements inserted in the newspapers to avoid dates clashing.

Monkstown's account books of October 1808 show that the Vestry knew that 'advertising pays': the event was placed in four different newspapers, with five insertions in the *Freeman's Journal* and *Saunders's News-Letter*, at a cost of £1-0-7, and six insertions in *The Correspondent* and *Dublin Journal*, at a cost of £1-1-8. A report of a typical charity sermon illustrates the fevour of the event (Warburton *et al.* 1818). Ladies, 'the most remarkable for their rank and beauty', were appointed as collectors. Every means was taken to ensure the success of the event; for example, neighbouring churches might be closed to ensure the attendance of their parishioners. Such crowds turned up that soldiers might have to keep order outside the church, while 'stewards with white wands to mark their authority' would keep the 'tumultuary congregation' quiet inside. Scant attention was paid to the service and 'scenes of irregularity' often occurred. But as soon as the preacher appeared at the top of the three-decker pulpit, 'every auditor (was) fixed in wrapt attention'. After the sermon, the beautiful ladies, each attended by a 'white rod' and a female attendant, would go from pew to pew, graciously taking up the collection on a silver plate. The collection from each pew was poured into a basin held by the female attendant and the plate presented empty to the next pew, so that everyone's donation was conspicuous. Based on the average curate's salary of £40, one would assume that the Monkstown Vestry was happy with the sums raised — £48-14-2½ in 1808 and £40-18-10½ in 1819. Often the amount would appear in the papers, with further appeals if it was not considered sufficient.

In 1857 in Monkstown charity sermons were preached every month (except January and June) for the following causes:

22 February	Association for Discountenancing Vice (later APCK)	£16-0-0
8 March	Additional Curates' Fund	£15-0-0
26 April	Church Missionary Society (CMS)	£32-0-0
28 May	Jews' Society	£16-2-6
22 July	Parochial Schools	£60-0-0
9 August	Protestant Orphan Society	£38-17-4
27 September	Irish Society	£20-0-0
7 October	Service of Humiliation for Indian Insurrection: Collection for Sufferers	£73-6-0
22 November	Parochial Schools	£45-0-0
December	Rathdown Hospital	£33-0-0

The previous year, 1856, there had also been collections for the Society for the Propagation of the Gospel (SPG), the Infants' School, the Lying-in Hospital and Kingstown School.

Poor Fund books and vouchers

Thanks to the painstaking record-keeping of the parish clerk, churchwardens, rector and curates, we know, nearly 200 years later, where every penny went. The Poor Fund books and vouchers are intimate historic documents. They are not just antiquated 'shopping-lists': they tell us about individuals who would otherwise be forgotten. They record the personal minutiae of the poor of the parish — the names, characteristics, occupations, illnesses and accidents, details of medical care, incidents of petty crime and articles of clothing (down to the 'v. gd. Horn Buttons' on the greatcoats supplied by the parish to the elderly men on the Poor List).

There are four Poor Fund books for Monkstown, covering the years 1803–15 and 1835–58. There is also an almost complete collection of Poor Fund vouchers from 1862–72. Inside the cover of the 1803 book are the words, 'Blessed be the Man, that provideth for the Sick and Needy, The Lord shall deliver him in the Time of Trouble'. In the notice for the Monkstown Poor Fund's charity sermon of 1815, printed in *Saunders's News-Letter* on 6 October, it was promised that 'From this Fund … Forty distressed and deserving widows, and Old Men, receive a Monthly Allowance of One Crown each, and comfortable Clothing every Christmas; the Labouring Poor are relieved during Sickness, with Bread, pecuniary Allowances and Wine, in addition to Medicines, and Advice … from that humane Institution, the Rathdown Dispensary'.

An entry in the Poor Fund book in April 1868 recorded: 'To Radford, poor water carrier, to enable him to buy a new donkey, by direction of Dr. MacDonnell, 10s'. The seemingly cheap cost of a donkey could lead one to be dismissive of such an apparently small contribution. But by the purchase of a new animal for the 'poor water carrier' the Poor Fund made his livelihood possible again. One shilling, the average day's wages for a labourer, would just about feed a family of six (8d a day were 'starvation wages'). It would have been impossible for the water carrier to purchase that donkey (over €120 in today's money) without the help of the parish. In the accounts that follow, as a rough 'rule of thumb', 2/6 in the 1840s, '50s and '60s had the purchasing power of €30 (i.e. one penny was approximately equivalent to €1).

A small box in the Monkstown Vestry Archives reveals, in a fascinating, almost voyeuristic way, what the parish did for the 'sick and indigent poor', irrespective of their denomination. Bundles of diminutive blue and white envelopes, tied together with coarse twine or thread, complement the Poor Fund books. There were originally twelve envelopes in each bundle, all labelled 'Poor Fund' in a neat copperplate script, with an envelope identified for each month, starting at April until the following March. Each envelope contains a wad of papers, tightly folded to fit; when unwrapped, each small collection — all carefully filed in chronological order for that particular month — has been joined together at one corner. The scraps of paper are of different sizes. Many are grubby and torn. These are the original 'vouchers' given by the Poor Fund to 'the deserving poor' of the parish.

Monkstown of yesterday must have been a bit like the Calcutta of today. 'The Sunday poor' thronged to the church ('To a Poor Idiot Boy at the Church Door, 10d'), accosted the minister and curates in the street or called at their homes, asking for financial help. If it was a small sum, the clergy usually helped immediately, keeping a record so that they could get repaid later by the parish clerk, who officially looked after the Poor Fund. For larger amounts, if they felt the request was reasonable and the person genuinely destitute, they jotted down on a scrap of paper the suppliant's name, the amount of money allowed and often its purpose, and signed and dated it. These vouchers on bits of paper were presented to the parish clerk by the suppliant, who would honour them.

The Poor Fund vouchers and ledgers illustrate the extent to which nineteenth-century parishes like Monkstown acted like the involved GP or social worker of today, while alternatively indulgent, authoritative or judgemental. In 1866–7, of the parish income of £838 raised mainly through collections, Monkstown spent over £380 through the Poor Fund (almost €120,000 today). Another £276 went to other charitable causes, mainly outside the parish. Thus some 78% of the parish's income went directly out again to charity.

Money poured into the Fund. Every Sunday a collection was taken up especially for the poor. Charity sermons were packed out and brought in huge sums. In addition, there were some large individual donations. Even magistrates and local judges found ways of helping by imposing fines for petty crimes that went directly into the Fund: 'Received from Mr. Jones of Seapoint, being Fines levied on Jingles No. 22 and 151, 12/8½' (20 October 1805); 'Received from the Resident Magistrate being a Moiety [half] of a Fine levied by him on a Coachowner for refusing to convey a Physician to the vicinity of the Blackrock, in a case of danger, £2' (9 April 1808); 'A Fine on a Person near Dunleary for having in his possession part of a Sheep and Wool, for which he could not properly account to the Magistrates, £2-10s' (14 February 1809); 'A Fine … for cutting Timber near Crinken, £1-0-0' (14 February 1809); and 'A balance deducted … from his carman for one barrel of coals found deficient in Coals delivered by them, 4/-' (31 January 1815).

Monkstown in Georgian and Victorian times had few of the 'fund-raising activities' of today: it was a case of straight donations of money, bolstered by hours of hard grind by the dedicated few who ministered at the grass roots, visiting the poor in their cabins, seeing what was necessary and making sure it was done, and risking the potentially fatal fevers endemic there. Some died as a result, especially during the years of the Great Famine (*see Chapter 15*).

Help for every misfortune — in life and death

The vouchers help to piece together an evocative picture of the Monkstown of over 100 years ago:

> '£1 to Joseph Thornton to assist in buying a horse' (5 October 1864)
> 'Mr. Hackett … please to give Mrs. Adams ten shillings to assist her in paying rent due by her … [signed] Ronald MacDonnell' (May 1868)
> 'Please give Alice Feris six shillings to assist her procuring clothes to fit her for a situation [domestic service]' (13 May 1868)
> 'Mr. Hackett … pay five shillings towards the expense of Thomas Murray's fare to Birmingham' (July 1868)

In May 1868, 'F. Ranson, Boot and Shoemaker of 108 Lower George's-St, Kingstown, Repairs neatly executed', made William Philips a pair of boots costing 4/6 out of the Poor Fund. It sounds as if William may have had to pawn them, as two months later there is another slip of paper, saying 'Mr. Hackett … give Mr. Higgins four shillings to assist in releasing W. Philips' clothing … Ronald MacDonnell' (July 1868). Other vouchers helped people during their illness: 'To Daniel Murray, for wine and nourishment during sickness (2 months), £1' (January 1868). Daniel must have made a good recovery for in February 1868 F. Ranson made him an expensive pair of boots costing 10/6. (Adults' shoes usually cost 8/-.) Another gentleman was slower to recover from his illness: 'Please pay John Corry the sum of £1 as he is sick and required to go to the country for change of air' (September 1855).

Other vouchers covered the fare to Chester or Birmingham (1868), 'the Rosborough family in distress' (30 July 1868), Christmas provisions, clothes and mountains of boots. On 18 May 1852 'two poor Prot. females' were given 10/- 'to assist them in emigrating to

America'. The adventurous Anna Smith was given a generous £3-10s for her 'outfit for Australia' in February 1857. Gold had been discovered there in 1851 and there was an acute shortage of women of marriageable age in the towns that had mushroomed around the mines.

In the Poor Fund books, we come across words no longer in common usage. For example, in December 1862, 'Bluchers for Mr. Hancock, 10/-' refer to a pair of strong, leather half-boots, considered better than the average boots (named after the Prussian commander Field-Marshal Von Blücher). In June 1868 the Rev. Ronald MacDonnell ordered the churchwarden, Mr Hackett, to 'pay blind Usher ten shillings for the purchase of rods to make baskets'. In July 'blind Usher', who was given the rods every month for some years, was also given a 'shift', or smock (£1-5-2), and a 'muffler', or scarf (1/9). The muffler could also be used as a blindfold and, in this context, may have been a covering to hide Usher's eyes, more likely in the summer than a scarf.

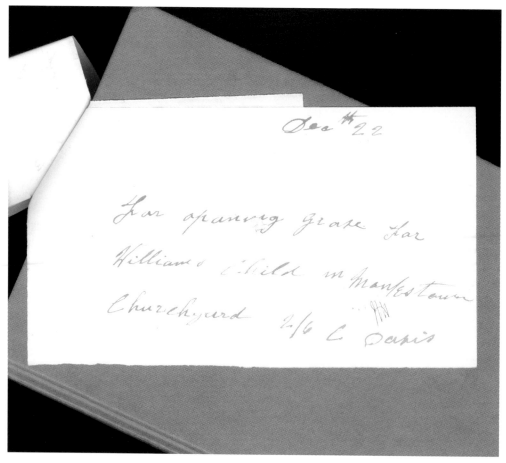

One of the hand-written vouchers of the grave-digger Christopher Davis, dated 22 December 1871, 'For opening grave for Williams child in Monkstown Churchyard, 2/6. C. Davis'. It is countersigned by the scribbled initials of the churchwarden, Harry Hodges.

While alive, the poor struggled to make ends meet; in death, the parish helped them too. In 1819 'a decent black pall for the use of the poor' was recycled during burials. In each of the bundles of Poor Fund vouchers there are torn scraps of paper written and signed by Christopher Davis, the grave-digger (1864–75) who had taken over from George Argue

(1810–64). Davis was paid 2/6 for each grave he dug for the poor, many of whom were children. A sample of his vouchers reveal the sad facts: 'For the Intering of Prodestant orphant child, 2/6' (October 1864), 'For opening a grave … still borne child' (July 1866) and 'For opening a grave for McAllister's Child, 2/6 … Cristopher Davis'.

When her father died, the bereaved daughter approached Dr MacDonnell, the incumbent, for help: 'Feb 2 … Mr. Hackett … give Eliza Morris one pound to defray expenses of her father's funeral … Ronald MacDonnell'. And two days later: 'Feb 4 1869 … For opening grave for George Morress [Morris], 2/6 … C..Davis'.

One note, dated 8 February 1855, read: 'Rev. Dr. Sir — I am the person whome maid the coffin for Wilhiam Graham's child. My charge is, Sir, 6s. Daniel Hickey, Kingstown'. This price was exorbitant — as a rule, coffins cost 2/6 for infants, 3/6 for children and 7/6 for adults.

Monkstown Parish Poor Fund had to pay for the burial of the destitute who died within the parish bounds: 'You are hereby required to allow the body of a male infant, name unknown, to be buried, on which I this day held an inquest. Dated the 6th day of June 1868. Henry Kelly [? name not clear], Coroner County Dublin.' Sadly, there were many 'unknowns': another baby boy was found in 'the Kill of Grange' three weeks later.

While the Poor Fund was doling out money for coffins and burials, the parishioners were 'assessed' (taxed) to raise money for this purpose. Every year the assessments brought in about £20 from the parishioners (and often a great deal more, for example £40 in both 1827 and 1828). This was a self-imposed obligation: according to the Hon. John Radcliffe, judge of the prerogative court and vicar general, whose opinion Archdeacon Lindsay sought in February 1823, 'there (was) a great difference of opinion' as to whether the parish should finance coffins. He himself thought that the 'charge (was) allowable when the Poor would otherwise be buried without them, (although) others (did) not'.

The Poor Fund book of 1803–15 gives a list of the regulations for admission to the Poor List. Anyone who begged, who could support themselves or was under 50 (unless they could prove 'Great bodily infirmity'), or was 'guilty of any Misconduct or Irregularity', or 'whose Character (could) not bear the strictest Scrutiny, as to Honesty, Sobriety, Quietness, and Industry according to Ability' was not eligible. Undoubtedly, many poor wretches could not fulfil these impossible requirements and were crossed off the list.

The 'widows and old men' on the Poor List had to be recommended by a parishioner who attended church regularly or was a contributor to the Poor Fund. Being on the Poor List was probably a life-saver for many. They were given food, 'comfortable clothing' at Christmas and 'one British crown … on the first Sunday in every month'. They had to present themselves at church, wearing the clothes bought by the Poor Fund, and would lose their allowance if there was not a valid excuse for not turning up. At Christmas these widows and old men were warmly kitted out: the men were given specially made greatcoats (2/8½ each), using 'v. gd. Horn Buttons', while the women received cloaks (1/3), bonnets, petticoats (5d) and 'black stuff quilted petticoats', or warm skirts (8/8). In 1868 the 34 aged and infirm on the Poor List were given between 1/- and 4/- every week, amounting to £220 over the year.

Although the Poor Fund was largely aimed at 'poor Protestants', some of whom were described as 'extreme cases of poverty', help was given to 'the poor in general throughout the United Parishes, under all the Accidents and Casualties to which they are subject: and in the Calamities which so frequently occur on this extensive and dangerous Coast'. And plenty of 'calamities' there were on 'this dangerous coast'. Two orphans whose parents were shipwrecked in 1812 were assisted with 2/2. When a particularly upsetting tragedy occurred there was usually a public 'subscription' (or collection) to which the Poor Fund contributed, such as 'for the Relief of the Families of Five Fisherman drowned' (10 February 1814), or 'for Thomas Burnet of Glanamuck towards rebuilding his house, accidentally consumed by fire, £1-10s' (10 January 1811), or 'for Joseph Hill who was robbed and wounded near Cabinteely, 7/6' (7 February 1816). A reward of 11/4½ was given to 'Peter White and six seamen for exertions in saving some Passengers in the Beresford Packet' (21 August 1803). The thatched cabins of the poor often needed repair. John and Elizabeth Smith, 'an aged couple' of Johnstown, were paid in full the cost of thatching their cabin in 1807 (11/4½), 1812 (11/4½) and again in 1815 (18/10). The language may be old-fashioned, but the problems of the poor sound very contemporary: 'To the Widow Whitmore of Blackrock with 6 children who was robbed, towards setting her up in business again' (1812).

There is no doubt that the parish saved many of the poor, regardless of denomination, from living in absolute destitution or from dying of starvation. The Poor Fund books show that, although every penny had to be religiously accounted for, the money was spent generously. Sometimes the assistance was eminently practical: 'To Richd. Williams for planting his Garden, 5/5' (17 April 1803), 'To Richd. Bryan (a Poor Man with a large family) towards repair of his cabbin, 11/4½' (6 March 1804), and 'To Richd. Bryan, a Poor Man, in aid of the Subscripn to buy him a Horse, 5/4' (7 December 1807). 'Charitable loans' were also given by the Poor Fund to enable people to purchase 'useful articles' which were then sold 'to earn subsistence' by the 'many aged and infirm, but industriously disposed persons'. These 'poor persons of established good character', who were unfit for manual labour, could 'earn their Bread by the Sale of Moral and Religious Tracts, Delph, etc'. In 1810, six people (five of them women) were supplied with a basket each (1/1) and a 'set' (i.e. 100) of 'Moore's Moral and Religious Tracts', costing 4 shillings.

There was a regular account with Johnston & Company, Machine Bread & Biscuit Makers, Ballsbridge Mills (the antecedents of Johnston, Mooney and O'Brien, the 'Favourite Family Pan'). Between 15 January 1814 and 13 June 1816, '1,744 loaves of bread were given to 705 poor persons in sickness etc. whose families consisted of 2,796 persons'. Over 50 years later the company was still supplying bread in Monkstown: in 1869 over 260 2lb loaves, costing 3½d and 3¼d each, were given to the children in Monkstown's Boys', Girls' and Infants' schools between 5 April and 28 May. Meanwhile, the school supplied breakfast each day; in April 1836 the Sunday School children breakfasted on bread and milk out of 'tin porringers'.

In April 1837 a dressmaker was paid to make some necessary clothes for the 'poor children of Monkstown church' — 'Corduroy for clothing, £2-14-2; Calico for lining, 12-0; Buttons, 10-0; Tailoring, 17-4; 4 yards long cloth, 3-4'. On 15 September that same year the Vestry clerk wrote precisely, 'Flannel and calico for inner clothing of poor children of Monkstown Female School, £2'.

234

Some medical details

Illness and accidents were so prevalent among the poor that from 1813 half the proceeds of the annual charity sermon for the Poor Fund went towards the Rathdown Dispensary, reported *Saunders's News-Letter* of 2 October 1815. Dr Thomas Arthure ran the dispensary until 1822, when Dr William Plant took over (*see Chapter 22*). The medical conditions are listed in the Poor Fund books. They include 'Andrew Smith, having his Leg cut by a Reaping hook, 2/6' (14 October 1812), the man who was 'injured by blasting a rock' (8 June 1816, possibly at Dalkey Quarry while blasting granite), the 'aged and infirm', 'with a disabled arm', 'with a scalded leg', 'prevented working by a hurt', 'blind', 'consumptive', 'the smallpox', 'with a broken collar bone', 'ill of an erysipelas on his leg' and many more. Most people seemed to stay at home during illness, but many still had to be brought to hospital in Dublin for diagnosis ('For a seat in a gingle to old Mrs Redmonds to get advice at the Hospital, 1/1', August 1804) or for treatment ('To send the Widow Keogh of Dunleary's child to an Hospital, 1/8', 27 February 1816, or 'Going to Lying-in Hospital and taken ill on the road, 5/-', 12 July 1808). Free tickets were given out to see a dispensary doctor: 'To Mr. Hiatt for seven Dispensary Tickets, £1-2s-9d' (1804). The mentally disturbed were apparently taken elsewhere: 'For the conveyance of a poor mad woman to the House of Industry' (19 May 1806). (The 'House of Industry' later became the Richmond Hospital.)

There are some early preventative measures and treatments: 'Paid John Williams of Dalkey for conveying in his Jingle the children of Jas. Williams twice to and from Town to be innoculated, 10/10' (8 July 1811).[1] Vaccination was first accepted in 1800 in England as a method of preventing smallpox. There were some unusual forms of treatment: the use of 'a quart of vinegar for patient with Fever to be rubbed with' (24 April 1804), 'a poor man attending salt water, 1/8' (8 July 1812), 'a flannel waistcoat for Brien in an Asthma, 4/4' (31 December 1803) or 'a yd of Flannel ordered for a strained back to Larry Conlon, 1/4½' (18 April 1804). Wine was freely dispensed when 'either ordered by Medical Persons, or is very evidently necessary' and the parish gave bountifully of supplies, as in the voucher of 12 July 1803 'for 1 Dozn of Port Wine for the Sick and carriage of Ditto, £1-11-1'.

If the main breadwinner of a family fell ill or died, it could spell disaster. Such families were often given a weekly allowance until the crisis was over: 'Fitzwilliam (a hard working man (his earnings 9-9 pr week) with a large family) in a Dropsey, unable to earn, allow 5-5 pr week, 20 weeks, £5-8-4' (September 1803), or 'Hacket, his leg broke, (allowed) 3-3 pr week for 6 weeks & 4-4 the 1st, £1-07' (18 September 1803). One-off emergency help was also provided: 'Towards repairing the house of James Moore of Williamstown injured by a storm, he being a poor man, afflicted with a palsy — and having a wife etc. to support, and having an excellt charr [character], 11/4½' (26 May 1809).

Poor Judy Murphy's illness was itemised in some detail. She first appeared in the Poor Fund book on 14 May 1804, when she was described as 'laid up in the rheumatism'. All through May and June weekly observations were entered describing Judy's condition, together with her allowance of 1/1. By July she was 'quite helpless', so was given 'further aid, 6/6'. The weekly notes continued all through August ('confined to her Bed a long time by sickness'), when the amounts increased to 2/6 weekly. In December we read that Judy 'suffered amputation of her leg'. Somehow, without anaesthetic or antibiotics, she survived this. In February 1805, still bedridden, she was given 'a Calico Bedgown and Flannel Petticoat' (17/9½). She disappeared from the Poor Fund book after that and her fate is unknown.

Charity in action

When the Rev. William Tew left Monkstown in July 1816, after sixteen years as curate, the churchwardens made a farewell speech, focusing on Tew's kindness to the poor: 'You have been the constant and assiduous friend of the poor, whose Fund you have long faithfully administer'd, whose Intreats you never neglected, and which has been this day exemplified by it appearing that you advanced your own money rather than let their wants to remain unsatisfied; and your attention to the Duties of Curate has been unceasing and meritorious'.

In January 1814 the public-spirited Mr Samuel Bewley (of the later Bewley's Oriental Cafés), a Monkstown parishioner, paid for the roads around Blackrock to be cleared of snow and then invited contributions, which he passed on to Monkstown Poor Fund (£5-10s-3d) and two other charities. Charles Haliday, another parishioner (who wrote *The Scandinavian kingdom of Dublin*, published in 1881), agonised over the conditions in which the poor lived. He fought to reinstate their bathing places along the shore, which had been taken away by the railway line of 1834, and to provide a clean water supply and drains for them. He died in 1866, probably of an infectious disease caught from beggars he was working with at the Mendicity Association.

As part of its charitable programme the parish set up a system of 'District Visitors', whereby 'a number of Ladies, Members of the Congregation, kindly undertake visiting the Sick Poor throughout the District'. In 1865 the Annual Report mentions nine such 'visitors'. In 1862 we come across the names of three philanthropic ladies — Miss Pim, Miss Williams and Miss Sharpe — who visited the poor and helped them financially if necessary, getting reimbursed later. Poor Fund vouchers refer to Miss Pim's visits: 'Pay Miss Pim five shillings for relief of Mrs. Elliot in Chandlers' Court … July 3rd, 1862'; in September Miss Pim visited Mrs Eliot twice and also two other houses in Chandlers' Court; the conscientious Miss Pim was still visiting in 1868 when, on 23 December, she brought Mrs Golins in a cab to and from hospital. 'Miss Pim' could have been Isabella, Charlotte or Jane Pim (aged 34, 26 and 22 respectively in 1862) of the Mission to Lepers (*see Chapter 22*) or one of the other Miss Pims resident in the parish.

Samuel Sproule was one of the first to leave a legacy to the poor: 'Samuel Sproule of Fleet St. in the City of Dublin Painter and Plaister now Oil and Colour Merchant' wrote his will on 25 February 1797, leaving £100 to Monkstown parish, to be placed out at interest, 'for the benefit of six old men or women of the Protestant religion who have been reduced in their circumstances and become unable to earn a livlihood'. Other legacies specifically benefiting the poor were left by Edward Atkinson (£200 in 1865) and Susan Carter (£1,000 in 1871).

The *Irish Ecclesiastical Gazette* of 19 November 1897 reported that 'Sunday last was

Hospital Sunday … St. Matthias' Church is likely to again head the list of contributors … Christchurch, Leeson Park … Baggotrath and Monkstown are also amongst the largest contributors to the fund, and there seems to be a friendly rivalry amongst these various churches as to which shall head the list in each year'.

Help for non-parishioners

The Poor Fund did not generally help those from outside the parish, but exceptions were sometimes made. A voucher dated 28 March 1803 records, 'A strange Woman in a fever on the Road, lodged and maintained during her illness, 10/2'. The parish found itself in a quandary about this policy during the bitter month of January 1823, when it decided to raise 'a fund for relieving the poor of (the) parish during the inclemency of the … season'. As a result a meeting was called 'of the Resident Inhabitants of the Parish of Monkstown', which met in Samuel Bewley's Dublin residence in Suffolk Street on 25 January. At this meeting, the churchwardens reported that they had been approached by 'several poor men stating themselves to have been employed in the Public Works'. These were some of the thousands of labourers working on the building of the harbour at Kingstown, who had been forced to stop work for two weeks due to the severe snow and frost (De Courcy Ireland 2001). In their subsequent letter to the Commissioners of Kingstown Harbour, the minister and churchwardens indicated that the parish Poor Fund could not possibly support people from outside the parish since funds were 'merely adequate to the relief of the permanent poor of the parish'. They asked for a contribution, but were told that the men should be able to survive without pay for two weeks.[2]

Introduction of the Poor Law

In 1838 the Poor Law was introduced to Ireland and Poor Law Unions were set up all over the country. Each Union had its own workhouse where relief was based. The workhouses were deliberately made as unattractive as possible because there was a real fear that good conditions in them might encourage a population explosion of the destitute. The introduction of the Poor Law made no obvious changes to the Poor Fund of Monkstown: the local workhouse is not mentioned in the record books and work with the poor continued without any appreciable decrease in demand. The Monkstown Poor List continued until 1936, when 'the Rector undertook to pay the recipients of the Poor List from funds at his disposal', from 1 July 1936 onwards.

Other charitable organisations

While the Poor Fund needed a sizeable network of men and women to administer it efficiently, an even larger group of committed parishioners ran other charitable

Report of the Monkstown
Coal Fund, 1866–7.

REPORT

OF THE

Monkstown Coal Fund and Charitable Association.

WINTER 1866-67.

First Distribution of Coals, December 6th, 1866.

Committee.

REV. R. MACDONNELL, D.D.	EDWARD ALEXANDER, ESQ.
REV. J. F. PEACOCKE.	GILBERT SANDERS, ESQ.
REV. H. JOHNSON.	JOSEPH GALLOWAY, ESQ.
REV. JOHN LYNCH.	THOMAS BELL, ESQ.
WILLIAM ANDREWS, ESQ.	CAPTAIN M. CAULFIELD.
KEITH HALLOWES, ESQ.	MAJOR MILLER, R.E.
MATHIAS KENNY, ESQ.	MR. R. BAILEY.
MAJOR-GEN. HANNYNGTON.	

Treasurer and Hon. Secretary—WM. ANDREWS, ESQ.

Assistant-Secretary—MR. P. HACKETT.   *Collector*—MR. JOHN HAZLEY.

At no more urgent period could the Committee submit to the kind sympathy of the Subscribers the Annual Report of the "Monkstown Coal Fund and Charitable Association" than at the present—a season of serious illness, and a time at which the poor require every comfort and aid, as well as provision, against distress that may arise during the severity of the coming Winter.

Viewing the relief that has been afforded throughout the Winter of 1865-66, your Committee are much gratified to state that considerable and certain benefit has been conferred.

Two Thousand Two Hundred and Fifty-three Bags of Coal, equal to One Hundred and Forty-one Tons, were distributed.

The system in the issue of Tickets has been found of great utility; and from the zeal and impartiality of your parochial Clergy, extremely poor and deserving families have not only been regularly supplied each day of issue, but the Coals were delivered free at their homes.

Cases of distress of all denominations have, on the recommendation of Subscribers, met with most impartial attention.

The expenditure, as shown by the account, has been in excess of the Subscriptions received, chiefly owing to the increased price of Coals.

The rate of the Contract for the ensuing Winter 1866-67 has so much increased, that your Committee venture to hope, that a liberal support will enable them to provide an equal, if not a greater issue than that of the past season.

The explanation given at the foot of the annexed Rules, the Committee trust, will satisfy the Subscribers of the mode adopted, and the Committee will scrupulously distribute to the deserving, the Tickets that the Subscribers do not retain for their own disposal.

First Distribution of Coals, December 6th, 1866.

organisations within the parish. The Coal Fund alone had a committee of fifteen. There was also the Dorcas Society, the Parochial Union Benefit Society and the Monkstown Protestant Orphan Society. In addition, the Lending Library and the Penny Bank were founded to help the poor. Although these societies helped Roman Catholics also, their primary allegiance was to members of the Church of Ireland.

The Coal Fund (c. 1858–1912)

One of the earliest surviving annual reports for the Coal Fund is that of 1858–9. It gives a list of its committee of fifteen, its rules and accounts, and names the subscribers and their donations. Its stated aim is 'to relieve the deserving poor of all denominations, by the distribution of Coal and (should prevalent distress require it) Meal either gratuitously or at reduced prices'. Between December 1858 and March 1859, 1,222 bags of coal were delivered free. Anyone who donated over 10 shillings to the Fund was entitled to recommend either one family or seven individuals for free coal, and had to fill in a form detailing the name, address, occupation, weekly income and number in the family. The amount delivered depended on the weather. In 1865–6, a 'Winter which was of more than ordinary severity', 156 tons of coal were delivered, whereas, during a more average winter, such as that of 1878, 101 tons were delivered to 116 Protestant families and 78 Roman Catholic families. The Coal Fund continued its work up until about 1912.

The Dorcas Society (1828–c. 1911)

This was one of the earliest charities in the parish. It was apparently launched in 1828 by Lady Anglesey, whose husband, William Henry Paget, 1st marquis of Anglesey (who lost his leg at Waterloo), had been appointed as lord lieutenant in February 1828.[3] As one of the Harbour Commissioners (from April 1828) the marquis was closely involved in the building of the new pier, so his wife was privy to the inside knowledge apparent in a letter, dated 25 September 1828, to the Harbour Commissioners. It asked them, on behalf of 'her Excellency the Marchioness of Anglesey', to allow 'the Ladies of the Anglesey Dorcas Institution of the Parish of Monkstown the use of the Magistrates' Room at the Police Office now unoccupied until such time as it may be required for its original purpose'. The Harbour Commissioners (including Lady Anglesey's husband) obviously had no objection.

The aim of the organisation was 'to benefit and encourage those whose lot in life is in many ways rough and full of care' by helping them to purchase sensible clothes cheaply. A Charity Bazaar ('Admission one shilling, children free') was held at the Anglesey Arms Hotel, Kingstown, on Monday 28 September 1829. Two days earlier, an advertisement in *Saunders's News-Letter* had suggested that 'Ladies and Gentlemen Visitors' should buy 'fancy articles … and ready made clothes in the shop … at a low price … to clothe their poor neighbours on their return home, and at the same time afford the means of employing the numerous widows and orphans of this parish whose applications for work are incessant'.

In the 1880s the organisation — now simply known as the Dorcas Society — was run on Saturdays in the Infants' School on Cumberland Street, Kingstown, by the ladies of the parish. The Annual Report of 1876 observed that 'a very considerable number of families, whose means barely suffice for a livelihood, dwell at the Kingstown or eastern end of this parish. To provide suitable clothing, even of the plainest sort, is to such, often a matter of the greatest difficulty and concern'. 'Poor needlewomen' were supplied with 'good and useful materials' at cost price, which they repaid in instalments according to their means. In 1881 there were 173 women on the Society's books, 150 of whom were also paid about seven shillings every three months.

Monkstown Protestant Orphan Society (1830–c. 1934)

One of the first parish Protestant orphan societies to have been founded in Ireland, the *Irish Ecclesiastical Gazette* of 11 October 1907 reported that 'the Monkstown Protestant Orphan Society (had been) working since the year 1830'. The national Protestant Orphan Society had been founded in 1828, probably triggered by the 1826 Vestry Act, which meant that the Vestry could no longer levy cess, or tax, for non-church purposes, such as the support of parish orphans. Thus the organisation had to be run on voluntary contributions. Its aim was 'to provide for the most destitute orphans, being Protestants, or whose surviving parent is a Protestant, diet, lodging, clothing and scriptural education, and finally to apprentice them to Protestant masters and mistresses', reported *Saunders's News-Letter* of 5 October 1830. By the 1870s the rules of admission to the Society had relaxed slightly: by then it admitted 'the children of mixed marriages, no less than those who … had two Protestant parents'.

In 1836 one of the girls, Catherine Duffy, was apprenticed to Mr Thomas Eustace (1834–40), the schoolmaster at Monkstown, and clothed in a new outfit for the occasion, costing a guinea (27 April 1836). The Society's Annual Report of 1845 recorded that James Malholm, aged fifteen, was apprenticed to 'a respectable ship owner' and added, 'having evinced a strong predilection for a sea-faring life, it was not thought prudent to oppose the boy's wishes'.[4]

If at all possible, the children were kept with their mother. If not, 'approved Protestant nurses' were employed. The children (on average about 30 in number) had to attend school every day, as well as Sunday school; if they were absent without a reasonable excuse, their nurses were 'admonished' or fined. However, 'rewards' for the children were also allowed for in the accounts and an annual 'feast' took place — like that of 1911, which cost £1-18-6. The 'feast' of 1876 must have been a much more lavish affair as it cost £3-17-10.

Apart from printing and postage, every penny donated to the Orphan Society went to the support of the children. The 1911 Annual Report gave an account of its six departing orphans: four of them found employment locally (at the Hibernian Marine School, a draper's firm in Kingstown, a dairy in Monkstown and in domestic service), while two boys were 'sent to Canada and favourably settled with well-to-do farmers in Ontario', the first of the orphans to be able 'to take advantage of the better prospects offered by the Colonies'.[5]

STORY OF TWO PARISH ORPHANS

From the Poor Fund books we can piece together the story of the Bird family of Monkstown. It was maintained by the parish for some years: Charlotte, the elder, for six years (1836–42), Anne for ten years (1836–46) and their widowed mother, who had been on the parish Poor List from 1835 or earlier and continued until 1842.

On 23 December 1835 Mrs Bird, along with 25 others on the Poor List, was given ten shillings as a 'Xmas Charity'. Soon afterwards, her elder daughter, Charlotte, was given into the care of a 'Mrs. Millin' (probably 'Miller', from subsequent entries), who was paid £5 a year (or 8/4 a month) for her keep. The family, who may have come from Delgany, Co. Wicklow, next appear in the books on 23 June 1836. The entry reads: 'Mrs. Miller for maintenance of Charlotte Bird for 4 months, £1-13s-4d. Mrs Bird for car hire to and from

Delgany, 4s.' Anne must have joined Charlotte in early 1837; when Mrs Fanagan took over from Mrs Miller, she was given the cost of a 'bedstead for the Birds, 5/-' on 7 February 1837.

Clothing, schooling and 'rewards' were extra, and money was not stinted, as the following entries show:

Flannel vests and flannel for vests, 9/6 (5 November 1836)
A.B. [Anne Bird] one frock, 5s (12 April 1837)
C.B. [Charlotte Bird] one pair shoes, 5s (13 April 1837)
A.B. and C.B. for two chemises, 2/6 (25 April 1837)
A.B. for p.coat [petticoat] and two chemises, 5s (18 May 1837)
A.B. and C.B. for repairing shoes, 1s (13 September 1837)
A.B. and C.B. for frocks 13yds print C [calico?], 8/8, calico for lining, 1/6, trimmings, 3½d (19 September 1837)

More must have been spent on Charlotte and Anne than the entries indicate since there are numerous 'general' entries in the books, such as:

Printed calico and lining for parish orphans, £1-4-3½ (14 December 1836)
Worsted for knitting stockings for do, 4-4 (14 December 1836)
Blue cloth for cloaks for Protestant orphans, £2-5-6 (28 January 1837)
Trimming for bonnets for Protestant orphans, 5-6 (22 May 1837)

Meanwhile, the Widow Bird was given one shilling a week and a 'quartern loaf' of bread (a 4lb loaf). The girls earned some pocket money by singing in church with six other 'poor girls', earning between 2/6 and 5/- each a month. Charlotte and Anne joined the group in October and November 1836 respectively. To ensure their attendance, anyone who missed a Sunday was 'fined for absence from singing, 1/6'. Boys occasionally joined the group from 1838.

The parish organised the girls' apprenticeships with Protestant mistresses: 'Grace Maholm as apprentice Fee with Anne Bird, £2-10s' (14 January 1840) and 'Jane Maholm, portion of fee with A. Bird, £2-10s' (11 January 1841). One of these ladies may have been the 'Mrs. Malhohn' who was 'assistant sextoness and bellows blower' at the church during 1834–55 (*see Appendix 5*).

Charlotte's maintenance apparently stopped in March 1842, four years before Anne, who was probably therefore four years younger. If Anne was twelve when she was apprenticed in 1840, the girls were maintained by the parish until they reached the age of eighteen (1842 for Charlotte and 1846 for Anne). The Widow Bird was taken off the Poor List in 1842. Charlotte continued to sing in church for another seven years, until 1849. Anne also continued to sing until July 1846, when she disappears from the Poor Fund records, probably because she had reached the age of eighteen.

On 27 May 1849, as the worst of the Great Famine was ending, 'Charlotte Bird, formerly parish orphan', was given £2 'to enable her and her mother to go to America'. Charlotte may have needed the money to pay for the ticket in advance as she was still singing in church during June and July of that year, collecting her 5/- each month. She finally disappeared from the records in August 1849. If the calculations are correct, she was now 25.

Monkstown Penny Bank (1877–c. 1912)

Founded in 1877, the Monkstown Penny Bank was 'established with the view of encouraging the Working Classes to lay by even small sums as a provision for future wants, and especially of teaching the young to cultivate in early life the useful habit of thrift'. The savings bank opened, like the Dorcas Society, on Saturdays in the Cumberland Street Infants' School, between 12 noon and 2pm 'for the benefit of the Poor of the Parish of Monkstown'.

Sums from one penny upwards could be deposited. In 1903 the bank met with some competition: a similar scheme was founded in Kingstown 'under Roman Catholic auspices' and many Catholics removed their savings as a result. The Select Vestry's Annual Report of 1904 tried to look on the bright side: it maintained that this was 'gratifying evidence that the benefits afforded by the Monkstown Penny Bank for so many years past to the poorer classes of the district are perceived, and its usefulness admitted'. The 1905 report regretted that lodgements had decreased by £200 because two other Penny Banks had opened in Kingstown. However, the 1906 report tried not to crow while informing its readers that the 'depositors' had increased again as most of the former savers had now returned.

The Workman's Lending Library (1876–c. 1904)

This library was founded in 1876, according to the Select Vestry's Annual Report of that year, 'to bring within convenient reach of the many hard-working families at the east end of the parish, a supply of useful literature. At the mere nominal charge of One Penny per month, books are lent out, and in cases of invalids gratis'.

Monkstown Parochial Union Benefit Society (1816–1970)

This society was set up as a form of voluntary health insurance. In 1884 it had 340 members 'divided into three classes, paying a weekly sum of 1s-1d, 6d, and 1d, for which they receive Medical advice and Medicine, with 12s, 5s, or 1s-6d weekly allowance when sick; and, in the event of death, their relatives are paid £5, £3 and £1-10s, according to class. The weekly payments are at a rate far more than sufficient to pay the expenses, and the balance is divided annually at Christmas after payment of all claims. The sum returned at the last Annual Meeting was £292-16s, being, in the first class, £2-5s-6d; in the second, £1-3s-6d; and 5s-6d in the third — the two first being self-supporting, but the last named assisted by donations.'

In 1846 'females' were admitted to a fourth class; the usual admission fee was waived and the weekly sum of one penny imposed. (In 1846 those in the third class paid an admission fee of 9d and thereafter 3d weekly.) Members found 'drunk and disorderly' were fined for the first two offences and faced expulsion for the third.[6]

Not surprisingly, the mortality and sickness rate was directly related to class: in 1869 the committee of the Society 'heartily congratulate(d) the First Class on their unprecedented freedom from illness, only one week's sick allowance having been drawn. In the Second Class, there has been but one death, and the Sick list is not nearly so serious as in the previous year. In the Third Class the number of deaths, and the heavy demands on its funds, are a source of much regret to the Committee ...' A 'pall and Hand-hearse' were lent to

242

members for funerals.

Things had improved markedly among the poor by 1903, although there was a sting in the tail: 'Class C [Third Class] continues to enjoy its wonderful immunity from illness, no sick money having been paid, and the one death which occurred in this class was of a member not "in benefit".'[7]

Parish foundlings

> *Foundling: A childe which is laid and found in the streete …*
> *or elsewhere, which they call commonly a foundling.*
> Withals' Dictionary, 1602

Monkstown's earliest Vestry book contains the following entries:

> Thursday the 19th day of April 1744
> For Margery Cabe paid her for nursing the parish foundling
> for half a year due ye 1st of Jan 1743,   1-0-0
> Sunday 28th March 1769
> For leaving a foundling in the Poor house,   2s-2d
> Mrs. Rathbone for nursing a Fondling left at the Church,   £2-2-2
> Fondling Hospital for Admission of d(itt)o,   £5-0-0

Who were these parish foundlings? In 1722 William King, archbishop of Dublin, wrote a letter exposing the widespread practice of abandoning newborn babies. But the House of Lords did not appoint a commission to investigate the situation until 1730. The reality was much worse than could have been imagined. When 'nurses' and churchwardens were interviewed, a chilling story emerged.

At this time the workhouse in Dublin, founded in 1704, catered only for abandoned or orphaned children over six years of age;[8] the younger ones were considered the responsibility of the parishes in which they were found. Each parish employed a nurse to look after any babies found abandoned within its boundaries. Her usual salary was £2 or £3 a year, but this was not enough to cover the cost of looking after the huge number of babies involved. So the nurse became a 'lifter'. When she went on her nightly walk around the parish and found a baby, she would 'lift' the child, bring it to a neighbouring parish and leave it there, usually with a sedative, diacodium (a syrup made from poppy-heads), in its mouth to stop it crying. If the baby was lucky enough to be found by the 'lifter' employed by the second parish before dying of cold and exposure, it might well be transported back to the original parish. This practice went on with the apparent knowledge of many of the churchwardens (Hayden 1943).

When 'lifting' babies became public knowledge, the resulting scandal compelled the authorities to turn part of the original workhouse into a Foundling Hospital for Deserted Infants. At its gate a 'turning-box' was installed. This was a cradle into which a baby could be placed, while the person bringing it could disappear discreetly after ringing a bell to summon the porter. This was not an Irish invention: these turning-box arrangements were found throughout Europe, as in France at the Ancien Hospice de Hautefort in Perigord, where the device was last used in 1847 (Taylor 1999), and in Italy at the Spedale degli Innocenti in Florence.

The parish, then, was responsible for its foundlings and for naming them. Many were landed with names that would have publicly identified them as parish foundlings, such as 'Mary Parrish, ore ye Parrish Child, was baptized one ye first day of July 1705' and, probably, the unimaginatively christened 'Mary Monks' in 1897. Charles Lindsay, perpetual curate of Monkstown (1815–55), delighted in more exotic surnames for the deserted infants he baptised. The Monkstown Baptismal Register of 1828–35 gives an entry for a child baptised on 31 March 1829: 'This child was found on the steps of Dr. Plant's house in Montpelier Place between the hours of 10 and 11 at night, on 21st March 1829 … and then appeared to be 3 days old. Her Christian name is Mary — I call her by the surname of Plantagenet to denote the place where she was found.' For another child, baptised on 4 August the same year, the entry reads: 'This child (Sarah Piers) deserted at Cherrywood — we gave it "Piers" for a sirname'.

Lindsay's curates followed suit: 'Barbara. Deserted child. March 1 1836. This child being found on the lands of Rochestown, I have called "Roche's-terre" alias Rochester. John Grant.' But sometimes their imaginations deserted them: 'January 28 1829. Elizabeth. This child was found at Mounttown, apparently about 6 months old, near the house of a man of the name of John Byrne — on which account we have given it the name of Johnbyrne.' Again, 'Mary. This child is a foundling being found in George's street, Kingstown — has been called for a surname "George"' (baptised 11 May 1834). 'Georgina King, foundling', who was baptised on 30 August 1840, was probably also found on George's Street.

In 1796, for the months of May, August and September, there are three sad little entries in the Monkstown Burial Register: all three read, 'A child from Dublin'. No name or age, and the almost accusatory tag, 'from Dublin', indicates that these were thought to have been infants from town, dumped in Monkstown. The relatively low numbers of foundlings baptised (between none and three a year) would appear to indicate that many babies died before being found. From 1848 to 1850 only two foundlings were baptised in Monkstown (remarkably few considering the size of the parish or Union of Monkstown — including Mounttown, Kingstown, Glenageary, Killiney, Dalkey, Blackrock, Cabinteely, Tullow and Kill-of-the-Grange).

Unfortunately, the Foundling Hospital was not a haven for the survivors. It took over a hundred years, and thousands of children's lives, before it was, quite rightly, closed down. Conditions there should have scandalised respectable Dublin society just as much as the custom of 'lifting' did in the first place. The figures speak for themselves: between 1750 and 1760, 7,781 babies were admitted to the Foundling Hospital. Of these, 3,797 died. Even worse statistics emerge from the infirmary of the hospital, where sick babies were sent: between 1791 and 1796, 5,716 babies were admitted — there was one survivor. The high death rate was due to mismanagement, cruelty and neglect, insufficient food and filthy conditions (Hayden 1943).[8]

Lady Arabella Denny, a relation of Judge Robert Day and friend of Grace La Touche, who were both Monkstown parishioners, did her best to change things in the Foundling Hospital during the 1760s and '70s (Butler 1946–7). She instigated feeding routines and financed better food, clothing and conditions. The survival rate improved markedly during her supervision, but after she died things became as bad as ever. In 1790, of 2,180 foundlings who were admitted to the hospital, 2,087 either died or could not be traced. From time to time there were investigations into conditions, but nothing was ever done. This appalling situation continued until 1 January 1830, when it was announced that the Foundling Hospital for Deserted Infants would close down forever by order of the lord lieutenant, as reported in *Saunders's News-Letter* on 2 October 1829.

CHAPTER 18

Raising money from pew rents

11th. (Lord's day.) To church into our new gallery, the first time it was used.
There being no women this day, we sat in the foremost pew and behind our
servants, and I hope it will not always be so, it not being handsome for our
servants to sit so equal with us.
The Diary of Samuel Pepys, 11 November 1660

'In one fashionable church with which we are acquainted, where pewdom reigns supreme, the clergyman, who is seldom or never seen by his poorer parishioners, is aptly styled "the apostle to the genteels".' So said the *Irish Ecclesiastical Gazette* on 13 August 1881 in its 'Church Notes' section. Whether this satirical remark referred to Monkstown Church is not known, but more than a year before, on 20 March 1880, the same newspaper had said with direct reference to Monkstown Church, 'Let the present assessment system, which is but another name for pew rents, be given up, and let all comers to the church, poor as well as rich, be placed upon an equality as regards worshipping in the House of God'.

Inequality between rich and poor

Today it seems iniquitous that at one time 'all comers … poor as well as rich' were apparently not considered equal 'as regards worshipping in the House of God'. But the warning of Jesus that those who loved 'the chief seats in the synagogues' would 'receive greater damnation' (Mark 12:38–40) apparently did not impinge on the comfortable 'upstairs–downstairs' world of the wealthy landed gentry of Monkstown. Besides, the selling and letting of pews was one of the chief ways of bringing in money to the church coffers — and probably one of the major talking points of the parish. Alexander Pope (1688–1744) listed the main topics of conversation of the country clergyman of his day:

> *Toast Church and Queen, explain the news,*
> *Talk with churchwardens about pews,*
> *Pray heartily for some new gift,*
> *and shake his head at Doctor Swift.*

Monkstown's 1789 Georgian ('pre-Semple') church had only 54 pews altogether, accommodating about 340 people seated. The church was very cramped: 'Forty of the pews may with inconvenience, which in such a place is perhaps with impropriety, each hold one person more, and the entire capacity of the church is, when inconveniently crowded, competent to 380 persons, seated in pews'. There were only six public pews, which were even narrower; as John Semple's report to the Vestry in 1823 said, 'but 2½ feet wide in which grown up persons cannot kneel'. Those six pews were free and 'for the use of the parish at large'. This apparently generous gesture actually meant that only a fraction of the majority — the hundreds of 'poor Protestants' — in the parish could attend church if they wanted a seat and nobody seemed at all concerned.

The dilemma, however, was that pew subscriptions, like the collection plates of today, brought in much-needed money, while public pews brought in none. The cost of the private pews depended on their size and position. In 1807, like today, front pews were less popular and therefore less expensive: the six front pews cost 11/4½ each, whereas pews 7 to 34 cost 18/5 (*see Appendix 6*). The pew-holders actually owned their pews: they were responsible for repairing them if necessary and could furnish them comfortably with cushions and kneelers. The ownership of a pew represented church membership — and consequent responsibilities. The Vestry minutes of 1817 record that 'each pew owner (was) asked for a subscription of one guinea each towards a hot air stove'.

One writer in the *Irish Ecclesiastical Gazette* of 13 August 1881 severely criticised pew-owners of the day, saying that they tended to look down on those in the public pews and that they were 'too dignified to kneel to Almighty God, too lazy to stand at the reading of the Gospel, and too sleepy to attend to the sermon'. Since their seat was waiting for them, they would be late for church and distract everyone else. He added the caveat that the clergyman in a pew-rented church could not speak freely: he 'must preach to please his hearers, not to teach them, or else his pews will empty, and his stipend dwindle away'.

When John Semple enlarged the 1789 church, making it three times bigger, he wrote on his plans that 'the pews in the West gallery and in the area of the Old Church (would) seat 400', whereas 'the enlargement (would afford) seated accommodation for 800 persons', so that, altogether, the 'new' church would hold 1,200 people. The Building Committee allocated four classes of pews, costing between £10 and £50 each, depending on their size and position in the church (*see Appendix 6*). This represented a steep escalation in their rent, designed specifically to bring in money for the building of the church. But it also created a further divide between those who could afford a pew and those who could not.

The new seating plans were put on view in the schoolhouse. Semple had labelled the pews from A to R, stating the number of people each could accommodate: 'A' pews could seat nine, 'B' seven, 'D' six and 'E' five. The Building Committee decided that there would be a ballot, or lottery, of pews to finalise the seatings. Each applicant was 'intitled to one (pew) in the new (church) at least equal in dimensions (to their pew in the old church) and as nearly as possible in the same relative position'. To fit the maximum number (and therefore bring in the maximum amount of money), the pews were crammed into the church, closely surrounding the central three-decker pulpit, so that there was only the width of one pew left clear on three sides of it. All the pews faced inwards towards the pulpit, including those in the transepts and in the small extension at the east end.

It was one of the churchwardens' responsibilities to allocate pews, so, as soon as they had

Semple's plans, they proceeded to sell them. Nowadays, the church tends to fill up from the back; in 1832 it was the other way around — the wealthy and titled sat towards the front, with the poor sitting in the free 'public pews' at the back. But, presumably to the churchwardens' disappointment, the hoped-for queues of pew-buyers did not materialise. In their newspaper notice announcing the opening of the new church on Christmas Day 1831, placed in *Saunders's News-Letter* of 13 December, the churchwardens, perhaps a little plaintively, stated that there were 'some pews still undisposed of, both in the galleries and body of the church'.

It was, however, the sale of the pews (and vaults) that raised the final amount necessary for the building of Semple's church (total cost of about £8,665; *see Chapter 5*). The allocation of seating had been haphazard before 1831, but now the churchwardens insisted that all the proper legalities should be observed 'which … (had) not hitherto been the case'. From that year a faculty had to be obtained from the Ordinary (i.e. permission from the bishop). By 14 March 1832 all the pews from 1 to 139 were allocated; the remaining 33 were allocated to the Building Committee as security against the final £426 owed to the builders.

The problem with pews

The 'fun' was only starting. The churchwardens' books, letters and documents demonstrate the incredible amount of time and energy they spent allocating pews, collecting 'subscriptions' and trying to sort out the legal wrangles that inevitably arose as a result. Pews were the property of their owner and could not be used casually by anyone else. They could be bought and sold, sub-let or even bequeathed in one's will. *Saunders's News-Letter* of 23 May 1840 carried the following advertisement:

> 'Monkstown Church. To be Sold, a pew in this church, well circumstanced. Apply to James Cowley, jun., Esq., 24, Temple-street.'

Again, in the same paper on 23 April 1849 it was announced:

> 'Monkstown Church. To be Sold by Auction, on Friday, the 5th of May, 1849, by order of the Executors of the late G. Wilson, Esq, one of the best Pews in the above extremely beautiful Edifice, capable of seating six persons. Mr. Downes, the grocer, who lives opposite the Church, has kindly permitted the Auction to be holden at his house. This Pew should be valued for £3 per Annum, and as there is no reserve the terms of sale are, as usual, cash. Sale to commence at Twelve o'Clock — Terms Cash. Thomas Dockrell, Auctioneer, Valuator and Undertaker, Kingstown.'

Pews could even be attached to the sale of a property. A notice in the *Dublin Evening Mail* on 23 April 1832 announced:

'To be let, for three years, Monkstown Castle [this refers to Monkstown Castle House, not the fourteenth-century castle) … NB A large pew in the New Church of Monkstown attached to the house.'

Pew-owners could get very irate if they found someone else in 'their' pew, even if they themselves never darkened the church door. A court case almost ensued in about 1832 over Pew No. 73, owned by Samuel Smith (son of George Smith, the stone contractor for Kingstown Harbour). Samuel used the pew until his death in about 1844, after which the pew remained unoccupied for ten or eleven years. Since it was vacant, the churchwarden, Major Winter, reallocated it in 1855 to Robert Giveen, who used it regularly and paid for any necessary repairs. But as far as the Smith family was concerned, the pew still belonged to Samuel's son, George. He, however, did not attend church. When he died, his son, William, found out that the pew was being used by Robert Giveen, by then (1857) a churchwarden. Although William Smith was actually a Roman Catholic and obviously did not intend to use the pew, he directed his attorney to write to Giveen, demanding that he should, as churchwarden, 'preserve said pew or seat from being interfered with or used by any person or persons whatsoever except authorized by the same William Smith'. Giveen found himself in an awkward position and sought legal advice, apparently successfully. A final note on the correspondence reads, 'Nothing further has since been done in the matter'.

Another problem with pews was that the influx of summer visitors to Monkstown and its surrounds (for the sea-bathing and other amenities) could not find seats in church. Pew-owners (and even those who claimed pew-ownership, like William Smith; *see above*) were not prepared to share their pews, whether they were attending services or not. Thus in August 1857 the Vestry decided to run a poster campaign to educate the public in the intricacies of pew-ownership. The sum of 12/6 was spent on printing 250 large posters, announcing new regulations:

'MONKSTOWN CHURCH
PROPRIETORS OF PEWS

Are particularly requested to accommodate as many as they possibly can in seats, as a great number of the Parishioners, who have been unable to procure Pews in the Church, and families who come to reside in this Parish in the Summer Season, cannot be provided with Seats in any other way.

"Those, who by purchase or otherwise are entitled to Pews, have, in fact, only a right of precedence in being shown into them, and lose it on every occasion that they absent themselves from the Church until after the first Lesson".

Brown's Ecclesiastical Law'

The churchwardens had an uphill battle as they tried to change the traditions of a century. They took legal advice several times and were told that they, as the churchwardens, were the only ones entitled to allocate pews (not the Vestry or incumbent or through inheritance) and that 'dealing and trafficking in pews' was 'illegal and should in future be discontinued and discountenanced'. This advice came from A.E. Gayer of 47 Upper Mount Street on 21 June 1858 and was recorded in the Easter Vestry Minute book of 1871–present.

In May 1858 the churchwardens fixed a notice on the church doors, asking parishioners to apply for pews only to them or to the parish clerk, Mr Hackett. But they were ignored. One of the members of the Building Committee for the 1831 church (who had been allocated pews at that time) was even threatening proceedings in the ecclesiastical courts against the churchwardens for interfering with his legal 'rights'. The churchwardens complained: 'There are numerous persons holding pews in the overcrowded church, who are in the habit of attending with regularity the performances of the services, but who do not occupy more than one or two sittings in the pews, leaving the remainder of the pew empty, some refusing to allow persons standing near to be admitted to the vacant seats until a portion of the service is gone through, others altogether refusing admission to persons who are strangers to them'.

Pew Allocation Book covering the years 1863–4.

The lawyers began to suggest that the beleaguered churchwardens should take legal steps against 'intruders' in the pews. Although they apparently never used this final lever, inch by inch the churchwardens got 'tough' and gradually reasserted their authority. In 1865 Molyneux Betham's younger brother, Sheffield, seems to have followed the new guidelines when asked to hold a seat while the owner departed for her summer holidays. The Churchwardens' Order book of 1865 records: 'No. 82, Mrs. Perry application to Captain Betham that her pew may not be filled during her absence for six weeks after 8th June 1865. No allocation to be made of Mrs. Perry's seat.' This request was honoured, but visitors were allowed to use Mrs Perry's pew in the meantime. Another case involved a Mrs Murphy, who was not allowed the 'entire of seat No. 88' as she had requested on the grounds that 'she (had) not a sufficient number to occupy seats'.

In 1872 the churchwardens sent a letter to every pew-holder, asking if they still wanted their 'sitting' and, if so, to forward the appropriate fee. The churchwardens further instructed the pew-holders that they would like to be informed if their present accommodation either exceeded or fell short of their actual requirements 'as there are many applicants for Sittings'. One of the replies said, 'Mr. Bate presents his compliments to Mr. Kincaid and to Mr. Hodges and in reply to their letter begs to say he will not retain the pew No. 19 hitherto occupied by him in Monkstown Church any longer. Mr. Bate wishes to mention that the furniture of the pew is his. [signed] 6 Longford Terrace, 27th January 1872'.

251

Removing inequality and the end of pew-ownership

It had been a gargantuan struggle, but the churchwardens were finally more or less in control of the church pews. But this was not the end of the story. The pews were still not 'free'; they were merely allocated for a yearly fee or rent (assessment) to a particular pew-owner by the churchwardens. Meanwhile, greater things were happening outside the environs of Monkstown. Public feeling was growing against the rent and sale of pews. The 'Free' Church in Great Charles' Street, Dublin, had been consecrated as early as 1828 and was 'open and free to all descriptions of persons, inhabitants of Dublin, during the time of Divine Service, especially for the accommodation of the poorer classes of inhabitants with liberty of entering therein and occupying the seats and pews' (Wallace 2001).

In 1884 the Vestry paid £103-2-9 to re-cushion the allocated pews in the main body of the church. In February 1903 it was suggested during a Vestry meeting that 'some effort should be made to make the occupants (of the 36 free sittings) more comfortable'. To fit these pews with mats and kneeling stools would cost £25. But the church roof needed immediate work done on it, so it was agreed to postpone the refurbishment of these pews since 'such expenditure (was) not justified'. However, it was pointed out that 'if it was a matter of principle, it should be carried out'. When an anonymous donor gave £20 towards the refurbishment, the Vestry sanctioned the remaining payment and announced, in the minutes of July 1903, that they had 'at last been enabled to remove the inequality in comfort between the free and the allocated sittings in the church'.

During the recession of the 1930s, members of the Vestry became extremely concerned about the parish finances as they saw the income from pew assessments falling every year. In 1935 they decided to organise a new system of voluntary giving in the form of weekly envelopes. An open letter was sent to the parishioners, followed up by a visit, explaining the two main ways of subscribing to the upkeep of the parish: an annual subscription to the Sustentation Fund (a fund set up towards the salaries of the clergy) and the new 'Free Will Offering Scheme'. In appealing for their help, it was said that 'no weekly offering is too small'. The system of pew assessments continued in parallel with the new envelope scheme, but was to be discontinued in 1938.

In October 1935 fifteen parishioners had joined the scheme and contributed £4-0s-3d between 20 October and 31 December. The following year 22 people gave £23-5s-3d. In the meantime, the organist, paid singers and parish secretary had all accepted a cut of 15% in their salaries (Annual Report, 1936). By 1938 there were 22 subscribers — three parishioners who gave 6d a week had left the parish, whereas one new subscriber of 3d a week had been gained. Things were picking up by 1944: the honorary treasurer of the Vestry noted that there were less 'coppers' (halfpennies and pennies) in the collecting plates, which was 'a good sign' (Easter Vestry minutes, 1944). In 1948 the Rev. Arthur Butler reorganised the envelope collection system, calling it the Monkstown Church Defence Association (or Alliance), 'designed to help Parishioners to subscribe to the Parochial and Sustentation Fund in a modern and convenient way'.

Pew allocations continued in conservative Monkstown right into the 1950s and there were 'long discussions' during Select Vestry meetings as to whether they should be

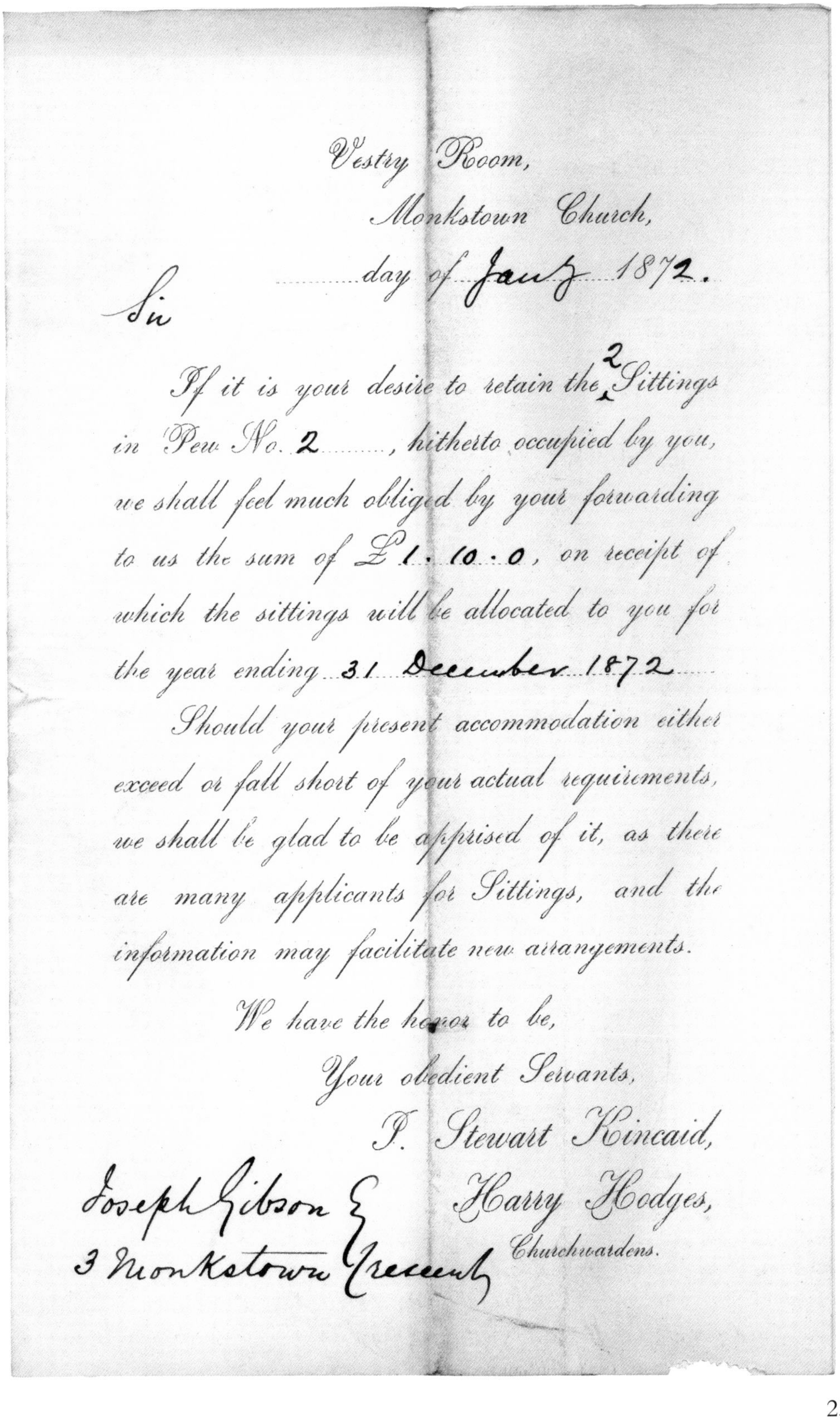

Vestry Room,

Monkstown Church,

_____ day of Jany 1872.

Sir

If it is your desire to retain the 2 Sittings in Pew No. 2 _____, hitherto occupied by you, we shall feel much obliged by your forwarding to us the sum of £1. 10. 0, on receipt of which the sittings will be allocated to you for the year ending 31 December 1872

Should your present accommodation either exceed or fall short of your actual requirements, we shall be glad to be apprised of it, as there are many applicants for Sittings, and the information may facilitate new arrangements.

We have the honor to be,

Your obedient Servants,

P. Stewart Kincaid,

Harry Hodges,

Churchwardens.

Joseph Gibson &

3 Monkstown Crescent,

One of the standard 1872 letters from the churchwardens to current pew-holders, this one completed and returned by Joseph Gibson of 3 Monkstown Crescent.

abolished. Eventually, in 1959, letters were sent to all 173 parishioners with pew allocations, asking for their views. The overwhelming majority were in favour of abandoning the system, and so in April 1959 pew allocations at last came to an official end.

There were some exceptions to this rule, but these were quite permissible. The Index to Sittings in April 1955 records that the two boarding schools in the parish, Brook House and The Hall, were asked to carry on sitting in the galleries as before, and the three front pews in the nave were to be kept for those who wanted to sit near the pulpit, presumably because they were hard of hearing. The girls of The Hall School occupied ten pews (Nos 130–139, with 50 'sittings') in the north gallery and the boys of Brook House had nine pews (Nos 107–115, 45 'sittings') in the south gallery opposite, while the children of the Claremont Institution for the Education of the Deaf and Dumb sat in Pew No. 152 (seven 'sittings') in the second row of the west gallery.

Fund-raising without pews

With the abolition of pew rents in 1959, the problem now was how to raise money for the church without this guaranteed source of income. At least when parishioners had forked out their annual subscriptions for pews they had felt that they were getting something for their money. Voluntary donations, on the other hand, were much more difficult to extract. Well-meaning parishioners and churchwardens did not necessarily possess financial skills; they soon found that raising money was fraught with difficulty.

This is well illustrated by one disastrous attempt to raise money in 1954 for the organ restoration fund. A 16mm 'sound film' of the 'Royal Tour of Australia' was hired, tickets printed and an operator hired. Mrs Smyly, who ran the 'Birds' Nest Home' orphanage, was invited to attend with 50 children, who were provided generously with sweets. The film was shown in the Knox Memorial Hall in two evening seatings, at 7pm and 9pm, on 5 and 6 August. The accounts for the two nights show:

Sale of tickets	£51-12-0	Gratuities (Bray & operator)	£2-0-0
Donation	1-0-0	Sweets (Birds' Nest)	15-9
	£52-12-0	Hire of film	27-0-0
		Printing tickets	2-5-0
		Revenue Tax	19-15-0
		Balance to credit of Organ Fund	16-3
			£52-12-0

Although the children had apparently enjoyed their treat and the Revenue Tax Office had its cut, the organ fund only made 16/3. This was obviously not the answer. And so Christian Stewardship was eventually introduced to Monkstown in 1982. Further Stewardship programmes took place in 1995 and 2001. As Mr Micawber cautioned in *David Copperfield*, 'Annual income twenty pounds, annual expenditure nineteen nineteen six, result happiness. Annual income twenty pounds, annual expenditure twenty pounds, nought and six, result misery'.

CHAPTER 19

Parish organisations

Today there are numerous organisations within Monkstown parish. Georgian Monkstown had no 'organisations' as such; all its energies revolved around the myriad functions of the Vestry, which would have listed helping the 'deserving poor' as one of its priorities. Victorian Monkstown, on the other hand, while still very concerned with charitable enterprises, was also keen on all-round self-improvement, especially from a spiritual point of view. The 1895 Spring programme for the Young Men's Christian Association (1878–*c.* 1911) is a good example.

Besides the religious talks, there were others on political and scientific subjects. Social meetings, debates, musical and literary evenings were held. Those who attended were given marking papers on which they marked the essays or debates out of ten, and prizes were awarded accordingly. In 1884 women had been allowed to attend the opening social evening for the first time, and 'the largeness of the attendance and the interest in the proceedings displayed by the visitors showed the wisdom of the Committee in making the experiment', reported the *Monkstown Herald* in November that year. By 1895 the men were debating 'That TCD should be open to Women' and listened to an essay on 'The New Woman'.

The YMCA meetings were gradually replaced by Bible classes: by 1901 there was a weekly Tuesday evening meeting in the Vestry, while another 'Bible Class for Young Men' was held on Sundays at 10.15am in the schoolhouse. Incredibly, by 1911 a third Bible class had started for this group on Friday nights.[1]

James Digges La Touche, the eldest son of William, was the first secretary of the Sunday School Society, founded in 1809. A Sunday school existed in Monkstown during the childhood of Thomas Rooke (b. 1825 and uncle of the later organist, B. Warburton Rooke), who returned to Monkstown as a curate in 1850–9. He started the afternoon Sunday school and by the time he left, in 1859, there were 38 teachers for the Sunday morning and afternoon classes.[2]

The Sunday School Calendar of 1880 would strike horror into the average child of

Spring programme of 1895 for YMCA meetings in Monkstown.

Monkstown Young Men's Christian Association.
FOUNDED A.D. 1879.
SEVENTEENTH SESSION—PROGRAMME FOR SECOND TERM.

Members meet every TUESDAY Evening, at 8 15 o'clock, in the Vestry Room attached to the Parish Church.

SCRIPTURE SUBJECTS.			LECTURE, ESSAYS, DEBATES, &c.	
1895.				
Feb. 5.—"Stephen,"	... ...	Acts vi.	ESSAY—"Competition,"	BARRY MEADE, B.A.
,, 12.—"Stephen's Defence,"	...	,, vii., 1-34.	DEBATE—"That all Raffling should be regarded as Gambling, and suppressed by law,"	*Aff.*—B. MEADE, B.A. *Neg.*—J. SIBTHORPE. G. B. PILKINGTON, B.A.
,, 19.—"The First Christian Martyrdom,"	...	,, vii., 35-60.	READINGS, ...	MEMBERS.
,, 26.—"Simon Magus,"	... ...	,, viii., 1-17.	ESSAY—"The Cultivation of the Imagination,"	The VICE-PRESIDENT.
Mar. 5.—"St. Peter and Simon Magus,"	...	,, viii., 18-40	ESSAY—"Progress,"	Sr. C. DOBBS, B.A.
,, 12.—PUBLIC LECTURE.			LECTURE—"The Birds we see and hear,"	Rev. C. W. BENSON, M.A.
,, 19.—"Conversion of Saul of Tarsus,"	...	,, ix., 1-19.	ESSAY—"Nature and the Supernatural," Part II.,	Prof. BARRETT.
,, 26.—"St. Peter's Miracles,"	... ...	,, ix., 20-43.	ESSAY—"The Glaciers of the Alps," ... (*Illustrated.*)	G. PIM, F.R.G.S.
Apr. 2.—"A Godly Soldier," ...	...	,, x., 1-23.	DEBATE—"That T.C.D. should be open to Women,"	*Aff.*—J. W. HOUGHTON. A. N. S. RICE. *Neg.*—The VICE-PRESIDENT. J. W. BALL, B.L.
,, 9.—"The Power of the Keys," ...	...	,, x., 24-48.	ESSAY—"An Art Ramble through Belgium and Holland,"	J. W. SIBTHORPE.
,, 16.—"Good out of Evil,"	... ...	,, xi.	ESSAY—"The New Woman," ...	J. W. GALLOWAY, B.A.
,, 23.—"God's Power and Man's,"	...	,, xii.	SHORT PAPERS by D. BEATTY, C. HOUGHTON and R. FLEMING.	
,, 30.—CLOSING MEETING.			MUSICAL and LITERARY EVENING, DISTRIBUTION OF PRIZES.	

☞ The regular and punctual attendance of Members is requested.

Donations and Subscriptions will be received by the Hon. Treasurer. Names of persons desiring to become Members may be sent to the Hon. Sec. Members willing to be appointed Speakers upon any particular Essay or Debate will kindly communicate with the Hon. Sec.

today. Prizes ('premiums') were awarded for the most assiduous and punctual of the children. Two or three verses had to be learned by heart each week and a subject studied from the Prayer Book (such as 'The Litany, Part 1') or from the Bible (such as 'Jeroboam, the Son of Nebat'). Sunday school did not replace the morning service; it occurred *before* the service and on Sunday afternoons. This meant that children were spending much of that day attending church and Sunday school.

The Rev. Arthur Stewart (son of the murdered missionaries Robert and Louisa Stewart; *see Chapter 22*) wrote: 'My earliest memories are of going to Sunday School, at Monkstown Church, followed by the Morning service at 11.30. We were given full measure in those days and so were seldom home before 2 o'clock — too long at our age. I think I can attribute to those long periods of inattention, when my mind was occupied with some story I had read, or in making up one of my own, that I have always had a difficulty in concentrating my mind on, and listening to, a sermon.'[3]

According to Miss Edith Dowse, during her father's long incumbency (1894–1929), 'It was the very mischief to get the children to go to Sunday school — the Plims [Plymouth Brethren] used to give them tea and buns [at a rival Sunday school] and we couldn't compete'.

There were several other non-charitable organisations or societies in the parish. For example, there was the Monkstown and Kingstown Scripture Readers' Society, which operated from 1874 to about 1878. It was part of the wider Scripture Readers' Society for Ireland, founded in 1822, which employed 'competent persons to read the Scriptures among the poor, and by familiar conversation, leading their attention to divine things' (*Thom's Dublin Directory*, 1853). In 1853, 84 readers were employed by the society, each with a specific district and under the supervision of a clergyman. In 1876 nearly 10% of the 'Protestant Episcopalian' population still admitted to being illiterate (1881 Census); the society apparently wanted to prevent any more loss to the 'Wesleyites', who were thought to be 'poaching' illiterate and naive members of the Established Church.

Cover of the calender for Afternoon Sunday School in 1880.

The Monkstown Society paid a generous annual salary of £84 (the two curates were being paid £100 each) to a 'scripture reader' to visit the homes of the Protestant working classes to read them passages from the Bible. According to the Select Vestry Report of 1876, the reader paid 1,708 home visits, 'not including many casual ones, or visits to the "Home" on Sunday evenings', and reported that 'the Protestants of the working classes seem improved both temporally and spiritually' (*Thom's Dublin Directory*, 1853).

The Parochial Lending Library operated from the Vestry rooms from about 1856 to 1946. It was open to subscribers only (5 shillings a year) for an hour every week. The twelve-page printed catalogue listed 335 books in 1856, including *A boy's adventures in Australia*, *Anna or a daughter at home*, *Taylor's Holy living and holy dying* and *The domestic habits of birds*.[4] By 1876 the list had grown to 1,160 books. By 1911 there were 1,600 books and the borrowing time had narrowed to 30 minutes between 12.30pm and 1pm. By 1946 the library 'had ceased to serve any useful purpose', so the books and three bookcases were 'disposed of'.[5]

Members of the Lay-Helpers' Prayer Union (1881–1918) prayed weekly for the clergy and all parish activities. A Communion service was held quarterly.

The Monkstown Association of the Church of Ireland Temperance Society (founded in 1878) had sixteen on its Executive Committee in 1883, when it began. Instructive lectures were given, such as the one in April 1884 (reported in the *Monkstown Herald*) by Dr Ridge, 'the eminent physician', who 'dwelt at considerable length on total abstinence, which, he demonstrated by statistics, resulted in improved health and longevity'. The Band of Hope catered for the young people. An account of their annual fête, from the *Monkstown Herald* of July 1885, gives a flavour:

'The annual flower show and industrial exhibition in connection with the Monkstown Band of Hope was held on Friday, the 17th of July, in the grounds of Monkstown Castle. This year, there were in addition athletic sports open only to members of the local Band of Hope of over two months standing. Various amusements were to be had on payment of a small fee in different parts of the ground, including Aunt Sally, swings and a shooting gallery. The day was fine up to about half past five in the afternoon when the rain began to come down in torrents, but by that time the greater part of the sports had been finished. A large number of people visited the fête, so that the Committee of the Temperance Society have reason to congratulate themselves on the success of the undertaking.'

The Choral Union was formed in 1883 'for the purpose of promoting a practical knowledge of Music, with a view to improving the Service of Praise in Public Worship'. The society had been proposed as early as 1877 (Select Vestry minutes, 29 January), but apparently did not get off the ground until the appointment, in 1882, of the eighteen-year-old B. Warburton Rooke, the new church organist. He conducted the group and one of its first concerts was reviewed in the *Monkstown Herald* of June 1884: 'Mrs. Joseph Robinson's Cantata, *God is Love*, was effectively rendered, the choruses being given with precision and the proper regard to light and shade'. After remarking that another section was 'of a miscellaneous character', the reviewer thought that 'Caldicott's chorus, *This is the House that Jack built*, formed a pleasing contrast to the more serious part of the programme and received a warm encore, which, however, was not responded to'. Sadly, the Choral Union was disbanded in about 1885.

The Men's Meetings were instituted in 1944. To quote G.A. Mackay's 1958 poem *Monkstown memories*, 'Then we had an innovation — Men's Meetings were the new sensation'. Harry Lidstone, the honorary secretary to the Select Vestry, had sent out dozens of letters to all the men in the parish: 'A meeting of the men of Monkstown Parish on Tuesday 18th April 8.15pm in the Knox Hall at which we hope to have an interesting and informal discussion on matters of general interest in connection with the life of the Parish. Being anxious to have as large and representative an attendance as possible, we would like you to make a very special effort to come along.'

Six apologies are filed with Mr Lidstone's original letter, including a postcard from 20 Longford Terrace, saying 'I cannot be present on the 18th, I am sorry but I always am at work in Dublin on Tuesday evenings. [Signed] Lennox Robinson'. But 30 to 40 others did turn up for that first Men's Meeting, when one brave parishioner read a paper on the 'somewhat gloomy and unpromising subject' of 'Hell: A recapitulation of some Victorian conceptions and beliefs', which led to 'a surprising discussion'. Perhaps Lennox Robinson (author, playwright and director of the Abbey Theatre from 1909 to 1956, and also a registered vestryman for 1944) eventually made it to the Men's Meetings, as they were subsequently changed to Wednesday nights, once a month during the winter.

Guest speakers were invited to speak on 'subjects of general interest'. This would be followed by an informal discussion. Mackay gave an entertaining description of the sessions in his poem, *Monkstown memories*:

> *Men, whose silence was a boast,*
> *Left the Mothers' Union at the post.*
> *The talks were good; the discussion free;*
> *We often chose to disagree.*
> *Thro' altercation, rich and ripe,*
> *Arthur just smiled and smoked his pipe.*

'Arthur', of course, refers to the popular rector of the day, Mr Butler. In 1958 he wrote of the success of the Men's Meetings, adding that 'it (was) obvious they (had) come to stay'. The five talks given in 1958 were on 'The Iona Experiment', 'How my life was changed', 'The Lambeth Conference of 1958' (by Dr George Simms, archbishop of Dublin), 'Psychology and day-to-day problems' and a 'Religious Brains Trust'.

This was not Dr Simms's first contact with the Men's Meetings of Monkstown. Several years earlier, the Rev. Arthur Butler had invited Jack White, a journalist with *The Irish Times*, to give a talk on 'The Church and the Media'. At the discussion afterwards, it was suggested that the Church of Ireland could play a more leading role in the media. Later, Jack White asked Mr Butler who he would recommend to write a religious column in his paper. George Simms, then bishop of Cork, was suggested. As a result, his Saturday column in *The Irish Times*, signed 'S', became an institution for nearly 30 years, over the period 1953–81 (Whiteside 1990). (Coincidentally, Butler's successor as rector was the Rev. Billy Wynne (1958–78) who, with Fr Francis MacNamara, OP, wrote a fortnightly column in *The Irish Times*, called 'Thinking Anew', from 1992 to 1999, published in book form in 2000.)

Extraparochial organisations

Giving outside the parish has been cited as a measure of a healthy parish. Monkstown has always had a tradition of generosity (*see Chapter 17*). The 1911 Annual Report of the Select Vestry listed the following 23 societies with a Monkstown branch. Interestingly, all these societies were represented in Monkstown by 22 women and one man; this was in the days when women could not attend or vote at Vestries or become churchwardens, yet they played their part effectively. The following list has been arranged alphabetically for ease of reference:

Army Scripture Readers' Society; Church Missionary Society; Church of England Zenana Missionary Society; Church of Ireland Temperance Society; Clergy Sons' Education Society; Colonial and Continental Church Society (especially for clergy emigrating to Canada); Continental Society; Deaf and Dumb, Adult Christian Association; Deaf and Dumb, Claremont Institution; Dublin University Fuh Kien Mission; Female Association (Working Party); Girls' Friendly Society; Hibernian Bible Society; Irish Church Missions and Schools; Irish Society; Island and Coast Society (formed in 1833 to help schools on the offshore islands and western seaboard); Medical Needs; Mission to Lepers in India; Mission to Seamen; Prison Gate Mission; The London Society for promoting Christianity amongst the Jews; Young People's Scripture Union; Young Women's Christian Association.

Before 1895 Monkstown had only an auxiliary branch of the Church Missionary Society (CMS). Then in 1896 the Monkstown CMS Association was founded as a direct result of the murders of the Stewarts in China (*see Chapter 22*). Monkstown soon became known for its outstanding support for the CMS. The *Irish Ecclesiastical Gazette* of 15 January 1897 noted, 'It is a curious coincidence, and perhaps worthy of note, that the two parishes in Ireland which return the largest sums to the CMS (according to the last report) viz., Monkstown, Co. Dublin and St Thomas', Belfast, are in charge of two brothers'. The 'two brothers' referred to were John Clarence Dowse, incumbent of Monkstown during 1894–1929, and his twin brother, William, incumbent of St Thomas's (and who had also been curate in Monkstown during 1886–92). Other curates of Monkstown also served with the CMS: Edward Goldsmith (1896–1902) went on to become organising secretary of the CMS Medical Fund and William Coulter (1924–32) became vice-president of the CMS (Wallace 2001).

In 1896 thirteen people worked on the committee or as collectors, and two of 'Our Own Missionaries' were supported — George Pilkington in Uganda and Ella Green in Mid-China. The following year Pilkington was murdered during a tribal squabble. By 1911, 23 parishioners were directly involved with the Monkstown CMS Association. There were now four of 'Our Own Missionaries' — the Rev. and Mrs C.M. Gough worked in India's Clarkabad, while the other two were medical missionaries in Persia's Isfahan, which was 'in a very disturbed state' at the time. That year the incredible amount of £1,436-8s-9d was raised in the parish for the CMS alone. This was not unusual: in 1903 £1,301 had been raised and £1,206 in 1904. The Monkstown CMS Association was replaced in 1926 by the Monkstown Missionary Union, which continued to be well supported in the parish. The Hall School, for example, raised money for missionary causes: in 1934 the school sent £25 to maintain a bed (called The Hall School bed) in Dr Schafter's Hospital in Isfahan. For about 20 years, from *c.* 1936 to *c.* 1957, Miss Doris Boyland, a former pupil of The Hall School who worked in India, was 'Our Own Missionary'. The Annual Missionary Sale is now an institution in Monkstown and raises large amounts for missions every year.

Monkstown's tradition of generosity continues. In 1997 Monkstown Missionary Union Allocations were as follows:

Bishops' Appeal (for the Third World)	£4,500
Leprosy Mission	£1,850
per Mrs Tracey	£180
Church Missionary Society	£2,000
Crosslinks	£500
Mothers' Union Overseas	£500
per Mothers' Union	£300
National Bible Society	£400
United Society for the Propagation of the Gospel	£400
Jerusalem and Mid.Eastern Society	£400
Society for the Propagation of Christian Knowledge	£500
South American Missionary Society	£400
Feed the Minds	£400

Dublin University Far Eastern Mission	£350
Missions to Seamen	£100
Church of Ireland Jews' Society	£100
Total	£12,880

The Vestry also contributed £250 towards the Peace Park at Menin Bridge in France (to commemorate Irish soldiers who died during the 1914–18 war) and £500 towards the appeal for St Colman's Cathedral in Cloyne.

Parish organisations from 1956 to present

The first edition of the *Monkstown Review* in 1956 listed the numerous parish organisations at that time:

> Badminton Club (Wednesdays and Fridays, Knox Hall). Founded in 1920.
> Brownies, 23rd South Dublin (Saturdays, Knox Hall, 11am)
> Choir (Fridays, Vestry, 8pm)
> Dramatic Society (Knox Hall). Founded in *c.* 1954.
> Girl Guides (Fridays, Hall School, 6.45pm). Founded in 1927.
> Guild of Youth (Tuesdays in Vestry, 8pm). Founded in *c.* 1938.
> Men's Meetings (3rd Wednesday in month, Knox Hall, 8pm). Instituted in 1944.
> Mothers' Union (first Wednesday in month, Vestry, 8pm). This organisation, founded in England, started in Raheny in 1887; the Dublin Association was formed in 1892 and the Monkstown branch was operating by 1919.
> Social Club (once per month in winter)
> Sunday School, with 22 teachers and 135 children: Kindergarten (Minor Hall of Knox Hall), Senior School (Main Hall of Knox Hall) and Boys' Bible Class (Vestry)
> Table Tennis Club (Mondays and Thursdays, Knox Hall, 7.45pm). Founded in 1934.
> Young Wives' Group (once per month, Rectory). Founded in *c.* 1956.

Two of the earliest children's organisations were the Wolf Cubs (*c.* 1929–31), the Girl Guides (*c.* 1927, closed, reopened *c.* 1969, closed) and the Rangers (*c.* 1927–34). Then in April 1972 the 39th Dublin (Monkstown) Scout Troop was launched, followed by the Cubs in March 1973. Both have, unfortunately, closed down since. In 1990 the Boys' Brigade, 6th Company, was founded by Carole Cullen. The 6th Company had originally been attached to the Mariners' Church, Dun Laoghaire, but was disbanded when the church closed in 1972. The boys were divided into two groups, according to age: the Anchor Boys and the Junior Section. They closed in 1995. Ladybirds operated from 1995 to 1988.

At the start of 2003, nearly 50 years later, many of these parish activities continued (table tennis, for example, is even held on the same evenings as in 1956) and new ones have formed:

261

Altar Guild (care of altar linen)

Bible Study (Tuesdays, 8pm)

Bridge Club (Thursdays, 10am–12.30pm)

C.S. Lewis Study Centre (lending library at west door)

Church Choir (Adult Choir, Mondays, 8pm), Junior Choir (Sundays, 10am) and 'Older group' of Junior Choir (Mondays, 7pm)

Flower-arranging group (rota of 20 people)

Healer Prayer Union (founded 1979, Monday after 2nd Sunday in month, 7.30pm)

Indoor Bowling Club (founded 1966, on Wednesdays and Fridays, September–April, 7.45pm)

Mothers' Union (1st Wednesday in month, October–April, 8pm)

Sunday Club (the new name for Sunday School, during 11.15am service)

Table Tennis Club (Seniors on Mondays, 8.30pm, and Thursdays, 7.30pm; Juniors on Mondays, 7.15–8.30pm)

Tuesday Club, a social club for the elderly (founded in 1990 by Pauline Huissoon)

Web site for parish founded by Fiona Deverell (www.monkstown. dublin.anglican.org)

The following organisations have come and gone over the years: Alpha Group (2001–2); Badminton Club (closed 2001); Boys' Brigade 6th Company (closed 1995); Brownies (closed 1999); Dramatic Society (closed in 1980s, reopened briefly 1994–5); Friends of Monkstown (1974–*c.* 1978); Girls' Friendly Society (*c.* 1924–43); Men's Meetings (closed *c.* 1958); Tuesday Club (closed 2003); the Women's Circle (in assocation with St Patrick's Roman Catholic Church, founded by Mrs Jennifer Dalton in 1992, closed 1996); Youth Club (formerly Guild of Youth, closed 2001).

PART 4:
'THOSE WHO HAVE GONE BEFORE'

CHAPTER 20

Carrickbrennan Graveyard and the resurrection men

Thus are poor servitors,
When others sleep upon their quiet beds,
Constrain'd to watch in darkness, rain and cold.
First Sentinel in Shakespeare's *Henry VI*

Today Carrickbrennan Graveyard is a haven of tranquillity. In a hollow in the middle of this sleepy churchyard the ancient parish church of Monkstown reposes, surrounded by leaning headstones. Within its walls a little slated house nestles. On a warm summer's evening the buildings seem to slumber to the tune of birdsong and the buzz of insects. But if those granite stones could speak we would hear a conflicting story — an ongoing saga of wanton destruction and plundering, even, on at least one occasion, the taking of life. That slated building inside the church is a watch-house, built for a specific reason: to prevent body-snatchers from digging up recently interred corpses.

Before the Anatomy Act of 1832, the only bodies available for dissection were those of executed criminals. In the numerous private anatomy schools of Dublin and further afield, demand exceeded supply — more bodies were needed. The nefarious business of the 'resurrection men' grew up. These body-snatchers plied their lucrative trade as they roamed the city graveyards at night, looking for freshly turned earth. The practice continued unabated for about 100 years, from the 1730s, but was at its height in the early 1800s. People were not as fastidious then; besides supplying medical students with bodies for dissection, hair was bought by wig-makers, teeth by dentists. Occasionally a fatal infection must have been transferred to the recipient, but this did not deter the illegal trade (Fleetwood 1988).

Although there were numerous reports of resurrection men in the newspapers of the time, the vast majority of grave robberies went undetected. It was not considered a crime to steal bodies: the courts could only impose sentence if the grave-clothes were stolen too. One 'Resurrection man extraordinary', reported *Saunders's News-Letter* of September 1829, went into a pub in Frederick Lane, where he left the wrapped-up corpse of a four-year-old child, 'grave clothes and all', under a seat while he sallied forth looking for a surgeon who would buy the body. When he returned, he was 'detained' and 'committed for the felony of the clothes'.

Bodies were also exported from Dublin to medical schools in London and Edinburgh. In Scotland parishes kept a very close eye on their graveyards, so bodies were harder to come by there and the Scottish route was particularly busy. The price depended on availability — in 1828 the going rate was a few shillings per corpse, while three bodies in December 1831 cost £38. Sometimes victims were murdered to provide fresh bodies. An entry in *Saunders's News-Letter* of December 1831 reported: 'Missing and supposed to be burked ...'. The term 'burking' came from the notorious Irishman, William Burke, who, with his friend William Hare, murdered tramps staying in their lodging house in Edinburgh and then sold their bodies to a Dr Knox for dissection.

The last thing the recently bereaved wished for their nearest and dearest was for their remains to fall into the hands of the anatomists. Mounting a constant guard over recent burials was the only sure way to prevent body-snatching. The city graveyards were particularly busy, especially the 'Hospital Fields'. There were rich pickings enough in Dublin; it would have seemed unnecessary to travel to Monkstown, several miles outside the city (and passing Merrion Graveyard on the way), and then run the risk of transporting a suspicious-looking object on the return journey. But the parish of Monkstown obviously thought itself at risk. The Vestry minutes of 14 August 1803 record that Catherine Perry and Anne Ward were paid 4/4 for watching the bodies of 'three drowned persons' buried in Carrickbrennan Churchyard.

Grave-diggers would sometimes earn extra money on the side by supplying the resurrection men. Sometimes they even did the digging for them: after all, they were experienced, had all the tools of the trade and the crucial 'inside knowledge'. For a substantial fee, the grave-diggers would turn a blind eye. The churchwardens were aware of these abuses of the system. When George Hughes became the grave-digger at Monkstown in 1826, the Vestry minutes record his precise orders: 'That it be an instruction to him that he dig the graves himself — and do not allow any person to dig for him, except it be in his own presence and under his own eye'. This cryptic command probably referred to the well-known practice of interring the body in a shallow grave so that it could be easily and quickly removed afterwards.

Desecrated and abandoned

In 1789 the church in Carrickbrennan was abandoned and the new Georgian church opened down the road. By then the old church had already fallen into 'ruin and decay' and this process was speeded up even further by its disuse. Stones were taken from the church for building and the graveyard was vandalised. In March 1826, reported *Saunders's News-Letter*, '... several tombs in the burial ground of the Church yard of Monkstown were attacked and mutilated, and the railings about them torn down, some parts of the same carried off, and others scattered about the Church yard'. The parishioners were appalled at the desecration. The Rathdown Association, most, if not all, of whom were parishioners, offered an enormous reward of £50 for any information leading to the conviction of those responsible, saying that they held 'such barbarous conduct in the highest degree of detestation and abhorrence ... which is so subversive of every principle of religion, morality and common humanity'. The Association met in John Armit's house, with James Price as

The watch-house was built between 1829 and 1831 as a precaution against the forays of the 'resurrection men' in Carrickbrennan Graveyard. It housed guards with blunderbusses and dogs in a crypt below.

secretary, both churchwardens of Monkstown.

A watch-house was built between 1829 and 1831 in order to protect the churchyard. Although the parish was 'strapped for cash' (Semple's church was still not completed and would cost more than £8,000), it still thought it essential to build the watch-house, so genuinely worried were the parishioners about body-snatching. It was constructed inside the abandoned church, using its stones, at a cost of £16-13s-4d (Ecclesiastical Commissioners 1837). The south and west walls of the old church were incorporated in the building and the west door blocked up. The church windows were bricked up where necessary and loop-holes knocked through each wall to enable watchmen inside to see in all directions and to use their blunderbusses if necessary. Dogs were kept in a crypt under the building and when they barked at intruders the watchmen could release them by pulling open a trapdoor from inside the watch-house (English 1987).

A watch had to be kept day and night for up to ten days after each burial. A fireplace was built to keep the guards warm during the long winter nights. September to November were the busiest months and as the evenings drew in the resurrection men had the cover of darkness for their gruesome activities. Anatomy lectures began in November after the long summer holidays, so there was a huge demand at this time. The body-snatchers were helped by the fact that the ground was still relatively soft; the frozen earth from December onwards made digging more difficult.

Besides dogs and guns, the graves themselves were designed as deterrents. On average, it might take less than an hour for two men to steal a body from a freshly dug grave. But a huge stone slab would need several strong men to shift it and disinterring the body could

267

take hours. High railings would not stop the determined, but could make things more difficult. Finally, lead coffins were harder to break open than wooden ones.

In spite of all these precautions, the resurrection men were apparently undeterred. On 11 October 1831 the following story appeared in *Saunders's News-Letter*:

> 'MANSLAUGHTER — On Saturday, a man, named Timothy Darby, died in Mercer's hospital, in consequence of a gun shot wound he received some time ago in Monkstown Church-yard, inflicted by a man named William Smith. They were both, along with others, engaged to prevent a corpse from being disinterred, which had been recently buried in the grave-yard, at the time of the fatal occurrence. Darby, a short time previous to his death, declared that the wound, of which he was dying, had been accidentally inflicted by Smith, who, however, was yesterday committed to stand his trial for manslaughter.'

The watch-house was obsolete within a short time. On 1 August 1832 the Anatomy Act became law in Ireland and bodies were allowed to be donated for teaching. Body-snatching was no longer profitable and those who were buried in Monkstown and elsewhere were allowed to 'rest in peace'. Simpler gravestones appeared again and the graveyard returned to its slumber. But not for long. Until they owned their own burial-grounds, Roman Catholics and 'dissenters' (Presbyterians and Methodists) were buried in churchyards belonging to the Church of Ireland, although their clergy were not allowed within the churchyard and no religious service could be held within its precincts. When Mary Anne Galbraith (aged 47) of Kingstown was buried in Carrickbrennan on 8 September 1849, it was recorded that 'Being a Dissenter no Clergyman (was) invited'.[1]

Occasionally this caused trouble. On 20 February 1856 the lord lieutenant's spokesman wrote to the archbishop of Dublin, Richard Whately, about an incident in which a dissenting minister, the 'Reverend J.D. Smith ... (was) refused permission to perform burial service in the church yard of the Parish of Monkstown' by Archdeacon William Fitzgerald, the incumbent. An act had already been passed in order to avoid such situations: it specified that an incumbent was supposed to write to both the lord lieutenant and the minister involved, giving his reason for refusing permission. The lord lieutenant was obviously afraid of the incident getting out of hand: his spokesman stated that 'in a case which his Excellency cannot but foresee may be the subject of public discussion and enquiry ... (he) was anxious that the Law should prove to be in all respects complied with'. He added that the act was 'manifestly intended for the relief of Dissenters' and if Fitzgerald's example was followed it would be '(rendered) a mere nullity'.[2]

In June 1856 a Mr Pollard-Urquhart asked a question in the House of Commons as to whether 'the government (was) ... aware that certain of the clergy of the Established Church in the diocese of Dublin had prohibited Presbyterian and Dissenting clergymen from holding any formal service at the interment of their people in the consecrated burial-ground, thereby compelling them, in some instances, to hold the funeral service on the highway, or wherever they best could?' A Mr Horseman replied that he was 'only aware of one case of the kind referred to by the honourable gentleman' and cited that of Archdeacon Fitzgerald. He added that the lord lieutenant had received a report on the incident, but had 'no power to proceed further, and the matter therefore dropped' (Hansard, 26 June 1856). From the correspondence it appears that the legalities were not complied with and it is not clear what happened subsequently. Archbishop Whately cannot have disapproved too much of Fitzgerald's actions since he was appointed bishop of Cork, Cloyne and Ross just over a year later.

In 1874 Carrickbrennan Graveyard was closed down.[3] It was full owing to recurring cholera epidemics (1832, 1849, 1861 and 1872). According to Rooke (1923), the church was vested in the Representative Church Body in 1879; the Commissioners of Church Temporalities 'would not vest in that body any burial ground separated from its church by a carriage highway', so Carrickbrennan Graveyard was taken into the care of the Corporation at that time. After that, only those with room still in family plots were allowed burial, the last of which took place in the 1950s.

Restoration of the graveyard

The neglected state of Carrickbrennan Graveyard in the early 1980s led to the setting up of the Carrickbrennan Restoration Group, chaired by Pat Walsh. Her friend, Valerie Smyth, a teacher at Dun Laoghaire's VEC (Vocational Education College), saw this as an ideal assignment for her students, which it proved to be; the project came first in the An Taisce 'Work for Ireland' competition of 1984. Between 1985 and 1986 the Restoration Group organised the major refurbishment of the graveyard, under the combined aegis of Dun Laoghaire Historical Society, AnCo and Dun Laoghaire Corporation, with the guidance of an archaeologist, Ms Linda Doran.[4] The gravestone inscriptions were copied and recorded in a computer database and the site of each burial marked on a detailed map. Damaged ironwork on tombs was repaired, the boundary wall and the entrance arch were rebuilt, ivy was removed from the church and a mature sycamore tree removed from the walls of the watch-house.

An ecumenical service marked the official reopening of Carrickbrennan Graveyard, at which the Rev. Kevin Dalton and Fr Vincent Quilter, parish priest of St Patrick's, officiated. Among those who attended were the O'Conor Don, David Andrews, TD, and Charles Haughey, TD. Joe English, a member of the Restoration committee, produced an informative booklet on the graveyard in about 1987, describing the work and listing the recorded burials.

There were so many burials that the church now lies in a hollow, the ground level raised by several feet owing to the thousands of interments. Among these are:

- 104 of the victims of the horrific *Rochdale* and *Prince of Wales* 1807 shipwrecks;
- four sailors from the *Ajax* who tried, in 1861, to rescue others from the *Neptune*, but were themselves drowned;
- Charles Haliday, the historian (d. 1866) and author of *The Scandinavian kingdom of Dublin*, published in 1881;[5]

- Joseph Holt (d. 1826), the rebel general of the 1798 insurrection;
- hundreds, without headstones, of cholera victims from the plague year of 1832 and those who died in the Great Famine of 1845–50;
- unknown numbers of Roman Catholics and 'dissenters', buried here until the 1820s.

Others who are buried in Carrickbrennan also have wall memorials inside Monkstown Church, such as Judge Robert Day, Justice Alexander Crookshank, Sir John Lees and Sir William Betham (*see Chapter 22*).

Besides the recorded attack in 1826, there must have been other forays into the graveyard to steal and damage headstones. Only eight of the 480 names in the first Parish Burial Register covering the years 1699–1786 have a surviving headstone (Guinness 1908). The earliest headstone, belonging to John Hall, only dates back to 1750 and there are only fifteen headstones from before 1800. Twelve of the 28 headstones dating from 1736 to 1835, listed by the local historian John D'Alton (1838b), are no longer there.

There are now 436 registered headstones in Carrickbrennan Graveyard, bearing the names of about 800 individuals. We know that thousands must have been buried here, most without any marker. But there were those like 'My Lady Mary Shears of Dunleary' (d. 1711), 'Ye Right Honorable the Lady Theudorah' (d. 1727) or the two children of Lord Ranelagh ('John Joens' [Jones] and 'Margret', who both died in 1769) who must surely have had imposing monuments. We can only speculate as to why these memorials are missing. A combination of vandalism, theft and wear and tear over the centuries have meant that nearly half of those headstones identified by D'Alton in 1838 have now disappeared without trace. Two years after D'Alton's visit, John Semple, Senior, architect of Monkstown Church, was buried in Carrickbrennan Graveyard (*see Chapter 6*). If he did have a monument over his last resting-place, it is no longer there.

CHAPTER 21

Of monuments and mourning

*We met … Dr. Hall in such very deep mourning that either
his mother, his wife, or himself must be dead.*
Jane Austen, in a letter to Cassandra Austen, 17 May 1799

Georgian grieving

How long should a woman be in mourning for her husband and vice versa? The Georgians had very definite rules on the subject, as reported in *Walker's Hibernian Magazine* of November 1786:

> 'A wife mourns for her husband, a year and six weeks; four months and a half in cambrick, the cloak, gown and petticoat of French stuff, four months and a half in crape and woollen, three months in silk and gauze, and six weeks in half-mourning. A husband for his wife, six months, … six weeks for the great and small weepers, six weeks after in woollen without weepers, six weeks in silk, and six more in half mourning.' ('Weepers' were conventional badges of mourning, such as long black hat bands or white linen or muslin cuffs.)

Other people anticipated their own passing. For example, Dr Benjamin Domvile (*see Chapter 22*) left two bequests of £100 in his will so that two gentlemen (one was the archdeacon of Dublin, Isaac Mann) could get 'mourning rings' made, to wear in his memory.

There are six Georgian wall monuments in Monkstown Church. That of Benjamin Domvile is the oldest, dating from 1774, and was probably brought from the old church in Carrickbrennan. The other five were erected in the 1789 Georgian church, the original church to be built on the present site: James Stewart (1798), William Digges La Touche (1803), William Browne (1813), Alexander Crookshank (1813) and Joseph Atkinson (1818).

In most of these monuments, there are common denominators:

- The monument is often superimposed on a black pyramid. Elizabethan and seventeenth-century tombs frequently carried obelisks; the eighteenth-century equivalent was a pyramid, which like the obelisk was also an antique motif and symbol of eternity.

- A coat of arms is displayed. Only members of the landed gentry, and therefore armigers, would have been in the position to afford such monuments.
- There is effusive praise for the departed, even if only a line.
- There are usually classical motifs on the memorial, such as draped female figures or urns. This was the age of the Grand Tour, which Joseph Atkinson, at least, had undertaken.[1] The aristocracy used these motifs to remind them of the sights they had seen in Italy, Greece and Egypt.
- Seventeenth-century tombs were often coloured; eighteenth-century monuments, however, were more restrained and kept to white marble on a black or grey background.

While the wealthy spent a great deal on lavish funerals and ceremonial, the poor could not even afford a funeral pall (a black or purple velvet cloth to cover the coffin). The Vestry of Monkstown therefore decided to buy one and lend it out as necessary. In 1763 £4 was spent in purchasing a funeral pall; a second one was needed the following year, costing only £2-18-4, but 'a bag for hold of same' was also bought, at a cost of 1s-7½d. In 1819 palls were still being provided: the Vestry minutes record that it was 'Resolved that a decent black pall for the use of the poor be provided by the church wardens'.

Victorian mourning

Understanding how death was observed in Victorian Ireland gives us an insight into the monuments erected for the dead. The story of the *Ajax* will serve as an example.

In February 1861 Captain J. McNeill Boyd (49) and four of his men from the coastguard ship the *Ajax* were drowned during a rescue attempt. Ironically, the men from the coal-boat *Neptune*, whom they were trying to help, survived. The description of the funeral of the sailors — Boyd was buried in St Patrick's Cathedral — helps to illustrate the sober pageantry associated with Victorian bereavement (Powell 1861):

> 'So calm was the surface of the harbour that the flags — hung half-mast high — drooped motionless above their long reflection in the glassy waters. The day was calm and beautiful. The bright sunlight of very early Spring lit up the waters of the bay ... The funeral was formed at the Revenue-yard, about two o'clock, and moved towards the place of burial, Monkstown churchyard [the present Carrickbrennan Graveyard], in the following order:— First came a firing party of Marines from on board the Ajax; next the band of the 26th Cameronians, performing the solemn strains of the "Dead March in Saul". Close to the band came the coffins, on a gun-carriage, drawn by sailors from the ship, followed by the whole of the Ajax crew, the cutter's men and boatmen two by two. Behind, marched the officers of the Ajax in full uniform, the chaplain, the Rev. Mr. Howe, and other clergymen accompanying the procession, which was closed by a hearse and a long line of vehicles. The procession extended for fully half-a-mile over the road taken. It was computed

that at least 6,000 or 7,000 persons attended. The quiet little parish churchyard at Monkstown was filled to overflowing while the coffins were being lowered, and the beautiful and expressive service for the dead was being read by the chaplain.

Every tree and every point capable of being used as a position for witnessing the ceremony was quickly seized on. At the close of the service, three volleys were fired, and the crowds dispersed.'

In 1843 an average funeral for the titled cost £500–£1,500; for the 'upper-class' £200–£400; and for the 'ordinary' middle-class family £50–£70. However, over the next 30 or 40 years the Victorian funeral became a status symbol. In the 1870s an expensive middle-class funeral could cost over £1,000 (over €94,000 in today's money), and frequently did. Poor families could be ruined in attempting to emulate the rich. By the 1880s more realistic values were reappearing, so that in 1894 the British medical journal *The Lancet* reported that funeral reform had been achieved and that £10–£15 would pay for a funeral 'in good taste and reverence, but without any extras'.

On the day of the funeral of the more affluent, proceedings would start at the house of the deceased. All the window blinds would be drawn. 'Mutes' would often stand on the front doorstep; paid by the undertaker and dressed in full mourning, they would maintain a solemn silence and walk in front of the hearse. The funeral procession was an extravagant affair: six black horses decorated with black ostrich feathers pulled the hearse, on which the coffin lay among mountains of flowers, under a huge canopy of more black ostrich feathers. Numerous coaches followed, with their blinds drawn, in strict order according to etiquette. The gentlemen wore full mourning dress, with black crêpe around their top hats, and the ladies were dressed in black, with black veils and gloves, handkerchiefs edged in black lace and even mourning fans made of black ostrich feathers. The ladies often did not carry on to the burial service, which was considered too much of an ordeal for the 'weaker sex'. The coffins were made of the finest polished oak or elm, embellished with elaborate brass handles and inscribed plates.

A feast was usually held at the house, either before or after the funeral. This again was an opportunity for lavish hospitality (even in the homes of the poor), since it was considered a disgrace if a magnificent meal was not provided for all the mourners.

Mourning lasted for at least a year and appropriate clothing had to be worn by everyone in the family, including the servants, according to the period after the death. Widows, parents, brothers and sisters would wear 'full' mourning for a year, followed by 'half' mourning for another year for widows and six months for the others. Grandparents had six months each of 'full' and 'half' mourning. Even underclothes were trimmed with black lace. Mourning jewellery was worn, consisting of black jet, cameo, pearls or lockets containing the plaited hair of the departed (Jalland 1996).

A huge business grew up around the trappings of Victorian bereavement. Not only the undertakers grew wealthy, but also architects, monumental masons, sculptors, coffin-makers, clothing shops, jewellers and even manufacturers of 'mourning' ear-trumpets edged with black silk for deaf ladies. Printers produced mourning cards, envelopes edged in black and black sealing wax. A large store, Jay's London General Mourning Warehouse, opened in

Regent Street in 1841, exclusively supplying 'all that is necessary for mourning'. Similarly, in Dublin, Ogilvy's Mourning Warehouse at 13 Grafton Street advertised 'an assortment of goods suitable for the Mourning required', and there were 'mourning departments' in all the larger stores.

Such extravagance and ceremony were the general rule unless someone, like Sir William Betham, stated categorically that he wanted none of it. His will, dated 30 October 1817, contained the clause: 'I wish to be buried ... in the most private way possible without expense, at least with as little expense as possible'.

When we realise the 'pomp and circumstance' associated with most Victorian funerals, the wall monuments in Monkstown Church do not seem so pretentious. There are over twenty of them, of different shapes and sizes, distributed over the walls of the building (along the nave and chancel, in both transepts and in all three galleries), spanning the years 1837 to 1901. Their ostentation was in proportion to the public display of grief. To the Victorians death was a part of life and they wanted to be reminded every Sunday of their loved ones; it was as if they were bringing their gravestones into church. In contrast, in our modern society there is almost a conspiracy that death does not exist. We want tidy unobtrusive cemeteries, with stones in neat rows, and do not value our old graveyards, like Carrickbrennan and Mount Jerome.

John Semple, Senior, the architect who enlarged the church in 1831, understood the importance of displaying the wall monuments. He knew that people would not be happy if they were disturbed; indeed, the Vestry minutes of 20 December 1823 record him as saying, 'Even the temporary violation of these monuments of living recollections ought not to be undertaken without caution, and could not be accomplished without regret'. Thus Semple tendered two possible plans to the Vestry. One of them, the 'abbey' plan, was designed with the monuments in mind: he pointed out that they could not be properly seen in a church with galleries and so suggested keeping the nave of the old Georgian church as a display area for the monuments, while building an extension to contain the galleries. Eventually, his alternative plan — the transeptal one — was chosen and all of the existing monuments had to be rearranged (*see Chapter 5*).

At least one contemporary visitor thought Monkstown was rather extravagant. As reported in the *Irish Ecclesiastical Gazette* of 20 March 1880, he expostulated: 'And as for the walls — we fancied ourselves inside Glasnevin or Mount Jerome mortuary chapels. We have seen many churches, churches dating centuries back, but we never saw any with the walls studded over to an equal extent with those sad memorials of the departed worthies of the place. Monkstown Parish must have been one of the most exceptionally favoured places in the world if all that is carved upon those stones be true.'

Only three of the twenty or so Victorian monuments (James Campbell, Robert Dudley Oliver and James Knight) are completely plain; all the others are embellished in some way. The writing is often on a white marble sarcophagus (Annie Arthure) or scroll (Charles Butler), with a black marble background, often pyramidal as with the Georgians. Coats of arms and classical urns are everywhere in evidence.

What was typically Victorian was the symbolism associated with death, which did not need any translation at the time. Accompanying this was the unwavering belief that death was not the end: 'They which sleep in Jesus will God bring with Him', says the monument of Cecil Russell. Symbols of death were inverted torches (the Rev. Thomas Goff), draped urns and sarcophagi. The monuments of Annie Arthure, Harcourt Lees and Edward Ward Drewe all depict a snake consuming its own tail; this was the 'ouroboros' and represented the continuing cycle of life and death, symbolising the Resurrection. The drooping daffodil on Richard Brown's monument might appear at first to represent the ephemeral nature of human life, but it, too, was a symbol of hope: even when the flower withered and died, the bulb in the ground was merely sleeping and the new blooms would emerge beautiful and full of life the following spring. The memorial scrolls carrying the names of the departed would remind readers, who were more familiar with their Bibles than most of us are today, that 'there shall in no wise enter (the holy city) ... but they which are written in the Lamb's book of life'.

The Victorians mourned publicly (Queen Victoria was the archetypal example of such grief, wearing black from Albert's death to the end of her life, some 40 years later). They also attached great importance to the outward trappings of bereavement. Often, to emphasise the depth of their sorrow, 'weepers' were carved on the monuments. Those of Richard Brown and Elizabeth Stewart in Monkstown, for example, show such grieving figures, representing the family bereft of their loved one.

Thomas Kirk, sculptor (1777–1845)

'Bust of the Bishop of Cork — Kirk, the celebrated sculptor, has lately executed a bust of our much respected and venerated Diocesan, which, for faithfulness of portraiture and design, equals the best works of this eminent artist. Cork Constitution', reported *Saunders's News-Letter* of 16 November 1843.

Three of Monkstown's memorial tablets were executed by Thomas Kirk, the man who also fashioned the 13-foot-high Portland stone statue of Admiral Nelson on top of the Pillar in 1809 (Henchy 1948). (This Dublin landmark in O'Connell Street was blown up by the IRA on 8 March 1966.) Thomas Kirk was born in Newry in 1777, the only son of Scottish parents, William Kirk and Elizabeth Bible.[2] They moved to Cork when Thomas was still a young boy. He went to Dublin where he studied in the art school run by the Dublin Society of Artists. Henry Darley, the builder employed by Gandon, first employed him and he started to carve marble mantelpieces. Soon he opened his own establishment in Jervis Street. After sculpting Nelson in 1809, he was chosen to execute the three neo-classical figures over the portico of the classical façade of the GPO in O'Connell Street; he created the three statues of Hibernia, Mercury and Fidelity in 1817, one year before the building was completed. Kirk was one of the founding members of the Royal Hibernian Academy (RHA) and was a professor of sculpture there. Indeed, he executed a bust of one of the most influential and powerful people involved in the building of Monkstown Church — Archbishop William Magee (*see Chapter 5*). This bust can now be seen in the Long Room of Trinity College. Other of his portrait busts are in the Royal Dublin Society and Royal College of Surgeons. His work proved so popular that before long he was being asked to make memorial tablets in churches all over Ireland. The three monuments in Monkstown Church were completed towards the end of his life, when he was in his sixties, and are memorials to Richard Brown

Richard Brown's monument (left) in Monkstown, sculpted by Thomas Kirk in the typical Victorian Greek Revival style. The grieving lady on Brown's monument is almost identical to that on Nathaniel Sneyd's monument (bottom left), today in the crypt of Christ Church, which was sculpted by Thomas Kirk (his 'masterpiece', according to Homan Potterton).

Detail of Brown's monument (bottom right). The inverted torch was a typical Victorian symbol for the extinction of life, seen on many of the wall monuments in Monkstown.

276

(1838), John Armit (1835) and Annie Arthure (1838). In small plain letters he carved on each 'T. Kirk Fecit'. He was known for his lifelike portrait busts, his attention to detail and sensitive handling of marble. Brown's monument is typical of Kirk's work: Victorian sentimentality portrayed through Greek Revival (Potterton 1975). The bereaved son and daughter, dressed in flowing Greek robes, stand weeping, supported by a pedestal on which stands an urn containing their father's ashes. On the tablet are inverted torches, reminding us that life is snuffed out in death, and a lily, which symbolises the Resurrection. About three years earlier Kirk had carved a fine monument — 'generally regarded as Kirk's masterpiece', according to Homan Potterton — to Nathaniel Sneyd in Christ Church Cathedral,

Thomas Kirk's monument in Mount Jerome, sculpted by his son, Joseph. Note the Masonic symbols of the skull and the Star of David.

which was subsequently relegated to the crypt.[3] The mourning woman on Brown's memorial is virtually identical to that on Sneyd's.

Thomas Kirk had married Eliza Robinson in March 1808,[4] shortly after the foundation stone of Nelson's Pillar was laid. Of his twelve children, his artistic talent was inherited by two of his sons, a daughter and a grandson, who also became well-known sculptors (Strickland 1913).[5] His eldest son, Joseph (b. 1821), executed four more of Monkstown's monuments — those of Anne Butler (1845), William Cusack (1851), Charles MacDonnell (1853) and Charles Lindsay (1855). He also sculpted many important statues, monuments (including the recumbent figure of Bishop Charles Lindsay, patron of Monkstown, in Christ Church Cathedral;[6] *see Chapter 3*) and portrait busts, while his most familiar works would probably be the four figures of Divinity, Law, Medicine and Science on the Campanile in Trinity College and his bronze bas-relief of the Siege of Seringapatam on the base of the Wellington Memorial in the Phoenix Park. As a final tribute, he sculpted the life-size figure of a woman carrying an urn on his father's tomb in Mount Jerome Cemetery. Thomas Kirk had died on 19 April 1845 (Strickland 1913). Certain symbols on Kirk's monument, such as the skull and the Star of David, indicate that he was a member of the Masonic Order (Langtry and Carter 1997).[7]

It was said of Thomas Kirk, 'He was a man of simple manners, honourable and upright in all his dealings and scrupulously exact and punctual in carrying out his contracts'.[8] I believe that this is how he would like to be remembered, rather than for his Nelson, whose damaged head in the Civic Museum is the only known surviving fragment on public display of a pillar which caused so much controversy.

The church vaults

Air-raid shelter, turf store, youth club and food kitchen — these have all found a home in the vaults of Monkstown Church. There were no vaults under the original 1789 church. When John Semple added the great north and south transepts in 1829–31, he also built vaults, twenty in total, beneath the church.

The decision to build vaults under the remodelled church took place in May 1830, about a year after building had already begun. It was then 'resolved ... that Vaults ... should be ... built under the Floor of the Church ... in a permanent and substantial manner of stone

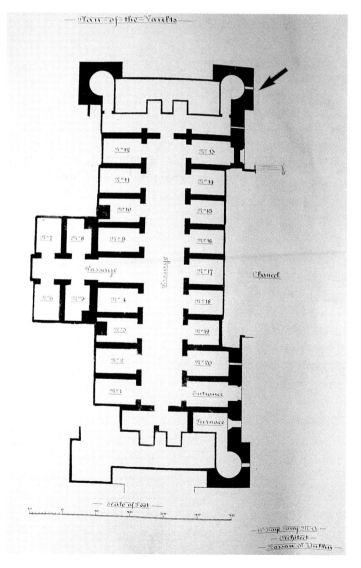

Plan of Semple's vaults, drawn by the architect William Kaye Parry of Nassau Street, Dublin. The present entrance is identified by an arrow.

and brick with Lime and sand, the door in (the) entrance wall ... to open outwards and such Vaults to have no kind of communication with the interior of the Church, and each of such vaults ... should be for ever set apart as and for the burial place of the person whether parishioner or stranger, who shall pay (£130) into the hands of John Armit [the treasurer of the Church Building Fund] ... for the use of the said parish to be appropriated towards the building and completing of said Church and the Vaults under same'.[9] There was to be no further charge, apart from the 'customary fees to the Clerke and sexton and for tolling the bell'. The indenture also stipulated that the bodies were to be encased in lead coffins.

This was a money-making exercise, pure and simple, in order to raise money quickly for the completion of the church, which was costing over £8,000. Each vault cost £130; £30 would cover the actual cost of the vault itself and the remaining £100 would go towards the church building fund. Twenty vaults would bring in £2,600 — a great sum in those days. Eight brick-lined vaults were built on each side of the central passage that ran from north to south under the transepts. This passage was interrupted on the west side by a side passage, which led to a further four vaults.

> 'Monkstown Church. To be Sold, a few Family Sepulchral Vaults, perfectly secured, and of a very superior description. The plan lies at the Office of Messrs. Carolin and Sons, Talbot-street, where the terms may be known.'

(The Carolins were the builders of Semple's church.) This advertisement appeared in the *Dublin Evening Post* on 10 December 1831, about two weeks before the church was officially opened. However, applicants for these 'superior' vaults did not come flocking and eventually those that were still unsold were reduced to £50 and offered to 'the publick' after the church was officially opened. The advertisement was rerun in *Saunder's News-Letter* in January 1832:

> 'To be sold, a few separate vaults of a very superior description and perfectly secured ... Purchasers will have their choice of the vaults according to priority. An early application is therefore recommended.'

A further advertisement, years later (on 27 September 1836), enthused about 'a peculiarly well circumstanced New Family Vault ... secured by three separate Locks and Iron Gates, built in solid Masonry, and so situated above ground as to be always perfectly dry'.

In 1874 a Vault Committee was set up to investigate 'the state of the vaults ... and on the claims of families exercising the right of sepulchre in these vaults so that the same may be correctly ascertained and recorded in the vestry books'. The minutes of 14 March also reported that 'the right of sepulchre (had) been exercised by only 11 of these families'.

In 1881 a new Local Government Act ordered that 'burials (were to) be discontinued and (were) prohibited in the Vaults under the Parish Church (Protestant) of Monkstown' from 1 September 1881. In the 50 years since 1831 there were said to have been 184 interments. No more burials were to be allowed in the public vaults, whereas some more would be permitted in the named private family vaults. A sheet of paper pasted inside the large wall safe in the Vestry Room quotes part of the Local Government order and lists the seven vaults where fourteen further interments could take place. There were strict provisos: 'No body (is to) be buried in any vault ... unless the Coffin be separately entombed in an air-tight manner; that is, by properly cemented stone or brick work which (is) never (to) be disturbed'. According to Mr Bartholomew Warburton Rooke, church organist (1882–1937), the last interment in the private vaults took place in about 1918. Meanwhile, the ex-army sexton, Mr Lewis (1905–28), who was considered 'a bit fierce' by Canon Dowse's children, used to bring them into the vaults for 'a spooky treat'.

For some years before World War II, Mr William Bray (sexton, 1928–56) would receive a postcard every July from England, announcing the imminent arrival of two elderly ladies. He would sweep the central passageway through the vaults and place two chairs and a small table there. When the ladies arrived, they were ushered into the vaults, provided with a couple of lanterns and left in peace for half an hour or so. They would always recompense the sexton with a 10-shilling note, before disappearing until the following July.[10] Whose vault they were visiting remains a mystery.

As stipulated in the original Vestry plans of 1830, there was no access to the vaults from within the church. The original entrance was through a fine segmental-arched doorway, now kept locked, on the external east wall of the south transept, to the right of the furnace door. A new entrance to the vaults was made in 1940 (to the right of the Vestry door at the back of the church; *see Parry's plan of vaults, p. 278*). This was done to facilitate an occurrence that would have been inconceivable to the original occupants. The Air Raid Precautions Authorities asked the Vestry for permission to use the vaults as 'an emergency public air-raid shelter'. The archbishop of Dublin, Arthur Barton, gave his permission and Dun Laoghaire Borough Corporation carried out the necessary alterations. These apparently involved the removal of some coffins from their original vaults and their reinterment. The empty vaults were then bricked up; their original wrought-iron gates were bought by the Corporation for £10 and apparently reused at the Temple Hill air raid shelters in Blackrock.[11] Finally, electric light was installed throughout the vaults. The Vestry's Annual Report of 1940 noted, 'While an excellent air-raid shelter has thus been provided for some 250 people, it is devoutly hoped that the necessity for its use will never arise'. And, apparently, it did not.

After the war, one of the churchwardens, William ('Billy') Lee, used to store his turf in the vaults. Canon Albert Stokes remembers that, as a curate in Monkstown (1946–51), he would travel up to the Featherbed in the Dublin Mountains to cut some of this turf with Billy.

More recently, between 1967 and 1998, the Parish Youth Club used the vaults as a venue. In 1999, when St Michael's Private Hospital closed down, the nuns stopped supplying meals to the homeless, so an Interchurch Care Group was set up (consisting of members of St Patrick's and St Michael's Roman Catholic churches and Monkstown Parish Church, with the help of the Society of St Vincent de Paul). This group took over the task of providing midday meals to the homeless in December 1999 and tables and chairs were set up in Monkstown's vaults for this purpose. In the first fifteen months 6,000 meals were served. The Eastern Health Board has since assumed responsibility for this work.

CHAPTER 22

'They are not dead but sleepeth'

Their bodies are buried in peace, but their name lives for ever.
Ecclesiasticus 44:1–14

In Monkstown we are especially conscious of that 'great ... cloud of witnesses' who have gone before — the church walls are 'studded over' with their monuments, while Carrickbrennan Graveyard is so crowded that the old church now sits in a hollow.

The wall monuments

Some 50 wall monuments crowd the walls of Monkstown Church (*see Chapter 21*). They commemorate the lives of over 100 Monkstown parishioners, dating from Dr Benjamin Domvile's monument of 1774 right up to the brass plaque of 1997 to the long-serving sexton Mr Ronnie Blay. They have been moved around over the years: Domvile's monument was originally in the old church in Carrickbrennan and was re-erected in the nave of the 'new' 1789 church, but had to be taken down again and repositioned in the north transept when John Semple remodelled that church over the years 1829–31. Other monuments were shuffled about when the chancel was added by McCurdy in 1862. The World War I memorial plaque, now in the south gallery, came from St John's of Mounttown when that church was sold in 1985; St John's other monuments were stored in Monkstown's vaults, where they remain to this day. It would be almost impossible to give them wall-space. One is reminded of lines from the poem 'The Borough' by the Rev. George Crabbe, published in 1840: 'We have mural tablets, every size, That woe could wish, or vanity devise'.

I have been forced to choose only a fraction of those who are commemorated in the church where they worshipped Sunday by Sunday but where they are now largely unknown. The choice has been serendipitous: their inclusion simply rests on whether old newspapers, wills and other random archives could be found to tell of their fragile existence. I am sure, for example, that Annie Scovell (whose memorial is on the east wall of the south galley), who grew up in 'Purbeck House' on Monkstown Road and died in Bombay, aged 26, had a story to tell, but I have not been able to find it.

Others have fascinating, well-documented histories. But space does not permit me to tell them in full. For example, the two MacDonnells, Charles and Frederick, brothers of the Rev. Ronald MacDonnell (rector of Monkstown, 1857–78), sailed to India to fight and die in the Sikh Wars. Although he must have been horribly mutilated by 'a musket-ball through the face' and the loss of his left eye at Sobraon in 1846, Charles went on to become captain and brevet major of his regiment in 1850. But, as his monument states, 'his health sank from the effects of continual active service under the sun of India', so he headed for home in time to marry Ellen Cotter two months before his early death on his birthday, 5 August 1853, aged 29 (MacDonnell 1889; Smith 1854–7). His younger brother Frederick — while second-in-command to Sam Browne (who later won a Victoria Cross and gave his name to the gun belt he invented) — was killed in action in 1858. Similarly, the uncles of Nicholas Robinson (the husband of former president Mary Robinson) are celebrated in two tablets in the old Georgian nave of the church — Douglas St Quentin Robinson ('Missing 6th August 1938 whilst flying on duty, aged 21 years') and Kenneth Basil Robinson ('Killed in action, 7th June 1944, aged 22 years').

There are two notable omissions among the wall memorials. Firstly, Robert Warren Stewart, the highly respected missionary and one of Monkstown's greatest sons, has been inexplicably forgotten. Secondly, Ralph Ward, churchwarden and one of the chief organisers (and possible architect) of the 1789 church, is also not represented; his suicide meant that he was buried at St Ann's rather than Monkstown (*see Chapter 14 for his biography*).

The following, then, are the stories of some of the others — a small group of extraordinary men and women who invested their talents and energies in an astonishing variety of ways.

Colonel Sir William Cox (1777–1864)

TO THE MEMORY OF A BELOVED HUSBAND
COLONEL SIR WILLIAM COX
LATE OF COOLCLIFFE CO. WEXFORD
WHO DIED 1ST JULY 1864
AGED 87 YEARS.
'WITH LONG LIFE WILL I SATISFY HIM AND
SHEW HIM MY SALVATION'

'He behaved remarkably well', said the duke of Wellington about William Cox. The sound of the explosion must have rung in his ears for days afterwards, the memory of its aftermath given him nightmares for years. More has been written in the history books about two days in William Cox's life than the rest of his life put together, during which he was caught up in one of the worst disasters of the Peninsular War (1808–14).

In 1804 Napoleon crowned himself emperor of France and in 1808 invaded Spain, crowning his brother, Joseph, king of Spain. The British sent troops to help the Spanish. Sir Arthur Wellesley, later the duke of Wellington, was made commander of the British forces and, with the help of the Spanish and a Portuguese army organised by the British, tried to drive the French out of Spain and Portugal.

At 6am on the morning of Sunday 26 August 1810, Lieutenant-Colonel William Cox heard the sounds he had been expecting: a heavy bombardment of artillery on the old walls of Almeida. William was a long way from 'Coolcliffe', Co. Wexford, where he had been born 33 years before. For the past sixteen months he had been the governor of Almeida, a garrison town in Portugal and one of two fortresses guarding that country's border with Spain. Almeida protected the crossings of the River Coa, which formed a natural barrier between Spain and Portugal. For twelve days French soldiers had waited outside the walls of Almeida. At first they attempted to dig ditches to provide an interconnecting system of trenches and so protect their guns and men, but the earth was so stony that sandbags and gabions (wickerwork baskets full of earth) had to be used as well. Day and night the French sappers dug in full view of the defenders who fired on them, but eleven batteries, armed with 65 heavy guns, were finally completed.

Inside the walls, in spite of everything, morale was high. Cox was an able officer and his men had confidence in him. Marshal Beresford, a British officer, commander-in-chief of the Portuguese army, praised Cox in a letter to Wellesley: 'Every officer and man gives the highest applause to his unremitting zeal and activity, encouraging all by his own example' (Wellington 1837). Cox and five other British officers commanded one regular and two militia regiments, a body of artillery and a squadron of cavalry, amounting to over 4,000 Portuguese soldiers (Oman 1908). They had plenty of guns, ammunition and food. As Wellington wrote later in one of his despatches, 'The garrison ... was in the best order and spirits, and had no thoughts of surrender, and expected to hold the place for two months'.

Wellington had given Cox his orders. Almeida played a crucial role in his strategic campaign plan. There were three possible routes into Portugal for the invading French army. As Wellington had hoped, the French chose the most northerly, which ran through Ciudad Rodrigo, a fortified town in Spain, and then Almeida. Wellington made his headquarters near Almeida and instructed Cox to hold the garrison for as long as possible. Ciudad Rodrigo held out for 42 days. Now Almeida was the last remaining obstacle between Napoleon's army, led by Massena, and Lisbon, the capital and seat of power. Wellington hoped that Almeida could hold out until the autumn rains, which would be to his advantage. As soon as Cox felt surrender was unavoidable, he was to signal to Wellington, who would bring his combined forces immediately to save the garrison.

That Sunday morning when Cox heard the bombardment was overcast and visibility was poor. The guns battering Almeida were only 500 yards away. All day the French continued to fire their shells into the town. Several houses caught fire. The civilians took shelter in bunkers under the ancient walls. By nightfall the artillery on the southern ramparts found that their gunpowder was getting low. Donkeys were brought into the castle courtyard to carry kegs of gunpowder back to the walls. The castle, old but immensely strong, had been chosen as the main magazine where most of the gunpowder and ammunition were stored. The soldiers tied the kegs on to the donkeys' saddles, leaving the door of the magazine open and more kegs just outside. One keg was damaged and left a trail of powder as it was carried to the donkey. A French shell fell in the courtyard and ignited the powder on the ground, which tracked back to the kegs standing at the door.

These exploded and, through the open door, set off the whole magazine.

The explosion could be seen and heard for miles. A French eyewitness wrote later in *Sprünglins Journal*: 'The earth trembled, and we saw an immense whirlwind of fire and smoke rise from the middle of the place. It was like the bursting of a volcano — one of the things I can never forget after 26 years. Enormous blocks of stone were hurled into our trenches, where they killed and wounded some of our men. Guns of heavy calibre were lifted from the ramparts and hurled down far outside them. When the smoke cleared off, a great part of Almeida had disappeared, and the rest was a heap of debris' (Oman 1908).

Five hundred British and Portuguese soldiers were killed instantly, including nearly all of the 200 artillerymen on the walls. Only one man survived in the courtyard to explain afterwards how the disaster had occurred. He had dived into an oven just before the main explosion. Cox was shaken but unhurt and ran to the ramparts to prevent the French from scaling the walls in the aftermath of the explosion. With the help of a Portuguese artillery officer, he managed to load the few undamaged guns and fire into the French trenches (Napier 1828–40). He kept the whole garrison up all night as the French continued their bombardment. He expected an attack at any minute.

At daybreak Cox was horrified to see the scale of devastation. There was a huge hole where the castle and cathedral had been; almost all the houses were roofless and the streets were blocked with debris. There was only enough gunpowder left for a day. Although he knew his situation was hopeless, he decided to delay for as long as possible, hoping that Wellesley could save the garrison as originally planned. But although the signallers on the western ramparts desperately tried to alert Wellesley's lookouts all morning, the weather was too hazy for them to be seen. Wellesley had heard the explosion, spotted the disappearance of the cathedral steeple and noted the times of firing, but did not know what had actually happened (Stothert 1812).

At 9am on Monday morning the French commander, Massena, sent his aide-de-camp, Pelet, to demand the garrison's surrender. The French were still unaware of the extent of the damage inflicted by the explosion. Its force had been directed in such a way as to demolish almost everything inside the walls while leaving them intact. So Cox blindfolded the French delegation and met them in one of the shelters under the walls. Pelet threatened that if the garrison did not surrender the French would attack and kill them all. Cox played down the explosion, describing it as a 'deplorable accident' that would not prevent him from continuing to fight.

While Cox was talking to Pelet, he was unaware that some of his men were talking to the enemy. General d'Alorna and some other Portuguese officers in the French army had emerged from the trenches and walked over to the walls, where they tried to persuade their fellow countrymen to give up. General d'Alorna recognised some of the Portuguese soldiers and assured them that if they continued to resist they would all be killed. By now most of the garrison was completely demoralised: they had seen their friends blown to pieces, they knew their stocks of gunpowder were hopelessly low and they wanted to surrender immediately.

To gain time, Cox decided to send Major José Bareiros, his chief of artillery, to the French with his demands and conditions. But, unknown to Cox, Bareiros had been in touch secretly with the French for some time and now told them the real state of affairs within Almeida. He remained with the French and joined their army immediately, where he was promoted to the rank of colonel. As a result of Bareiros's information, Massena refused all Cox's proposals and at 7pm began to bombard the town again.

Cox's Portuguese lieutenant-governor, Bernardo Costa, and some other officers now approached him and tried to persuade him to raise the white flag, threatening that if he did not they would open the gates of Almeida to the enemy. Single-handed, Cox could no longer resist, and so at 10pm he finally had to capitulate. Massena agreed that the regular troops should be sent to France as prisoners of war, while the British officers and the three militia regiments should return home 'on parole' (on condition that they did not serve in the war again). On the morning of 28 August the British troops marched out of Almeida.

As soon as he heard of the surrender, Wellesley wrote, 'I cannot express how much I am disappointed at this fatal event', but he agreed that 'it was impossible to expect Col. Cox should continue the defence of the place after the unfortunate occurrence ... and I am happy to add, that all of the accounts which I have received ... concur in applauding the conduct of the Governor throughout the siege'. He added in another letter, 'Even the enemy acknowledge that he behaved remarkably well' (Wellington 1837). Wellesley had hoped that Almeida would delay the French for several months; instead the fortress had fallen after five weeks. Within a month the British army was retreating towards Lisbon.

During the autumn of 1810 there was a special commission on traitors. D'Alorna and his fellow Portuguese officers who had fought on the French side were found guilty of high treason and condemned to death. Cox's second-in-command, former Lieutenant-Governor Bernardo Costa, was captured in 1812 and shot as a traitor. In 1814 Wellesley defeated the French at the Battle of Toulouse. Napoleon abdicated and the Peninsular War was over. Sir Arthur Wellesley returned to a hero's welcome in London and was given the title of 'Duke of Wellington'.

Cox returned to London on parole. In 1815 he was made a Knight of the Tower and Sword of Portugal, which was a decoration founded in 1808 to reward loyalty and service to Portugal. On 13 August 1816 he was knighted by the prince regent, later George IV, at Carlton House. Retiring on half-pay, he returned home to Ireland and was promoted to colonel in 1819. In 1820 he married Anna Hickson;[1] John William was born in 1821, followed by Sarah Julia. (John later became a general in the British army and served in the Crimean War.) Colonel Sir William Cox became the sheriff of King's County (Offaly) in 1825 (Boase 1892). He lived in Monkstown, at 6 Longford Place and 2 Belgrave Square, East, for the last five years of his life (Dublin directories, 1859–64) and, with his wife, was buried in the old graveyard at Carrickbrennan.

In 1906 Sir Charles Oman explored the ruins of Almeida. He wrote: 'Almeida has never recovered from the disaster of 1810 ... Open spaces are frequent and some of the more important buildings — especially the old palace of the governor — stand in ruins. Others show solid 17th or 18th-century masonry on the ground floor, and flimsy modern repairs above, where the upper stories were blown away by the explosion. The cathedral has never been properly rebuilt, and is a mere fragment. The place ... remains in a state of decay. The walls stand just as they were left ...' (Oman 1908).

Judge Alexander Crookshank (1736–1813)

On Tuesday 14 December 1813 an obituary appeared in *Saunders's News-Letter*. Alexander Crookshank's friends and relations must have been distressed when they read it, for it merely stated: '… His character is too well known to require any comment; and it only remains to be said, that as he led an upright and useful life, so his end was that of the pious and resigned Christian'. This single sentence was the sum total written after a long life spent in, as we shall see, faithful public service.

His monument in Monkstown went to the other extreme, giving the standard Georgian hyperbole:

SACRED TO THE MEMORY OF
ALEXANDER CROOKSHANK
LATE OF THE CITY OF DUBLIN ESQR.
HE FILLED THE SITUATION OF A JUDGE
OF THE COURT OF COMMON PLEAS IN IRELAND
FOR SEVENTEEN YEARS WITH ABILITY AND INTEGRITY.
AS IT PLEASED GOD TO GRANT HIM A LONG LIFE
SO DID HE RENDER IT BOTH USEFUL AND HONORABLE
HE WAS AN UPRIGHT JUDGE A STEADY FRIEND
AND A SINCERE CHRISTIAN.
HIS AFFLICTED WIDOW AND CHILDREN
WHO KNEW HIS VALUE AND REVERED HIS VIRTUES
HAVE ERECTED THIS SMALL BUT SINCERE TRIBUTE
TO THE MEMORY OF HIS DEPARTED WORTH.
HE DIED THE 10TH DAY OF DECEMBER 1813 AGED 77 YEARS.

Alexander Crookshank was born in 1736, was elected MP for Belfast from 1777 to 1783 and then justice of the court of common pleas in Dublin from 1784 to 1800 (Ball 1926). He and his wife, Esther, had eight children. They lived at 'Newtown Park', a beautiful late eighteenth-century house, still standing, in Blackrock, although it was then surrounded by twelve acres (Bence-Jones 1990). (Sir John Lees was their next-door neighbour, in 'Blackrock House'.) They also owned a townhouse in Leinster Street, where Judge Crookshank was living at the time of his death. Both he and Esther (d. 1825) are buried in Carrickbrennan Graveyard, with their grand-daughters, Harriet and Mary, who died 'of fever' in 1843 (English 1987). A huge flat stone, to deter grave-robbers, covers their grave. It is supported by stone pedestals at each corner and enclosed by iron railings.

Burke's *Landed gentry of Ireland* tells us that the Crookshanks came to Ireland from Aberdeenshire in the seventeenth century. Esther's father, grandfather and great-grandfather were all aldermen of Derry. John, her great-grandfather (coincidentally also named Crookshank), fought in the Siege of Derry, when he was in charge of a 'train of artillery'.

Although the journalists of the day were economic with their obituaries, they and their readers found many of the more sordid or brutal court cases absorbing. But from these details we find out more about the character and humanity of Judge Alexander Crookshank. For example, while in Cork in September 1785, he had to preside over the trial of two prisoners who were accused of brutally raping an 'unhappy girl, not above seventeen years old'. The unfortunate girl had been accused of stealing from her master, but, 'after an honourable acquittal', was waiting in the 'nunnery' (the female wing of the gaol) before her release. Under some pretext, she was persuaded to leave it and walked straight into the clutches of her attackers. Crookshank seems to have dealt with both victim and accused with compassion and fairness. As reported in *Walker's Hibernian Magazine* on 6 September 1785, 'Judge Crookshank behaved towards the prosecutrix with the greatest humanity and tenderness, giving at the same time the unhappy culprits every indulgence and opportunity for a defence'. Apparently they could produce no convincing defence, so were 'capitally convicted' (i.e. they received the death sentence, which was the usual penalty for rape and out of the judge's hands).

For once, a Georgian epitaph seems to have been substantiated: 'He was an upright judge, a steady friend and a sincere Christian'.

Judge Robert Day (1746–1841)

SACRED TO THE MEMORY OF
ROBERT DAY ESQUIRE
LATE SECOND JUSTICE OF THE COURT OF KING'S BENCH IN
IRELAND.
HE WAS THIRD SON OF THE REVD JOHN DAY OF LOHERCANNON IN
THE CO. OF KERRY
AND OF LUCY HIS WIFE DAUGHTER OF MAURICE FITZGERALD
KNIGHT OF KERRY.
HE DIED 8TH FEBRY 1841 IN THE 95TH YEAR OF HIS AGE.
HE WAS AN ELOQUENT ADVOCATE, AN ABLE LAWYER
AND A JUST AND MERCIFUL JUDGE.
HIS AFFECTIONATE WIDOW ERECTED THIS MONUMENT
AS A SLIGHT TRIBUTE TO HIS MANY VIRTUES
AND IN THE HOPE OF HIS RESURRECTION TO ETERNAL LIFE
THROUGH OUR LORD JESUS CHRIST.

Robert Day was a man of contrasts — a member of the Ascendancy, he spoke Irish fluently; Grattan's best friend but politically opposed to him; 'a just and merciful judge' (so says his monument) who sentenced many to a cruel death; considered himself completely Irish yet courted an English girl against his parents' wishes; a pillar of the Establishment but kept a mistress when his wife became ill; a devout pillar of the Church of Ireland who married a Roman Catholic; a patriotic Irishman yet completely loyal to the British Crown; friend to the greatest in the country yet completely unpretentious.

The third son of the Rev. John Day, rector of Listowel, Day was the grandson of the 14th knight of Kerry, Maurice FitzGerald, through his mother, Lucy. In keeping with local custom, he was fostered until he was seven years old in an Irish-speaking farmer's family, one of his father's tenants, which gave him a lifelong love of farming. He then attended the Catholic Master Casey's school at Banna during the years 1753–60 (O'Carroll 1998).

Kept over a lifetime, the diaries of Robert Day — judge, politician, Volunteer, generous host, eloquent writer, and prime mover in the building of Semple's Monkstown Church — are detailed and candid, and provide a fascinating insight into contemporary life in Ireland. He is commemorated by two impressive monuments — one in the south transept of the church and the other in Carrickbrennan Graveyard, where he is buried with his two wives.

When he was thirteen he won a scholarship to Trinity College, Dublin, where he met Henry Grattan. Both boys were members of the 'Hist' (Historical Society), Grattan's introduction to debating. Later, they went to the Temple in London for five years before being raised to the Bench in Ireland.

While in London, Grattan and Day shared rooms for three years and became friends with a fellow Irishman, Oliver Goldsmith. Day met and fell in love with Mary ('Polly') Pott, the daughter of Dr Percival Pott, a surgeon in London's St Bartholomew's (after whom Pott's Fracture is named). Both families were unhappy with the match — Day's because they wanted him to marry a girl from the local Kerry gentry (a 'Kerry cousin') and Mary's, according to Day, because of 'violent anti-Irish prejudice which operated against the match, and the phlegmatic caution which, in all matters of business, is characteristic of an Englishman' (Day 1938). The Potts may also have suspected his motives, in view of Mary's £50,000 dowry.

In 1784 Day wrote, 'Happily, all objections are now at an end'. He married Mary Pott in London and then brought her home to Kerry to meet his family. The couple made their new home at 17 North Frederick Street, which was then in one of the most fashionable parts of Dublin. This was the era of the duke of Rutland, when Dublin society was at its most glittering. Their only child, Elizabeth, was born the next year. She later followed the conventions and married her 'Kerry cousin', Sir Edward Denny, writer of the hymn 'Light of the lonely pilgrim's heart'.

Day was a member of the Irish Volunteers, an armed Protestant force of about 80,000, formed in the 1770s ostensibly to guard the country in the event of a French invasion when the British regiments left to deal with trouble in America. The list of resolutions of the Kerry Volunteers was drawn up in Day's handwriting. F. W. Wheatley's famous picture of the Irish parliament in 1780 includes uniformed Volunteers: Grattan is standing in the centre behind a table, while Day, with Lady Crosby at his side, leans over the balcony overhead. (This picture can be seen in the vestibule of the Bank of Ireland, College Green.) The Volunteers helped Grattan to win from the British government in 1782 a Declaration of Independence. This so-called Grattan's Parliament lasted until 1801. It was an independent parliament, which fought for Catholic Emancipation and freed Irish trade from English control. While Grattan opposed the Union with Great Britain, Day supported it, at least initially; by 1827 he seemed to regret it, remarking wryly in his diary, 'Oh how wretched all public places look in Dublin since the Union! Not an individual in the House above the condition of a shopkeeper'.

Day was an eloquent speaker and writer. His diaries are so personal and candid (such as his critical description of the Lindsays; *see Appendix 1*) that it seems unlikely that he thought they would be read by others and so are all the more interesting. (Day's diaries are today in the Royal Irish Academy; *see Select Bibliography*.) He kept copies of his addresses to juries and to prisoners in the dock, as well as newspaper cuttings of his speeches. His Charge to the Grand Jury of County Dublin in January 1797 was widely read and admired in his day as far afield as Yorkshire, where 'many gentlemen … at their own expense reprinted that excellent speech, & directed many hundreds of copies thereof to be distributed in this Riding'. Day dedicated a copy of his Charges to Grattan, writing on the flyleaf: 'In proud acknowledgement of his long and flattering friendship unmoved amidst the shock of politics and party, and a token of just respect for fine talents, public integrity and private honour' (Day 1808). This strong mutual regard and affection lasted until Grattan's death in 1820.

The 1798 insurrection signalled the death-knell of Grattan's Parliament. Day acted on the special commission set up after the rebellion and had to pass judgement on Oliver Bond, who had been caught red-handed with more than a dozen others at a meeting of the United Irishmen in his house at Lower Bridge Street. The jury took seven minutes to find Bond guilty of high treason. Day pronounced the sentence: 'You, Oliver Bond, are to be taken from the place in which you stand to the gaol from whence you came, and thence to the common place of execution, there to be hanged by the neck, but not until you are dead, for while you are yet living, your bowels are to be taken out and thrown in your face, and your head is to be cut off, and your head and limbs to be at the King's disposal' (Gilbert 1861). Later Bond was conditionally pardoned, but died in Newgate Prison, following a seizure. Although Day's sentence seems bloodthirsty to modern minds, he considered it a necessary evil. On 3 August 1801 in Omagh he lamented, 'Here I have the pain for the first time this circuit to pass a capital sentence' (Day 1938).

With the Union, Day dropped politics and concentrated on his legal career, although he was responsible for getting the duke of Wellington, as Arthur Wellesley, returned as a member of parliament for Tralee in 1807. (Wellington never took this seat, but instead represented the Isle of Wight.) Day mixed with the greatest in the land, yet always signed his name as plain 'Rob Day' on legal documents or at the Monkstown Vestry, which he somehow found time to attend regularly. On visits to England he was invited to 'Bushy Park', where the duke of Clarence (later William IV) and his mistress, Dorothea Jordan (*see below*), entertained him to dinner; later they would ride around William's farm at Esher, sharing their common love of farming (Day 1938).

Day regarded himself as a good friend of Daniel O'Connell; their paths crossed frequently in their respective roles of judge and barrister, and O'Connell was often a guest at Day's table. However, we find O'Connell after one of Day's judgements giving a darker side of the judge: he wrote in a letter, dated 29 November 1804, to his wife that he thought Day 'fully justified what Sigerson formerly called him — a mass of corruption'. He added, 'I know, my heart, you will not say a word of this to anyone. The mention of it may injure me, and in fact Day has never been unfriendly to us' (O'Connell 1972).

In 1816 Day served as the judge at the assizes of Tralee, when Rowan Cashel was tried for killing his rival in a duel. Such a death was considered to be murder by this time, but Judge Day delivered a most controversial summing-up to the jury. He attacked the law, saying, 'I must deprecate, that this law should countervail the laws of the land, and that we unfortunately cannot oppose this despotic law'. The jury found Cashel 'not guilty' and he was acquitted. The case was reported in the *Limerick Evening Post* on 3 April 1816 and in *The Times* of London on 15 April. Afterwards Day's behaviour was criticised. It was said that he was personally involved, that he was distantly related to Cashel and was also canvassing on behalf of his grandson against one of the victim's relations. Day's retirement in 1818 was said to have been as a result of this public outcry. Sir Robert Peel, later British prime minister, supported Day by saying that he 'acted in a manner most consistent with the dignity of the situation that he held, and with his duties both as a judge and as a Christian' (Hansard, 1818).

Day's name occasioned witticisms: he was very tall and, on being seen out walking with a short friend, Sir Arthur Clarke, a friend joked, 'There goes the longest Day and the shortest knight'. In the front of one of Day's bound volumes of his 1797 Charges he stuck a small cutting from an English paper, which read: 'An Hibernian having been found guilty of a burglary before Mr. Justice Day, in Ireland, shrewdly observed that he had lost by Day what he had got by night'.

In April 1823, after 49 years of marriage, many of them apparently spent as an invalid, his wife Mary (née Pott) died, aged 76. Day wrote in his diary, 'O fatal and unhappy day! The wife of my bosom is gone! The partner of all my cares and comforts for nigh on half a century'. The following year, Day, then aged 77, married his long-time mistress, Mary Fitzgerald, a Catholic and the daughter of a doctor, who was considerably younger. Two sons had already been born to the couple: John Robert (b. 1797) and Edward. Day wrote about the marriage in his diary: 'This event took place on Monday 21st June 1824 in the presence of Robert Hitchcock, Baggot St., Barrister at Law, and his son, Robert, an attorney'. (He had made sure that lawyers were present as witnesses to prove the validity of the marriage.) He also inserted an official announcement in the *Freeman's Journal* on 18 August 1824: 'Robert Day, Esq., late one of the Judges of the King's Bench in Ireland to Mary, daughter of the late B. Fitzgerald, Esq., MD of Bandon'. The union was very happy, according to his diaries: 'We return to our beloved Retreat tired of 5 days City Life' (entry on 10 November 1827). When he was over 80 he still loved good food and conversation, and wrote in his diary about the 'agreeable party dinners' that he and his wife gave for fourteen or more at a time.

Although a poor preacher might put him off church ('I do not go to church and why? I do not hear a word of the sermon, bad delivery and my thick hearing. Our chaplain Edward gives us prayers at home'[2]), bad weather did not. His diary entry on Sunday 11 March 1827 reads: 'Turns out most severe day so violent a shower of hail drifted into the face of the horses and carriage returning from church that it was with great difficulty the horses could be prevented from wheeling round and upsetting us'.

Judge Day lived at 'Loughlinstown House' for the last 45 years of his long life. (He rented it from the Domviles, whose family home it had been since the eighteenth century; *see below.*) On Sundays he travelled all the way to Monkstown, his nearest church, which must have been an uncomfortable carriage journey for an elderly man over the hills on bumpy roads. He would leave his wife off at Kingstown or Cabinteely for Mass. In 1836 he was at the 'dedication of the new Catholic Chapel there [Cabinteely] with General Sir George Cockburn ... the parson and a few more heretics. The dear Miss Byrnes [direct descendants of Henry Cheevers of Monkstown Castle] made room for Mrs. Day and self in their pew'. It was probably largely through Day's protracted 'negotiations' with Archbishop Magee that the Monkstown chapel of ease at Killiney, St Matthias's, was finally built in 1835 (*see Appendix 1*).

Day was elected chairman of the first Building Committee of Monkstown Church during its planning and construction by Semple. He was 85 when the church was opened in 1831; at the age of 90 he translated Erasmus. He died in his 95th year and his widow buried him beside his first wife in Carrickbrennan Graveyard. She erected the wall monument in Monkstown Church to his memory, seen today in the south transept. Eight years after his death, she, too, was laid to rest beside him in Carrickbrennan. Day's sons were both ordained in the Church of Ireland. They took their mother's name initially; John Robert was ordained as John Robert Fitzgerald, but took the additional name of Day after his father's death, as he had requested in his will (Leslie 1940).

Dr Benjamin Domvile (1711–74)

Sacred to the Memory of **BENJAMIN DOMVILE, D.D.**
who was born May 19th 1711, and died October 18th 1774.
He entertained the deepest sense of the importance, and
exerted the most conscientious diligence in the discharge
of his sacred office; his discourses addressed to the
understanding and the heart were so powerfully enforced by
animated language and strength of reasoning that he was
justly admired as the most persuasive preacher of his time.
Equally respected in private life, his filial piety, conjugal
affection and tender regard to all his family were most
exemplary. Invariable in friendship, unbounded in
benevolence, the great object of his constant
endeavours was to promote the honour of God
and the happiness of mankind.
This humble Monument was erected by
his grateful and afflicted Widow.

Benjamin Domvile started out in life as Benjamin Barrington; he died Benjamin Domvile. His huge wall monument (almost 9 feet high) is the oldest in Monkstown Church, dating from 1774; it must have dominated the small church at Carrickbrennan, where it would have hung before being transferred to the nave of the new Georgian church, built in 1789 on the present site, and then resited to its present position in the north transept of Semple's 1831 church.

Benjamin was one of four cousins whose lives became intimately connected, children of the three daughters of Sir Thomas Domvile of Templeogue (*Burke's Irish Family Records* 1976). Benjamin, son of Sir Thomas's daughter Margaret and Benjamin Barrington, was born in Cork in 1711. After a conventional schooling, he entered Trinity College, Dublin, aged fifteen, in 1725, was awarded his Bachelor of Arts in 1730 and his MA in 1733 (Burtchaell and Sadleir 1935). He probably kept in touch with his three cousins: Henry (son of his aunt Bridget and Lord Barry of Santry) and Charles and Anna-Maria (the two children of his other aunt, Elizabeth, and Admiral Christopher Pocklington). Perhaps he took a more than cousinly interest in Anna-Maria.

The escapades of Benjamin's cousin, Henry Barry, Lord Santry's son, were public knowledge. He was a leading member of Dublin's notorious Hell Fire Club, feared for its reckless and anti-social behaviour. Dean Swift wrote to Lady Santry in about 1730, 'from friendship', advising her to get her spoilt son into line. He followed up his letter by calling on her, but gave up after being refused admission four times by Henry's offended mother (Adams 1883).

In 1738 Benjamin Barrington was ordained and safely making his way up the ecclesiastical ladder. But Swift's warning about his cousin, Henry Barry, was unfortunately prophetic. Henry had succeeded to his father's title four years earlier. Now Lord Santry, he had used his sword in a drunken rage, fatally wounding a porter called Laughlin Murphy in a Palmerstown pub. Murphy died seven weeks later. Seven months after that, Henry, Lord Santry, was tried for murder by his peers — a jury of 23 earls, viscounts and barons of the realm. Since the House of Lords was too small for the hearing, the House of Commons had to be used instead. Shocked Dubliners heard of the unprovoked attack. But they were even more shocked when Lord Santry was found guilty, his estates confiscated and he was sentenced to death by beheading, albeit with a unanimous appeal for mercy (Gilbert 1861). The axe was purchased. The former Lord Santry and his inevitable fate were on everyone's lips. But two months after the trial news circulated that he had somehow managed to escape his come-uppance. His uncle, Sir Compton Domvile of Santry and Templeogue, intervened on his behalf. Sir Compton happened to be the proprietor of Templeogue, through which Dublin's water supply ran, and so found himself in a strong bargaining position. He threatened to cut off the water to Dublin unless his nephew was spared. The gamble paid off. Henry was granted a royal pardon: he escaped the axe and had his estates restored, but lost his title. He left Dublin and went to live in Nottingham. By now, Dr Benjamin Barrington had been prebendary of Tynan for several years. His cousin, Anna-Maria Pocklington, was still unwed.

Henry died eleven years later, aged 41, leaving all his estates to the uncle who had saved his life. This was the year when Dr Benjamin Barrington ('justly admired as the most persuasive preacher of his time') published the sermon he had delivered to the Irish House of Commons on 5 November 1745 (Cotton 1849). When Sir Compton Domvile died in March 1768 he, in his turn, left his Santry estates to his nephew, Charles Pocklington, son of his youngest sister, stipulating that he was to adopt the Domvile name and coat of arms. Sir Compton's death also led to a sudden upheaval in the life of Dr Benjamin Barrington, the bookish 'confirmed bachelor' of 57 and dean of Armagh for the previous five years. By Sir Compton's death, Dr Barrington became the 'heir at law and inheritor of the estates' of his uncle, William Domvile of Loughlinstown, who had died in 1763, and therefore also assumed the Domvile name and coat of arms.

Now called 'Benjamin Domvile', he immediately left Armagh, swapping its deanery for the vicarage of St Ann's in Dublin's

The memorial of Dr Benjamin Domvile, 'the most persuasive preacher of his time', dates from 1774 and is the oldest wall monument in Monkstown Church today. Set in the north transept and measuring some 9 feet high, it originally hung in Carrickbrennan Church, was then moved to the 'new' 1789 Georgian church and finally came to rest in Semple's 1831 church of today.

Dawson Street. There, on 4 April 1768, he married his cousin, Anna-Maria Pocklington, the sister of Charles and niece and heir of Sir Compton Domvile.[3] (Coincidentally, the Monkstown Easter Vestry was held on the same date and 'The Revd. Doct. Benjamin Domvil' was appointed as one of the governors of the new Monkstown Charity School. Presumably, since it was his wedding day, he did not attend.) Over the next month Dr Domvile, possibly celebrating both his marriage and his inheritance, published several notices in the April 1768 issues of the *Freeman's Journal*, announcing donations to various charities: £25 annually to the Society for Relief of Widows of Clergymen in the Diocese of Dublin; £10 to the perpetual curate of Monkstown, Thomas Heany, 'to be by him distributed among the industrious poor of the Parish of Monkstown and its Union, without making any distinction on Account of their Religion, Profession or particular Attachment'; £20 annually to Mercer's Hospital to support a bed; £10 each to the 'industrious poor' of Kilsallaghan, Finglas and Drumcondra; and 10 guineas to the 'Alms Houses belonging to the Baptists Meeting in Swift's-Ally for Widows and aged poor'.

Just over a year after his marriage, Benjamin made his last will and testament,[4] 'being of sound mind, but allarmed by some symptoms of (his) approaching dissolution'. After ensuring that his aunt, Elizabeth Barrington, was provided for during her lifetime and making a few bequests, mainly charitable, he left the residue of his fortune to his 'dear and well beloved wife, Anna-Maria'. Those disquieting 'symptoms' which provoked his will were probably part of the same illness to which he referred in a letter three years later to his friend Sir William Lee: 'I am I think perfectly recovered, at least as much as I can ever expect after such a long illness and at this advanced Period of Life' (he was 61).[5] Benjamin had followed Sir William's advice and dosed himself with his friend's 'favourite Medicine, James' Powder' for his 'ugly distemper' (possibly a skin disease). He told Sir William that he now felt 'better than ever'. He wrote from Bath, where he was staying with Anna-Maria, who was taking the water there. (Dr Robert James (1703–76) invented the powder that was called after him, whose main function was to reduce temperature. It was very popular in the mid-1700s and early 1800s, still being advertised enthusiastically in *Saunders's News-Letter* on 22 May 1826.)

In 1773 Dr Domville was made rector of Bray and prebendary of Rathmichael (Cotton 1848; Wallace 2001) and lived in 'Cherrywood House', which was the glebe house for Rathmichael. He died the following year, in 1774. He was buried with his parents at St Bride's Church in Dublin, as he had requested in his will, 'privately and early, without ringing of bells'. If, as his wall monument proclaims, he was 'the most persuasive preacher of his time', it is a great pity that, among the other requests in his will, he asked his friend Dr Isaac Mann, archdeacon of Dublin, to inspect his 'papers, manuscripts, sermons and letters', and then burn them.

Benjamin Domvile never lived at Loughlinstown House, the Domvile family seat, but Anna-Maria moved there six years after his death and her nephew, Mr Francis Savage, made improvements to the house and grounds. A later tenant (1796–1841) was Judge Robert Day (*see above*), another Monkstown parishioner (Turner 1987) who also enthused about Dr James's Powders ('I take my panacea for all complaints, James's powders and castor oil diluted with whiskey, and health is completely restored'). Loughlinstown House finally passed out of the hands of the Domviles in 1963 with the death of Colonel Alexander, who had married the widow of Barry Domvile, last of the junior branch of the family in Ireland. Today, it is the headquarters of the European Foundation for the Improvement of Living and Working Conditions, bought from the previous owner, Sir John Galvin.

Colonel Edward Ward Drewe (1782–1862)

SACRED
TO THE LOVED MEMORY
OF A BRAVE PENINSULAR
AND WATERLOO SOLDIER
EDWD. WARD DREWE
LATE MAJOR UNATTACHED
WHOSE REMAINS REPOSE
IN A VAULT
BENEATH THIS CHURCH.
OBIIT FEBY 20TH 1862
O God the Lord the strength of my Salvation,
Thou hast covered my head in the day of Battle.
Psalm CXL.VII.V

This verse from the Psalms[6] was not metaphorical as far as Edward Drewe was concerned. As a young man he had fought in a battle of which it was said, 'It is usual, upon the conclusion of a battle, to ask, "Who's dead?" So terrible was the Battle of Waterloo that the question asked was, "Who's alive?" '

Drewe was a lieutenant of the 27th Regiment, the Royal Inniskilling Fusiliers, which guarded a crucial crossroads during the Battle of Waterloo. When they were first ordered to their battle position, on high ground and therefore terribly exposed, 'every man grasped his fire-lock and moved forward with a decided firm and confident step'. They formed into a battle square and faced cavalry charges, musket-fire and heavy cannister-fire from a nearby battery. Musket balls in the head or trunk were usually fatal, and in the limbs usually meant amputation. Cannister wounds literally cut men to pieces.

When the French saw how important the regiment's position was they attacked even more ferociously, but the 27th held firm. Major-General Sir John Lambert, second-in-command after the duke of Wellington, wrote in a letter to Major-General Sir James Kempt on 19 June 1815 that he was 'perfectly satisfied with the conduct of every individual'; he praised the men's 'steady and gallant conduct' while they were 'unavoidably exposed for several hours to a galling fire'. Sir James reported to Wellington that same day: 'I found it absolutely necessary to increase our fire by moving up ... the 27th regiment ... but it was unavoidably much exposed. The regiment behaved nobly and suffered exceedingly' (Wellington 1863).

'Suffered exceedingly' was an understatement. Nearly 70% were killed or wounded at their positions. Out of 698 men, 105 were killed outright and 373 wounded 'severely', including Lieutenant Edward Drewe (reported in *Saunders's News-Letter* of 7 July 1815). On the evening of the battle, Wellington surveyed the field and saw dozens of young men mown down, still lying in their battle-square formation. He later said that they had 'saved the centre of (his) line at Waterloo'.

On Drewe's monument, set on the south wall of Monkstown's chancel, the prestigious Waterloo medal is hanging conspicuously under his sword and helmet, which bears the regimental number, '27', picked out in gold. The winged figure of Victory is stamped on the medal; she holds a branch of olive in one hand and a branch of palm in the other. Below Drewe's coat of arms is the motto *Sub cruce salus* ('Under the cross of salvation'). The Waterloo medal was the first to be awarded by the British government to all men, regardless of rank. It was also the first campaign medal given to the next-of-kin of men killed in action and to have the recipient's name impressed around the edge by machine. Naturally, veterans like Drewe were enormously proud to wear it and copies were even made for their wives.

In the early 1800s one-third of the British army was Irish. Most of these men were enlisted and Catholic. However, many of the officers were Anglo-Irish, such as Wellington himself (born in Merrion Square) and Edward Drewe. Of the Irish officers, 80% belonged to the Church of Ireland. Officers had to be wealthy since their pay was considered an honorarium. In 1820 Drewe, then a lieutenant, would have earned nine shillings a day, while his basic officer's uniform cost nearly £135. After the Battle of Waterloo the army was reduced in size and Drewe, like many other officers, had a choice of retiring on 'half pay' or selling his commission. Drewe decided to retire, but had to make offers of service

295

occasionally in order to be considered for promotion. In 1837 he was made major of the Connaught Rangers and in 1859 became their colonel.

After his life in the army, Edward Drewe retired to 'Valetta House' at 17 George's Street, Lower, in Kingstown, one of the 'handsome seats and pleasing villas' mentioned in Lewis's *Topographical dictionary* of 1837. ('Valetta House' was directly behind the present Dun Laoghaire Library; demolished in the 1960s, the site is now a multi-story carpark.) Drewe was elected a town commissioner in 1845, overseeing 'paving, watching, lighting, regulating and otherwise improving the town of Kingstown', where he lived until his death at the age of 80. He continued to attend Monkstown Church. In Brooke's *Recollections* (1877), Colonel Drewe was 'a noble-looking and gallant old Artillery officer, who had seen much service'; his pew was in the front of the gallery and 'it was a picture to see his military and erect form standing during the psalmody … the face of the veteran embrowned and worn with the hue of foreign clime and service'.

Drewe was proud of his army career: before Waterloo he had served under the duke of Wellington during the Peninsular War (1808–14). But his moment of glory in the Battle of Waterloo had meant most to him and this was what his wife tried to capture in the monument she erected to his memory.

Dorothea Goff (1846–70)

A beautiful white marble monument, dusty and broken into several pieces, leans against a brick wall in the vaults of Monkstown Church. It commemorates an intriguing young woman called Dorothea. The inscription reads:

Edward Ward Drewe's wall monument celebrates his military career — the number '27' on the helmet indicates his regiment (the 27th, Royal Inniskilling Fusiliers). The prestigious Waterloo medal, stamped with the winged figure of Victory, was awarded to him for service in that battle.

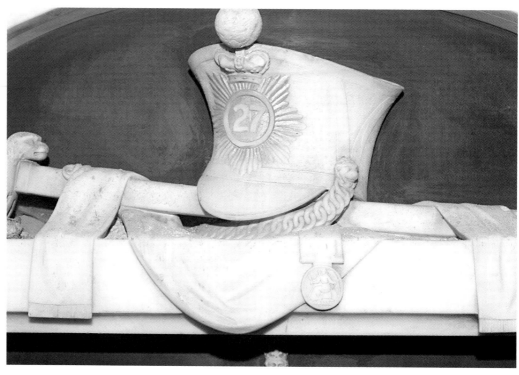

IN
AFFECTIONATE REMEMBRANCE OF
DOROTHEA
WIFE OF
THOMAS WM GOFF ESQR
OF CARRIGLEA, KILL-OF-THE-GRANGE,
AND ELDEST DAUGHTER OF THE LATE
LORD AUGUSTUS FITZCLARENCE
DIED MAY 15TH 1870, AGED 24 YEARS.
HER REMAINS
LIE IN BROMPTON CEMETERY, LONDON,
BUT HER MEMORIAL
BELONGS TO THIS CHURCH
WHERE SHE DELIGHTED TO WORSHIP
AND TO PRAISE GOD IN HIS SANCTUARY.
'Weep not, she is not dead, but sleepeth', St Luke VIII, 52
'Them also which sleep in Jesus will God bring with Him', I Thess IV, 14

The church where Dorothea 'delighted to worship' was actually St John's of Mounttown, not Monkstown Parish Church, but when that church was sold in 1985 its wall monuments, church furniture and stained-glass windows all came to Monkstown. The monuments are stored in the church vaults to this day.

Dorothea's husband was Thomas William Goff, the eldest son of the Rev. Thomas Goff, who, as Wallace (2001) tells us, was prebendary of Kilrane (Ferns) (1806–19), curate of Coolock and Raheny (1810) and vicar of Tallaght and Whitechurch (1813–30). With his wife Anne[7] he had moved to 'Carriglea' on Kill Avenue in about 1836 (Laffan 1987). This house, built in 1826, had a walled garden with greenhouses and lay in an estate of over 37 acres 'of improved ground, well planted, commanding extensive views', as reported in *Saunders's News-Letter* of 1 June 1826. (It has since been incorporated into the Dun Laoghaire College of Art, Design and Technology on Kill Avenue, near Baker's Corner.) Diagonally opposite 'Carriglea' was the first glebe house of Monkstown, built in 1797 (today called 'Fairholme'; *see Chapter 11*). Kill Avenue was formerly known as 'Goff's Avenue' and is still lined by some of its original beech trees (Pearson 1998).

On the death of his father, Thomas Goff was left a very wealthy young man. He owned a house at Oakport in County Roscommon, as well as 'Carriglea' and huge estates in Galway and Roscommon. He became a captain in the 7th Dragoon Guards, high sheriff for Roscommon (1858) and MP for Roscommon (1859), and had his own coat of arms confirmed (1859).[8] These trappings of wealth, leadership and privilege were essential for a young man who was to choose a bride from even higher up the social scale. His intended was Dorothea FitzClarence, who was, as her monument tells us, the eldest daughter of the Rev. Lord Augustus FitzClarence, rector of Mapledurham in England. Dorothea and Thomas were thus both 'rectory children'. But while Thomas's grandfather had been a wealthy Anglo-Irish landlord from County Roscommon, Dorothea's had been a king (albeit an illegitimate line).

William, the duke of Clarence (later to become William IV), had a long-standing relationship with the beautiful Irish actress known as Dorothea Jordan (originally Dorothea

The broken wall monument of Dorothea Goff (née FitzClarence) reflects the fact that she died young at the age of 24, possibly in childbirth. She was named after her grandmother, the famous Irish actress Dorothea Jordan (formerly Bland) and the long-time mistress of the duke of Clarence (later William IV).

Bland). The relationship carried on for over twenty years and the couple lived openly together at 'Bushy Park' in London. They were accepted together publicly, entertained lavishly and raised ten children, called the FitzClarences (Aspinall 1951). Dorothea was the favourite of Sir Joshua Reynolds and of Byron, who thought she was 'superb'. Her brilliant stage career was matched by her controversial private life. At the age of twenty she was seduced by her Dublin manager and fled, pregnant, to England. There she changed her name to Jordan, suggested apparently because she had 'crossed the water'. London audiences loved her, especially one young man, Richard Ford, with whom she lived and bore three children.[9] The duke of Clarence met her and was smitten from that moment on; indeed, *The Morning Post* of July 1791 remarked satirically, 'We hear from Richmond that an illustrious youth has at length passed the ford, yet is not likely to be pickled by a legal process' (Ziegler 1971).

Interestingly, two Monkstown parishioners met Dorothea, or Mrs Jordan as she was known. Judge Robert Day dined with the couple at 'Bushy Park' and was shown around the Duke's Esher estate by William, who shared Day's passion for farming (Day 1938). Sir Joseph Atkinson, the well-known dramatist and former high sheriff of Dublin (who lived in 'Melfield', the present Music School in the grounds of Newpark School, Blackrock), also knew Mrs Jordan and invited her to Dublin in 1809 to act in the theatre he managed (Aspinall 1951).

Of William and Dorothea's ten children, Augustus FitzClarence was the second-youngest. He had tried the navy as a career, but it was not to his liking so he went into the church instead. His father was not enamoured with this change and was heard to remark, 'I am not very fond of the Church'. However, Augustus was ordained rector of Mapledurham, married and raised a family. His eldest daughter was Dorothea, named after her grandmother.

We can only speculate as to where Thomas Goff and Dorothea met, but it was presumably on one of Thomas's visits to England. In 1864, when Dorothea was eighteen, she and Thomas were married and the couple came to live at 'Carriglea', where Thomas's widowed mother, Anne, was apparently still living.[10] It was natural that Thomas and Dorothea should attend the new church of St John's in Mounttown (built in 1860) rather than Monkstown, since it was

'Carriglea', on today's Kill Avenue, was built in 1826 within an estate of some 40 acres and was the family home of the Goffs from 1836. It is now part of the Dun Laoghaire College of Art, Design and Technology.

much closer to their home. Three children were born to the couple — Muriel Helen in 1865 and the twins Ethel Anne and Thomas Clarence Edward (called after both his grandfathers) in 1867. But then, in 1870, tragedy struck the little family, when Dorothea, aged only 24, died, apparently while on a visit to England. The cause of death is unknown, but childbirth must be high on the list. Thomas, her bereaved husband, erected a white marble monument to her memory on the wall of St John's, probably one of the first in the church and the only one to be mentioned in its later history (published in 1911) written by the rector, the Rev. Ralph Harden (1895–1910), who was himself married to a Goff (Wallace 2001).

Meanwhile Thomas's mother, Anne Goff, continued to attend Monkstown Church, sitting in the family pew (No. 132[11]) in the north gallery where she could see the wall monument of her husband, the Rev. Thomas Goff, who had died in 1844, and their three children. After her death, in 1877, her monument joined theirs.

Dorothea's grandmother, Mrs Jordan, had come to a sad and undignified end. In 1811, when she was nearly 50, putting on weight and nearing the end of her stage career, William, duke of Clarence, realised that it was time for him to produce a legitimate heir. His father, the king, George III, was considered to be 'mad', while his brother George, the prince regent (later George IV), was childless. William was next in line to the throne. Dorothea had to go. The press was openly critical:

> 'What! Leave a woman to her tears?
> Your faithful friend for twenty years.
> One who gave up her youthful charms,
> The fond companion of your arms!' (Ziegler 1971).

Mrs Jordan went to live in Paris, where she died a year later in penury.

William found it difficult to find a willing yet suitable wife. Even though he was heir to the throne, he was stout, unpolished and in debt, but perhaps the greatest deterrent to any potential wife was his family of ten difficult children, the FitzClarences. However, Adelaide of Saxe-Meiningen (after whom the Adelaide Hospital is called) agreed to become the duchess of Clarence and later his queen. Sadly, her own children all died as babies or were stillborn. Adelaide was a kind and generous woman, described by her husband as 'beloved and superior', who cared for the FitzClarences and for her niece as if they were her own. She wrote to her sister-in-law, the duchess of Kent, 'My children are dead, but your child lives, and she is mine too'.

That child was Victoria, the only surviving legitimate heir of the children of George III. If Victoria had died before producing her huge family, it has been suggested that George, the eldest FitzClarence, could have been crowned George V.

Lieutenant Colonel William Hoey (1815–54)

> *Now is the stately column broke,*
> *The beacon-light is quench'd in smoke,*
> *The trumpet's silver silver sound is still,*
> *The warder silent on the hill!*
> Sir Walter Scott talking about William Pitt

SACRED
TO THE MEMORY
OF MY DEAR HUSBAND
WILLIAM FRANCIS HOEY
LIEUT. COLN. COMMANDING XXXTH REGT
BORN AUGUST 3RD 1815
DIED IN THE CRIMEA
SEPTEMBER 25TH 1854

'BLESSED ARE THE DEAD WHICH DIE IN THE LORD'
REV XIV:18

The meaning of a broken column was probably clear to anyone entering a church in the last century. Now, such symbolism seems to be a foreign language. In the Bible, Judges 16:29–30 says:

> 'And Samson took hold of the two middle pillars upon which the house stood ... of the one with his right hand, and of the other with his left. And Samson said, "Let me die with the Philistines". And he bowed himself with all his might; and the house fell upon the lords, and upon all the people that were therein. So the dead which he slew at his death were more than they which he slew in his life.'

Thus a broken column came to symbolise 'Fortitude', one of the four 'cardinal virtues', signifying courage, endurance and strength. It also meant death in the prime of life. When Samson pulled the house down on top of himself and the Philistines he died, but in his death he was victorious.

We know from the inscription on William Hoey's wall monument that he was the commanding officer of the 30th Regiment. Regimental flags form a backdrop to his tablet and the word 'Alma' is enclosed in a laurel crown over the broken column. The Battle of Alma was fought — and won — on 20 September 1854. Hoey died five days afterwards. Like Samson, he was victorious in death.

The Battle of Alma was the decisive battle of the Crimean War (Gibbs 1963). If it had been lost, the British and French would have had to leave the Crimea. Because they won, they advanced and laid siege to the fortress and naval base of Sebastopol, which eventually fell. The battle was won against all the odds. But

'Alma', the broken column and the regimental flags on William Hoey's wall monument all tell of the death of this officer, the 'idol of his regiment', at the tragically young age of 39, after the Battle of Alma in the Crimea.

instead of feeling elated, the soldiers felt totally downhearted: they had seen friends killed or die in agony. Many were ill with cholera. In his diary, Lord George Paget quoted the duke of Wellington, 'Next to a battle lost, there is nothing so dreadful as a battle won'.

It took two days to bury the Allied and Russian dead in huge pits. Then the wounded and sick were carried on jolting litters for three miles to the ships, where the surgeons worked on them, amputating limbs without anaesthetic, but able to do little else owing to inadequate medical supplies. There were no bandages or splints, no morphine or chloroform, and no shelter. At Varna, where the army had embarked for the Crimea, chaotic organisation meant that there were not enough ships to accommodate the men, with their cumbersome equipment and baggage animals. An order was made to abandon tents, bedding, medicine chests, cooking equipment, 1,200 officers' horses and 4,000 baggage animals; most of the animals starved to death (Woodham-Smith 1950).

After the long, uncomfortable journey to the sea, the wounded and sick, including Russian officers, were crammed into hospital transports. On some ships the only medical attendants were soldiers' wives. The ships were filthy and so crowded that the few surgeons could hardly move among the lines of sick and dying men (Hibbert 1961). Far more died of dysentery and cholera than from their wounds (78% died from disease, 9% from wounds and 13% were killed in action).

It was not only the wounded who caught cholera. Healthy young soldiers like William Hoey were struck down too. Dublin's *Freeman's Journal* carried this notice in 1854:

'It is with feelings of the deepest regret ... that we have to announce the death, from cholera of (this) brave and distinguished officer [William Hoey]. He ... endeared (himself) to many of our readers ... by the warmth and amiability of his character, while his known talents as an officer, and distinguished gallantry in the field ... rendered him the idol of his regiment. We insert the following extract of a letter from (a fellow) officer ... in reference to his decease, cut off, as he was, in the flush of victory and in the prime of manhood: — "The poor Colonel is dead. He died about three days ago of cholera, having been only 24 hours ill. I am very sorry for him, for he was a gallant fellow ... It is a melancholy thing to think that, by escaping the murderous fire of the 20th, (he) should ... be cut off by the worst enemy we have to contend with. Poor Hoey! he was a fine fellow" ' (Smith 1854–7).

The Crimean War dragged on until February 1856 and a peace treaty was signed that March. To commemorate the Battle of Alma, Alma Terrace in Rathmines first appeared in the 1856 Dublin directory and Alma Road and Alma Place in Monkstown in 1859.[12]

This following passage appeared in the *Dublin Medical Press* on 17 January 1855:

'Let the names of the glorious dead, who perished of their wounds on the Alma hill-side — of those, too, who pined away in the foetid holds of the transports on their passage to Constantinople ... be comforted; the means of saving their precious lives were all prepared, duly labelled and carefully stored away beneath the bales and boxes of a stupid and obstructive purveyor in the village of Balaklava! ... When sick there has been no medicine, when wounded no hospital, and they have perished like dogs, in the trenches, and outside their tents.'

William Digges La Touche (1747–1803)

'His wonderful humanity and boundless generosity', his 'recognition of the existence and goodness of providence', his 'mind glowed in gratitude to God for every benefit', whose 'universal benevolence was ever active' — these are some of the tributes paid to William Digges La Touche, writer, diplomat, banker and philantropist. For a fuller biography of this extraordinary man, *see Chapter 14* on 'Monkstown's churchwardens'.

William Digges La Touche served the British government in the city of Bassora in southern Persia (today's Basra in southern Iraq) for almost twenty years (1865–84). He was a popular and sensitive diplomatic representative. Five years after he left Basra, an English traveller called Major John Taylor passed through the town on his way to India. William La Touche's praises were still being sung, particularly because of his part in saving many lives during the Siege of Basra. Taylor wrote:

'No man ever deserved better at the hands of the Arabs, or was more highly respected and esteemed amongst them, than Mr. La Touche. His wonderful humanity and boundless generosity to the unhappy captives of Zebur [a town about twelve miles west of Basra] had gained him their warmest affection.

When Bussora was besieged by the Persians, he sheltered within his own walls and under the English flag, the principal people with their wives and families. And when the miserable inhabitants of Zebur, according to the custom of the Persians to persons taken in war, became the slaves of their opponents, he ransomed them without distinction, at his own expense' (Urwick 1868).

A touching legacy in William La Touche's will read:

'To Coja Petrus Millick of Bassora in Arabia — £100 as a small token of my regard for him and my sense of the attachment which he shewed unto me as well as to my late friend, Henry Moore.'[13] (Henry Moore had been William's predecessor as British resident, or diplomatic representative, to Bassora.)

After his death in 1803, Grace Digges La Touche had a fine marble monument to her husband's memory set on the east wall of the south transept in Monkstown. Many years later, Ronnie Blay, sexton of Monkstown Church for over twenty years until his death in 1997, related how, one dark winter morning in late 1975, he went into the church and found himself tripping over pieces of masonry on the floor. When he turned on the lights, he found that the front of the La Touche monument had fallen to the floor, chipping a corner of the font beneath as it did so. Apparently, the iron pegs fixing the marble inscription to the monument had rusted over the years and expanded, causing the tablet to shatter and fall. The front of the monument was repaired with cement and a simple dedication added: 'In Memory of William Digges La Touche, Died 8th November 1803'. This is what is seen today in the church. But then, in November 2002, members of a Vestry work party, including the author, found the original marble tablet in a passageway of the church vaults. Although shattered into about twenty pieces, the writing is still pristine and the marble in excellent condition. The author carefully reassembled the fragments and, although the upper section is the most damaged, most of the inscription can still be read (suggestions for some of the missing words are included in square brackets below). The whole is a fitting tribute to this great man.

Sacred to the Memory of
WILLIAM DIGGES LA TOUCHE ESQRE
Whose Character combined __rrect__ _orals and genuine Piety [? Morals]
In Publick Life, Many __eady, Disinterested;
Neither the Slave of Party nor the Dupe _____ction, [? of Faction]
In Times the most turbulent and ___l; [? cruel]
He promoted judiciously and effectually th__ ____entatiously.
The Prosperity of his fellow Citizens, and _____llity of his Country. [? the tranquillity]

In Private Life, Upright and _____, Mild, and Benevolent;
A kind Husband, a tender Father, a gentle Master, imparting
to the Poor, not only his Bounty but his Counsel and Protection.

He sympathized with the Feelings, conciliated the Affections,
and promoted the Happiness of all with whom he was connected.

Temperate amidst Eastern Luxury,
unseduced by the temptations of Power and Wealth;
He filled an important situation at Bussora for 18 Years,
where he did not amass Riches,
But ransom'd Many from Captivity;
He reconciled the differences and relieved the wants of the Natives,
adorning and recommending the Character of a Christian;
Thus, his Faith was not only firm but practical,
working by Love;
Not only by his Lips but by his Life He glorified God.
Death came on him unexpected, but we may
humbly hope it did not find him unprepared.
He departed this Life on the 8th November 1803,
In the 57th Year of his Age

wishing to transmit to Posterity, an Example,
so worthy of Imitation, this Marble
has been inscribed to his Beloved Memory,
by Her who best knew his worth.

Similar sentiments on William Digges La Touche were expressed in his obituary in *Faulkner's Dublin Journal* on 12 November 1803:

'Died, on Tuesday morning, at his house in Stephen's Green, William Digges La Touche Esq — a man whose life was a continued scene of unsullied purity and Christian virtue; in whose bosom charity, delighted, dwelled; by whom the widow's tears were wiped away, and the orphans' sorrows stilled; whose universal benevolence was ever active in pouring oil into the wounds of affliction, and binding up the care-worn heart. Possessed of an ample fortune, acquired in a foreign clime by strict uprightness and with the poor man's blessing, he considered it as a loan from Heaven, and so applied it that, whether in his native land, in the West Indies, or in Arabia's sands, the name of 'Latouche' [sic] shall be remembered with gratitude and love, whilst Mercy and true Christianity (to whose blest abodes his spirit hath departed) demand the tribute of admiration and of praise.'

The Times of London was blunter:

'Wm. Digges Latouche, Esq., the richest of that family, is dead. He was seized with an apoplectic fit yesterday, in the Royal Exchange, and dropped down senseless.'

Sir John Lees (1737–1811)

Sir John Lees's wall memorial in Monkstown Church extols his virtues:

SACRED TO THE MEMORY OF THE LATE
SIR JOHN LEES, BARONET
WHAT HE WAS AS A HUSBAND, A FATHER AND A
CHRISTIAN IS DEEPLY ENGRAVEN IN THE MEMORY
OF HIS SURVIVING FAMILY AND FRIENDS, AND HIS
GREAT PUBLIC AND PRIVATE CHARACTER WILL REMAIN
LONG AFTER THIS FRAIL MONUMENT SHALL PERISH
AND BE FORGOTTEN, A MEMORIAL WHICH IS RATHER
INTENDED AS A GRATEFUL AND DUTIFUL OFFERING
OF THE FILIAL AFFECTION AND PIETY
OF SIX AFFLICTED SONS
THAN TO BE THE RECORD OF HIS VIRTUES
TO POSTERITY.
HE DIED UNIVERLY LAMENTED
BY ALL RANKS
AND DESCRIPTIONS OF PEOPLE
THE 3 OF SEPTEMBER A:D: 1811
AGED 74 YEARS

A more fitting inscription might be the lines from Shakespeare's *Henry IV*, 'Adieu, and take thy praise with thee to heaven! Thy ignominy sleep with thee in the grave, But not rememb'red in thy epitaph!' In reality, Lees was unscrupulous, self-motivated and a swindler, who feathered his own nest and that of his relatives over many years. However, he was undoubtedly an able man and a busy one — appointed in 1767 as private secretary to Lord Townshend, the lord lieutenant of Ireland, and subsequently to his successor, Lord Harcourt; secretary of the Irish Post Office in 1774; usher of the Black Rod in the Irish House of Commons in 1780; and under-secretary of the War Department in Ireland in 1781. In 1790 he set up a very efficient system of post roads throughout Ireland, carrying mail coaches. In between his business dealings he served as churchwarden in Monkstown for at least eleven years, between 1784 and 1796, and was one of the prime movers behind the building of the 1789 Georgian church on its new site (the present location). For a fuller biography of Sir John Lees, *see Chapter 14* on 'Monkstown's churchwardens'.

The Rev. Sir Harcourt Lees (1776–1852)

'The united powers of this world, or a view of all those tortures that ever distinguished and rendered horrible the Inquisition, could not deprive me of my firmness, or affect the determination of a mind inaccessible alike to influence or terror.' So wrote the Rev. Sir Harcourt Lees, the eldest son and heir of the influential and powerful Sir John Lees (*see above*), in one of his many pamphlets, entitled 'A cursory view of the present state of Ireland', published in January 1820.

Firm and determined are two words that certainly describe Harcourt Lees. He and his neighbour, Lord Cloncurry (Valentine Lawless), did everything possible to stop the Dublin

The Rev. Sir Harcourt Lees, painted by T.C.Thompson, RHA, was perhaps a more likeable rogue than his father, Sir John Lees. Although rector of Killaney in County Down for over 40 years, Harcourt Lees was resident at 'Blackrock House'. A prolific pamphleteer, who saw 'popish plots' everywhere, he was not averse to holding out for £7,500 compensation from the Dublin–Kingstown Railway Company to run the line through his property in the early 1830s.

to Kingstown railway running through their properties, which took in a considerable portion of the shoreline at Blackrock. Harcourt Lees lived in the family home of 'Blackrock House', while Cloncurry lived in 'Maretimo', both on Newtown Avenue. The railway was given the royal assent in 1831 by an act of parliament and the company was able to proceed by compulsorily purchasing land along the route, except for the Blackrock stretch with its two formidable landowners. They seemed untouchable, and the following extract from *Saunders's News-Letter* of 24 October 1831 goes some way towards explaining why: 'His Excellency the Marquis of Anglesey [the lord lieutenant] with the Marchioness and family, took their departure from the Marine villa of Sir Harcourt Lees, Blackrock, on Friday, and proceeded to Lyons, the seat of Lord Cloncurry, on a visit for a few days'.

As time went on, however, both these gentlemen, good parishioners of Monkstown, were enticed to part with their land by the offer of huge sums of money — £7,500 for Sir Harcourt and £3,000 for Lord Cloncurry. Both landowners also ensured that parliament had inserted some very strict conditions in the act, favouring them. For example, the railway company was forced to build tunnels (so that the railway line would be unobtrusive), ventilating shafts where appropriate and also 'ornamental' works that would add value to their land. These works included 'fishing and bathing lodges, a camera obscura [literally, a dark chamber] tower, a boat-slip with pier and harbour, and iron-latticed bridge ... across the railway to the sea ... executed in the very best style of Italian architecture, the stone finely-chiselled and moulded granite obtained from Seapoint cliffs' (*The Irish Builder,* 15 June 1887). Today, the neglected remains of these works can be seen, just to the north of Seapoint, as a small classical 'temple', a pier and harbour, an open-air bathing pool and a granite cut-stone bridge over the railway.

Who was this Sir Harcourt Lees, who could intimidate the Dublin–Kingstown Railway Company and even the mighty British parliament? Besides being the eldest son and heir of Sir John Lees, the influential secretary of the Irish Post Office (*see above*), he was also 'the redoubtable, the renowned, the dreaded and the dreadless Sir Harcourt Lees'. This alliterative epithet sounds as if it would be more at home in a music hall than in the conservative *Dublin and London Magazine* of March–December 1825. The Rev. Sir Harcourt Lees took himself extremely seriously and would have been horrified to hear that others, by and large, did not. An imaginary conversation between Sir Harcourt and a diarist (who called himself 'The Hermit in Ireland') was recorded in the same article which, even if partly tongue-in-cheek, gives a hint of how Sir Harcourt was regarded by others. The 'conversation' goes as follows. Sir Harcourt asserts, '... The Protestants, sir, have a right to look to me as a leader; — my splendid services — my sterling honesty — my tried intrepidity — and my sacred character as a minister of the Gospel'. ' "Minister of the Gospel!" thought I. I looked at Sir Harcourt and struggled with my countenance.'

In a letter to Daniel O'Connell in 1821, Sir Harcourt stated his *raison d'être*:

> 'My life ... Sir, is devoted to the service of my religion, my ill-used venerated Sovereign, and my endangered country, and with my latest breath I will defend and protect them and will declare myself, in defiance of every danger and every difficulty, the determined advocate of the rights and privileges of the Established Apostolic Church, and the constitutional Advocate of a Protestant King, and Protestant Ascendancy in both Church and State.'

In an address to the King's Friends that same year, Sir Harcourt said: 'May this gratifying memorial of my humble exertions be engraved upon my tomb-stone, it is the only honor that I desire to obtain in this world, or would give one farthing for the personal enjoyment of, and as it has proved the legitimate source of my chief happiness in this life, so will the recollection of my having, at least, endeavored to deserve the proud distinction, console me at the final hour of my dissolution.'

Harcourt Lees was called after Lord Harcourt, the viceroy, to whom his father, Sir John, had been private secretary. (Other of Sir John's sons were also called after notables, such as 'Townshend' after the lord lieutenant of that name and 'Thomas Orde' after the duke of Rutland's secretary.) Harcourt entered Trinity College, Dublin, at the age of seventeen and stayed there for two years (1794–6). He then transferred to Trinity College, Cambridge

(1796), from where he graduated with his MA in 1802.[14] He was appointed prebendary of Fennor (Cashel) and also of Tullycorbet (Clogher), which he held until 1806. Then he became rector and vicar of Killaney in County Down, which position he held for the rest of his life.[15]

When his father died in 1811, the Rev. Harcourt Lees, at the age of 35, succeeded him and moved into the family home of 'Blackrock House'. The following year he married Sophia Lyster, with whom he had four sons and four daughters. Only occasionally visiting his glebe house, 'Essexford', in County Down, it was his 'most excellent, religious, and estimable curate' who looked after the parish for him. When the Whig politician Lord King gave a speech in the House of Lords claiming that 6,000 out of 10,500 clergy were non-resident, Sir Harcourt had the gall to write a letter contradicting these facts. (It was published in *Saunders's News-Letter* of 10 and 17 February 1831.)

Because the Irish Post Office was monopolised by various members of his family, Sir Harcourt was able to carry on a huge correspondence, his elastic conscience allowing him to use his brother Edward's frank and therefore escape any mail charges. Harcourt took over the Writing Office — with its secretaries and stationery — as his copying office, from where he would dictate articles (his writing was indecipherable) for *The Antidote*, an anti-Catholic newspaper, as well as numerous letters to the press. He was well known as an 'uncompromising supporter of the Protestant Constitution in Church and State', who spent most of his time and energy writing letters to the newspapers and churning out what looked like hate-mail in his anti-Catholic pamphlets. He was such a larger-than-life character that he was almost a figure of fun, so that 'the Catholics harboured no malice against him; they (thought) him harmless'. *The Times* of London, too, had obvious reservations about him: 'We insert a crazy kind of letter from Sir Harcourt Lees addressed to the Popish Prelates and priesthood of Ireland. Yet is there, to a certain degree, "method in the man's madness"?'

Catholic Emancipation was becoming more and more likely, and Sir Harcourt was determined to stop it in its tracks (just as he'd tried with the railway). He genuinely believed that it would lead to the ruin of both Ireland and England, so he used every method he could to prevent it, often of questionable morality, believing that the end justified the means. He was prepared to resort to arms if necessary and would have regarded such a conflict as a 'just' war. *Saunders's News-Letter* of 8 October 1827 published one of his letters, in which he said,

> 'As to Ireland, Sir, it may gratify you to learn, that I have at this moment about 270 thousand men ready to rise in support of the King's Government and the Reformed Church, on reading one line from my pen. And when I think it necessary to write THAT LINE, I would strongly recommend every Radical scribe and Whig Renegade to take care how he crosses the path of, Sir, Yours, H.L.' (He had already been indicted for incitement to violence in 1824, but the prosecution had failed.)

Harcourt thought that his battle was a single-handed one: that everything depended on him, the self-appointed 'protector of the Protestants of Great Britain and Ireland': 'Without

(the) steady adoption (of his wise measures) no human power can save Ireland, and indeed Great Britain from eventual destruction — I will soon dispose of Popery and priestcraft, with Bolivar O'Connell and every future agitator in this land of holy Roman Saints and revolutionary associated mountibanks.'

One of his 'wise measures' was the foundation, in 1825, of the Benevolent Orange Society in Dublin, a splinter group of the main Orange Order (Senior 1966); it only lasted until 1828. He believed in a 'popish plot', an international Catholic conspiracy to annihilate Protestants, and therefore petitioned the House of Lords in 1829 not to allow the 'Romish Ascendancy Bill' (the Catholic Emancipation Bill) to go forward, claiming that he had proof of 'a treasonable conspiracy existing in these British islands, in conjunction with the American revolutionists, the objects contemplated being the possession of the Canadas by General Jackson, the exciting simultaneous insurrection in the north of England and Ireland, the extirpation of the Protestants and the re-establishment of Popery in the latter country.'

But, in spite of his fears as regards Catholicism, Harcourt could still say: 'Some of my most esteemed friends are of the latter religion; although I think them in error, and wish to correct them. Religious topics I avoid, and in conversation or society, never introduce them.' And again, in his June 1820 pamphlet entitled *Nineteen pages of advice to the Protestant freemen and freeholders of Dublin*, he states: 'Many years of deep and awful research into the

The Dublin to Kingstown railway was opened in 1834. This charming engraving, one of a series, shows the stretch from the Martello tower at Seapoint around the coast to Kingstown. From right to left: the recently completed Monkstown Parish Church, the first houses of Clifton Terrace, the small cottages of Tully's Row, possibly the Lime Kiln with its smoking chimney (close to the site of the present railway station), the Salthill Hotel and, in the distance, the houses of Kingstown around the Old Harbour.

mysteries of this extraordinary code of false religion and blasphemy, entitle me to give this solemn advice to my deluded and deceived brethren. Individually I bear them no enmity, but to their creed I swear eternal hostility; some of my dearest friends are Roman Catholics — I lament their errors, and I wish to save them from perdition: but no private friendship shall ever induce me to risk the peace and happiness of my Country.'

Interestingly, his obituary, published in the *Gentleman's Magazine* of March 1852, accepted that 'his manliness and truth brought him into conflict with several opponents; not one of whom, however, even in the fiercest heavings of the controversial surge, ever questioned his sincerity, or the genuine goodness of heart which, like a golden sand, lay at the bottom of the tide'. I suspect that the inscription on his wall monument in Monkstown — in stark contrast to that of his father — was mostly true:

SACRED TO THE MEMORY OF
THE REVD SIR HARCOURT LEES BART
BORN IN DUBLIN 29TH NOVR 1776,
DIED AT BLACK ROCK HOUSE, 7TH MARCH 1852,
AGED 75 YEARS.

HONORABLE, GUILELESS AND TRUE
IN ALL THE PUBLIC AND SOCIAL RELATIONS OF LIFE,
HE WAS AN AFFECTIONATE HUSBAND
A KIND INDULGENT FATHER AND A SINCERE FRIEND,
HIS HAND WAS EVER OPEN TO ASSIST THE UNFORTUNATE
AND TO RELIEVE THE DISTRESSED
AND DURING A LONG AND ACTIVE LIFE
HE WAS DISTINGUISHED AS THE UNCOMPROMISING SUPPORTER
OF THE PROTESTANT CONSTITUTION IN CHURCH AND STATE.

AS A TRIBUTE OF LOVE AND ATTACHMENT
TO THE PARTNER AND COMPANION OF 39 YEARS;
THIS MONUMENT
IS ERECTED BY HIS SORROWING WIDOW.
'The memory of the Just is Blessed.'

Intriguingly, Harcourt Lees's influence reached even to America. In 1827 the 'Harcourt Episcopal Parish' in Kenyon College, Ohio, was founded and named after him. The bishop of Ohio, also president of the college, subsequently built a house for himself at Kenyon, calling it 'Harcourt Place'. The bishop's home later became the Harcourt Place School for Boys, until the 1880s, when it became the Harcourt Place Seminary for Young Ladies and Girls. It closed in 1936 during the Great Depression.

Harcourt's intransigence even followed him beyond the grave. An envelope exists, addressed to a 'Miss H. Lees' (probably Helen Lees, his daughter), franked with the date '1861' and with a distinctive wax seal on the back, bearing the Lees crest and the injunction underneath, 'No Popery'.[16] This was undoubtedly Sir Harcourt's seal — the satisfying Parthian shot delivered after each vituperative missive.

Sir Harcourt was not afraid of anybody or anything, and, after an arson attack on his house, knew the risks he was taking. In his *Nineteen pages* pamphlet of June 1820, he wrote, 'It is incredible, the number of anonymous letters I have received threatening me with assassination, unless I ceased writing against popery'. For three years, in his pamphlets and letters, he publicly insulted Lord Wellesley, the lord lieutenant, who was married to a Catholic and supported Catholic Emancipation. At a Dublin ball they finally met face to face: 'The most noble and puissant Marquis shot his fine and indignant eyes into the soul' of Sir Harcourt. He, in return, treated Wellesley with 'jocular disdain ... blending the grin of an ostler with the acrimony of a divine'. The encounter was the talk of Dublin (Brynn 1978).

Although he was conservative, he was not conventional, least of all in his dress. The diarist, 'The Hermit in Ireland', of the *Dublin and London Magazine* of March–December 1825, in describing his attire reported that Sir Harcourt 'was dressed as usual — spatterdashed to the knees — buckskinned to the hips — the small hat covered with oiled silk, and the black coat buttoned even to the chin.' ('Spatterdashed' referred to leggings of cloth or leather, worn to keep the trousers from getting splashed, especially while riding.)

Sir Harcourt worked hard ('I never was lethargic at any moment of my existence'), but he played hard too. He liked to hunt, which was simply 'not done' by the clergy of his day. For example, it was said of the archdiocese of Dublin in 1831 that 'amongst its hundreds of clergymen we are assured no man could fix his finger on a huntsman, a card-player, or a ball-frequenter'.[17] But Sir Harcourt's incumbency was in the diocese of Clogher, so he was not included in this sedate company. Not alone did he commit the impropriety of hunting ('this most cheerful and innocent amusement'), but this incongruous man of the cloth — who was continually lambasting Catholics in the newspapers — boasted, in his pamphlet *L'Abeja, or a bee among the Evangelicals* of 1 January 1820, that he hunted and even dined with 'a priest'; he went on to describe his companion as 'well informed and really enlightened ... a man for whom I had a great regard'.

But it would be naïve to assume that he was harmless, as one 'Ribbon Agent' apparently did, to his cost. One night Sir Harcourt found him in his house, trying to persuade the servants to assassinate him. Sir Harcourt chased the intruder out of the house and later boasted in a letter to Daniel O'Connell (dated 1 May 1820) that he 'was lucky enough to leave a pretty severe fracture on (his head) as he was making his escape, breaking (his) gun across it'. Several nights later, the family dog woke everyone with its barking. This time the house had been set on fire, but everyone escaped unharmed. As a result, Sir Harcourt was very security-conscious. A contemporary writer, in the *Dublin and London Magazine* of March–December 1825, after praising the 'beautiful situation (of Blackrock House) at the upper end of the town', added, 'There is something heavy, however, in the external appearance of the place; the lofty gates lined with sheet iron, trebly barred and closed at all hours, indicate something like fear or uneasiness in the mind of the man who deems them necessary'. But, from what I have read of him, I think his fears — which, after all, had been proved valid — were for his young wife and eight children rather than for himself.

For a finale, we will let Sir Harcourt speak for himself in his own inimitable style, remembering that he never used one word when he could use ten. In his January 1820 pamphlet *A cursory view of the present state of Ireland*, he wrote on the topic of 'being slandered in the newspapers':

> 'I am now on the eve of leaving Town, and have desired my Bookseller to forward all your future Newspaper Effusions — Criticize and abuse me if you choose it, in my absence; but depend upon it, I will come down on you in an evil hour, some time or other, if by your noisy railings at Vestries or scurrility against myself, you presume to take up those columns that will soon be much better occupied in repudiating the brilliant Orations of Gentlemen who will ever inform, though they may not possibly convince. Think of the Hebrews — and for the present, farewell. Vive, vale, cave me titubes, Mandata que frangas.'

[This is a quotation from Horace's *Epistulae* 1, 13, 19; it should actually read, *Vade, vale, cave ne titubes mandataque frangas*, which means 'Go, farewell, be on your guard, lest you stumble and break my Commandments'.]

Archdeacon Charles Lindsay (1790–1855)

> *Do not, as some ungracious pastors do,*
> *Show me the steep and thorny way to heaven,*
> *Whiles, like a puff'd and reckless libertine,*
> *Himself the primrose path of dalliance treads*
> *And recks not his own rede.*
> Shakespeare's *Hamlet*

The parish of Monkstown was the 'jewel in the crown', described in the *Irish Ecclesiastical Gazette* of 20 March 1880 as 'formerly ... one of the pet pieces of preferment which the archbishops of Dublin had in their gift'. Monkstown was one of the wealthiest parishes in Dublin (*see Chapter 17*). The figures at Disestablishment proved this: out of 91 Dublin bishops and incumbents, the amount of commutation (or compensation) agreed upon for Monkstown (£10,195-5s-1d, equivalent to over €960,000 in today's money) was the next greatest after that of the archbishop of Dublin, Archbishop Trench (£93,045-11s-8d, almost €9 million today). The two curates of Monkstown were paid £3,868 and £3,041 a year, while the rector of Booterstown got £2,183 (Commissioners of Church Temporalities in Ireland 1875).

Nepotism was rife in the late 1700s and early 1800s. If you knew, or, more significantly, if you were related to, someone in power, you could get appointed to a parish like Monkstown. On 12 June 1815 a young Oxford graduate of 25 called Charles Lindsay was nominated to Stillorgan parish by his father, who happened to be 'Charles, by Divine Providence, Lord Bishop of Kildare, Dean of the Cathedral Church of the Holy and Undivided Trinity [Christ Church]'. Exactly a week later he resigned (Ingram 1997). Why? Singleton Harpur, the resident perpetual curate at Monkstown, had died in office unexpectedly and was buried on 17 June 1815. Three days after the burial, Lindsay was nominated to Monkstown, again by 'Charles, by Divine Providence', and was licensed as perpetual curate on 23 June 1815.[18] This was rapid processing by any standards, but one must

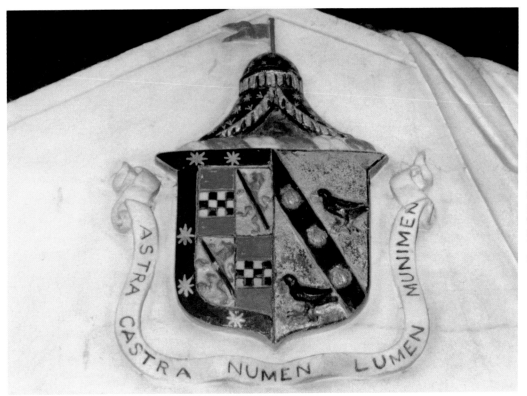

One of the longest-serving incumbents of Monkstown (1815–55), Charles Lindsay's wall monument, sculpted by Joseph Kirk, proudly displays the family coat of arms, with the rhyming motto meaning 'The stars my camp, God my light and protection'.

remember that the dean of Christ Church was also the patron of Monkstown up until 1846 and had the right to appoint the perpetual curates (*see Chapter 3*). Having secured such a plum job, Lindsay stayed in Monkstown until his death, 40 years later. In the meantime, in 1829, he was appointed to St Mary's, the second richest parish out of the 102 in Dublin. As incumbent of these two parishes alone, some six miles apart, Lindsay was one of the wealthiest clergymen of his day. In addition, later in his career he was appointed prebendary of St Michael's and St John's (both Christ Church Cathedral) and as one of the lord lieutenant's chaplains in 1835.

The nepotism employed in Lindsay's appointments was commonplace prior to the 1830s, when church reform in this area really began. His father's own appointments — first as personal secretary to Lord Hardwicke, lord lieutenant of Ireland, then as bishop of Killaloe and finally as bishop of Kildare — had been engineered by his brother-in-law, who happened to be Lord Hardwicke (Akenson 1971). Perhaps the title 'Charles, by Divine Providence' rings a little hollow.

Charles Lindsay (grandson of the earl of Balcarres on his father's side and Thomas Fydell of Boston on his mother's) was born in Cambridge and educated at Harrow. While still a student at St John's College, Cambridge, Lindsay contracted a sexually transmitted disease, probably syphilis. His father explained the embarrassing situation in a frank but obviously cross letter, dated 18 March 1812:

'The Medical Gentleman whom my son consulted on his late visit to London
assured him that the cutaneous disorder with which he is afflicted does not

313

communicate except by contact of bodies in bed, at least in the state he saw it. I should not on any consideration have desired him to return had there been any chance of mischief to the other students, and I hope with proper confinement and good purification he will be quite free from this disgraceful malady in a few days.'

The infection did no damage to the career prospects of the 22-year-old Lindsay Junior, who was appointed prebendary of Kildare in 1815 and then second canon by his father, who had been elected bishop there in 1804.

Charles Lindsay Senior and Junior were proud of their noble ancestry. The nomination papers of Monkstown curates were signed by 'Charles, by Divine Providence, Lord Bishop of Kildare'. All are stamped with one of four different seals — the coat of arms and crest to which he was entitled as a bishop and his own crest. But the one used most often, and therefore, presumably, his favourite, was his personal coat of arms, which is displayed in all its splendour on his son's wall monument in Monkstown Church. Underneath runs the rhyming motto, *Astra, castra, numen, lumen, munimen*, meaning 'The stars my camp, God my light and protection'.

Joseph Kirk, son of Thomas, sculpted this wall monument to Archdeacon Lindsay in 1855. (He also made the larger-than-life recumbent statue of his father, Bishop Lindsay, in 1846, seen today in the north aisle of Christ Church Cathedral; *see Chapter 3*.) The inscription below the coat of arms reads:

IN A VAULT
ON THE S.E. SIDE OF THIS CHURCH
WHICH OWES ITS ERECTION
TO HIS PIOUS EXERTIONS
RESTS THE BODY OF
THE VENBLE **CHARLES LINDSAY**
ARCHDEACON OF KILDARE
FOR 40 YEARS PERPETUAL CURATE
OF THE UNION OF MONKSTOWN
AND FOR 26 YEARS RECTOR
OF ST MARY'S DUBLIN
HE WAS THE ELDEST SON
OF THE LATE HONBLE CHARLES LINDSAY
BISHOP OF KILDARE
AND ELIZABETH HIS WIFE
ONLY DAUGHTER
OF THE LATE THOS FYDELL ESQR M.P.
AND DEPARTED THIS LIFE ON
THE 23RD OF APRIL 1855 AGED 64
'Blessed are the pure in heart for they shall see God'.
MATT. C.V.V.VIII.

Even if we find Lindsay's appointment to Monkstown a little suspect, we have to give him credit, as those who erected his memorial did, for 'his pious exertions'. It is interesting to realise that this was the second Semple church he had seen through. Lindsay was appointed to St Mary's in 1829; in 1830 St Mary's Chapel of Ease ('the Black Church') was built. Meanwhile, Monkstown Church was under construction and eventually opened in 1831. Lindsay was the clergyman on the spot and had to see the whole gigantic project through in spite of lack of funds and support, and the 'political' machinations with the archbishop of Dublin, William Magee, who seemed to be taking an inordinate interest in his parish (*see Chapter 5*).

The Lindsays, father and son, were not popular. Judge Robert Day, who was chairman of the first Building Committee for Semple's Monkstown, did not approve of either of them. He did not bandy his words when describing the two in his diary during November 1827 as 'that wrong-headed fellow Archdn Lindsay our Rector' and 'that contemptible conceited worldling the Bp of Kildare'.[19] Judge Day was having an ongoing battle with both men about the building of the chapel of ease at Killiney (*see Appendix 1*). The Lindsays were unpopular in other circles, too. For example, the *Dublin Evening Post* of 7 February 1832 published a letter from an irate writer, who described himself as 'A Kingstonian', in which he called Lindsay Junior 'a pluralist, a non-resident, and sinecurist', and was cynical about the Lindsays' motivation being for 'the public good, or a love of religion'.

Charles Lindsay had married Anne Rowley, of 'Priory Hill', Huntingdonshire, on 28 September 1819 (Hughes 1889) and baptised his only child, Caroline Frances, on 17 January 1822 when she was five weeks old. During his 40 years' incumbency they lived in the glebe house at Kill, which Lindsay had found 'in very bad order' and had renovated, at his own personal expense, to the tune of '£2,400 British' (*see Chapter 11*). Curiously, Lindsay's wife, Anne, is missing from his monument. A letter among the Vestry archives clears up any mystery: two years after his death she was living in Brighton, where she probably died. She wrote to someone in Monkstown (probably one of the churchwardens) about the three Lindsay pews, which her husband had bequeathed to 'the Protestant poor of Monkstown for ever'.[20] One was a £50 pew in the second row of the south gallery and the other two were in the north transept downstairs, where the family servants had sat.

A further indication of Lindsay's concern for the poor was demonstated in a letter of his to the Commissioners of Kingstown Harbour, dated 1826, asking them to employ his tenant, John Murphy, 'not only because he happens to be my tenant for a small house and acre of Glebe land, but because he is a sober, honest, industrious man with a wife and 5 children, and pays rent and taxes'.[21]

Admiral Robert Dudley Oliver (1766–1850)

> *He that will learn to pray, let him go to sea.*
> Outlandish proverbs, selected by Mr George Herbert, 1651

Sailors will be familiar with the Beaufort Wind Scale, but are unlikely to know that had it not been for Admiral Robert Dudley Oliver of Monkstown it would never have been invented. In July 1791 a seventeen-year-old midshipman was climbing from a small boat in Portsmouth harbour onto his ship. His later account reads, 'In foolish eagerness I stepped upon the gunwhale, the boat of course upset, and I fell into the water, and not knowing how to swim, all my efforts to lay hold either of the boat or of the floating sculls were useless'. After a few minutes, his splashing was noticed and the alarm raised. 'The first lieutenant instantly and gallantly jumped overboard, the carpenter followed his example,' and together managed to haul the young man to safety (Friendly 1977). The young midshipman was Francis Beaufort (who later became chief hydrographer of the Royal Navy[22] and invented the wind scale that bears his name) and the first lieutenant was Robert Dudley Oliver.

Both men were Irish, which was not unusual at the time since there were a great number of Irish officers and men in the British army and navy. Both were also second sons of clergy — Beaufort of the Rev. Daniel Beaufort, rector of Collan and Navan, and Oliver of the Venerable John Oliver, the archdeacon of Ardagh. In a letter to a friend, 34 years later, Beaufort described his drowning incident in detail (Friendly 1977); it is one of the first descriptions of 'a near-death experience' and was discussed widely at the time.[23] (Nowadays, these experiences are more common with improved resuscitation techniques.)

From the age of sixteen Francis Beaufort had kept a meteorological journal. This was the basis of his later wind scale, whose first recorded use was on the *Beagle*, with Charles Darwin on board, one day after leaving Plymouth on a British scientific expedition. The date was 21 December 1831, which, in the context of Monkstown, was four days before Semple's church was opened.

Robert Dudley Oliver had been sent to sea at the age of thirteen by his father, the archdeacon of Ardagh. He found himself, with other young midshipmen (including Prince William, later William IV, then aged fourteen), aboard the *Prince George en route* for Gibraltar, which was under siege. On the way there, they intercepted a Spanish squadron of nine ships and a hair-raising battle was fought at night during a storm and dangerously close to land; six Spanish ships were captured and one sunk. The *Prince George* sailed on and successfully relieved Gibraltar.

During 1803 and 1804 Oliver (by now a captain) was busily occupied off the coast of France and in the Mediterranean. He captured numerous enemy French ships, blockaded the French coast and bombarded Le Havre (O'Byrne 1849). By the summer of 1805 he returned to Portsmouth to put his ship, the *Melpomeme*, into dock for vital repairs. In September Admiral Nelson, also at Portsmouth, received news of the arrival of the French at Cadiz and decided to leave immediately to confront them. Captain Oliver hurried around to Nelson's lodgings at the George Hotel to say that he would be held up until his ship was repaired. Nelson exclaimed optimistically, 'I hope you will come in time to tow some of the rascals'. Oliver's ship joined the British fleet off Trafalgar the day after the battle — and Nelson's death — and did in fact help to tow some of the captured ships home.

Perhaps another reason for Oliver's reluctance to leave Portsmouth was that he was unwilling to leave Mary, his new bride, whom he had married in June 1805. She was the only daughter of Sir Charles Saxton, the commissioner of the Royal Dockyard at Portsmouth. After his marriage, Oliver returned to service in the navy for a further nine years and then retired to live at 'Baron Hill' in Dalkey. Three sons were born to the couple: Robert, John and Richard (who, like his father, became an admiral).[24]

Oliver was promoted to rear-admiral in 1819, vice-admiral in 1830 and admiral in 1841.

He died at the age of 84. The chaplain to the Mariners' Church, Forbes Street,[25] Mr Andrew Campbell, took his funeral service and he was interred in the vaults of Monkstown Church. A brass plaque was erected on the north wall of the chancel to commemorate him. It reads:

IN MEMORY OF
ROBERT DUDLEY OLIVER,
ADMIRAL OF THE RED SQUADRON IN HER MAJESTY'S FLEET.
BORN 31ST OCTOBER 1766. DIED 1ST SEPTEMBER 1850.
INTERRED BENEATH THIS CHURCH. ALSO OF
MARY,
HIS WIFE, DAUGHTER OF CAPTAIN SIR CHARLES SAXTON, BART:
R.N.,
WHO DIED 16TH JUNE 1848, AGED 68,
AND WAS BURIED AT THE CHURCH OF ST. PETER, DUBLIN.

The Pim sisters: Isabella, Charlotte and Jane

> *I thank God for the Leprosy Mission and its workers. It was the inspiration*
> *and dedication of the Mission to Lepers, as it then was,*
> *which gave me the example and courage to begin my work.*
> Mother Teresa of Calcutta, 1974[26]

A headstone in Deansgrange Cemetery records the deaths of the three Pim sisters, founders of the Mission to Lepers in 1878:

Isabella Pim, Alma Monkstown, December 7 1904
Also her sister Charlotte Elizabeth, November 17 1912, 'A Succourer of Many'
Also her sister Jane, December 3 1924

The three Pim sisters of Alma Road rarely strayed outside Monkstown all their lives. Daughters of the wealthy James Pim of Monkstown Castle House, these Victorian ladies founded an organisation which is now worldwide and has helped millions. The Pims' involvement began when Charlotte Pim made friends at school with Alice Grahame, a boarder from Abbeyleix. As it happened, Alice was also close friends with a young man called Wellesley Bailey.

However, Wellesley sought adventure before settling down and, like thousands of other young men in the 1860s, was lured to the Australian gold fields. About to embark on the long sea voyage, the twenty-year-old Wellesley was delayed by fog at Gravesend and, remembering a promise made to Alice that he would attend church whenever possible, he went to a service. There he heard a verse from Isaiah:

'And I will bring the blind by a way that they knew not ... I will make darkness light before them, and crooked things straight.'

Years later, Wellesley admitted that he was moved by these words, but found the pull of

317

Alma House, the Monkstown home of the Pim sisters, and headquarters of the Mission to Lepers from 1874 to 1921.

the Australian gold fields stronger. Unlucky there, he moved on to New Zealand, where he tried his hand at breaking wild horses. Then he headed for New Caledonia, a group of islands in the Pacific. Eventually he returned home, but not to stay. For his next venture, he sailed to India, where he found less exciting work teaching children at the American Presbyterian Mission at Ambala in northern India. By now, he and Alice were engaged and he wrote long letters home to her. After the day's teaching, Wellesley visited the little leper colony nearby, where mutilated and crippled outcasts lived in poverty. In his letters he told Alice how helpless and frustrated he felt at their plight (Fancutt 1974).

Alice told Charlotte and her sisters, Jane and Isabella, of Wellesley's concerns. In 1871 Alice left her home in Blackrock and sailed for Bombay, where she and Wellesley (25) were married in the cathedral. However, after a couple of years the Indian climate had taken its toll on her and Wellesley was advised to bring her home to Ireland for a holiday.

In September 1874, the Pim sisters invited Alice and Wellesley (now 28) to their home, 'Alma House' at 3 Alma Road, Monkstown, for tea. Wellesley held his audience captive as he told of his work among the lepers. Charlotte (36) suggested that he retell his story at the Friends' Meeting House nearby, on the following Sunday, 6 September 1874, which he did. (Although the Pims were Church of Ireland, they had many Quaker relations and friends.) Charlotte told Wellesley that she would undertake to raise £30 a year (almost €2,750 in today's money) to support his work and asked him to write something about it. To her consternation, 2,000 sixteen-page booklets arrived; she had envisaged 100. However, the booklet, entitled *The penny beggar*, had to be reprinted again and again. Money flooded in from all directions: £527-12-10 (about €50,000) was raised in the first year alone.

However, there was still no effective treatment for leprosy: little could be done for its victims, apart from improving their living conditions and so making their lives more comfortable. The breakthrough came in 1874, when a Norwegian scientist, Armauer Hansen, discovered the bacillus responsible (which was named after him). Back in India, Wellesley wrote in his account book in May 1875, 'To coolies marking site, 5 annas = 6d'. It was the beginnings of the first hospital for lepers built with money from Dublin. Then in 1878

Wellesley returned to Ireland to discuss further action and the first committee meeting of the Mission to Lepers was held, with Charlotte Pim as honorary secretary. Its aim was 'for the purpose of considering the best way of bringing spiritual and temporal relief to as many poor outcast lepers in India as possible'. The work of the Mission spread quickly, largely owing to the indefatigable efforts of Charlotte Pim. As Wellesley wrote:

> 'There is one thing … of which there can be no doubt, and that is that the largest share in the success of those efforts was Miss Pim's. Her entire devotion and untiring energy carried all before them. No one could be in her presence for long without hearing something of the lepers' (Fancutt 1974).

Isabella was the first of the Pim sisters to die, in 1904, aged 76. When Charlotte died, aged 76, in 1912, she had been the honorary secretary of the Mission to Lepers for 38 years. Jane, the youngest sister, took over the position and served until her death, at the age of 84, in 1924 — the Jubilee year of the Mission. (Alice Bailey, wife of Wellesley Bailey, also died the same year.)

Wellesley Bailey was the superintendent of the Mission to Lepers and 'Alma House' (the Monkstown home of the Pim sisters) its headquarters until his retirement in 1917, when William Anderson took over. The committee met for the 175th, and last, time at 'Alma House' in 1921, when the headquarters of the Mission to Lepers was moved to London. Wellesley continued as honorary superintendent until his death in 1937, aged 91. He had seen the work of the Mission grow from basic care for the first 40 patients at Ambala, India, in 1874 to tens of thousands being treated effectively in 33 countries. In 1954 over 66,000 patients were treated, of whom 7,550 became disease-arrested.[27] By 1982 the Leprosy Mission (the name was changed in 1966) spent £3 million treating 300,000 patients (*The Irish Times*, December 1982).

Wellesley Bailey had written in 1924:

> 'The Mission to Lepers, I am accustomed to think, is "a building not made with hands". God has been the Builder and the Founder thereof; and because of that fact, the Mission has gone on prospering and will prosper. To His Name alone, we will give all praise and glory.'

In August 1959, in an article in the *Church of Ireland Gazette*, 'Cromlyn' (a pen name for the Rev. Canon John Barry) stressed the interdenominational aspect of the Mission to Lepers. He pointed out that the Presbyterian Baileys had first told of their work in a Church of Ireland home and then in a Friends' Meeting House; that, in the first years of the Mission, money had been sent to Anglicans in Kashmir, German Lutherans in East India, American Presyterians in the Punjab, Congregationalists in the Kumaon Hills and Travancorr, and the Swiss Reformed Church in Malabar. He 'deplored' the lack of any 'visible evidence' in Monkstown Church that the worldwide Mission to Lepers had originated in the parish and suggested 'a small plaque … placed somewhere near to the fourth pew from the front', where the Pims had sat regularly.

Cromlyn's article was discussed at the next meeting of the Select Vestry, on 9 September 1959. Over the following months the Vestry agreed on a suitable memorial. On Sunday 20 March 1960 an interdenominational service commemorated the founding of the Mission to Lepers in Monkstown 86 years earlier and a brass plaque was dedicated.[28] Located on the left wall as one enters the church through the west door, it reads:

THIS PLAQUE IS DEDICATED TO
THE GLORY OF GOD
AND TO THE MEMORY OF
ISABELLA, CHARLOTTE AND JANE PIM
WHO WORSHIPPED IN THIS CHURCH,
AND IN WHOSE HOME, ALMA HOUSE, MONKSTOWN,
THE MISSION TO LEPERS
WAS FOUNDED IN SEPTEMBER 1874.

In 1974, the centenary year, Dr George Simms, world president of the Leprosy Mission since 1967, departed on a six-week tour of India, Thailand, Nepal, Hong Kong and Ethiopia, visiting Leprosy Mission establishments.[29] On his return, centenary celebrations were held in London, at which the Rev. Billy Wynne represented Monkstown. Monkstown also held its own centenary service on Sunday 28 April, with the archbishops of Dublin and Armagh both attending, as well as clergy and laity of other countries and denominations.[30] An annual service has been held ever since.

Lamprene, one of the main drugs for leprosy, was developed in Trinity College, Dublin, under the auspices of the Medical Research Council of Ireland. The team responsible won the UNESCO Science prize in 1980 (*The Irish Times*, December 1982).

Miss Edith Dowse remembers that one of the Pim sisters — probably Jane — had rather a novel method of befriending the rector's little daughter: she would lift her long gown, revealing a pocket full of sweets sewn into her petticoat.

Dr William Plant (1790–1875)

He was ... considered by the great men of his day
(Crampton, Graves and others) ... as a physician and surgeon of the first order.
The Medical Press and Circular, 10 November 1875

In 1831 Ireland was visited by an unwelcome guest — cholera. Whole families were wiped out by the disease; doctors and clergy attending the sick died in their hundreds. In Monkstown Dr William Plant had to tackle the deadly disease alone. As the only physician in the area, he 'had the whole weight of the labour attendant on such a fearful epidemic, yet he never flinched'.

This was not William Plant's first encounter with epidemic fever. Soon after qualifying at the Apothecary's Hall in Dublin, he was appointed apothecary to Dr Steeven's Hospital. Here he found himself in the middle of one of Dublin's frequent epidemics, which mainly attacked the poor who lived in terrible conditions in squalid overcrowded tenements. The 1817–19 fever epidemic was his 'baptism by fire'; in the fever wards of Dr Steeven's, he learned how to treat the disease. Although Dr John Crampton, the physician in charge, would make daily visits, it was Plant who was responsible for 'the details of the supervision' of about 100 patients (Kirkpatrick 1924). Dr Crampton referred approvingly to the 'exertions' of Plant, 'who, at an imminent hazard, gave up almost the whole of his time to those fever wards, and to enforce those measures of arrangement so judiciously planned'. Inevitably, Plant contracted cholera himself, but recovered.[31]

The mortality rate in Dr Steeven's Hospital was lower than in any other Dublin hospital, in spite of a higher turnover of patients (Crampton 1819). In August 1819 the fever wards of Dr Steeven's were closed as the epidemic had run its course. Plant continued as the hospital apothecary, gaining experience under doctors and surgeons whose names are still well known, including Abraham Colles, Sir Philip Crampton and Sir Henry Marsh.

The son of a 'gentleman farmer' from County Meath, eighteen-year-old William Plant had arrived in Dublin in 1808, determined to become a doctor. After a stiff examination in Latin, Greek, English and Maths, he was allowed into the Apothecary's Hall, one of Dublin's many medical schools. Medical training then was haphazard, attendance at lectures non-compulsory, bedside teaching non-existent. Plant learned through experience. He had to serve an apprenticeship of five years with a Mr Holmes for his licence to the Apothecary's Hall.

Apothecaries then were like GPs to the poor. They alone were allowed to dispense medicine; there was a sizeable fine of twenty guineas if this rule was flouted. In 1842, of the 2,500 doctors in Ireland, 1,174 (47%) had passed through the Apothecary's Hall. Although it was admitted that the examination to the Apothecary's Hall was 'as searching and as extended as that of many an MD', 'proper' doctors looked down on apothecaries. The *Dublin Medical Press* of 29 December 1852 maintained that doctors 'could never expect their medical men to compound medicine; they have never served their time to any apothecary, and it would be a degradation to them'.

The year 1822 was a busy one for William Plant. He resigned from Dr Steeven's and obtained, from Trinity College, Dublin, his licence to practice medicine. He was appointed physician and surgeon to Rathdown Dispensary (Medical Directory, 1876). Somehow, that year, he found time to get married. His bride of eighteen years was Jane Morgell;[32] Plant was 32. Two years later their first child was born, John Floyd Alexander, followed by two girls, Charlotte (b. 1828) and Sophia Lees (b. 1834),[33] and another boy, William Charles (b. 1836).[34]

But Plant had little time for family life, so busy was he administering to the sick of the parish. Rathdown Dispensary dealt with a huge catchment area — from Merrion to Three Rock Mountain, and from Foxrock to Killiney, including Kingstown. As the only doctor, Plant would have treated the rich and titled who were moving into the area, but the bulk of his work was 'for the relief of the sick poor' (*see Chapter 17*). The Rev. Beaver Blacker gives us a description of the conditions under which most of Plant's patients lived: 'The number of poor in this parish [Booterstown] amounts to upwards of 700; and owing to the contiguity, filth, and wretchedness of their numerous and crowded cabins, particularly in the lanes at Booterstown, Williamstown, Merrion-Avenue, etc., fever and other contagious diseases would readily spread. The poor here are all of the labouring class; during summer and part of autumn many derive some support from attending bathers, but in winter few have any employment' (Blacker 1874).

The Rathdown Dispensary had been running for ten years when Dr Plant took over in 1822. Thomas Arthure, MD, had been his predecessor.[35] Dr Plant ran two branches of the dispensary: the Blackrock branch in Newtown Avenue and the Monkstown branch from the gatelodge of his home called 'Plantation', a fine Georgian house (now 'Gortmore') on Monkstown Road. The dispensary had its own governing body and raised money by public subscription. Charity sermons, beloved by fund-raisers in those days, helped to bring money into its coffers: over £40 in September 1819. During the building of the west pier, the Kingstown Harbour Commissioners contributed ten guineas annually during the years 1826–8 and 1831 to the Rathdown Dispensary (as well as to the Kingstown Dispensary and Mercer's Hospital) towards the treatment of sick or injured men working on the harbour.[36] An enormous number of patients (28,424) were seen and treated during its 23 years in existence. Between 1820 and 1821, 1,282 patients were seen at the dispensary, costing the princely sum of £228-14-10½, approximately 3s-7d per patient. Over the same period the dispensary's income was £266-2-5, so the accounts remained 'in the black'.

A cholera pandemic, originating in India, reached Europe in 1831. The newspapers charted its progress as it came nearer and nearer Ireland. In October 1831 an act of parliament was passed: in the event of the disease entering Ireland, Boards of Health and Officers of Health were to be appointed, medical depots and hospitals or hospital tents to be established, carriages to be provided for the exclusive use of affected patients, and parishes to supply 'cleansing houses' — all by 25 March 1832 (or earlier if cholera hit Ireland before then). Vestries began to meet all over Dublin to prepare for the worst.

On 20 October 1831 Lieutenant William Hutchinson, the Harbour Master, presented a letter to the Harbour Commissioners. It was signed by Charles Lindsay, perpetual curate of Monkstown, and 44 'Clergymen and gentlemen, Inhabitants of the Union of Monkstown', and asked the Harbour Board to make representations on their behalf to the lord lieutenant for the building of a local hospital, 'where the diseased poor of this extensive parish (could) receive proper and daily medical and surgical advice and attention with the necessary comforts of cleanliness and nourishment which their miserable cabins and wretched poverty preclude'. The letter-writers also reminded the Board of the 'numerous accidents which (were) of frequent occurrence to the labouring poor ... and more particularly the men employ'd in the great work under (its) management' (i.e. the building of the harbour). Lives had been lost, they said, because of the distance to the nearest hospital in Dublin.

The secretary of the Harbour Board immediately penned an enthusiastic letter, endorsing the idea of a Monkstown hospital, to Sir William Gosset (under-secretary to the lord lieutenant), asking him to approach the lord lieutenant on their behalf. They had 'no doubt but His Excellency (would) be pleased to sanction' both the building of the hospital and their contribution of £100 towards it. Ten days later a letter from Sir William arrived, saying that the 'law advisor of the Crown' had advised that 'the funds applicable to the Harbour could not be appropriated to building an Hospital' and that Archdeacon Lindsay and his fellow-signees should instead apply to the new Commissioners of Public Works.[37]

Lieutenant Hutchinson had to communicate the bad news. As soon as they heard that the Harbour Board could not support them, Archdeacon Lindsay and the churchwardens called a parish meeting. The notice in *Saunders's News-Letter* on 17 November 1831 announced: 'The Church-Wardens of the Parish of Monkstown request a Meeting of the Parishioners, on Friday the 18 of November, Instant, at Ten o'Clock in the Forenoon, at Monkstown School-house, for the purpose of taking into consideration what precautionary measures it may be best to adopt in this parish, for providing against the contigency of the Pestilential Disorder (which has already shewn itself in the North of England), ultimately finding its way into this country. Fenton Hort and John Murphy, Church-Wardens. 14th November 1831.' No Vestry minutes survive to tell us whether this meeting ever took place or what happened at it, but it seems that plans for a hospital were shelved. From the evidence of later events, it seems that the 1831 act of parliament, stipulating that Boards and Officers of Health be appointed, was ignored, according to the report in *Saunders's News-Letter* on 18 November 1831.

In the spring of 1832 cholera reached Dublin. The papers alternated between panic-mongering and refusing to admit its existence. The *Dublin Evening Mail* of 16 April 1832, for example, stated, 'There is no cholera in Dublin. We re-assert it most emphatically'. But sick patients, mainly from the crowded slums, were beginning to crowd into the hospitals. The same paper that had 'emphatically' denied the existence of the epidemic now had to eat its words; an article on 25 April described:

'the processions of patients throughout the streets, guarded by bodies of horse and foot police, and surrounded by hundreds of idle and disorderly persons, en route to an Hospital, situated at the extreme end of the city, and at a considerable distance from the quarters in which the lower orders reside, is shocking to humanity. Yesterday, several skirmishes took place between the mob and the police, contending for litters in which unfortunate victims to the disease were placed — the common people having taken the monstrous idea into their heads that their friends will be made away with in the Hospital, and their bodies handed over to the Surgeons for dissection ...'

Before the Anatomy Act became law in August 1832 it was not unreasonable to fear such a fate; bands of 'resurrectionists' or 'resurrection men' roamed the graveyards, digging up newly interred bodies and selling them to the medical schools of Dublin (*see Chapter 20*). Fear and ignorance bred violence, as seen in the report in the *Dublin Evening Post* of 26 April:

'A mob collected last night in Chapel Lane ... and destroyed a temporary shelter erected there for the reception of cholera patients. The police were attacked in several places yesterday and in one instance vitriol was thrown on them.'

Kingstown, because it was a port, was one of the first places to be hit. A suspected case was seen in April 1832 by two doctors, Dr Thomas Rumley and Dr William Stokes. When they made their diagnosis of 'asiatic cholera', they were attacked by a mob and narrowly escaped with their lives (Kearns 1996). Between April and July 1832 there were 89 cases in Kingstown, of which 36 died. In the same period 1,688 died in the Dublin catchment area. On 17 May the Harbour Commissioners acknowledged that 'a disease of a contagious character' had hit Dublin and admitted the possibility of its spread into the vicinity of Kingstown. They donated ten guineas to the Kingstown Dispensary 'on the condition that the same shall not be considered as a precedent to ground further applications upon'.[37]

But nothing further was done. A very critical editorial appeared in the *Dublin Evening Post* on 7 July 1832, accusing the 'People of Kingstown' of 'gross and ... culpaple as well as fatal negligence' for failing to take any steps to halt the progress of the disease, while, in spite of

> 'all the efforts which the local and medical authorities can use ... the City of Dublin is losing (patients) at the rate of about 500 a week ... But the People of Kingstown, forsooth, would persuade the world that they "bear a charmed life" and that plague and pestilence, though at their door, cannot reach them! But it has reached them as we have seen — and with all appurtenances and means to boot, with a thriving, and in other respects, an intelligent and wealthy population, they have not, at this moment, established a Local Board of Health — they have not hired a house for a hospital — they have not engaged any medical men — but the poorer people are suffered to sicken, to recover, or to die, as the case may be, in their own houses — or they are sent perhaps seven miles into town in cholera cots ... They should forthwith, therefore, constitute a Board of Health, engage medical men, and hire a place for a hospital on the spot.'

This article had the desired effect. Five days later, a newly elected Board of Health met in Monkstown Vestry room. As a result of that meeting, Mr Frederick Parker, the chairman, wrote to the Kingstown Harbour Commissioners asking for permission to use the 'sheds on the North side of their yard' to house patients stricken with cholera; they were to be fenced off from the yard and a new entrance made. He also asked for ground on which to build a temporary 'Cholera Hospital'. The Commissioners, 'taking into consideration the awful calamity of this disease at present infecting Kingstown', gave permission for this building to be 'erected on the ground near Glastool Quarry' (the present People's Park). It was to be enclosed by a stone wall 'so as to secure it from all passengers'.[38] If it was built at all, this structure was probably pulled down when it was no longer of any use.

Meanwhile, plans were afoot again for a hospital in Monkstown. The last discussion on this subject was towards the end of 1831, when the idea had been shelved. Now, on 13 November 1833, a lease was taken out on a site on Pakenham Road for a sixteen-bed hospital, to be called Rathdown Fever Hospital (later renamed Monkstown Hospital; *see below*). By 1834, £500 had been collected. The four trustees were Archdeacon Charles Lindsay, Dr William Plant, Lieutenant William Hutchinson (the Harbour Master) and William Disney (churchwarden). The hospital opened officially in March 1835, primarily treating fever cases. Dr William Plant was in charge as the 'attending physician', assisted by a nurse (paid 7s per week) and an assistant (at 3s per week). Later an apothecary was

Monkstown Hospital, pictured in about 1910, was originally opened as Rathdown Fever Hospital in March 1835, with Dr William Plant as medical superintendent from that year until his death in 1875. The hospital closed down in 1987 and was demolished two years later. The old 'Juggy's Well' (railed in, bottom right of picture), used as a public water supply for centuries, is now covered over by the 'Monkstown Gate' development.

employed to help Dr Plant — Joseph Finnucane (from 1851 to 1854) and Dr O'Flaherty (from 1856 to 1874). The dispensary, or outpatients' department, dealt with anyone who presented themselves.

During its first year (1835) 81 patients were admitted (three of these died), while 1,148 attended the dispensary as outpatients ('externs') and 196 were seen in their homes. By 1837 the numbers had increased considerably: 277 patients were admitted (sixteen died), 1,712 were seen as outpatients and there were 521 home visits (State Papers Ireland 1840). The total cost of running the hospital was £150 a year in the 1840s. During the Great Famine year of 1848 the hospital committee observed that the 'sick poor' were anxious to gain admission to the hospital, 'where they were humanely and skilfully treated'. The death rate was one in every 45 cases admitted, which was good during the Famine years. Being a doctor was a risky business during any epidemic, involving close contact between doctor and patient. During the earlier 1833 epidemic nearly 25% of Irish doctors succumbed. Later, during the epidemic that accompanied the Famine, two local doctors died within a few months of each other — Dr John Houston (aged 43) and Dr Clement Taylor (28), surgeon to Dalkey Dispensary, in August and October 1845 respectively (*see Chapter 15*).

The 1848 Dublin directory gives us a thumbnail sketch of the hospital: 'Here is the Rathdown Dispensary and Hospital, maintained by subscription, and serves for the whole barony of that name, of which it is in the centre. It consists of 4 wards, in each of which are 8 beds, with all necessary medical attendance.' The building itself was two-storey over basement, with two wards on each of the first and second floors, accommodating 32 patients

325

in all (although sometimes the patients had to sleep two to a bed).

Besides his GP work, Dr Plant also undertook other duties; for example, the Monkstown Vestry minutes of 1822 mention 'Dr Plant for attending an inquest, £1-2-9'. He also involved himself in community work: he was a justice of the peace and, in 1863, first chairman of the newly formed Blackrock Commissioners, responsible for such things as street lighting and the public water supply (*Kingstown Journal*, 1863).

In October 1866 cholera visited Kingstown again. One of the very first to fall ill was a seaman called Hughes of the *Munster*, a Holyhead steamer. Dr Plant's refusal to admit him to Rathdown Hospital reached *The Times* of London, which ran a story on 16 October proving acutely embarrassing to the Kingstown authorities and leading to a Poor Law Medical Inquiry. The lord lieutenant's spokesman reprimanded Dr Plant in an open letter to the newspaper on 7 November. The story apparently was that Mr Howell, the secretary of the City of Dublin Steampacket Company, had been told that a sick man was being landed on the pier at Kingstown. He hurried there to find that Hughes had already been taken on a hand-cart to Rathdown Hospital, only to be refused admission. Howell found him lying outside the hospital gates, wrapped in blankets, and went to Dr Plant's home to remonstrate with him. Plant, aged 78 at this time, explained that 'he dared not admit the man, in consequence of a decision come to by the committee not to admit such cases'. Howell tried to get Hughes, who was nearly moribund at this stage, taken to the Union Workhouse in Bray, 'but no cabman could be induced to do the job, not even for £2'. Eventually he managed to organise transport in a furniture van to Bray, where Hughes died that evening. The circumstances surrounding Hughes's death galvanised the Sanitary Committee of Kingstown to set up a highly efficient medical service for cholera patients, including their admission to Rathdown Hospital, if necessary.

This unfortunate episode does not seem typical of Dr Plant, who, from all the available evidence, worked heroically at the dispensary and then at Rathdown Hospital for all of his long life. According to his obituary, he continued working until 'almost the very last day of his life'. Even in his 80s he was 'on call'. At 5am one Sunday morning, when he was 82, he was summoned to deal with an emergency: the *Kingstown and Bray Observer* of 14 May 1870 reported that:

> 'a woman named Lucy Butler, residing in No. 25 Old Dunleary [one of the houses near the Purty Kitchen], met with an accident on Sunday morning which nearly resulted fatally from weakness brought on by loss of blood. It seems that about three o'clock in the morning she got up to light a candle, her foot slipped on a piece of an onion, when she was thrown violently forward, her right temple coming in contact with the rim of an iron pot, cutting it severely. No medical aid being at hand, the poor woman continued bleeding for a couple of hours until she was taken to the Rathdown Hospital where Dr. Plant promptly arrested further hemorrhage. The doctor stated that the woman had a very narrow escape from bleeding to death.'

Dr William Plant died on 24 October 1875, leaving about £3,000 to his wife Jane (née Morgell).[39] He was buried in Carrickbrennan Graveyard in her family plot. His monument, in the chancel of Monkstown Church today, carries this inscription:[35]

SACRED
TO THE MEMORY OF
WILLIAM PLANT ESQR
M.D. & J.P.
IN THIS COUNTY
WHERE HE LIVED FOR 54 YEARS
ESTEEMED & HONORED
IN HIS PROFESSION
HE DIED AT HIS RESIDENCE
PLANTATION MONKSTOWN
OCTOBER 24th 1875
BELOVED REVERED & LAMENTED
AGED 87 YEARS.

'LOOKING UNTO JESUS, THE AUTHOR
AND FINISHER OF OUR FAITH.'
HEB. 12th CHAP. 2ND VERSE.

ALSO JANE PLANT HIS WIFE
DIED DECEMBER 27th 1889
AGED 85 YEARS.

After the death of Dr Plant, the hospital committee decided, in 1876, to enlarge the premises. Dr Joseph Beatty (godfather of Dr Desmond de Courcy-Wheeler, the last physician of the hospital) was appointed in 1878 and oversaw the expansion of the hospital, which was renamed 'Monkstown Hospital' at this time. (The name 'Rathdown Hospital' had to be changed because Loughlinstown Hospital was then called the 'Rathdown Union Hospital' and the two were easily confused.) Monkstown Hospital was 'rebuilt (in) 1880, containing 20 beds, (was) supported by voluntary contributions, and receive(d) patients without religious distinction' (Dublin directory, 1896).

The medical superintendents at Monkstown Hospital over the years were Dr William Plant (1835–75), Dr Joseph Beatty (1878–1919), Dr Robert de Courcy-Wheeler (1919–56) and Dr Desmond de Courcy-Wheeler (1956–87). The dispenser to the hospital (according to a 1910 photograph, published in *St Patrick's News* of June 1981) was George Lane McCormack, who had opened his pharmacy in Monkstown in 1884. (It is a treat to enter this pharmacy today, where many of the original fittings have been retained, such as the deep, wooden drawers for dispensing medicines, the old glass bottles and porcelain jars, still with their labels intact; the name of 'Lane McCormack' was changed recently.)

After World War I, Monkstown parishioners raised enough money to endow a ward, 'the Monkstown Ward', in memory of those from the parish who had died during the war (Annual Report of Select Vestry, 1921). Over the following years the hospital was further extended. By 1944 there were 25 beds. 'There are general, surgical, gynaecological, dental, throat, ear and nose departments. Also X-ray, violet-ray and massage (departments).' The hospital was closed down on 31 July 1987, along with a number of other Dublin hospitals (such as Mercer's and Sir Patrick's Dun's) and was demolished in 1989. The 'Monkstown Gate' apartments have since been built on the site.

The Rev. Robert Warren Stewart (1850–95) and Louisa Stewart, née Smyly (1852–95)

'Simplicity was perhaps his most striking characteristic. He was absolutely without guile. He had strong convictions, and could express them strongly and hold them tenaciously; but there was not an atom of pretentiousness about him.' This is how the Rev. Eugene Stock described Robert Warren Stewart in the memoriam written by W. E. Burroughs in October 1895. Robert Warren Stewart had been born into one of the most distinguished families of Monkstown. He had a privileged childhood, surrounded by all the trappings of wealth and culture. Who could have envisaged his violent end and that his last resting place, 45 years later, would be thousands of miles away, in the English Cemetery at Fuh-chow, China, beside his wife Louisa and their two small children, Hilda and Herbert?

Robert's father, James Robert Stewart, must have been an influential figure in the life of his family. He was a larger-than-life personality, who had strong leadership qualities and inspired the admiration and affection of others. In his obituary he was described as 'the kindest of friends, the wisest of counsellors, and the most liberal of benefactors'. He was one of the trustees of the Mariners' Church in Kingstown for nearly 50 years — from its opening in 1837 until his death on 10 December 1889 at the age of 84.[40] This kindly man was the grandson of the first Lord Longford (Edward Michael Lord Baron Longford), who had, with Lord de Vesci, given the site for Monkstown Parish Church in 1785 (*see Chapter 4*). James's mother, the Hon. Elizabeth Pakenham, was the eldest child of Lord Longford.

Robert Warren Stewart of the Church Missionary Society set up a three-tiered educational system in southern China, with dozens of village schools for children, secondary schools and a theological college at Fuh-chow (opened in 1883), called 'Trinity' after his Alma Mater in Dublin. Born at 11 Longford Terrace, a great-grandson of Lord Longford, he was murdered, along with his wife and two of his children, at Hwa-sang in 1895.

His father, Henry Stewart, had been the land agent for the Longford and de Vesci estates during the years 1813–51 and James followed in his footsteps, carrying on the business from his offices at 6 Leinster Street. (Elizabeth's sister, Kitty, married the duke of Wellington.) The history of the Longford family and *The Stewarts of Killymoon and Tyrcallen* can be found on Anthony Maitland's website, www.anthonymaitland.com.

Robert Warren Stewart was born on 9 March 1850, the ninth in a family of fourteen. As child after child was born every year or two, the family home at 11 Longford Terrace must have become more and more crowded. By 1853 there were eleven children, which, with the usual quota of servants, may well have been the signal to move to the larger 'Monkstown House' on

Monkstown Avenue (now a Community Centre). By 1857 the Stewarts had moved to 'Gortleightragh' on Sloperton, a huge house with a large garden and plenty of room for the Stewart children and, later, grandchildren. (During World War II it became the German Legation.) In 1865, when Robert was fifteen, his mother, Martha, died, aged 51.[41] He was educated at Marlborough College and Trinity College, Dublin, where he was a gold medallist (Burroughs 1895). After graduating in 1873, he went to study law in London. While there, he had a conversion experience during a service at Holy Trinity Church in Richmond, which changed his life. Instead of becoming a lawyer, he decided to become a missionary: he entered the Church Missionary Society (CMS) Theological College at Islington and was ordained in St Paul's Cathedral.

Robert returned home to Dublin, where he asked his childhood friend, Louisa Smyly, to marry him and to go with him to China as a missionary. Louisa was born in 1852 and, like Robert, was the ninth child in a large family (of eleven). The Smylys of Dublin were a deeply devout and philanthropic family. Her father was Dr Josiah Smyly, surgeon of the Meath Hospital, and her mother was Ellen Franks, the founder of the Smyly Homes for Children.[42] Ellen had founded a day school for poor children in 1852 (the year Louisa was born). Gradually, she established orphanages for boys and girls, and the 'Bird's Nest' for infants (the large, creeper-clad building is still there today, on York Road, Dun Laoghaire). By 1870 up to 1,000 children were cared for in 'Mrs. Smyly's Homes and Schools'. Two of Louisa's brothers became eminent doctors (Sir Philip Crampton Smyly, surgeon in ordinary to Queen Victoria, and Sir William Josiah Smyly, master of the Rotunda). Her great-nephew, Dr Philip Crampton Smyly, is today the curator of the Maritime Museum, housed in the converted Mariners' Church in Dun Laoghaire.

On 7 September 1876 Robert and Louisa were married in St Stephen's Church, Upper Mount Street, Dublin, and sailed for China nine days later.[43] Robert had been asked to found a theological college at Fuh-chow in the province of Fukien in southern China and to act as its principal. But he was to experience an uphill struggle: as soon as the new buildings were built inside the walled city, they were deliberately burned down. Stewart had been careful to seek advice about building in accordance with the principles of Feng Shui, but the problem may have been that he unwittingly transgressed against ancestral property rights. He built his college again, this time outside the city, and it was officially opened in 1883 (Burroughs 1895). The *Irish Ecclesiastical Gazette* of 29 November 1884 reported that Stewart's theological college could 'accommodate 50 students, each having a small room to himself, and the large hall, set apart for Divine Service and fitted up as a chapel, (could) when needed, seat some 250'.

Stewart's plan was to establish a self-supporting native church. But because there was widespread illiteracy in China, he had to set up a three-tiered educational system first. He travelled around the district, visiting each village ('itinerating', as he dubbed it). He promised to supply a teacher to each village if there were at least ten children, both boys and girls, who were willing to learn and if a room was available. By 1884 he had set up 38 village schools with 479 scholars, with seventeen young men going on for ordination. Many more schools would be established over the years (in one year alone he set up 96 village schools). He would hold regular inspections of the schools. The brightest boys were sent on to secondary school and then to Stewart's theological college at Fuh-chow. It took years, but gradually young

Chinese men were trained as teachers and catechists, some of whom were ordained (Burroughs 1895). A description of these activities is contained in one of R.W. Stewart's annual letters to the CMS, dated 6 March 1895 (reproduced in the Memorial Number of the *Dublin University Missionary Magazine* in October 1895). Stewart had also solved 'that most puzzling problem' of what to do with the boys he had educated who were not suited to teaching or mission work. For them he founded an Industrial School, which proved extremely popular, according to the 'Missionary Intelligence' column in the *Irish Ecclesiastical Gazette* of 29 November 1884.

Louisa's input was important to her husband's work in China. Being familiar with her mother's work and the running of the Smyly Homes back in Dublin, it is thought that Louisa helped to set up the Chinese primary schools based on the Smyly Day Schools. She also started a training college for 'Bible-women'.

Meanwhile, Robert and Louisa's own family was growing. The eldest three were boys: Arthur (b. 1877), Philip (b. 1879) and James (b. 1881). In 1881 Arthur and Philip were sent home to their grandfather, James Robert, and Aunt Emily at 'Gortleightragh'. James joined them, aged three, in 1884. Arthur explained the reason for this in his unpublished autobiography:[44]

> 'Life in the Far East was a continual struggle against illness, and before long the dreaded malaria fever had me in its grip. No knowledge then of mosquito or quinine and all the little Mother could do was to put me in a bath of warm water, gradually filling up with cold water to bring the temperature down. But this could not go on for long and, to save life, the doctor ordered that I and my brother Phil, or Pelik, as the Chinese called him, should be sent to England, or rather Ireland, as it happened.'

The Chinese women could see how difficult it was for Louisa to part with her three boys: the day after Arthur and Philip left, they were heard to remark, 'Su Sing sang wong has grey hairs today' (Bradshaw 1895). Two more children were born, Mildred (b. 1882) and Kathleen (b. 1884).

Much of the support from the churches at home was due to the Stewarts' long letters. Louisa, especially, devoted hours to writing thousands of letters to those who supported their work in Ireland, England, Canada and Australia.[45] In 1884 the Stewarts returned home to see their children, to recharge their batteries and to publicise their work, returning to China the following year. In 1888 Robert had to return home again, on sick leave: he was dangerously ill with chronic dysentery, a common problem in southern China at the time. This meant that he was probably at home when his father, James Robert, died in 1889, aged 84. When Robert eventually recovered, he and Louisa began an exhausting tour of meetings around Ireland and England; in 1892 Robert travelled with the Rev. Eugene Stock, editorial secretary of the CMS, to Australia and New Zealand to make their work known, to encourage more recruits and to raise money. In less than seven months the two men spoke at over 300 meetings and services, according to *The Church Missionary Gleaner* of September 1895. Stock later said of Robert Stewart, 'The more I was with him, the more I loved him. I do not say he was faultless, but I do say a more unselfish and Christ-like character I never met' (Burroughs 1895).

Robert's meetings in Dublin galvanised the students at Trinity College to support mission work abroad (Gwynn *et al.* 1936). Because Robert was a TCD graduate, they chose his mission in China, calling it the 'Dublin University Fukien Mission', and Robert's college in Fukien was called Trinity College, Fukien.[46]

Robert Stewart realised the potential of women missionaries in China — not just as support for their husbands, but as independent missionaries. As W.J. Smyly explains, 'The story was told of a Red Indian practice of carrying fire from one wigwam to the next — that a single fire brand would go out but two held together would keep each other alight and start the new fire. This was compared to a husband and wife team at a distant mission station, keeping each other's flame alight and doing the work together.'[47] Young women missionaries were sent out in pairs in the same way and, in the future, Robert and Louisa's own children would travel to China in pairs, to support each other.

Over the next ten years Robert Stewart's talks were to influence 30 young women, largely from the Church of England Zenana Missionary Society (CEZMS), an offshoot of the CMS, to join the Fukien Mission. Among the first of the Irish recruits were two sisters from Booterstown, Hessie and Inie Newcombe, who volunteered for the CEZMS after hearing the Stewarts and travelled to Ku-Cheng in 1886 to work with them. The *Irish Ecclesiastical Gazette* of 23 September 1892 announced that Miss F.R. Burroughs, of 'Rokeby', Blackrock, was to sail for Fuh-Chow in October that year; her brother, William, was the incumbent of the Mariners' Church, Kingstown, and subsequently became central secretary of the CMS in London (Wallace 2001). Robert's first sermon in Melbourne prompted two sisters, Nellie and Topsy Saunders, to volunteer as CEZMS missionaries and they, too, followed the Stewarts to China.

Two more boys, Herbert (b. 1889) and Evan (b. 1892), were born while the Stewarts were at home. The following year they returned to China, arriving on 1 September 1893. Their four youngest children travelled in the care of their nurse, seventeen-year-old Lena Yallop (who had come from the Elliott Home[48]), and the CEZMS ladies on the regular P&O route, while their parents took a detour, via Canada, where they addressed yet more meetings. The three older boys, Arthur, Philip and Jim, stayed behind in order to attend Haileybury College in Hertfordshire.

Robert Stewart returned to a new post: he was now in charge of the CMS station at Ku-Cheng, which was 100 miles north-west of Fuh-chow. The missionary compound there consisted of boys' and girls' boarding schools, an orphanage (for abandoned baby girls) and missionary living quarters, and stood on a hill outside the city walls. The missionaries met with immediate opposition. But they carried on stoically, working closely with the CEZMS women, who lived in pairs in the district, wearing Chinese dress, learning the language and working among the Chinese women. Several of these missionary women were talented linguistically and, encouraged by Robert Stewart, worked on a translation of the New Testament into the Fuh-chow vernacular. He had developed a system of printing this in Roman characters.

Missionaries were unpopular in China because their work was thought to undermine traditional customs, such as the early marriage of girls and the binding of their feet. In opening orphanages for abandoned baby girls, raising them as Christians and educating them, the missionaries were flouting another tradition. They did not bind the feet of these girls and so, in Chinese eyes, they were unmarriageable; as a result, many of these educated women went on to become missionaries to their own people.[45]

In 1894 war broke out between China and Japan. China was defeated, leading to riots and indiscriminate hostility towards foreigners, especially the missionaries, who were accused of introducing foreign customs and ideas. In March 1895 there was such unrest in the district caused by a fanatical anti-foreign sect, the Tsi-li or 'Vegetarians', that Robert Stewart and the other CMS missionaries left their compound to take refuge in the walled city of Ku-Cheng, which had already closed its gates. The missionary group had to climb over the city walls by ladder. Soon the situation became so dangerous that the British consul advised the missionary women and children to travel to Fuh-chow, 100 miles south, for safety. A few months later, in June, it was considered safe enough for them to return home (Hibernian Church Missionary Society 1896).

Every July and August, the missionaries would close their school in Ku-Cheng and escape the stultifying heat by moving to a little village called Hwa-sang ('Flowery Hill'), six miles away and a long steep climb (over 900m or 3,000ft) up the mountainside. They stayed there in a small group of isolated houses some distance from the village. August 1st, 1895, was little Herbert Stewart's sixth birthday and a picnic was planned for the afternoon. His sisters, Mildred (12) and Kathleen (11), decided to get up early, about 6am, with Herbert, to pick flowers to decorate the house. While they were on the hillside near the house, they heard a large crowd of people approaching, banging drums and blowing horns. They thought a colourful Chinese procession was approaching and ran to meet it, but instead found themselves caught up in a frightening mob. The children were terrified. One man seized Kathleen by the hair and began to beat her, but she managed to flee back to the house with the others.

The crowd of over 80 men followed the children and burst into the house, brandishing their swords and clubs. They killed Robert and Louisa Stewart, who were still in their bedroom. The children locked themselves into their bedroom, where Mildred pushed Kathleen under the bed. Mildred was about to hide there too, but realised that the attackers would know they were in the room because of the locked door, so she lay on top of the bed and opened the door, hoping that no-one would look under the bed. The men came into the room, looked for valuables and then pulled the bedclothes off Mildred and slashed at her knee, badly injuring it. Evan, in his cot, stood up and shouted at the men 'so boisterously that they left him alone', apart from a blow on the head, which was said to have caused the stutter he developed later.[45]

Nellie and Topsy Saunders from Melbourne, who were staying with the Stewarts while they learned the language, were killed next. The mob then left to attack the five missionary women in the house nearby. Kathleen crawled out from under her bed to find the house on fire. After finding her parents' bodies, she helped her brothers and sisters out of the burning house one by one. She found one-year-old Hilda, only just alive, under the body of her dead nurse, who had tried to protect her. Six-year-old Herbert was also badly hurt. The children took refuge in the home of an American missionary nearby. Four of the five missionary women had been killed — Hessie Newcombe from Booterstown, Elsie Marshall and Flora

Stewart, clergydaughters from England, and Annie Gordon from Melbourne. The only survivor, Flora Codrington, had been left for dead.

A warning about a likely attack then arrived: a pastor at Ku-Cheng had heard about the conspiracy the evening before, but did not send the message until the following morning. It arrived 30 minutes too late. The survivors set off for Fuh-chow, 100 miles away, the following afternoon, after sending a messenger ahead to raise the alarm. The first 15–20 miles were difficult and distressing, as the party negotiated the steep mountainside through the night, carrying the charred remains of the Stewarts and the other bodies in coffins, and the injured in chairs. A motor launch was sent from Fuh-chow to the nearest point on the River Min to transport them on the final stage. The journey took two days: Herbert died on the way and the baby on arrival. At 5am on 6 August the ten victims were buried in the English Cemetery at Fuh-Chow. On the coffin of Robert and Louisa were the words from II Samuel 1:23: 'Lovely and pleasant in their lives, and in their death they were not divided'. Mildred was critically ill for months but eventually recovered, though she was left with a limp for the rest of her life.[45]

Chinese soldiers were sent to protect the personal property of the Stewarts at Ku-Cheng, but they looted the house instead. A week later, a missionary hospital near Canton was demolished by a mob, but the missionaries there escaped. Miss Burroughs (of Blackrock) had stayed at Fuh-chow and so escaped the massacre. All European missionaries were ordered to Fuh-chow until things had quietened down. The British government demanded that those responsible for the massacre should be brought to justice and the missionaries protected. In spite of some initial official resistance, the British and Americans were eventually allowed to hold an official consular inquiry: about twenty of the ringleaders were caught and executed, and the viceroy of Cze-Chuen Province was stripped of his rank for failing to protect the missionaries, as reported in *The Irish Times* of 1 October 1895. Meanwhile, at home, packed churches prayed for the church in China. The CMS held a prayer meeting in London's Exeter Hall on 13 August, attended by 'a vast assembly from all parts', according to the *Church Missionary Gleaner* in its September 1895 issue. The CMS refused to accept any monetary compensation for the loss of their missionaries (Stock 1899).

The massacre caused an unprecedented interest in Christianity in China, where adult baptisms in the Fuh-chow district rose by 50%, from 503 in 1895 to 753 in 1896 (Hibernian Church Missionary Society 1896). Missionary recruitment soared at home. Even before the deaths in China the CMS was well supported in the Monkstown area. The Rev. W.E. Burroughs, incumbent (1876–95) of the Mariners' Church in Kingstown (and brother of Miss Burroughs, who had narrowly escaped death in China), reported in 1893 that 'the five Kingstown churches' had raised more for the CMS 'than from all the rest of Dublin City and County put together'.[49] In 1895 Monkstown raised £800 for the CMS — the largest contribution in Ireland, reported the *Church Missionary Gleaner* in March 1896.

In 1895 Mr Burroughs was appointed central secretary of the CMS in London. He suggested that a Stewart Memorial Fund should be set up, starting the fund himself with the huge sum, for that time, of £50. He preached at Monkstown on 8 September, raising £35-10s in aid of the 'Ku Cheng Martyrs' Memorial Fund' — seven times the usual Sunday

Louisa Stewart (née Smyly) is celebrated today in a stained-glass window in Liverpool Cathedral. She is one of 21 'Noble Women' remembered and represents 'The noble army of martyrs'. At the base of the window, Galatians 6:2 is quoted — 'Bear ye one another's burdens'.

collection.[50] People in all parishes gave generously — £2,500 was collected in the first month alone. It was largely through the support of Irish parishes, galvanised by Mrs Ellen Smyly, Louisa Stewart's mother, that by 1897 there were 200 'little day-schools' in China (Stock 1899). Instead of a wall monument or memorial window, the money was spent on projects that would have been dear to the hearts of Robert and Louisa Stewart: the education of their six surviving children, the support of the day schools in Fuh-kien started by Robert Stewart and the production of a dictionary and grammar, using his romanised characters (Hibernian Church Missionary Society 1896).

A list was later published showing the level of contributions to the fund from various parishes; the top six were Monkstown; St John's, Mounttown; St Matthias's, Sandford; St Thomas's, Belfast; Zion Church, Rathgar; and the Mariners' Church, Kingstown. It is perhaps not surprising that Monkstown should be top of the list or that its neighbouring parishes of St John's and Kingstown contributed so generously: the Stewarts and Smylys were well known and highly regarded in the area. William Dowse, the incumbent of St Thomas's, Belfast, was the twin brother of John Dowse, the incumbent of Monkstown at the time, and had also been curate in Monkstown from 1886–92, a period coinciding with the Stewarts' home visit. The curate at Zion Church, James Haythornthwaite, was the associate secretary for Southern Ireland CMS for 1891–4 (Wallace 2001).

Today, Louisa Stewart is commemorated in Liverpool Cathedral. Stained-glass windows in the Lady Chapel there celebrate the lives of 21 'Noble Women', such as 'Grace Darling and all courageous maidens' and 'Elizabeth Barrett Browning and all who have seen the infinite in things'. Louisa represents 'the noble army of martyrs'; she is depicted in the window on the staircase leading down to the Lady Chapel. Here, in 1995, the CMS marked the centenary of her death, with her granddaughter, great-granddaughter and two great-great-grandchildren present. Louisa knew that she and Robert might be martyred. She once said, 'If it should ever be that we meet our deaths by violence, let no one think that God has in any way failed us. We are nowhere promised that His servants may not be called upon to suffer, even to die for His sake, Who died for us. What we are promised is that, living or dying, we cannot be separated from Him; and that under all circumstances He will be sufficient.'

In Ireland there is no memorial to Robert or Louisa Stewart, not even in the church most closely associated with them. It is a tribute to them that their faith lived on in their children, five of whom returned to China as missionaries, and in the Chinese schools and translation of the New Testament, whose lasting influence can never be fully known. The last word should perhaps be left with John Gregg, archbishop of Dublin, who in 1938 at the General Synod of the Church of Ireland said: 'May the Church of St Patrick, of St Columba and St Gall and St Canice, of Robert and Louisa Stewart ... may our ancient Church of Ireland ever be true to her glorious ancestry, and may she ever realise that her supreme purpose, for which she was founded by her Saviour Christ, is to preach His Gospel to all mankind'.

The Rev. James Robert Stewart (1881–1916)

A fearless son of a fearless father.
Obituary in the *Proceedings of the CMS for Africa and the East, 1915–16:*
West China Mission

Picture the scene. Northern France, 1920. Row upon row of identical crosses, over 3,000, fill the military section of the town cemetery at Bethune. Beside one of these crosses stands a young Chinese man, carefully taking photographs. The name on the cross — 'The Rev. James Robert Stewart' (Commonwealth War Graves Commission, www.cwgc.org).

James Stewart (or Jim, as he was usually called) was born in China on 7 January 1881 to the Irish Church Missionary Society missionaries the Rev. Robert Warren Stewart and his wife Louisa (née Smyly).[42] When he was three Jim joined his two older brothers, Arthur and Philip, who were living with their grandfather, James Robert Stewart, and his daughter Emily (the children's beloved 'Tem') at 'Gortleightragh' in Monkstown. Arthur later wrote of his Aunt Emily in his autobiography (unpublished), 'Poor Tem must have had a trying time with us, for we were not only shy but extremely nervous and delicate'.[44] When James Robert Stewart died in 1889, 'Gortleightragh' was left to his son James. Although Tem's younger brother, George, was the official guardian of the children, she was determined to continue to look after them while their parents were in China, so she bought 'Brighton Lodge' on Seafield Avenue as a home for the children.

Arthur recalls:

'Like many another, Grandfather made a mistake in his will because he left Tem only a small amount, feeling sure that she would marry. He had reason to think so because she always had suitors round her, but he did not realize how deeply

335

she was attached to her brother Bob [Robert Warren Stewart] and that for his sake she was prepared to make a home for his children. Hence, when suitors applied, they were told that they would have to take on a ready made family of three lusty boys and after 1895 this family grew to six. This was too much of a good thing and, as Tem refused to give us up, she devoted the rest of her life to looking after us, and devotion it truly was. No Mother could have done more for her own children than Tem did for us, and I look back to those years with deepest gratitude and memories of happy days.'

In 1893 Jim, then aged twelve, joined his brothers at Haileybury College, a public school in Hertfordshire. From that time on the boys were only home for holidays. During the summer of 1895 Jim and Philip went to the Isle of Man with their 'other' grandmother — Louisa's mother, Ellen Smyly, the founder of the Smyly Homes. There the boys heard news that would influence the rest of their lives. During the first weekend of August 1895, the grim news arrived by cable to the Church Missionary Society's (CMS) headquarters in London (the message was encoded as a system of numbers that had to be translated from Chinese characters and then turned into English). Though somewhat garbled, the message was tragically clear: a mob of Chinese fanatics had overrun the little missionary station at Hwa-sang, killing the 'foreign devils' and torching their houses. Over 5–10 August 1895 *The Irish Times* ran the story of the massacre in detail: eleven of the fifteen were dead — Jim's parents, Robert and Louisa Stewart; his little brother, Herbert, and baby sister, Hilda; the children's nurse, Lena Yallop; and six young missionary women (Nellie and Topsy Saunders, Hessie Newcombe, Elsie Marshall, Flora Stewart and Annie Gordon). Only one woman (Flora Codrington) and three children (Mildred, Kathleen and Evan) had survived. When Mildred recovered from her serious leg injuries, she, Kathleen and Evan left China for Monkstown, to join their older brothers, Arthur, Philip and Jim, at 'Brighton Lodge'. On Sundays the family attended Sunday school and church at Monkstown. Kathleen was confirmed in Monkstown Church in 1901 at the age of seventeen and Mildred (aged twenty) the following year.[51]

Soon after returning to school in 1895, Jim became seriously ill with TB. Doctors recommended a warmer climate, so Jim, aged fourteen, was sent to Australia to stay with a CMS friend of his father's. His obituary stated that he first 'matriculated at Trinity College, Dublin' (CMS 1916); this was the entrance exam to TCD, which Jim never actually entered.[52] About eight years later he returned to Ireland, 'not only fully restored to health, but so led by the Spirit that he had passed safely through a period of doubt ... became President of the Christian Union in Sydney, studied for Ordination at Moore [Anglican Theological] College in Sydney, and arrived home ready to take a curacy at Shirley, near Southampton. Mildred joined him there until a few years later, when both joined the CMS and went to West China'.[53]

Like his father, Jim had a natural affinity for young people and especially for young Chinese people. The new university at Chengtu opened a diocesan hostel in September 1910 and Jim was appointed as its warden. Here he taught English and Bible study to the students. Mildred worked at Chengtu with Jim, later marrying the Rev. Reg Taylor, another CMS missionary in Chengtu. Arthur, their older brother, was also ordained and became warden (1909–30) of the CMS St Paul's School in Hong Kong (Hewitt 1977), assisted by his sister, Kathleen, who had grown into 'a ravishingly beautiful' woman.[45] She married Canon Ernest

Martin, while Arthur and Evan married the two daughters of Bishop Lander of Hong Kong and worked at St Paul's School as masters and wardens. Thus, extraordinarily, five of the six surviving Stewart children had followed their parents to China, four of them into the mission field.

Jim was keen that a CMS hostel should be built on the university campus at Chengtu. He offered a personal loan for the purchase of a site and had just begun negotiations in 1915 when he decided to return home. War had broken out in Europe the year before and he felt that he could not stay in China while thousands of his compatriots were dying at home.[54] He joined up as a temporary chaplain to the Second Battalion of the Worcestershire Regiment and set off for France. On Sunday evening, 2 January 1916, he was taking a funeral service just behind the firing line when a shell exploded nearby. He was killed instantly.[55] His death was a setback for the West China mission. In his seven short years there he had made a lasting impact and was seen as a future church leader. It was said that C.T. Song, the bishop of Western Szechwan, had become a Christian because of the 'sheer goodness' of Jim Stewart (Hewitt 1977). The money he had left towards educational purposes in his will was used to buy a site for a CMS hostel at Chengtu, eventually completed in 1927.

In 1920 a young Chinese man called James Yang-chu Yen travelled to the town of Bethune in northern France to find the grave of his friend, Jim Stewart. Yang-chu Yen had worked with Jim at the Chengtu hostel, as his assistant 'Chinese sub-warden', and under his guidance (and subsequently Arthur's) had entered the University of Hong Kong. He had taken the name 'James' as his baptismal name in honour of his friend and mentor. After graduating, Yang-chu Yen went to Yale and then completed his postgraduate studies at Princeton.

In a letter to the *Church Missionary Gleaner* on 2 February 1920, Yang-chu Yen recalls how, on arrival in Bethune, he had approached the mayor to discover the whereabouts of Jim Stewart's grave, only to be told that there were no records available of the 40 cemeteries around the town. (The mayor was mistaken: the Stewart family had been notified of the grave's location in 1919.[56]). Yen writes:

'I was in despair. Finally we had to resort to the process of looking for the grave from cemetery to cemetery until we could locate it. So we agreed to start with the one right in the city. We were still worrying about the matter when the car stopped at the military section of the cemetery. The wonderful thing was that no sooner had the car stopped than my friend's chauffeur called out at the top of his voice: "What is that cross?" It was no other than the cross on Rev. James Stewart's grave. I almost broke down with the sudden joy and relief at finding it. It would have been my life's regret if I had been to France and had failed to see the grave of my heroic and Christlike friend. That hour at the grave was to me a memorable hour, which I shall remember as long as I live. I prayed there as fervently as I knew how. I asked God that I might live worthy of my friend and brother. We took a few pictures of the grave. Mr. Stewart's portrait, along with the photograph of his grave, will be to me a constant inspiration for Christlike living.'

Jim Stewart's grave (Ref: II.L.11.) is in the Commonwealth Section of the Bethune Town

Cemetery, which was designed by Sir Edwin Lutyens. Another memorial to him, in the form of a brass plaque, hangs in the chancel of Monkstown Church. It reads:

IN MEMORY OF
REV. JAMES ROBERT STEWART B.A.
REPRESENTATIVE OF THIS PARISH IN W. CHINA
TEMPORARY CHAPLAIN TO THE FORCES
KILLED IN ACTION AT CAMBRIN, FRANCE
JAN 2ND 1916 AGED 35 YEARS

'GREATER LOVE HATH NO MAN THAN THIS — THAT
A MAN LAY DOWN HIS LIFE FOR HIS FRIENDS'

ERECTED BY HIS FELLOW CHAPLAINS

Jim Stewart would have been proud of his friend, James Yang-chu Yen. The work of this man was to become legendary. He 'dedicated his whole life (to working for the peasant people of the Third World) through his International Institute for Rural Reconstruction (IIRR)'.[54] He also 'transformed the organisation of public medicine in China and created the pattern which still exists today'.[45] And all this because he had found in the life of Jim Stewart 'a constant inspiration for Christlike living'.

Monkstown parish war memorials

> *We can truly say that the whole circuit of the earth is girdled with the graves of our dead ... and, in the course of my pilgrimage, I have many times asked myself whether there can be more potent advocates of peace upon earth through the years to come, than this massed multitude of silent witnesses to the desolation of war.*
> King George V, Flanders, 1922

During the Great War of 1914–18, 155 men and women from Monkstown volunteered for service — 28 never returned. The overall Allied death rate was 10% (Harris 1968); the death rate among Irish soldiers was 16% (Cronin 1989), but in Monkstown the rate was 18%.

On 25 June 1920 the *Church of Ireland Gazette* published the following article:

'On Sunday, at morning service in Monkstown Church, the Dean of Christ Church [the Very Rev. Harry Vere White] unveiled a mural tablet erected by the parishioners to the memory of some 28 members of the congregation who lost their lives during the Great War. The memorial of these brave men is a handsome emblazure sculptured in stone and red alabaster, erected on the south wall within the chancel. The architectural design is by Mr. R. Caulfeild Orpen. The work was carried out by Messrs. Sharp and Emery, Dublin. The ceremony of unveiling and dedication took place during Divine Service, which was conducted by the rector, Canon J.C. Dowse, MA, assisted by the

Very Rev. the Dean of Christ Church Cathedral and Rev. Dr. G.R. Elliott, curate of Monkstown Parish.'

Among those 28 names were six sets of brothers and two clergymen. The Rolls of Honour in the transept porches of Monkstown Church today record that sixteen soldiers won nineteen distinctions between them, including ten MCs, three were 'mentioned in despatches', two won DSOs, one the DSC, one the Croix de Guerre, one was 'mentioned for services in Mesopotamia' and one was 'Commended for Gallant Conduct and Devotion to Duty'. Not included on the Rolls of Honour is the posthumous award to Edward Chaytor Millar for 'gallant and distinguished conduct in the field'.

The British Empire entered World War I on Tuesday 4 August 1914. Two days later, on 6 August 1914, Canon John Dowse, rector of Monkstown (1894–1929), held a 'Special Service of Intercession' at 8pm. This was the first of these services, which were to continue for over four years. Thereafter services of intercession were held every Wednesday at 12 noon and 8.15pm.[57] The rector's daughter, Edith Dowse (born in 1899 and still in good health in 2003), remembers attending every Wednesday evening.

Within a few weeks of war breaking out, three new Irish divisions were formed — the 10th, 16th and 36th. The 16th was mainly Nationalist and Catholic, the 36th was drawn from the Ulster Volunteer Force (UVF), while the 10th was a mixture of Protestant and Catholic, and included the 7th Royal Dublin Fusiliers. It was the first division raised in Ireland to be sent to the Front and, although its men had no previous military experience, they participated in some of the heaviest fighting of the war. As John Redmond, the leader of the Irish Nationalist Party, said, the 10th Division was 'the first definitely Irish Division that ever existed in the British Army'. He emphasised the importance of this — 'For the first time in history, (Ireland had) put a national army in the field … for the express purpose of defending Ireland' (Jeffery 2000).

Below are the stories of four young men from Monkstown who died during World War I, three of them at Gallipoli.

- **Edward Chaytor Millar**, Reg. No. 14645, Sergeant, 'D' Company, 7th Battalion, Royal Dublin Fusiliers, killed in action at Gallipoli, on Monday 9 August 1915, aged 28.
- **Charles Edward Dowse**, Reg. No. 14185, Lance-Corporal, 'D' Company, 7th Battalion, Royal Dublin Fusiliers, killed in action at Gallipoli, on 16 August 1915, aged 19.
- **Henry Harvey Dowse**, Lieutenant, RAF, died of influenza in hospital at Genoa, N. Italy, following gunshot wounds, 10 November 1918, aged 25.
- **Richard McClatchie**, Able Seaman 209542, HMS *Goliath*, killed in action 13 May 1915.

Gallipoli was Churchill's idea. The plan was to lead a naval expedition to take the Gallipoli Peninsula and eventually Constantinople (now Istanbul). The campaign was a disaster from the start, with old battleships and cruisers, due to be scrapped, being used for the invasion. The end result was the loss of about 50,000 British, French, Australian and New Zealand forces and 66,000 Turks, with nothing at all gained strategically. Two separate waves of Royal Dublin battalions were sent to Gallipoli in 1915: the first in April 1915 and the second, with the 6th and 7th Battalions – including many young men from Monkstown – in August 1915.

To go back a year, on 11 September 1914 Dubliners opened *The Irish Times* and read:

> 'To the Irish Rugby Football Volunteers, I am keeping my Battalion open for you to join. Come in your 'platoons' [50 men]; 'mess', 'drill', and work together, and, I hope, fight the common enemy together. The 1st City of Dublin Cadets are joining me as a body. I am waiting for YOU, but I cannot keep open long. Come at once, TO-DAY. Enlist at Great Brunswick Street (ask for Major Ward). Signed, G. Downing (Lt.-Colonel) (late captain 1st Monkstown XV (1883), Commanding 7th (Service) Battalion RDF [Royal Dublin Fusiliers].'

Many Monkstown parishioners immediately recognised the name of Geoffrey Downing — captain of the 1st XV of Monkstown Rugby Football Club in 1883. The club aimed high: they played a match against the officers of the Channel Fleet 'as a wind-up to the season' in April 1900 and won by a goal and a try to nil. They travelled to England in 1902 and 1903 to play matches against Oxford, Cambridge and the Royal Naval College at Greenwich. Undeterred by five defeats, this parish club beat the Royal Navy College in November 1903.[58] One of Downing's friends was the barrister F.H. Browning, who was also president of the Irish Rugby Football Union (IRFU) in 1913–16 (Morgan 1999).[59]

A few weeks previously, in August 1914, Lord Kitchener, another Irishman, had, in similar words to Downing, called for 100,000 volunteers. He had urged groups of men who were 'accustomed to work together or play together' to 'enlist together and form their own section, platoon or company'. The idea was that 'comrades in arms' would fight better together.[60] Within a week or two of Kitchener's appeal, F.H. Browning sent a circular to the Dublin rugby clubs, asking them to encourage their members to volunteer. On getting an enthusiastic response to his letters, he founded a volunteer corps, called the Irish Rugby Football Union Volunteer Corps, which had its headquarters at Lansdowne Road. Browning contacted Geoffrey Downing, who had just been appointed commanding officer of the Royal Dublin Fusiliers, and asked him to form a 'Pals' company, 'D' Company, for members of the rugby clubs. Downing immediately sent the letter to *The Irish Times* and waited for developments.

On 14 September 1914 in *The Irish Times*, Downing wrote about what happened:

> 'I went to Lansdowne Road on Thursday afternoon, when Mr. Browning, the President of the IRFU, gave me an opportunity of addressing the members of the Union who had volunteered for active service. After speaking to them for a few minutes, they all, with one accord, elected to join the 7th RDF [Royal Dublin Fusiliers], and a more splendid set of young men I have hardly ever seen. I think 89 came forward but I am assured that double and treble that number will follow them. With this "advance guard" of real, true-hearted volunteers I can see in the very near future the makings of one of the finest

battalions that Ireland has ever produced, and I feel a proud man to have the honour of commanding them.' He added, 'We hear that the foe do not like the bayonet. God help them if this lot ever have the luck to charge them, when properly trained in the use of it'.

Over the next week, *The Irish Times* reported on the progress of the battalion. On 16 September 1914, 110 men left for the Curragh to train, among them members of Monkstown Rugby Football Club. They marched from Trinity College, down Dame Street and along the quays to Kingsbridge Station (now Heuston). The streets were thronged with their friends and the public, giving them a huge send-off. Handkerchiefs fluttered from nearly all the windows in College Green and Dame Street. They reached the Curragh at 5pm in pouring rain and were greeted with a short welcoming talk from their new commanding officer, Lieutenant Colonel Downing. Over the next five months, those young men were turned into soldiers. They entered 'D' company as barristers, civil servants, stockbrokers, insurance agents, business men, doctors, solicitors and students of engineering, art, divinity and medicine. By April 1915 they were considered nearly ready to face the enemy. The Royal Dublin Fusiliers were affectionately called the 'Old Toughs'; the 'Pals' of D Company quickly became known as the 'Young Toffs' (Hanna 1917).

There is a widely held belief that proportionately more Protestants than Roman Catholics joined up in the Great War, but the figures belie this. Of the recruits who enlisted in Dublin between August 1914 and March 1915, there were 6,850 Roman Catholic men and 1,908 Protestants. This represented 3.86% and 3.92% respectively of their male populations (Cronin 1989). At the end of December 1914, the Annual Report of the Monkstown Select Vestry reported, 'Some 66 of our Parishioners have answered the call of their King to join the army fighting for the liberty of Belgium and the freedom of the world. Their names will be seen on the boards in the Church porches. The Vestry desire the prayers of the Parishioners on their behalf, and especially for their safe return.'

One of the 66 was Edward Chaytor Millar, aged 27 (born 6 June 1887, confirmed in Monkstown in 1904), the fourth son of Fitzadam Millar, a churchwarden on several occasions (*see Appendix 4*) and parochial nominator of Monkstown Church. His uncle, Richard, was the architect of the Knox Memorial Hall, opened in 1904. While at Trinity College, Edward had rowed for the Junior Eight for two seasons and then worked in the family vintner firm of Millar & Co. The Millar family lived in 'Windsor House', a fine Georgian house today, near the end of Monkstown Avenue. Edward was a member of Monkstown Rugby Football Club and of their 1st XV in 1913 and 1914. In September 1914, just after arriving at the Curragh, he was promoted to sergeant. His older brother, George, was a doctor, serving with the Royal Army Medical Corps (Lecane 1997).

Three sons of Canon John Clarence Dowse, rector of Monkstown, joined up at the same time as Edward Chaytor Millar — John, Henry and Charles Dowse. John was 23 years old, Henry ('Harry') was 21 and Charles ('Charlie') was 19. (Their younger brother, Richard Victor (17), was still at school[61] and their sister, Edith (15), was a pupil at The Hall School in Monkstown.) John had qualified as a doctor at Trinity College in 1914 and immediately entered the Royal Army Medical Corps (RAMC) for service in France. Harry, his younger brother, was already at Trinity College (University of Dublin War List 1922);[62] on enlisting,

The Dowse family in 1907 — (from left to right) Henry ('Harry'), Canon J. Dowse, John, Mrs Henrietta Dowse, Charles ('Charlie'), Edith and Richard.
Below: Edith Dowse pictured at her 100th birthday party in 1999. Her silver medal from the president of Ireland the following year was engraved with the words 'A witness to 3 centuries', acknowledging her extraordinary achievement of having lived in three centuries—the nineteenth, twentieth and twenty-first.

he progressed rapidly from lance corporal (17 September 1914) to corporal (28 September) to sergeant in March 1915 (Hanna 1917). Charlie was 6ft 2in. and had left school at Trent College, Derbyshire, in 1913; when the call to arms came, he was staying with some cousins in the country, learning the basics of farming with a view to emigrating to Canada and taking up the farming life there. In January 1915 he was promoted to lance corporal.

On 16 April 1915, after exactly seven months of training, the commanding officer, Lieutenant General Sir Bryan Mahon (a Galway man), inspected the 10th Division at the Curragh for the first time (Johnstone 1992). Several weeks later the 10th set off for Basingstoke in Hampshire for their final training. They were inspected by King George V and Queen Mary, and a few days later by Lord Kitchener. The king told Mahon 'how pleased (he) was to have an opportunity of seeing the 10th Irish Division, and how impressed he was with the appearance and physical fitness of the troops' (Cooper 1918).

342

At the beginning of July the men were issued with tropical gear: pith sun helmets, slacks, puttees (strips of cloth wound around the leg between the ankle and knee) and khaki drill shirts. They departed for Liverpool, where boats were waiting to take them to the Greek Islands, *en route* for Gallipoli. While they waited there for further orders, they swam in warm seas and basked in sunshine, although the 'down side' was that many fell ill in the debilitating heat, had to eat fly-infested food and suffered from a shortage of fresh water (Cooper 1918). On 4 August the order came to embark at 9am the following morning; before dawn that day, the men attended services of Holy Communion or Mass before embarking on packed ferries, which sailed immediately for Gallipoli.

The men of the 10th Division were not the first to arrive at Gallipoli. The Allies had landed there unopposed in February 1915. In April that year two landings were attempted: each was resisted strongly by the Turks, led by German officers, and there were huge casualties. The Allies could not drive the Turks off the high ground above the beaches, while the Turks could not dislodge the Allies below on the beaches. A stalemate was reached, so the Allies sent for reinforcements — enter the 10th.

The 6th and 7th Battalions of the Royal Dublin Fusiliers arrived off Suvla Beach on the Gallipoli Peninsula before dawn on 7 August 1915. 'D' Company landed 239 men. Nine days later, 131 (55%) were dead (Cooper 1918). The whole operation was chaotic. The Hon. Sir Frederick Stopford, the commanding officer, stayed on board his boat, unwell. Brigadier Sitwell replaced him; he gave orders to attack and then withdrew them, while crucial hours slipped away. Many of the men were feeling ill after their cholera vaccinations; most were hungry, thirsty or had diarrhoea. The scorching sun and dust-filled wind made conditions difficult, and the Turkish snipers (many of them women) picked off the officers with deadly accuracy; they also trained their guns on the wells, where dozens of thirsty soldiers lost their lives. (According to Curtayne (1972), the soldiers learned to practise 'the Gallipoli stoop', as they tried to avoid being hit.) Initially there were only three Turkish battalions opposing the much larger Allied force. If Sitwell had attacked immediately he would probably have succeeded, but he dithered. Men were allowed to bathe, while Turkish reinforcements were speeding towards the area.

On 14 August orders at last came to attack Kireç Tepe Sirti, a ridge overlooking Suvla, which was now strongly defended by the enemy. The 15 and 16 of August were two days of needless slaughter. In spite of incredible bravery, the men could not compete against the superior numbers of Turks who, unlike them, were familiar with the terrain and the heat, and had excellent leadership: their Turkish leader, Mustafa Kemal (or Atatürk, the father of the Turks, as he was called later), became the legendary first president of Turkey in 1923 until his death in 1938. The Turks held the higher ground and picked off the soldiers easily as they advanced up the ridge with no cover. Francis Ledwidge, the famous Irish war poet who was there, wrote later to Lord Dunsany, saying 'It was Hell! Hell! No man thought he would ever return. Just fancy out of D Company, 250 strong, only 76 returned' (Curtayne 1972). Ledwidge himself was to die in Flanders in 1917.

Anxious family and friends back in Ireland scanned the headlines of *The Irish Times* during August and September 1915. The first report of the Suvla Bay landing appeared on 26 August: it did not identify the troops involved and the list of those in the Roll of Honour under 'Dardanelles' (one column to the right), dated 19 August, included no Royal Dublin Fusiliers (RDF). Two days later, on 28 August, the landing of the 7th Battalion of the RDF was reported (nearly three weeks after it had occurred) and a letter printed from one of its members, Lance-Corporal Norman Brown, a clergyman's son, who had been wounded on the first day and was now hospitalised in Alexandria.[63] The following day, in the special Sunday edition issued by *The Irish Times* during the war, under the headline '7th Battalion Complimented', an extract from another soldier's letter was printed. Victor Jefferson (of 44 Grosvenor Road, Rathmines) had written: 'You will have to excuse the writing, as we are at present on top of a mountain'.

Still no 7th Battalion casualties had been announced. Then on 30 August a headline appeared in the paper — 'Sergeant Edward C. Millar'. It was the announcement of his death and read:

> 'In August last he was among the first to join the "D" (Footballers') Company, and, like several others who enlisted at that time, refused to take a commission. From several sources, it is reported that he died a most gallant death. He was a prominent footballer, having played for Monkstown for several seasons. Most of the Monkstown 1st XV were serving in the same company with him...'

We can imagine the anxiety of the Dowse family when they heard about Edward Millar's death and waited and prayed that their own three sons would come home safely.

At the bottom of the same newspaper's page, extracts were printed from a letter written by Colonel Downing (who had been wounded in the foot by a Turkish sniper on 15 August) to his wife (Hanna 1917).[64] He wrote:

> 'We ... arrived here ... on the 7th. What a day it was! We fought from early morning to dark, and the 7th RDF made a great name for itself; they did splendidly, and I am so proud of them. I got a message from General ____ [censored] ... that it was imperative that Hill 53 should be taken before sundown (now Dublin Hill). I was the senior Colonel in the attacking line, and told him it should be done. We captured it at 7.30 (just as it was getting dark), and the Turks fled from it, and we gained the front line of trenches ... We have gained a great name for the capture and for the splendid regiment which I have the honour to command.'

In one of the many letters printed over the following weeks, one of Downing's men, Private Frank M. Laird, wrote of his commanding officer's behaviour:

> 'The shrapnel was dropping pretty sharply there, and I saw Colonel Downing [who was a tall, well-built man] with a stick in his hand, standing up as cool as a cucumber, while everyone else, of course, was rubbing his respective nose on the ground and making himself as small as possible' (*The Irish Times*, 16 September 1915).

On 31 August, under the headline 'Irish Valour in Gallipoli', a fuller account of the first week was given by Captain Poole Hickman, who had taken over from Colonel Downing

(Dungan 1997). He wrote a detailed account of the action in which Millar, 'one of my best sergeants', was killed: 'He died gallantly and his name has been sent forward for recognition' (*The Irish Times*, 31 August 1915). Poole Hickman himself (an eminent barrister in civilian life) was killed shortly after Millar, on 16 August, while leading a bayonet charge over the crest of Kireç Tepe Sirti (Hanna 1917). Apparently 'D' Company was asked to carry supplies to an English brigade that had run out of ammunition; Millar was killed while calling on the soldiers to 'stand firm'. He was posthumously 'mentioned in despatches' for his 'gallant and distinguished conduct in the field'.

During the beginning of September 1915, 'Dublin Recruiting Week' was held in a special effort to reach 'a class of young men [professional and middle class] who have hitherto avoided these recruiting rallies'. Meetings were held all over Dublin, including Kingstown, and were well attended. According to a report in *The Irish Times* on 11 September 1915, Mr M.F. O'Brian, chairman of the Kingstown Urban Council, said that:

> 'already fifty Kingstown camp recruits had been sent to join the main battalion …The Kingstown workingmen had done very well. But they did not want to have it said of those fine young fellows, of whom they saw so many, that they had left it to the workingmen to fight their battles. It would be far better for these young men, instead of killing time, that they should kill something that was worth the killing. It would be well if these young men would exchange the golf ball for an equally sporting ball, the bullet. They wanted these young men to follow the example of Canon Dowse's son, of Herbert Findlater, who was an MA and a solicitor, and of young Brett, and of a score of others who had entered amongst the ranks. (Applause)…'

Those at that meeting did not seem to know that Lance-Corporal Charles Dowse had already been killed — on 16 August, several weeks earlier. The notice had appeared in *The Irish Times* on 4 September:

> 'We regret to learn of the death in action … of Lance-Corporal Charles Edward Dowse (who) … was the third son of Canon and Mrs. Dowse … and was aged 19 years and ten months.'

The Dowse family always went to the Firth of Clyde in Scotland for the month of August, where Canon Dowse did a holiday locum tenens. On their arrival home, Charles Strong, the curate, broke the news to them of Charlie's death. He had been shot in the head while storming the Kireç Tepe Sirti ridge on 16 August; his height (6ft 2in.) had made him an easy target. He was not the only one — 25 other 'Pals' in 'D' Company were also killed in action that day and a further seventeen wounded (Morgan 1999).

A few days later the Dowse family received more bad news: Charlie's elder brother, Harry, had been seriously wounded in the chest on 7 September and was invalided out of Gallipoli. When he recovered, he joined the Army Service Corps, but finding it too boring (as his sister Edith recalls) he joined the RAF (139th Squadron). On 16 October 1917 Harry was shot down over France while acting as an observer in an FE2B. He was slightly

Lieutenant Henry (Harry) Dowse, RAF, survived being shot down over France (right) on 16 October 1917, only to die the day before the Armistice (10 November 1918) after sustaining serious injury in a crash-landing in northern Italy.

wounded and had to stay in the open all night until help arrived.[65]

As the war progressed, Canon Dowse often jotted down comments in the 'Notes' section of the Monkstown Preachers' book. In March 1918 the Germans launched three huge offensives on the Western Front. On 1 April that year Canon Dowse initiated additional 'special Intercessions in connection with the Great Battle', every day at noon, underlining the words 'Great Battle' twice. On 28 May he wrote, 'Great advance of Germany on West Front'. The months passed and then, on Monday 11 November 1918, at noon, there was a 'Thanksgiving and Intercession service for the signing of the armistice in the 1914–8 [sic] war'. Canon Dowse took the usual intercessional service at noon on the 12th. On the evening of the 13th, Canon Dowse did not turn up as usual to a meeting of the Select Vestry. Instead, the shocked members of the Vestry heard harrowing words from William Tatlow, the rector's churchwarden. Lieutenant Henry Dowse had died on 10 November 1918, the day before the Armistice. Harry had been the gunner in a two-man plane (a Bristol Fighter) that crash-landed after being shot down over Italy on 30 October. The pilot managed to get out alive; Harry had been injured with gunshot wounds and was brought to hospital where he died, eleven days later, of pneumonia (Henshaw 1995). He was buried in Grave No. II.A.7 in Staglieno Cemetary, Genoa (Commonwealth War Graves Commission, www.cwgc.org).

Mr Tatlow 'referred in very feeling terms to the lamented death while on active service in Italy of Lieutenant Harry Dowse, RAF, the son of their esteemed Rector, and proposed the following Resolution which was recorded by Herbert D. Vaughan, People's churchwarden, and passed in silence, all the members standing:

That we, the members of the Select Vestry ... before adjourning, as a mark of respect and condolence, desire to tender our heartfelt sympathy to Canon and Mrs Dowse and family, on the loss of their dearly loved son Harry, who has given his life in the service of his King and Country in the great world war. We commend them to the unfailing comfort of the God of all Consolation.'

The following Sunday, 17 November, 'Special services of Thanksgiving for the Armistice' were held and the bishop of Cork preached at the 7pm service.

Dr John Dowse, the eldest son of Canon Dowse, a doctor in the Royal Army Medical Corps (RAMC), survived the Great War, aged 27. He was awarded a military cross in 1916 and a Bar in October 1918 (University of Dublin War List 1922).[66] During World War II he became inspector of medical forces in the Middle East, commandant of the RAM College in 1948 and was promoted to the position of major-general. He was a popular and highly respected member of the Council of the British Medical Association and died in 1964.

F.H. Browning, president of the IRFU since 1913, who had asked Geoffrey Downing to form a 'Pals' Company from members of Dublin's rugby clubs, was shot by the IRA at Easter 1916 in Northumberland Road while walking back to Beggars' Bush Barracks with his volunteers (dubbed, by Dubliners, the 'Gorgeous Wrecks', from the 'Georgius Rex' on their armbands). He died of his wounds. Buried in Deansgrange Cemetery, his memorial inscription reads:

'He will live in the memory of all as an honourable comrade and true and distinguished sportsman who by his untiring efforts and splendid patriotism obtained from his corps over 300 recruits for His Majesty's Forces during the Great European War'.[67]

Caricature of Lieutenant John Dowse of the Royal Army Medical Corps, drawn in 1914 by Private Charles Carlin.

Over 21,000 of those who were killed at Gallipoli have no known grave.[68] On the tip of the peninsula today stands the Helles Memorial, which commemorates men from Great Britain, Ireland, India and Australia, including Charles Dowse and Edward Chaytor Millar (Panel 190–196). The memorial is an obelisk, over 30 metres (100 feet) high, and can be seen by ships passing through the Dardenelles (www.battlefields1418.50megs.com). A memorial erected at Anzac Cove in 1934 bears these words of Atatürk, the Turkish leader who led the attack at Gallipoli:

'Those heroes that shed their blood and lost their lives ... You are now lying in
the soil of a friendly country. Therefore rest in peace ... You the mothers who
sent their sons from far away countries, wipe away your tears. Your sons are now
lying in our bosom and are in peace. After having lost their lives on this land
they have become our sons as well' (Morgan 1999).

Another tragic loss of life for a young Monkstown man occurred in 1915 with the death
of Richard McClatchie, Able Seaman 209542 of HMS *Goliath*. In 1914 this ageing battleship
(originally built in 1897 for the China Station, with a shallow enough draught to allow her
to use the Suez Canal) was dispatched to the East Indies for escort duties, but was
transferred to the Dardanelles in April 1915 to support the landings around Cape Helles. In
the early hours of 13 May, while anchored in Morto Bay, a Turkish torpedo-boat destroyer
crept towards the *Goliath*, hidden by a dense fog (Denham 1981; Liddle 1976). At 1.15am
three dull thuds were heard on the *Cornwallis*, another ship anchored some distance away,
and then the cries of men struggling in the water. HMS *Goliath* quickly turned turtle and
sank within two minutes, trapping hundreds of men below. Of her 800 crew, 570 were lost,
including Richard McClatchie from Monkstown (Commonwealth War Graves
Commission, www.cwgc.org).

The diary of a midshipman who survived tells the story vividly; it was published in 1916
under the title *From Dartmouth to the Dardanelles: A midshipman's log edited by his mother*. An
extract reads:

'Some of the midshipmen were already standing on the deck in their pyjamas
... the ship was now heeling about 5 degrees to starboard and I climbed up the
port side. It was nearly pitch dark ... a crowd gathered along the port side "Boat
ahoy! Boat ahoy!" they yelled, but as the ship listed more and more and there
was no sign or sound of any approaching vessel, the men's voices seemed to
get hopeless. Inside the ship everything which was not secured was sliding
about and bringing up against the bulkheads with a series of crashes ... She had
heeled over to about 20 degrees, then she stopped and remained steady for a
few seconds. In the momentary lull the voice of one of our officers rang out
steady and clear as at "divisions", "Keep calm, men. Be British!" Then the ship
started to heel rapidly again and I felt sure there was no chance of saving her.
I turned to jump overboard ... Raising my arms above my head I sprang well
outboard and dived. Just before I struck the water my face hit the side of the
ship. It was a horrid feeling sliding on my face down the slimy side and a
second later I splashed in with tremendous force, having dived about 30 feet.
Just as I was rising to the surface again, a heavy body came down on top of
me. I fought clear and rose rather breathless and bruised.'

The midshipman swam away from the suction of the sinking ship and watched her go
down. He tried to swim towards the *Cornwallis*, but was swept away by a strong current as
he heard the cries of the drowning become fainter. He and several others with him were
eventually spotted by the searchlights of HMS *Lord Nelson* and rescued.

Most members of the Royal Navy who died in action, like Richard McClatchie, have no
known graves. After the 1914–18 war, the Admiralty Committee recommended that three

identical memorials to commemorate these men should be erected at each of the three manning ports in Britain: Chatham, Plymouth and Portsmouth. The name of Richard McClatchie, along with 7,000 other sailors, was cast on a bronze panel (Ref. 9, 6, 5) on the Plymouth Naval Memorial, which stands on the Hoe looking directly across towards Plymouth Sound. An inscription reads:

> IN HONOUR OF THE NAVY AND TO THE ABIDING MEMORY
> OF THOSE RANKS AND RATINGS OF THIS PORT WHO LAID
> DOWN THEIR LIVES IN THE DEFENCE OF THE EMPIRE AND
> HAVE NO OTHER GRAVE THAN THE SEA.

A suitable memorial

In October 1917, at the Dublin Diocesan Synod, John Henry Bernard, archbishop of Dublin, suggested that, 'after the war, a simple dignified tablet' should be placed in every Church of Ireland church. He felt strongly that 'the names of men who fought together and died together, whether they were Churchmen, Methodists, Roman Catholics, or Presbyterians (should) be honoured together'. This was reported in the *Bray & South County Dublin Herald* on 20 October 1917.

On 8 January 1919 the Monkstown Select Vestry discussed the most suitable memorial to the 28 men of their parish who had been killed. Among the possibilities were a brass plate, a new east window and a 'large Celtic Cross in the Church grounds'. In view of the unsettled political situation at the time, it was thought (according to Edith Dowse) that any method of commemoration outside the church, such as a cross in 'The Ring' (the small roundabout in front of the church), ran the risk of being desecrated. Eventually, Richard Caulfeild Orpen was asked to design a War Memorial in the church; at a cost of £175, this took the form of 'a handsome emblazure sculptured in stone and red alabaster, erected on the south wall within the chancel', carved with the names of the 28 young men who died in World War I.

Besides the War Memorial in the church, the parishioners also raised money to endow a bed in Monkstown Hospital in memory of those who had 'made the Great Sacrifice'. A newspaper clipping (undated) admits that, instead of the £500 they needed to endow a bed, 'times being bad and money scarce, they could only raise £300'. This £300 was given to the Hospital Board 'to be used for the good of the hospital' and a ward named 'the Monkstown Ward', which 'would stand as long as the hospital stood as a memorial to those who died'. On 18 November 1921 the archbishop of Dublin, the Most Rev. Dr John Gregg, unveiled a brass mural tablet in the hospital: 'In lasting and loving memory of the men of the Parish and Congregation who gave their lives for King and Country in the Great War, 1914–1918' (Annual Report of Select Vestry, 1921).

At St John's in Mounttown on Sunday 31 October 1920 the dedication took place of a two-light War Memorial window of stained glass (made by Douglas Sons & Co. of Belfast) and a brass plaque, bearing the names of the fifteen young men from the parish who had died in the Great War (*Church of Ireland Gazette*, 19 November 1920). Their names are displayed 'in the order in which they fell'.[69] Both memorials came to Monkstown Church

349

in 1985 when St John's was sold and were reinstalled there. The two-light window was split in two and placed in the north and south transepts, while the brass plaque was set on the west wall of the south gallery, to the left of the window (*see Chapter 8*).

On Remembrance Sunday, 9 November 1958, a War Memorial to the seven parishioners who died in World War II was dedicated in Monkstown Church. Again designed by Richard Caulfeild Orpen, it is a white marble plate mounted on dark limestone and has been placed to the right of the World War I Memorial in the chancel.

On Remembrance Sunday every year, the names of all Monkstown and St John's parishioners who were killed in both world wars are read aloud.

Monkstown's dead: 1914–18

Benjamin Lawrence Birchall
Leslie W. Callaghan
Arthur N. Callaghan
Valentine A.B. Cranwill
Charles W. Darcus
Hugh Cathcart
Henry Harvey Dowse
Charles Edward Dowse
Douglas H.L. Fergusson
James A. Godfrey
Robert Kinston Gray
John C. Hannon
Norman L. Hannon
George W.D. Lawder

Isaac Long
Geoffrey Clogstoun Martin
Richard Archer W. Martin
Edward Chaytor Millar
Henry John Moore
William Morris Dobbs
Richard McClatchie
Robert H.B. McCombie
Harry McCombie
James G. McCormick
John H.G. McCormick
Walter L. Prentice
Alfred G.F. Simms
James R. Stewart

Monkstown's dead: 1939–45

Thomas Edgar Aplin
Robert Joseph Gordon Campbell
Richard Reynolds Irvine
Thelma Daphne Jackson

Robert George Marks
Reginald Vere Massey Odbert
Kenneth Basil Robinson

St John's dead: 1914–18 (listed in the order in which they fell)

Samuels, Lt. A.M.O'D
Homan, Capt. H.L.
Hinds, Lt. R.W.G.
Burgess, Capt. R.B.
Stokes, Pt. A.E.
Morrison, Lt. R.C.
Homan, Pt. C.E.
Worthington-Eyre, Lt. L.G.

Blackmore, J., Second Hand
Dowse, R.H., Chief Engineer
Warren, Pt. W.
Warren, Pt. G.F.
Sutton, Capt. R.T.
McClure, Pt. W.
Milling, QM. Sergt. I.O.

Endnotes

Full details of sources and publications are given in the Select Bibliography.

What they have said about Monkstown Church

1   This information is cited in the booklet on Kilternan Church (1976).
2   Ken Bray (of Weston-Super-Mare) to the Rev. Kevin Dalton, 13 December 1997.

Chapter 1: Origins of Monkstown

1   There is a framed pencil drawing hanging in the Vestry today entitled 'Monkstown Church as opened 19th August 1789', signed by 'A. Downs'. (This date is actually incorrect; the church was consecrated on Sunday 30 August 1789.) On the back of the picture is written, 'Presented to the Young Men's Christian Association at Monkstown by Alexander Downs, who read an Essay on "Monkstown Parish in the Olden Time" at the meeting 7th December 1880'. This essay has, unfortunately, not survived so we have no idea of its content.
2   Christ Church Deed No. 150, *c.* 1294.

Chapter 2: Carrickbrennan Church

1   'Archbishop Bulkeley's Visitation of Dublin, 1630', *Archivium Hibernicum*, Vol. VIII (new series), Maynooth, 1941.
2   In 1615 Henry Cheevers, as the great-great-grandson of Sir John Travers, owned the advowson of Carrickbrennan Church.
3   'Royal Visitation of Dublin, 1615', *Archivium Hibernicum*, Vol. VIII (new series), Maynooth, 1941.
4   A 'perpetual curate' was a post that came into being after the Reformation. It was described as 'perpetual' because the curate's licence could only be revoked by his bishop, and not by his lay rector (patron or owner of the parish) and, in addition, the position could be endowed. Previously, monks had been temporary curates, in unendowed posts.
5   Visitation of Archbishop William King, 8 May 1723, Representative Church Body Library.
6   Order of Council for Changing the Scite [*sic*] of the Church of Monkstown, 1 October 1787, among Monkstown loose papers (1775–1907), Representative Church Body Library.

Chapter 3: Patrons of Monkstown

1   Christ Church Chapter Act 12, Representative Church Body Library.
2   Christ Church Deed No. 51, *c.* 1240: 'Luke, archbishop of Dublin, confirms to the Prior and Canons of the Holy Trinity, Dublin, the church of the Holy Trinity with its cemetery, Klunken [Clonkeen or Kill-of-the-Grange] with the chapel of Karobrenan [Carrickbrennan, or Monkstown], Kylbekenet [*Cill Begnet*, or Dalkey], Killeny [Killiney], Telach [Tullow] and the chapel of Stachlorgan [Stillorgan].'
3   'Royal Visitation of Dublin, 1615', *Archivia Hibernia*, Vol. VIII, 1941.
4   Monkstown loose papers (1775–1907), Representative Church Body Library.

Chapter 4: The Georgian church

1   The reasons for moving the church to a new site were recorded in June 1808, possibly because the book containing the Vestry minutes for the years 1778 to 1804 was missing.
2   Irish Parliamentary Debates, January–September 1785, Vol. IV.
3   Indenture of 30 July 1785 between Lords Longford and de Vesci, the Rev. Philip Tracy and his wife Anne, and the Monkstown churchwardens, Sir John Lees and Ralph Ward.
4   Act of Consecration of 1789 among Monkstown loose papers (1775–1907), Representative Church Body Library.
5   Indenture of 1 July 1806 between Lords Longford and de Vesci, Singleton Harpur (perpetual curate, 1804–15) and the churchwardens, William Browne and John Armit.
6   Letter from Archbishop Robert Fowler to the Rev. Dr William Jephson, 15 August 1789, in Visitations of Dublin and Glendalough (1788–91), Representative Church Body Library.
7   *The Dublin Chronicle*, 3 September 1789; *Walker's Hibernian Magazine*, 1789, p. 502.
8   MacDonnell, H.H.G. 1889, some notes on the Graves family, with thanks to Professor Davis Coakley.

9 For example, in the *Journal of the Royal Society of Antiquaries of Ireland* 1899 and Ball 1902.

10 Archdeacon Charles Lindsay to Archbishop Richard Whately asking permission to hold a second Vestry on 19 April 1836, Monkstown loose papers (1775–1907), Representative Church Body Library.

11 Brian (Bryan) Bolger Papers, National Archives; Vestry minutes of 16 April 1805, 7 April 1806 and 30 March 1807.

12 John Semple's report to the Monkstown Vestry, 1823.

13 The 'Schedule of Books and Documents in Vestry Safe, December 1857' includes the 'Device of the Espinasse pew', but does not indicate its date, Representative Church Body Library (Monkstown Vestry Archives).

Chapter 5: The archbishop and the architect

1 Papers and diaries of Judge Robert Day, *c.* 1780–1839, Royal Irish Academy.

2 John Armit of 'Newtown Park', Blackrock, was a wealthy army agent and banker, as well as secretary of the Ordnance Board (Bence-Jones 1990); he also served as Monkstown's people's churchwarden from 1804–7.

3 Certificate of Notification, dated 31 March 1826, in Monkstown Vestry Minute book 1805–29, Representative Church Body Library (Monkstown Vestry Archives).

4 A careful search by Shirley O'Brien in *Saunders's News-Letter*, the usual newspaper used for such advertisements, up until September 1826 did not turn up Semple's advertisement for estimates.

5 This supposition is supported by the date of the last Vestry meeting in the Vestry room (held on 19 February 1829); thereafter meetings were held in the schoolhouse (24 February, 2 March, 8 April, 20 April and 19 May), presumably because the church itself was unusable owing to construction.

6 The *Evening Packet* of 31 December 1831, reporting on the opening of Semple's church on Christmas Day 1831, said: 'We do not remember ever to have witnessed greater anxiety in worshipping the Lord, than the poorer brethren manifested on Sunday last, when they, for the first time during a period of three years, were accommodated properly; there were fully four hundred poor present'.

7 Entry of February 1825 in Whitechurch Vestry Minute Book 1824–33, Representative Church Body Library.

8 John Armit's letters, dated 7 October and 11 October 1830; among Monkstown loose papers (1775–1907), Representative Church Body Library.

9 According to the Ecclesiastical Commissioners' *Diocese of Dublin: revenues and patronage of benefices, No. 56, Monkstown Union* (1837), the final cost was £9,222 (£4,615 as loan from the Board of First Fruits, £1,200 from the 'late archdeacon of Dublin' [*sic*; this should be the late archbishop of Dublin, i.e. William Magee], and £3,407 raised by private subscription).

Chapter 6: Who designed Monkstown Church?

1 *A list of persons who suffered losses of property in 1798*, National Library (Main Reading Room).

2 *Index to the act or grant books and to original wills of the Dublin Diocese*, Vol. 1 (1270–1800), shows the marriage of John Semple to Mary Russell; the Monkstown Register of Baptisms 1835–48, Marriages 1836–42 and Burials 1835–54 shows that Mary Semple died in 1843, aged 72 (so was born in 1771), Representative Church Body Library (Monkstown Vestry Archives).

3 Memorial of an Indented Deed dated 15 April 1805 between Elizabeth Bryan and John Semple, and Indented Deed of Declaration of Trust dated 17 July 1805 between John Semple and James Edwards (referring to lease above), Registry of Deeds.

4 Monkstown Vestry Minute book 1805–29 gives a list of householders in 1806, with 36 names mentioned, including 'John Semple, 11 acres'.

5 *Edward Semple*, in Burtchaell and Sadleir (eds), *Alumni Dublinenses*: Edward Semple, son of John Semple, architect, 18 on 4 Oct. 1813;
John Semple, in *Dublin Evening Post*, 9 June 1849: 'In the matter of John Semple, College Green … and of Monkstown and Donnybrook … a Bankrupt … The Bankrupt is now about 49 years of age';
James Semple, in *King's Inns Admission Papers, 1607–1867*: James Semple, third son of John Semple of Fairyland, was said to be 33 on 29 July 1838; also in Burtchaell and Sadleir (eds), *Alumni Dublinenses*: James Semple, son of John architectus, was said to be 19 on 3 June 1822; died on 23 July 1869, aged 67;
Mary Semple, in Death certificate, General Register Office: Mary Semple died 24 Oct. 1874, aged 65;
Kate Semple, in Death certificate, General Register Office: Kate Semple died 28 Aug. 1882, aged 68;

Isabella Semple, in St Mary's, Donnybrook Marriage Register: Isabella Semple ('full age') married William Lynar on 22 Oct. 1817.

6   Anyone living in Monkstown parish, whether Protestant, Catholic or 'dissenter', was a parishioner and therefore entitled to attend Vestries called for non-church or secular issues, such as the repair of the roads or supervision of public houses.

7   Suggestion by Stephen Devaney.

8   The 'Reception Committee' received four estimates for the building of the 'King's Room' on 20 July 1821; the banquet for George IV was held there on 23 August (*Ancient Records*, Vol. XVII, pp 397, 402; Annual Register 1821, *Chronicle*, p. 131).

9   The Ecclesiastical Commissioners replaced the Board of First Fruits in 1834.

10   The Marlborough Street premises were the same, but the number changed from 21 to 20.

11   Leaflet issued by Dublin City Archives, entitled *Freedom of the City of Dublin*.

12   *Index to the act or grant books and to original wills of the Dublin Diocese*, Vol. 2 (1800–58).

13   There is no record of Jane's baptism in the Donnybrook Baptismal Registers, which may have been an oversight. However, she was married from 78 Heytesbury Street, her father was listed as John Semple (of same address) and her age at death gives a birth date of *c.* 1844.

14   Donnybrook Baptismal Registers, 1825–36 and 1836–58, Representative Church Body Library.

15   Lady Gilbert 1891–1944, Vol. XIX; *Pettigrew & Oulton Directories*, 1832–43.

16   *King's Inns Admission Papers, 1607–1867*.

17   Death certificate, General Register Office: died on 23 July 1869, at 78 Heytesbury St; *James Semple*, bachelor, 67, barrister; of disease of liver and stomach, about three months uncertified; John Semple of 78 Heytesbury St present at death.

      Death certificate, General Register Office: died on 24 October 1874, at 4 Tivoli Terrace, south; *Mary Semple*, spinster, 65; cause of death: apoplexy, three days certified; informant: Anne Griffith (who could not sign her name) present at death, of 4 Tivoli Tce, S.

      Death certificate, General Register Office: died on 11 October 1880; *Edward Semple*, married, 85, clergyman; died of natural causes, six months uncertified; William Gibson of Kesh present at death.

      Death certificate, General Register Office: died on 28 August 1882, at 4 Tivoli Tce; *Catherine Semple*, spinster, 68, lady; of disease of stomach, four weeks certified; Sarah Argue of 4 Tivoli Tce present at death.

18   Death certificate, General Register Office: died on 15 October 1882, at 6 Ontario Terrace, Portabello; *John Semple*, widower, 81, civil engineer; cause of death: age and contusions from fall, 28 days certified, bed sores, 14 days certified; informant: John George Semple, son, present at death, of 6 Ontario Terrace, Portabello.

19   *Memorial inscriptions of Deansgrange Cemetery*, Vol. 4, South Section, 2000.

20   Information from staff at Mount Jerome Cemetery.

21   Marriage certificate, General Register Office: at the parish church of St Peter in the City of Dublin, on 5 July 1870; Henry Thomas Brownrigg, full age, bachelor, Esq., MD; of 40 Sandford Rd, father: Henry Thomas Brownrigg, merchant, to Jane Semple, full age, spinster, of 78 Hetesbury St, father: John Semple, C.E.

22   Death certificate, General Register Office: died on 17 September 1873, at 40 Sandford Rd, Henry Thomas Brownrigg, married, 29, physician, surgeon and apothecary; paralysis, three days certified; T.H. Brownrigg of 40 Sandford Rd present at death.

23   Death certificate, General Register Office: died on 15 September 1920, at 2 Marine Tce; James Charles Semple, married, 69, gentleman; of carcinoma of colon, cardiac failure, eight hours certified.

24   Marriage certificate, General Register Office: Meta Larella Staunton (daughter of Charles Frederick Staunton, gent, of Hybla, 18 York Rd, Kingstown) married James Charles Semple, widower, architect & C.E., son of John Semple, architect & C.E., on 27 June 1919, in Monkstown Church. Meta Semple died 22 April 1936, aged 64, of heart failure, buried in grave A25-274, Mount Jerome.

25   Christ Church Chapter Minute Books, Vol. XI, Representative Church Body Library.

26   The *Cork Examiner*, 7 June 1844, reports the investigation by Sir William Lynar, RM, while attending the Birr Sessions, of the murder of James Stapleton, 1 June 1844. The *Evening Packet*, 5 February 1845, reports the investigation into the murder of Captain McLeod, RM, by Sir William and four other magistrates.

27   Craig (1990), McDermott (1990) and Allen (1993) all credit John Semple, Junior, as the more important of the two architects; Scott Richardson considers the older Semple as more important, possibly because

of the Tarragona link (which compares Semple's diaphragm arches in Kilternan Church with those of the Cistercian monastery at Poblet, near Tarragona in Spain).

28 There are several glebe houses among the Semple drawings of church buildings, Representative Church Body Library.

29 *Dublin Penny Journal*, account of Simmons-Court Church.

30 Quoted by Henry Hill in his Notebook, No. 1, Cork Public Museum.

31 Dictionary of National Biography, Vol. XIII; File on James Cavanah Murphy in 'The Alfred Jones Biographical Index', Irish Architectural Archive.

32 Study of the Vestry minutes for the parish of Wexford, 1662–1871, Vol. 32, revealed that a Vestry called on 13 April 1824 resolved that the building committee for the proposed new church in Selskar Churchyard was to meet 'the Architect of the Board of First Fruits' (i.e. John Semple). A gift of £900 and a loan of £600 had already been granted. The church opened by 17 April 1827. I am grateful to Patrick Farrell who suggested that Selskar was a Semple church.

33 Semple drawings of church buildings, Representative Church Body Library.

34 Letter, dated 11 February 1825, written on behalf of the archbishop by his son, the Rev. Thomas Percival Magee, to the Vestry of Whitechurch: 'I write his Grace's final determination about Whitechurch from which his Grace *will not alter* "accommodation for Three Hundred sittings below and a *capability of a Gallery* …" ' [original emphasis]. Whitechurch Vestry Minute Book 1824–33, Representative Church Body Library.

Chapter 7: McCurdy's chancel and other changes

1 Letter to author from Patrick Farrell, 11 September 2000.

2 This estimate was found on a single sheet among the Vestry archives; Thom's Dublin Directory of 1858 lists 'John Lynch, builder, 22 Richmond St, S'.

3 Monkstown loose papers (1775–1907), Representative Church Body Library.

4 Architects' drawings of churches, Portfolio 15, Representative Church Body Library.

5 *The Irish Builder*, 15 September 1885, p. 256; File Mc46 (John McCurdy) in 'The Alfred Jones Biographical Index', Irish Architectural Archive.

6 Ralph Harden in his 1911 book *St John's, Monkstown* [Mounttown] quotes the Rev. John Lynch as saying on 21 December 1868, 'Several of our friends have expressed a wish to see the lower part of the Chancel below the window-sills, plastered and painted in some way similar to the Chancels of the Parish Church [i.e. Monkstown] and the Mariners' with a text of Scripture going around at the head'.

7 File D93 (Thomas Drew) in 'The Alfred Jones Biographical Index', Irish Architectural Archive.

8 *Irish Builder and Engineer,* Jubilee Number, 1909; memorial brass to Sir Thomas Drew in Christ Church Cathedral.

9 Death certificates, General Register Office: Thomas Drew, 71, knight; cause of death: operation and heart failure. William Mansfield Mitchell, 67, architect; cause of death: arteriosclerosis two years, cardiac degeneration six months.

10 *Irish Builder*, Vol. XXIII, No. 525, p. 317, 1 November 1881.

11 Vestry minutes of 6 March 1946, 10 April 1946, 8 May 1946, 18 September 1946, 9 October 1946 and 12 February 1947.

Chapter 8: Stained-glass windows

1 Marriage settlement of Ellen Jordan and William C. Garner, 31 August 1847, from will of Richard Jordan (d. 15 November 1854), National Archives.

2 Dublin directories, 1854.

3 *King's Inns Admission Papers, 1607–1867.*

4 Dublin directories, 1858.

5 Will of William Cathcart Garner, late of Richview, d. 3 October 1875, National Archives.

Chapter 9: The Monkstown organs

1 1862 plan of chancel by Welland and Gillespie shows position of organ and fireplace, Monkstown loose papers (1775–1907), Representative Church Body Library.

2 Vestry Minute Book 1847–1924, Mariners' Church, Kingstown, Representative Church Body Library.

3 Letter dated 31 October 1965 from R.E. Meates to E.G. Barton, in private collection of W.G. Ebbs.

4   William Morgan, FRCO, to the Rev. Kevin Dalton, 7 April 1997: Richard Benson was born in 1849 in Dublin. He died in 1922 in Norwich, aged 73. A month or so earlier his youngest daughter, Elizabeth, had given birth to her fifth child, Robert Runcie, later archbishop of Canterbury.

5   Will of William Telford, died 31 January 1885, effects £3,038-15s-6d, National Archives.

6   According to Barton's *The Parish of Monkstown* (written *c.* 1950s and in the private collection of W.G. Ebbs), Gray & Davison built other Dublin organs, including St Bartholomew's; the Chapel Royal, Dublin Castle; Christ Church; Rathgar; Kirwan House (now in Crumlin Church); Christchurch, Leeson Park; and the Mariners' Church in Kingstown.

7   Letters from E.G. Barton to Mr Mackenzie, dated 23 October 1953 and 13 November 1954.

8   Letter from E.G. Barton to Mr Mackenzie, dated 25 October 1954.

9   Letter from Chas. Lythgoe of Rushworth & Dreaper Ltd, Organ Builders, of Liverpool to Mr William Ebbs, Monkstown organist, dated 30 December 1964.

10   Letter from R.E. Meates to Mr E.G. Barton, dated 1 October 1965.

Chapter 10: The Knox Memorial Hall

1   Private collection, Knox family tree.

2   Between 1800 and 1853, out of 76 Knox marriages twelve were to other Knoxs, according to the *Index to the act or grant books and to original wills of the Dublin Diocese* (1899).

3   *King's Inns Admission Papers, 1607–1867.*

4   *Burke's Irish Family Records*, 5th edition, 1976.

5   Will of Edward Chaloner Knox, Probate 3 June 1896.

6   An undated slip of paper, handwritten in pencil and found in the Select Vestry book of 1890–1905, states: 'The erection of a P.H. [parochial hall] this year in com. of the D.J. [Diamond Jubilee] of her Majesty Q.V. was then discussed and postponed for further par. [particulars] to be obtained and laid before the Select Vestry.'

7   Entry on Richard Chaytor Millar in Irish Architectural Archive Biographical Index of Irish Architects (database).

8   Arms of Knox, National Library (Manuscripts Section).

9   Gravestone 19/K1/S in Deansgrange Cemetery.

10   'The Friendly Room', *St Patrick's News*, Monkstown Parish, No. 11, April 1980.

11   SPADE stands for 'St Paul's Area Development Enterprise'.

12   Information from Mrs Cecil Wynne.

Chapter 11: Incumbents and curates

1   *The Irish Times* of 27 February 1901 reported some 400 mourners at the funeral of George Francis Fitzgerald. Among those who attended were the Church of Ireland and the Roman Catholic archbishops of Dublin; Lord Plunkett represented the lord lieutenant; the lord chancellor; the provost of Trinity; Dr John Pentland Mahaffy; and Sir Howard Grubb. Members of TCD Boat Club carried the coffin into Trinity Chapel and other students carried it to the hearse, which proceeded to Mount Jerome for the burial.

2   *Irish Ecclesiastical Gazette*, 20 November 1866.

3   Information from the Rev. Kevin Dalton.

4   The rest of Irving Caesar's lyrics also apply to Billy Wynne: 'I'm a very ordinary man, trying to work out life's happy plan. Doing unto others as I'd like to have doing unto me. When I find a very lonely soul, to be kind becomes my only goal. I feel so much better when I tell them my philosophy: I want to be happy …'

5   Information from Mrs Cecil Wynne.

6   Monkstown loose papers (1775–1907), Representative Church Body Library.

7   Visitation of Archbishop William King, 8 May 1723, Representative Church Body Library.

8   Indenture between the archbishop of Dublin, William King, and the Rev. Allan Maddison, dated 8 November 1728.

9   'Royal Visitation of Dublin, 1615', *Archivium Hibernicum*, Vol. VIII (new series), Maynooth, 1941 (*Clonkine alias Grange. Owinus Ellis curatus. Ecclesia et cancella bene*, 'Clonkeen alias Grange. Owen Ellis curate. Church and chancel in good repair'); 'Archbishop Bulkeley's Visitation of Dublin, 1630', *Archivium Hibernicum*, Vol. VIII (new series), Maynooth, 1941.

10   House of Commons Journal, Vol. XI, Petition No. 69 (petition to parliament in 1785 for £1,000 for the new church 'of the United Parishes of Monkstown and Kill').

11   Visitations of Dublin and Glendalough, Representative Church Body Library.

Chapter 13: The role of the Vestry

1   'From an act to … amend the laws which regulate the levy and application of church rates and parish cess', 7° Georgii IV, Chap. 72, 31 May 1826.

2   25° Geo III, Chap. 50, Sect. 3.

3   Visitations in the diocese of Kildare by Bishop Charles Lindsay (1804–8), Representative Church Body Library.

4   The Queen v. churchwardens of Monkstown, Pembroke Estate Papers, National Archives.

Chapter 14: Monkstown's churchwardens

1   Churchwardens' accounts, 1813 in Vestry Minute book of 1805–29, Representative Church Body Library (Monkstown Vestry Archives).

2   Vestry Minute book of 1871–present (Easter Vestry), 1 April 1921, Representative Church Body Library (Monkstown Vestry Archives).

3   The first female churchwarden in Ireland was elected in 1954, in Donaghadee parish, Co. Down (*Church of Ireland Gazette*, 21 May 1954).

4   Blackrock Association, Minute Book … 1782–97, National Library (Manuscripts Section).

5   Information from Mrs Cecil Wynne: descent traced through Wallace's *Clergy of Dublin and Glendalough* (2001) *and Burke's Peerage and Baronetage*, Vol. II, 106th edition, 1999.

6   Catalogue of Manuscripts, La Touche gifts, Trinity College, Dublin (Manuscripts Department).

7   Library Minute Book, containing entries on gifts of Persian letters and manuscripts from William Digges La Touche, Trinity College, Dublin (Manuscripts Department).

8   Stewart-Watson Almanacks of 1793–1803 record that William D. La Touche was on the Grand Canal Company's court of directors, deputy chairman in 1794 and chairman in 1795 and 1800.

9   The Rev. James Dunn published parts of this sermon in 1804 under the title *Extract from a sermon, preached at Monkstown church, the Sunday after the death of William La Touche, Esq.*

10   Register of Baptisms 1835–48, Marriages 1836–42 and Burials 1835–54 records that Harriette Betham, 32, of Rockford House, Monkstown, was buried 18 October 1853, Representative Church Body Library (Monkstown Vestry Archives).

11   Ball (1902) says that Betham died at Stradbrook, while both Phair (1972) and Betham's obituary (in the *Gentleman's Magazine*, Vol. 40, December 1853) state '… at his residence, Rochfort [*sic*] House, Blackrock'. The burial entries in the Monkstown register for both Sir William and his daughter, Harriette, give 'Rockford House' as their address.

12   On 11 February 1789 a letter was read in parliament, part of which read: '… (among) names either fictitious or of Persons irregularly placed on the (payment) Lists were three servants of Mr. Ward …', in the *Journal of the House of Commons*, 1789–90, Vol. XIII, Appendix CXLVI.

Chapter 15: Parish officers

1   'A List of the several Families, in the Parish of Monks Town and its United Parishes … dated March the fifth, 1766 — by the Revd. Mr. Thomas Heany, the Parish Minister, Appendix D.', contained in *The Register of the Union of Monkstown, Co. Dublin, 1669–1786* (Guinness 1908).

2   I am grateful to Rob Goodbody, who has noticed, among some nineteenth-century architectural drawings, two cow houses with narrow doorways, one only 3 feet wide. He queries, 'Perhaps 19th-century cattle were slimmer?'

3   Information from former occupant of house overlooking the pound in Stepaside.

4   Dr Clement Taylor, according to his gravestone in Carrickbrennan, was the last surviving son of his widowed mother and 'fell a victim to malignant fever'.

5   'On the nineteenth of Novr 1807, the ship Rochdale and the ship the Prince of Wales were wrecked off the Coast near Sea Point & Black Rock and on the Sunday and week after 104 Bodies were buried in Monkstown Church yard — and 6 in Dalkey Church yard', Register of Baptisms 1804–31, Marriages 1805–27 and Burials 1805–27, Representative Church Body Library (Monkstown Vestry Archives).

Chapter 16: Schools of the parish

1   Visitation of Archbishop William King, 8 May 1723, Representative Church Body Library.

2   Curiously, the ground leases for the church and school are more than 100 years apart: that for the church dates from 1806 and for the school 1915. The Select Vestry minutes of 10 May 1961 record: 'Letter from Messrs. Stewart and Sons, Leinster St., Dublin, Agents for Lord Longford and De Vesci Estates, confirming that ground for the building of Monkstown church was leased on 1st July 1806 for ever, free of rent; also that ground, on which the school stands, was leased on 10th September 1915 to the Diocesan Board of Education for a term of 900 years, subject to a yearly rent of one shilling'.

3   Information from the 'Parochial Returns', in Appendix 22 (pp 596–7) of the Commissioners of the Irish Education Inquiry, *Irish Education Inquiry, Second Report*, 1826.

4   Monkstown Boys' and Girls' National Schools, records of (ED9/25516), National Archives.

5   D'Alton in his *History of the County of Dublin* (1838) says that 205 children attended Monkstown school in 1834, which was 'assisted by £12 from the National Board and £8 from the RC priest'.

6   Monkstown Boys' and Girls' National Schools, records of (ED9/22230), National Archives.

7   Miss Elizabeth Bradley had taught for 11½ years in the Infants' School before she was made principal.

8   The building of Tullow Church is reported in the *Dublin Builder* of 1 November 1860; the church was consecrated on 14 April 1864, as reported in the *Irish Ecclesiastical Gazette* of 20 April 1864.

Chapter 17: A wealthy and generous parish

1   Stewart's Dublin Directory of 1802 mentions that children of the poor were vaccinated free 'in the evenings during April and September at the Dispensary for the Infant Poor', 26 Exchequer St (opened 1800), while Thom's Directory of 1853 records 'on Tuesdays and Fridays (11–3) at the Cowpock Institution', 67 Upper Sackville St (opened 1804).

2   Letter from minister and churchwardens of Monkstown to Kingstown Harbour Commssioners, asking for contribution to the Poor Fund, Minutes and Correspondence of Kingstown Harbour Commssioners (1815–36), National Archives.

3   Lord and Lady Anglesey's complicated matrimonial situation resulted in seventeen children between them. Both had been married before and had then eloped with each other and married in 1810, following a duel, a celebrated court case and divorces from their respective partners. In addition to Lord Anglesey's eight children by his first wife and Lady Anglesey's four children by her first husband, the couple had five children with each other.

4   1845 Annual Report of Monkstown Protestant Orphan Society in Haliday Pamphlets Collection, Royal Irish Academy.

5   Annual Reports of Select Vestry, 1870, 1876 and 1911.

6   1846 Report of Monkstown Parochial Union Benefit Society in Haliday Pamphlets Collection, Royal Irish Academy.

7   Annual Reports of Select Vestry, 1869, 1884 and 1903.

8   'Foundling Hospital and Workhouse, 1704', *The Irish Builder*, 15 August 1897.

Chapter 19: Parish organisations

1   Select Vestry Reports for the years 1881, 1896, 1901 and 1911.

2   Address in January 1859 to the Rev. Thomas Rooke on his resignation, signed by 38 Sunday School teachers.

3   Hand-written autobiography of the Rev. Arthur Stewart, with thanks to his daughter, Margaret, and her husband, Professor David Ride.

4   1856 Catalogue in Haliday Pamphlets Collection, Royal Irish Academy.

5   Easter Vestry minutes of 25 April 1946; Select Vestry minutes of 8 September 1946.

Chapter 20: Carrickbrennan Graveyard and the resurrection men

1   Register of Baptisms 1835–48, Marriages 1836–42 and Burials 1835–54, Representative Church Body Library (Monkstown Vestry Archives).

2   Monkstown loose papers (1775–1907), Representative Church Body Library.

3   The date of 1874 is given by English (1987). But Carrickbrennan Graveyard may have been closed earlier: the *Kingstown and Bray Observer* of 25 February 1871 reported that at a meeting of the guardians

of Rathdown Union, 'A communication was read respecting the closing up of Monkstown and other overcrowded burial places in the union …'.

4   *St Patrick's News*, Monkstown parish, September, November and December 1984; June and October 1985.

5   Charles Haliday lived at 'Monkstown Park', now the Christian Brothers' College (CBC) on Mounttown Road, Upper, just around the corner from Carrickbrennan Graveyard.

Chapter 21: Of monuments and mourning

1   *The Cyclopaedian Magazine and Dublin Monthly Register*, September 1808, pp 481–3.

2   Homan Potterton, in his *Irish church monuments* (1975), gives Thomas Kirk's date of birth as 1781; in the Dictionary of National Biography, based on information from his son, Joseph, the date given is 1777.

3   During their restoration of Christ Church Cathedral (1870–7) the architects, Street and Drew, moved the monuments down to the crypt (*Irish Builder*, 15 February 1886, p. 59).

4   *Index to the act or grant books and to original wills of the Dublin Diocese*, Vol. 2 (1800–58).

5   'Boys at Play', a portrait of four of the sons of Thomas Kirk, RHA, by George F. Mulvaney, RHA (on loan from the RHA), can be seen in the ESB Museum.

6   Christ Church Chapter Act Books, Vol. 12, Representative Church Body Library.

7   'Architects who were members of Masonic Lodges', from the Librarian, Masonic Hall, Molesworth Street, Dublin.

8   Dictionary of National Biography, Vol. XI, pp 203–4.

9   Conveyance, dated 14 March 1830, between the Venerable Archdeacon Charles Lindsay, Fenton Hort and John Murphy, Esqs (churchwardens), and Benedict Arthure, Esq.

10   Information from Eric Mackenzie.

11   Letters from the Air-Raid Precautions Officer, 9 August and 27 December 1940.

Chapter 22: 'They are not dead but sleepeth'

1   *Index to the act or grant books and to original wills of the Dublin Diocese* (1899) gives 'Anna Hickson', whereas William Cox's obituary, in the *Gentleman's Magazine* (Vol. 217, July–December 1864), says he married 'the youngest daughter of the late Robert Dixon, Esq. of Dingle, Co. Kerry'.

2   Judge Robert Day had four close relatives called Edward Day, who were also clergy: his younger son, his eldest brother (the archdeacon of Ardfert), his uncle (the rector of Tralee) and his grand-nephew (the rector of Sligo).

3   Copy of the Rev. Benjamin Domvile's settlement made on his intermarriage with Anna-Maria Pocklington, dated 9 April 1768, National Library (Manuscripts Section).

4   Benjamin Domvill [*sic*], Will and Grant 1774, National Archives.

5   Benjamin Domvile to Sir W. Lee, 17 December 1772, National Archives.

6   The inscription 'Psalm CXL.VII.V' on the wall memorial should actually read 'Psalm CXL.V.VII', indicating Psalm 140, verse 7.

7   *Index to the act or grant books and to original wills of the Dublin Diocese*, Vol. 2 (1800–58), records the marriage licence of the Rev. Thomas Goff and Anne Caulfield in 1826; will of Anne Goff, late of 'Carriglea'.

8   Confirmation of arms to the descendants of the Rev. Thomas Goff and Anne Caulfield, and to his son, Thomas William Goff, of Oakport, Co. Roscommon, 7 January 1861, National Library (Manuscripts Section).

9   Dictionary of National Biography, Vol. X.

10   Dublin street directories, 1855 and 1864.

11   'A Record of the Allocations of All the pews in the Parish Church for the year ending on Easter Monday the 28th March 1864', Pew Allocation book, 1863–4, Representative Church Body Library (Monkstown Vestry Archives).

12   It is also possible that Alma Road was called after the solicitor and developer Thomas Alma, according to Pearson (1998).

13   Will of William Digges Latouche [*sic*], National Archives.

14   *Alumni Cantabrigienses*, compiled by J.A. Venn, Part II (1752–1900), Vol. IV, Cambridge, 1951.

15   Dictionary of National Biography, Vol. XI.

16   Letter to Miss H. Lees, 1861, Representative Church Body Library.

17   Extract from the obituary of Archbishop Magee in the *Christian Examiner*, Vol. XI, January–December 1831.

18   Licence of Charles Lindsay, Monkstown loose papers (1775–1907), Representative Church Body Library.

19   Papers and diaries of Judge Robert Day, *c.* 1780–1839, Royal Irish Academy.

20   Letter from Anne Lindsay, 21 March 1857, Representative Church Body Library (Monkstown Vestry Archives).

21   Kingstown Harbour Commissioners, *Minutes and Correspondence of, 1815–36*, National Archives.

22   Beaufort was later asked to arbitrate on the width of the entrance to Kingstown Harbour; Rennie's suggested 430 feet was enlarged to 800 feet.

23   Letter to William Hyde Wollaston, published in 1847 in autobiography of Sir John Barrow (Friendly 1977).

24   *Burke's Irish Family Records*, 5th edition, 1976.

25   Oliver had laid the foundation stone for this church on 18 July 1832, recorded in 'Historical Annals of Dublin' in Thom's Dublin Directory 1833.

26   Mother Teresa speaking at St Paul's Cathedral Parish Hall, Calcutta, to mark the centenary of the Leprosy Mission, from a Church of Ireland press release, 28 January 1974, Leprosy Mission pack, Representative Church Body Library.

27   Service sheet for dedication of plaque to Mission of Lepers in Monkstown Church on 20 March 1960, Leprosy Mission pack, Representative Church Body Library.

28   Order of Service, Leprosy Mission pack, Representative Church Body Library.

29   Church of Ireland press release, 16 April 1974, Leprosy Mission pack, Representative Church Body Library.

30   Centenary Thanksgiving Service, Order of Service, Leprosy Mission pack, Representative Church Body Library.

31   Dr John Crampton (1819) wrote, 'With the exception of (Dr Harvey) and myself, all those concerned in the attendance on the patients caught the disease … none of the nurses, none of the porters, barbers, or those occupied in … tending on the sick escaped …'.

32   *Index to the act or grant books and to original wills of the Dublin Diocese* (1899): Jane died aged 85 in 1889 (wall tablet), so was born *c.* 1804.

33   *Saunders's News-Letter* of 19 September 1857 reported that Miss S. Plant won first prize in the Monkstown Archery Club's competition for lady members ('a gold necklet, with arrow pendant and turquoise feathers, made by Mr. Johnson of Suffolk St.').

34   Register of Baptisms 1835–48, Marriages 1836–42 and Burials 1835–54, Representative Church Body Library (Monkstown Vestry Archives).

35   Kirkpatrick Archive, Royal College of Physicians of Ireland. According to Kirkpatrick and the obituary in *The Medical Press and Circular*, 10 November 1875, William Plant was born in 1790. But his wall memorial in Monkstown Church states that he was 87 years of age when he died, which would make his date of birth 1788. Unfortunately, there are no other readily available sources of information to verify the date.

36   *Royal Harbour of George IV Commissioners' Transactions, 1826*, National Archives (OPW I/8/6/4).

37   *Minutes and Correspondence of the Kingstown Harbour Commissioners, 1815–36*, National Archives (OPW 1/8/6/5).

38   *Royal Harbour of George IV Commissioners' Transactions, 1826*, National Archives (OPW8/KIN/1091(10, 11)).

39   Will of William Plant, National Archives.

40   Mariners' Church, Kingstown, Vestry Minute Book, 1847–1924, Representative Church Body Library.

41   Martha Eleanor Stewart, daughter of Richard B. Warren, QC, died 4 May 1865. A memorial window was erected in her memory in the Mariners' Church, Kingstown, in 1867 (*Irish Builder*, 15 April 1867).

42   Private collection, Smyly family tree; memorial brass in Christ Church Cathedral, Dublin.

43   Information from Professor and Mrs W.D.L. Ride (Margaret Ride is the daughter of the Rev. Arthur Stewart, the eldest son of Robert Warren Stewart).

44   Private collection, Arthur Stewart's hand-written autobiography (unpublished).

45   Letter to author from W.J. Smyly, 9 March 2002.

46   The name of the 'Dublin University Fukien Mission' changed in 1952 to the 'Dublin University Far Eastern Mission'.

47   Letter to author from W.J. Smyly, sometime journalist in Hong Kong, who while there met Evan

Stewart, the youngest surviving member of the Stewart family, a distinguished officer in the Hong Kong Volunteer Force during the battle for Hong Kong in 1942 and later colonel of the regiment.

48   The Elliott Home is now incorporated into 'Glensilva', Monkstown, along with the other 'Mrs Smyly's Homes' of the Bird's Nest, Boys' Home and Children's Fold.

49   Mariners' Church, Kingstown, papers, 1838–1978, Representative Church Body Library.

50   Monkstown Preachers' book 1894–1912 records the 11.30am service on Sunday, 8 September 1895; the normal Sunday collection for the 11.30 service was between £5 and £8. Representative Church Body Library (Monkstown Vestry Archives).

51   Monkstown Preachers' book 1894–1912, Representative Church Body Library (Monkstown Vestry Archives).

52   If this information is correct, Jim would have been only fourteen or fifteen years old, a very young age to sit the matric.

53   From Arthur Stewart's unpublished autobiography (private collection). James Stewart's obituary (CMS, 1916) adds that he was ordained in 1904 by the bishop of Winchester, served as curate at St James, Shirley, Hants, until 1907 when he left for China.

54   Prospectus of the James R. Stewart Memorial Fellowship, International Institute for Rural Reconstruction (Maria Berl Lee). Information from Professor and Mrs W.D.L. Ride.

55   Church Missionary Gleaner, 1 March 1916; The Irish Times, 'Ireland's Roll of Honour', 23 January 1916; Ireland's Memorial Records, 1914–18, Dublin, 1923.

56   The family were notified on 24 January 1919; information from Margaret Ride (daughter of Arthur Stewart) and Prof. David Ride.

57   Monkstown Preachers' book July 1912–December 1934, Representative Church Body Library (Monkstown Vestry Archives).

58   The London Times, 18 and 20 November 1902, and 9, 10 and 11 November 1903.

59   Browning was also a half-back for Dublin University in 1888–9, 1889–90 and 1890–1, and for Wanderers, and an international cricketer who scored two half-centuries against the 1905 Australians in College Park (Morgan 1999).

60   Notice in The Irish Times on 11 September 1914: 'Young Men of Dublin, Your King and Country Call You. Comrades in Peace, Comrades in War. Dublin Men, serve with Your Friends …'

61   Richard Victor Dowse was called 'Victor' because he was born in the year of Queen Victoria's Diamond Jubilee; he was always known as Victor or Vic, never Richard (information from Mrs Elizabeth Sharp-Paul).

62   The Dowse family believe that Harry would have been ordained into the ministry of the Church of Ireland.

63   Letter, dated 17 August 1915, from Lance-Corporal Norman Brown, son of the Rev. John Irwin Brown. Before the war he had been assistant professor of modern languages at Beirut College in Syria. He wrote a graphic account of his single day in action, advancing under shrapnel fire with 'men falling all around'.

64   Colonel Downing's letter to his wife was sent to the Irish Times by his friend, F.H. Browning.

65   Letter to author from Mrs Elizabeth Sharp-Paul, daughter of Richard Victor Dowse and niece of Miss Edith Dowse, 2 December 2002.

66   'For conspicuous bravery in France while evacuating wounded under heavy artillery and machine-gun fire', obituary of Major-General J.C.A. Dowse, with thanks to Mrs Elizabeth Sharp-Paul.

67   Grave U 27, Memorial inscriptions of Deansgrange Cemetery, Vol. 4, South Section, 2000.

68   Of the 21,000 killed at Gallipoli, 18,985 were sailors, soldiers and marines from the United Kingdom, 248 soldiers were from Australia and 1,530 soldiers were from the Indian Army.

69   Inside the front cover of the copy of Harden's St John's (1911) in the Representative Church Body Library is a notice announcing the 'Unveiling of the War Memorial'.

Appendices

Appendix 1: Other churches in Monkstown parish

1   Letter from the Rev. Ronald MacDonnell to Mr Samuels of the Representative Church Body on 11 June 1866, stating that 'Mr. Slater [*sic*, referring to Charles Sleator, perpetual curate of Killiney] ... was acting on his own responsibility — I had told him verbally, and stated on paper, that I would be glad if he could convert his chapel of ease into a district parochial church, but I did not believe he could', Monkstown loose papers (1775–1907), Representative Church Body Library.

Appendix 2: Specifications of the Monkstown organs

1   R.E. Meates to Mr E.G. Barton, 31 October 1965, in private collection of W.G. Ebbs.

2   Private collection (W.G. Ebbs).

3   1898 Dedication Service Sheet, with specification of organ, in private collection of W.G. Ebbs.

4   1966 Service Sheet, with specification of Meates's rebuild, in private collection of W.G. Ebbs.

Appendix 4: Monkstown's churchwardens

1   Colonel Prowse had replaced Colonel William Browne by 20 October 1808, according to an advertisement for a charity sermon in the *Freeman's Journal*.

2   Names of the 1861 churchwardens discovered on letter to Archbishop Richard Whately about chancel, 19 March 1862, Monkstown loose papers (1775–1907), Representative Church Body Library.

3   According to the address presented to Chancellor Dowse on his retirement, William Tatlow had replaced Mr Jameson by 1 October 1829.

4   *Monkstown Review* records Mitchell (P) instead of Greville.

Appendix 7: Gifts and memorials to Monkstown Church

1   *Church of Ireland Gazette*, 10 December 1932; Annual Report, 1932.

Chronology

This chronology deals with events, both major and minor, in the history of Monkstown, its churches and further afield. The Vestry minutes provide the main source of events to do with the church and quotations from them are included below.

600–700	Approximate dates for St Mochonna.
798	Sacking of the monastery on Inis Patrick by Vikings.
1030	Church of the Holy and Undivided Trinity (forerunner of Christ Church Cathedral) founded by Sitric, Norse king of Dublin, and Donatus (Dúnán), the first bishop of Dublin.
1139	Founding of the Abbey of the Blessed Virgin Mary (St Mary's Abbey) by the Benedictines.
1147	St Mary's Abbey becomes Cistercian.
1163	Laurence O'Toole invites the Canons Regular of St Augustine, an Arrouasian order, to take over the Church of the Holy Trinity, which becomes a priory.
1171	Lands of Carrickbrennan confirmed to St Mary's Abbey by Henry II.
1172	The Normans invade Ireland.
1174	Henry II confirms all grants made to St Mary's before the arrival of the Normans.
1178	Kill-of-the-Grange (Clonkeen), Tullow and Killiney granted to the Priory of the Holy and Undivided Trinity.
1185	Carrickbrennan, with its chapel and tithes, confirmed to St Mary's Abbey by King John.
1189	The chapel of Carrickbrennan, with its tithes and liberty to present a chaplain, confirmed to St Mary's Abbey by Pope Clement III.
1219	The church of Kill-of-the-Grange given to Ralph de Bristol, the prebendary of Clonkeen (one of the prebends of the new cathedral of St Patrick's), with 40 marks.
1220	Ralph de Bristol claims the tithes of the grange of Monkstown and also those of lands close to it. The monks of St Mary's agree to pay de Bristol half a mark of silver each year and five marks for his legal expenses.
1240	Archbishop Luke of Dublin substitutes Ballymore for Kill-of-the-Grange, so that the latter becomes the sole property of Holy Trinity (later Christ Church). Archbishop Luke confirmed to the Priory of Holy Trinity the churches of Kill-of-the-Grange, with the chapels of Monkstown, Dalkey, Killiney, Tully and Stillorgan.
1294	In a taxation of the diocese of Dublin, it is noted that the 'temporalities [property] of the monks at Kylmohennok [Kill Mohonnóc] waste, and of same monks at Karrygbrekane [Carrickbrennan] nothing on account of war; chapel there not sufficient for a chaplain'.
1307	The chapel of Carrickbrennan confirmed to St Mary's Abbey by Pope Clement V.
1312	William, abbot of St Mary's, his monks and servants, pardoned by the Crown for having negotiated with Irish enemies of the king to obtain restitution of goods carried away from the granges of the abbey at Monkstown and Bullock.
1343–6	The accounts of John Comyn, seneschal of Christ Church, and of John Chamburleyn, bailiff, indicate a busy, well-organised manor at Clonkeen (Kill-of-the-Grange), where life went on as normally as possible in spite of the ever-present threat of raids by the 'wild Irish': carpenters (2d a day), smiths, ploughmen (1d a day), blacksmiths, builders, farmers, etc. were all employed, as well as 'two men watching for two nights on the mountain top for fear of the Irish, 4d'. Similar situation prevails around the grange of Monkstown, run by the monks of St Mary's.
1346	Account roll of the Priory of the Holy Trinity notes, 'Shoes for Andrew keeping the tithes at Karrybrenan, 8d'.
	St Mary's Abbey is granted the right to tolls from fishing boats at Bullock.

1348–9	The Black Death appears in Ireland.
1349	Abbot of St Mary's volunteers to equip and maintain two mailed horsemen and six light horsemen (*hobellers*) near Monkstown, to support the garrison at Bray.
1363	William and Walter Walfre sued by the abbot of St Mary's for destroying the lands of Monkstown granted to them.
1370	An argument occurs about the right of Thomas Minot, the archbishop of Dublin, to visit the St Mary's group of churches in his diocese, including Carrickbrennan.
1372	The monks of St Mary's concede and agree to obey the archbishop and pay him six marks of silver a year.
1390	Stillorgan 'burned and laid waste by adjoining enemies of the mountains'.
1415	The manor of Carrickbrennan, which had been seized by the Crown for 'all felonies, conspiracies and transgressions', is restored to St Mary's.
1430	Booterstown 'destroyed, burned and devastated'.
1488	Monkstown, with Dalkey, Booterstown, Kill-of-the-Grange and Bullock, said to be within the Pale by an act of parliament.
1539	Dissolution of the Monasteries by Henry VIII throughout Britain and Ireland.
	Dissolution of St Mary's Abbey in Dublin.
	The Priory of the Holy Trinity dissolved and reconstituted as Christ Church Cathedral.
	In the town of Monkstown there are four houses and thirteen cottages. At the grange of Monkstown there is a 'chief mansion with three towers, surrounded by stone walls' (with William Kelly as bailiff) and two cottages. Residents include John Gavan, James McShane, John O Moran, William Fullam, Walter Coleman, John Long, Denis O'Finn, Thomas McMyles, Patrick Frynde, Patrick Bayley, David Vengill, James Cogan, John and William Lacy, John Taylor, Patrick Gygin, Hugh White and Simon Brown.
1543	'Carrickbrenan alias Monckenton, and the rectory of the same' leased to Sir John Travers, master of the king's ordnance in Ireland, by Fiant No. 310 of Henry VIII.
1545	The manor of Monkstown had a castle and sixteen houses; the grange of Monkstown had 'a capital messuage, surrounded by stone walls and three towers' and three cottages.
1546	'Grant to John Traverse, Esq. … Carbrynan alias Monketon the grange and capital messuage [Monkstown Castle]', by Fiant No. 460 of Henry VIII.
1577	The advowson (the right to choose a vicar) of Carrickbrennan Church confirmed to James Eustace, Viscount Baltinglass (patron of Monkstown).
1615	Royal Visitation of Dublin, 1615, states: 'Carrickbrennan: No curate in charge, therefore [the parish] was sequestered' (*Carragh Brennan Nullus curatus comparuit, ergo sequestratur*).
1630	Tullogh was 'somewhat ruined by the late stormes. The roof of the chauncel (was) almost downe'. Clonkeen, alias Grange, was 'somewhat uncovered with the late stormes'. At Dalkey, 'the church (was) ruinous, the chauncell hath no roofe'. Killiney's 'church and chauncell … wanteth a roofe and ornaments'. Monkstown (i.e. Carrickbrennan) alone was the only church in the neighbourhood 'in good repairacon, but wants decencie and some necessaries within'.
1641	The insurrection of 1641 begins. South Dublin overrun by the rebels — Kill-of-the-Grange curate's wife and maid hanged; vicar of Dalkey and Killiney murdered; battle at Deansgrange; the siege of Carrickmines.
	The Civil Survey of Monkstown reports: 'There is on the p'misses one old Castle newly repaired with a Barne, Two garden plotts & an Orchard; one Mill in use worth in 1640 Seaven poundes; There is a small Creek for a haven; the Jury value the Buildings at three hundred poundes being repaired by Lieutenant Generall Ludlow; there is alsoe a parish Church in repaire. There is on the p'misses a Small scrubby wood, with a few Ashtrees.'
1647	Book of Common Prayer abolished by Oliver Cromwell. The Directory to be used instead.
1649	Arrival of Cromwell in Ireland. The massacre of Drogheda.
1653	Walter Cheevers evicted from Monkstown Castle, which is given to Edmund Ludlow (Cromwell's

general of horse and a strict Puritan).

1654   The tithes of Monkstown belong to Christ Church.

1657   Down Survey shows parishes in half-barony of Rathdown, including those of Kill (the Dean's Grange) and Monkstown.

1659   Population of Monkstown is 64 (eleven English and 53 Irish).

1660   Restoration of Charles II. Walter Cheevers reinstated as owner of Monkstown Castle.

1664   There are sixteen householders in Monkstown, owning 23 hearths between them, as the Hearth Money Rolls show:

Walter Cheevers	6	John Lasseys	1
Thomas Chidwick	2	Richard Hinnikan	1
Peirce ye Smith	2	Daniell Connor	1
Richard Boshan	1	Farrall Murphy	1
Nicholas Murphy	1	Garrett Samon	1
John Farran	1	Murtagh Cane	1
Thomas ye Slater	1	Murtagh Coman	1
Henry Crosse	1	Robert Squire	1

1666   31 householders in Monkstown, including Asbill, Chambers and Dixon.

c.1667   Cheevers moves to his tower house in Dalkey (Goat Castle) and rents Monkstown Castle to Edward Corker, MP for County Dublin.

1668   Edward Corker rebuilds Carrickbrennan Church.

1669   The first parochial register of the Union of Monkstown.

1690   Battle of the Boyne.

1691   Allan Maddison appointed to Monkstown as district and perpetual curate (1691–1741).

1694   Visitation of Archbishop Narcissus Marsh (of Marsh's Library) to Monkstown.

1725   Allan Maddison lists the five parishes in the Union of Monkstown, with their 22 townlands:
Monkstown: Monkston, Donlary, Newtown on ye Strand [Blackrock], Thomas town and Bullock.
Kill: Stilorgan, Killmacud, Little Newton [Newtown Park], Dean's Grange,
Kill o' ye Grange, Cornelscourt, Rochestown and Balincloa.
Tullogh: Mulchans-town, Glanamuck, Leopards-town, Carrickmaine, Loghanstown and Brennans-town.
Killiney: Killbogget, Loghlinstown.
Dalkey: Dalkey.

1737   First silver chalice and paten provided for Carrickbrennan Church.

1740–1   Severe winter, so cold that the Liffey is frozen enough to skate on; some 13–20% of the population die from starvation and disease.

1741   Thomas Heany appointed to Monkstown as district and perpetual curate (1741–69).

1742   First performance of 'Messiah' by Handel at Fishamble Street.

1744   Monkstown's earliest Vestry Book begins, recording work and maintenance to the church at Carrickbrennan. For example, 'For glazing ye Church Windows, paid Thos Seymor, £1-2-8; For flooring 2 seats and sceiling ye church, paid Joseph Smith, £1-0-3; For whitewashing and painting the Church, 11s 4½d'.

1748   A new north–south aisle built in Carrickbrennan Church 'for the more convenient accomodation of the parishioners'.

1753   'A stocks (built) in the parish of Monkstown, £2-10.'

1756   'The Bay and Harbour of Dublin [map] drawn from an actual survey taken by Geo. Gibson, Surveyor and Hydrographer, under the inspection of his father Robert Gibson, teacher of mathematics, a native and citizen, 1756' depicts Monkstown Castle and Carrickbrennan Church surrounded by trees and fields. Less than twenty houses cluster around Old Dunleary (present-day 'Purty Kitchen' area).

1760	St Brigid's, Stillorgan, built.
1762	Stillorgan and Kilmacud severed from Monkstown.
1766	Heaney's Census shows 196 Protestants (54 families) and 570 'Papists' (121 families) resident in the parish of Monkstown.
1767	A pier and coffee house built at Dunleary, still a tiny fishing village.
1769	Thomas Robinson appointed to Monkstown as district and perpetual curate (1769–75).
1772	Monkstown's parish pound (for stray animals) rebuilt at a cost of £4–13.
1775	John Hely appointed to Monkstown as district and perpetual curate (1775–8).
1777	Carrickbrennan Church declared 'insufficient for the congregation' and 'ruinous'.
1778	Edward Ledwich appointed to Monkstown as district and perpetual curate (1778–80).
1780	John Forsayeth appointed to Monkstown as district and perpetual curate (1780–2). Monkstown Castle for sale: described as 'the second-best residence in Dublin'.
	Visit of Austin Cooper, antiquarian, to Monkstown; he describes the Carrickbrennan church as 'very plain and small … Here are no Old Tomb Stones or any thing in that way, but a very Old Yew Tree mostly decayed, & measuring in Diamr. 3 ft. 6 In'.
1781	The Act of Council for the Perpetual Union of Monkstown states that the six parishes (Monkstown, Kill, Dalkey, Killiney, Bullock and Carrickbrennan) were 'contiguous and episcopally united', that there was 'one church … in the parish of Monkstown' where 'the parishioners … (could) conveniently resort for divine service' and that, in order to support the upkeep of a glebe house and clergyman, the parishes would have to form a union. The annual yearly income was given for each parish (making a total of £151-17s) as follows:

Monkstown and Bullock	£75-10s
Kill	£29
Dalkey	£25-10s
Killeeny otherwise Killeen	£7-5s
Carrickbrennan	£14-12s

The Act noted that 'if the said parishes should at any time hereafter be disunited, the Income arising from the said parish of Monkstown would not be sufficient to support the Incumbent and keep up the necessary Repairs of the said (glebe) House and Offices'. (There was actually no glebe house in any of the parishes yet, although Forsayeth had been told to build one by Robert Fowler, archbishop of Dublin, in 1780.) Viscount Lifford, the lord chancellor, '(did therefore) hereby Order and Direct that the … parishes of Kill, Dalkey, Killeeny otherwise Killeen, Bullock and Carrickbrennan be united for ever to … Monkstown and erected into one parish by the Name of the perpetual Cure or Parish of Monkstown with all Parochial Rights'.

Monkstown Castle and demesne (c. 20 acres) still up for sale (advertised in *Saunders's News-Letter* in April and October).

1782	William Jephson appointed to Monkstown as district and perpetual curate (1782–91).
1785	Foundation stone of the new Monkstown Parish Church laid by the duke of Rutland on 1 September on new site acquired from Lords Longford and de Vesci (the present site).
1787	Order of Council for changing the site of the Church of Monkstown (from Carrickbrennan Road to its present site, facing down Monkstown Road). An act of parliament confirmed that the 'site (of the church which had been) … changed to the piece of ground granted by the Lords of the Manor … should be for ever after deemed and taken to be the Parish Church of the said parish'.
1789	The new Georgian church is consecrated on Sunday 30 August by Robert Fowler, archbishop of Dublin. Church accommodates 340 worshippers.
1791	John Ryves appointed to Monkstown as district and perpetual curate (1791–9). Monkstown schoolhouse built.
1797	Monkstown glebe house built on 2-acre site in Kill (opposite Baker's Corner today) belonging

to Monkstown parish. John Ryves is first incumbent to live there.

1799   Marmaduke Cramer appointed to Monkstown as district and perpetual curate (1799–1802).

1802   James Dunn appointed to Monkstown as district and perpetual curate (1802–4). Montpelier Parade built, the first of the grand terraces of Monkstown.

1804   Singleton Harpur appointed to Monkstown as district and perpetual curate (1804–15).

1805   'Painting and whitewashing church, £20.' 'Bricklayer's bill for repairs to old churchyard [Carrickbrennan], £7-2-10.'

1806–7   A list of Church of Ireland 'residents' in the five parishes in the Union of Monkstown given in the Vestry Minute book of 1805–29:

	1806	1807
Monkstown	36	70
Killiney	16	17
Dalkey	30	28
Tullow	47	46
Kill	66	69
	195	230

These '195' in the United Parishes of Monkstown must mean 195 heads of households rather than people. (Heany had counted 196 Protestants in the Union in 1766.) With a conservative average of four people per household, this would mean about 780 Protestants in the Union of Monkstown in 1806.

1806–8   Wall built by George Smith (future stone contractor for Dunleary Harbour) to enclose church grounds, widening of road and 'other improvements', totalling £542-9-5.

1807   The *Rochdale* and the *Prince of Wales* wrecked at Seapoint and Blackrock in November; 385 drowned, buried in Carrickbrennan and Merrion graveyards.

1808   Petition for asylum harbour in Dublin Bay signed in Monkstown Church by the nobility and gentry of Rathdown. A list of the 'Proprietors of seats' shows that only 44 pews in the church were owned by one or more people. *Saunders's News-Letter* of 22 October carried the following appeal for the annual charity sermon: '… the benevolent assistance of the parishioners is most earnestly requested … particularly of those who, by their residence in town during the Winter, are prevented contributing to relieve the wants, and to alleviate the distresses which at that season of the year are felt with such accumulated severity by the Poor of this neighbourhood.'

1809   'For painting the church, £16-5-10½.'

1811   'Repairs to church roof, £50; painting and glazing church, £22-2-7; painting outside of church, £5-13-9.'

1813   Monkstown was said to have 'a more numerous population of the established religion than in any other part of Ireland … The church accommodates all the nobility and gentry of a very rich and populous vicinity: it is, therefore, always much crowded'.
'Paid P. Byrne for 31 loads of gravel for Entrance of the Church, £1-0-8.'

1815   Charles Lindsay appointed to Monkstown as district and perpetual curate (1815–55). He spends '£2,400 British' of his private funds in repairing the glebe house at Kill, where he lives for the next 40 years.

1816   'A marble font and fitting, £6-0-9.'

1817   The lord lieutenant lays the first stone of Dunleary Harbour's east pier; although most of the east and west piers were completed by 1821, building continued until 1859. The project employed about 1,000 labourers.
Each pew owner is asked to subscribe a guinea towards a new 'hot air stove' for the church.

1818   'To Geo. Simpson, Slater, for keeping the Church Roof in order as p(er) agreement for 10 yrs from 1816, £3-8-3.' 'To 3 Copper Collecting Boxes, £2-7-0.' 'To John Walker for 3 Boards painted with the Ten Commandments, the Lord's Prayer and Creed in Gold letters, £22-15-0.'

1820	Rennie's map of Old Dunleary, showing cluster of houses around the site of the present 'Purty Kitchen'. An English tourist wrote of Monkstown, 'Here is a Castle; and the Church is a handsome modern edifice, frequented for public worship by all the gentry of this rich and populous vicinity'.
1821	George IV ascends throne after the death of his father, 'the mad King George'. He was crowned in July and came to Ireland on a State visit in August, landing at Howth on 12 August and departing from the east pier in Dunleary on 3 September. Dunleary renamed 'Kingstown' in his honour. For a month before his visit the country erupted in a flurry of activity: John Semple & Son built 'the King's Room' (the Round Room) next to the Mansion House for a State dinner and the Harbour Commissioners employed 'upwards of 500 men … in repairing the roads in the vicinity' of the new harbour.
	In Monkstown, the Vestry purchase a flag ('Expense of Flag and erecting do on Steeple in honor of His most Gracious Majesty's Visit to Ireland — Geo 4th, £6-11-6½') to fly from the church tower and Archdeacon Lindsay organises a party for local schoolchildren in the church grounds.
1822	'Bryan for 48 loads of Sea Gravel round Church, £2; Edward Ford for rolling do, 3/4; For painting the church, £20-4-10; Perrin for Upholstery Work in fitting up and ornamenting the Church, £58-17-0. (Note: This demand is considered great, but Mr. Perrin has proposed to submit it to the decision of two competent persons in the trade.)'
1823	John Semple, Junior, on behalf of his father, presents two plans to the Vestry for the enlargement of Monkstown Church.
1825	Kingstown changing rapidly. With the building of the Royal Harbour of George IV, domestic buildings, including 'some eligible houses, calculated for retired residences, began to spread in every direction … Enclosures have been made, and agriculture has claimed its dues on cheerless plains, lately productive chiefly of furze and heath. The want of wood will long be felt, in efforts towards the improvement of this neighbourhood, as regards its ornamental character; but the sea-views present some of the boldest features of the bay … and the village will, probably at no distant day, expand into a town of much fashionable resort.'
1826	'A second door … to facilitate egress and regress of the congregation, £24-18-4.'
1827	'Lamps for lighting the church, £35.'
1828	'Candles for Evening Service, £8.' 'Stove flue and chimney, £46.'
	Henry William Paget, lord lieutenant and marquis of Anglesey, had 'a beautiful house near Monkstown in order to be near the Royal Charlotte Yacht which his Lordship commands' (*Saunders's News-Letter*, 28 March).
	The workmen on the pier complain to the Harbour Commissioners of the 'exorbitant price of provisions … and (that) house rent (was) very dear'. Their wages increased from 2/9½ to 3/6 per day.
1829	Building of Monkstown Church begins with Semple & Son, diocesan architects.
1831	Semple's Monkstown Church opens for worship on Christmas Day, 25 December 1831. Built to accommodate 1,200 worshippers. The building receives some praise and much criticism. There are 2,424 members of the Established Church in Monkstown parish (plus Kill, 281; Dalkey, 104; Killiney, 115; Bullock, 213), making a total of 3,137 in the Union. Average Sunday attendance at church is 1,300, which was 'increasing'.
	The *Dublin Evening Post* of 29 November 1831 gives a 'daily account … of the entire traffic on the present road from 6 o'clock in the morning until 9 at night, since the 11th February last, for 37 weeks, ending 30th October: 29,256 private carriages; 5,999 hackney coaches; 113,945 private jaunting cars; 149,754 public cars; 20,070 gigs; 40,485 saddle horses; 58,297 carts'.
1832	New organ installed, in west gallery as before (cost £392), and dedicated in September by Charles Lindsay, dean of Christ Church, bishop of Kildare and patron of Monkstown.
	Building of the railway from Dublin to Kingstown begins.
1834	First locomotive train, the 'Hibernia', runs from Westland Row to Salthill — 22½ minutes, at the cost of 1s, 8d and 6d for a single fare, for first, second and third class respectively (opened to the public on 17 December 1834). Opening of the Salthill Hotel, beside the railway station.

In 1834 the *parish* of Monkstown consisted of 3,103 Churchmen, 178 Presbyterians, 116 other Protestant Dissenters and 10,741 Roman Catholics, making a total of 14,138.

In the *Union* of Monkstown (the parishes of Monkstown, Kill, Killiney, Dalkey and Tullow), there were 3,816 Churchmen, 186 Presbyterians, 141 other Protestant Dissenters and 14,583 Roman Catholics. If the figure of 1,300 said to attend church in 1831 is accurate (out of a possible 3,816), this means that 34% were church-goers.

The seven daily schools in the *parish* had on their books 476 boys and 311 girls, and 45 'others' (sex not specified). The thirteen daily schools in the *Union* had 763 boys and 541 girls.

1835 Monkstown Hospital opened, under supervision of Dr William Plant.

Monkstown chapel of ease at Killiney (present St Matthias's) built.

'By Cash, paid Alexr. Riggs, for car hire & carriage of Lamps, from Monkstown to Dublin, 5-0; By Cash, paid Alexr. Hilton for putting up Lamps in Monkstown Church, 4-10.'

The convict ship, the *Essex*, lay in Kingstown Harbour that year, awaiting the transportation of convicts (up to 275 at any one time). There, in its cramped hold, little Agnes Smith (2½ years of age) died and was brought to Carrickbrennan Graveyard to be buried on 2 February 1835.

1836 'Paid Mr. West for Plated Patten, £2-2-0; Paid Hiram Murray for glazing 52 squares of glass, £2-12-0.'

1841 The *Parliamentary Gazetteer* of 1845 gives the following description of Monkstown and environs: 'The whole district is one of the most luscious and lively portions of the southern sea-board of the bay of Dublin; and is principally disposed in towns, villages, gay hamlets, clusters of villas, and the gardens and mimic demesnes of a profusion of neat and fashionable residences … The shore extends from the NW end of Blackrock to within 3 furlongs of the village of Dalkey; and is richly variegated with Blackrock, Kingstown, and Bullock, the harbour of Kingstown, the Dublin and Kingstown railway, the creeks of Scotchbay and Sandycove, 3 Martello towers and a great number and divers of both small natural features of beauty and tasteful touches of artificial decoration. The principal part of the atmospheric railway is within the limits … Some of the most noticeable of the numerous seats, villas and cottages ornées, are Maritimo, Seapoint-house, Salthill-house, Templehill, Rockfield-house, Stradbrook-house, Melfield, Monkstown-house, Monkstown-castle, Ashton-park, Bloomsbury, Longford-lodge, Highthorn, Corrig-house, Avondale, Glenagarey-house, Burnfield, Anglesea, Lesly-cottage, Castle-park, Glasthule-house and Minor's-hill.'

The article also gave the numbers attending for the different denominations:

Monkstown parish church:	1,300 (seating capacity, 1,200)
Presbyterian church:	300
Quaker meeting-house:	60
Roman Catholic chapel of Kingstown:	1,500
Roman Catholic chapel of Cabinteely:	600
Roman Catholic chapel of Blackrock:	300
Conventual chapel in Kingstown:	500

1842 Lawson's *Gazetteer of Ireland* describes Monkstown as 'improving and fashionable'. It added, 'Monkstown is a gem of a place — pleasant, fashionable, and gay, containing the most elegant and first-rate society'.

1843 Date of 'Bishop window' installed on east wall of north transept and its counterpart in the south transept.

1844 As ground landlords, Lords Longford and de Vesci stipulate that houses built on their lands must be of a consistently high quality; for example, a house in De Vesci Terrace should be completed 'in a good and workmanlike manner, with good and sound materials'. The lessee was to build the house 'two storeys high at the least, besides the basement storey … and shall and will, at least once every alternate year … paint or colour the exterior front wall and porticos … Portland stone colour and none other, under a penalty of £5'.

1848 Terraced houses, such as Longford Terrace and Clifton Terrace, going up along the seafront at Monkstown. The Dublin Directory of that year describes a scene of 'innumerable seats and villas, encircled in demesnes, or adorned with shrubs and gardens, abound; other residences approximating to, or on the line of the road to Kingstown, in beautifully aligned terraces front the sea, or command fine views of the Dublin and Wicklow mountains'.

Monkstown Church, too, wins some unaccustomed praise (maybe it was beginning to 'grow' on people): 'The church of Monkstown, in the later English Style, stands on the right of the road to Kingstown, and is an imposing if not a handsome structure, and very neatly fitted up within'.

1849	The estate agent and auctioneer, Thomas Dockrell, a Monkstown parishioner, enthuses about living in Monkstown in *Saunders's News-Letter* of 24 May: 'The views of Howth, Dublin Bay, Kingstown Harbour with all its attractive aquatic sports, salubrious air, and select society unite in producing the most fascinating neighbourhood of any in Europe'. While extolling a house on Monkstown Avenue, he claims, 'Monkstown Avenue being principally inhabited by the Society of Friends [Quakers], it is unnecessary to say more in its favour'.
1851	'Mr. Daniel for lighting Church with Gass, £12-0-6'.
1855	William Fitzgerald appointed to Monkstown as district and perpetual curate (1855–7).
	'To Edward Bryson for claining snow of the roofe And gutters of Monksetoun Chursh, 10/-, paid Feb the 21st 1855.'
1856	Addition of chancel suggested for Monkstown Church. No support, idea dropped.
1857	Ronald MacDonnell appointed to Monkstown as district and perpetual curate (1857–78). Idea of chancel again suggested. Public outcry this time, so idea dropped again.
	Purchase of 'Iron safe, 16/-'.
1858	Hodges of Dublin cast the church bell, weighing approximately 15 cwt; it is 44 inches in diameter across the mouth and has a 55-foot bell-pull.
1860s	Horse-drawn trams appear in Monkstown.
1861	Foundation stone laid for St Patrick's Roman Catholic Church, across the road from Monkstown Church. Designed by Pugin and Ashlin. Opened in 1866.
1862	Addition of chancel to Monkstown Church, designed by John McCurdy. Organ moved from west gallery to new 'organ room' on north side of chancel.
1864	'42 loads of Killiney gravel from P. Goggins, at 2/6 per load (£5-5s); wheel-barrow (13/-).'
1866	Memorial window to Sir William Betham installed in south transept.
1867	'Laying down of the Hot water pipes' and a thermometer (1s) 'for use of Church' installed.
1868	Church painted inside. Some 'old doors of pews' sold for £1-5s.
1869	A clock (£10) was fixed in place (probably in the west gallery) by a carpenter for £1-10s-9d.
1870	Well-attended Vestry about the Central Sustentation Fund (£1,141 contributed in 1870).
1871	Disestablishment of the Church of Ireland (1 January). The names of 146 registered vestrymen are placed on the Register; the first select vestrymen, synodsmen and nominators are elected.
	New 'carpet windows' installed at east end of chancel. 'Upholstery for the pulpit, reading desk, kneeling stools, £28-8s-4d; three flights of winding stairs to galleries, £23-18s.'
1872	New Telford & Telford organ installed in chancel's 'organ room'. Donated at a cost of 'over £700' by an anonymous donor (later found to be Thomas Hone of 'Yapton', Monkstown).
1874	Founding of Mission to Lepers by the Pim sisters of 'Alma House', Monkstown.
	'4 (oak) handrails for the wall side of (the transept) stairs' fitted at a cost of £11-10s. 'To an Extra Heavy Table on stand[?ard] framings with two extra large falling leaves, made of first class pitch pine French polished, £6-6-0, J.J. Byrne & Sons, Cabinet-makers & Upholsterers, June 5, 1874.'
1875	Jordan Memorial windows installed, flanking Betham Window in south transept.
	Carrickbrennan Graveyard taken over by the Poor Law Guardians.
1876	Monkstown glebe in Kill sold, valued at £2,000.
1878	Joseph Peacocke appointed as incumbent of Monkstown (1878–94).
1879	Garner Memorial windows installed in north transept.
	The marriage of Edward Carson and Sarah Annette Kirwan in Monkstown Church celebrated on 19 December by Carson's old schoolmaster, the Rev. F. Hewson Wall.

1881	Church roof repaired, a new boiler (£93) installed, schoolhouse renovated. Local Government Act orders that burials in Monkstown vaults be discontinued (except for fourteen further private interments).
1883	Drew and Mitchell make modifications to McCurdy's chancel, mainly decorative, including stone arcading on east wall, elaborate carved reredos, new Communion rails and encaustic tiles in sanctuary.
1884	Internally, Semple's entrances into the north and south transepts are blocked up and a new wide central doorway installed, to ease congestion in narrow porches. The body of the church was re-pewed according to Drew and Mitchell's plans, so that all the seating faced the chancel, and the 'allocated' pews were recushioned (£103). New heating installed throughout. Wooden steps to chancel replaced by stone steps. Tiling of central aisle.

The *Monkstown Herald* announced in October that 'the telephone has been erected between Dublin and Kingstown, and is, we believe, in operation'. |
1885	The brass eagle lectern and two prayer desks were presented.
1886	The clock in the west gallery (installed in 1869) is removed and sold.
1887	External woodwork of church painted. Four-line verse from I Corinthians 11:26 inscribed on panels of reredos. A 'dado in oils around the body of the church' painted. Chancel repainted. Pews in the west gallery 'remodelled'. Total cost for internal decoration, £60.
1889	Monkstown Select Vestry decide to have Semple's narrow ogee doorways into the north and south transepts widened by Drew for £210. An 'ornamental' noticeboard of pitch pine is erected at the west door for £8.
1890	The two new transept porches are tiled (£20).
1891	Canon Peacocke donates Royal Doulton tiles for chancel.
1893	Lighting and ventilating of all three galleries carried out (£67-10s).
1894	John Clarence Dowse appointed as incumbent of Monkstown (1894–1929).
1895	Rainwater drains installed.
1896	Electric trams reach Monkstown.
1897	'2 brass hand rails down chancel steps.'
1898	New Gray & Davison organ (£1,041-10s) installed and dedicated on 17 November by Dr Joseph Peacocke, archbishop of Dublin and former curate and incumbent of Monkstown.

North and south galleries are raised several feet higher (£600).

Letter to the editor of *The Irish Times* on 10 November from L.B. Penrose of 2 New Brighton, Monkstown, on the 'State of Seafield Avenue':

'Sir — I think it is quite time to draw the attention to the proper authorities to the disgraceful state of Seafield Avenue. Since the Tramway Company commenced their operations on the Monkstown Road, nearly all the heavy traffic goes by way of Seapoint Road and Seafield Avenue with the result of making the latter place well-nigh impossible for vehicles.

I would also like to point out to the Society for Prevention of Cruelty to Animals that it is quite time for them to put one of their inspectors on the avenue to prevent the inhuman treatment of some of the poor horses which have to drag heavy loads on the hill. Only today, I saw several horses being barbarously beaten, simply because the wheels of the carts got into ruts, and they were not able to pull them with the loads.

This state of things grows worse every day, and I think something should be done to alter it.'

The first petrol car in Ireland (a 3.5hp Benz Convertible) seen — and heard — in Monkstown, driven by its proud owner, Dr Colohan of Blackrock. |
| 1900 | Queen Victoria visits Dublin. Monkstown Church 'handsomely decorated' for her entry into Dublin, past the church. |
| 1901 | The Dockrell Memorial Porch (£190-9s) at the Vestry entrance, designed by Parry, was built by Maurice E. Dockrell in memory of his father, Thomas Dockrell (d. 1880). The Select Vestry held protracted discussions about draughts and stuffiness. It was 'decided to direct Shannon, the sexton, to see that the temperature does not rise under the galleries beyond 52° and in the chancel |

beyond 60°. Dr Adeney undertook to provide nine thermometers for use in the church'.

1902   Plans for the Knox Memorial Hall, the new parochial hall, submitted by architect Richard Chaytor Millar to Monkstown Fabric Committee. Best tender from builder Mr Christopher Jolley accepted, £2,500 agreed.

Miss Edith Dowse (b. 1899), daughter of the rector, Chancellor Dowse, recalls parishioners from inner-city Church of Ireland parishes, such as St Thomas's, being entertained 'for a day in the country' at Monkstown, which was 'a great treat and variety to them'; during the day, in the 'delightful surroundings of sea and verdure', they collected wild flowers, walked on the west pier and along 'the pretty shaded roads' (*The Irish Times*, 19 June 1902). Miss Dowse remembers these annual excursions, when a tram would be hired to bring these poor families for a day at the seaside. After a dinner of 'meat and cabbage', they would spend a few hours at Seapoint, return to the Knox Hall for tea and depart for home with a bunch of flowers.

1903–15 Miss Edith Dowse recalls the Monkstown of her childhood. Frequent trams trundled along Monkstown Road, one of which ran over the rectory dog; a return fare to Dublin cost 7d. Milk was delivered to the door in 'a sort of watering-can'; if you bought a pint, you were given a tilly (a little extra) 'for the cat'. The grocer came to the rectory every day, often when nothing was strictly necessary, so 'Cook' would have to think of something to buy. Edith was initially taught at home by a governess called Miss Cooper. When Edith asked her questions, she was invariably answered with 'Deary knows'. Usually, Chancellor Dowse used his bicycle to get around the parish, but occasionally would hire a horse-drawn 'cab' (tied up at 'The Ring'), owned by a Mr Walsh, for trips further afield with the family. The Dowses always went to the Firth of Clyde in Scotland for the month of August.

1903   A pinnacle falls from the north-west turret of the church and the architect's subsequent report states that the main tower, turrets and battlements require extensive repairs and the fillets of the roof gutters need cementing as soon as the weather improves. The Vestry decides that the finials of the towers must be 'made safe at once, the matter being urgent'. First meeting of a special committee to raise money for these repairs; its nine members contribute £150 between them.

1904   Knox Memorial Hall officially opened on 28 June by Dr Joseph Peacocke, archbishop of Dublin. Property secured by a 5½-foot wall and railings built in front of the hall, costing £138-14s-6d. Side and rear boundaries fenced in for £21-16s-4d.

1905   'Churchville' acquired through the will of Miss Mary Anne Battersby.

1906   'Churchville' 'put in thorough repair including the addition of a bathroom if possible'. 'That Churchville be let at an annual rent of £40, tenant paying all taxes and keeping the interior of the premises in good repairs and condition.'

1907   'New rails for the chancel steps, £8.'

1910   'Improved lighting … by the incandescent system (£40-15s) resulting in greatly improved atmospheric conditions through the abolition of over 100 gas burners.'

1911   Inside of church painted ('the decorative colour plan designed by Mr. Caulfeild Orpen, architect, harmonises with the building, and in dignity, simplicity, and lightness of effect'), at cost of £345-4s-6d. (Orpen's colour scheme seems to have returned to that used before 1898.) Ventilation was improved and work carried out on the organ. Umbrella-holders installed at the end of each pew downstairs.

1912   Doors in north and south galleries installed. Umbrella-holders installed in gallery pews.

1914   'The most momentous year in living memory', when 66 parishioners 'answered the call of their king to join the army fighting for the liberty of Belgium and the freedom of the world'. Between 1914 and 1918, 155 men from Monkstown parish joined up; 28 of them died. Rolls of Honour hung in the church porches, listing those in the services.

1916   Easter Rising starts on 24 April in Dublin. Monkstown's Sunday evening service was moved from 7pm to 6pm during May 'in consequence of Rebellion' and the Easter Vestry was postponed until 1 June.

1918   Last interment in private vaults of Monkstown Church.

1920   Money collected for parish war memorials goes towards the World War I Memorial Tablet in the chancel and the 'Monkstown Ward' of Monkstown Hospital.

1921   Women first attend the Easter Vestry and the first woman (Miss Mabel Kough) is elected to the Select Vestry.

1922   'A general exodus' from the parish to England, including Captain R. Magill, the Misses Galloway and Dr Robert Lynn Heard. The latter was churchwarden during 1903–4 and lived at 'Carnsore' (today's 'Glensilva') with his family of six sons and two daughters.

1925   Church wired for electricity, costing £297. (This was early: the streets of Dun Laoghaire were not lit by the ESB until 1932.)

1926   Church grounds spread with Killiney gravel at 9/6 per ton (Bray gravel was 12/- per ton). 'Boring beetle' found in the roof timbers of the church and treated with carbolinium, £50.

1929   John Oulton appointed as incumbent of Monkstown (1929–31).

1931   Harold Forde appointed as incumbent of Monkstown (1931–45).

1932   Centenary Service held on 11 December to commemorate opening of Semple's Monkstown Church. (In fact, it should have been held twelve months earlier, in 1931. In March 1932 research instigated by B. Warburton Rooke discovered that the actual opening date was 25 December 1831.) Various gifts presented to church by parishioners and friends, including a silver chalice, two silver patens and a 'carved oak Holy Table and matching credence table' (both designed by Richard Caulfeild Orpen and echoing the design of the east 'carpet windows'), all in memory of Chancellor Dowse (d. 1930). Gifts dedicated by Dr John Gregg, archbishop of Dublin, at the service. The Vestry inserted an advertisement in the *Church of Ireland Gazette*, offering the 'old' Communion table free of charge to another church. The Rev. R.H. Thompson of Kilcoman Rectory, Milltown, Co. Kerry, replied and the Vestry agreed to send the table to Castlemaine Station by train, contributing half the cost of £3-10-0 for packing and carriage.

1934   Telephone installed in rector's residence.

1935   Weekly Free Will Offering Scheme initiated, a form of voluntary giving by parishioners.

1936   Church debt of £289 causes concern: 'The financial position of the parish still gives cause for much anxiety … A voluntary reduction of 15% in their salaries has been accepted by the Organist, Secretary and professional members of the Choir, at the request of the Select Vestry.'

1938   The Infants' School at Cumberland Street is 'surrendered by the Diocesan Board of Education to Lords Longford and de Vesci for £250'. A new rectory at 5 Brighton Terrace acquired. First glebe wardens appointed. Pew assessments discontinued.

1940   New boiler installed in the Knox Memorial Hall (£60).

1941   New church boiler installed (£290-12s-5d). Major repairs to the 1898 Gray & Davison organ.

1942–50   Protracted discussions during Vestry meetings on how to 'eliminate draughts from the church' — by blocking up ventilators, sealing around radiators, hanging curtains at gallery doors and keeping all doors shut during services.

1943   A large hole appears in the garden of 'Churchville' (owing to subsidence). The Claremont Institution for the Education of the Deaf and Dumb, originally located in Glasnevin (1819–1943), moves to 'Carrick Manor', Monkstown (closes in 1978).

1945   Death of the incumbent, Harold Forde. Rectory at 5 Brighton Terrace sold and purchase of new rectory, 'Winton Lodge', 62 Monkstown Road. Arthur Butler appointed as incumbent of Monkstown (1945–58).

1948   The Rev. Arthur Butler reorganised the envelope collection system, calling it the Monkstown Church Defence Association (or Alliance). Knox Memorial Hall 'completely redecorated and renovated' (£170–£180). The Young People's Union renamed 'Discoverers of the Way' and 'flourished' under the adventurous Miss Ada Boyland (who went on a canoeing trip to the north of Canada and was 'the first white woman in Timbuctoo', according to Miss Edith Dowse).
Valuation of church for insurance purposes: church building £41,000; stained-glass windows £1,000; organ £5,000; monuments £4,000; pews, pulpit, bell, reading desk, etc. £4,500; chancel ornament and decoration £950. Total: £56,450.

1949   Robing of the Choir. The last Dublin city tram (the '252') travelled from Nelson's Pillar to

Blackrock on Sunday morning, 10 July 1949.

1950   Publication of *Where monks walked: the story of Monkstown* by the Rev. A.E. Stokes, curate of Monkstown. Cost of £32-10s-6d to print 1,000 copies.

1951–3   The 'Children's Church' set up in the north transept. A reconditioned piano purchased.

1952–3   Repair to bell and belfry floor (£313) after collapse owing to accumulated weight of pigeon dung. In November 1952 the bell was rehung for 'slow swinging' by Gillett & Johnston of Croydon, England. Repairs to dry rot in Knox Memorial Hall and 'boring beetles' in the roof (£300). In October the Choir had 42 members: the leader, Mrs Hazlett, twenty sopranos, six contraltos, five tenors and ten basses.

1953   'Floodlights' for church paid for by the Borough An Tostal Committee (£80). Restoration of Gray & Davison organ by Evans & Barr (£297) under supervision of Mr E.G. Barton. Chancel redecorated (£236). Valuation of church for insurance purposes (excluding organ and piano), £89,000. Average weekly collection, £23-17-3.

1954   Heating of church and Knox Memorial Hall changed from coke furnace to automatic oil fuel heating (£595). Interior of church redecorated by Sibthorpe & Son (£796-13-6). Organ repairs (£145). Three wooden boxes made (£129) for water containers and glasses, so that 'fresh water … was available at each of the three doors for the convenience of worshippers attending the Sunday services'. Two parishioners, Cecil Faull and Richard Groves Large, ordained (Large appointed curate of Monkstown in 1954).

1956   The Sunday School has a superintendent and eighteen teachers, with 115 children on roll. The first parish newsletter, the *Monkstown Review*, printed, replacing the previous 'Annual Report and Accounts'. Cost of £60 to print 850 copies.

1957   The Guild of Youth debated the motion 'That the youth of today is degenerate'.

1958   William (Billy) Wynne appointed as incumbent of Monkstown (1958–78).

1959–66   Major work carried out on church roof under supervision of architect, Wilson P. Guard, also a parishioner. The ends of the timber trusses supporting the slated roof over the nave and transepts 'rested on a continuous timber wall-plate built into the masonry walling. There was extensive wet-rot in these timbers. The Hartigan Bros. devised an ingenious way of supporting one truss at a time to enable the decayed ends to be cut away and stiffened with metal plates or supported on concrete supports formed so as to project out from the walling. The decayed wall-plate was cut out where possible and replaced with concrete.' The main roof timbers were also treated for woodworm. (In January 1985 Wilson Guard wrote in the 'Fabric Report': 'The church and the Fabric Committee were extremely fortunate in having the services of the skill and practical knowledge of the Hartigan Bros. in carrying out the roof timber repairs. They worked in their own time with the minimum of equipment to produce practical results at a fraction of the cost of such work today.')

1959   Long tradition of pew allocation (ownership of pews) abolished in April for 'new method of free seating'.

1962   Extension built to 1791 Parish schoolhouse (£7,500); opened by Dr G.O. Simms, archbishop of Dublin.

1964   Robing of Junior Choir. Both choirs sang together for the 90th anniversary of the Mission to Lepers.

1965   Dun Laoghaire Corporation acquires 2 perches (*c.* 7 square yards) 'on south side of church grounds alongside boundary wall from the main yard gate to the small gate used by the school' (£175 compensation) and 18 square yards 'on south side of school yard alongside the south boundary wall' (£50 compensation) for road improvement and widening. Church wall and entrance gates resited at expense of Corporation.

The 'You're Welcome' series of social events started by incumbent Billy Wynne.
Further restoration of Gray & Davison organ by Meates & Son, under supervision of Mr E.G. Barton (as with the 1953 work).

1966   Freehold of Knox Memorial Hall purchased from landlords (£117).
The 'heavy outer doors of north and south porches' are removed and stored in the vaults. Pews at

west door removed. A new church noticeboard (£40-5s) installed, designed by architect and parishioner Wilson P. Guard, who also designed a 'proposed garden room' on the site of the present Bicentenary Memorial Garden, but this was decided against.

Organ restoration completed (£3,500).

1967   New wooden floor in Knox Memorial Hall installed and the 'Minor Hall' transformed into the 'Friendly Room'.

New church seat coverings purchased. Church vaults rewired and converted as a venue for Parish Youth Club. In July the taoiseach, Jack Lynch, opened Monkstown Fête, to raise money for the organ fund (£1,370 raised and total debt wiped out). Mr Lynch said on the occasion, 'The close positions of the Parish Church and St Patrick's across the road is noteworthy. We think of that road less and less as a dividing line and more and more as a way of contact between the churches.'

1968   Road widening. Church wall resited.

1970   Repairs, decoration and external pointing to chancel (£4,404). Formation of a Junior School of Music under Miss Pomeroy.

1971   Church floodlit in time for Christmas. New entrance gates to church fitted (17ft gates, £27-10s; 13ft, £25-10s).

1972   'Reconstruction of sexton's apartments' in schoolhouse (£1,184). The 39th Dublin (Monkstown) Scout Troop founded. Song School (Schola Cantorum) inaugurated by Mr John C. Kearon, principal of Monkstown Parish School.

1973   Heating installed in Knox Memorial Hall (£750). The Rev. Charles Wanguba from West Kenya seconded to parish for six months.

1974   Centenary of the Mission to Lepers (now called the Leprosy Mission). 'The Lay Contact Movement … is developing satisfactorily; the Friends of Monkstown inaugurated, with Sir John Betjeman as patron.' Its purpose was to raise funds for the upkeep, repair, improvement and maintenance of the parish buildings; disbanded *c.* 1978.

1975   'May in Monkstown' inaugurated, a fortnight of music with well-known artists performing, planned as an annual event. Valuation of church for insurance purposes: church £250,000; 'Churchville' £15,000; Knox Hall £40,000; school £40,000; church plate £400.

1976   Valuation of rectory, £25,000. Alterations to the Knox Memorial Hall (£4,721).

1977   New church boiler installed.

1978   Interior decoration of church (£1,025) and improved lighting in church (£440).

1979   Kevin Dalton appointed as incumbent of Monkstown (1979 to present). Renovations to schoolhouse and caretaker's flat (£37,350). Rectory repairs (£17,500).

1981   Rendering of rectory (£1,829). Service broadcast on Christmas Day (150th anniversary of the opening of Semple's church). Part of west gable repointed (£750).

1982   The Christian Stewardship scheme inaugurated on 7 March.

St. John's, Mounttown, closed to public worship on 31 July and the parish united with Monkstown on 1 August. General Vestry meeting held on the instructions of the Diocesan Council on 29 September (64 attended) for the 'coming together of two parishes in a new United parish' and to elect at least three parishioners from St. John's parish to the new Vestry.

1983   Amplification system installed in church.

1984   250 copies of the Alternative Prayer Book (APB) bought for £1-50 each.

On Sunday 2 December St John's silver is stolen. On Sunday night, 9 December, thieves break into Monkstown Vestry, force open the safe and steal all the church silver. A silver paten is found eight months later in a ditch in Wicklow.

The DART reaches Monkstown.

The Diocesan Employment Bureau opens in the Knox Memorial Hall.

1985   St John's Church, hall and sexton's house sold (£150,000) to the Order of St Pius X. St John's rectory and land sold at auction (£90,000). St John's World War I memorial plaque and two-light stained-glass window given to Monkstown Church, as well as its wall monuments. Repairs to church roof (£8,000). 170 more APB books bought for the church.

1986   New Communion silver purchased. Knox Memorial Hall rewired (£11,850) and roof repaired (£3,850). Live morning service televised on 22 June. Iron gate fitted at Vestry door. Monkstown Parish School closes down on 31 December, after almost 200 years.

1987   Church rewired (c. £25,000). Monkstown Hospital closes down. Service broadcast on 21 June. A Broadwood Baby Grand piano, 50 years old, purchased for Vestry rooms (£1,750). New Choir robes purchased. Two more silver patens recovered from the 1984 robbery.

1988   Church floodlights replaced (£463). 'Churchville' sold (£20,400).

1989   Bicentenary of consecration of 1789 Georgian church. Service televised. Year-long celebrations and fund-raising events include a garden fête, 'All Priests' show, a team quiz set by Fr Vincent Quilter, an antique and art auction, an ecumenical service (preacher Fr Michael Hurley, SJ, of the School of Ecumenics), the Village Day on 16 September, a Bicentenary Ball, parish consultations led by the Rev. Herbert O'Driscoll, culminating in a thanksgiving parish Communion (broadcast). The sum of £57,000 was raised over and above the normal parish income; the profits were divided between Our Lady's Hospice in Harold's Cross and restoration work on the church. Also that year the Bicentenary Memorial Garden opened behind the church (£6,000). Church rewiring completed (c. £28,385) and new carpeting laid (£1,397). Interior of church repainted (c. £40,000).

1990   Organ repairs (£11,044). The Tuesday Club, a social club for the elderly, founded by Pauline Huissoon.

1991   Repairs to chancel roof (c. £10,000).

1992   A ramp built up to the church (£2,619) for wheelchair access, using granite stones from the old Carrickbrennan Graveyard. The Monkstown Women's Circle founded by Mrs Jennifer Dalton, with a committee from both Monkstown Parish Church and St Patrick's Roman Catholic Church.

1993   The curates' house, at 2 Grange Crescent, Kill-of-the-Grange, purchased.
Storm damage sustained to stained-glass windows (£22,000) in south transept.
'Music in Monkstown' (Junior Choir and Organ School) established.

1993–7   Refurbishment of Knox Memorial Hall.

1997   Monkstown 'Educate Together' National School opens on 1 September.

1998   'Monkstown 1200' held on 26 September as a Village Day to commemorate the coming of the monks to Monkstown. Opened by the president, Mrs Mary McAleese, £21,000 was raised, which was divided among three projects: Monkstown School building restoration, the releading of St Patrick's stained-glass windows and the Monkstown 'Educate Together' National School. Services were broadcast on Good Friday and Easter Sunday. £12,000 was donated to the Christ Church Appeal and a further £8,000 promised over the next four years.

1999   Alarm system installed in church (£2,000–£2,500). Vaults converted into a centre for supplying midday meals to the homeless by the Interchurch Care Group (parishioners of St Michael's, St Patrick's and Monkstown), with the help of the Society of St Vincent de Paul. In the first fifteen months 6,000 meals provided.

2000   C.S. Lewis Study Centre opened by the Right Hon. David Bleakley, CBE.

2001   Watercolour of Monkstown Church by Esme McDowell hung in Friendly Room, dedicated to the memory of Mrs Dorrie Martin, who had looked after the room for over 35 years.

2002   Changeover to the euro. Select Vestry concerned that giving to the church would drop if parishioners gave the same amount in euro as they had in pounds. Parish information campaign run, culminating with a dinner (free of charge) and social occasion. The end result was that giving in Monkstown rose by 25% (in other Dublin churches it dropped markedly).

2003   Plans made for a major refurbishment of Monkstown Church (target of c. €2 million).

APPENDICES

Appendix 1

Other churches in the original parish of Monkstown

Over a period of 35 years, between 1835 and 1870, eleven churches sprang up (two of them 'chapels of ease'), and three 'rooms' were used for services, within the original Union of Monkstown:

1835	St Matthias's Church, Killiney (Ballybrack)
1836–7	The Mariners' Church, Kingstown
1836	The Bethel Episcopal Free Church, Kingstown (present Christ Church)
1843	St Patrick's, Dalkey
1851	Christ Church, Carysfort, Blackrock
1855	The Mission Room, Corrig Avenue, Kingstown
1859	Trinity Church, Killiney (present Holy Trinity Church)
1860	St John's, Mounttown
1861–3	Room for Divine Service at Connell's Court [Cornelscourt]
1860–4	Room at Kingston Grove, Ballycorus Road, for Divine Service during the building of Tullow Church
1864	Tullow Church, Brighton Road, Foxrock
1864	St John's, Kill-of-the-Grange
1867–8	St Paul's, Glenageary
1870	All Saints', Carysfort Avenue, Blackrock
1898–1909	The Mission Room in Mr Long's house in Monkstown Farm

Of these fourteen places of worship, by 2003 one church has been demolished (Christchurch, Carysfort, Blackrock), the future of another is uncertain (the Mariners', Dun Laoghaire) and one is no longer used by the Church of Ireland (St John's, Mounttown). The 'rooms' have closed down. The remaining eight churches are still in use.

It falls outside the subject of this book to give an account of all these churches, except for brief references in the text where relevant to Monkstown. However, as the first chapel of ease of Monkstown, St Matthias's Church in Killiney (Ballybrack) deserves some attention.

St Matthias's Church, Killiney (Ballybrack), 1835

The establishment of this, the first chapel of ease of Monkstown, in 1835 triggered a protracted battle between the archdeacon of Kildare, Charles Lindsay, who was also the perpetual curate of Monkstown (1815–55), and some of his wayward parishioners. Chapels of ease were sometimes built when parishioners lived a long way (originally six miles) from their parish church. They were usually only used for 'Morning and Evening Prayer, the Sacraments of Baptism and the Lord's Supper — but not for Confirmation, Matrimony or Burial of the Dead'. A bishop usually endowed them with tithes for the officiating curate. The setting up of the chapel of ease at Killiney was facilitated by the passing of an act on 23 June 1827 to 'amend the Laws in force in Ireland for Unions and Divisions of Parishes … and to make further provision with respect to the erecting (of) Chapels of Ease'.

The driving force behind the Killiney chapel of ease was probably the 71-year-old Judge Robert Day, a Monkstown parishioner and formerly one of the most powerful judges in Ireland (*see Chapter 22*). Through his connections, he was in an ideal position to engineer the act safely through the appropriate channels. Day lived at 'Loughlinstown House' and wanted a church that was closer than Monkstown. One suspects that Judge Day knew — and rather relished the fact — that he was opening a veritable Pandora's box. His diaries (now in the Royal Irish Academy) make it abundantly clear that he did not see eye to eye with either Bishop Lindsay (patron of Monkstown) or his son, Archdeacon Charles Lindsay (the perpetual curate of Monkstown).

There are indications that Archdeacon Lindsay could antagonise people. Judge Day described him as 'wrong-headed'. From Lindsay's remark in the Monkstown Baptismal Register of 1822 it would also appear, reading between the lines, that he was at odds with the parishioners of Booterstown: he said at the time, 'It is to be observed … that in the present state of church discipline many things may be done in Booterstown without my knowledge or that of the Archdeacon of Dublin'. Lindsay also seems to have had problems in Killiney: in 1824, when he gave the Monkstown Vestry 'some old accts and duplicate leases' that had been in his possession, he included a lease 'of the premises at Killiney', adding these words in the Vestry book, 'out of which we have now been ejected'. Unfortunately, there are no further clues to explain this apparent act of subordination, which was only the first of many.

During the summer of 1827, obviously thinking that they had been fobbed off for too long, the parishioners took things into their own hands. When Archdeacon Lindsay departed on his protracted holiday, a group of his parishioners living in Killiney began to meet for services, apparently in a private house, knowingly flouting his authority. According to *Saunders's News-Letter* of 16 October 1827, on his return Archdeacon Lindsay threatened 'legal proceedings' against his recalcitrant parishioners and posted a notice on the door of 'the temporary building in which Divine Service had been performed'. It read:

> 'Killiney, Sunday, October 14, 1827 — The congregation who have
> hitherto attended this place of worship are requested to take notice,
> that in consequence of the prohibition of the Incumbent of the Parish
> of Monkstown, Divine Service cannot be celebrated here as usual.'

Saunders's News-Letter added that although Lindsay's 'prerogative was invaded by the establishment of a house of prayer within his jurisdiction; invasion of right there could be none, for the officiating clergyman received neither tithes nor dues'. The following day an anonymous letter, written by 'A friend to Truth and Honour' (and obviously, too, of the Lindsays), appeared in the same newspaper, claiming that Archdeacon Lindsay was 'perfectly justified in the step he took'. He thought that the parishioners' move was premature, claiming that the Lindsays should have been given more time to organise the building of the chapel of ease. The writer said that they 'had been aware of the necessity for a place of worship in Killiney' because of 'the distance in the best of seasons, and the inclemency of winter weather'. They had therefore agreed to the building of two new chapels of ease, at Killiney and Dalkey, had arranged for their endowment and nominated two curates (? Bonrue/Bonvie to Killiney and Crooke to Dalkey) in readiness. However, while Archdeacon Lindsay was away, 'a Calvinistic Conventicle [a word meaning a clandestine irregular religious assembly] … had gotten foot in the neighbourhood (and) … had made a few female converts'. The report continued, 'A private house (was) opened in a hasty (and) unbecoming manner, for Divine Worship. A new Curate (was) placed there: not the nominee of the Rector …'

Meanwhile, the exasperated Judge Day (chairman of the first Building Committee for the enlargement of Monkstown Parish Church, being designed by Semple & Son; *see Chapter 5*) jotted in his diary for November 1827:

> 'I have been negotiating while in town between the Abp [Archbishop] of Dublin & that wrong-
> headed fellow Archdn Lindsay our Rector about re-opening our Place of Worship at Killiney,
> & hope to have succeeded. Lindsay & that contemptible conceited worldling the Bp of Kildare
> his father will seek an Act of Plt enabling Him to Endow a Perpetual Cure w/in Land in Dalkey
> & the Abp will License our Conventicles [also means place of assembly but without the
> derogatory implications, but Day is probably writing with 'tongue in cheek'] as a Chapel of Ease
> & require the Archdn to appoint a Curate or in default thereof His Grace will re-appoint the 2
> Clergymen who before gratuitously did duty there. This week I trust will conclude the
> discussions amicably. Beati pacifice.'

Saunders's News-Letter reported the happy outcome on 26 December 1827:

> 'Killiney Church was reopened on Sunday for the celebration of Divine Worship, when a
> congregation of over 100 persons was assembled, although the notice did not exceed a few
> hours. The Rev. Mr. Bonvie [?] preached an excellent sermon.'

Since the chapel of ease at Killiney was not built until 1834, the 'temporary building' shut down by Archdeacon Lindsay just two months before must be the 'Killiney Church' referred to in the article.

On 27 January 1828 a notice was displayed on the main door of Monkstown Church:

> 'You are requested to take notice that a vestry will be held … on the 5th day of February …
> for the purpose of obtaining and giving the consent of the parishioners in vestry assembled to

the building and maintainance of a Parochial Chapel of Ease at or near Killiney in this Parish pursuant to the provisions of an Act of Parliament for that purpose first had and obtained.'

On 5 February that year, the Monkstown Vestry 'resolved that we do hereby authorize the Minister and Church wardens on the part of the Parishioners to express and declare their consent in writing to the building, and to the maintainence by parochial assessment of a Chapel of Ease at or near Killiney, and to have the same transmitted and duly witnessed before the two Houses of Parliament'. Judge Day smugly reported in his diary, 'Our little chapel of ease is reopened and we muster a comfortable congregation'.

On 4 March 1828 the Killiney Chapel (Ireland) Bill was discussed in the House of Commons. Henry Grattan did not support it, arguing that 'the chapel was not wanted, and (that) the erection of it would only bring about much unnecessary expense on the parish of Monkstown'. However, a Mr Moore opposed him, maintaining that 'the vestry of Monkstown, the perpetual curate [Charles Lindsay] and the Rector [Bishop Lindsay, the Bishop of Kildare] … had all agreed' that the chapel was necessary because the present church 'was not large enough to contain the parishioners', as reported in *Saunders's News-Letter* of 8 March 1828. All this was going on just at the time when Monkstown Church itself was on the drawing-board and being designed to fit a congregation of 1,200 (*see Chapter 5*).

And so, on 15 July 1828, 'An Act for erecting a Chapel of Ease at Killiney in the Parish of Monkstown in the County and Diocese of Dublin, and for providing for the due Celebration of Divine Service therein' (9° Georgii IV Cap 52) was passed. The relevant passage reads:

'Whereas the Parish of Monkstown … has of late Years become very populous, and a considerable Number of Inhabitants reside at Killiney in the said Parish, at a Distance of Two Miles and upwards from the Parish Church, which is not sufficiently large to accommodate the increasing population of said parish; and the Parishioners dwelling in the Neighbourhood of Killiney aforesaid are very much in need of a particular Place of Worship nearer their Homes … And whereas many Inhabitants of the said Parish have expressed an earnest Desire that said Chapel of Ease should be forthwith erected … for Morning and Evening Prayer, the Sacraments of Baptism and the Lord's Supper — but not for Confirmation, Matrimony or Burial of the Dead — to continue to be solemnised in the Parish Church only …'

The next step was the endowment of land for the curate of the new chapel of ease. In November 1828 'the Twelve Acres, part of the Furlongs in Dalkey' were granted to Killiney; this land was originally designated for the glebe house of Monkstown and sold for 'five shillings sterling' by Archbishop William King of Dublin to the Rev. Allan Maddison of Monkstown one hundred years earlier (*see Chapter 11*).

Charles Sleator was the first curate of Killiney, from 1828 until 1843, when he was made perpetual curate until his death in 1868. For the first eight years, until the new chapel of ease, to be called St Matthias's, was completed in 1835, the Rev. Sleator had to take services in a 'temporary church'. In 1831 it was reported that two Sunday services were held in summer and one in winter, with a congregation of about 170, which was said to be 'increasing', according to the 1st Report in 1835 of the Commissioners of Public Instruction. In 1834 Frederick Darley was commissioned to design the new Killiney church. His plan was submitted to the Monkstown Vestry at Christmas that year, recorded in the minutes as: 'Killiney Church, Plan of the enclosed Pews. 26th Dec. 1834. Fredk. Darley, Junr. Archt. This plan of part of Killiney Chapel of Ease was this day submitted to a Vestry legally convened, in the Vestry Room of Monkstown Church, and the Pews were allocated to the several purchasers as therein marked. Charles Lindsay, Minister. J. Murphy, George Jackson, Church Wardens.'

A Mr Dixon (probably Richard Dixon, the teacher of Clonkeen School at Kill-of-the-Grange) was appointed as the new 'Chapel Clerk', starting from 4 February 1834 with a salary of £7-10s. (This position and wage would have been the equivalent of that of the parish clerk in Monkstown.) A sextoness was employed from the same date — Mrs Mary Robinson at a salary of £3-15s per annum. The new Chapel of Ease was consecrated in April 1835, to serve Killiney, Ballybrack and Dalkey. The design was critised years later by the Rev. Robert B. Stoney in his series of articles on 'Dublin suburban churches', published in the *Irish Ecclesiastical Gazette* during 1880; he said that Killiney was 'the usual orthodox small country edifice … (where) the Communion Table was under this window, and the rails came out in the form of a bow between the desk and the pulpit, thus completely blocking up the east end and making minister and people almost touch each other during service'.

In 1866 it seems that Charles Sleator attempted to convert his chapel of ease into a parish church. This was against the specific advice of the Rev. Ronald MacDonnell, the somewhat irascible incumbent of Monkstown (1857–78).[1] In the 1870s William J. Welland enlarged St Matthias's by building on a chancel and transept. The Rev. Robert Stoney, continuing his outspoken articles in the *Irish Ecclesiastical Gazette*, thought that the church should 'be made uniform throughout', by adding a second transept and organ chamber, so that the choir could sit in the chancel. St Matthias's did, indeed, became a parish church, in 1876 — eight years too late for Charles Sleator.

Appendix 2

The Monkstown organs

Specification of first organ (*c.* 1789)

'It consists of a Principal, Twelfth, Fifteenth, Open and Stopt Diapasons, Flute, Cornet and Sequealtra [*sic; recte* Sesquialtera]. It stands twelve feet high and nine feet broad, in a handsome mahogany case', reported *Saunders's News-Letter* of 27 March 1832.

Abridged specification of 1832 organ[1]

Two manual organ, with Gothic case, measuring 15ft x 12ft x 6ft 6ins, with 18 stops and 1,134 pipes. Builder's name unknown.

Great Organ	GG to G	11 stops
Swell Organ	Tenor D to G	7 stops
Pedal Organ	Double Open 16'	(one octave)

3 couplers and 3 composition pedals

This organ was sold to the Free Church, Cork, in 1872. A new set of pedals, CCC to D, 27 notes, was added when it was erected there and the opening recital (December 1872) was given by Dr Marks of St Fin Barre's Cathedral.

Specification of 1872 organ[2]

Built by Telford & Telford, three manual organ with 28 stops and 1,940 pipes. Present whereabouts unknown.

Swell Organ

Open Diapason	8'
Hohl Flute	8'
Octave	4'
Flute Harmonic	4'
Fifteenth	2'
Mixture 17.19.22	(3 ranks)
Cornopean	8'
Oboe	8'
Tremulant	

Great Organ

Bourdon	16'
Double Gamba	16'
Open Diapason	8'
Salicional	8'
Rohr Flute	8'
Octave	4'
Flute Harmonic	4'
Twelfth	2⅔'
Fifteenth	2'
Mixture 19.22.26.29	(4 ranks)
Trumpet	8'

Choir Organ

Dulciana	8'
Viol di Gamba	8'
Lieblich Gedact	8'
Flute Harmonic	4'
Piccolo Harmonic	2'
Clarionet	8'

Pedal Organ

Grand Double Open Diapason	16'
Bourdon	16'
Open Diapason	8'

Couplers

Swell to Great
Swell to Choir
Swell to Pedal
Great to Pedal

5 composition pedals
Mechanical action throughout

Specification of 1898 organ[3]
Built by Gray & Davison, three manual organ with 32 stops and 1,952 pipes.

Swell Organ			Choir Organ	
Bourdon	16'		Gamba	8'
Open Diapason	8'		Clarinet Flute	8'
Lieblich Gedact	8'		Dulciana	8'
Gamba	8'		Wald Flute	4'
Keraulophon	8'		Fifteenth	2'
Voix Celeste	8'		Corno Di Bassetto	8'
Echo Dulciana	8'			
Flauto Traverso	4'		**Pedal Organ**	
Flageolet	2'		Open Diapason	16'
Mixture 15.19.22	(3 ranks)		Bourdon	16'
Cornopean	8'		Violoncello	8'
Oboe	8'		Trombone	16'
Vox Humana	8'			
Tremulant			**Couplers**	
			Swell Octave	
Great Organ			Swell to Great	
Double Diapason	16'		Swell to Choir	
Open Diapason	8'		Swell to Pedal	
Stopped Diapason	8'		Great to Pedal	
Gamba	8'		Choir to Pedal	
Principal	4'			
Harmonic Flute	4'		6 thumb pistons	
Fifteenth	2'		10 composition pedals	
Mixture 12.15.19	(3 ranks)		Tracker action to manuals	
Posaune	8'		Pneumatic action to pedals,	
			drawstops and pistons	

The present organ[4]
The 1898 organ, as rebuilt by R.E. Meates & Son in 1965–6, has 39 stops and 2,158 pipes.

Swell Organ			Choir Organ	
Open Diapason	8'		Gamba	8'
Lieblich Gedact	8'		Clarinet Flute	8'
Gamba	8'		Dulciana	8'
Keraulophon	8'		Wald Flute	4'
Voix Celeste	8'		Nazard	2⅔'
Principal	4'		Fifteenth	2'
Flauto Traverso	4'		Corno Di Bassetto	8'
Flageolet	2'			
Mixture 19.22.26	(3 ranks)		**Pedal Organ**	
Contra Fagotto	16'		Open Diapason	16'
Cornopean	8'		Bourdon	16'
Oboe	8'		Echo Bourdon	16'
Clarion	4'		Octave	8'
Tremulant			Violoncello	8'
			Bass Flute	8'
Great Organ			Super Octave	4'
Double Diapason	16'		Choral Bass	4'
Large Open Diapason	8'		Trombone	16'
Open Diapason	8'			
Stopped Diapason	8'			

Couplers

Gamba	8'	Swell Octave
Principal	4'	Swell to Great
Harmonic Flute	4'	Swell to Choir
Fifteenth	2'	Swell to Pedal
Mixture 12.15.19	(3 ranks)	Great to Pedal
Posaune	8'	Choir to Pedal
		19 thumb pistons
		7 toe pistons
		Tracker action to manuals
		Electro-pneumatic action to pedals, draw-stops and pistons

Monkstown's organists

c. 1789–1825	Peter Alma (36 years)
1825–7	Edward Alma
1827–8	Ernest Crofton
1828 (Easter–June)	Henry Hooper
1828–34	Mr Jephson
1834–46	Frederick Hankin
1846–71 (January)	Henry Toole (25 years)
1871 (February)	Temporary organist: James Taylor
1871–82	Francis Quin
1882–1937	Bartholomew Warburton Rooke (55 years)
1937–41	George Rothwell
1941–90	William Gabriel Ebbs (49 years)
1991 (1 January to present)	Siobhán Kilkelly

Telford & Telford Organ Builders

An article in *The Dublin Builder* of 1 April 1860 describes a visit to Telford & Telford's 'extensive manufactory':

'Mr Telford was engaged making the working drawings for (St Catherine's Church) and we cannot conceive an occupation requiring more universal information and skill than a clever organ builder. He must have practical knowledge as an architect, engineer, carpenter, joiner, worker in metals; be versed in music, acoustics, pneumatics, and mechanics … [A detailed description followed of the shop floor] … We were much gratified with the bustle and business tone pervading the building. On the ground floor some men were engaged casting the metal in sheets to make the metal pipes. This metal is a compound of tin and lead, and is melted in a cauldron holding about a ton and a half. When properly mixed and ready, it is poured into a box, which is moved along a bench, leaving behind it a sheet of liquid metal, of the requisite thickness, on a lining of ticken. The pipes are cut out of these sheets, turned on mandrils, and soldered up. Others were engaged on a large bellows; some at the case and training; others at the sound-boards and action; every portion of the instrument being made on the premises, with the exception of the keys. Drawings are first made of every portion of the instrument, and then each part is allotted to that particular branch. Numerous hands are busily employed on an organ for His Grace the Duke of Leinster, at Carton …'

Appendix 3

Monkstown's clergy

I am indebted to W.J.R. Wallace for his monumental *Clergy of Dublin and Glendalough* (2001), from which I have unashamedly pirated biographies of the Monkstown clergy.

District and perpetual curates (PC)

1615	**Byrn**, Morris (? Morgan): non-resident, sequestered.
1630	**Lloyd**, William Morris: also curate in Killiney and Dalkey.
1639	**Davis**, John: also curate in Carrickbrennan.
1642	**Foxwith**, Randolph: licensed 1 July 1642.
1670–85	**Ward**, Thomas (?–1695): possibly the same Thomas Ward who was later dean of Connor and deprived of his deanery for adultery.
1685–91	**Dean (Deane)**, William (1650–91): licensed with Kill, 3 June 1685.
1691–1741	**Maddison**, Allan (1663–1741): licensed PC to Monkstown and Kill, 26 April 1691.
1741–69	**Heany**, Thomas (1706–69): licensed PC to Monkstown, Kill, Dalkey and Stillorgan, 12 February 1741.
1769–75	**Robinson**, Thomas (1735–97): licensed 22 February 1769.
1775–8	**Hely**, John (1738–78): nominated 22 August; licensed 28 August 1775.
1778–80	**Ledwich**, Edward (1753–?): licensed 19 December 1778.
1780–2	**Forsayeth**, John (1736–85): nominated and licensed 8 March 1780.
1782–91	**Jephson**, William (1734–91): nominated and licensed 18 March 1782.
1791–9	**Ryves**, John William Dudley (1716–1801): nominated 21 December 1790; licensed 21 January 1791; buried Killiney Old Graveyard (copied in 1895–6): 'Here lieth the Remains of the Revd. Dudley Ryves. Late Minister of the Parish of Monckstown & its Unions. Departed this Life March ye Second 1801.'
1799–1802	**Cramer**, Marmaduke (1739–1802): nominated 14 February; licensed 29 February 1799.
1802–4	**Dunn**, James (1767–1838): nominated 16 July; licensed 20 July 1802; resigned 17 September 1804.
1804–15	**Harpur**, Singleton (?–1815): nominated 28 September; licensed 9 October 1804.
1815–55	**Lindsay**, Charles (1790–1855): nominated 20 June; licensed PC to Kill, Dalkey, Monkstown and Killiney, 23 June 1815.
1855–7	**Fitzgerald**, William (1814–83): licensed 13 May 1855.
1857–78	**MacDonnell**, Ronald (1825–89): licensed 8 April 1857; resigned 19 September 1878.

Incumbents

1878–94	**Peacocke**, Joseph Ferguson (1835–1916): nominated 16 October; instituted 25 October 1878; had served as curate (1863–73).
1894–1929	**Dowse**, John Clarence (1856–1930): nominated 28 June; instituted 9 July 1894.
1929–31	**Oulton**, John Ernest Leonard (*c.* 1887–1957): instituted 13 November 1929.
1931–45	**Forde**, Harold Giles (*c.* 1890–1945): instituted 4 February 1931.
1945–58	**Butler**, Arthur Hamilton (1912–91): instituted 28 November 1945.
1958–78	**Wynne**, Richard William (Billy) Maurice (1919–2000): instituted 16 September 1958.
1979–present	**Dalton**, Kevin (1932–): instituted 2 February 1979, the 27th incumbent.

Curates

1699	**Tollett**, Marcus
1709	**Meredith**, William (1661–?)
1731–8	**Babe**, George (1703–75)
1737–40	**Gibson**, Matthew (1712–40)
1740–4	**Dickinson**, Daniel (1715– ?)
1762–5	**Wright**, Henry (?–1773)
1768–9	**La Nauze**, Alexander (1744–69)
1770–7	**Andrews**, John (1731–77)
1771	**Towers**, Anthony
1773–4	**Ashe**, Isaac (1750–1834)
1775–85	**Beatty**, Edward (?–1818)
1785–92	**Burrowes**, John (?–1797)
1793	**Burrowes**, Robert (1759–1841)
1799	**Robinson,** George (1765–?)
1800–2	**Dunn**, James (1767–1838)
1801–16	**Tew,** William (1770–1830)
1817	**McKenna**, Hill
1818	**Galwey,** Charles (1802–88)
1821	**Kinahan,** John
1824–7	**Mahaffy**, Nathaniel Brindley (1799–1855)
1827	**Grier**, Samuel
1829	**Roberts,** Walter Cramer (1802–?)
1830–5	**West**, John (1805–90)
1832–43	**Grant**, John (1804–58)
1836–54	**Williams**, John St George (1806–?)
1843–5	**Sanders**, Francis Alexander (1818–92)
1845–7	**Stepney**, Henry Paisley Herbert (1816–?)
1850–9	**Rooke**, Thomas (1825–89)
1854–7	**Mulloy**, William James (1816–88)
1857–8	**Fawcett**, John
1859	**Grogan**, John (1816–99). Although he was not licensed for Monkstown, according to the registers, Grogan took services from January to May 1859.
1859–63	**Hobson**, William Thomas (1833–97)
1860–2	**Clare**, Mervyn Archdall (1832–?)
1863–73	**Peacocke**, Joseph Ferguson (1835–1916)
1864–8	**Johnson**, Henry (1836–1906)
1868–78	**Palmer**, Abraham Henry Herbert (1843–?)
1874–5	**Alcock**, Alured (1816–93), locum (1 October, for twelve months) for Dr Ronald MacDonnell, who was advised by his doctor to rest.
1874–8	**Kennedy**, James Houghton (1842–1924)
1878–86	**Mahaffy**, Gilbert (1850–1916)
1886–92	**Dowse**, William (1856–1939)
1892–3	**Mervyn**, Frederick William (1858–1933)
1894	**Gibbon**, William Monk (1864–1935)
1894–5	**Goff**, John Richards (?–1951)
1896–1902	**Goldsmith**, Edward James
1902–3	**Rogers**, Travers Guy (1876–1967)
1903–6	**Buchanan**, Louis George (1870–1952)
1906–9	**Phair**, John Percy (1876–1967)
1909–15	**Strong**, Charles Henry (1869–1964)
1916–24	**Elliott**, George Ruddell (?–1933)
1924–32	**Coulter**, William Henry (1895–1977)
1932–5	**McGinley**, John Barnhill Smith (1905–80)

1935–7	**Butler**, Arthur Hamilton (1912–91)
1938–40	**Cooper**, William Gough Porter (1915–90)
1940	**Colin,** D.E., temporary curate for about five months, between Cooper's enlistment and Kennedy's ordination.
1941–4	**Kennedy**, Thomas Henry (?–1970)
1944–5	**Ruskell**, T. George Arnold
1946–51	**Stokes**, Albert Edward (1921–)
1951	**Hipwell**, Trevor Senior (1923–95)
1952–4	**O'Driscoll**, Thomas Herbert (1928–)
1954–7	**Large**, Richard Groves (1932–85)
1958–60	**Tuckey**, John William Townsend (1919–)
1960–2	**Levingston**, Peter Owen Wingfield (1931–)
1962–6	**Henderson**, James Edward (1928–93)
1966–8	**Hyland**, Cecil George (1938–)
1969–71	**Pike**, William Prenter (1941–)
1972–6	**Clarke**, John Percival (1944–)
1976–9	**Hammond**, James Francis (1948–97)
1980–2	**Muir**, David Trevor (1949–)
1986–90	**Dowd**, Garfield (Gary) George (1960–)
1993–5	**Neill**, Stephen Mahon (1969–)
1999–2001	**Hayden**, Mark Joseph James (1968–)

Appendix 4

Monkstown's churchwardens

The following list of churchwardens for 1706–2003 has been compiled from several primary sources, including the Vestry minutes, Annual Reports of Vestry, Rural Dean's Visitations, *Monkstown Reviews* and newspapers of the day. The succession of churchwardens for the period 1737–77 was abstracted from *The Register of the Union of Monkstown, Co. Dublin, 1669–1786* (Vol. VI), published by the Parochial Register Society of Dublin (Guinness 1908), and also checked in the Vestry book of 1744–77. Spellings have been kept as in the original documents. Efforts were made to discover Christian names for those churchwardens within living memory. 'R' and 'P' refer to the rector's churchwarden and the people's churchwarden respectively.

1706	Thomas Hoult and John Baxter
1737	John Laight and Oliver Bray
1738–42	*No information available*
1743	Samuel Gravill and James Byrne
1744	Thomas Maguire and Michael Gilligan
1745	William Syddon and Joy Whitmore
1746	*No information available*
1747	George Byrne, Esq. and Lewis Roberts, Esq.
1748	George Byrne, Esq. and Lewis Roberts, Esq.
1749	Lewis Roberts, Esq. and Robert Towson
1750	John Alleburn and Robert Towson
1751	Simon Johnson and John Davis
1752	Thomas Archbold of Dalkey and John Fawcett of Brenanstown
1753	Edward Maunsell, Esq. and Henry Gavin
1754	Michael Cullen and William Fearis
1755	Hugh Jones and Joseph Mills, Junr.
1756	Charles Coleman and John Watson
1757	James Ford
1758	*No information available*
1759	William Delamain and John Roberts
1760	Isaac Espinasse, Esq. and George Glover, Esq.
1761	Isaac Espinasse, Esq. and George Glover, Esq.
1762	Robert White, Esq. of Monkstown and William Medcalf of Stillorgan
1763	Sir George Ribton, Bart and Robert White, Esq.
1764	Jacob Sherrard of Dalkey and William Garstin of Newtownpark
1765	The Hon. Henry Loftus and Michael Byrne, Esq.
1766	Charles, Viscount Ranelagh and Luke Mercer, Esq.
1767	Charles, Viscount Ranelagh and Luke Mercer, Esq.
1768	Ralph Ward, Esq. and John Mapas, Esq.
1769	Anthony Grayson, Esq. and Richard Robinson, Esq.
1770	Robert Barry, Esq. and Isaac Espinasse (resigned in May and George Marjoribanks elected instead)
1771	William Roseingrave, Esq. of Dunleary and John Sproule (appointed 1 April; resigned 8 April; Capt. John Aldercron appointed instead)
1772	Henry Shawe, Esq. of Dunleary and James Condron, Esq. of Newtownpark
1773	Robert Towson of Killiney and Samuel Grevill of Laughanstown
1774	Isaac Espinasse, Esq. (resigned 6 June; John Watson, Esq. appointed instead) and John McDermott, Esq.
1775	Peter Warren of Kill and J. Sherwood of Killiney
1776	Frederick Flood, Esq. and James Shiel, Esq.
1777	Robert Byrne, Esq. and Thomas Ridgate Maunsell, Esq.

1778–81	*No information available*
1782	Ld Ranelagh and Lt John Parnele
1783	Pat Bride
1784	John Lees and Ralph Ward
1785	John Lees and Ralph Ward
1786	*No information available*
1787	Sir Nicholas Lawless, Bart and John Lees, Esq.
1788	Ld Viscount Ranelagh and John Lees, Esq.
1789	John Lees, Esq. and Robert Ashworth
1790	William Digges Latouche and John Swan, Esq.
1791	John Lees, Esq. and John Swan, Esq.
1792	John Lees, Esq. and Robert Alexander, Esq.
1793	John Lees, Esq. and Robert Alexander, Esq.
1794	John Lees, Esq. and Robert Alexander, Esq.
1795	John Lees, Esq. and Robert Alexander, Esq.
1796	John Lees, Esq. and Robert Alexander, Esq.
1797–1803	*No information available*
1804	Major General John Pratt and John Armit
1805	Major General John Pratt (R) and John Armit (P)
1806	Colonel William Browne (R) and John Armit, Esq. (P)
1807	Colonel William Browne (R) and John Armit, Esq. (P)
1808	Alderman W.H. Archer (R) and Colonel William Browne (P)[1]
1809	Alderman John Cash (R) and Alderman W.H. Archer (P)
1810	John Creathorne (R) and Nicholas Kildahl (P)
1811	John Creathorne (R) and Nicholas Kildahl (P); resigned in June 'on account of going to reside in Dublin'; George Casson (P) appointed instead
1812	William Disney, Esq. (R) and George Maunsell, Esq. (P)
1813	James Digges Latouche, Esq. of Sans Souci (R) and Edward Matthews, Esq. (P)
1814	William Palmer, Esq. (R) and Robert Alexander, Jun. Esq. (P)
1815	William Palmer, Esq. (R) and Robert Alexander, Jun. Esq. (P)
1816	Sir William Betham (R) and George Waller, Esq. (P)
1817	Sir William Betham (R) and George Waller, Esq. (P)
1818	Sir William Betham (R) and George Waller, Esq. (P)
1819	Richard Espinasse (R) and Sir Richard Steele, Bart (P)
1820	Sackville H. Lovett, Esq. (R) and Ford Leathley (P)
1821	Luke Tinkler, Esq. (R) and James Price (P)
1822	Luke Tinkler, Esq. and James Price
1823	George Earl Gregg and Benjamin Grierson
1824	George Earl Gregg and William Hamy
1825	Arthur Perrin, Esq. and Henry Kyle
1826	Major Henry Leslie and William Hutchinson of Bullock
1827	Major Charles Pratt of Stoneville and Henry Forde of Monkstown
1828	William Hanks, Esq. and John Swift Emerson, Esq.
1829	The Honourable John Jones and Captain E. Stratford Kirwan of Monkstown House, Sproule's Avenue
1830	Fenton Hort and John Murphy
1831	James Price and Henry Forde
1833	John Murphy and George Jackson
1834	William Disney and Joseph Kincaid
1835	Henry Cash and John Vance
1836	John Williamson and Alexander Boyle
1837	*No information available*
1838	John Busby and Basil Orpin
1839	Colonel Pratt and John Murphy, Esq.
1840	Benjamin Grant and Charles Haliday
1841	Captain Joseph H. Gardiner and John E. Hyndman, Esq.

1842	Edmond Atkinson and Horatio Nelson Wallace, Esq.
1843	Edmond Atkinson and Horatio Nelson Wallace, Esq.
1844	William Andrews and Thomas Dixon
1845	Henry Samuel Close and Lieut-Colonel Charles Pratt
1846	William Woodroofe, Esq. and James Vance, Esq.
1847	John Galloway and Horatio Nelson Wallace
1848	J. Harrison and Elias Arnold
1849	Elias Arnold and Surgeon Thomas Belton
1850	George Williamson and Galloway
1851	J. Kincaid and Joseph Finucane
1852	Twigg
1853	Murdock Green and Charles Butler, MD
1854	Charles Copland and Robert C. Lee
1855	Major F. Winter and Adam Millar
1856	John Mallet Williamson, Esq. and Robert Wilson
1857	Molyneux Cecil John Betham and Robert Giveen
1858	Henry Colles (R) and Augustus Arthur, Esq. of Sloperton (P)
1859	Joseph Kincaid and Keith C.H. Hallowes
1860	*No information available*
1861	Gilbert Saunders, Esq. (R) and Henry Andrews (P)[2]
1862	Augustus Arthur, Esq. (R) and Captain Molyneux Betham (P), resigned and replaced by his brother, Captain Sheffield Betham (P)
1863	Lieut-Colonel Robert Waller (R) and John Mallet Williamson, Esq. (P)
1864	Colonel Robert Waller (R) and John Mallet Williamson, Esq. (P)
1865	Captain Sheffield Philip Fiennes Betham (R) and John Galloway, Jun. (P)
1866	Captain Sheffield Philip Fiennes Betham (R) and William Parry (P)
1867	Captain Sheffield Philip Fiennes Betham (R) and William Parry (P)
1868	Captain Sheffield Philip Fiennes Betham (R) and Arthur Rotheram (P)
1869	Evory Carmichael (R) and Thomas Dockrell (P)
1870	Evory Carmichael (R) and Thomas Dockrell (P)
1871	James Stewart Kincaid (R) and Harry Hodges (P)
1872	James Stewart Kincaid (R) and Harry Hodges (P)
1873	Captain Sheffield Philip Fiennes Betham (R) and W.H. Robinson (P)
1874	Captain Sheffield Philip Fiennes Betham (R) and W.H. Robinson (P)
1875	Henry S. Watson (R) and Joseph Galloway (P)
1876	Joseph Galloway (R) and John E. Madden (P)
1877	John E. Madden (R) and Richard H.M. Orpen (P)
1878	Richard H.M. Orpen (R) and John Kempster (P)
1879	James Stewart Kincaid (R) and John Kempster (P)
1880	James Stewart Kincaid (R) and William Mansfield Mitchell (P)
1881	Joseph Galloway (R) and Fitzadam Millar (P)
1882	Joseph Galloway (R) and Fitzadam Millar (P)
1883	Richard Pim (R) and Captain Edward Chaloner Knox (P)
1884	Richard Pim (R) and Captain Edward Chaloner Knox (P)
1885	James Robert Stewart, Jun. (R) and Francis Johnston (P)
1886	James Robert Stewart, Jun. (R) and Francis Johnston (P)
1887	John Kempster (R) and William Robert Bruce (P)
1888	John Kempster (R) and William Robert Bruce (P)
1889	Fitzadam Millar (R) and Arthur Marrable (P)
1890	Fitzadam Millar (R) and Arthur Marrable (P)
1891	Joseph Galloway (R) and Arthur Rotheram (P)
1892	Joseph Galloway (R) and Arthur Rotheram (P)
1893	Francis Johnston (R) and Guy Brabazon Pilkington (P)
1894	W.J. Johnston (R) and Guy Brabazon Pilkington (P)
1895	Richard Pim (R) and R. Blair White (P)
1896	Richard Pim (R) and R. Blair White (P)

1897	R. Blair White (R) and Joseph J.H. Carson (P)
1898	Fitzadam Millar (R) and Joseph J.H. Carson (P)
1899	Fitzadam Millar (R) and John Galloway (P)
1900	Charles Kough (R) and John Galloway (P)
1901	Charles Kough (R) and John Kempster (P)
1902	Greenwood Pim (R) and John Kempster (P)
1903	Greenwood Pim (R) and Dr Robert Lynn Heard (P)
1904	Dr Walter Ernest Adeney (R) and Dr Robert Lynn Heard (P)
1905	Dr Walter Ernest Adeney (R) and Guy Brabazon Pilkington (P)
1906	Richard Pim (R) and Guy Brabazon Pilkington (P)
1907	Richard Pim (R) and Guy Brabazon Pilkington (P)
1908	Joseph A.Hayes (R) and R. Blair White (P)
1909	Joseph A.Hayes (R) and Colonel George C. Dobbs (P)
1910	Richard Pim (R) and Fitzadam Millar (P)
1911	Arthur Benjamin Watson, LL.D (R) and John Kempster, C.E. (P)
1912	Dr Walter Ernest Adeney (R) and William Tatlow, MA (P)
1913	Dr Walter Ernest Adeney (R) and William Tatlow, MA (P)
1914	Guy Brabazon Pilkington (R) and Herbert W. Jones, MA (P)
1915	Herbert W. Jones, MA and R. Blair White (P)
1916	R. Blair White (R) and Lieut-Col H.F. Macartney (P)
1917	Lieut-Col H.F. Macartney (R) and Herbert D.Vaughan (P)
1918	Arthur Fitzmaurice (R), died Oct; William Tatlow (R) elected instead; Herbert D. Vaughan (P)
1919	Dr Robert Cecil de Courcy Wheeler (R) and R. Blair White (P)
1920	Dr Robert Cecil de Courcy Wheeler (R) and Arthur A. Greene, MA (P)
1921	Walter Ernest Adeney, D.Sc (R) and Arthur A. Greene, MA (P)
1922	Dr Walter Ernest Adeney (R) and William R. Twigg (P). During Dr Adeney's absence for a few months, William Tatlow took his place.
1923	Charles Craig Scott (R) and William R. Twigg (P)
1924	Charles Craig Scott (R) and Captain F.E. Pim (P)
1925	William F. Wells (R) (died during office; replaced by Kenneth C. Bailey (R)); Captain F.E. Pim (P)
1926	Kenneth C. Bailey, D.Sc, FTCD (R) and Arthur A. Greene, MA (P)
1927	Ernest Frederick Noel Taylor, PASI (R) and H.W. Lea (Buddy) (P)
1928	Ernest Frederick Noel Taylor, PASI (R) and H.W. Lea (Buddy) (P)
1929	R.I.A. Jameson (R)[3] and Frederick Ernest Bermingham (P)
1930	Arthur A. Greene (R) and Frederick Ernest Bermingham (P)
1931	Walter Ernest Adeney, D.Sc (R) and Vincent Allman Smith (P)
1932	Vincent Allman Smith (R) and William Boulton Conyngham (P)
1933	Dr H.W. Parke (R) and William Boulton Conyngham (P)
1934	Cecil R. Ridgeway (R) and Arthur E. Snow (P)
1935	Robert Hudson (R) and Arthur E. Snow (P)
1936	Victor Ormsby McCormick (R) and William J. Bell (P)
1937	William Boulton Conyngham (R) and William J. Bell (P)
1938	Henry (Harry) Charles Lidstone (R) and John E. Commins (P)
1939	Edwin H. Bermingham (R) and John E. Commins (P)
1940	Arthur E. Coe (R) and Henry (Harry) Charles Lidstone (P)
1941	Ernest Frederick Noel Taylor (R) and Henry (Harry) Charles Lidstone (P)
1942	Arthur E. Snow (R) and Vincent Allman Smith (P)
1943	Ivan Franklin (R) and William (Billy) H.R. Lee (P)
1944	Edwin H. Bermingham (R) and William (Billy) H.R. Lee (P)
1945	John Thomas Keegan (R) and Geoffrey A. Mackay (P)
1946	John Thomas Keegan (R) and T.N. Long (P)
1947	J. Edward (Ted) O'Callaghan (R) and Thomas N. Long (P)
1948	Robert Evan Felton (R) and Thomas N. Long (P)
1949	J.G.B. Lamb (R) and Charles H. Mitchell (P)

1950	William (Billy) H. Lee (R) and Charles H. Mitchell (P)
1951	Sidney A. Henchie (R) and William (Bill) H. Walker (P)
1952	H.E. St George McClenaghan (R) and William (Bill) H. Walker (P)
1953	R.J.G. Parr (R) and T.C. Percy Kellett (P)
1954	Charles H. Mitchell (R) and T.C. Percy Kellett (P)
1955	Brian H.T. Taylor (R) and James B. Hartigan (P)
1956	Robert (Bob) J. Clinton (R) and Arthur Edgerton Ashmore (P)
1957	Arthur Edgerton Ashmore (R) and William G. McClatchie (P)
1958	C. Garrett Walker (R) and Alfred William Groves (P)
1959	Arthur E. Snow (R) and Francis F. McClatchie (P)
1960	William H. Orr (R) and Richard G. Mallet (P)
1961	Charles H. Mitchell (R) and William H. Orr (P)
1962	George A. Goff (R) and Peter E. Greville (P)[4]
1963	David R. Felton (R) and Leslie G. Andrews (P)
1964	Leslie G. Andrews (R) and John (Jack) Teggin (P)
1965	David C.M. Mitchell (R) and Lewis E. Thornton (P)
1966	Edwin R. Gorsuch (R) and Thomas (Tom) E. Aplin (P)
1967	George E. Dyke (R) and William (Bill) G. McClatchie (P)
1968	A.E. Smythe (R) and George E. Dyke (P)
1969	John (Jack) Teggin (R) and John D. Glenn (P)
1970	Charles B. Comyns (R) and John Eric Mackenzie (P)
1971	William J. Bell (R) and Marinus Huissoon (P)
1972	William H. Walker (R) and David Richard Felton (P)
1973	David Richard Felton (R) and William H. Walker (P)
1974	Timothy A.F. Chavasse (R) and Charles H. Mitchell (P)
1975	Thomas E. Aplin (R) and Thomas A. Walton (P)
1976	Brian H.T. Taylor (R) and Thomas A. Walton (P)
1977	David Rowell (R) and Robert (Bob) V. Fitzgerald (P)
1978	Edward (Ted) F.N. Seymour (R) and John L. Wynne (P)
1979	Robert (Bob) V. Fitzgerald (R) and John L. Wynne (P)
1980	William H. Deverell (R) and Lewis E. Thornton (P)
1981	David Little (R) and Timothy W.F. Gibson (P)
1982	David Rea (R) and Mrs Louise (Lou) Lowe (P)
1983	Marinus Huissoon (R) and Mrs Helen (Nell) Watkins (P)
1984	Mrs Helen (Nell) Watkins (R) and Kevin Keogh (P)
1985	Clive Cathcart (R) and Derek Dowling (P)
1986	Helen (Nell) Watkins (R); Brian Gorsuch (P) resigned June; Marinus Huissoon (P) appointed instead
1987	Lynn McCutcheon (R) and Eileen Kennedy (P)
1988	G. Derek Browne (R) and David Todd (P)
1989	William H. Deverell (R) and Robert J. Gray (P)
1990	David Davis (R) and Frederick W. Gray (P)
1991	David Davis (R) and John Burns (P)
1992	Thomas E. Aplin (R) and Lionel M. Hastings (P)
1993	Joan Talbot (R) and Jackie Orr (P)
1994	Jackie Orr (R) and Colm T. Greene (P)
1995	Colm T. Greene (R) and Elizabeth (Liz) Neill-Watson (P)
1996	Angus H.M. Macdonald (R) and Elizabeth (Liz) Neill-Watson (P)
1997	Elizabeth (Liz) Neill-Watson (R) and Angus H.M. Macdonald (P)
1998	Joyce Todd (R) and Colm T. Greene (P)
1999	Lyndon McCann (R) and Thelma King (P)
2000	Lyndon McCann (R) and Roger Hill (P)
2001	Gillian Donnelly (R) and Roger Hill (P)
2002	Gillian Donnelly (R) and Shirley Watchorn (P)
2003	Shirley Watchorn (R) and Derek Simpson (P)

Appendix 5

Parish officers

Parish and Vestry clerks

1702–8	William Hall (parish clerk), married to 'Ellenor'; children: 'Elinor' (b. 1702/3), Abigail (b. 1708 d. 1711/12) and Rachel (b. 1710). Died 7 May 1713.
1723	'There is a parish clerk licensed & lives in ye parish & performs his Duty well', said Allan Maddison's report in the Visitation of 1723.
1744–5	Richard Handberry (Vestry clerk), £2 a year.
1745–7	James Robinson (parish and Vestry clerk), £2 a year.
1747–72	Edward Lansdale (parish and Vestry clerk, bell-ringer, coal-measurer), married Elizabeth Smith of Dublin City on 11 February 1768, buried 24 July 1772.
1773–82	Robert David of Black Rock (parish and Vestry clerk, bell-ringer), married to Hannah; children: Henrietta (b. 1772), Hugh (b. 1775), Mary (b. 1777) and Christopher (b. 1780).
1776–7	William Johnston (Vestry clerk; also parish pound-keeper and bell-ringer).
1787–8	David Christian (parish clerk and 'English schoolmaster').
May 1788	John Kearney ('par clke & 'English schoolmaster, to be licd').
1794–5	James Collins (parish clerk and schoolmaster).
1797–1834	John Abbott (parish and Vestry clerk, schoolmaster), married Mary. Died 8 November 1863.
1834–55	Thomas Eustace (parish clerk, schoolmaster 1834–40, grocer and undertaker), earned £35 a year for being parish and Vestry clerk in 1847. (Eustace had been the schoolteacher at Stradbally in 1824 and Vestry clerk in Donnybrook in 1825–6, where he earned 13 guineas a year). Died 17 July 1855, aged 54.
1849	M. Cranston (Vestry clerk).
1855–72	Peter Hackett (parish clerk and schoolmaster).

Parish beadles

1806–19	James McDonald (also grave-digger and sexton, 1803–9, and bell-ringer)
1818–26	Samuel Overin
1826–c. 1829	George Hughes (also grave-digger)
1854–63	William Martin (also parish constable)
1864 (May–August)	Ward
1864 (August)–c. 1875	Christopher Davis (also grave-digger)

Parish constables

1807	John Dunbar and Thomas Brenan (£10 per annum) for the Union of Monkstown. Thomas Connors, Alexander Watson and George Hanlon for Dunleary Quay.
1808–29	Richard Martin (£12 per annum)
1854–63	William Martin (also parish beadle)

Parish pound-keepers

1759	Wm Simmons
1762	Thomas Carrol
1762– c. 1772	Edward Lansdale

1772 (7 December)	Robert David
1775–6	William Johnston (also Vestry clerk and bell-ringer)
1805–18	John Dunbar

Sextons and other church officials

1744–57	Eleanor Hall, sextoness, 'for washing the church linnen, £1' (probably the daughter of William Hall, parish clerk, 1702–8).
1757–9	Elizabeth Hall, sextoness, £2 (daughter-in-law of Eleanor Hall).
1759–60	Mrs Elizabeth Range ('for washing the Linnen and Cleaning the Church, £2').
1761–9	Rachel Dunn, church cleaner, widow of Patrick Dunn; children: Thomas (b. 1750), Patrick (b. 1755) and 'Vallintien' (b. 14 February 1757).
1769–87	Rachel Monks (née Dunn), sextoness, £6 per annum, married Charles Monks (b. 1769); child: Araminta (b. 1775). Died 1787.
1776	Hannah David, temporary sextoness, three months (wife of Robert David, parish and Vestry clerk and bell-ringer, 1773–82).
c. 1800–9	Anne Cross, sextoness, 13 guineas per annum in 1805, pension of £10 per annum (1809–15).
1803–9	James McDonald (also grave-digger, bell-ringer and beadle).
1805	Mrs Elizabeth Perry, organ-blower, £4-11s per annum.
c. 1810–64	George Argue, also grave-digger, lived at 8 Albert Place, 5 Alma Place (1859–61) and 3 Alma Place (1862–4), married Phoebe; children: George (b. 1828), Robert (b. 1829; d. 1831), Henry (b. 1831) and Robert (b. 1834). Died December 1870, aged about 90.
1809–35	Mrs Mary Abbott, sextoness, £9-15s per annum in 1834 (wife of John Abbott, schoolmaster).
1817–23	Richard Martin (also parish constable).
1819–23	Samuel Overin, Senior (also parish beadle 1818–26).
1819–23	Elizabeth Mahalm, organ-blower.
1834–5	Mrs Maria Jones, assistant sextoness, £3-5s per annum.
1834–5	Mrs Arnold, assistant sextoness, £3-5s per annum in 1834.
1835–71	Mrs Arnold, sextoness.
1834–55	Mrs Grace Malhohn (Mahalm), assistant sextoness and bellows-blower, £6-6-0 in 1834.
1835	Margaret Riggs, assistant sextoness, £2 per annum.
1834–5	Alexander Riggs, assistant sexton and bell-ringer, £12-10s per annum.
1835–63	Mary Arnett, sextoness, 16 guineas half-year's salary in 1837, lived at 1, 2 and 3 Alma Place ('Sextons' Cottages') during 1859–72. Died, aged 'about 80', May 1872.
1853–7	Mrs Cardle (Condle, Condell), 'third sextoness', £5-4s per annum.
1853–74	Charles Riggs, assistant sexton, bell-ringer, bellows-blower, £1-16s in 1853, £8 in 1874 (son of William Riggs, carpenter), married Selina Murray on 10 March 1870.
1854–75	Christopher Davis, also beadle, cleaned churchyard, grave-digger and caretaker of Clonkeen School.
1855	Edward Bryson, 'for clearing snow off Church, 10/-'.
1855	Mrs Clements
1855	Mrs Gurd
1855	Mrs Williams
1856	William Graham
1856–7	Mr and Mrs Armstrong
1857	John Moffitt, assistant sexton, 'for posting bills in Church, 5/-'.
1865	Mr Hall, 'duties [in Monkstown Church], £2 for the month'.

1864–95	William Moxham, described as 'verger' in *Thom's Directory* of 1880, living at 'Longford House', earned £15-3-4 in 1869, retired in 1895 on pension of £10 per annum.
1864–71	Mrs Mary Anne Graham, assistant sextoness.
c. 1869–70	Samuel Tomkins, £3 per annum.
1871–7	Mrs Mary Anne Graham, sextoness, 14/- per week in 1875. The Select Vestry minutes of 10 September 1877 record, 'That the sum of 9 shillings be presented to Mrs Graham as a retiring pension in consideration of her long services as sextoness of Monkstown Church'.
1871	Bayly, 'for 3 Sundays attending at church door at 2/6 for each Sunday'.
1871–7	George Shannon, assistant sexton in North Gallery.
1877–1905	Mr and Mrs George Shannon, sexton and sextoness. Responded to advertisement in the *General Advertiser* of 15 September 1877:

'Wanted for important church near Dublin, Man and his wife to act as Sexton and Caretakers; must be Irish Church; salary £1 per week, with apartments, coal and gas; characters must bear the strictest investigations. Apply, stating ages, with copies of testimonial and references.'

In 1895 the Shannons' salary was increased to £60 per annum; Mrs Shannon was to take over her husband's place 'on the N side [of the church]'. On their retirement, the Shannons were given a pension of 15/- per week during their joint lifetime or 7/6 for the surviving partner if one died, 'in consideration of the long and faithful services of George Shannon and his wife'. |
1890–3	Edward Long, also bell-ringer and organ-blower, £8 per annum.
1893–5	Irvine, assistant sexton, £6-10s per annum.
1893	Henderson (£6 per annum), Mrs Adams (£6-10s per annum), Mrs Knight (£18-4s per annum) and Morris (*c.* 8 guineas per annum).
1899–1954	Edward Simpson, assistant sexton, £12 per annum in 1909. Simpson was in charge of the church coke boilers for 53 years; in 1934, for sixteen fires at 2/6 each, he earned 40/-; in 1954 oil heating was installed.
1905–28	Mr and Mrs Lewis. In 1909 Mr Lewis's salary was raised to 30/- per week. He was paid £1 in 1925 for cleaning the gutters on the church roof, but frightened the Select Vestry on 11 November 1925 into recommending 'that a peremptory order be given to him that he was not in future to go upon the roof … or mount ladders to any height'. The Lewises were given a grant of £25 on their retirement. Miss Edith Dowse recalls, 'Mr Lewis had 6 sons and a very elegant wife. It was a sight to behold to see her walking up the aisle with the collection plate. She had a very good figure, in spite of her six sons'. Miss Edith Dowse also remembers Mr Lewis, who was a former army man, as being 'a bit fierce', although he would show the rectory children around the vaults as 'a spooky treat'.
19??–21	Arthur Long, also bell-ringer.
1928–56	Mr and Mrs William Bray. He was a former chief petty officer in the Royal Navy for 22 years. Two of his sons rang the church bell; one of them, Edward, joined the Royal Navy in 1947 and was accidentally killed, aged twenty, in 1948 on board HMS *Vanguard* in Malta (plaque on north wall of nave) and is buried in the RN Cemetery in Malta. Another son, Ken, has fond memories of his youth 'on top of the church catching pigeons to keep as pets' (*see p. xxiii*).
c. 1934–*c.* 1943	Thomas Long, probably also bell-ringer.
c. 1934–*c.* 1943	Mrs Woods, church cleaner.
c. 1934–6	Mrs Massey, church cleaner.
c. 1934–Oct. 1940	John Gray, assistant sexton. The Select Vestry suggested that his 'long and faithful service … should be recognised in a tangible form'.
1936–8	Miss Moore, church cleaner.

1946–83	Mrs Fox, church cleaner, £1-2-6 per week (five mornings) in 1949, £2-15s per week in June 1974, £14 in January 1982 (with £25 Christmas and Easter gratuities). Died in office, April 1983.
1949–86	Harry Bailey, appointed as assistant sexton in the south transept; main duties were to keep the doors properly closed and ensure that visitors were provided with books. Salary of 2/6 per Sunday, in addition to his pay for ringing the bell. By 1977 bell-ringing was his only duty (£2 per week, £7 in 1985). Died 1986.
1956–72	Frederick George Farr was appointed on William Bray's resignation, out of nineteen who applied for the post. Farr's starting salary in 1956 was £260 per annum and a free house (he and his wife lived in the schoolhouse). Mrs Cecil Wynne recalls stories being told of his cockney wit. He once caught some boys acting suspiciously in the front porch of the church, where coats were hanging. 'What are you looking for?' Fred demanded. 'Nothing!' came the answer. 'Well, I hope you found it!' he replied. While Billy Wynne was robing in the Vestry before a wedding, in the company of a nervous bridegroom, he asked Fred, 'Have you any advice to give this young man?' 'Yes', replied Fred, 'Don't!' He died in April 1972; £20 was sent to Monkstown Hospital in his memory.
1972–3	William Henry Arthur Sanderson, formerly sexton of the Mariners' Church, appointed 1 May 1972. Died January 1973.
1973–4	Stephen Black (12 May 1973–December 1974), lived in the schoolhouse with his wife and two children.
1975–97	Ronald (Ronnie) Lydmur Blay (1908–97). He lived in the sexton's apartment in the schoolhouse (advertised on 3 January 1975 as 'Spacious Flat, modernised and decorated'). Starting salary of £516 per annum and free house. Mr Blay always wore a black gown during services; this dated from as early as December 1863, when the Vestry minutes record, 'To a sexton's gown, £1-5-0'. In his 'Sexton's Agreement, 14 September 1975', it was stipulated that Mr Blay should 'wear sexton's gown at all major services, including baptisms, marriages and funerals'. Brass plaque on west wall commemorates him: 'In memory of Ronnie Blay, sexton of this church for over 20 years until 1997'.
1984 (Feb.)–c. 1986	Mrs Douglas, church cleaner, £15 per week.
c. 1995–2002	Mrs Elizabeth (Liz) Neill-Watson, church cleaner. Also parish secretary (c. 1998–2003).

School principals

1787	David Christian
1797–1834	John Abbott
1834–40	Thomas Eustace
1840–c. 1848	William Clarke
c. 1853–80	Peter Hackett
1881–1915	John Morrison
1915–26	John McAdoo
1926–7	Mr W.J. Whittaker
1927–36	Mr S.W. Power
1936–48	George Armstrong
1948–64	Richard (Fred) Rountree
1964–73	Mr J.C. Kearon
1973–85	Miss Patricia Hadnett
1985–6	Mrs Meta Morton

Appendix 6

Pew-holders

Names of pew-holders and costs (1807–8)

1	John Dwyer, Esq.	11/4
2	Hans Riddall, Esq.	11/4
3	John Creathorn, Esq.	11/4
4	Mrs Cassidy	11/4
5	Mrs Southwell	11/4
6	Mrs Dignan	11/4
7	Mr Geo. Smith	18/5
8	Mrs Domville	18/5
9	Mr Hodgekinson	18/5
10	Mrs Cummins	18/5
11	Mr Kirk	18/5
12	Mr De Olier	18/5
13	Lord Clonmelle	18/5
14	Joseph Atkinson, Esq.	18/5
15	Alex Crookshank, Esq.	18/5
16	Lady Ranelagh	18/5
17	Col Sankey	18/5
18	John Swan, Esq.	18/5
19	Mrs Keller	18/5
20	Rev. O. Miller	18/5
21	Lord Cloncurry	18/5
22	Mrs W.D. Latouche	18/5
23	Mr Aldercrown	18/5
24	Lord De Vesci	18/5
25	Alder(ma)n Cash	18/5
26	Rob(er)t Alexander, Esq.	18/5
27	Rob(er)t Ashworth, Esq.	18/5
28	Alder(ma)n Archer	18/5
29	Mrs Byrne	18/5
30	Stanly, Esq.	18/5
31	Alder(ma)n Read	18/5
32	Jas. Dance, Esq.	18/5
33	Sir John Lees, Bart	18/5
34	John Armit, Esq.	18/5
35	*To be sold*	
36	Mr Gray	7/7
37	Sir Allen Johnston	7/7
38	John J. Henry, Esq.	7/7
39	Col W. Browne	7/7
40	Benj(ami)n Kearney, Esq.	7/7
41	Col Richardson	7/7
42		
43		
44	Sir John Lees, Bart	7/7
45		
46	Mr Kimmis	7/7
47		

| 48 | Mr Cranfield | 7/7 |
| 49 | Mr Purdon | 7/7 |

The sale of pews

On 13 June 1825 there was an auction of pews to raise money for the new Monkstown Parish Church, being designed by Semple. Resolutions were drawn up on the sale of these pews, including the following classification and rules:

> The pews proposed for sale (are to) … be divided into 4 classes —
> The first class, holding 7 each in the Front of the new Gallery, to consist of 10 pews marked AK at 50£ each pew.
> The second class, holding 6 each in the back of the new organ gallery, to consist of 8 pews marked [left blank] at 25£ each pew.
> The third class, holding 4 each in the back part of the new gallery, to consist of 12 pews marked E at 20£ each pew.
> The fourth class, holding 2 each in the back part of the new organ gallery, to consist of 2 pews marked F at 10£ each pew.
>
> That each person not being a proprietor of a pew in the old church wishing to purchase a 1st class pew shall pay 25£ for it on or before the day of ballotting, and the remaining 25£ on or before the 1st day of June 1825.

Appendix 7

Gifts and memorials to Monkstown Church

This list has been compiled from Vestry minutes, Service sheets and Cantwell and Cantwell (1990). Every effort has been made to make it as comprehensive as possible.

1872	Telford & Telford organ, presented by Thomas Hone, inaugurated 1 March.
1883	Chancel reredos, presented by 'FH' (Mrs F. Hart).
1885	Oak prayer desk, presented by the Young Ladies' Bible Class. Oak seat, presented by the Young Men's Christian Association (YMCA). Brass eagle lectern, presented by John and Joseph Galloway, in memory of their parents, John (d. 1866) and Eliza (d. 1844).
1891	Chancel tiles, presented by Canon Joseph Peacocke.
1893	Brass book stand, engraved 'Laus Deo', in memory of Mary Galloway (d. 1893, wife of Joseph Galloway).
1901	Dockrell Memorial Porch erected as entrance to Vestry rooms, presented by Maurice Dockrell in memory of his father, Thomas Dockrell, JP (d. 1 March 1880).
1932	11 December (Centenary Service) Chancellor Dowse Memorial: Carved oak Holy Table and matching credence table, both designed by Richard Caulfeild Orpen; also marble base enlarged; silver chalice and two silver patens.[1] All gifts presented by parishioners and friends.
1936	Forde Prayer Book, presented by the Rector and Mrs Harold Forde in grateful remembrance of Mrs Forde's restoration to health (1 November).
1942	Alms dish in memory of Mrs Margaret Sidford, presented by her daughter, Mrs Martin, 5 Brighton Tce, Sandycove; dedicated Sunday evening, 4 January. Markers for the Service books and lectern Bible, embroidered by Mrs Fitzmaurice. Hymn book and prayer book for the reading desk, in memory of their mother, Mrs Twigg, presented by the Misses Twigg. Pulpit Bible, given by Mr William Boulton Conyngham. Complete set of new Communion linen, from the Guild of Youth.
1945	A set of felt liners for the collection plates, in memory of Mrs Sidford, presented by her daughters, Mrs Martin and Mrs Fulton.
1946	'A complete set of book markers', in memory of Mr W.J. Smalldridge, presented by Mrs Smalldridge and family (13 November). Two silver flower vases for the table in the Childrens' Choir, in memory of their mother and brother, the late Rev. Frank Snow, presented by Miss Snow and her brothers.
1947	Oak reading desk (to match the 1885 desk) in memory of the Rev. H.G. Forde; dedicated 22 June. Radiogram and records, presented by Mrs Bradbury.

1949	Brass jug for the baptismal font, presented by Miss Vaughan, 'to replace one stolen some years ago'. Lectern for Childrens' Choir, in memory of two parishioners, presented by the Rev. Gough Cooper; dedicated Sunday 13 February. Holy Communion linen, presented by Miss Flood, Mrs King-Irvine and Mrs McCrea. Flower vases, presented by Mrs Brindsley Sheridan. Holy Table covering, presented by Mrs Hudson. Prayer book and markers, presented by Mrs Carroll. Improvements to choir stalls: Messrs A.E. Snow and Bell.
1950	Two prayer desks (constructed by Messrs Scott), presented by Mrs Conyngham and Mrs Hurse, in memory of William Boulton Conyngham and Percival Henry Hurse; dedicated Sunday 12 February. Jackson Bible, in memory of Robert Tennant Jackson, presented by his wife and children (6 February).
1951	'Burse' (purse or bursary) and 'veils', in memory of Mr E. Meredith and of his daughter, Mrs Betson; dedicated 24 June. Holy Communion rails, in the Children's Church, in memory of James and Prudence Miller. Platform for Communion table, presented by Mr E. Gray. Carpet of red felt for sanctuary, presented by the Mothers' Union in memory of Mrs Miller. Bible and markers, presented by the Girl Guides in memory of Mrs Miller. Window glass, presented by Mr Gorsuch. Three mats, presented by Mrs Russell.
1952	£100 towards the organ repair, from Mrs Lander, late of 'Mount Temple'.
1956	Authorised Version of the Bible in memory of Dr R.T. Jackson.
1962	Brass alms dish, presented anonymously.
1973	Prayer desk, in memory of Samuel H. Colton, 'treasurer of Monkstown Parish for over 24 years, until the day he died, November 8th 1971, presented by those who served with him on the Select Vestry', dedicated 1 July.
1974	Dwelling-house at 10 Lansdowne Park, Dublin 4, presented by Hilda Stirling (on 24 November) to the Friends of Monkstown 'to be used for the upkeep of the fabric of Monkstown Church primarily, and secondarily towards the maintainance of the residence or stipend of the Rector of Monkstown'. The house was sold for *c.* £5,000 in 1977.
1975	*The following all dedicated on 21 December:* Books for organist, in memory of Mr John Keegan. Books for clergy, in memory of Mr Owen Wynne, brother of Billy Wynne. Credence table, in memory of Alfred and Phoebe Mallet.
1977	Silver box for bread at Communion services, presented by Mr Francis McClatchie, resident in Canada; dedicated 26 June.
1983	Carpeted area and carved table at the west end in memory of Miss Vaughan, from the Old Girls of The Hall School. The two rear pews were removed to accommodate the table, behind which a plaque was fixed.

1985   Bookcase (made from a pew) on south wall of chancel from the Select Vestry in memory of Frank Hartigan (d. 8 October 1978), 'who reinforced the roof trusses of this church'.

1994   West doors of church, in memory of Ben Carnegie (1913–89), erected by his family and friends; dedicated 10 April.

1997   'Plain brass cross, without any inscription thereon, behind the communion table', presented by Howard Robinson of Dorset. (Licence granted by Archbishop Walton Empey on 30 October.)

The following silver items were dedicated on Sunday 12 October 1997. Besides bearing the names of those in whose memory they were given, they carry the inscriptions that were on the original church silver, stolen in 1984.

A silver flagon and private Communion set, in memory of Henry Brough and all the Brough family.
A silver flagon, in memory of Mary Keogh.
Two silver chalices, in memory of Edwin and Ethel Gorsuch.
Two silver chalices, in memory of John Glynn and Jean Hammett Irvine.
A silver paten, in memory of Vera and Lewis Budd.

Choir Scholarship, in memory of Joan McWilliams (née Aplin), Choir Leader *c.* 1956–93. Brass plaque on choir stall commemorates her association of over 40 years with Monkstown Choir.
A book and CD of common lectionary readings, and altar frontals in memory of Peter Wood.
Altar linen, in memory of Ronnie Blay.
A cross and candlesticks, in memory of Audrey Kennedy and the Rev. Tom Kennedy.

2001   *The following all dedicated on Sunday 6 May:*
Communion linen, in memory of Canon Billy Wynne (rector, 1958–78).
Choir robes, in memory of Marjorie and Ernest Bell.
Choir and pew hymn books, in memory of Dolly and Bob Bell, by Margaret, Peter and family.
A piano, in memory of Eileen Ball (1914–98).

Picture credits

The author would like to thank the following for permission to reproduce photographs or other material belonging to them, for giving permission for photographs to be taken, or for taking photographs.

Tom Aplin: p. 135; The Board of Trinity College, Dublin: p. 40; Janet Cooke, p. 221; Dalkey Heritage Centre: p.150; the Rev Kevin Dalton: p.xxiii; Julian Deale: p. 162; Dr Desmond De Courcy Wheeler: p. 325; Stephen Devaney: pp 56, 59, 88, 89, 104, 119 (btm), 121 (left), 130, 140, 150, 157; 232; Jarrold Publishing by Peter Smith Photography: p. 334; The Keeper of the Manuscripts, National Library of Ireland: p. 153; The Manager of the Heraldic Museum, National Library of Ireland: p. 191; Monkstown Vestry Archives: pp xxii, 18, 34 (top), 36, 42, 52, 60, 80, 117, 119 (top), 121 (left), 123, 125, 130, 140, 142 (top and btm), 143, 144, 150, 157, 160, 164, 208, 232, 238, 251, 253, 256, 257, 278; The National Library of Ireland: 153, 288 (right), 306, 309; Arthur Ogilvie: 37, 93, 94, 99, 276 (top), 301, 313; Michael Pegum: pp 110, 111; An Post: p. 187; Representative Church Body Library: pp 84, 86, 87; David and Margaret Ride: p. 328; Elizabeth Sharpe-Paul: pp 131, 141, 342 (top), 346, 347; Phyllis Taylor: p. 342 (btm); Mella Travers: pp 4, 146; Tommy Walsh: pp 17, 60, 74, 75, 107 (right), 121 (right), 132, 142 (btm), 143, 144, 164, 293, 288 (left), 296, 298.

Stephen Devaney also digitally enhanced the following: pp xxii, 24, 32, 34 (top), 52, 58, 88, 89, 103, 123, 140, 150, 325.

The author took the following photographs: pp 5, 22, 34 (btm), 40, 58, 66, 95, 97, 99 (btm), 107 (left), 142 (top), 151, 154, 170, 191, 204, 206, 215, 267, 276 (btm left and right), 277, 299, 318.

SELECT BIBLIOGRAPHY

Acheson, A. 1997 *A history of the Church of Ireland, 1691–1996.* Columba Press/APCK, Dublin.

Adams, B.W. 1883 *History and description of Santry and Cloghran parishes, Co. Dublin.* Mitchell & Hughes, London.

Adams, R.H. 1971 *The parish clerks of London.* Phillimore & Co., Chichester.

Addleshaw, G.W.O. and Etchells, F. 1958 *The architectural setting of Anglican worship.* Faber & Faber, London.

Akenson, D.H. 1971 *The Church of Ireland, ecclesiastical reform and revolution, 1800–1885.* Yale University Press, London.

Allen, C. 1993 The Semple Temples: the church architecture of John Semple and Son (unpublished 4th year Architecture dissertation, Richview Library, University College, Dublin).

Annals of Ulster (2nd edn), Vol. I, with an Introduction by Nollaig Ó Muraíle (Edmund Burke, Dublin, 1998).

Anon. 1666 *A form of consecration or dedication of churches and chappels, together with what may be used in the restauration of ruined churches, and expiation of churches desecrated or prophan'd.*

Anon. 1897 Foundling Hospital and Workhouse, 1704. *The Irish Builder* (15 August 1897).

Archbishop Bulkeley's Visitation of Dublin, 1630. *Archivium Hibernicum* (new series) **VIII** (Maynooth, 1941).

Archdall, M. 1873 *Monasticon Hibernicum.* W.R. Kelly, Dublin.

Aspinall, A. (ed.) 1951 *Mrs Jordan and her family, being the unpublished correspondence of Mrs Jordan and the duke of Clarence, late William IV.* Arthur Barker, London.

Ball, F.E. 1899 Some residents of Monkstown in the eighteenth century. *Journal of the Royal Society of Antiquaries of Ireland* (5th series) **IX**.

Ball, F.E. 1902 *A history of the County Dublin. Part First, Monkstown, Kill-of-the-Grange, Dalkey, Killiney, Tully, Stillorgan and Kilmacud.* Thom, Dublin. (Reprinted by Gill & Macmillan, Dublin, 1979.)

Ball, F.E. 1926 *The judges in Ireland, 1221–1921,* Vols I–II. John Murray, London.

Ball, F.E. and Hamilton, E. 1895 *The parish of Taney.* Hodges Figgis, Dublin.

Barry, J. 1970 Guide to records of the Genealogical Office, Dublin. *Analecta Hibernica* **26**.

Bence-Jones, M. 1990 *A guide to Irish country houses.* Constable, London.

Benson, L.D. (ed.) 1988 *The Riverside Chaucer.* Oxford University Press.

Beresford, Col H. de la Poer 1977 *The book of the Beresfords.* Phillimore & Co., Chichester.

Best, R.I. and Lawlor, H.J. (eds) 1931 *The Martyrology of Tallaght.* Henry Bradshaw Society, London.

Betham, E. (ed.) (n.d., possibly 1905) *A house of letters.* Jarrold & Sons, London.

Betjeman, Sir J. 1954 *Poems in the porch.* SPCK, London.

Betjeman, Sir J. 1982 *Church poems.* Pan Books, London.

Blacker, B. 1874 *Brief sketches of the parishes of . . . Booterstown and Donnybrook.* Herbert, Dublin.

Boase, F. 1892 *Modern English biography. Vol. I, A–H.* Netheron & Worth, Truro.

Bowen, D. 1978 *The Protestant crusade in Ireland, 1800–70.* Gill & Macmillan, Dublin.

Bowen, E. 1951 *The Shelbourne.* Harrap & Co., London.

Bradley, P. 1996 A case study of a Huguenot family: La Touche. In M.D. Evans (ed.), *Aspects of Irish genealogy II.* Irish Genealogical Congress Committee, Dublin.

Bradshaw, H. 1895 Louisa Stewart. In Rev. T.A. O'Morchoe (ed.), *Dublin University Missionary Magazine,* Memorial Number (17 October 1895).

Brady, A. 2000 De Vesci Terrace, Kingstown (unpublished thesis, Diploma in Fine Art, Institute of Professional Auctioneers and Valuers, Dublin).

Brewer, J.N. 1825 *The beauties of Ireland,* Vol. 1. Sherwood Jones & Co., London.

Bric, M.J. 1986 The tithe system in eighteenth-century Ireland. *Proceedings of the Royal Irish Academy* **86C**, 271–88.

Broderick, D. 1996 *An early toll-road: the Dublin–Dunleer turnpike, 1731–1855.* Maynooth Studies in Local History. Irish Academic Press, Dublin.

Brooke, R.S. 1877 *Recollections of the Irish church.* Macmillan, London.

Brooke, W.G. (ed.) (n.d.) *The churchwarden's guide* (10th edn). Knight & Co., London.

Brooks, C. and Saint, A. (eds) 1995 *The Victorian church, architecture and society.* Manchester University Press,

Manchester and New York.

Brynn, E. 1978 *Crown and Castle, British rule in Ireland, 1800–1830*. O'Brien Press, Dublin.

Burke's Irish Family Records (2 vols) (5th edn) (Burke's Peerage Ltd, London, 1976).

Burke's Landed Gentry of Ireland (4th edn) (Burke's Peerage Ltd, London, 1958).

Burke's Peerage and Baronetage (106th edn), Vol. II (Burke's Peerage Ltd, London, 1999).

Burn, R. 1809 *The ecclesiastical law*, Vols I and IV. London. (Reprinted by Milliken, 1842.)

Burroughs, W.E. 1895 In Memoriam: Robert Warren Stewart. In Rev. T.A. O'Morchoe (ed.), *Dublin University Missionary Magazine*, Memorial Number (17 October 1895).

Burtchaell, G.D. and Sadleir, T.U. (eds) 1935 *Alumni Dublinenses*. Alex Thom & Co., Dublin. (Reprinted by Thoemmes Press, 2001.)

Butler, B.B. 1946–7 Lady Arabella Denny, 1707–1792. *Dublin Historical Record* **IX** (1).

Butler, B.B. 1953 John and Edward Lees. *Dublin Historical Record* **XIII** (3 and 4).

Cantwell, B. and Cantwell, I.T. 1990 *Memorials of the dead, Vol. XI: South Dublin*.

Chart, D.A. 1907 *The story of Dublin*. Dent, London.

Clark, K. 1974 *The Gothic Revival: an essay in the history of taste*. John Murray, London.

Clarke, A. 1989 Varieties of uniformity: the first century of the Church of Ireland. In Diana Woods and W.J. Sheils (eds), *The churches, Ireland and the Irish*. Ecclesiastical History Society, Dublin.

Cloncurry, Lord 1849 *Personal recollections of the life and times, with extracts from the correspondence of Valentine Lord Cloncurry*. James McGlashan, Dublin.

CMS 1916 *Proceedings of the CMS for Africa and the East, 1915–16: West China Mission*. Church Missionary Society, London.

Coincraft's Standard Catalogue of the coins of Scotland, Ireland, Channel Islands and Isle of Man (Coincraft, London, 1999).

Commissioners of Church Temporalities in Ireland 1875 *Report 1875*. Thom, Dublin.

Commissioners of Church Temporalities in Ireland 1880 *Report 1869–80*. Thom, Dublin.

Commissioners of the Irish Education Inquiry 1825 *Irish Education Inquiry, First Report*. Dublin.

Commissioners of the Irish Education Inquiry 1826 *Irish Education Inquiry, Second Report*. Dublin.

Commissioners of National Education 1892 *58th Report (1891)*. Thom, Dublin.

Commissioners of Public Instruction (Ireland) 1835a *1st Report 1835*. HMSO, London.

Commissioners of Public Instruction (Ireland) 1835b *2nd Report 1835*. HMSO, London.

Cooper, B. 1918 *The Tenth (Irish) Division in Gallipoli*. H. Jenkins, Dublin.

Cotton, H. 1848 *Fasti Ecclesiae Hibernicae: The succession of prelates and members of the cathedral bodies in Ireland. Vol. II: The province of Leinster*. Hodges & Smith, Dublin.

Cotton, H. 1849 *Fasti Ecclesiae Hibernicae: The succession of prelates and members of the cathedral bodies in Ireland. Vol. III: The province of Ulster*. Hodges & Smith, Dublin.

Crabbe, Rev. G. 1840 *The Borough: a poem*. Charles Daly, London.

Craig, M. 1982 *The architecture of Ireland from the earliest times to 1880*. Batsford, London.

Craig, M. 1990 John Semple and his churches. *Irish Arts Review: Yearbook, 1989–90*.

Craig, M. 1992 *Dublin, 1660–1800*. Penguin Books, London.

Crampton, J. 1819 *Fever report, Steevens Hospital, containing a brief account of the late epidemic in Dublin, from September 1817 to August 1819*. Hodges & McArthur, Dublin.

Crawford, J. 1996 *St Catherine's Parish, Dublin, 1840–1900: portrait of a Church of Ireland community*. Maynooth Studies in Local History. Irish Academic Press, Dublin.

'Cromlyn' 1959 A strange and exciting story. *Church of Ireland Gazette* (14 August 1959).

Cromwell, T. 1820 *Excursions through Ireland*, Vol. II. Longman, London.

Cronin, P. 1989 *South County Dublin and East Wicklow during the 1914–18 War*. Foxrock Local History Club, Pamphlet No. 23.

Cullen, C. 1997 Ronnie Blay — an appreciation. *Monkstown Parish Newsletter* (January 1997).

Cullen, L.M. 1969 The smuggling trade in Ireland in the eighteenth century. *Proceedings of the Royal Irish Academy* **67C**, No. 5.

Curran, C.P. 1977 The architecture of the Bank of Ireland, part II: 1800–1946. *Quarterly Bulletin of the Irish Georgian Society* **XX**, Nos 3 and 4 (July–December 1977). (Reprinted by courtesy of the Bank of Ireland.)

Curtayne, A. 1972 *Francis Ledwidge — a life of the poet, 1887–1917*. Martin Brian & O'Keeffe, London.

D'Alton, J. 1838a *The memoirs of the archbishops of Dublin*. Hodges & Smith, Dublin.

D'Alton, J. 1838b *The history of the County of Dublin*. Hodges & Smith, Dublin. (Reprinted by Tower Books, Cork, 1976.)

Dalton, K. 2003a *That could never be*. Columba Press, Dublin.

Dalton, K. 2003b Rector's Letter. *Monkstown Parish Newsletter* 4 (3).

Davis, H. (ed.) 1948 Irish tracts and sermons, 1720–1723. In *The prose works of Jonathan Swift*, Vol. IX. Blackwell Publishers, Oxford.

Davis, R.H. 1901 *With both armies in South Africa*. New York.

Day, E.B. 1938 *Mr Justice Day of Kerry, 1745–1841*. Pollard & Co., Exeter.

Day, R. 1808 *Seven charges delivered to the the Grand Juries of the County of Dublin (1793–98)*. Dublin.

De Breffny, B. and Mott, G. 1976 *The churches and abbeys of Ireland*. Thames and Hudson, London.

De Courcy Ireland, J. 2001 *History of Dun Laoghaire Harbour*. Caisleán an Bhúrcaigh, Dublin.

Denham, H.M. 1981 *Dardanelles: A midshipman's diary, 1915–16*. John Murray, London.

Devaney, S. 1994 The Corporation of Dun Laoghaire's 1991 Development Plan Listed Structures: Architectural Heritage of the Borough of Dun Laoghaire (1930–93). Database, Dun Laoghaire Corporation.

Dickson, D. 1997 *Arctic Ireland: the extraordinary story of the Great Frost and forgotten famine of 1740–41*. White Row Press, Belfast.

Dickson, D. 2000 *Ireland, 1660–1800*. Irish Academic Press, Dublin.

Dictionary of national biography (22 vols). Oxford University Press, Oxford.

Donnelly, Bishop N. 1907 *History of Dublin parishes*, Vol. I, Part IV. Catholic Truth Society, Dublin.

Dooney, L. 1988 Trinity College and the War. In David Fitzpatrick (ed.), *Ireland and the First World War*. Lilliput Press and Trinity History Workshop, Dublin.

Drew, Sir T. 1899 Dublin for the architectural student. *The Irish Builder* (15 October 1899).

Drew, Sir T. 1908 *A report on the decayed stonework at Christchurch of the Holy Trinity at Dublin in 1908* [pamphlet]. Dublin.

Dublin City Archives *c.* 2000 *Freedom of the City of Dublin* [leaflet]. Dublin.

Dublin directories (various years), published by Stewart-Watson; Pettigrew & Oulton; Thom; Watson.

Dun Laoghaire Genealogical Society 1994 *Memorial inscriptions of Deansgrange Cemetery: Vol. I, SW Section*. (See also Genealogical Society of Ireland 2000.)

Dungan, M. 1997 *They shall grow not old: Irish soldiers and the Great War*. Four Courts Press, Dublin.

Dunn, Rev. J. 1804 *Extract from a sermon, preached at Monkstown church, the Sunday after the death of William La Touche, Esq*. William Porter, Dublin.

Ecclesiastical Commissioners (Ireland) 1824 *Money levied for building and repairing of churches in Ireland, part II*. Thom, Dublin.

Ecclesiastical Commissioners (Ireland) 1837 *Diocese of Dublin: revenues and patronage of benefices. No. 56, Monkstown Union*. Thom, Dublin.

Ecclesiastical Commissioners (Ireland) 1838 *Fourth Report, 1837*. Thom, Dublin.

Ecclesiastical Commissioners (Ireland) 1868 *Reports of Ecclesiastical Commissioners, 1868. Schedule V: Benefices, Monkstown*. Thom, Dublin.

Edwards, N. 1990 *The archaeology of early medieval Ireland*. Batsford, London.

English, J. (ed.) *c.* 1987 *Carrickbrennan, Monkstown*.

Erck, J.C. (ed.) 1830 *Ecclesiastical register, 1830*. R. Milliken, Dublin.

Fancutt, W. 1974 *With strange surprise*. Leprosy Mission, London.

Fiants of Elizabeth I. *The twenty-second report of the Deputy Keeper of the Public Records in Ireland* (Thom, Dublin, 1890). (Fiant No. 3146: 1577, re Church of St Mochonna of the Grange of Carrickbrennan, alias Monkstown, County Dublin.)

Fiants of Henry VIII. *The seventh report of the Deputy Keeper of the Public Records in Ireland* (Thom, Dublin, 1875). (Fiant No. 310: 1543, re Lease of Carrickbrennan, alias Monkstown, and the rectory of the same to John Travers . . . for 21 years at a rent of £24-5-2; Fiant No. 460: 1546, re Grant of Monkstown Castle to John Travers.)

Fitzgerald, B. (ed.) 1953 *Correspondence of Emily, duchess of Leinster. Vol. II (1731–1814)*. Stationery Office, Dublin.

Fitzgerald, W. 1885 *Lectures on ecclesiastical history* (edited by William Fitzgerald and John Quarry) (2 vols). John Murray, London.

Fleetwood, J. 1951 *The history of medicine in Ireland*. Browne and Nolan. (Reprinted by Skellig Press, Dublin, 1983.)

Fleetwood, J. 1988 *The Irish body snatchers*. Tomar Publishing, Dublin.

Fletcher, Sir B. 1938 *A history of architecture on the comparative method* (10th edn). B.T. Batsford, London.

Ford, A. 1997 *The Protestant Reformation in Ireland, 1590–1641*. Four Courts Press, Dublin.

Fowler, J.T. (ed.) 1894 *Adamnani Vita S. Columbae* (edited from Dr W. Reeves's 1857 text). Clarendon Press, Oxford.

Fox, M.D. 1990 *The Green Square: H.M. 27th (Inniskilling) Regiment of Foot at Waterloo*. Gravesend, Kent.

Frazer, W. 1888 On the Dublin stocks and pillory. *Proceedings of the Royal Irish Academy* (Series II) **II** (1879–88).

Friendly, A. 1977 *Beaufort of the Admiralty*. Hutchinson, London.

Galloway, P. 1983 *The Most Illustrious Order of St Patrick, 1783–1983*. Phillimore & Co., Chichester.

Gaskin, J. 1878 *Irish varieties*. Patrick Traynor, Dublin.

Genealogical Society of Ireland 2000 *Memorial inscriptions of Deansgrange Cemetery: Vol. 4, South Section*. (See also Dun Laoghaire Genealogical Society 1994.)

Georgian Society of Ireland 1912 *The Georgian Society records of eighteenth century domestic architecture and decoration in Dublin* (5 vols). Dublin University Press. (Reprinted by Irish University Press, Shannon, 1969.)

Gibbs, P. 1963 *The Battle of Alma*. Weidenfeld & Nicolson, London.

Gilbert, Sir J.T. 1861 *A history of the City of Dublin*, Vols I–III. Duffy, Dublin.

Gilbert, Sir J.T. (ed.) 1884 *Chartularies of St Mary's Abbey* (2 vols). Alex Thom, Dublin.

Gilbert, Lady (ed.) 1891–1944 *Calendar of ancient records of Dublin* (19 vols). Dollard, Dublin.

Gilbert, M. 1994 *The First World War*. Weidenfeld & Nicolson, London.

Goodbody, R. 1993 *On the borders of the Pale*. Pale Publishing, Bray.

Grenham, J. 1999 *Tracing your Irish ancestors* (2nd edn). Gill & Macmillan, Dublin.

Grey, E. 1971 *The noise of drums and trumpets: W.H. Russell reports from the Crimea*. Longman, London.

Grey, W.J. 1959 South Dublin revisited. *Focus* (February 1959).

Grindle, W.H.W. 1989 *Irish cathedral music*. Queen's University, Belfast.

Grindle, W.H.W. 1991 *… And organs and singing*. Dublin.

Grosart, Rev. A.B. (ed.) 1874 *The complete poems of Christopher Harvey* [including 'The Synagogue']. London.

Guinness, H.S. (ed.) 1908 *The Register of the Union of Monkstown, Co. Dublin, 1669–1786* (Parochial Registers, Vol. VI). Parochial Register Society of Dublin, Exeter and London.

Gwynn, A. 1949 Origins of St Mary's Abbey. *Journal of the Royal Society of Antiquaries of Ireland* **LXXIX**.

Gwynn, R.M., Norton, E.M. and Simpson, B.W. 1936 *'T.C.D.' in China: a history of the Dublin University Fukien Mission, 1885–1935*. Dublin. (Reprinted 1986.)

Haliday, C. 1881 *The Scandinavian kingdom of Dublin*. Thom, Dublin. (Reprinted by Irish University Press, Shannon, 1969.)

Hall, F.G. 1949 *History of the Bank of Ireland*. Hodges Figgis, Dublin.

Hanna, H. 1917 *The Pals at Suvla Bay*. Ponsonby, Dublin.

Hansard, T.C. (various years) *Parliamentary Debates* (3rd series). London.

Harden, Rev. R. 1911 *St John's, Monkstown: the story of an Irish church*. Hodges Figgis, Dublin.

Harris, H. 1968 *The Irish regiments in the First World War*. Mercier Press, Cork.

Harrison, M. 1980 *Victorian stained glass*. Barrie & Jenkins, London.

Hayden, M. 1943 Charity children in 18th century Dublin. *Dublin Historical Record* **V** (3).

Healy, F.J. 1914 Origin and antiquity of pounds. *Journal of the Cork Historical and Archaeological Society* (Series 2) **XX**.

Henchy, P. 1948 Nelson's Pillar. *Dublin Historical Record* **10** (1).

Henshaw, T. 1995 *The sky their battlefield*. Grub Street, London.

Herbert, M. 1988 *Iona, Kells and Derry: the history and hagiography of the monastic familia of Columba*. Clarendon Press, Oxford.

Hewitt, G. 1977 *The problems of success: a history of the Church Missionary Society, 1910–1942*, Vol. II. London.

Hibbert, C. 1961 *The destruction of Lord Raglan: a tragedy of the Crimean War 1854–55*. Longman, London.

Hibernian Church Missionary Society 1896 *82nd Annual Report (1895)*. HCMS, Dublin. (Also in Representative Church Body Library (315/3/7/13).)

Hibernian Church Missionary Society 1917 *102nd Annual Report (1916)*. HCMS, Dublin. (Also in

Representative Church Body Library (315/3/7/17).)

Historical Manuscripts Commission 1876 *5th Report*, Nos 16 and 17, p. 254 [letters from William Digges La Touche to Sir Robert Ainslie, 17 March and 14 May 1782]. HMSO, London.

Hostettler, J. 1997 *Sir Edward Carson: a dream too far*. Barry Rose Law Publishers, Chichester.

House of Commons (Ireland) 1785 *Journal of the House of Commons* **XI**, Petition No. 69 [petition to parliament in 1785 for £1,000 for the new church 'of the United Parishes of Monkstown and Kill'].

House of Commons (Ireland) 1789–90 *Journal of the House of Commons* **XIII**, Appendix CXLVI.

Hughes, K. 1972 *Early Christian Ireland: introduction to the sources*. Hodder & Stoughton, London.

Hughes, Rev. S.C. 1889 *The Church of St John the Evangelist, Dublin*. Hodges & Figgis, Dublin.

Index to Probate and Administration Calendars, 1858–1982 (Thom, Dublin, various years).

Index to the act or grant books and to original wills of the Dublin Diocese (Appendix to the Twenty-sixth Report of the Deputy Keeper of the Public Records in Ireland), Vol. 1 (1270–1800) (Thom, Dublin, 1895).

Index to the act or grant books and to original wills of the Dublin Diocese (Appendix to the Thirtieth Report of the Deputy Keeper of the Public Records in Ireland), Vol. 2 (1800–58) (Thom, Dublin, 1899).

Ingram, J.A. 1997 *The cure of souls, a history of St Brigid's Church of Ireland, Stillorgan*. Mahon Printing Works, Dublin.

Ireland's Memorial Records, 1914–18 (Committee of the Irish National War Memorial, Dublin, 1923).

Irish Architectural Archive Biographical Index of Irish Architects [largely based on 'The Alfred Jones Biographical Index']. Database, Irish Architectural Archive, Dublin.

Irish Church Hymnal (Dublin, 1966).

Irish Parliamentary Debates **IV** (January–September 1785) (Dublin, 1785).

Jalland, P. 1996 *Death in the Victorian family*. Oxford University Press, Oxford.

James, F.G. 1961 Irish smuggling in the eighteenth century. *Irish Historical Studies* **12** (48).

Jeffery, K. 2000 *Ireland and the Great War*. Cambridge University Press, Cambridge.

Johnston, T.J., Robinson, J.L. and Wyse Jackson, R. 1953 *A history of the Church of Ireland*. APCK, Dublin.

Johnstone, T. 1992 *Orange, green and khaki*. Gill & Macmillan, Dublin.

Journal of the Association for the Preservation of the Memorials of the Dead in Ireland **VIII** (1–4) (Dublin, 1913).

Joyce, W. St J. 1912 *The neighbourhood of Dublin*. M.H. Gill & Son, Dublin.

Keane, E., Phair, P.B. and Sadleir, T.U. (eds) 1982 *King's Inns Admission Papers, 1607–1867*. Irish Manuscripts Commission, Dublin.

Kearns, J.B. 1996 Dr Rumley and the Kingstown cholera 1832. *Dun Laoghaire Borough Historical Society Journal* **5**.

Kennedy, B.P. 1988 *South County Dubliners and the making of independent Ireland*. Foxrock Local History Club, Pamphlet No. 22.

Kennedy, R.T.C. 1968 The administration of the diocese of Dublin and Glendalough in the eighteenth century (unpublished M.Litt. thesis, Trinity College, Dublin).

Kenny, C. 1978 *A glance back: a brief history of Monkstown Lawn Tennis Club (1877–1978), including a history of the County Dublin (Monkstown) Archers (1846–77)*. Monkstown Lawn Tennis Club.

Kilternan Parish Church 1976 *Kilternan Church 1826–1976*. Dublin.

Kirkpatrick, T.P.C. 1924 *The history of Doctor Steevens' Hospital, 1720–1920*. University Press, Dublin.

Lacey, B. 1997 *Colum Cille and the Columban tradition*. Four Courts Press, Dublin.

Lacy, T. 1863 *Sights and scenes of our fatherland*. Simpkin, Marshall & Co, London.

Laffan, M. 1987 *Carriglea, from country demesne to college of art*. Foxrock Local History Club, Pamphlet No. 20.

Langtry, J. and Carter, N. (eds) 1997 *Mount Jerome — a Victorian cemetery*. Mount Jerome Historical Project, Staybro Publications in association with MJHP.

Larmour, P. 1992 *The Arts and Crafts Movement in Ireland*. Friar's Bush Press, Belfast.

Lawson, J.P. 1842 *The gazetteer of Ireland*. Edinburgh.

Lecane, P. 1997 Windsor, Monkstown. *Dun Laoghaire Borough Historical Society Journal* **6**.

Lecky, W.E.H. 1913 *A history of Ireland in the eighteenth century*, Vols III and V. Longman, London.

Lees, Rev. Sir H. 1820a *L'Abeja, or a bee among the Evangelicals*. Underwood, Dublin.

Lees, Rev. Sir H. 1820b *A cursory view of the present state of Ireland*. Underwood, Dublin.

Lees, Rev. Sir H. 1820c *Nineteen pages of advice to the Protestant freemen and freeholders of Dublin*. Underwood, Dublin.

Lees, Rev. Sir H. 1821 *A compendium of Sir H. Lees' anti-popish works*. Underwood, Dublin.

Leprosy Mission 1974a *The spreading tree.* Leprosy Mission, London.

Leprosy Mission 1974b *Greater things still — 100 years of the Leprosy Mission.* Leprosy Mission, London.

Leslie, Rev. J.B. 1929 *Clogher clergy and parishes.* Enniskillen.

Leslie, Rev. J.B. 1933 *Ossory clergy and parishes.* Enniskillen.

Leslie, Rev. J.B. 1934 Elphin clergy and parishes. (Unpublished; in Representative Church Body Library.)

Leslie, Rev. J.B. 1940 *Ardfert and Aghadoe clergy and parishes.* Dublin.

Lewis, S. 1837 *A topographical dictionary of Ireland comprising the several counties, cities, boroughs, corporate, market, and post towns, parishes and villages, with historical and statistical descriptions,* Vols I and II. S. Lewis & Co., London.

Lewis-Crosby, Very Rev. E.H. (n.d.) *Christ Church Cathedral, Dublin: a short history.* Dublin.

Liddle, P. 1976 *Men of Gallipoli.* Allen Lane, London.

Luce, F. 1997 *SPADE — the vision that became a reality. A short account of the work of the Diocesan Employment Bureau, 1983–1997.* Diocesan Employment Bureau, Dublin.

Lycett-Green, C. (ed.) 1997 *John Betjeman: Coming Home: an anthology of his prose, 1920–1977.* Methuen, London.

Mac Cóil, L. 1977 *The book of Blackrock.* Carraig Books, Blackrock.

McDermott, M.J. 1990 Notable Irish architectural families. No.10: the Semples. *Irish Architect* (September/October 1990), 65–7.

MacDonnell, H.H.G. 1889 *Some notes on the Graves family.* Browne and Nolan, Dublin.

McEnery, M.J. and Refaussé, R. (eds) 2001 *Christ Church deeds.* Christ Church History Series, Vol. 8. Four Courts Press, Dublin.

McFarlan, D.M. 1990 *Lift thy banner: Church of Ireland scenes, 1870–1900.* Dundalgan Press, Dundalk.

McNeill, C. (ed.) 1943 *The Tanner letters: original documents and notices of Irish affairs in the 16th and 17th centuries.* Stationery Office, Dublin.

McNeill, C. (ed.) 1950 *Calendar of Archbishop Alen's Register, c. 1172–1534.* Royal Society of Antiquaries of Ireland, Dublin.

Mac Shamhráin, A.S. 1996 *Church and polity in pre-Norman Ireland: the case of Glendalough.* An Sagart, Maynooth.

Mahaffy, J.P. 1912 *The Georgian Society records of eighteenth century domestic architecture and decoration in Dublin. Vol. IV. Furnishings of Georgian houses in Dublin.* Dublin University Press, Dublin. (Reprinted by Irish University Press, Shannon, 1969.)

Mason, W.M. 1820 *The history and antiquities of the Collegiate and Cathedral Church of St Patrick, near Dublin.* Dublin.

Medical directories (various years).

Miller, A.D. 1955 *A bridge of compassion.* Mission to Lepers, London.

Mills, J. (ed.) 1996 *Account roll of the Priory of the Holy Trinity, Dublin, 1337–1346.* Four Courts Press, Dublin.

Mollan, C., Davis, W. and Finucane, B. 2002 *Irish innovators in science and technology.* Royal Irish Academy, Dublin.

Monkstown Parish Church 1964 *Why we need to spend £4,000 on the organ, and how you can help* [leaflet].

Monkstown Parochial Schools 1866 *Annual report for year ending December 31 1865.* White, Dublin. (Available in National Library, Main Reading Room.)

Morgan, G. 1999 The Dublin Pals. (Paper read at a conference on 'Ireland and France: Heroism in Sport', Trinity College, Dublin, 9 July 1999.)

Murphy, J.C. 1813–16 *The Arabian antiquities of Spain: a description of the Alhamrā at Granada.* Cudell & Davies, London. (Reprinted by Procyta, Granada, 1987.)

Napier, Sir W. 1828–40 *History of the War in the Peninsula and in the south of France, from the year 1807 to the year 1814* (6 vols), Vol. III. T. & W. Boone, London.

Numskull, N. 1832 *An essay on the rise and progress of architectural taste in Dublin.* Dublin.

O'Brien, E. 1988 Churches of south-east County Dublin, seventh to twelfth centuries. In G. Mac Niocaill and P.F. Wallace (eds), *Keimelia — studies in medieval archaeology and history in memory of Tom Delaney,* 504–24. Galway.

O'Byrne, E. 1996 Betham and Lodge. In M.D. Evans (ed.), *Aspects of Irish genealogy II.* Irish Genealogical Congress Committee, Dublin.

O'Byrne, W.R. 1849 *A naval biographical dictionary.* John Murray, London.

O'Connell, M.R. (ed.) 1972 *The correspondence of Daniel O'Connell, 1792–1814*, Vol. I. Irish University Press, Dublin.

O'Carroll, G. 1998 Robert Day: his background and his career to 1798 (unpublished MA thesis, University of Limerick).

O'Carroll, G. 2001 Judge Robert Day, 1746–1841. *North Munster Antiquarian Journal* **41**.

O'Donovan, J. 1864 *The Martyrology of Donegal*. Thom, Dublin.

O'Dwyer, F. 1989 The foundation and early years of the RIAI. In J. Graby (ed.), *150 years of architecture in Ireland*. Royal Institute of Architects of Ireland, Dublin.

O'Hanlon, Rev. J. 1875 *Lives of the Irish saints*, Vol. I. Duffy & Sons, Dublin.

Oman, C. 1908 *A history of the Peninsular War. Vol. III: Siege of Almeida*. Clarendon Press, Oxford.

O'Rafferty, T. 1999 *The Seapoint and Salthill story* (revised edn). Monkstown, Dublin.

Ó Riain, P. 1977 St Finnbarr: a study in a cult. *Journal of the Cork Historical and Archaeological Society* **82**, 63–82.

Ó Riain, P. 1983 Cainnech alias Colum Cille, patron of Ossory. In P. de Brún, S. Ó Coileáin and P. Ó Riain (eds), *Folia Gadelica. Essays presented by former students to R.A. Breatnach*. Cork University Press, Cork.

Pakenham, T. 1972 *The year of liberty*. Panther Books, London.

Parliamentary Gazetteer of Ireland, Vol. II (D–M) (A. Fullarton & Co., Dublin, 1845).

Payne, B. 1709 *The parish clerk's guide*. Benjamin Motte, London. (Reprinted by John Marsh, London, 1731, with further reprints in 1752 and 1778.)

Pearson, P. 1998 *Between the mountains and the sea*. O'Brien Press, Dublin.

Pender, S. (ed.) 1942 *Census of Ireland, circa 1659*. Stationery Office, Dublin.

Pepys, S. 1978 *The diary of Samuel Pepys* (3 vols). Everyman's Library, London.

Phair, P.B. 1972 Sir William Betham's manuscripts. *Analecta Hibernica* **27**.

Philips, W.A. 1933 *History of the Church of Ireland. Vol. I: The Celtic church*. Oxford University Press, Oxford.

Pitkin Guide 2002 *The stained glass of Liverpool Cathedral*. Jarrold Publishing and Liverpool Cathedral, Liverpool.

Plunkett, Count 1909 James Cavanah Murphy. *The Irish Builder and Engineer* **LI** (10) (15 May 1909).

Potterton, H. 1975 *Irish church monuments, 1570–1880*. Ulster Architectural Heritage Society, Belfast.

Powell, G.R. 1861 *The gale of Saturday, 9th of February 1861, with full particulars of the loss of Captain Boyd and seamen of HMS Ajax*. McGlashan & Gill, Dublin.

Price, L. (ed.) 1942 *An eighteenth-century antiquary: the sketches, notes and diaries of Austin Cooper (1759–1830)*. John Falconer, Dublin.

Quane, M. 1961 Carysfort Royal School, Co. Wicklow. *Journal of the Royal Society of Antiquaries of Ireland* **91**, Part II.

Quilter, V. 1987 A short ecclesiastical history of Monkstown. In J. O'Sullivan and S. Cannon (eds), *The book of Dun Laoghaire*. Blackrock Teachers' Centre, Dublin.

Quilter, V. *c.* 1987 Chapter 1. In J. English (ed.), *Carrickbrennan, Monkstown*.

Rankin, J.F. 1997 *Down Cathedral*. Ulster Historical Foundation, Belfast.

Rathbone, H. 1901 Report on the second exhibition of the Arts and Crafts Society in Dublin, 1899. *Journal and Proceedings of the Arts and Crafts Society of Ireland* (1901).

Refaussé, R. (ed.) 1994 *The register of the parish of St Thomas, Dublin, 1750–1791*. Representative Church Body Library, Dublin.

Refaussé, R. 2000 *Church of Ireland records*. Irish Academic Press, Dublin.

Reville, W. 2001 The Irish Father of Television. *The Irish Times* (6 September 2001).

Reynolds, M. 1983 *A history of the Irish Post Office*. Dublin.

Richardson, D.S. 1983 *Gothic Revival architecture in Ireland*, Vol. I. Garland Publishing, New York and London.

Robins, J. 2002 *Champagne and silver buckles: the viceregal court at Dublin Castle, 1700–1922*. Lilliput Press, Dublin.

Royal Visitation of Dublin, 1615. *Archivium Hibernicum* (new series) **VIII** (Maynooth, 1941).

Russell, P. 2001 Patterns of hypocorism in early Irish hagiography. In J. Carey, M. Herbert and P. Ó Riain (eds), *Studies in Irish hagiography: saints and scholars*. Four Courts Press, Dublin.

Samaritans 1995 *Twenty-five years of listening: the story of the Samaritans in Dublin, 1970–1995*. Dublin.

Scantlebury, C. 1958–61 A tale of two islands. *Dublin Historical Record* **15–16**, 126–8.

Semple, G. 1873 [Extracts from his 1776 book *Building in water* serialised in *The Irish Builder*,

June–November 1873, in articles entitled 'The old builders: their methods and materials'.]

Senior, H. 1966 *Orangeism in Ireland and Britain 1795–1836*. Routledge & Kegan Paul, London.

Seymour, St J.D. 1921 *The Puritans in Ireland*. Oxford University Press, Oxford.

Simington, R.C. 1945 *The Civil Survey, AD 1654–1656, Vol. VII: County of Dublin*. Stationery Office, Dublin.

Simms, G.O. 1957 John Ernest Leonard Oulton. *Trinity, An Annual Record* **IX**.

Simms, G.O. 1983 *Tullow's story*. Select Vestry of Tullow Parish, Carrickmines.

Smith, H.S. (ed.) 1854–7 *The Military Obituary for 1853, 1854, 1855 and 1856*. London.

Stanford, W.B. and McDowell, R.B. (eds) 1971 *Mahaffy: a biography of an Anglo-Irishman*. Routledge & Kegan Paul, London.

State Papers Ireland, Accounts and Papers 1801–1852, Vol. 48 (1840).

Stock, E. 1899 *History of the Church Missionary Society*, Vol. III. London.

Stokes, A.E. 1950 *Where monks walked: the story of Monkstown*. APCK, Dublin.

Stokes, G.T. 1895 The antiquities from Kingstown to Dublin. *Journal of the Royal Society of Antiquaries of Ireland* (5th Series) **25**.

Stoney, Rev. R.B. 1880 Dublin suburban churches. *Irish Ecclesiastical Gazette* [series of articles].

Stothert, W. 1812 *A narrative of the principal events of the campaigns of 1809, 1810 and 1811, in Spain and Portugal*. P. Martin, London.

Strickland, W.G. 1913 *A dictionary of Irish artists* (2 vols). Maunsel, Dublin and London.

Sumner, W.L. 1952 *The organ: its evolution, principles of construction and use*. Macdonald, London.

Taylor, Dr J. 1999 Abandoning babies safely [letter]. *British Medical Journal* **319** (11 December 1999).

The traveller's new guide through Ireland (John Cumming, Dublin, 1815).

Trimble, W.C. 1876 *The historical record of the 27th Inniskilling Regiment*. W. Trimble, Enniskillen.

Turner, K. 1983 *If you seek monuments: a guide to the antiquities of the barony of Rathdown*. Rathmichael Historical Society, Dublin.

Turner, K. 1987 *Rathmichael: a parish history* (ed. G.O. Simms). Rathmichael Parish.

University of Dublin War List 1922 (Hodges Figgis & Co., Dublin, 1922).

Urwick, W. 1868 *Biographic sketches of the late James Digges La Touche, Esq*. John Robertson & Co., Dublin.

Venn, J.A. (ed.) 1951 *Alumni Cantabrigienses, Part II (1752–1900)*, Vol. IV. Cambridge.

Wallace, W.J.R. (ed.) 2001 *Clergy of Dublin and Glendalough*. Ulster Historical Foundation, Belfast.

Warburton, J., Whitelaw, J. and Walsh, R. 1818 *History of the city of Dublin* (2 vols). T. Cadell and W. Davies, London.

Watchorn, D. 2003 The Cloncurry Ascendancy. *Dublin Historical Record* **LVI** (1).

Webster, C.A. 1920 *The diocese of Cork*. Guy & Co., Cork.

Wellington, Duke of, 1837 *Despatches. Vol. IV: Peninsular War* (edited by Lieut-Col. Gurwood). John Murray, London.

Wellington, Duke of, 1863 *Supplementary despatches, correspondence and memoranda* (edited by his son), Vol. 10 (1815). John Murray, London.

White, N.B. (ed.) 1943 *Extents of Irish monastic possessions, 1540–1541*. Irish Manuscripts Commission, Dublin.

Whiteside, L. 1990 *George Otto Simms: a biography*. Colin Smythe, Gerrards Cross, Bucks.

Williams, H. (ed.) 1948 *Swift: Journal to Stella*, Vol. II. Oxford University Press, Oxford.

Williams, J. 1994 *Companion guide to architecture in Ireland, 1837–1921*. Irish Academic Press, Dublin.

Wills and Administrations (Thom, Dublin, various years) (available in National Archives).

Wills, J. 1875 *The Irish nation: its history and its biography*, Vol. IV (II: Ecclesiastical series). A. Fullarton & Co., London.

Woodham-Smith, C. 1950 *Florence Nightingale*. Constable, London.

Wynne, B. and MacNamara, F. 2000 *Called to think anew* (edited by Bernard Harris). Irish Times Books, Dublin.

Wynne, M. 1975 Stained glass in Ireland, principally Irish stained glass, 1760–1963 (unpublished Ph.D thesis, Trinity College, Dublin).

Yates, N. 1991 *Buildings, faith and worship — the liturgical arrangements in Anglican churches, 1600–1900*. Clarendon Press, Oxford.

Ziegler, P. 1971 *King William IV*. Collins, London.

ARCHIVAL AND MANUSCRIPT SOURCES

Cork Public Museum
Henry Hill Notebook, No. 1.

Dun Laoghaire Genealogical Society, Archives
(now called the Genealogical Society of Ireland)
Deansgrange Cemetery burial records (microfilm, 1865–1970).
International Genealogical Index.

General Register Office, Dublin
Certificates of Births, Marriages and Deaths.

Gilbert Library (Dublin City Archives)
Dublin City Assembly, Freedom Rolls, Vol. 5 (1774–1819) and Vol. 6 (1820–41).

Irish Architectural Archive, Dublin
Alfred Jones Biographical Index, with files on Thomas Drew (D93), John McCurdy (Mc46), William Mitchell, James Cavanah Murphy, John Semple Sr (S31) and John Semple Jr (S32).
Sibthorpe & Son Ltd: photographs of interior of Monkstown Church (17/93 Y2 and Y3) and drawings of interior of Monkstown Church (78/22 (A12)).

Monkstown Vestry Archives
See Representative Church Body Library.

National Archives, Dublin
Brian (Bryan) Bolger Papers (2/476/17).
Census Returns, 1901 and 1911.
Domvill [*sic*], Benjamin: will and grant, 1774 (T.1396).
Domvile, Benjamin: letter to Sir W. Lee, 17 December 1772 (M.3418).
Jordan, Richard: will (T.13436).
Latouche [*sic*], William Digges: will (T.8189 and T.8188).
Lees, John: letters to and from Lord Townshend, May–December 1772 (M.5040).
Lindsay, Charles, bishop of Kildare: will (T.7789 and T.7790).
Kingstown Harbour Commissioners: minutes and correspondence, 1826–32 (OPW8/KIN/285; OPW1/8/6/4; OPW1/8/6/5; OPW8/KIN/542; OPW8/KIN/971(4); OPW8/KIN/1091(10,11)).
Monkstown Boys' and Girls' National Schools, records (ED9/17879; ED9/22230; ED9/25516).
Monkstown Parish Fête, 8 July 1967, invitation to the taoiseach to perform opening, Department of the Taoiseach, Private Office Files (98/8/128).
Pembroke Estate Papers, the Queen v. churchwardens of Monkstown (1011/6/36).

National Library of Ireland, Dublin: Main Reading Room
A list of persons who suffered losses of property in 1798 (JLB 94107).
Holmes, John: 'The organ in Ireland. Part I: Organ builders', 1984 (ILB 04 P7).
List of subscribers for building and maintaining a parish school at Monkstown, 1791 (L.O. Folder 8 (28)).
Notice of a Charity Sermon, by the Rev. Dudley Ryves, in the Parish Church of Monkstown, on Sunday 21 August 1791 (L.O. Folder 8 (31)).
Taylor, Alexander: sketch of coast from Blackrock to Bray (microfilm, N.919, p. 994).

National Library of Ireland, Dublin: Manuscripts Section
Blackrock Association, Minute Book . . . 1782–97 (MS 84).
Domvile, Rev. Benjamin: copy of the settlement made on his intermarriage with Anna-Maria Pocklington, dated 9 April 1768 (MS 7316).
Goff: confirmation of arms to the descendants of Rev. Thomas Goff and Anne Caulfield, and to his son,

Thomas William Goff, of Oakport, Co. Roscommon, 7 January 1861 (GO MS 108).

Knox: arms of (GO MS 810).

La Touche, William: account book, 1786–98 (MS 19,898).

Longfield, John: 'A survey of Kill of the Grange, Co. Dublin, the estate of the dean of Christ Church', 1814 (16G 41 (19)).

Mercer, Luke: 'A description of the sea coast of the kingdom of Ireland with all the principal harbours, creeks and rivers adjoining to sea ports', written *c*. 1768 (MS 13,259).

Office of Public Works, Dublin

File on Carrickbrennan Church.

Private collections

Argue family research on the Argue family, Dublin (13 June 1988).

Coey, Michael: 'George Francis Fitzgerald' (unpublished paper, 2000).

Ebbs, W.G. (organ documents): E.G. Barton, 'The Parish of Monkstown', ten-page hand-written summary (n.d., *c*. 1950s); Dedication Service Sheet (1898), with specification of organ; Monkstown Choir, list of members, October 1952; R.E. Meates & Son, specification and tender, 1965; R.E. Meates to E.G. Barton, letters dated 31 October 1965 and July 1966; letter from Rushworth and Dreaper, 1964; Service Sheet (1966), with specification of Meates's rebuild; Telford and Telford organ (1872), specification.

Knox family tree.

Smyly, Crampton, Stewart, Franks, etc. families: illustrated family trees.

Stewart, Arthur: hand-written autobiography (unpublished).

Wynne, Billy: unfinished autobiography, written in 1980–1.

Registry of Deeds, Dublin

Memorial of an indented deed dated 15 April 1805 between Elizabeth Bryan and John Semple (B 566, p. 475, No. 384798).

Indented deed of declaration of trust dated 17 July 1805 between John Semple and James Edwards (referring to lease above) (B 577, p. 175, No. 385874).

Religious Society of Friends' Historical Library, Dublin

Pim families.

Representative Church Body Library, Dublin

(Documents with an asterisk are listed here for convenience, but remain in the custody of the parish.)

Architects' drawings of churches, Portfolio 15 (with McCurdy's drawings of 1862 chancel).

Christ Church Chapter Act Books, Vol. 12 (C6/1/12).

Christ Church Chapter Minute Books, Vol. XI, pp 134–77.

Donnybrook Baptismal Registers, 1825–36 (MIC. 277) and 1836–58 (MIC. 278).

Donnybrook Vestry Minute Book, 1825–53 (P.246/5/1).

Lees, Miss H.: letter to, 1861 (94/142).

Lees, Rev. Sir Harcourt: letter to, 1825 (D1/45/5).

Leprosy Mission Pack.

Lindsay, Bishop Charles: letter from, 18 March 1812 (39/6).

Mariners' Church, Kingstown, Vestry Minute Book, 1847–1924 (P.368/05/1), including 'Report of the Charities Committee for the year 1889'.

Mariners' Church, Kingstown, papers, 1838–1978 (P.0368/27/1).

Monkstown loose papers, 1775–1907 (66) and 1909–79 (67), including Annual Reports of Select Vestry for 1904–65 (various years).

Monkstown Vestry Archives:

Annual Reports of Select Vestry: 1869, 1870, 1876, 1878–9, 1881, 1883–5, 1894, 1896–1909, 1911–28, 1930–2, 1934.

Annual Reviews (replaced Annual Reports): 1957–8, 1961–3.

Applotment book, May 1848 (giving list of rate-payers, addresses, acreage and tax payable).

Barton, E.G.: 'The Parish of Monkstown', ten-page hand-written summary (n.d., *c.* 1950s).

Church Fees book, 1866–86.

Coal Fund Reports: 1853–5, 1858–60, 1865–70, 1879–80.

Leases and indentures (arranged by date): lease of part of Dalkey (2 acres 10 perches) to James Rose for 31 years, 29 September 1827; indenture re the vaults, March 1830; indenture, June 1834; lease of premises at Kingstown used as Infants' School and Savings Bank, April 1857; lease of ground at rear of Monkstown Church, October 1864; indenture, 13 October 1864; indenture re lease in Kingstown, 29 April 1891; indenture re £9,955 in stock left by William Hone the younger to Monkstown Church, 5 August 1885, also 20 August 1897.

Mackay, G.A.: 'Monkstown memories', poem written on the departure of the Rev. Arthur Butler, 1958.

Maps of Monkstown: Ordnance Survey map of Monkstown and environs, with boundaries of the 'proprietary church of St John, Monkstown' marked in red; written note detailing boundaries on N, S, E and W, signed by the Rev. R. MacDonnell, 17 October 1866; Sherrard and Brassington, 'A survey of ground contiguous to the Parish Church of Monkstown . . .' (1806).

Miscellaneous: Alphabetical list of 690 parishioners (*c.* 1980); The Argue Family, Dublin; Choir members, 1978, 1980; Church Fête in The Hall school grounds, 1967; 'Churchville' papers; expenses allowed by the Ecclesiastical Commisioners 1834–41; forms for obtaining coffins at the expense of the parish of Monkstown, January and February 1850; Inquest/Coroner's book, 1849–51; Inventory of Parish Records in small and large Vestry safes (dated February 1993); letter from Anne Lindsay, 21 March 1857, re Archdeacon Lindsay's pews; letters re vaults being converted into air-raid shelter, 1940; papers from Officers of Health, 1849; parish legacies and bequests; redecoration of church interior, 1954; repairs to chancel, 1970; road-widening scheme, 1964 (church boundary walls); Schedule of Books and Documents in Vestry safe, December 1857; statement to police re deserted child, December 1858; subscription list of William Riggs for Monkstown New Church (no date); Sunday School calendars, 1861, 1876; testimonials of Mr Peter Hackett (August 1864); truss repair drawings by Hartigan Bros; YMCA programme, 1884, 1895.

Monkstown Herald (local history pamphlets): October 1884, November 1884, January 1885, July 1885.

Monkstown Parochial Benefit Society (leaflet), December 1878.

Monkstown Parochial Schools: registers for various years; accounts book 1858–69; alterations and extensions, 1962–3, 1979; papers re school extension.

Pew-holders: letters re pews (1858, 1872); Pew Allocation book, 1863–4; list of pew-holders, 1869; index to sittings, 1955.

Plans of Monkstown Church (arranged by date):
Semple, 30 April 1829, 'Plan showing the ground floor and gallery pews of the enlarged church of Monkstown'; 1832, Plan of Monkstown Church, with seating plan and pew holders;
Plan of galleries, showing pew numbers (undated); Plan of seating (after 1862); W. Kaye Parry, Architect, 28 June 1881, Plan of the Vaults; Dun Laoghaire Borough Council, 1954, rebuilding of church boundary wall.

Poor Fund books: 1803–15; 1835–41; 1841–54; 1855–8.

Poor Fund vouchers: 1862–3, 1863–4, 1864–5, 1866–7, 1868–9, 1870–1, 1871–2.

Preachers' books: August 1834–June 1845; January 1852–November 1855; December 1855–August 1860; August 1860–January 1867; January 1867–January 1869; January 1869–December 1880; 1894–1912; July 1912–December 1934; December 1934–November 1947; November 1947–March 1996; March 1996–present★.

Presentation book to Dr Robert Lynn Heard, 1922.

Register of Baptisms 1679–1783, Marriages 1676–1785 and Burials 1669–1786; Register of Baptisms 1804–31, Marriages 1805–27 and Burials 1805–27; Register of Baptisms, Marriages and Burials 1827–35; Register of Baptisms 1835–48, Marriages 1836–42 and Burials 1835–54; Register of Baptisms 1848–53, 1853–8, 1858–84; Register of Marriages 1842–5, 1845–7, 1847–53, 1858–63, 1863–7, 1867–71, 1873–7, 1877–87, 1887–99; Register of Burials 1854–60, 1860–5, 1865–93.

Rooke, B. Warburton: notebook with notes for lecture given in 1923.

Rooke, B. Warburton: album with photographs and notes for diascope lecture given in 1923 and 1932.

Schedule of Books and Documents in Vestry Safe, December 1857.

Select Vestry Minute books: January 1871–September 1877; December 1877–April 1890; 1890–1905;

April 1918–December 1949; January 1950–July 1968; September 1968–June 1988; 1988–present★.
Vestry Minute books: 1744–77; 1805–29; 1871–present (Easter Vestry minutes, including material dating from 1858)★.
Semple drawings of church buildings.
Visitations of Dublin and Glendalough, for the years 1703–10, 1714–22, 1727–30, 1734–41, 1747–8, 1777–84, 1788–91, 1802–3, 1806, 1814, 1817, 1821–2, 1824, 1838–41 and 1852 (MIC. 12-21).
Visitations in the diocese of Kildare by Bishop Charles Lindsay (1804–8), Memorandum Book of, including copies of letters to recalcitrant clergy (MS8).
Visitation of Archbishop William King, 8 May 1723 (D6/41).
Walker, C. Garrett: Paper to mark the 140th anniversary of the death of Sir William Betham, 1993.
Walker, C. Garrett: The Knox Memorial Hall, 1992.
Whitechurch Vestry Minute Book, 1824–33 (P.0504/05/1).

Royal College of Physicians of Ireland, Dublin
Kirkpatrick Archive, biographical details of Irish doctors.

Royal Irish Academy, Dublin
Day, Judge Robert: papers and diaries, *c.* 1780–1839 (MSS 12.W.7–17).
Haliday Pamphlets Collection (including Monkstown Protestant Orphan Society's Annual Report for 1845 and Monkstown Parochial Union Benefit Society's Report for 1846).

St Iberius's Church, Wexford
Vestry Minutes for the parish of Wexford, 1662–1871, Vol. 32.

Trinity College, Dublin: Manuscripts Department
Catalogue of Manuscripts, La Touche gifts (Ref. Nos 1552, 1564, 1577, 1578 and 1587).
Library Minute Book, recording gifts of Persian letters and manuscripts from William Digges La Touche (MUN/LIB/2/1).

NEWSPAPERS, JOURNALS AND PERIODICALS CONSULTED

Analecta Hibernica; *Annual Registers*; *Architectural Magazine* (London); *Aspects of Irish Genealogy*; *Bray & South County Dublin Herald*; *British Medical Journal*; *Christian Examiner*; *Church of Ireland Gazette*; *Church Missionary Gleaner*; *Cork Examiner*; *Correspondent*; *Cyclopaedian Magazine and Dublin Monthly Register*; *Dublin Chronicle*; *Dublin Builder*; *Dublin Evening Mail*; *Dublin Evening Post*; *Dublin Gazette*; *Dublin Historical Record*; *Dublin and London Magazine*; *Dublin Medical Press*; *Dublin Penny Journal*; *Dublin University Magazine*; *Dun Laoghaire Borough Historical Society Journal*; *Evening Packet*; *Faulkner's Dublin Journal*; Foxrock Local History Club publications; *Freeman's Journal*; *Gentleman's Magazine*; *Hibernian Gleaner* (1895–1916); *Hibernian Magazine*; *Irish Architect; Irish Arts Review*; *Irish Builder*; *Irish Builder and Engineer*; *Irish Building*; *Irish Churchman*; *Irish Ecclesiastical Gazette*; *Irish Times*; *Journal of the Cork Historical and Archaeological Society*; *Journal of the Royal Society of Antiquaries of Ireland*; *Kingstown Journal*; *Kingstown and Bray Observer*; *Medical Press and Circular*; *Monkstown Herald*; *Monkstown Parish Newsletters*; *North Munster Antiquarian Journal*; *St Patrick's News*; *Pue's Occurrences*; *Saunders's News-Letter and Daily Advertiser*; *Sentimental and Masonic Journal*; *The Times*; *Trinity, An Annual Record*; *Walker's Hibernian Magazine*.

WEBSITES

Battlefields of World War I, 1914–18 (www.battlefields1418.50megs.com).
Church of Ireland (www.ireland.anglican.org).
Commonwealth War Graves Commission (www.cwgc.org).
Genealogy site by Antony Maitland (www.anthonymaitland.com), including The Stewarts of Killymoon and Tyrcallen, Source: T559/36, p. 86, Public Record Office of Northern Ireland (PRONI).
The Irish Times (www.ireland.com).
The Round Room of Dublin's Mansion House (www.theroundroom.ie).

INDEX